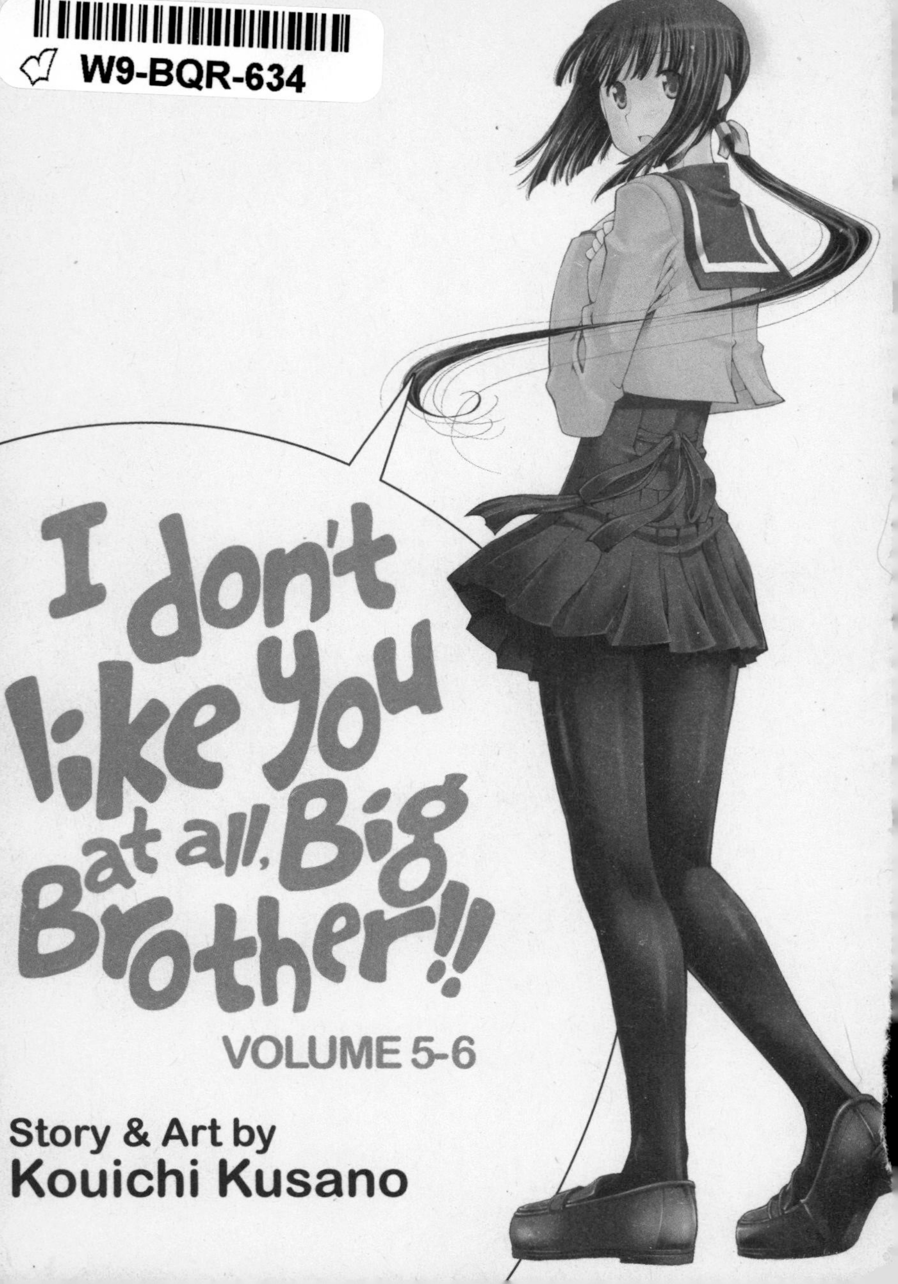

I don't like you at all, Big Brother!!

VOLUME 5-6

Story & Art by
Kouichi Kusano

I don't like you at all, Big Brother!!

VOLUME 5-6

story & art by Kouichi Kusano

STAFF CREDITS

translation	Nan Rymer
adaptation	Bambi Eloriaga-Amago
lettering	Roland Amago
layout	Mheeya Wok
cover design	Nicky Lim
proofreader	Katherine Bell, Janet Houck
editor	Adam Arnold
publisher	Jason DeAngelis
	Seven Seas Entertainment

ONIICHAN NO KOTO NANKA ZENZEN SUKIJANAIN DAKARA NE!! VOL.5-6
Copyright © KOUICHI KUSANO 2008 All rights reserved.
First published in Japan in 2008 by Futabasha Publishers Ltd., Tokyo.
English version published by Seven Seas Entertainment, LLC.
Under license from Futabasha Publishers Ltd.

ISBN: 978-1-937867-11-9

Printed in Canada

First Printing: July 2013

10 9 8 7 6 5 4 3 2 1

FOLLOW US ONLINE: www.gomanga.com

READING DIRECTIONS

This book reads from *right to left*, Japanese style.
If this is your first time reading manga, you start
reading from the top right panel on each page and
take it from there. If you get lost, just follow the
numbered diagram here. It may seem backwards
at first, but you'll get the hang of it! Have fun!!

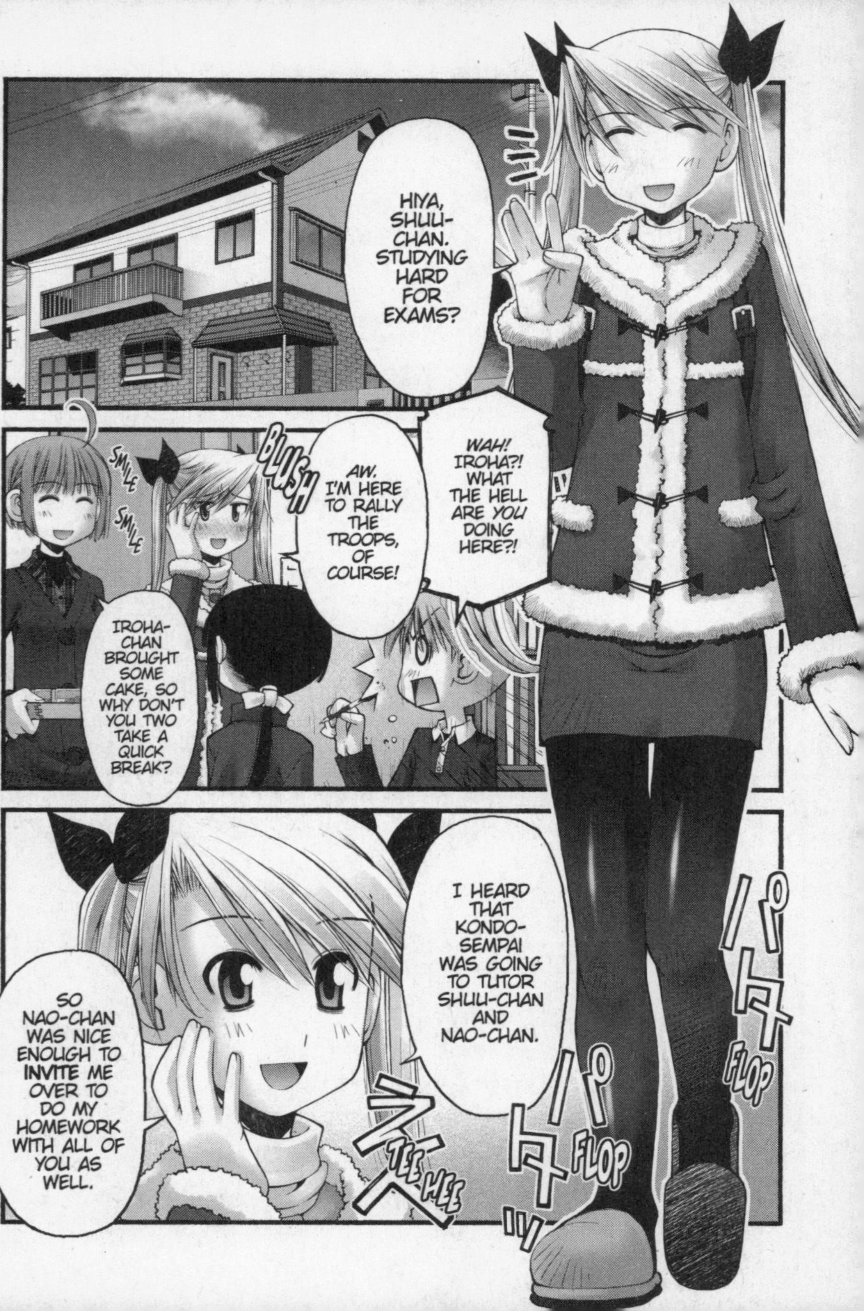
HIYA, SHUU-CHAN. STUDYING HARD FOR EXAMS?
WAH! IROHA?! WHAT THE HELL ARE YOU DOING HERE?!
AW. I'M HERE TO RALLY THE TROOPS, OF COURSE!
BLUSH
SMILE SMILE
IROHA-CHAN BROUGHT SOME CAKE, SO WHY DON'T YOU TWO TAKE A QUICK BREAK?
I HEARD THAT KONDO-SEMPAI WAS GOING TO TUTOR SHUU-CHAN AND NAO-CHAN.
SO NAO-CHAN WAS NICE ENOUGH TO INVITE ME OVER TO DO MY HOMEWORK WITH ALL OF YOU AS WELL.
TEE HEE
FLOP
FLOP

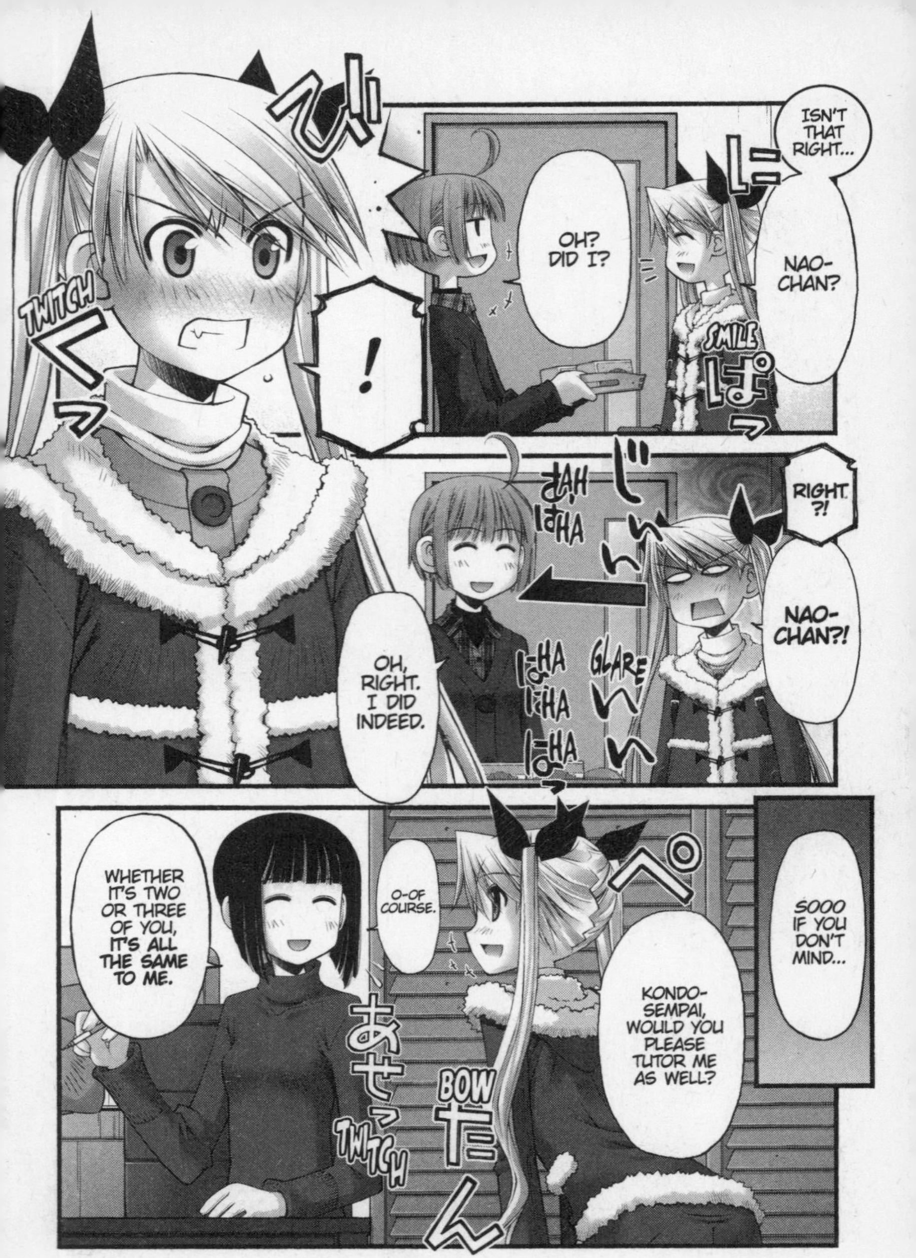

ISN'T THAT RIGHT...
NAO-CHAN?
SMILE
OH? DID I?
RIGHT.?!
NAO-CHAN?!
GLARE
AH HA HA
OH, RIGHT. I DID INDEED.
HA HA HA
!
TWITCH
SOOO IF YOU DON'T MIND...
KONDO-SEMPAI, WOULD YOU PLEASE TUTOR ME AS WELL?
BOW
O-OF COURSE.
TWITCH
WHETHER IT'S TWO OR THREE OF YOU, IT'S ALL THE SAME TO ME.

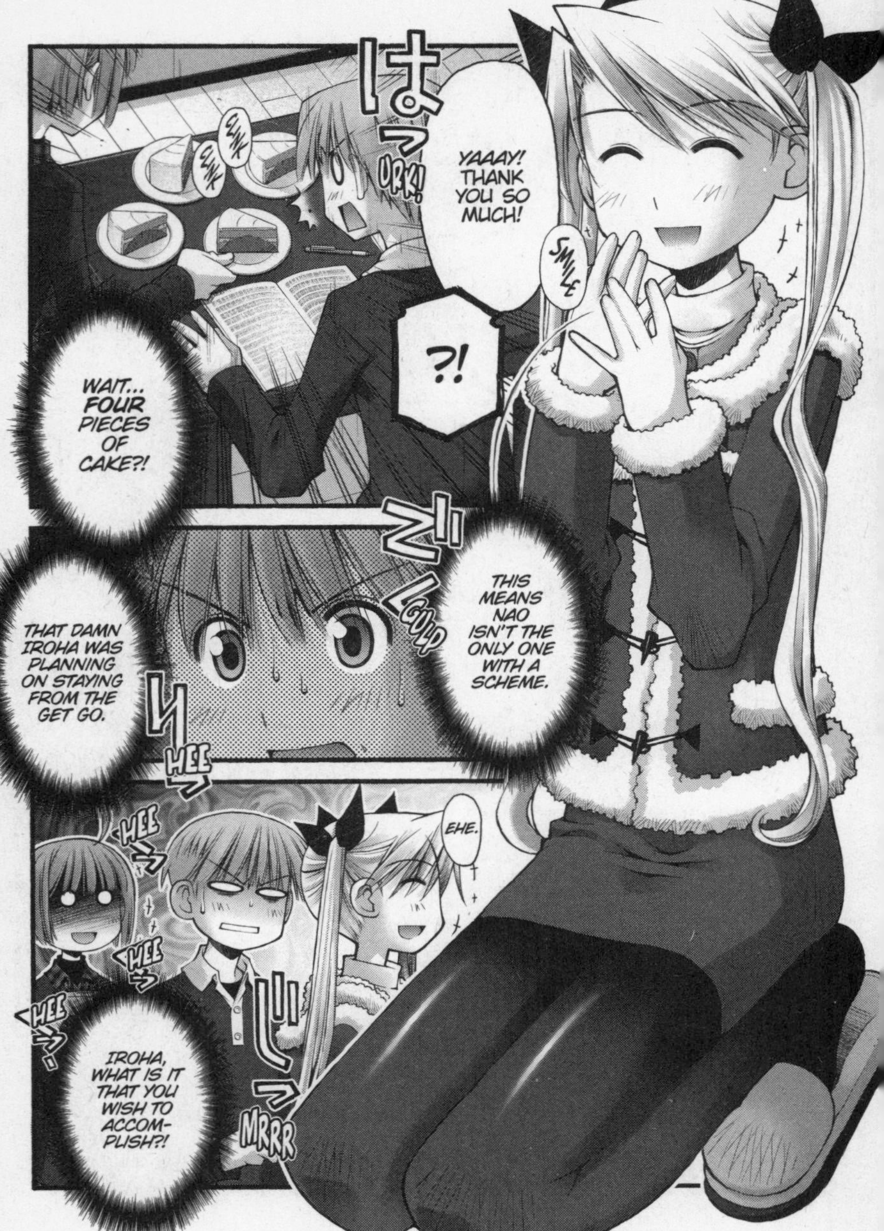
YAAAY! THANK YOU SO MUCH!
SMILE
はっ
ORK!
CLINK
CLINK
?!
WAIT... FOUR PIECES OF CAKE?!
GULP
THIS MEANS NAO ISN'T THE ONLY ONE WITH A SCHEME.
THAT DAMN IROHA WAS PLANNING ON STAYING FROM THE GET GO.
HEE
EHE.
HEE
HEE
HEE
MRRR
IROHA, WHAT IS IT THAT YOU WISH TO ACCOMPLISH?!

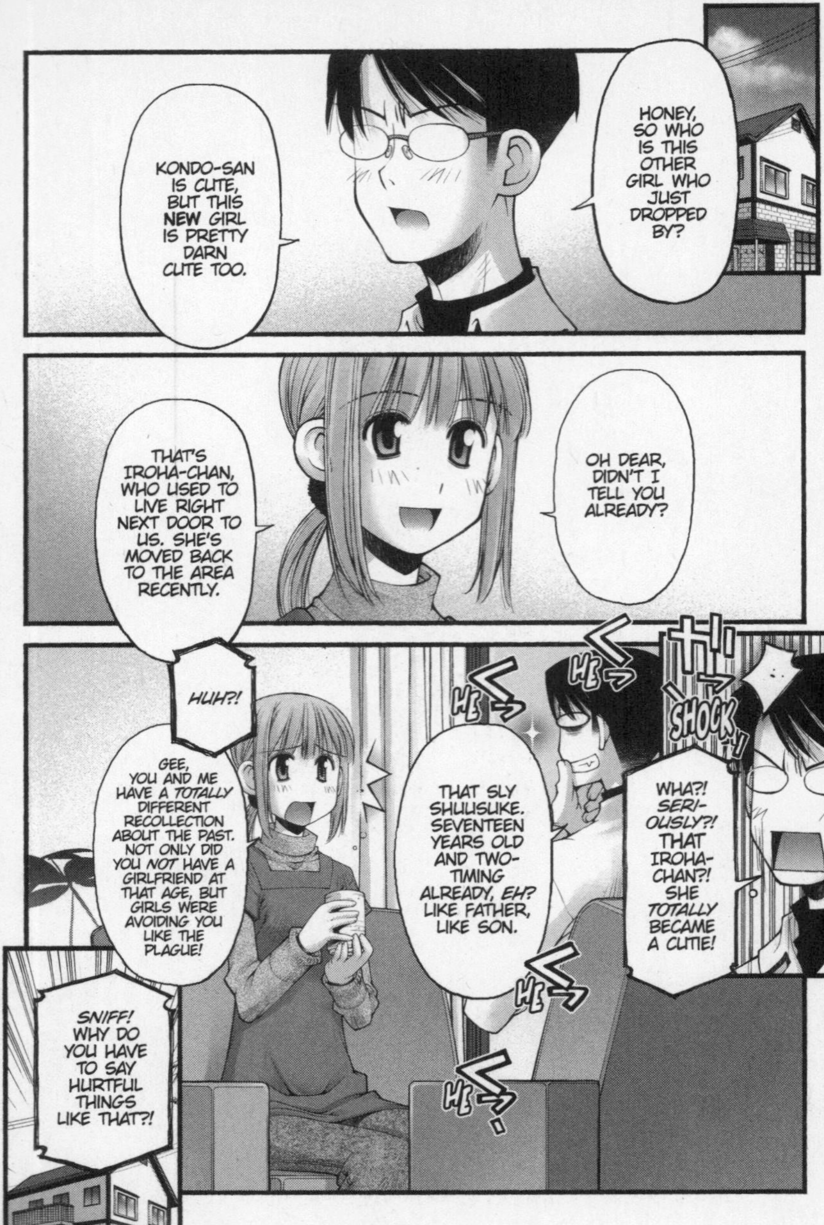
HONEY, SO WHO IS THIS OTHER GIRL WHO JUST DROPPED BY?
KONDO-SAN IS CUTE, BUT THIS NEW GIRL IS PRETTY DARN CUTE TOO.
OH DEAR, DIDN'T I TELL YOU ALREADY?
THAT'S IROHA-CHAN, WHO USED TO LIVE RIGHT NEXT DOOR TO US. SHE'S MOVED BACK TO THE AREA RECENTLY.
SHOCK
WHA?! SERIOUSLY?! THAT IROHA-CHAN?! SHE TOTALLY BECAME A CUTIE!
HE HE HE HE HE
THAT SLY SHUUSUKE. SEVENTEEN YEARS OLD AND TWO-TIMING ALREADY, EH? LIKE FATHER, LIKE SON.
HUH?!
GEE, YOU AND ME HAVE A TOTALLY DIFFERENT RECOLLECTION ABOUT THE PAST. NOT ONLY DID YOU NOT HAVE A GIRLFRIEND AT THAT AGE, BUT GIRLS WERE AVOIDING YOU LIKE THE PLAGUE!
SNIFF! WHY DO YOU HAVE TO SAY HURTFUL THINGS LIKE THAT?!

CHAPTER 28 Splash Country Strategery and Lust

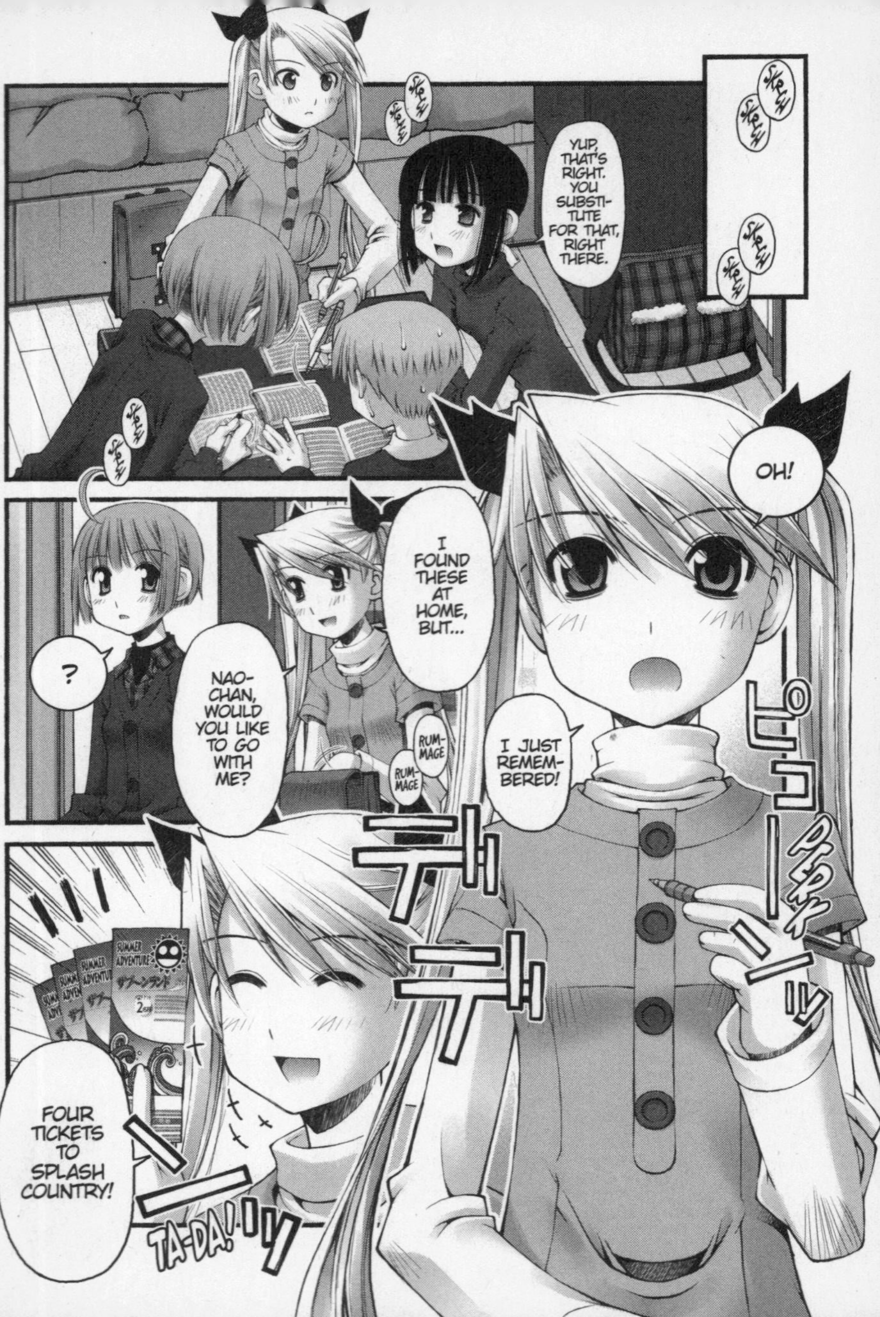
SKRCH
SKRCH
YUP, THAT'S RIGHT. YOU SUBSTITUTE FOR THAT, RIGHT THERE.
SKRCH
SKRCH
SKRCH
SKRCH
SKRCH
SKRCH
OH!
I JUST REMEMBERED!
PERK
I FOUND THESE AT HOME, BUT...
NAO-CHAN, WOULD YOU LIKE TO GO WITH ME?
RUMMAGE
RUMMAGE
?
SUMMER ADVENTURE
FOUR TICKETS TO SPLASH COUNTRY!
TA-DA!

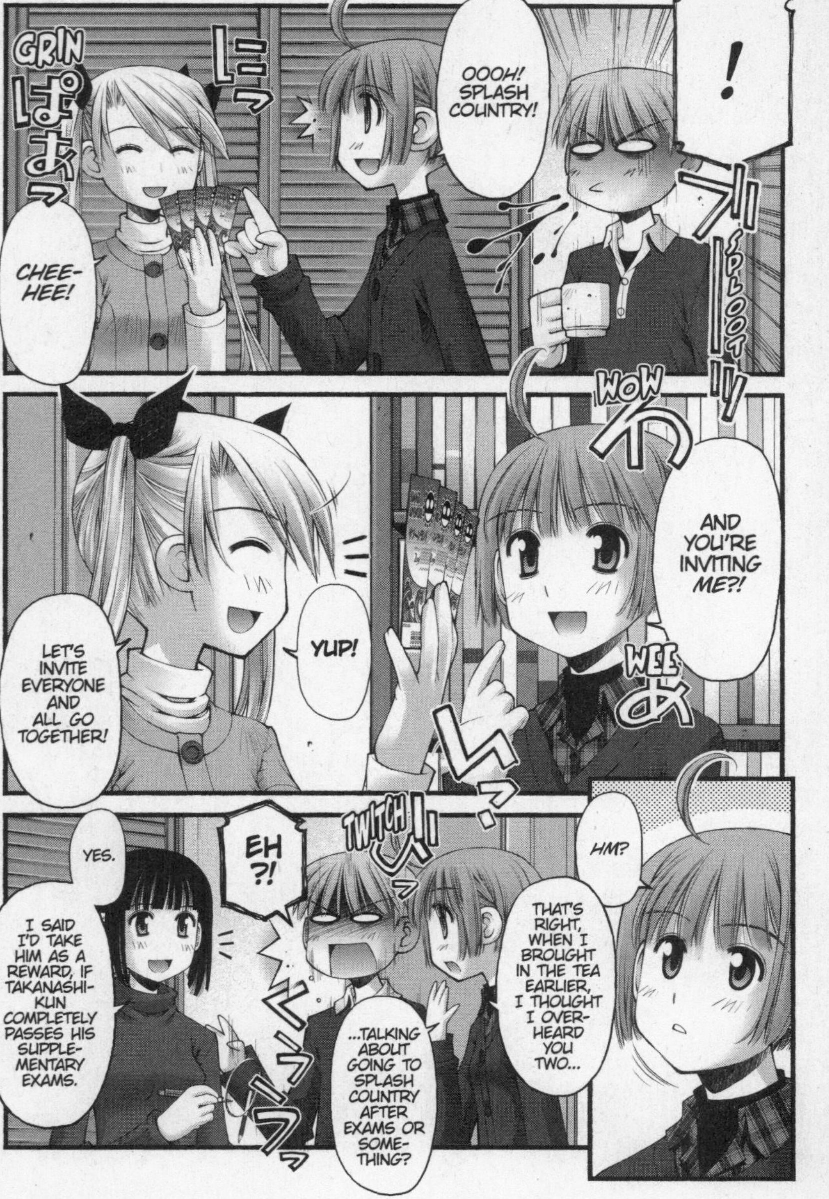
!
SPLOOT!!!
OOOH! SPLASH COUNTRY!
GRIN
CHEE-HEE!
WOW
AND YOU'RE INVITING ME?!
WEE
YUP!
LET'S INVITE EVERYONE AND ALL GO TOGETHER!
HM?
THAT'S RIGHT, WHEN I BROUGHT IN THE TEA EARLIER, I THOUGHT I OVERHEARD YOU TWO...
...TALKING ABOUT GOING TO SPLASH COUNTRY AFTER EXAMS OR SOMETHING?
TWITCH
EH?!
YES.
I SAID I'D TAKE HIM AS A REWARD, IF TAKANASHI-KUN COMPLETELY PASSES HIS SUPPLEMENTARY EXAMS.

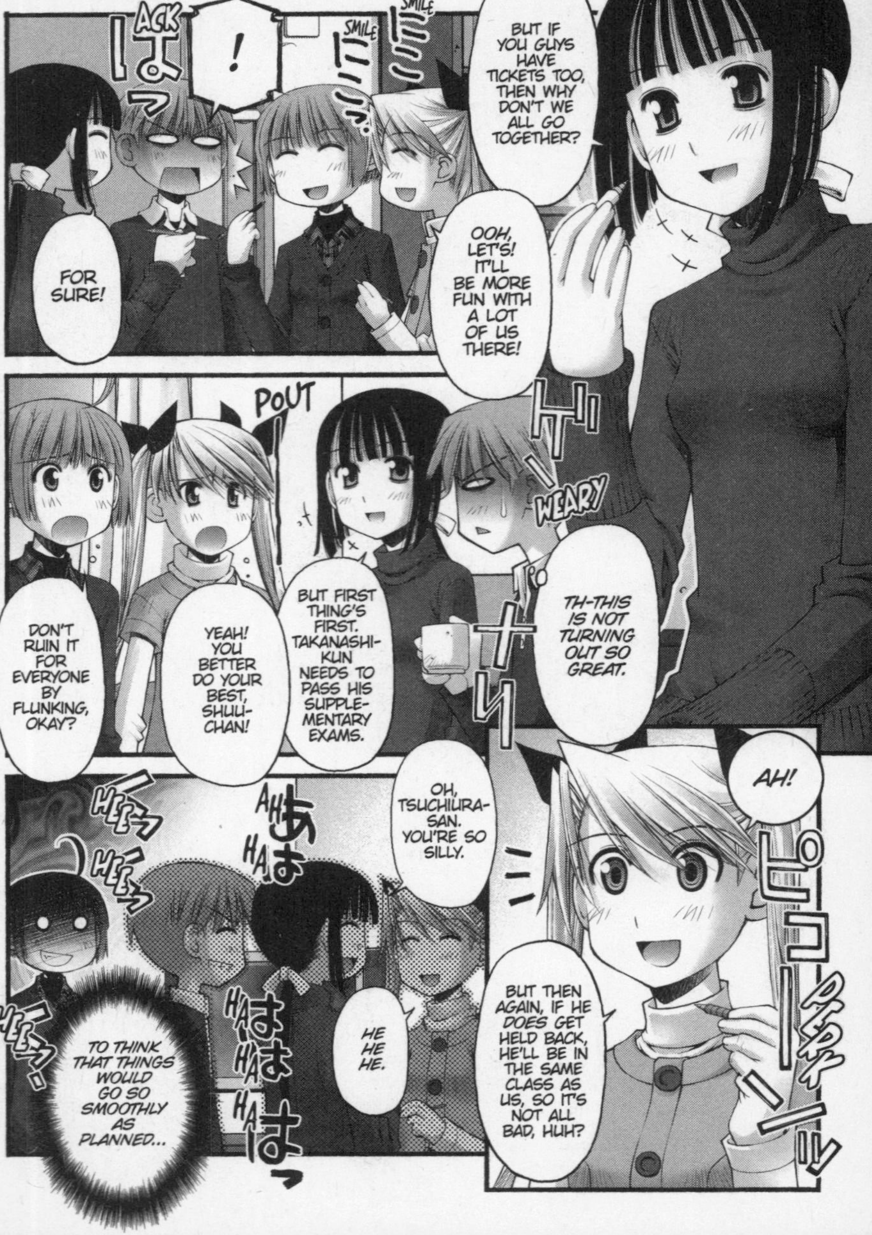
BUT IF YOU GUYS HAVE TICKETS TOO, THEN WHY DON'T WE ALL GO TOGETHER?
SMILE ニコ
SMILE ニコっ
!
ACK はっ
OOH, LET'S! IT'LL BE MORE FUN WITH A LOT OF US THERE!
FOR SURE!
WEARY
TH-THIS IS NOT TURNING OUT SO GREAT.
POUT
BUT FIRST THING'S FIRST. TAKANASHI-KUN NEEDS TO PASS HIS SUPPLE-MENTARY EXAMS.
YEAH! YOU BETTER DO YOUR BEST, SHUU-CHAN!
DON'T RUIN IT FOR EVERYONE BY FLUNKING, OKAY?
AH!
PERK ピコーン
OH, TSUCHIURA-SAN. YOU'RE SO SILLY.
BUT THEN AGAIN, IF HE DOES GET HELD BACK, HE'LL BE IN THE SAME CLASS AS US, SO IT'S NOT ALL BAD, HUH?
AH HA HA HA HA あはははっ
HE HE HE.
HEE HEE HEE
TO THINK THAT THINGS WOULD GO SO SMOOTHLY AS PLANNED...

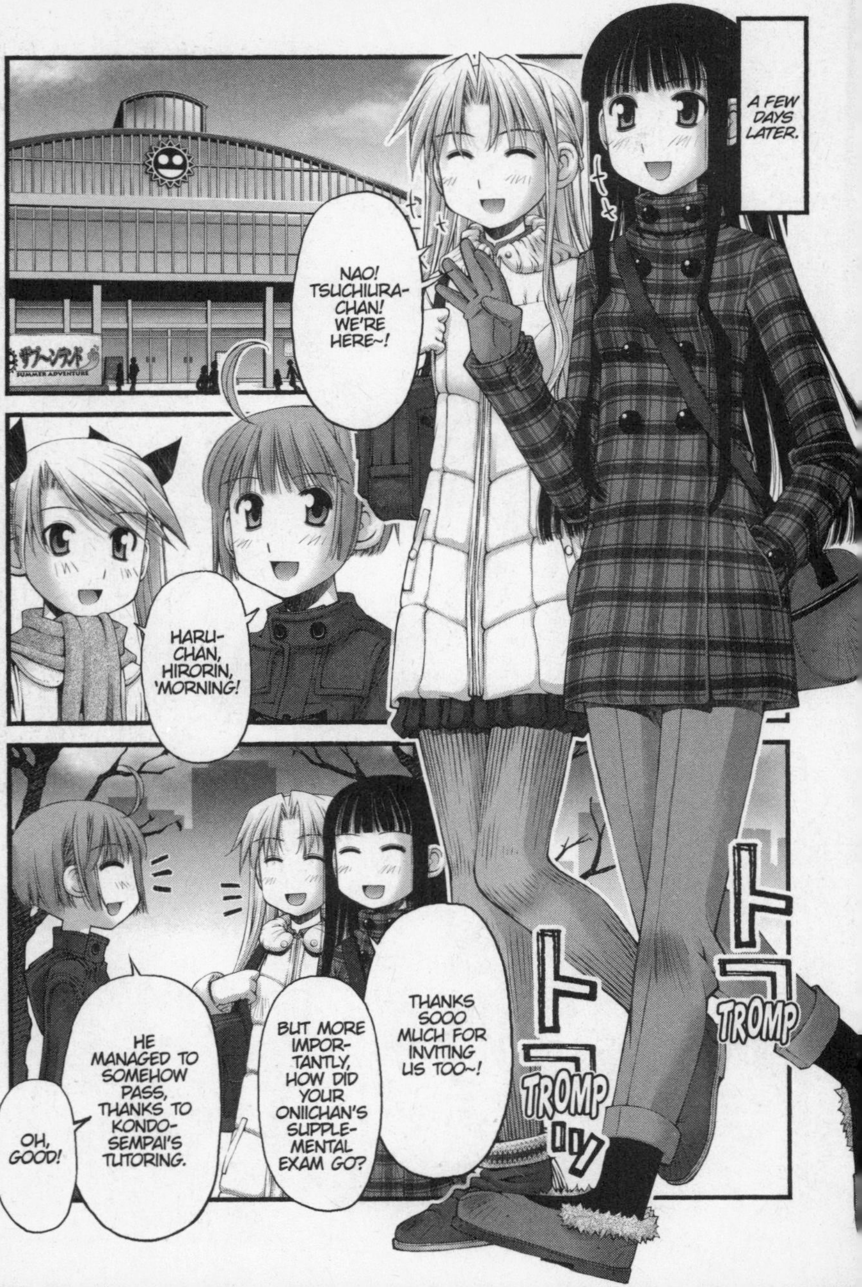
A FEW DAYS LATER.
NAO! TSUCHIURA-CHAN! WE'RE HERE~!
SUMMER ADVENTURE
HARU-CHAN, HIRORIN, 'MORNING!
TROMP
TROMP
THANKS SOOO MUCH FOR INVITING US TOO~!
BUT MORE IMPORTANTLY, HOW DID YOUR ONIICHAN'S SUPPLEMENTAL EXAM GO?
HE MANAGED TO SOMEHOW PASS, THANKS TO KONDO-SEMPAI'S TUTORING.
OH, GOOD!

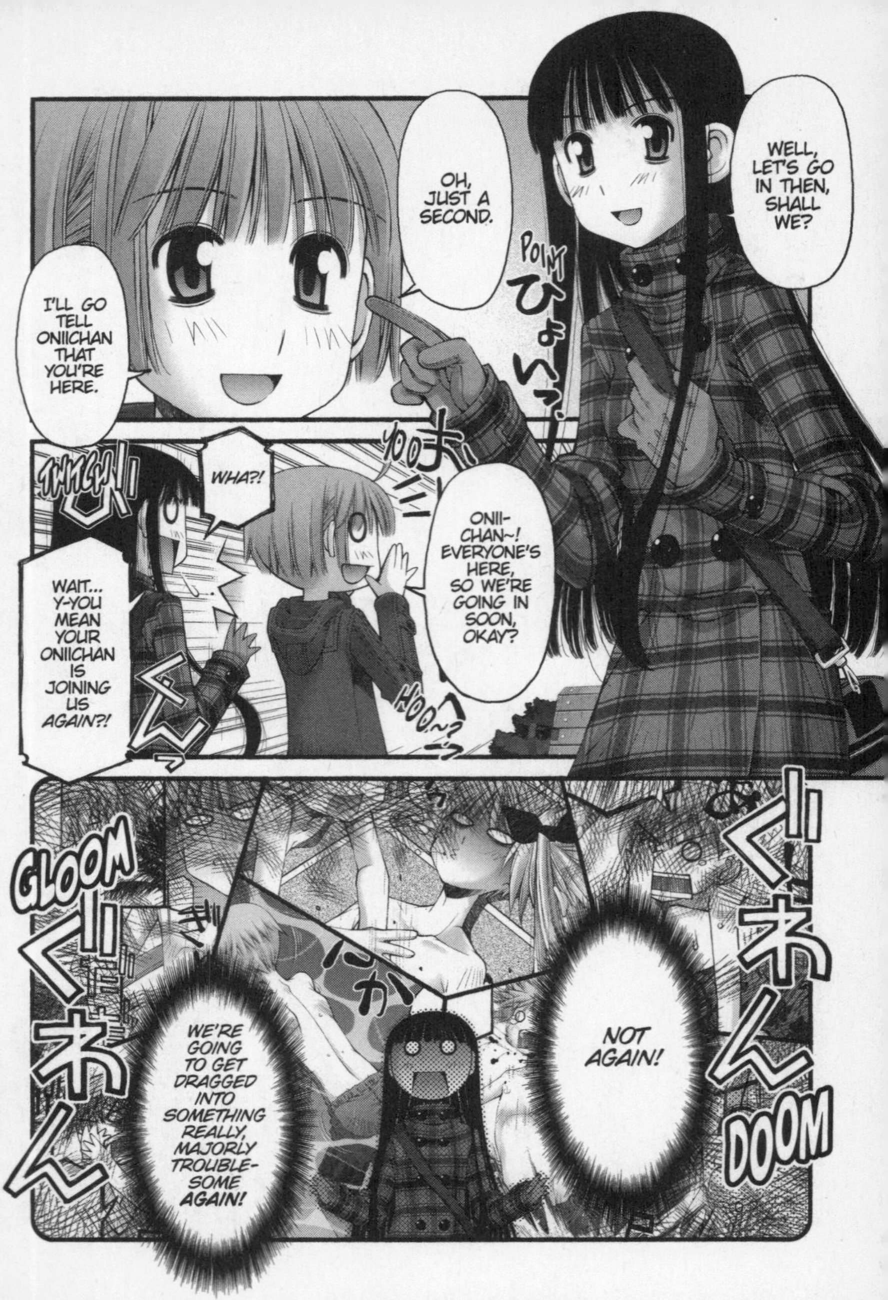
WELL, LET'S GO IN THEN, SHALL WE?
OH, JUST A SECOND.
POINT
I'LL GO TELL ONIICHAN THAT YOU'RE HERE.
YOO
ONII-CHAN~! EVERYONE'S HERE, SO WE'RE GOING IN SOON, OKAY?
HOO~?
WHA?!
WAIT... Y-YOU MEAN YOUR ONIICHAN IS JOINING US AGAIN?!
DOOM
NOT AGAIN!
GLOOM
WE'RE GOING TO GET DRAGGED INTO SOMETHING REALLY, MAJORLY TROUBLE-SOME AGAIN!

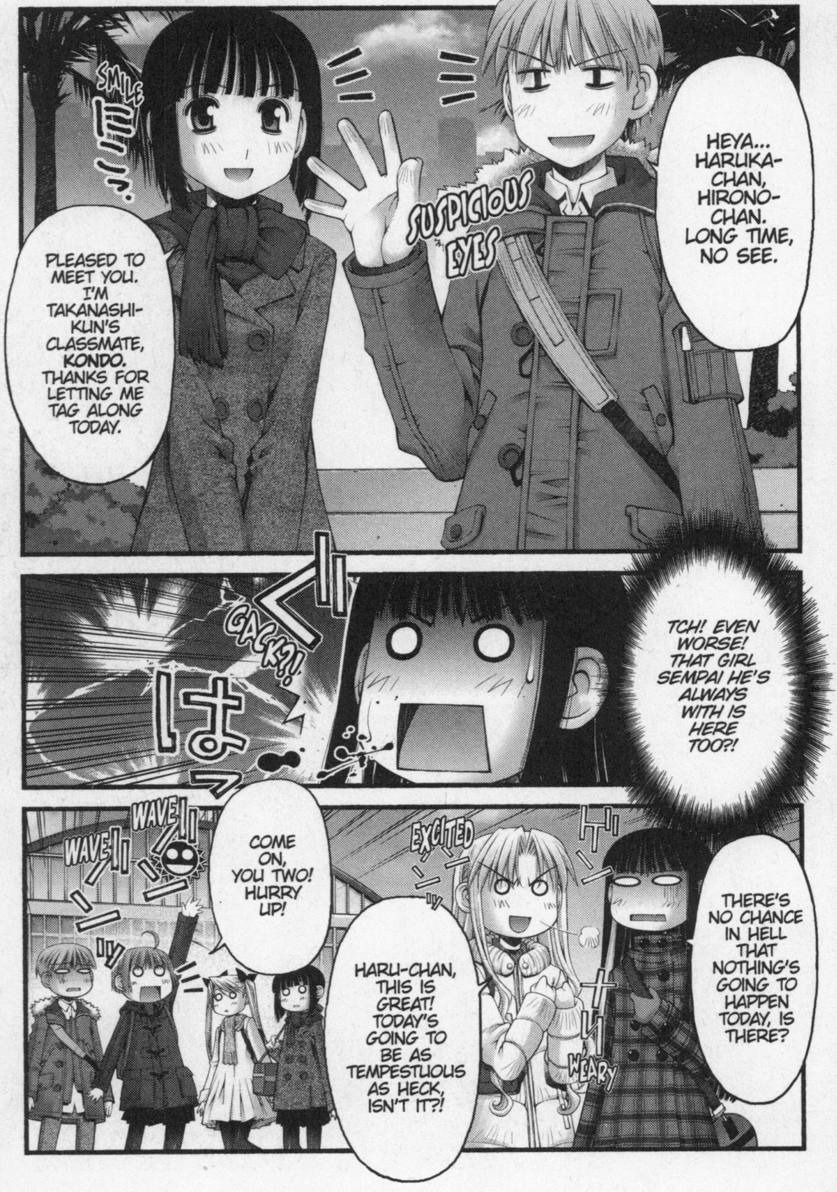
HEYA... HARUKA-CHAN, HIRONO-CHAN. LONG TIME, NO SEE.
SUSPICIOUS EYES
SMILE
PLEASED TO MEET YOU. I'M TAKANASHI-KUN'S CLASSMATE, KONDO. THANKS FOR LETTING ME TAG ALONG TODAY.
TCH! EVEN WORSE! THAT GIRL SEMPAI HE'S ALWAYS WITH IS HERE TOO?!
GACK?!
THERE'S NO CHANCE IN HELL THAT NOTHING'S GOING TO HAPPEN TODAY, IS THERE?
WEARY
EXCITED
HARU-CHAN, THIS IS GREAT! TODAY'S GOING TO BE AS TEMPESTUOUS AS HECK, ISN'T IT?!
COME ON, YOU TWO! HURRY UP!
WAVE
WAVE

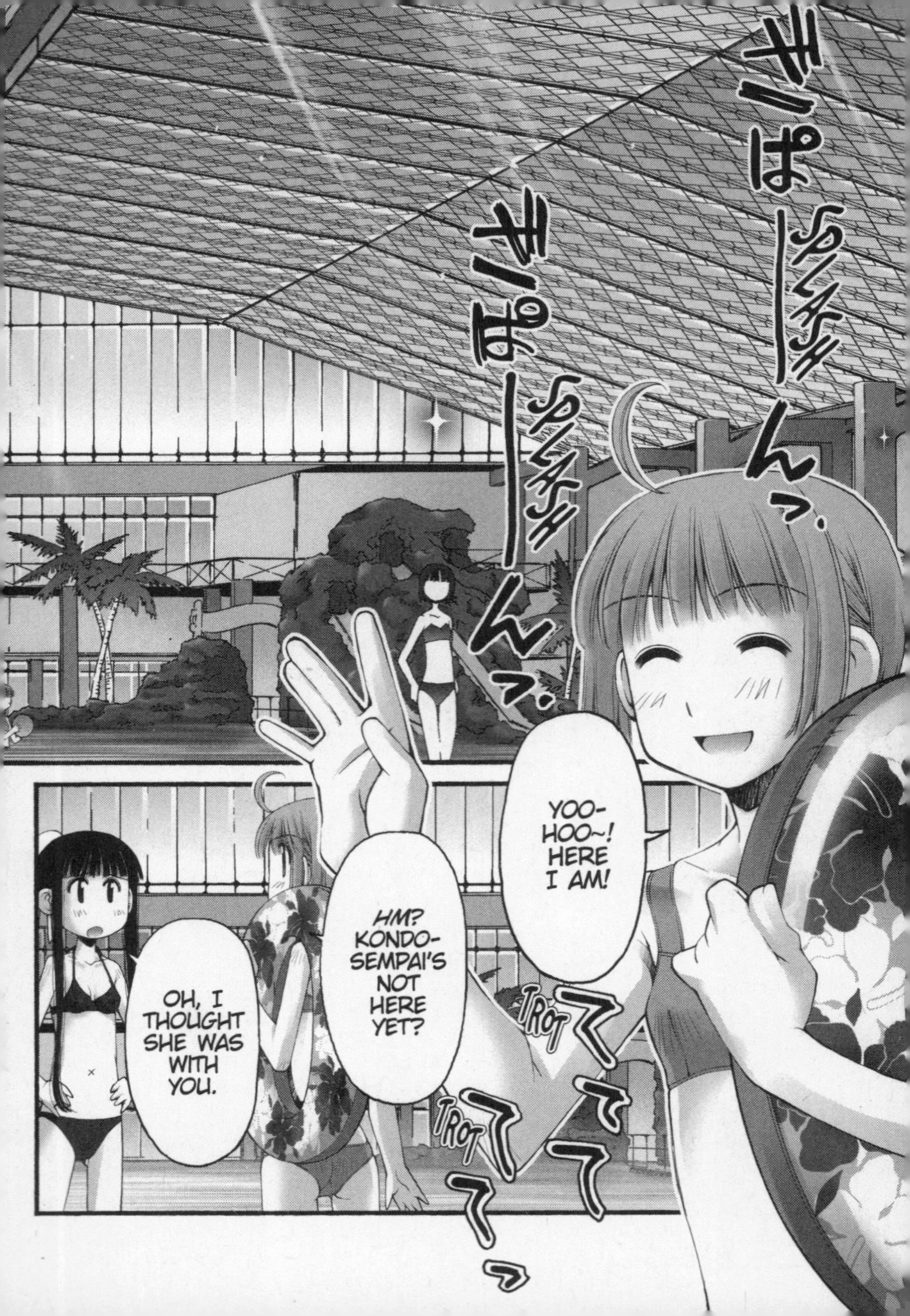
SPLASH
SPLASH
YOO-HOO~! HERE I AM!
TROT
TROT
HM? KONDO-SEMPAI'S NOT HERE YET?
OH, I THOUGHT SHE WAS WITH YOU.

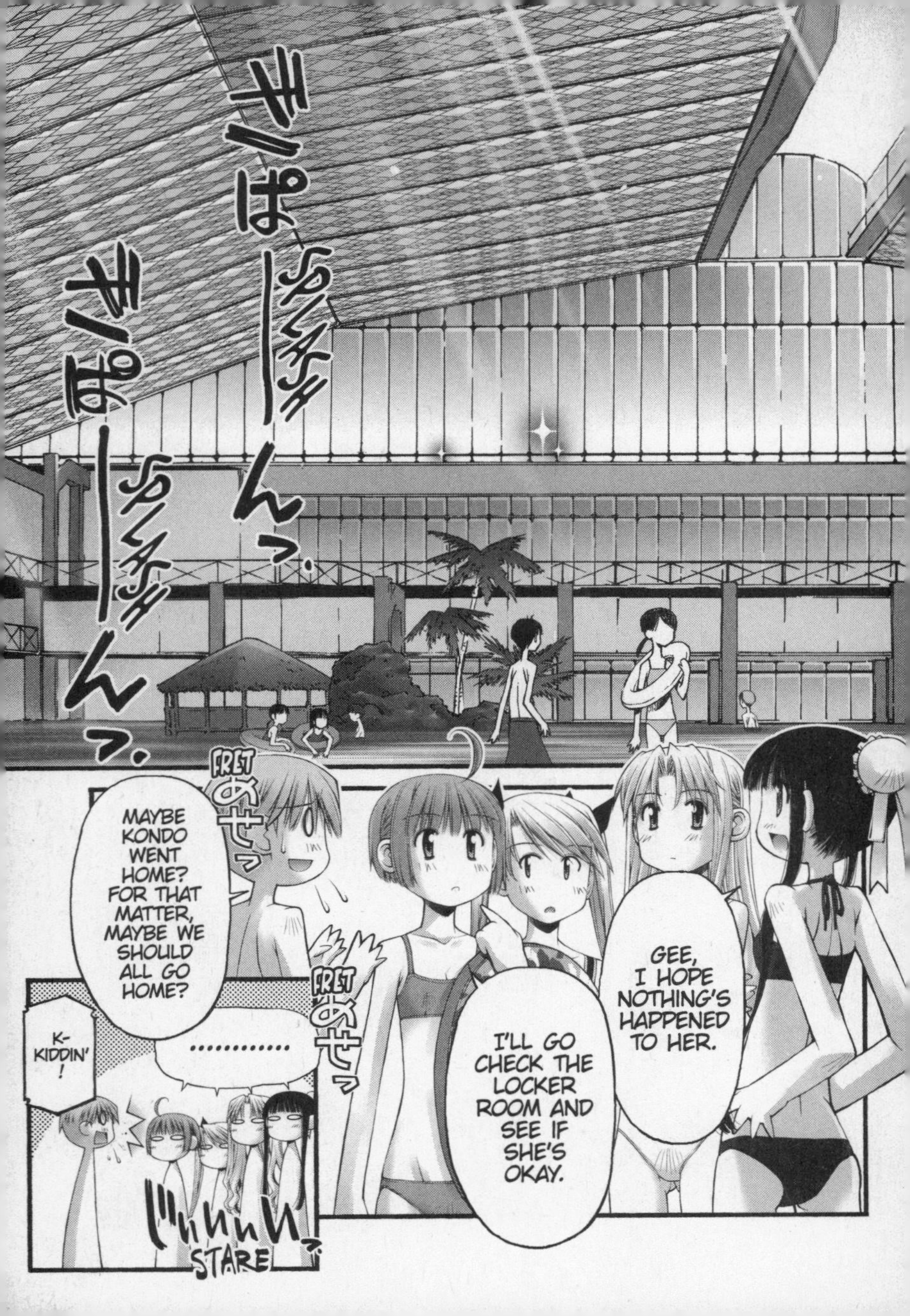
ざぱーんっ
SPLASH
ざぱーんっ
SPLASH
GEE, I HOPE NOTHING'S HAPPENED TO HER.
I'LL GO CHECK THE LOCKER ROOM AND SEE IF SHE'S OKAY.
あせっ
FRET
MAYBE KONDO WENT HOME? FOR THAT MATTER, MAYBE WE SHOULD ALL GO HOME?
あせっ
FRET
....
K-KIDDIN'!
じぃぃぃぃっ
STARE

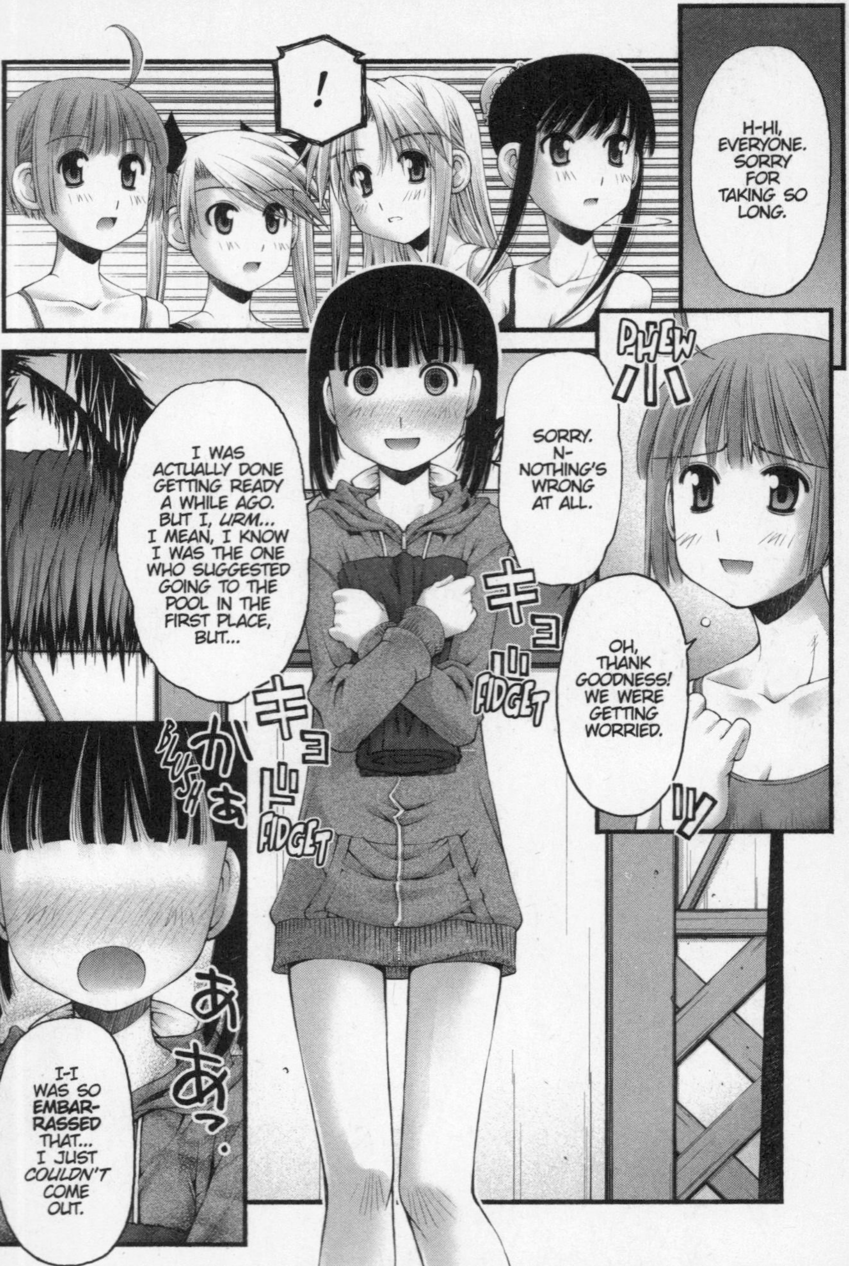
H-HI, EVERYONE. SORRY FOR TAKING SO LONG.
!
PHEW
SORRY. N-NOTHING'S WRONG AT ALL.
OH, THANK GOODNESS! WE WERE GETTING WORRIED.
I WAS ACTUALLY DONE GETTING READY A WHILE AGO. BUT I, URM... I MEAN, I KNOW I WAS THE ONE WHO SUGGESTED GOING TO THE POOL IN THE FIRST PLACE, BUT...
キョド
FIDGET
キョド
FIDGET
かぁ
BLUSH
あぁっ
I-I WAS SO EMBARRASSED THAT... I JUST COULDN'T COME OUT.

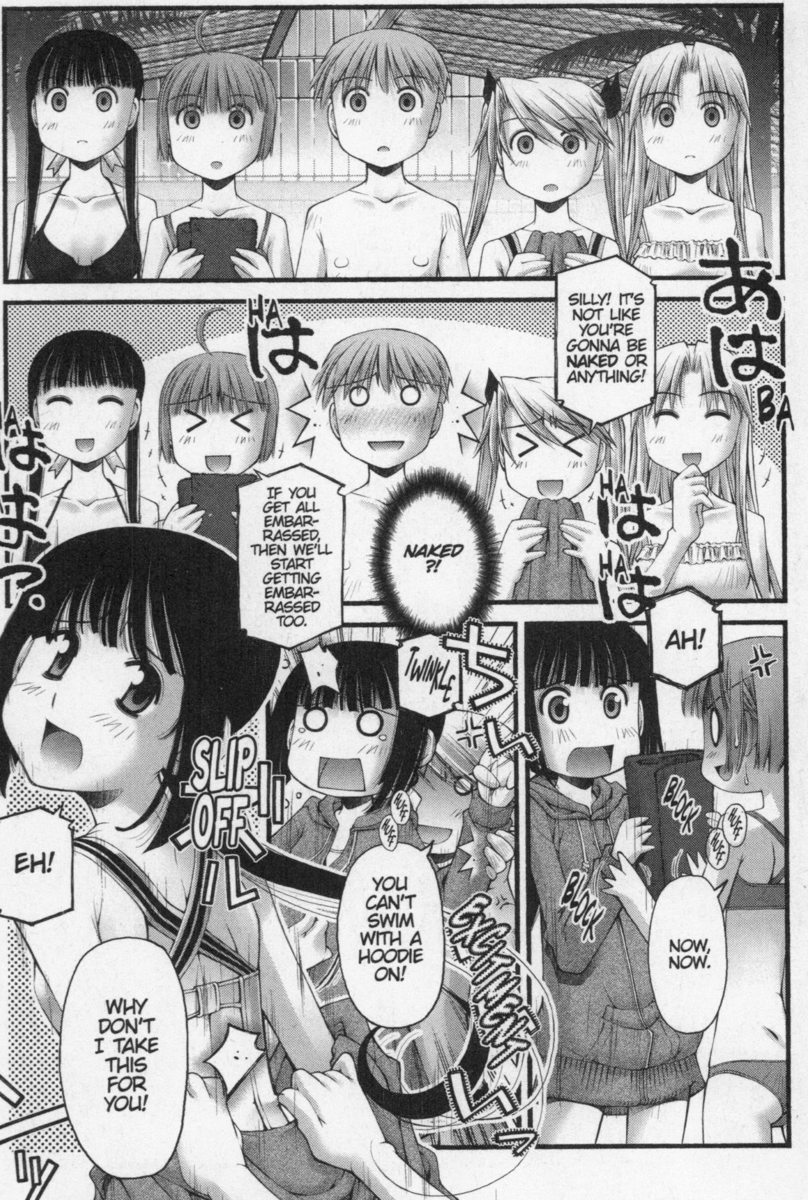
あは BA
SILLY! IT'S NOT LIKE YOU'RE GONNA BE NAKED OR ANYTHING!
HA は HA は
NAKED ?!
IF YOU GET ALL EMBARRASSED, THEN WE'LL START GETTING EMBARRASSED TOO.
HA は
HA は HA ぱァ。
AH!
TWINKLE
BLOCK
BLOCK
HUFF HUFF
NOW, NOW.
YOU CAN'T SWIM WITH A HOODIE ON!
HUFF HUFF
SLIP OFF
EH!
WHY DON'T I TAKE THIS FOR YOU!

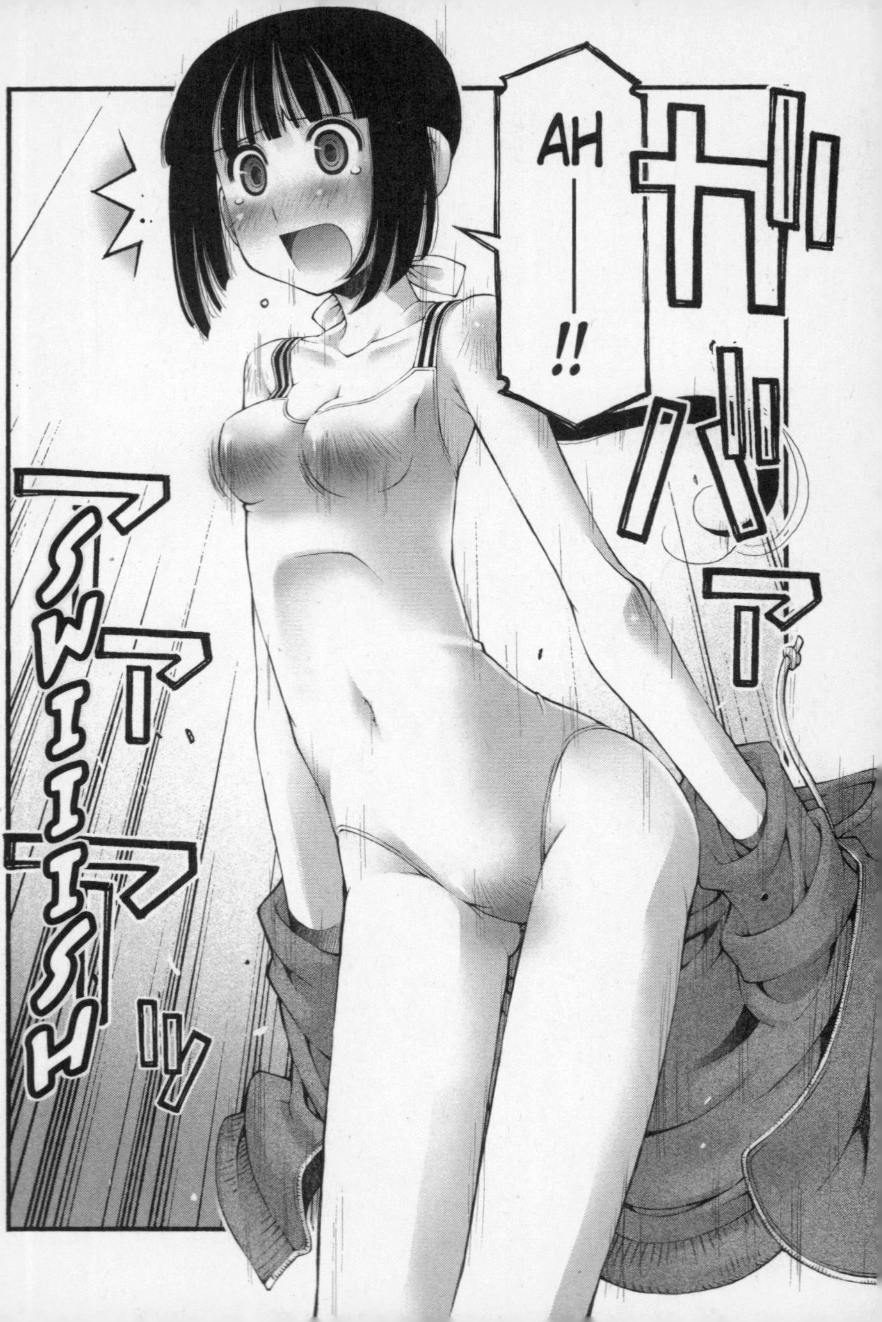
ガバァ
AH—!!
SWIIISH

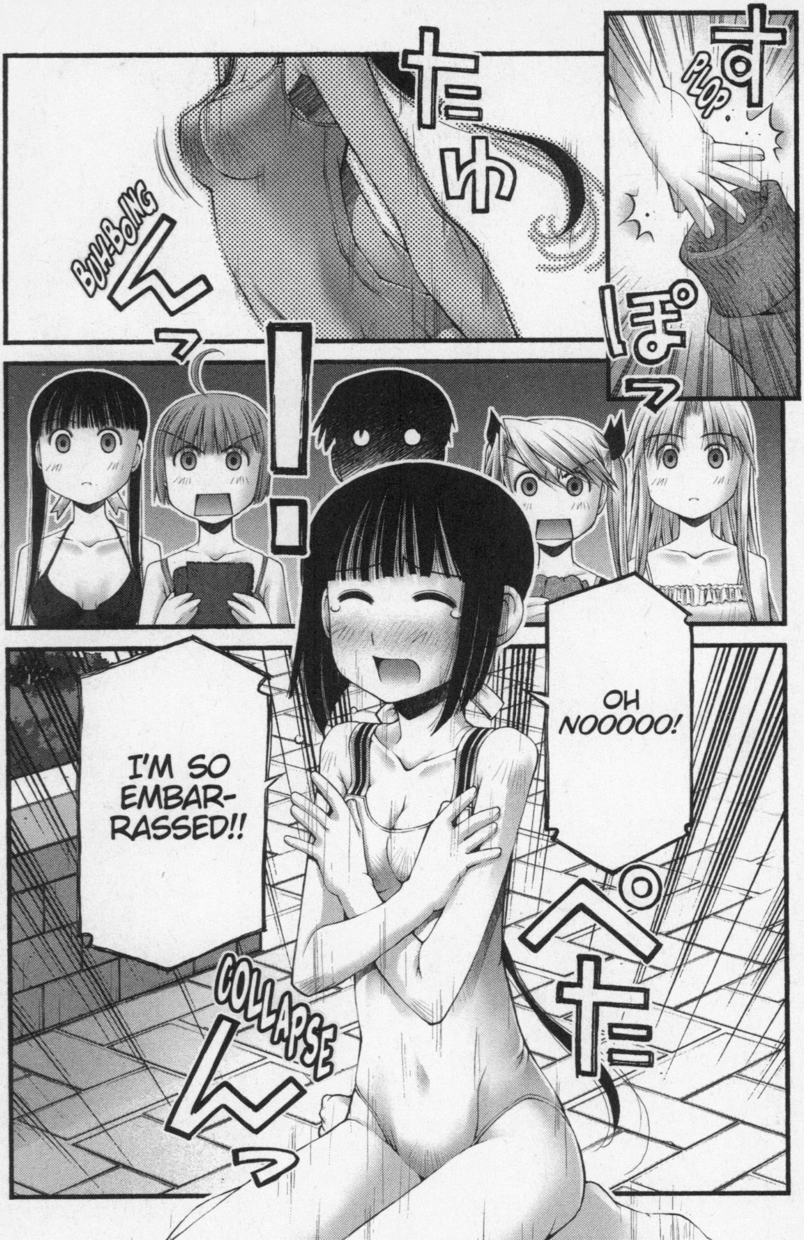
すぽっ
PLOP
たゆんっ
BUH-BOING
!!
OH NOOOOO!
I'M SO EMBARRASSED!!
ぺたんっ
COLLAPSE

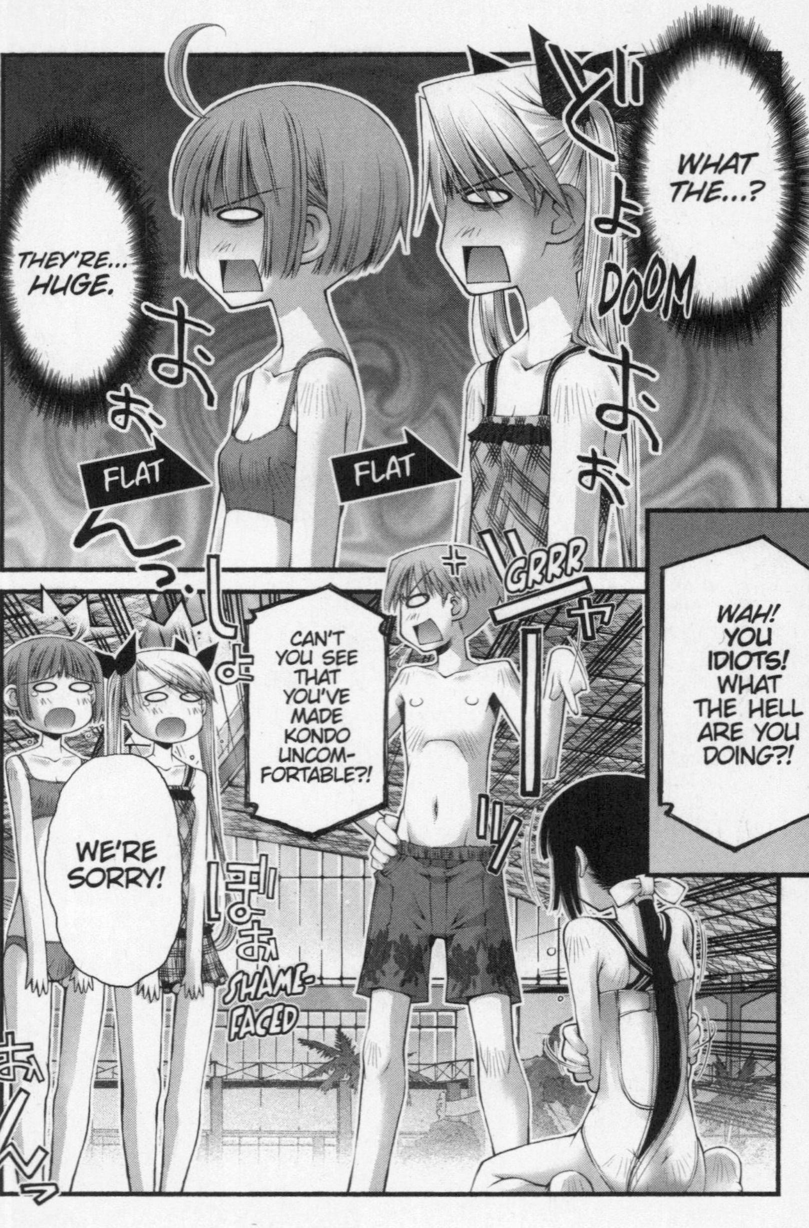
WHAT THE...?
DOOM
THEY'RE... HUGE.
FLAT
FLAT
WAH! YOU IDIOTS! WHAT THE HELL ARE YOU DOING?!
GRRR
CAN'T YOU SEE THAT YOU'VE MADE KONDO UNCOM-FORTABLE?!
WE'RE SORRY!
SHAME-FACED

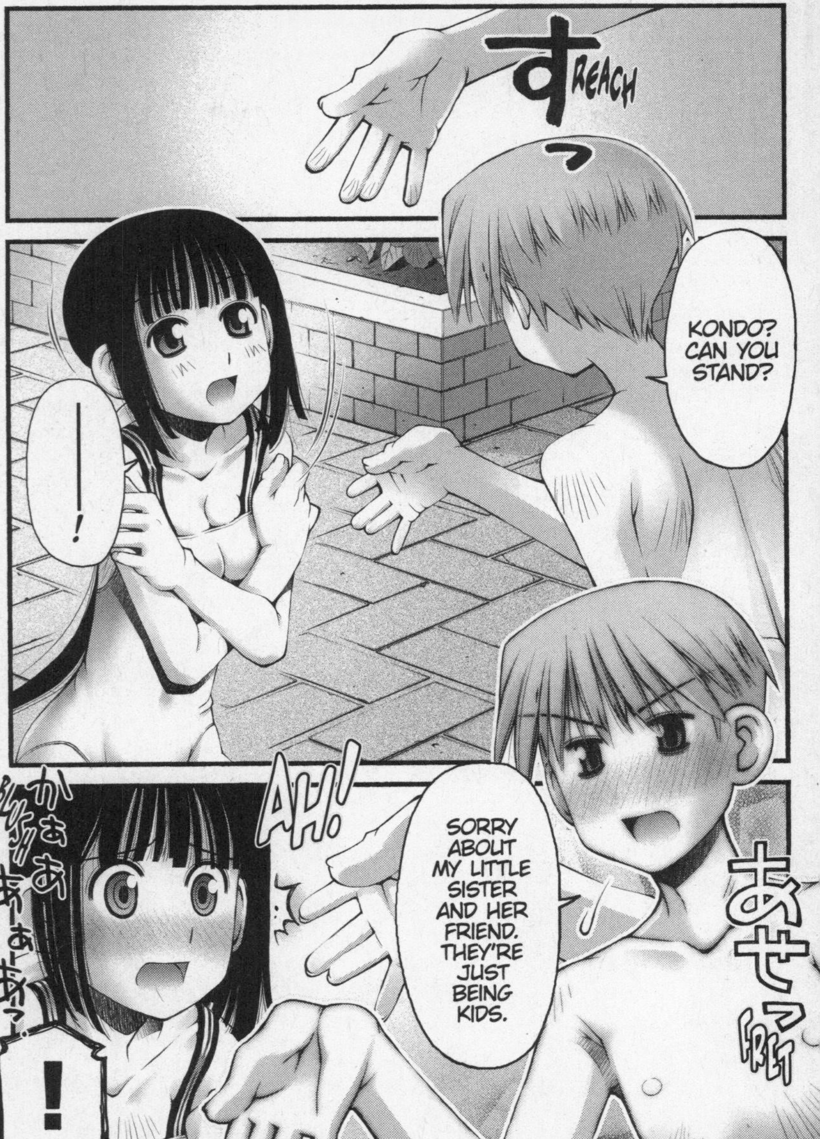
すっ
REACH
KONDO? CAN YOU STAND?
—!
あせっ
FRET
SORRY ABOUT MY LITTLE SISTER AND HER FRIEND. THEY'RE JUST BEING KIDS.
AH!
かぁぁ あーあーあっ
BLUSH
!

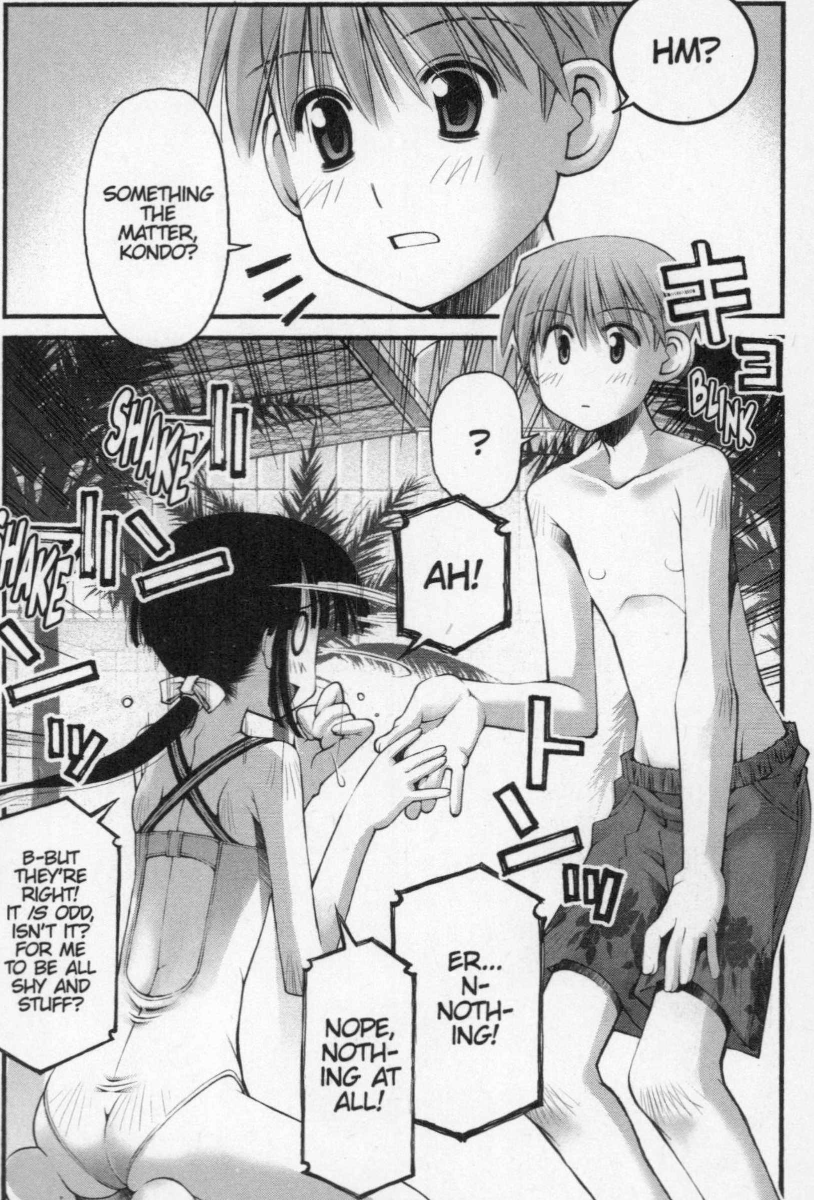
HM?
SOMETHING THE MATTER, KONDO?
キョ
BLINK
?
SHAKE
SHAKE
AH!
ト
ER... N-NOTHING!
NOPE, NOTHING AT ALL!
B-BUT THEY'RE RIGHT! IT IS ODD, ISN'T IT? FOR ME TO BE ALL SHY AND STUFF?

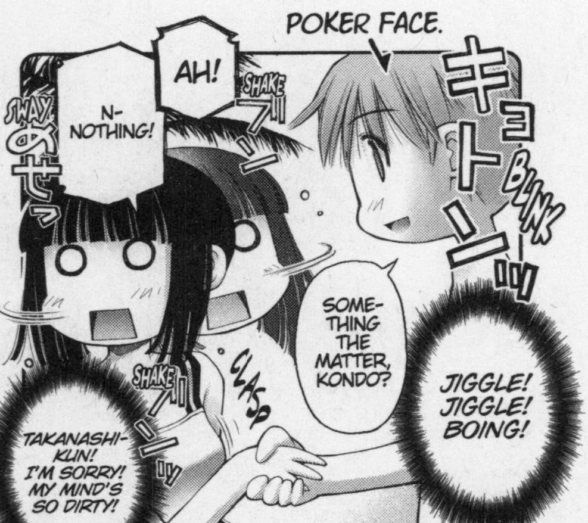
POKER FACE.
BLINK
AH!
SHAKE
N-NOTHING!
SWAY
SOMETHING THE MATTER, KONDO?
JIGGLE! JIGGLE! BOING!
CLASP
SHAKE
TAKANASHI-KUN! I'M SORRY! MY MIND'S SO DIRTY!

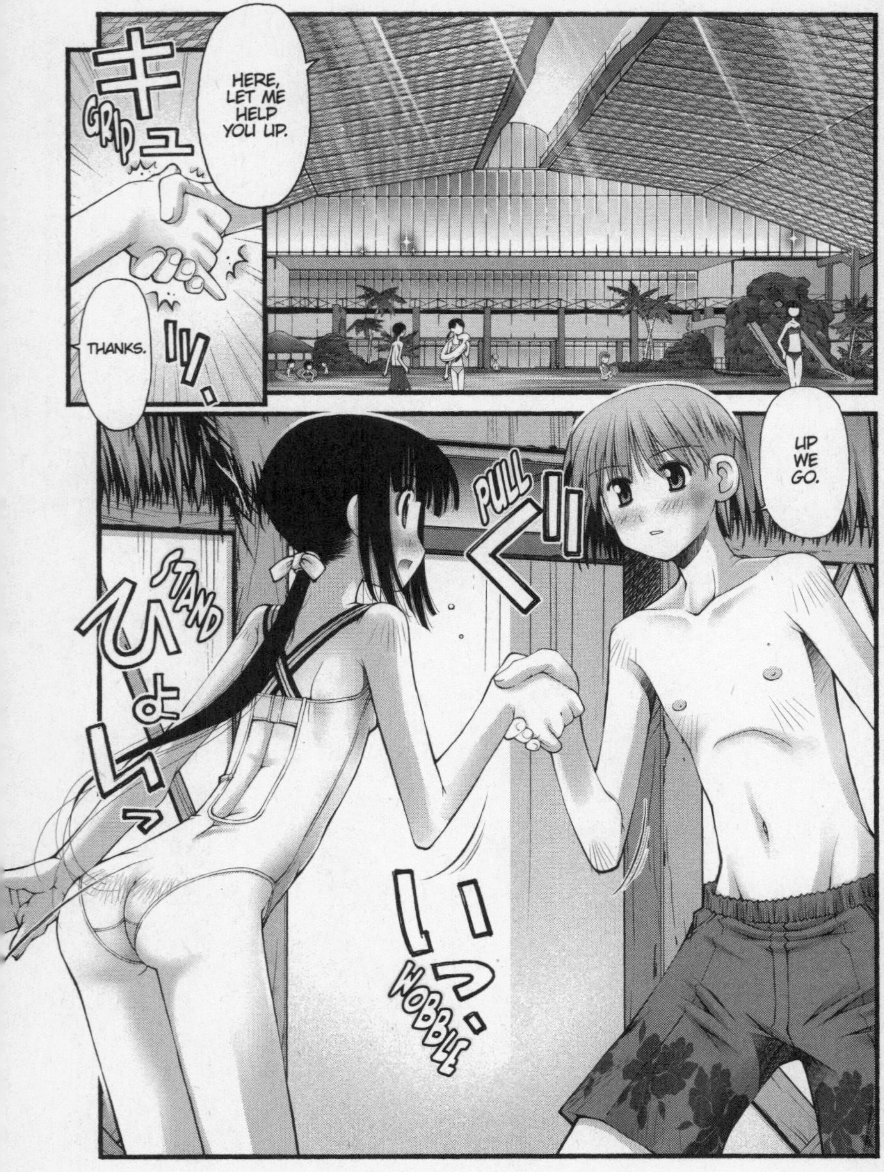
HERE, LET ME HELP YOU UP.
キュ
GRIP
THANKS.
ぃッ
UP WE GO.
ぐぃ
PULL
ひょこ
STAND
いっ
WOBBLE

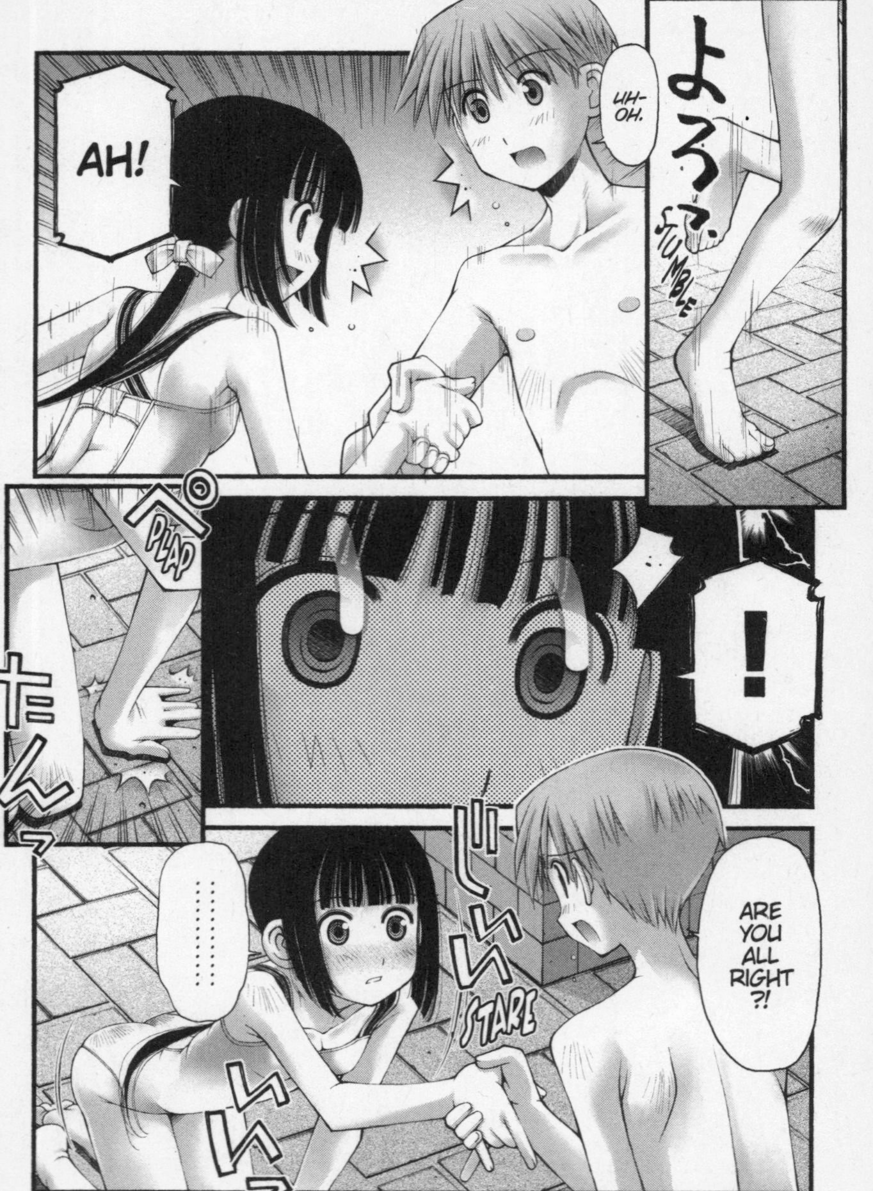
よろっ
STUMBLE
UH-OH.
AH!
!
ぺ
PLAP
たんっ
ARE YOU ALL RIGHT?!
じぃぃぃぃっ
STARE
……

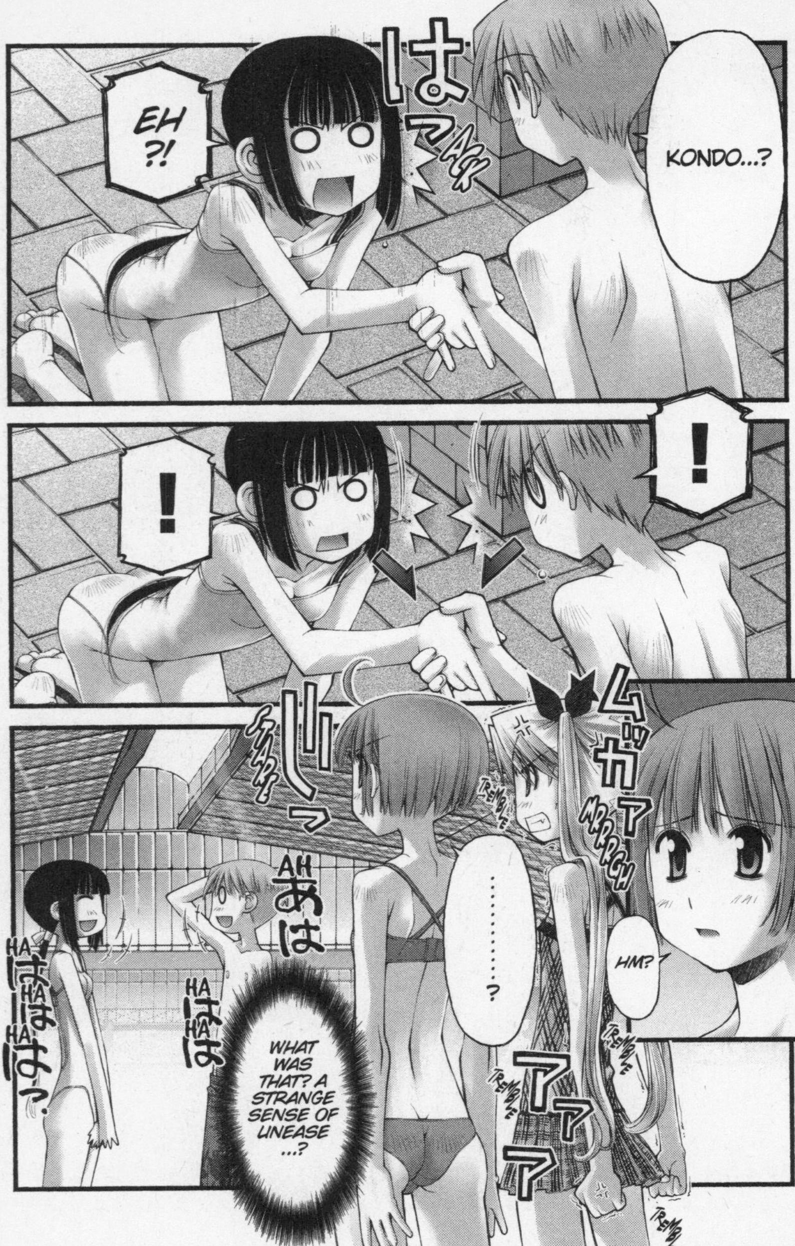
KONDO...?
はっ
ACK
EH ?!
!
!
HM?
ムッカァ
MRRRGH
TREMBLE
......?
じーしっ
STARE
WHAT WAS THAT? A STRANGE SENSE OF UNEASE ...?
TREMBLE
TREMBLE
アァァ
TREMBLE
あは
AH
ははは
HA HA HA
はははっ
HA HA HA

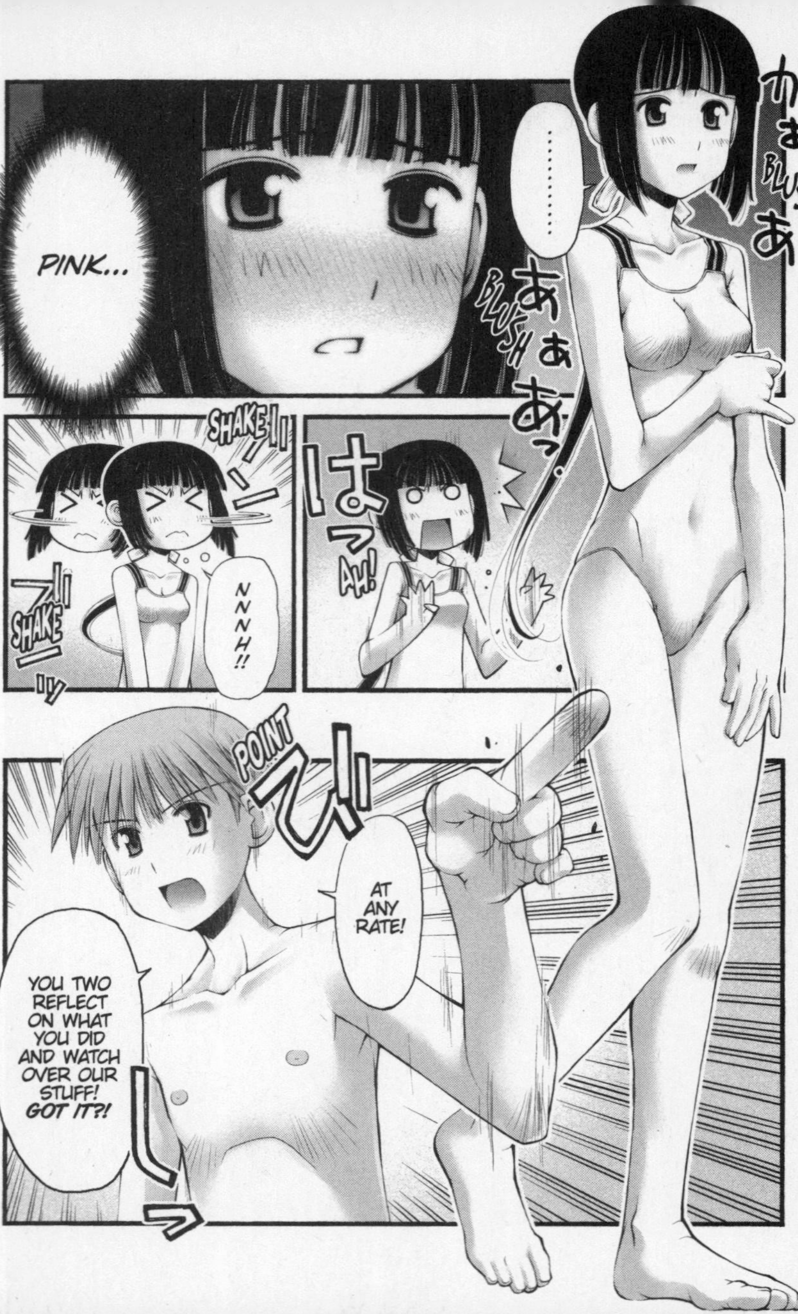
……
かぁあ
BLUSH
あぁぁあっ
BLUSH
PINK...
はっ
AH!
SHAKE
NNNH!!
SHAKE
POINT
ぴ
AT ANY RATE!
YOU TWO REFLECT ON WHAT YOU DID AND WATCH OVER OUR STUFF! GOT IT?!
しっ

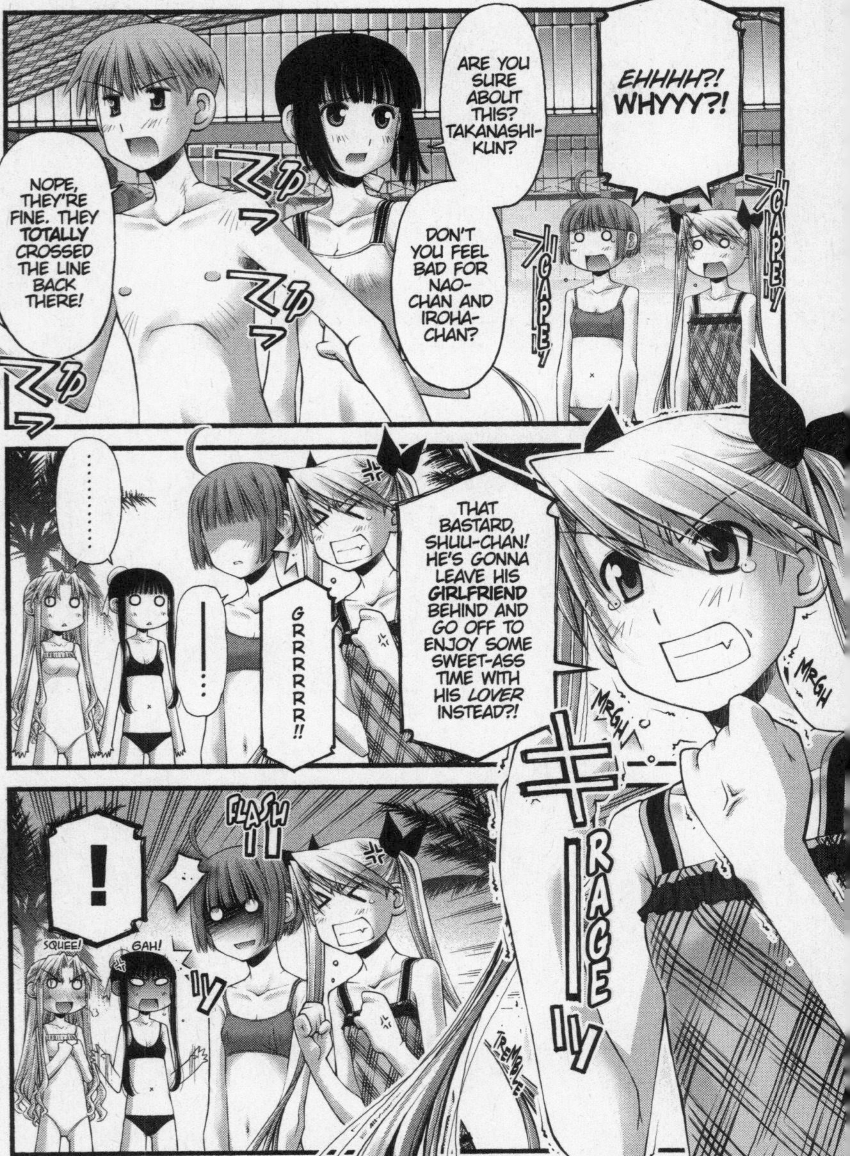
EHHHH?! WHYYY?!
GAPE!
GAPE!
ARE YOU SURE ABOUT THIS? TAKANASHI-KUN?
DON'T YOU FEEL BAD FOR NAO-CHAN AND IROHA-CHAN?
NOPE, THEY'RE FINE. THEY TOTALLY CROSSED THE LINE BACK THERE!
THAT BASTARD, SHUU-CHAN! HE'S GONNA LEAVE HIS GIRLFRIEND BEHIND AND GO OFF TO ENJOY SOME SWEET-ASS TIME WITH HIS LOVER INSTEAD?!
MRGH
MRGH
RAGE!
TREMBLE
GRRRRRR!!
......
......!
FLASH!
!
SQUEE!
GAH!

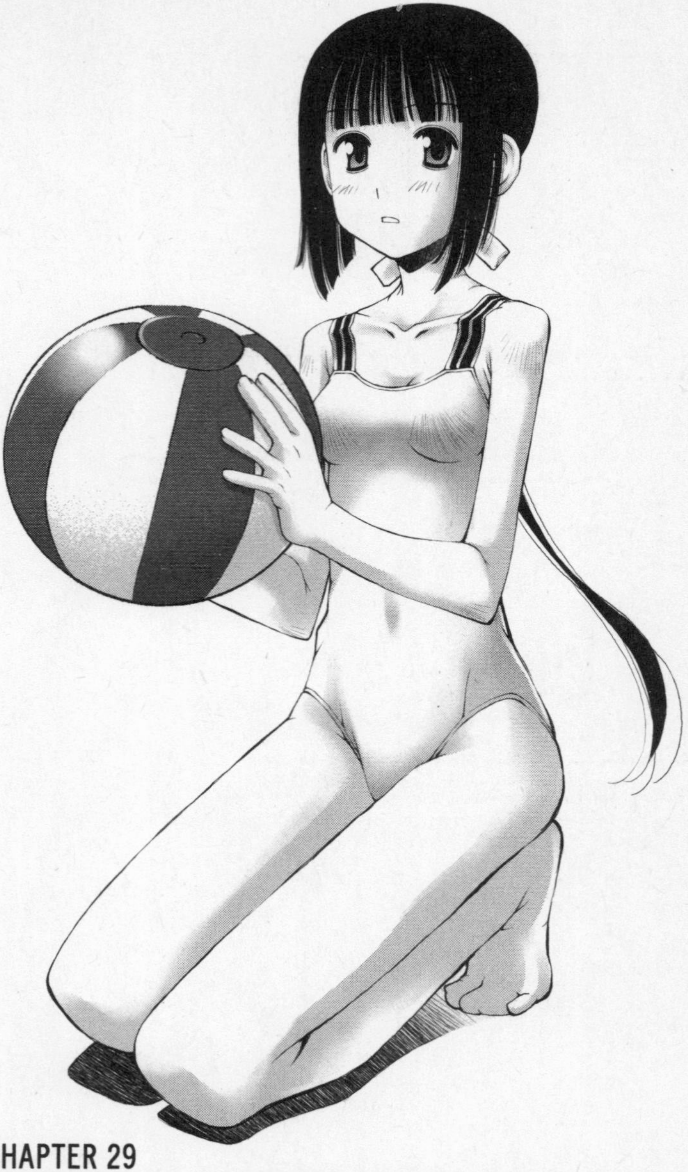

CHAPTER 29

A Beautiful and Sensitive Protuberance

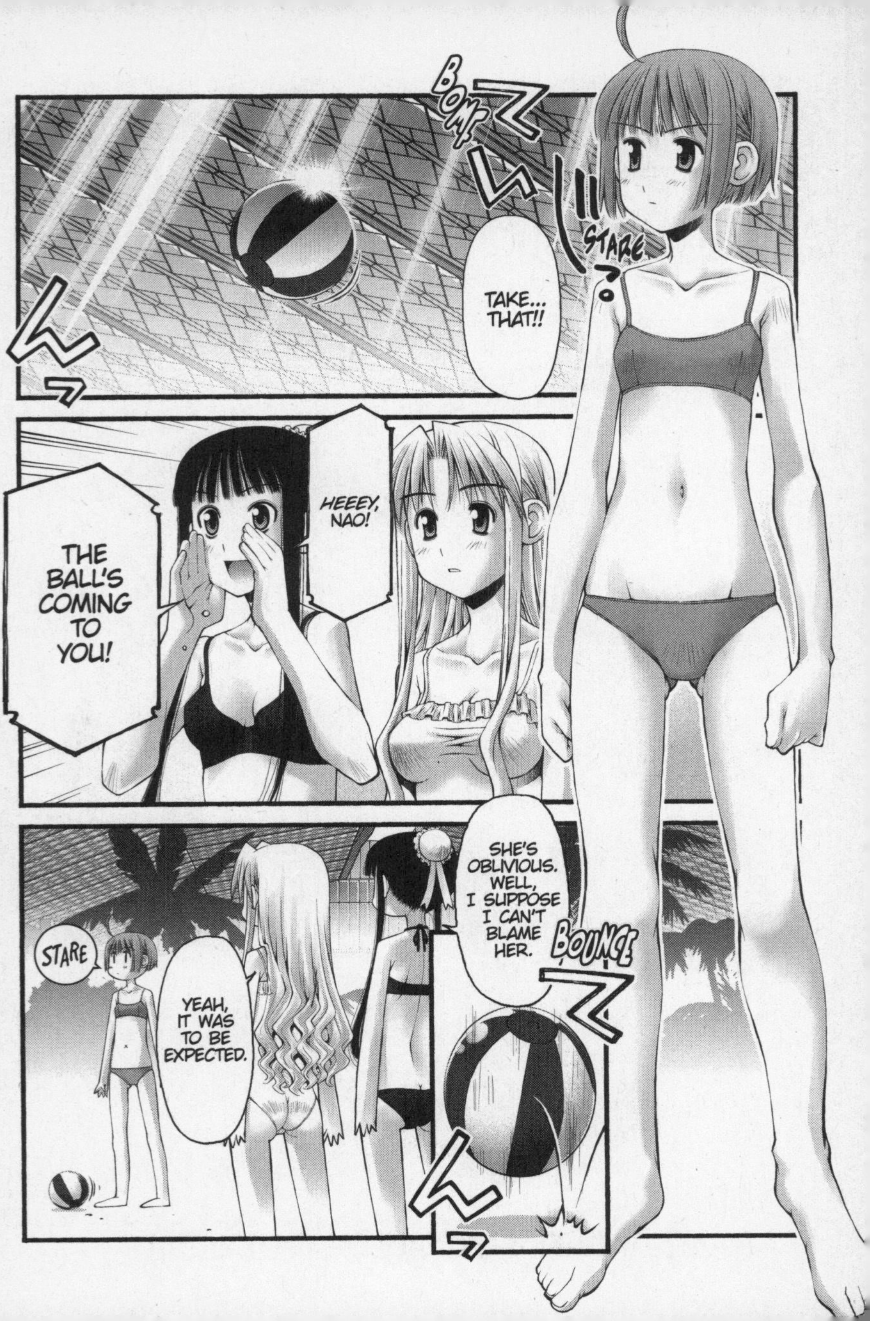
BOMF
TAKE... THAT!!
STARE
HEEEY, NAO!
THE BALL'S COMING TO YOU!
SHE'S OBLIVIOUS. WELL, I SUPPOSE I CAN'T BLAME HER.
BOUNCE
YEAH, IT WAS TO BE EXPECTED.
STARE

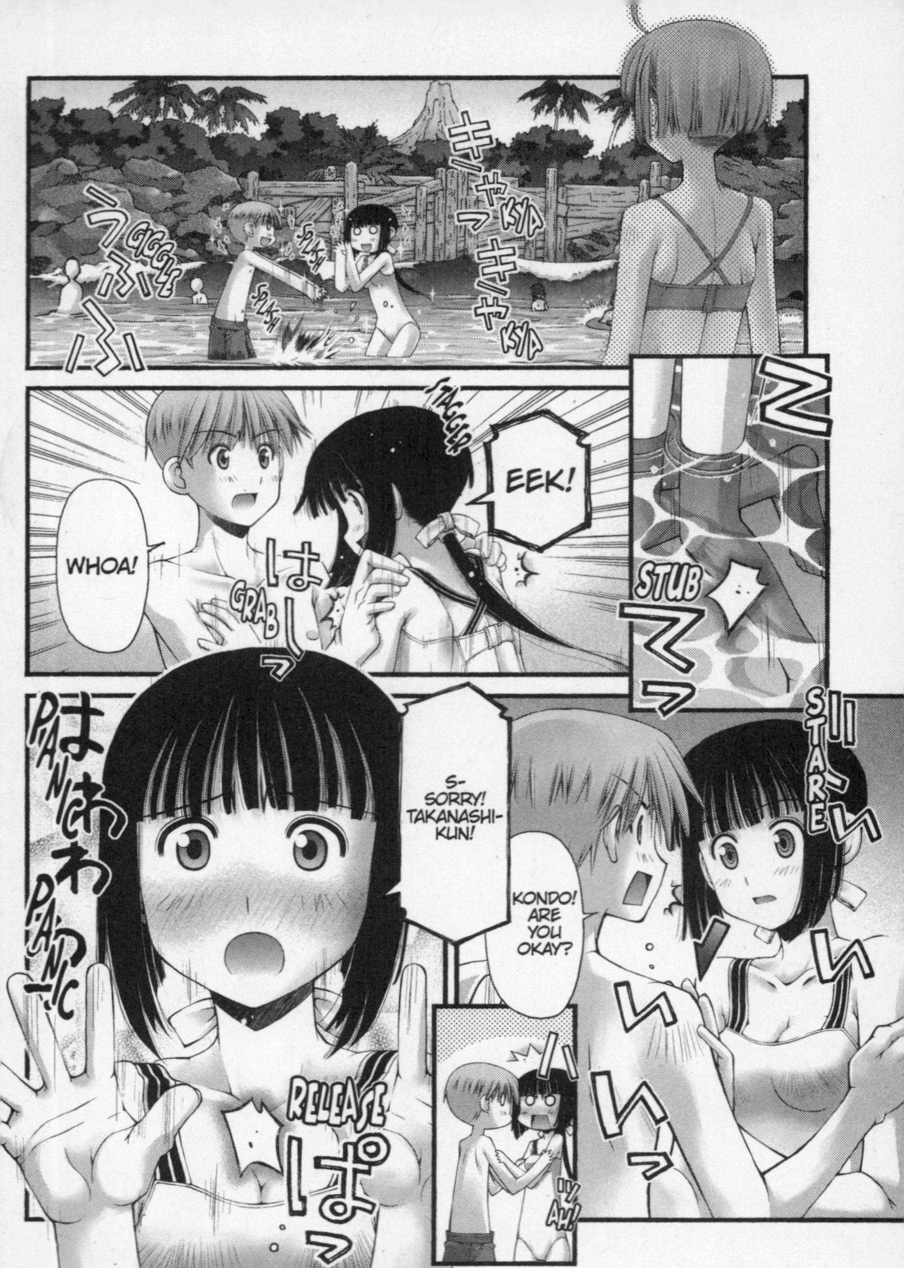

キャッキャッ
KYA KYA
SPLASH
SPLASH
うふふ
GIGGLE
STUB
STAGGER
EEK!
WHOA!
はしっ
GRAB
STARE
KONDO! ARE YOU OKAY?
AH!
S-SORRY! TAKANASHI-KUN!
はわわ
PANIC PANIC
ぱっ
RELEASE

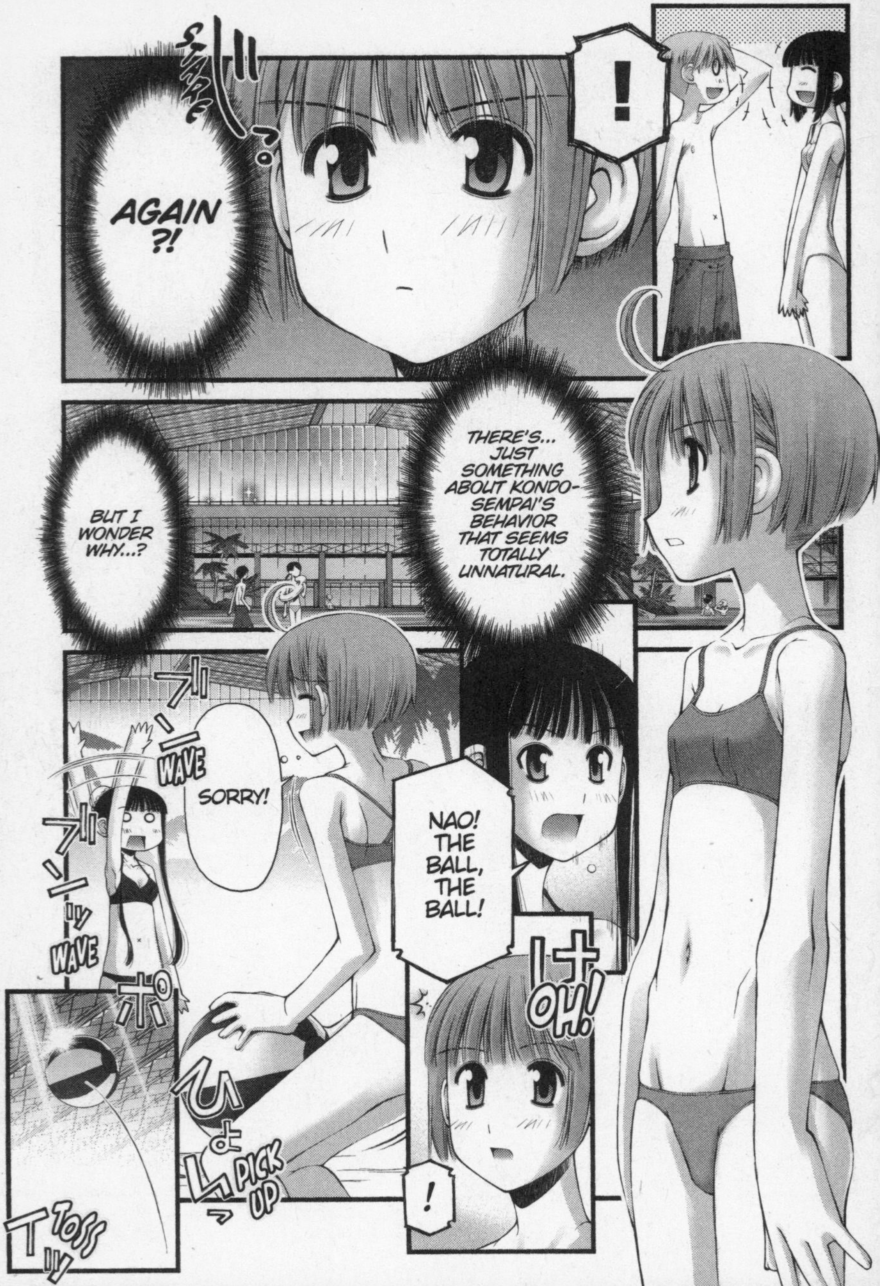
!
STARE
AGAIN ?!
THERE'S... JUST SOMETHING ABOUT KONDO-SEMPAI'S BEHAVIOR THAT SEEMS TOTALLY UNNATURAL.
BUT I WONDER WHY...?
NAO! THE BALL, THE BALL!
OH!
!
SORRY!
WAVE
WAVE
PICK UP
TOSS

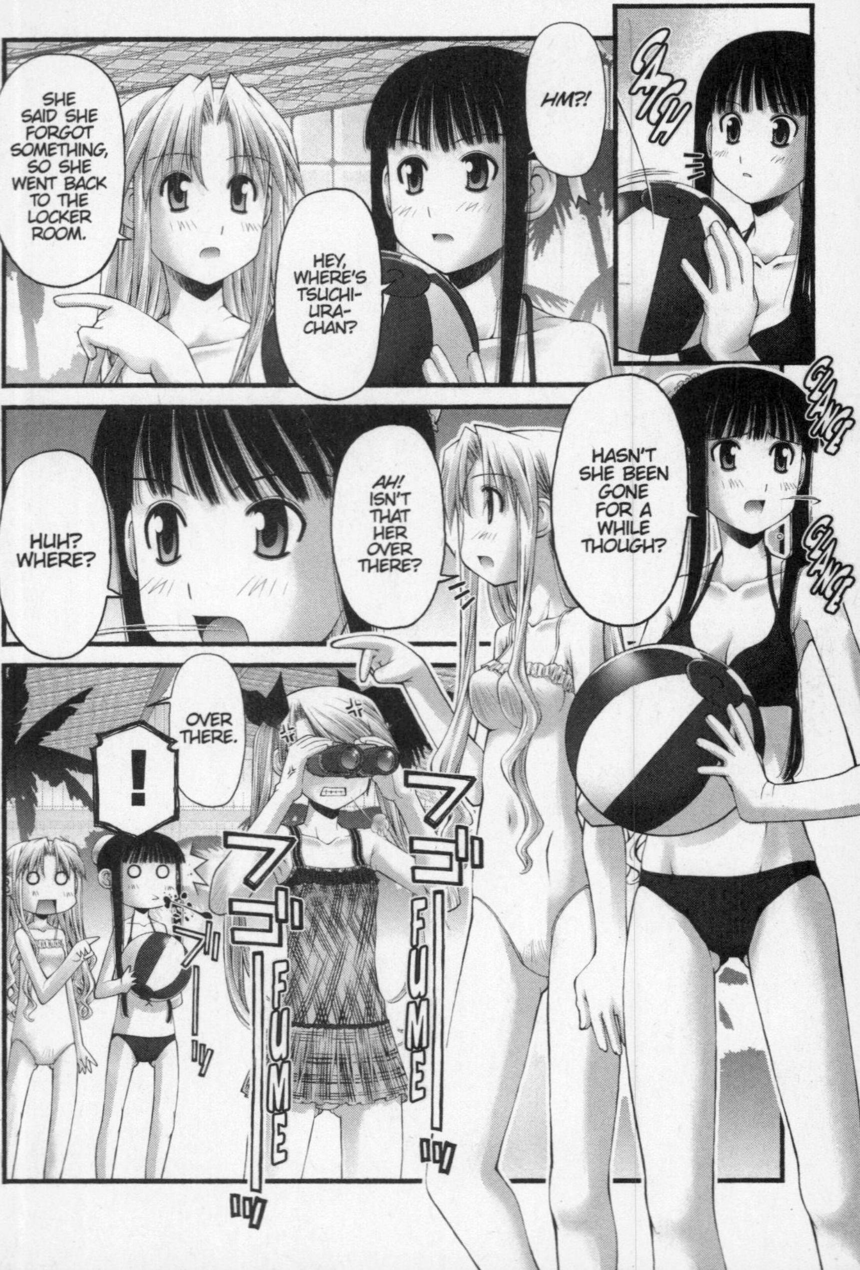
CATCH
HM?!
HEY, WHERE'S TSUCHIURA-CHAN?
SHE SAID SHE FORGOT SOMETHING, SO SHE WENT BACK TO THE LOCKER ROOM.
GLANCE
GLANCE
HASN'T SHE BEEN GONE FOR A WHILE THOUGH?
AH! ISN'T THAT HER OVER THERE?
HUH? WHERE?
OVER THERE.
!
FUME
FUME

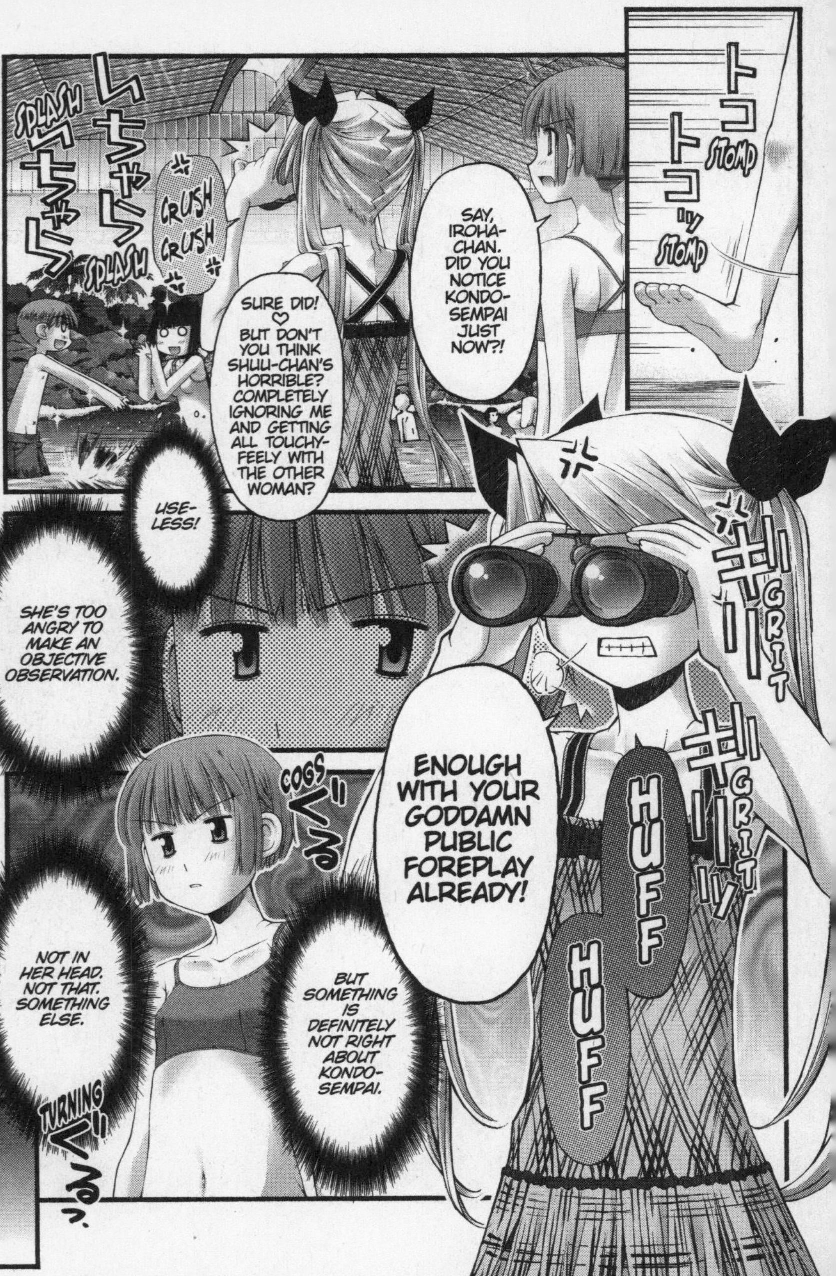
STOMP
STOMP
SAY, IROHA-CHAN. DID YOU NOTICE KONDO-SEMPAI JUST NOW?!
SURE DID! ♡ BUT DON'T YOU THINK SHUU-CHAN'S HORRIBLE? COMPLETELY IGNORING ME AND GETTING ALL TOUCHY-FEELY WITH THE OTHER WOMAN?
CRUSH CRUSH
SPLASH
SPLASH
GRIT
GRIT
ENOUGH WITH YOUR GODDAMN PUBLIC FOREPLAY ALREADY!
HUFF
HUFF
USE-LESS!
SHE'S TOO ANGRY TO MAKE AN OBJECTIVE OBSERVATION.
COGS
BUT SOMETHING IS DEFINITELY NOT RIGHT ABOUT KONDO-SEMPAI.
NOT IN HER HEAD. NOT THAT. SOMETHING ELSE.
TURNING

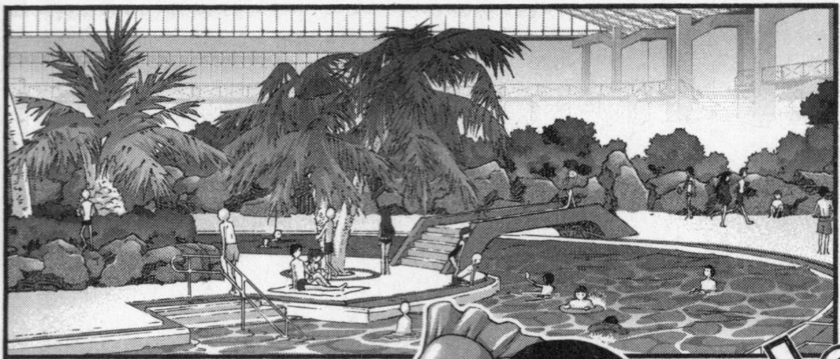

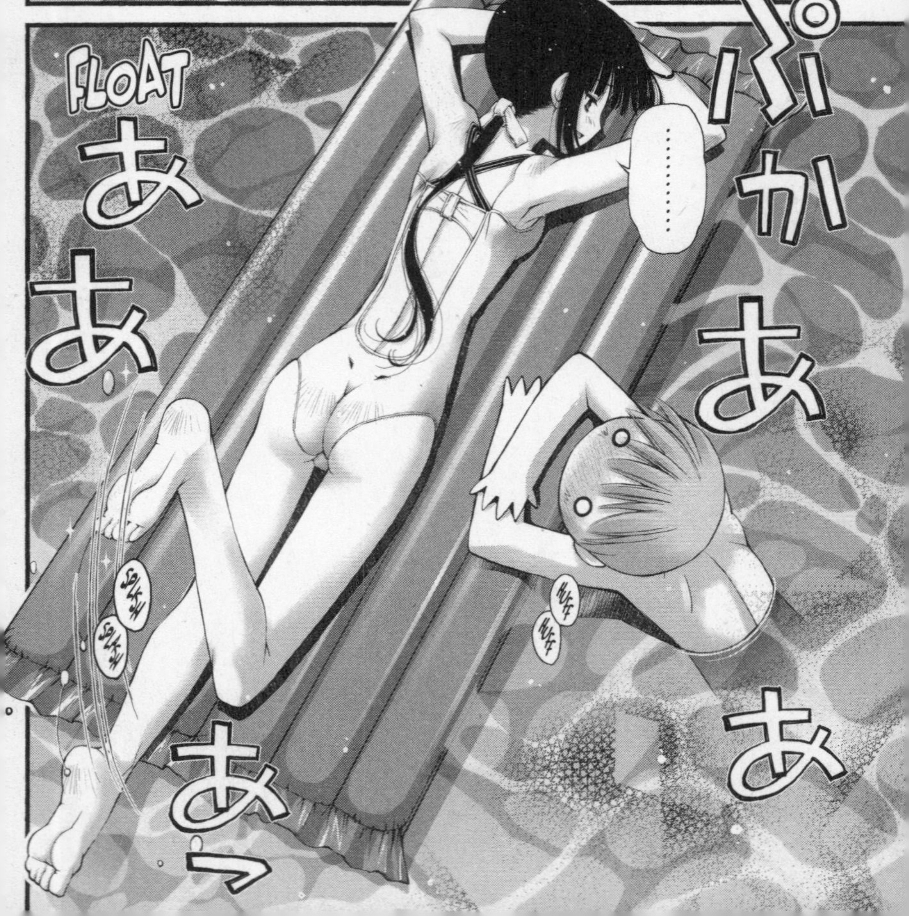
ぷかーあ
あ
……
HUFF HUFF
FLOAT
ああ
SPLSH SPLSH
あっ

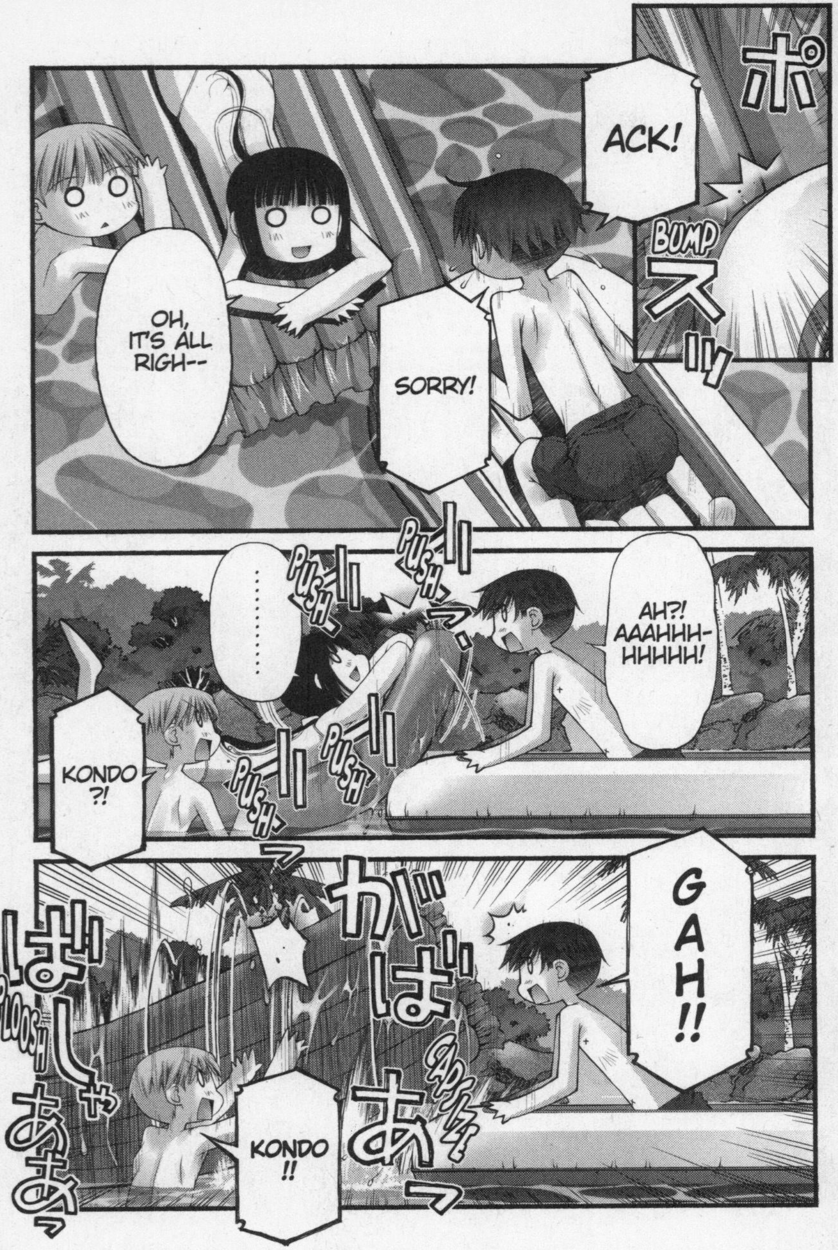
ポスッ
ACK!
BUMP
SORRY!
OH, IT'S ALL RIGH--
AH?! AAAHHH-HHHHH!
PUSH
PUSH
......
PUSH
PUSH
KONDO?!
GAH!!
がばぁっ
CAPSIZE!
KONDO!!
ばしゃあぁっ
SPLOOSH

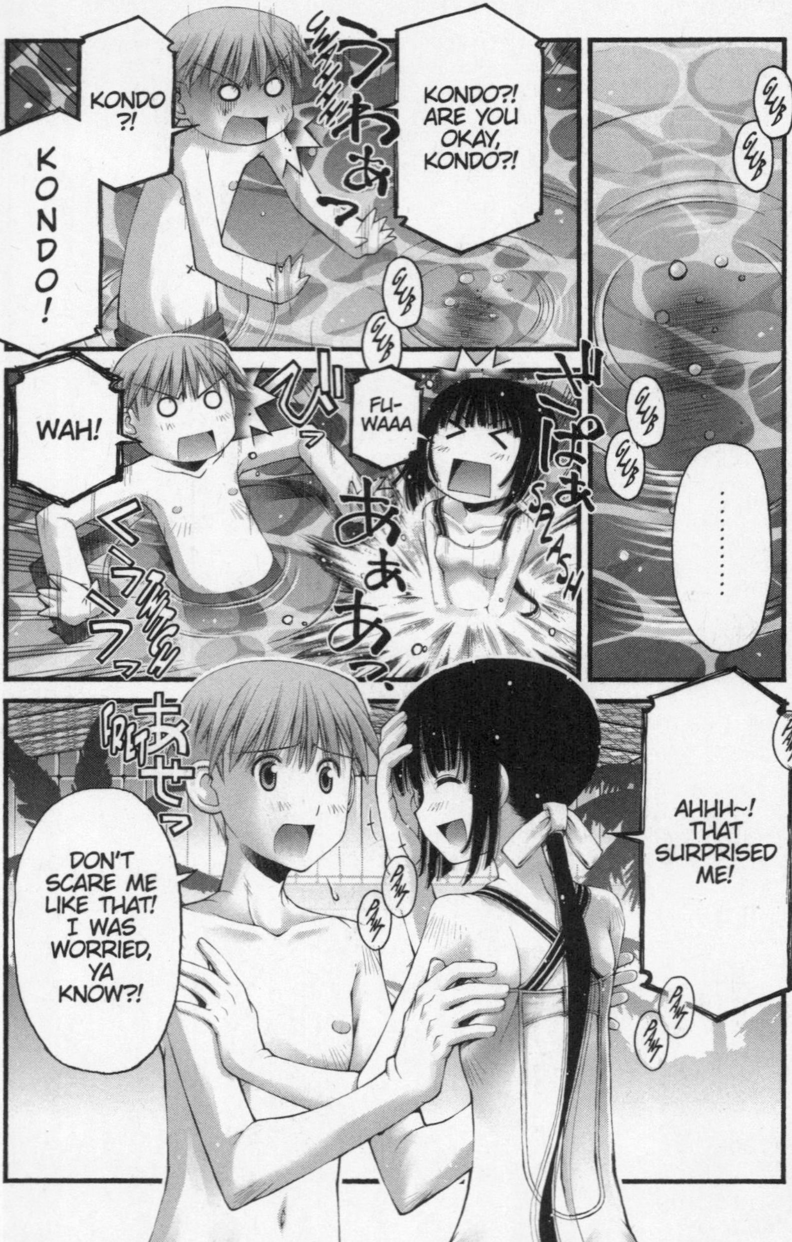
GLUB
GLUB
GLUB
GLUB
......
KONDO?! ARE YOU OKAY, KONDO?!
KONDO ?!
KONDO!
GLUB
GLUB
SPLASH
FU-WAAA
WAH!
PAW
PAW
AHHH~! THAT SURPRISED ME!
PAW
PAW
DON'T SCARE ME LIKE THAT! I WAS WORRIED, YA KNOW?!
PAW
PAW

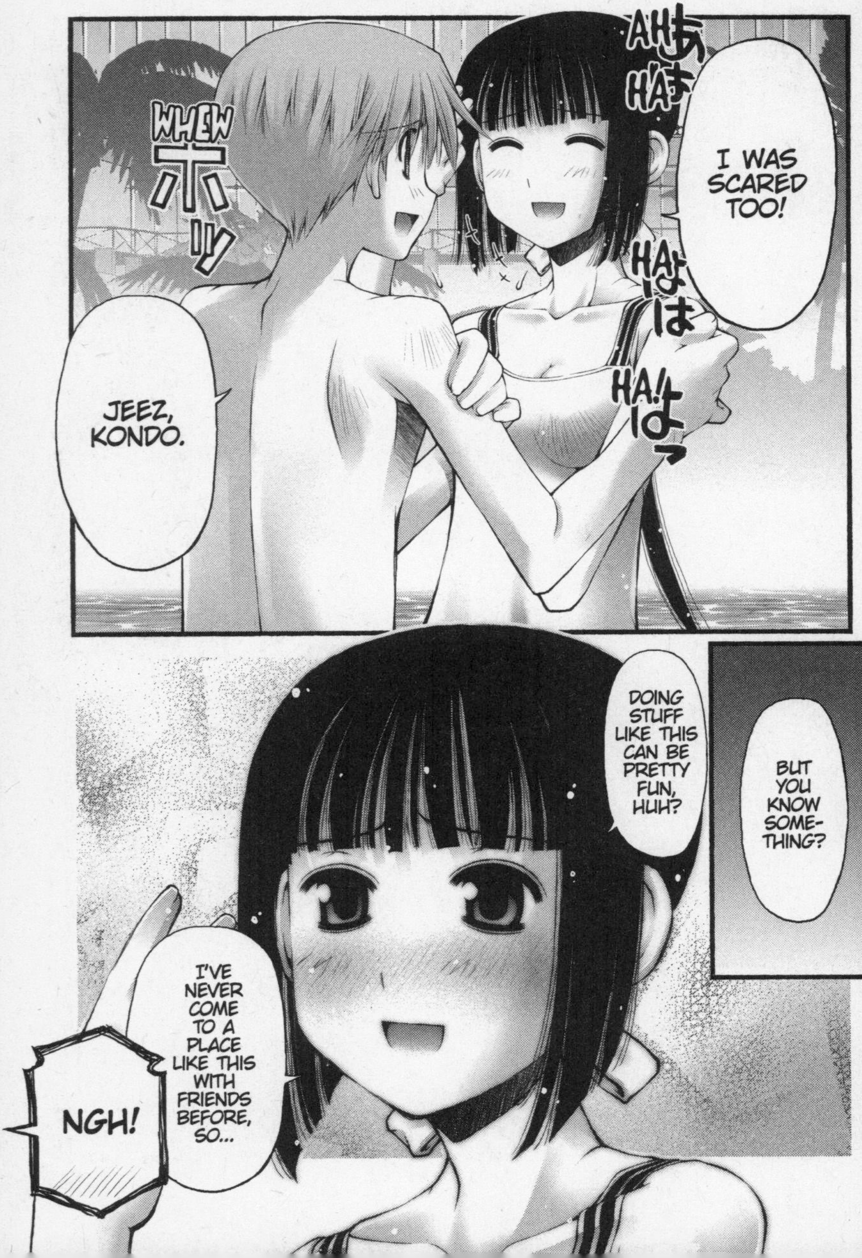
AH HA
I WAS SCARED TOO!
HA は
HA! はっ
WHEW ホッ
JEEZ, KONDO.
BUT YOU KNOW SOME-THING?
DOING STUFF LIKE THIS CAN BE PRETTY FUN, HUH?
I'VE NEVER COME TO A PLACE LIKE THIS WITH FRIENDS BEFORE, SO...
NGH!

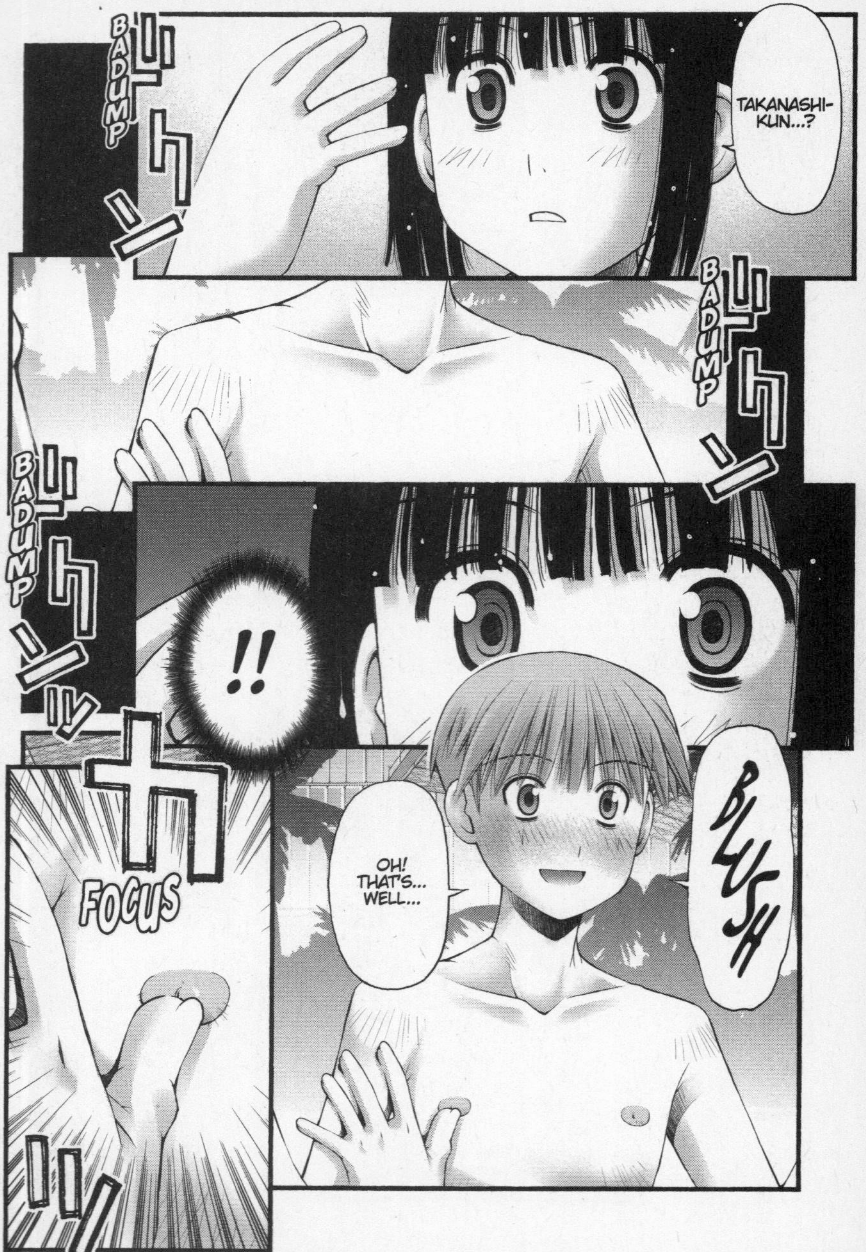
TAKANASHI-KUN...?
BADUMP
BADUMP
!!
BADUMP
BLUSH
OH! THAT'S... WELL...
FOCUS

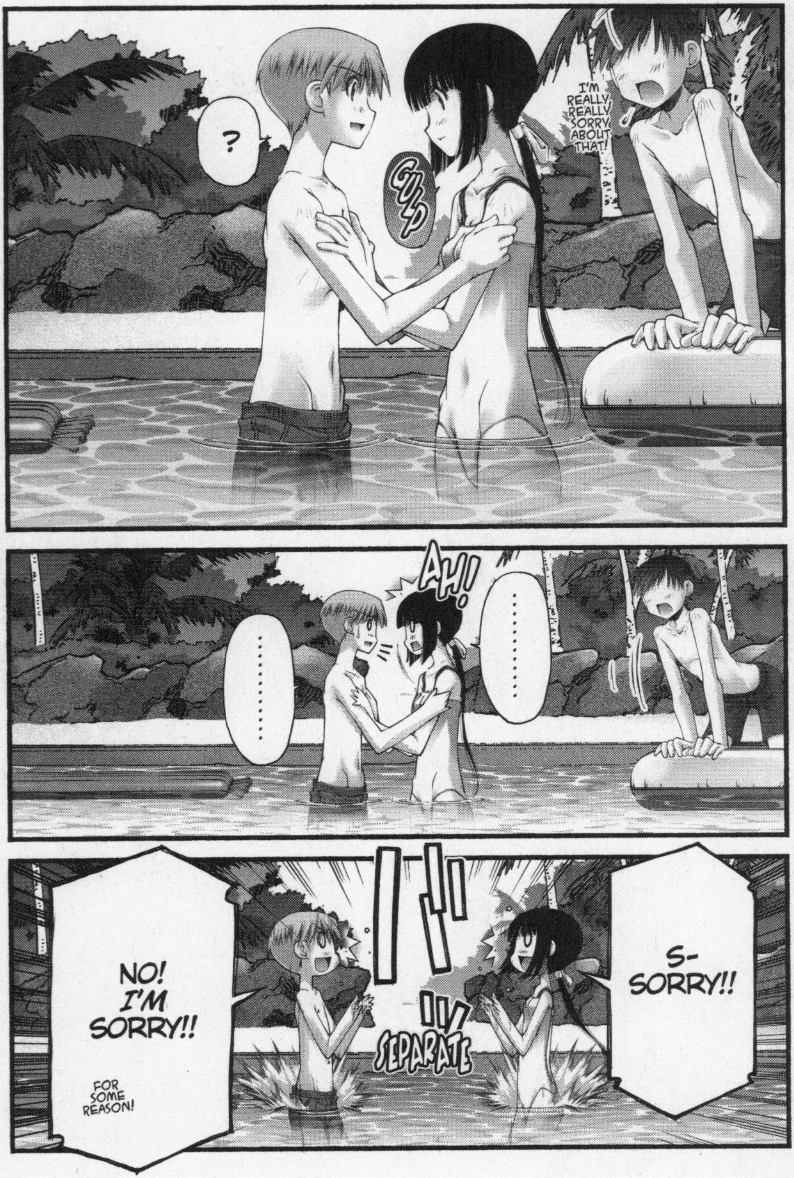
I'M REALLY, REALLY SORRY ABOUT THAT!
GULP
?
AH!
......
......
S-SORRY!!
SEPARATE
NO! I'M SORRY!!
FOR SOME REASON!

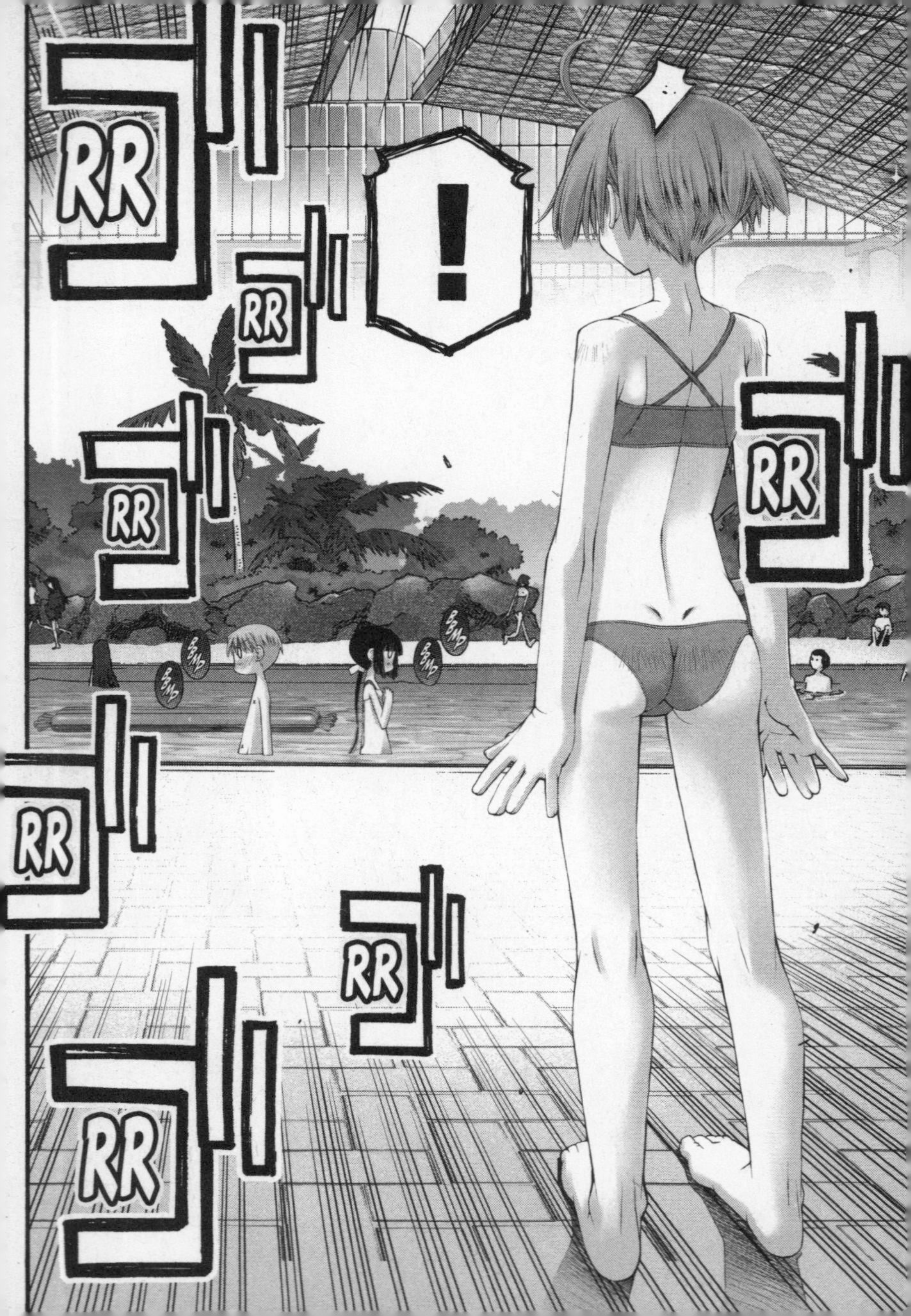
RR
RR
!
RR
RR
BBMP
BBMP
BBMP
BBMP
RR
RR
RR

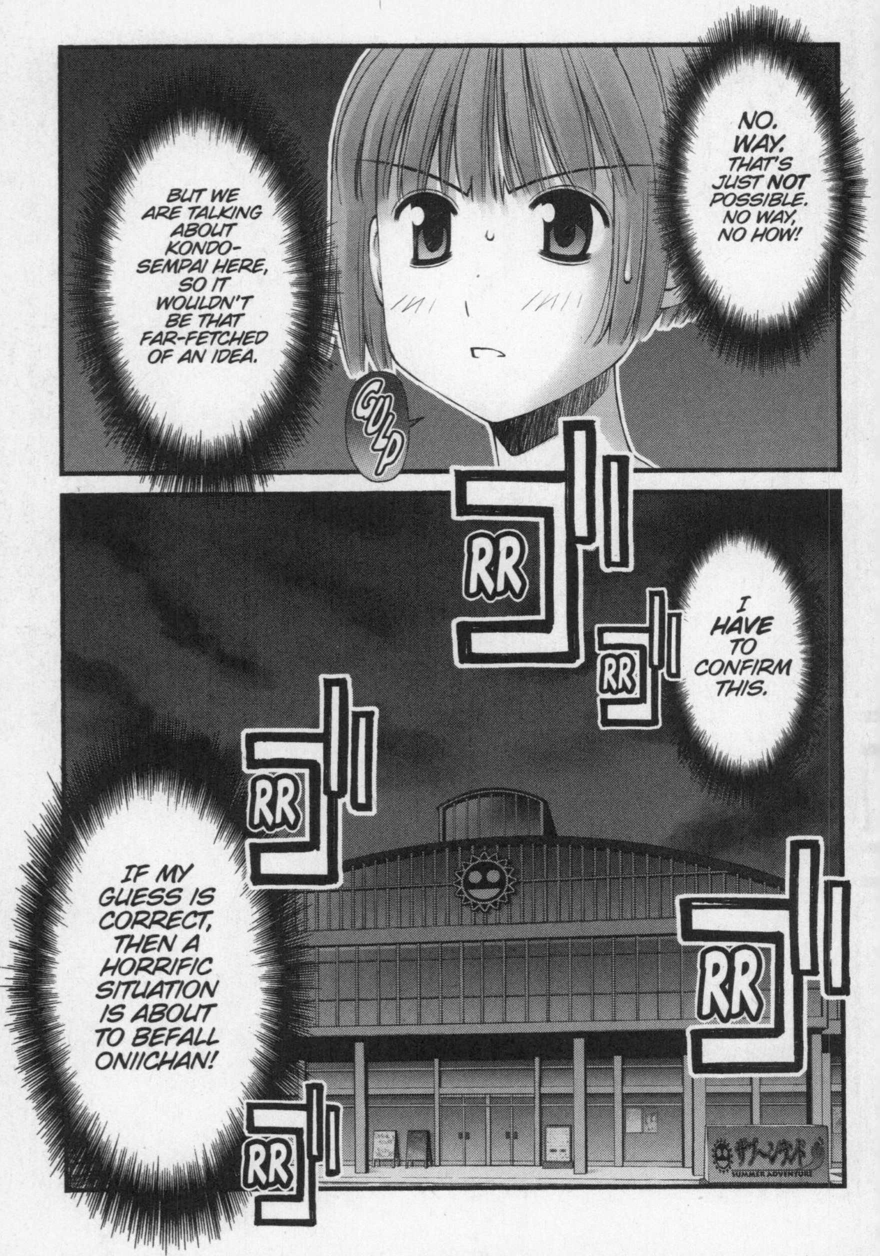
NO. WAY. THAT'S JUST NOT POSSIBLE. NO WAY, NO HOW!
BUT WE ARE TALKING ABOUT KONDO-SEMPAI HERE, SO IT WOULDN'T BE THAT FAR-FETCHED OF AN IDEA.
GULP
RR
I HAVE TO CONFIRM THIS.
RR
RR
RR
IF MY GUESS IS CORRECT, THEN A HORRIFIC SITUATION IS ABOUT TO BEFALL ONIICHAN!
RR

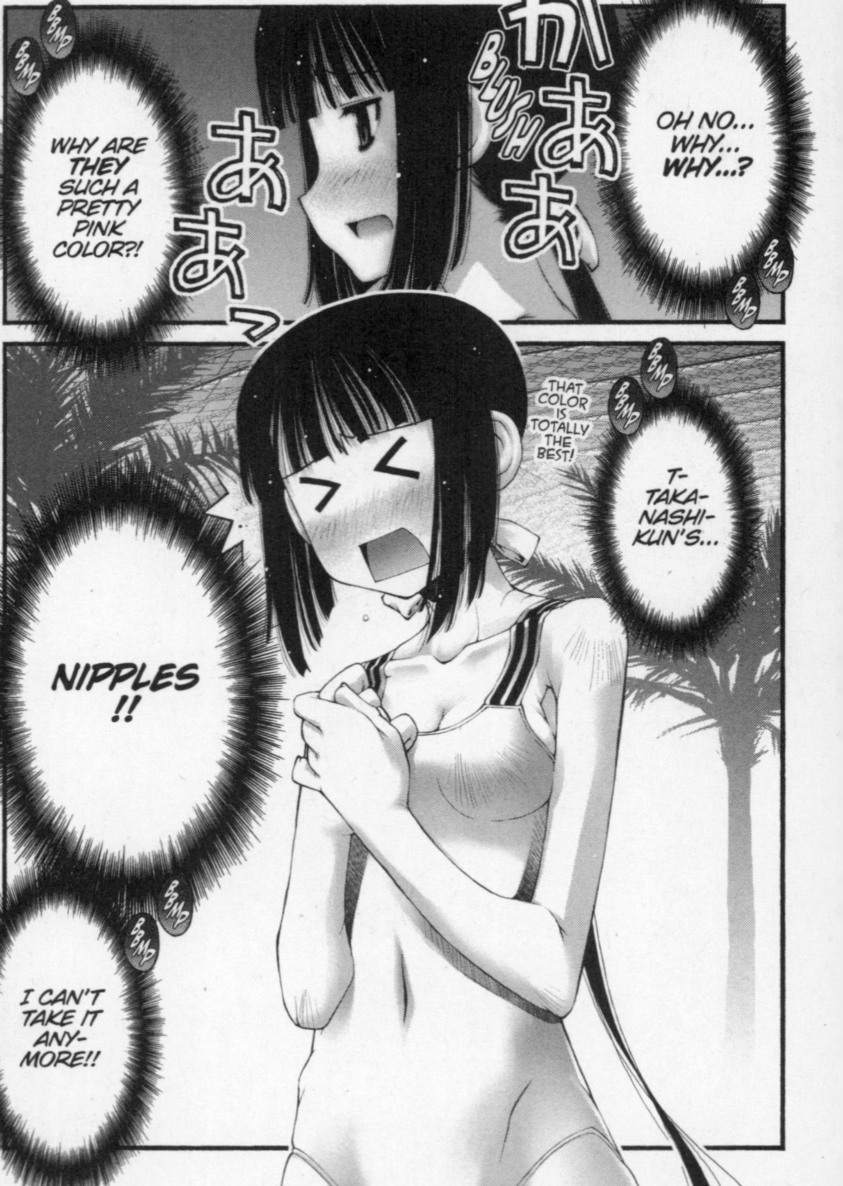

BBMP
BBMP
OH NO... WHY... WHY...?
かあああああっ
BLUSH
WHY ARE THEY SUCH A PRETTY PINK COLOR?!
BBMP
BBMP
BBMP
BBMP
THAT COLOR IS TOTALLY THE BEST!
T-TAKANASHI-KUN'S...
NIPPLES!!
BBMP
BBMP
I CAN'T TAKE IT ANYMORE!!

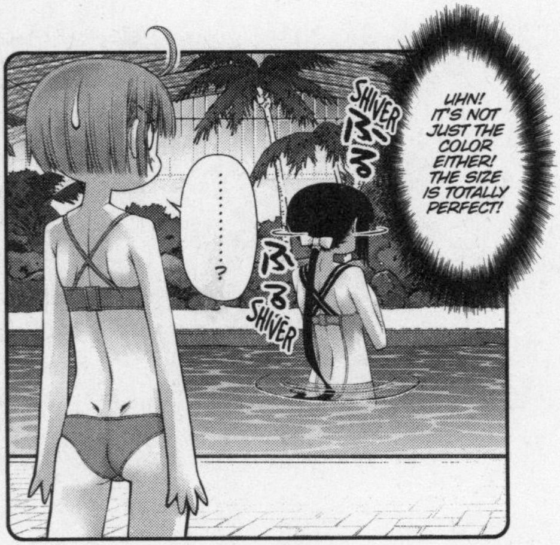
UHN! IT'S NOT JUST THE COLOR EITHER! THE SIZE IS TOTALLY PERFECT!
SHIVER ぶる
ぶる SHIVER
.........?

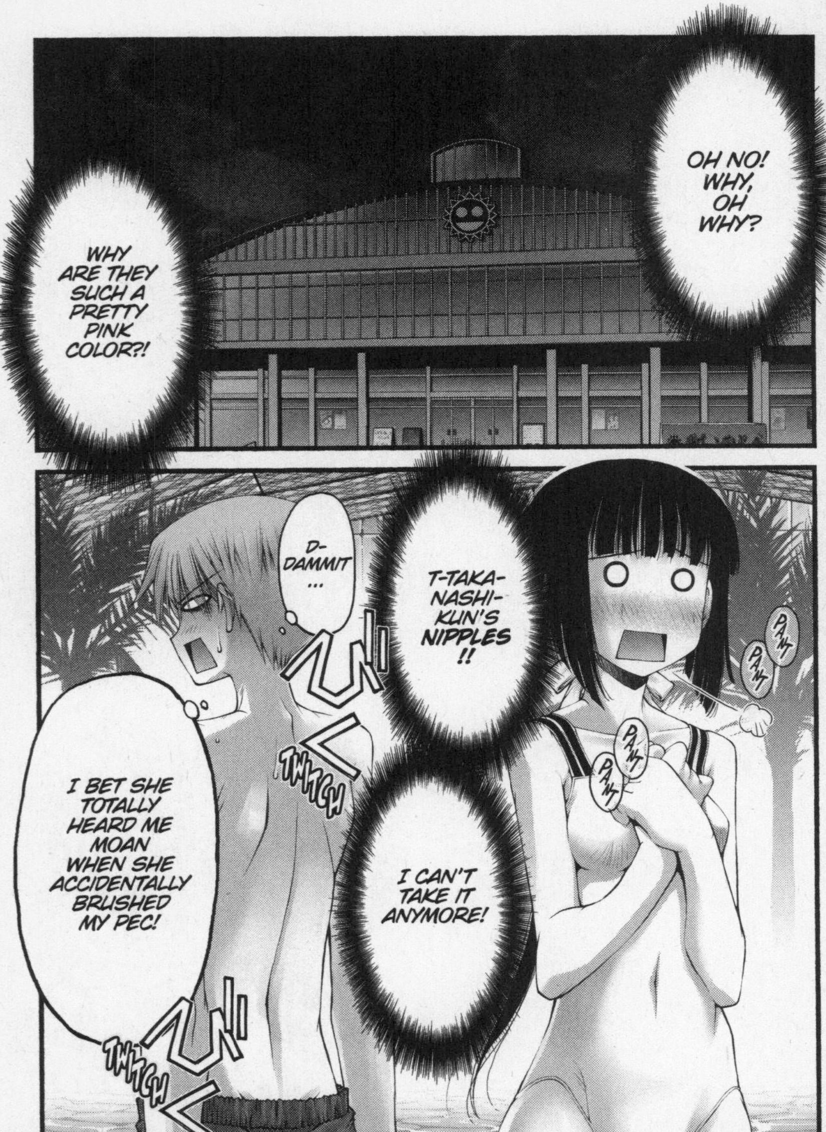
OH NO! WHY, OH WHY?
WHY ARE THEY SUCH A PRETTY PINK COLOR?!
T-TAKA-NASHI-KUN'S NIPPLES!!
PANT PANT PANT
PANT PANT
I CAN'T TAKE IT ANYMORE!
D-DAMMIT...
TWITCH
I BET SHE TOTALLY HEARD ME MOAN WHEN SHE ACCIDENTALLY BRUSHED MY PEC!
TWITCH

CHAPTER 30
That Which is Dear to a Big Brother

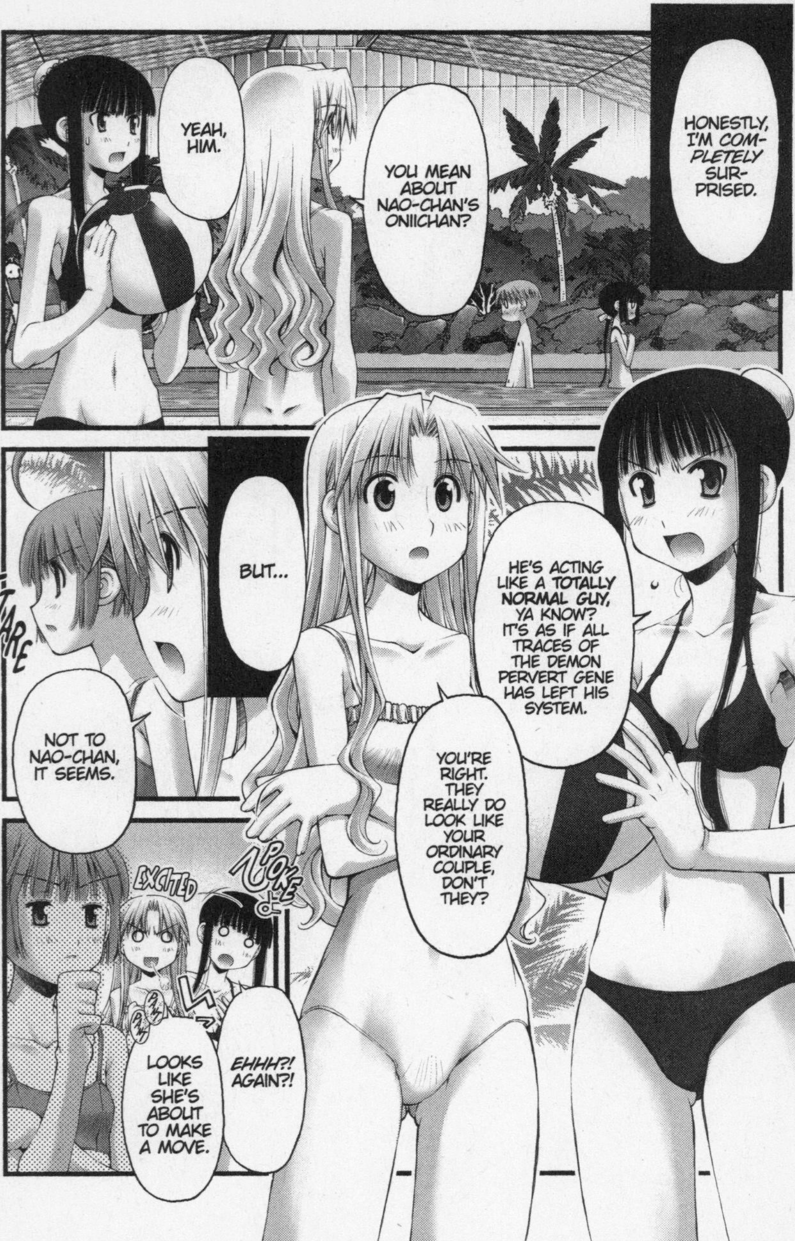

HONESTLY, I'M COMPLETELY SURPRISED.
YOU MEAN ABOUT NAO-CHAN'S ONIICHAN?
YEAH, HIM.
HE'S ACTING LIKE A TOTALLY NORMAL GUY, YA KNOW? IT'S AS IF ALL TRACES OF THE DEMON PERVERT GENE HAS LEFT HIS SYSTEM.
YOU'RE RIGHT. THEY REALLY DO LOOK LIKE YOUR ORDINARY COUPLE, DON'T THEY?
BUT...
STARE
NOT TO NAO-CHAN, IT SEEMS.
POKE
EXCITED
EHHH?! AGAIN?!
LOOKS LIKE SHE'S ABOUT TO MAKE A MOVE.

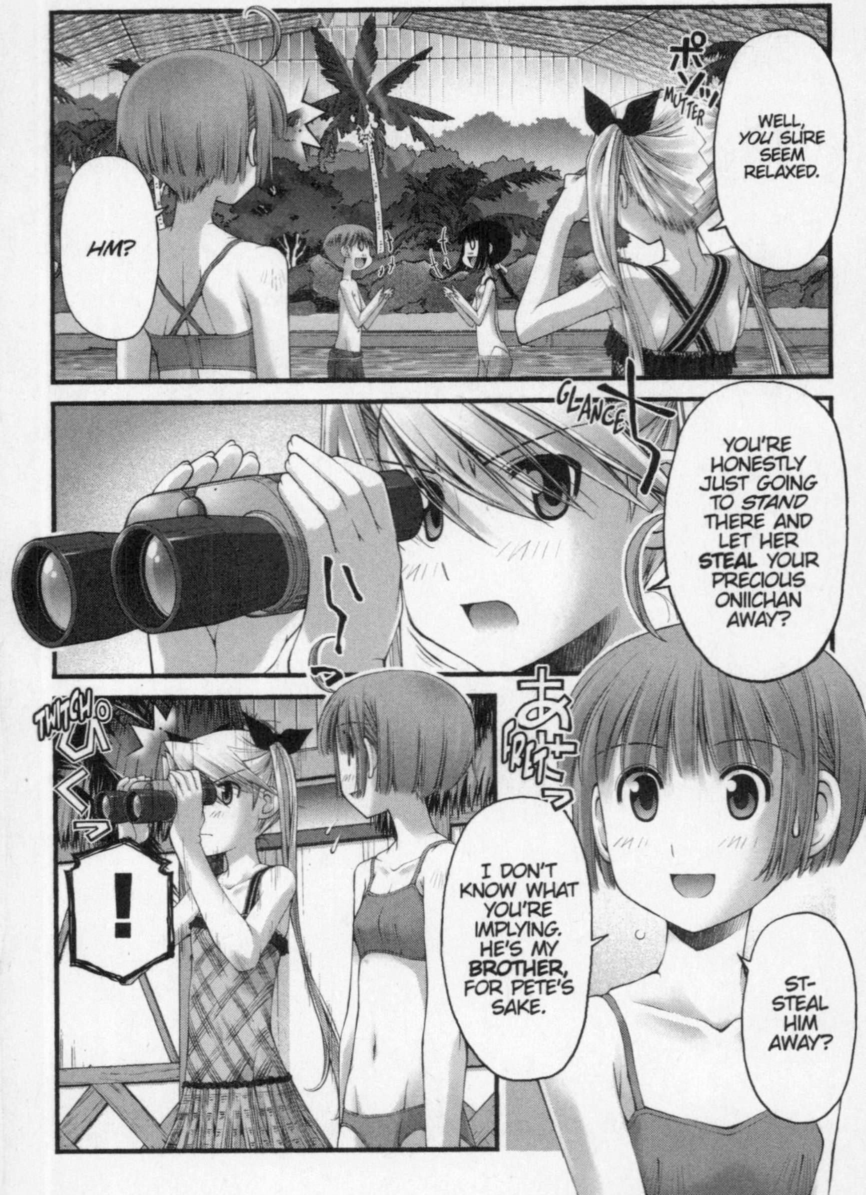
MUTTER
WELL, YOU SURE SEEM RELAXED.
HM?
GLANCE
YOU'RE HONESTLY JUST GOING TO STAND THERE AND LET HER STEAL YOUR PRECIOUS ONIICHAN AWAY?
FRET
ST- STEAL HIM AWAY?
I DON'T KNOW WHAT YOU'RE IMPLYING. HE'S MY BROTHER, FOR PETE'S SAKE.
TWITCH
!

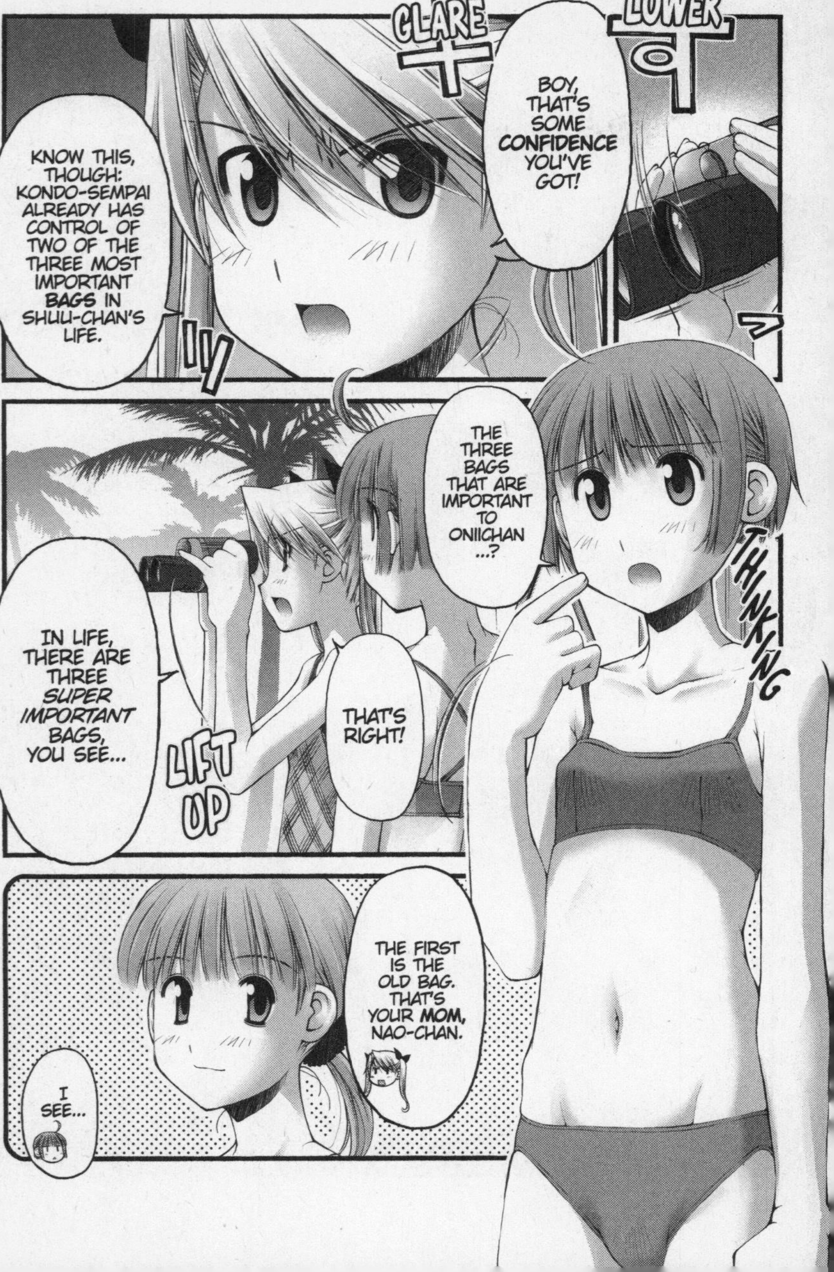
LOWER
BOY, THAT'S SOME CONFIDENCE YOU'VE GOT!
GLARE
KNOW THIS, THOUGH: KONDO-SEMPAI ALREADY HAS CONTROL OF TWO OF THE THREE MOST IMPORTANT BAGS IN SHUU-CHAN'S LIFE.
THE THREE BAGS THAT ARE IMPORTANT TO ONIICHAN ...?
THINKING
THAT'S RIGHT!
IN LIFE, THERE ARE THREE SUPER IMPORTANT BAGS, YOU SEE...
LIFT UP
THE FIRST IS THE OLD BAG. THAT'S YOUR MOM, NAO-CHAN.
I SEE...

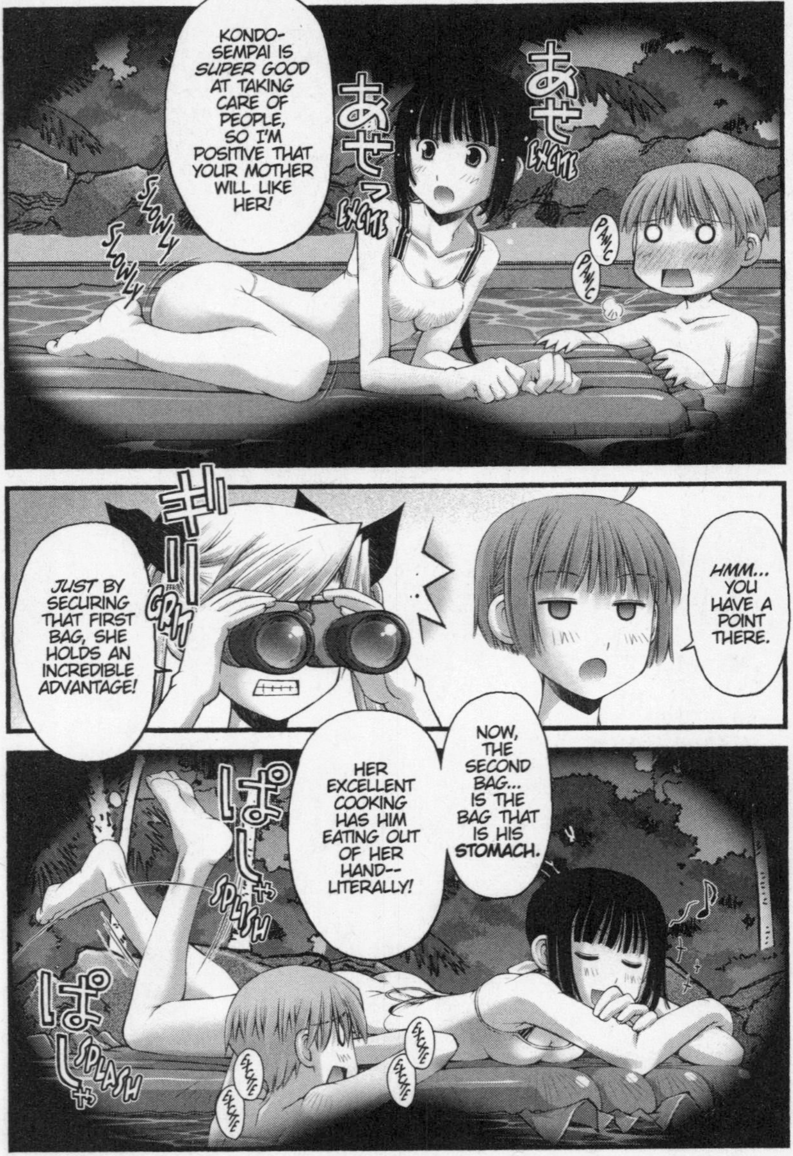

あせ
EXCITE
PANIC
PANIC
あせっ
EXCITE
KONDO-SEMPAI IS SUPER GOOD AT TAKING CARE OF PEOPLE, SO I'M POSITIVE THAT YOUR MOTHER WILL LIKE HER!
SLOWLY
SLOWLY
HMM... YOU HAVE A POINT THERE.
ギー
GRIT
JUST BY SECURING THAT FIRST BAG, SHE HOLDS AN INCREDIBLE ADVANTAGE!
NOW, THE SECOND BAG... IS THE BAG THAT IS HIS STOMACH.
HER EXCELLENT COOKING HAS HIM EATING OUT OF HER HAND-- LITERALLY!
ぱしゃ
SPLASH
ぱしゃ
SPLASH
EXCITE
EXCITE
EXCITE
EXCITE

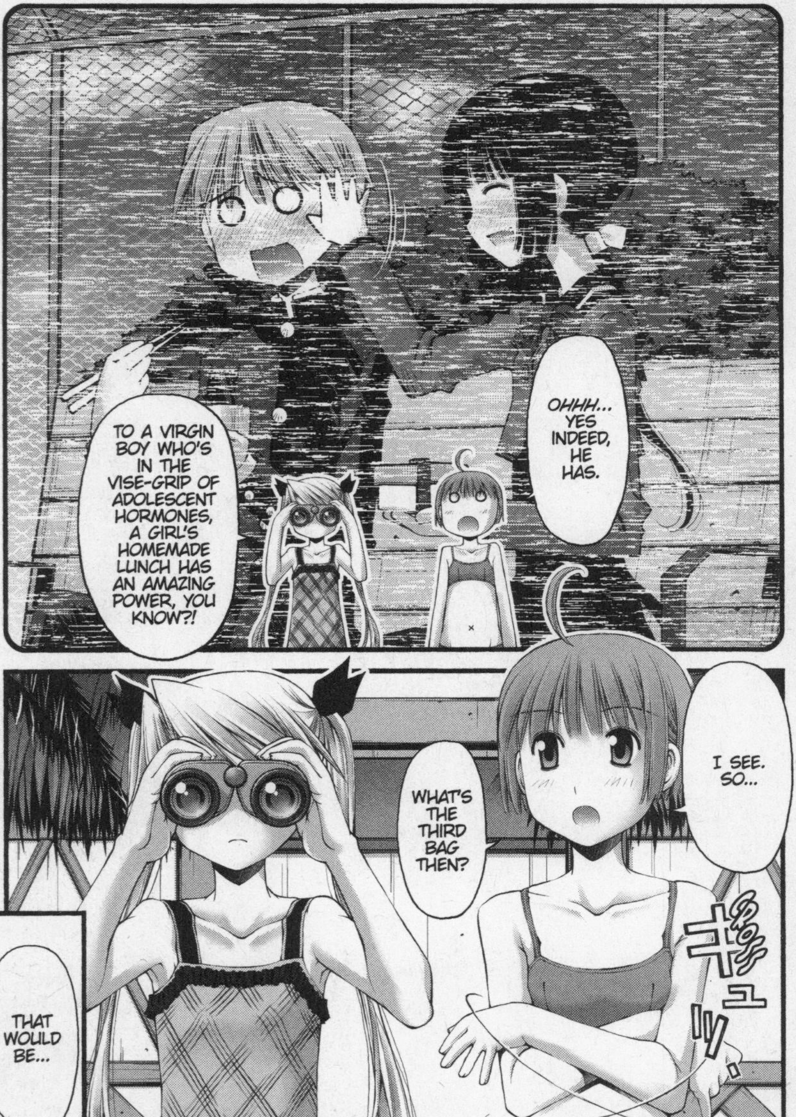
OHHH... YES INDEED, HE HAS.
TO A VIRGIN BOY WHO'S IN THE VISE-GRIP OF ADOLESCENT HORMONES, A GIRL'S HOMEMADE LUNCH HAS AN AMAZING POWER, YOU KNOW?!
I SEE. SO...
WHAT'S THE THIRD BAG THEN?
CROSS
ギュッ
THAT WOULD BE...

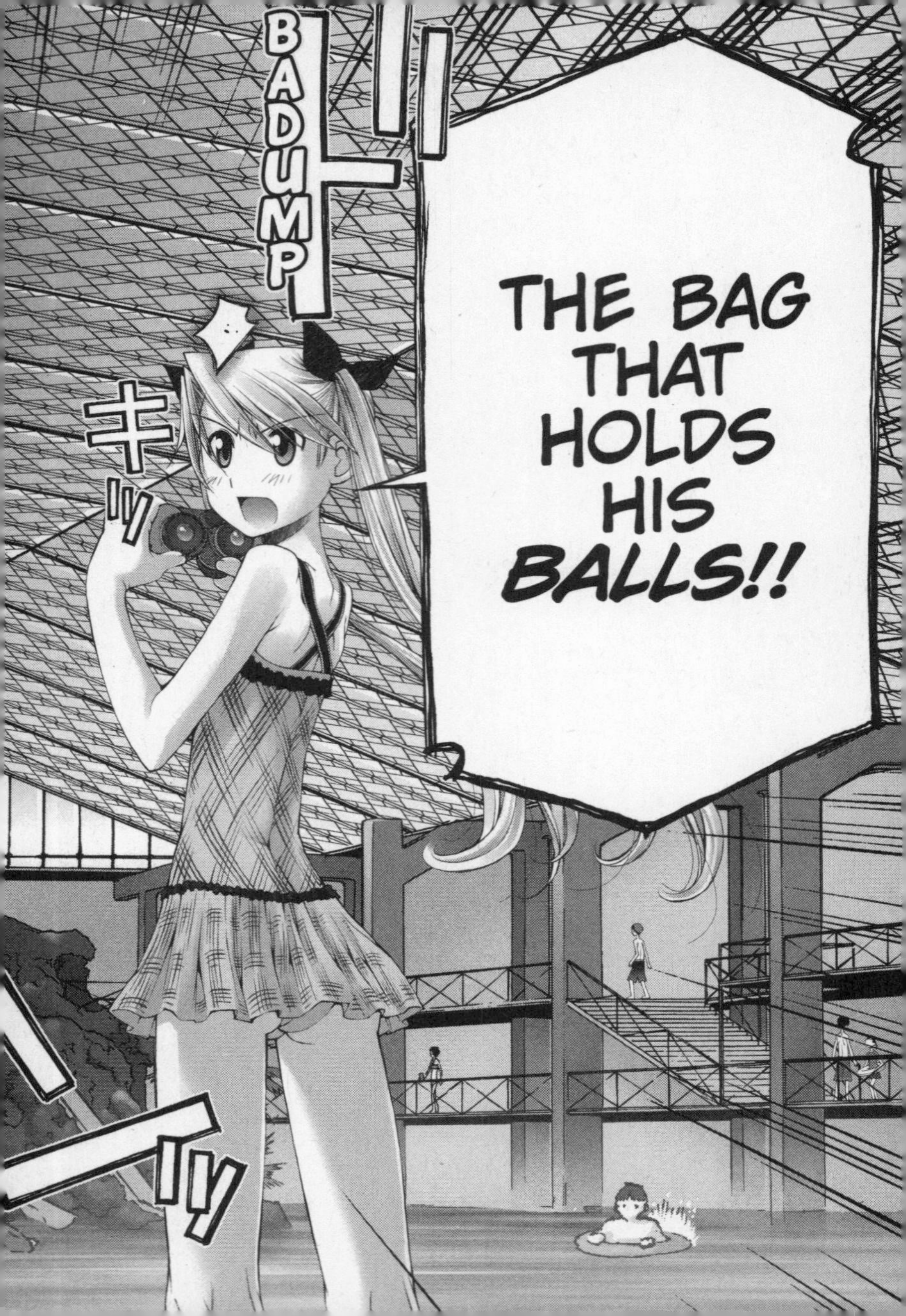
BADUMP
キ
THE BAG THAT HOLDS HIS BALLS!!

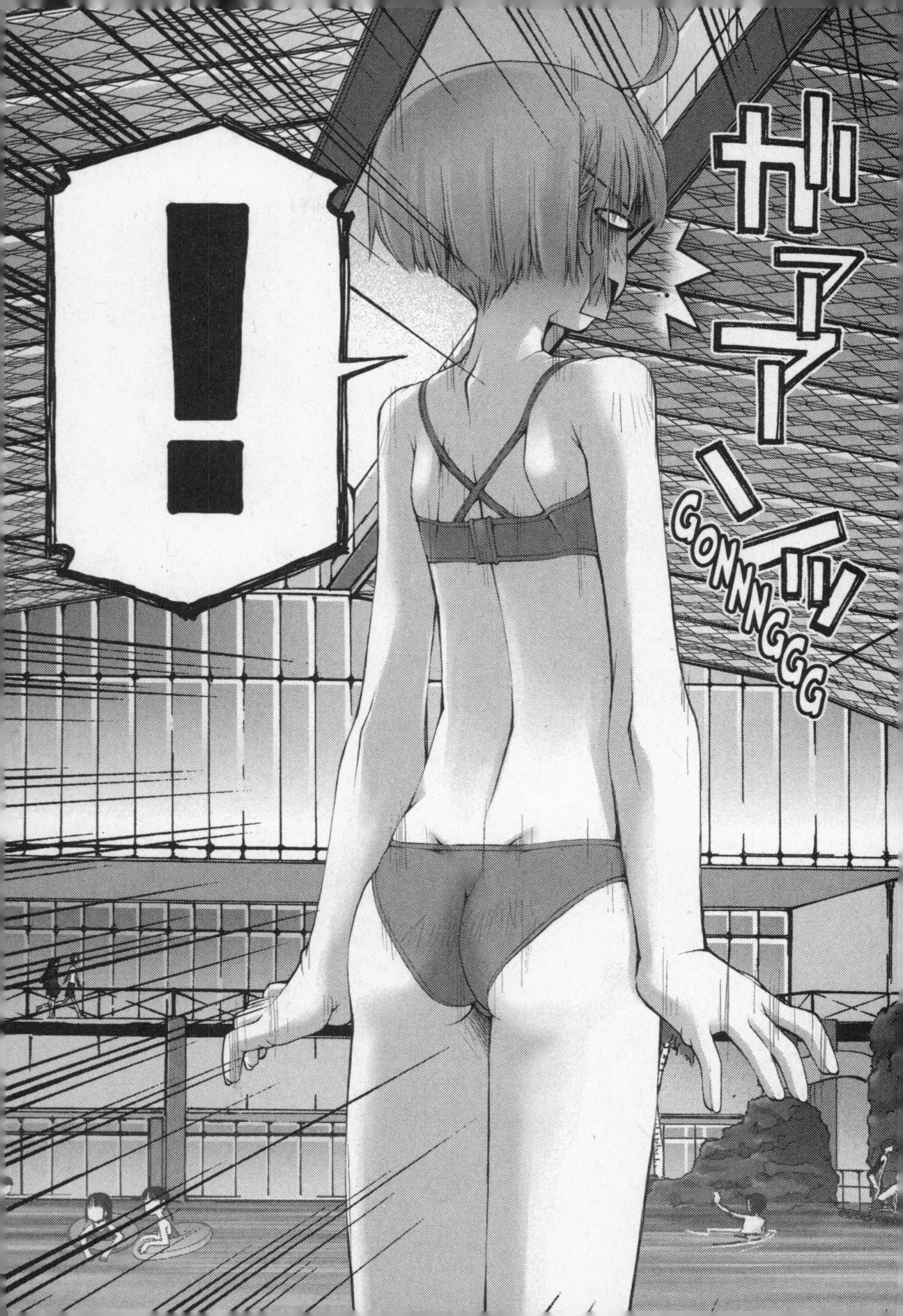
ガアーンッ
GONNNGGG
!

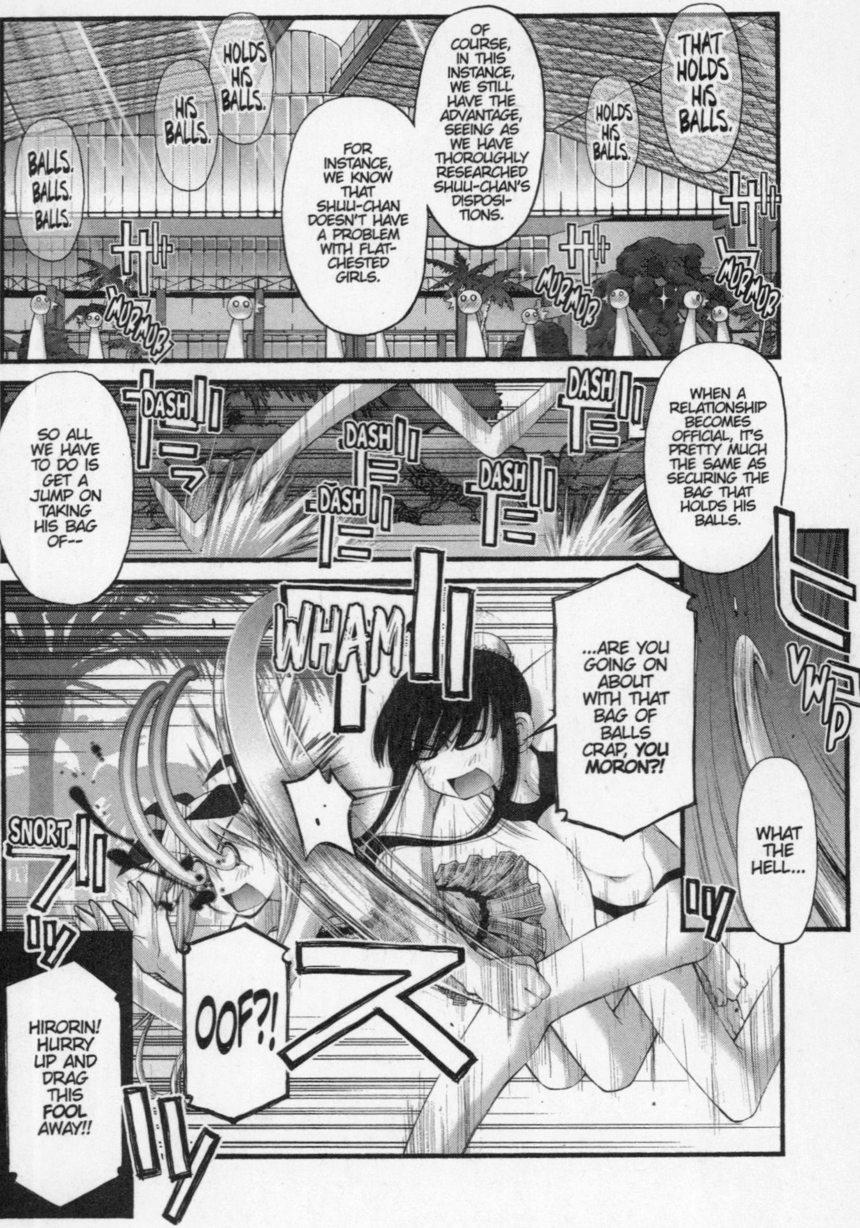
THAT HOLDS HIS BALLS.
MURMUR
HOLDS HIS BALLS.
MURMUR
OF COURSE, IN THIS INSTANCE, WE STILL HAVE THE ADVANTAGE, SEEING AS WE HAVE THOROUGHLY RESEARCHED SHUU-CHAN'S DISPOSITIONS.
FOR INSTANCE, WE KNOW THAT SHUU-CHAN DOESN'T HAVE A PROBLEM WITH FLAT-CHESTED GIRLS.
HOLDS HIS BALLS.
HIS BALLS.
BALLS. BALLS. BALLS.
MURMUR
WHEN A RELATIONSHIP BECOMES OFFICIAL, IT'S PRETTY MUCH THE SAME AS SECURING THE BAG THAT HOLDS HIS BALLS.
DASH
DASH
DASH
DASH
DASH
SO ALL WE HAVE TO DO IS GET A JUMP ON TAKING HIS BAG OF--
VWIP
WHAT THE HELL...
...ARE YOU GOING ON ABOUT WITH THAT BAG OF BALLS CRAP, YOU MORON?!
WHAM
SNORT
OOF?!
HIRORIN! HURRY UP AND DRAG THIS FOOL AWAY!!

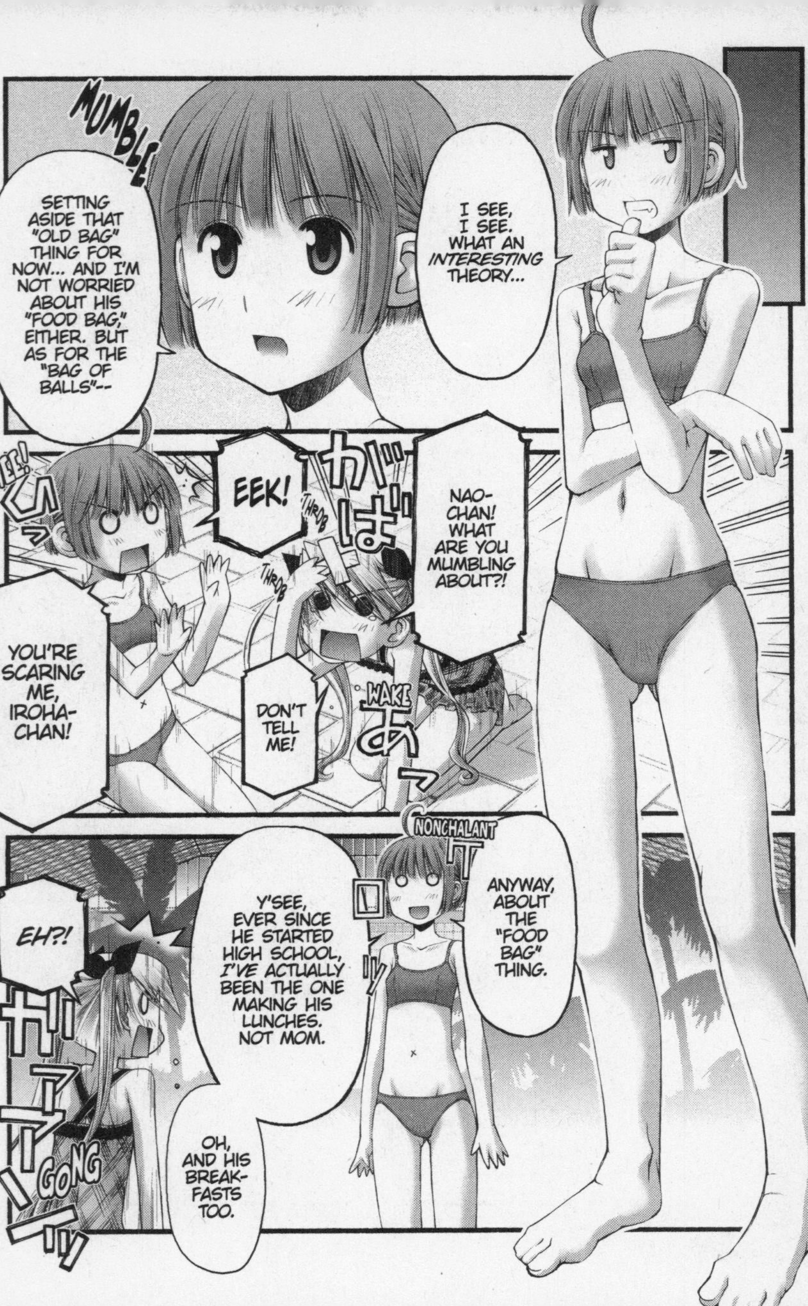
I SEE, I SEE. WHAT AN *INTERESTING* THEORY...
MUMBLE
SETTING ASIDE THAT "OLD BAG" THING FOR NOW... AND I'M NOT WORRIED ABOUT HIS "FOOD BAG," EITHER. BUT AS FOR THE "BAG OF BALLS"--
NAO-CHAN! WHAT ARE YOU MUMBLING ABOUT?!
がばっ
THROB
THROB
EEK!
HIEE!
ひっ
DON'T TELL ME!
WAKE
YOU'RE SCARING ME, IROHA-CHAN!
NONCHALANT
ANYWAY, ABOUT THE "FOOD BAG" THING.
Y'SEE, EVER SINCE HE STARTED HIGH SCHOOL, *I'VE* ACTUALLY BEEN THE ONE MAKING HIS LUNCHES. NOT MOM.
OH, AND HIS BREAK-FASTS TOO.
EH?!
GONG

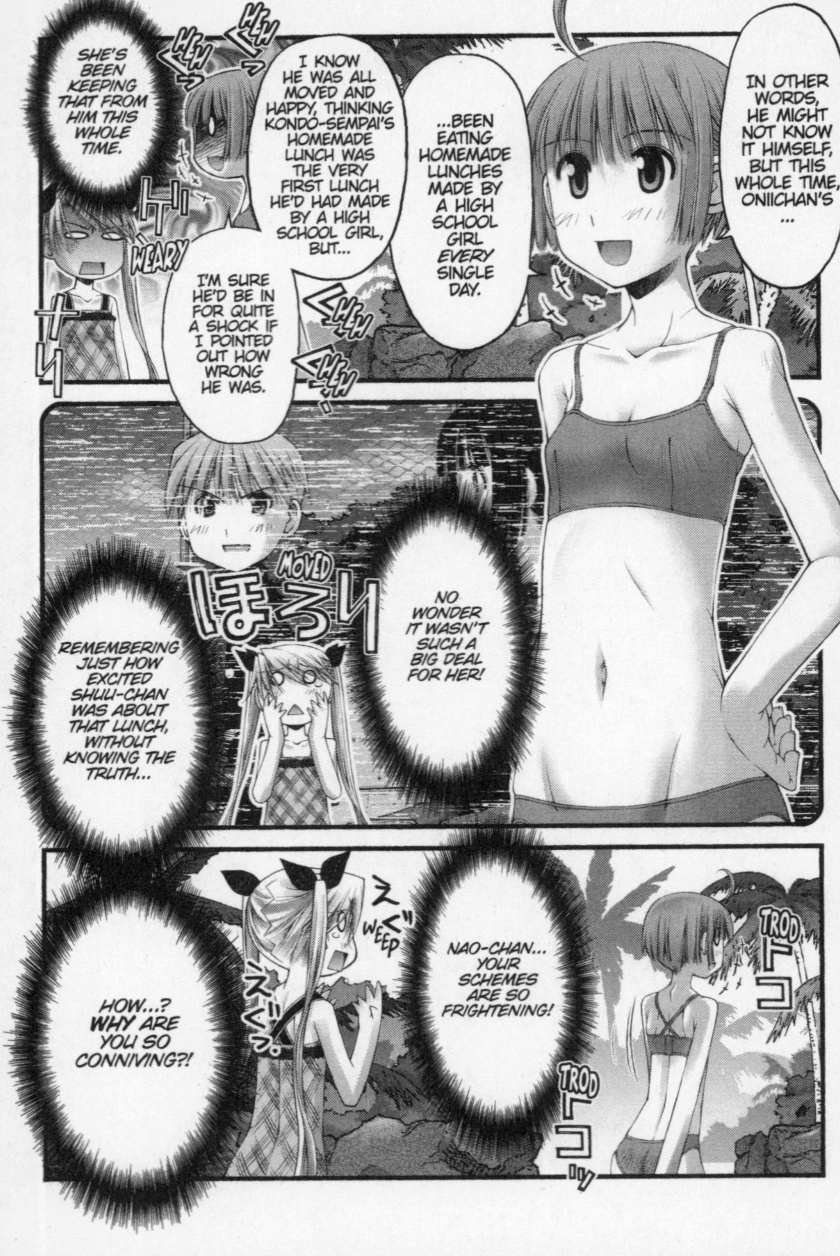
IN OTHER WORDS, HE MIGHT NOT KNOW IT HIMSELF, BUT THIS WHOLE TIME, ONIICHAN'S ...
...BEEN EATING HOMEMADE LUNCHES MADE BY A HIGH SCHOOL GIRL EVERY SINGLE DAY.
I KNOW HE WAS ALL MOVED AND HAPPY, THINKING KONDO-SEMPAI'S HOMEMADE LUNCH WAS THE VERY FIRST LUNCH HE'D HAD MADE BY A HIGH SCHOOL GIRL, BUT...
I'M SURE HE'D BE IN FOR QUITE A SHOCK IF I POINTED OUT HOW WRONG HE WAS.
HEH HEH
HEH HEH
SHE'S BEEN KEEPING THAT FROM HIM THIS WHOLE TIME.
WEARY
MOVED
ほろり
NO WONDER IT WASN'T SUCH A BIG DEAL FOR HER!
REMEMBERING JUST HOW EXCITED SHUU-CHAN WAS ABOUT THAT LUNCH, WITHOUT KNOWING THE TRUTH...
TROD
トコ
TROD
トコ
NAO-CHAN... YOUR SCHEMES ARE SO FRIGHTENING!
WEEP
HOW...? **WHY** ARE YOU SO CONNIVING?!

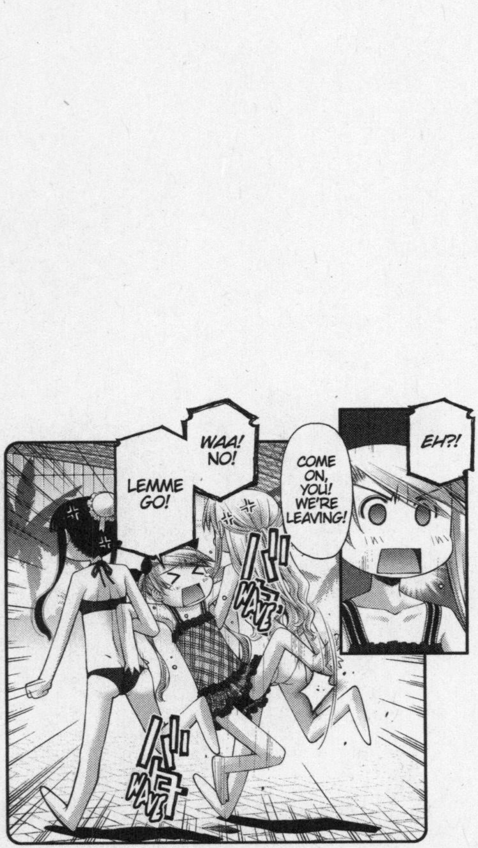
EH?!
WAA! NO!
COME ON, YOU! WE'RE LEAVING!
LEMME GO!
WAVE
WAVE

I don't like you at all, Big Brother!!

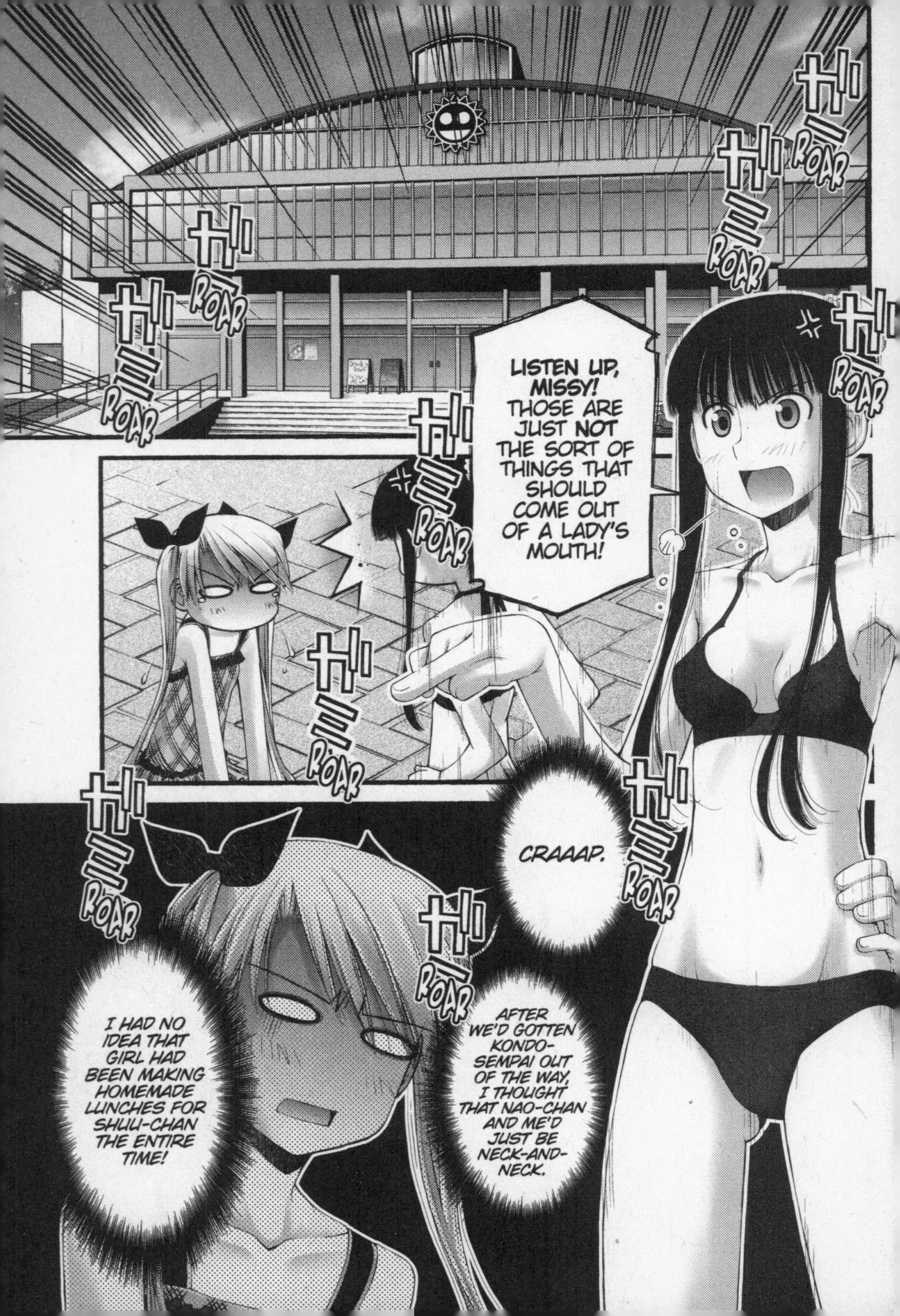
ROAR
ROAR
ROAR
ROAR
ROAR
LISTEN UP, MISSY! THOSE ARE JUST NOT THE SORT OF THINGS THAT SHOULD COME OUT OF A LADY'S MOUTH!
ROAR
ROAR
ROAR
CRAAAP.
ROAR
AFTER WE'D GOTTEN KONDO-SEMPAI OUT OF THE WAY, I THOUGHT THAT NAO-CHAN AND ME'D JUST BE NECK-AND-NECK.
ROAR
I HAD NO IDEA THAT GIRL HAD BEEN MAKING HOMEMADE LUNCHES FOR SHUU-CHAN THE ENTIRE TIME!

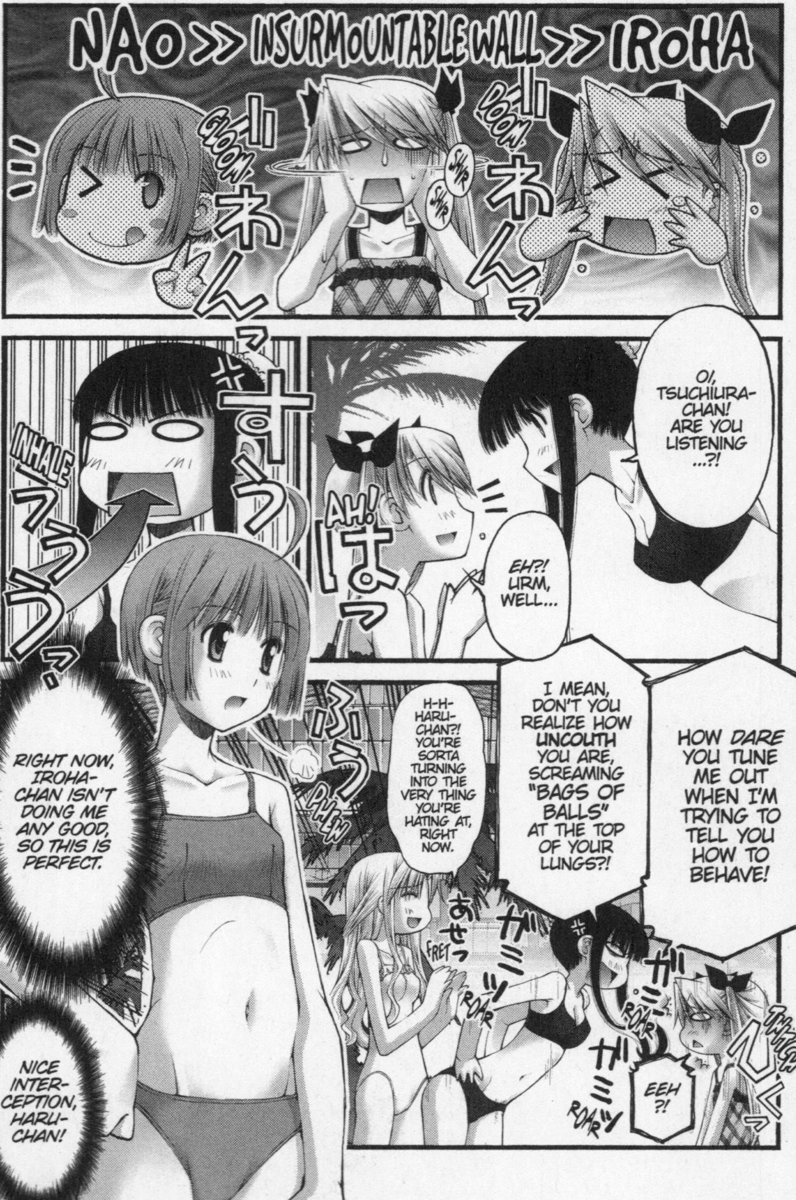
NAO >> INSURMOUNTABLE WALL >> IROHA
DOOM
わんっ
SHIR SHIR
GLOOM
わんっ
OI, TSUCHIURA-CHAN! ARE YOU LISTENING ...?!
EH?! URM, WELL...
AH! はっ
すう
INHALE
ううぅっ
HOW DARE YOU TUNE ME OUT WHEN I'M TRYING TO TELL YOU HOW TO BEHAVE!
I MEAN, DON'T YOU REALIZE HOW UNCOUTH YOU ARE, SCREAMING "BAGS OF BALLS" AT THE TOP OF YOUR LUNGS?!
TWITCH
ガミ ROAR
EEH ?!
ガミッ ROAR
ガミッ ROAR
H-H-HARU-CHAN?! YOU'RE SORTA TURNING INTO THE VERY THING YOU'RE HATING AT, RIGHT NOW.
あせっ FRET
ふう PHEW
RIGHT NOW, IROHA-CHAN ISN'T DOING ME ANY GOOD, SO THIS IS PERFECT.
NICE INTER-CEPTION, HARU-CHAN!

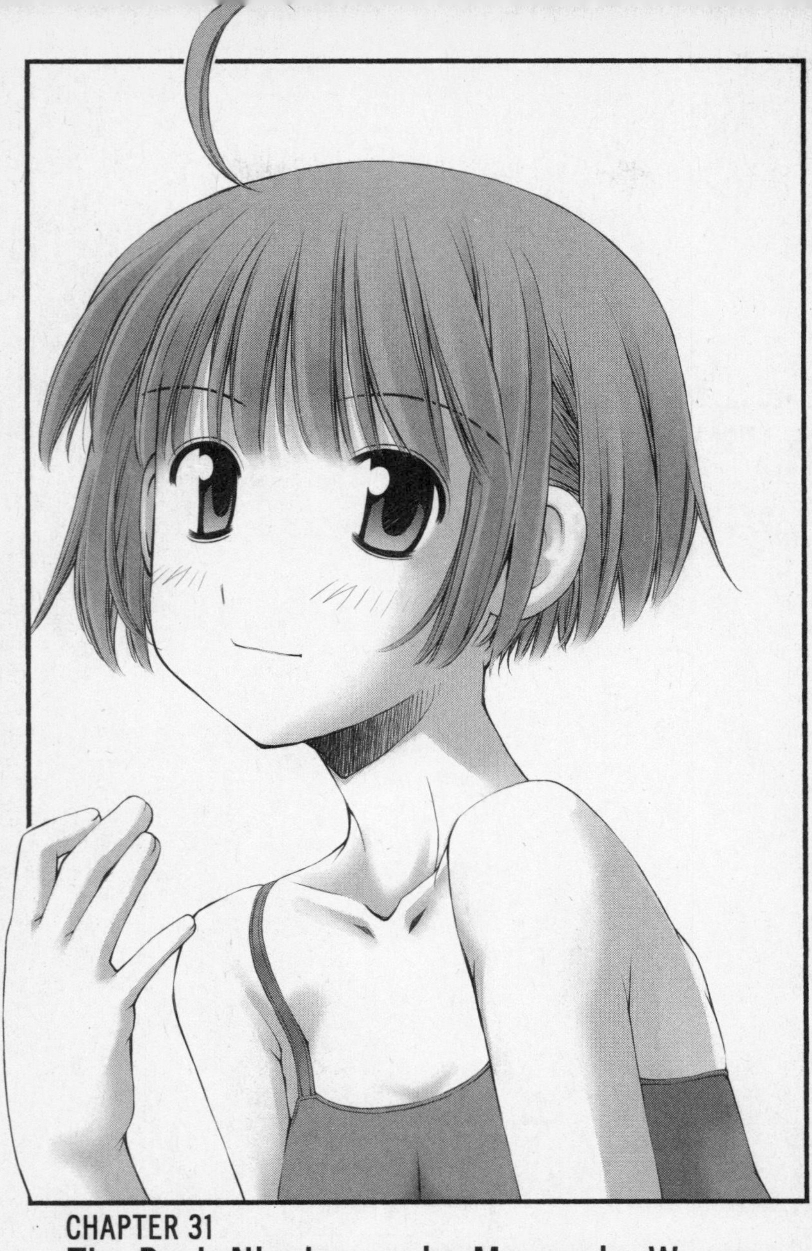

CHAPTER 31
The Pool, Nipples, and a Man and a Woman

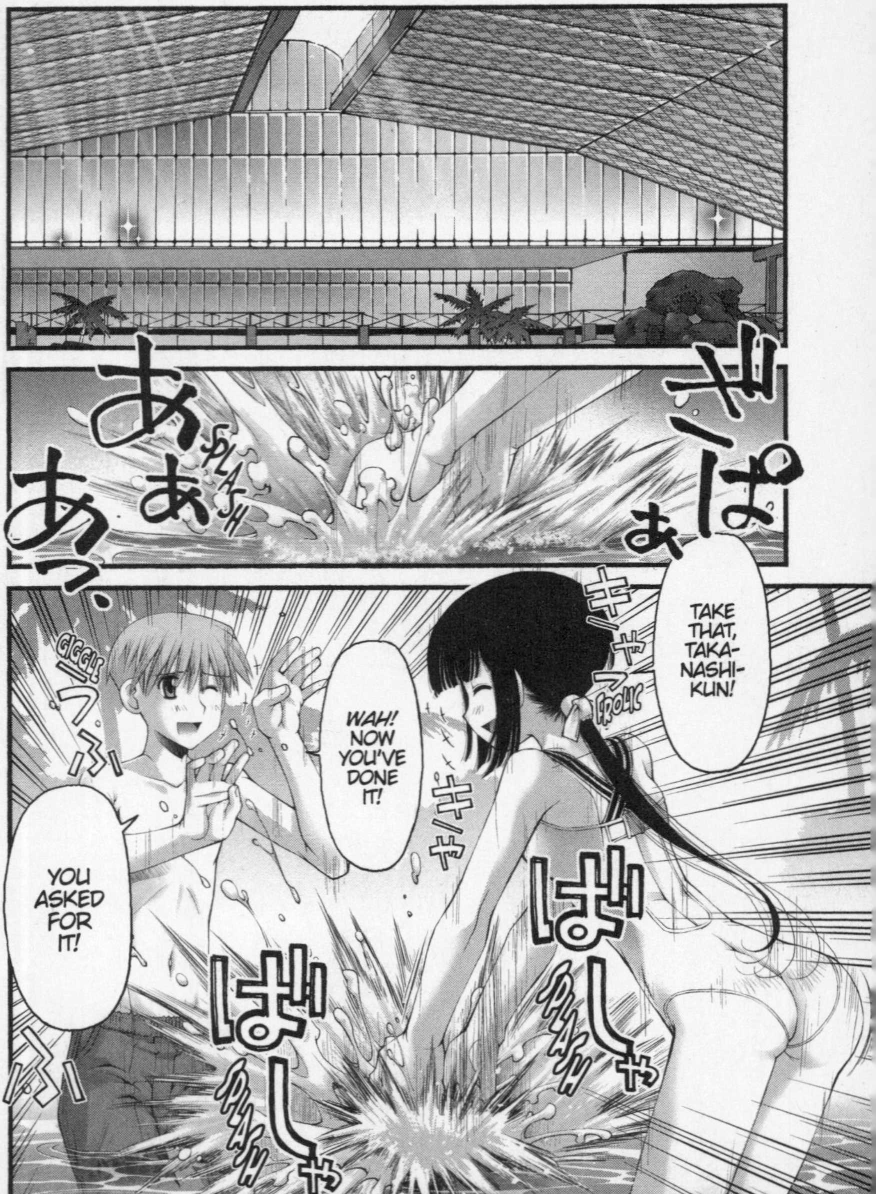
ざぱぁ
あああっ
SPLASH
TAKE THAT, TAKANASHI-KUN!
キャッ
FROLIC
WAH! NOW YOU'VE DONE IT!
キャ
ばしゃ
SPLASH
ばしゃっ
SPLASH
GIGGLE
ふふ
YOU ASKED FOR IT!
ふふ

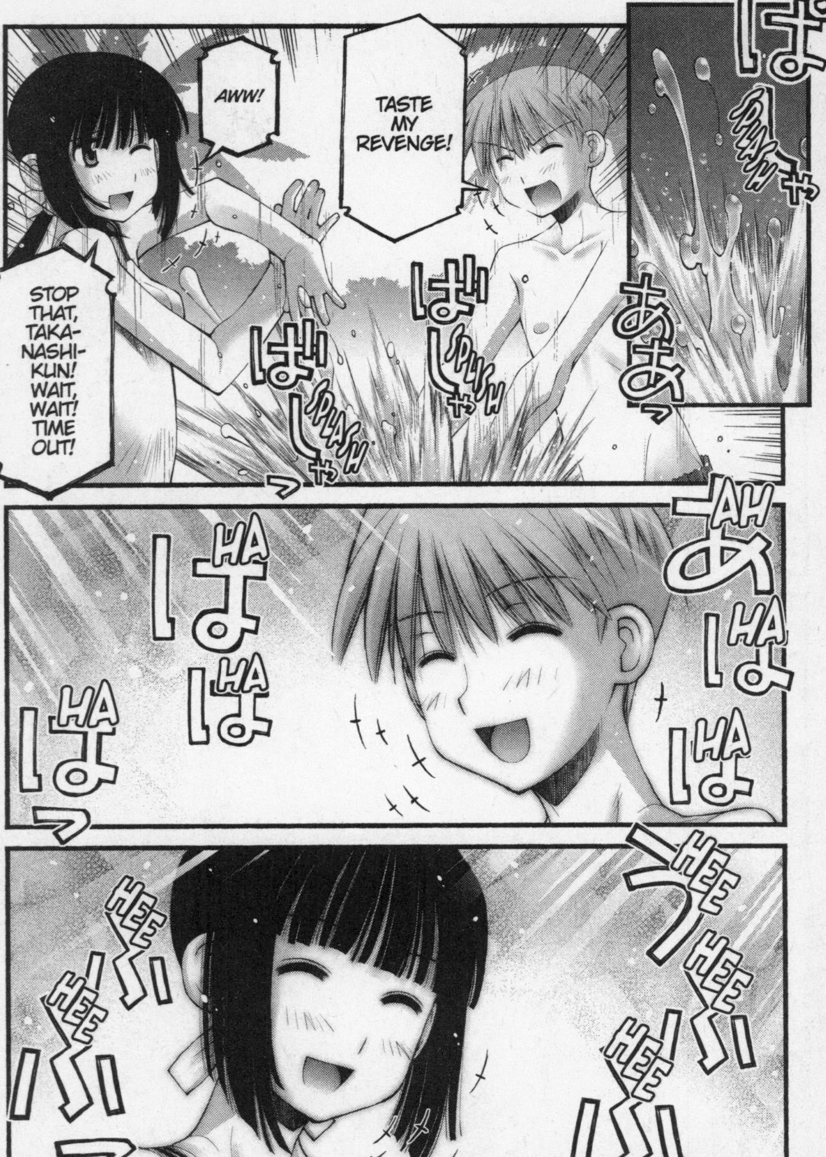
ぱしゃ
SPLASH
あぁっ
TASTE MY REVENGE!
AWW!
STOP THAT, TAKA-NASHI-KUN! WAIT, WAIT! TIME OUT!
ばしゃ
SPLASH
ばしゃっ
SPLASH
あははは
AH HA HA
ははは
HA HA HA
うふふ
HEE HEE HEE
ふふふっ
HEE HEE HEE

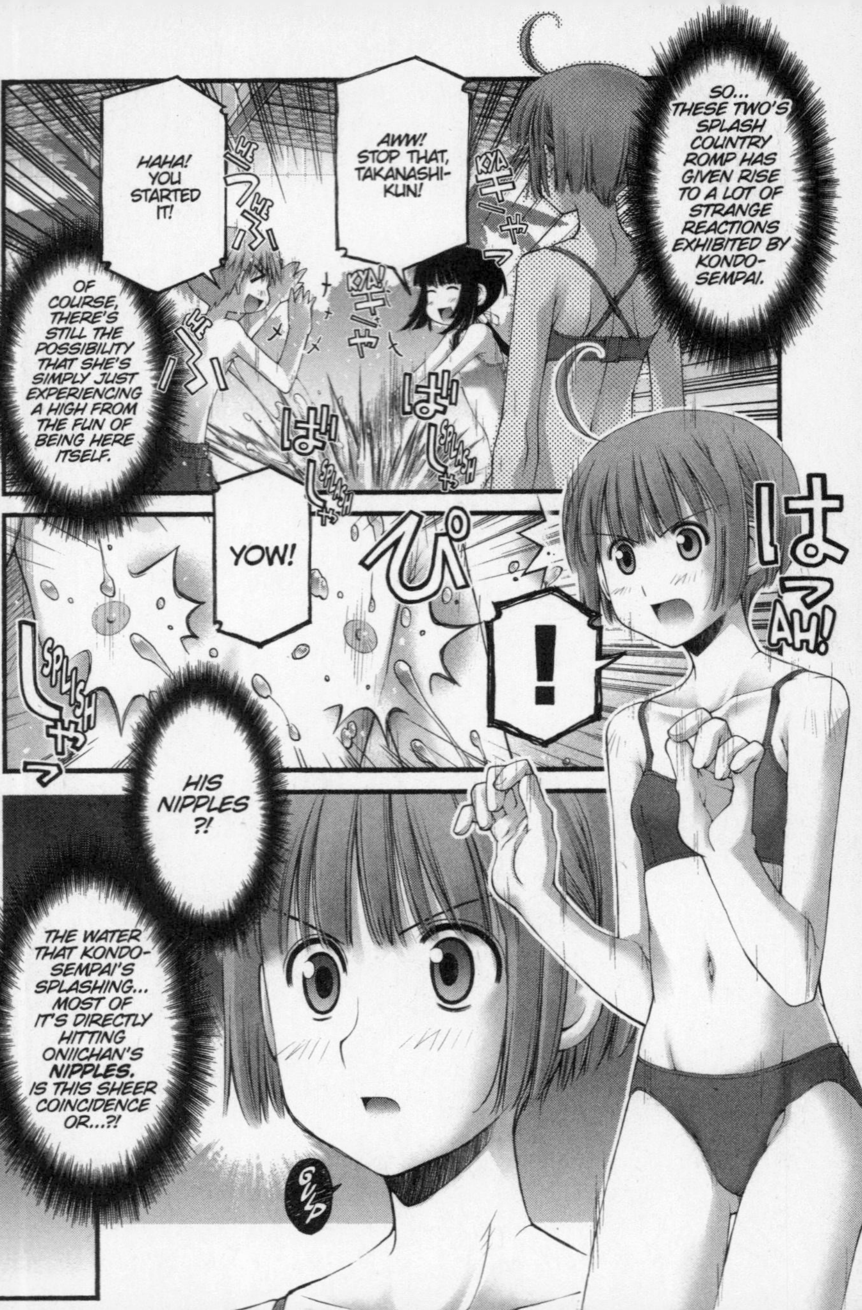

SO... THESE TWO'S SPLASH COUNTRY ROMP HAS GIVEN RISE TO A LOT OF STRANGE REACTIONS EXHIBITED BY KONDO-SEMPAI.
KYA
AWW! STOP THAT, TAKANASHI-KUN!
KYA!
HAHA! YOU STARTED IT!
HE
HE
OF COURSE, THERE'S STILL THE POSSIBILITY THAT SHE'S SIMPLY JUST EXPERIENCING A HIGH FROM THE FUN OF BEING HERE ITSELF.
HE
SPLASH
SPLASH
AH!
!
YOW!
SPLASH
HIS NIPPLES ?!
THE WATER THAT KONDO-SEMPAI'S SPLASHING... MOST OF IT'S DIRECTLY HITTING ONIICHAN'S NIPPLES. IS THIS SHEER COINCIDENCE OR...?!
GULP

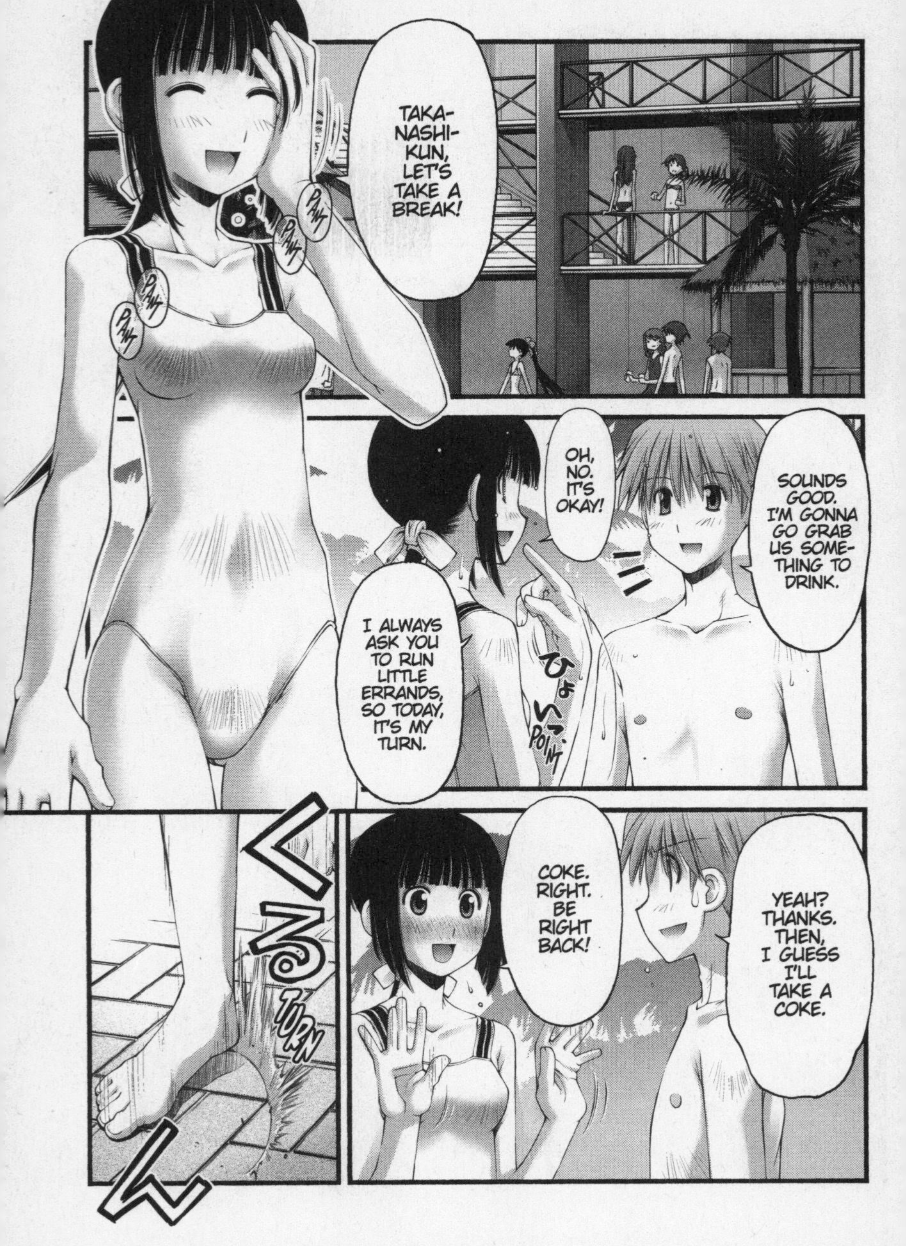
TAKA-NASHI-KUN, LET'S TAKE A BREAK!
PAW PAW PAW PAW PAW
SOUNDS GOOD. I'M GONNA GO GRAB US SOME-THING TO DRINK.
OH, NO. IT'S OKAY!
POINT
I ALWAYS ASK YOU TO RUN LITTLE ERRANDS, SO TODAY, IT'S MY TURN.
YEAH? THANKS. THEN, I GUESS I'LL TAKE A COKE.
COKE. RIGHT. BE RIGHT BACK!
TURN

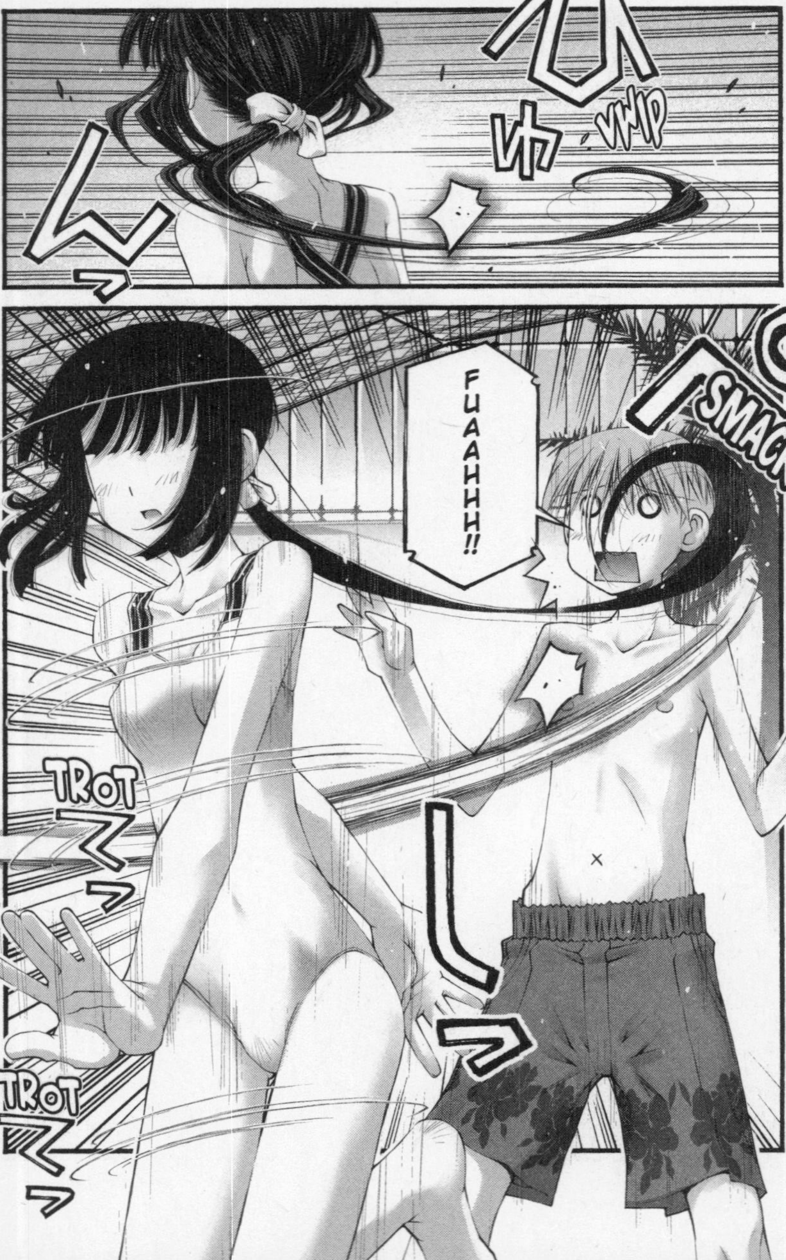
VWIP
SMACK
FUAAAHHH!!
TROT
TROT

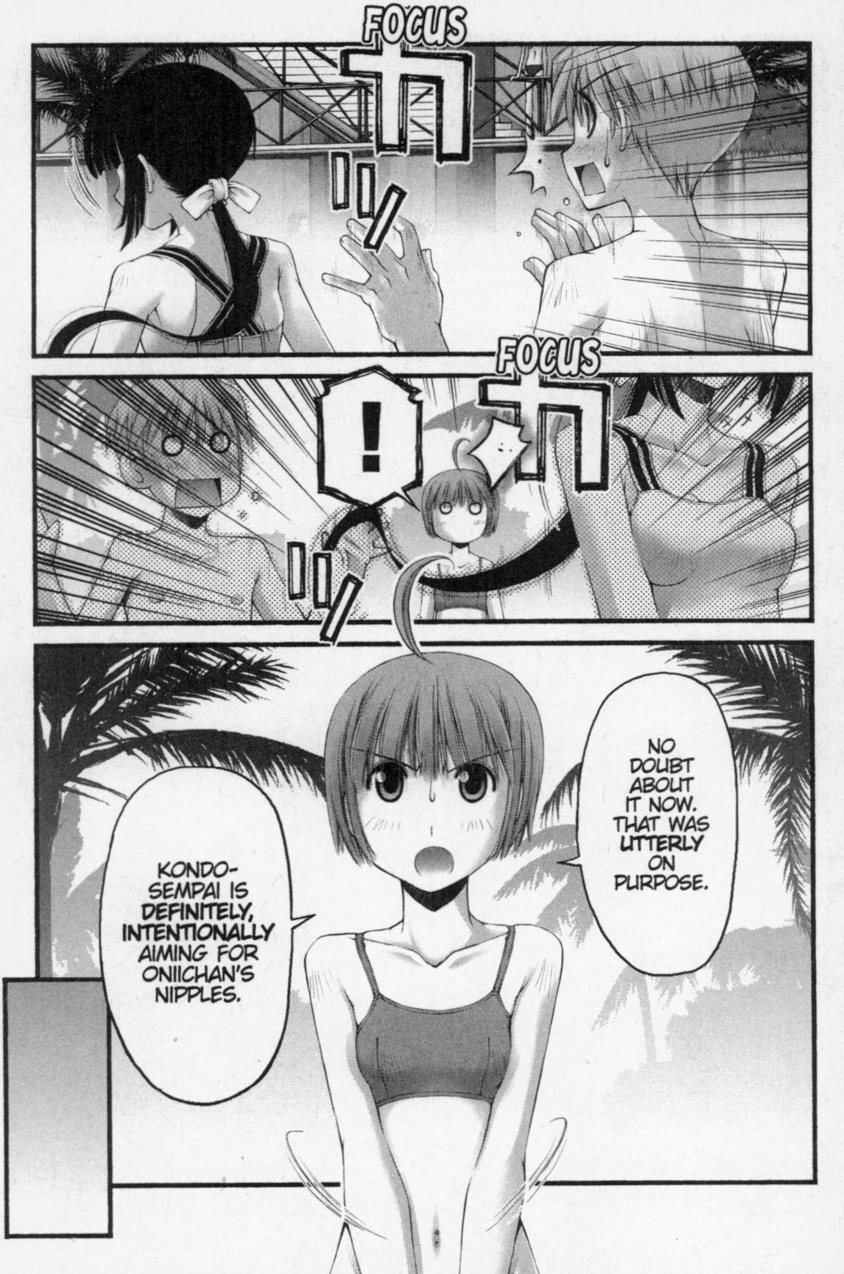
FOCUS
カ
FOCUS
カ
!
NO DOUBT ABOUT IT NOW. THAT WAS UTTERLY ON PURPOSE.
KONDO-SEMPAI IS DEFINITELY, INTENTIONALLY AIMING FOR ONIICHAN'S NIPPLES.

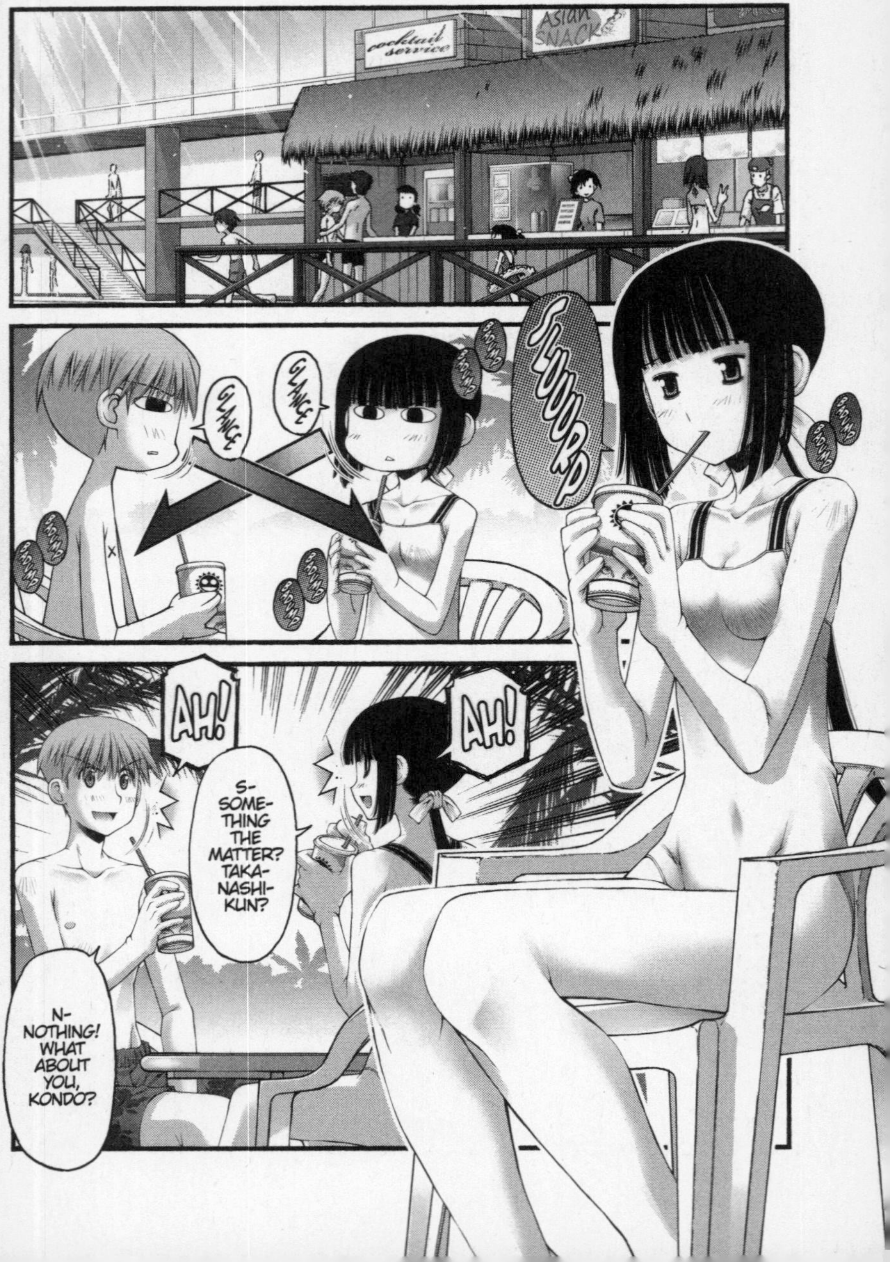
Asian SNACK
cocktail service
SLUUURP
BADUMP BADUMP
BADUMP
GLANCE
GLANCE
BADUMP BADUMP
BADUMP BADUMP
AH!
AH!
S-SOMETHING THE MATTER? TAKANASHI-KUN?
N-NOTHING! WHAT ABOUT YOU, KONDO?

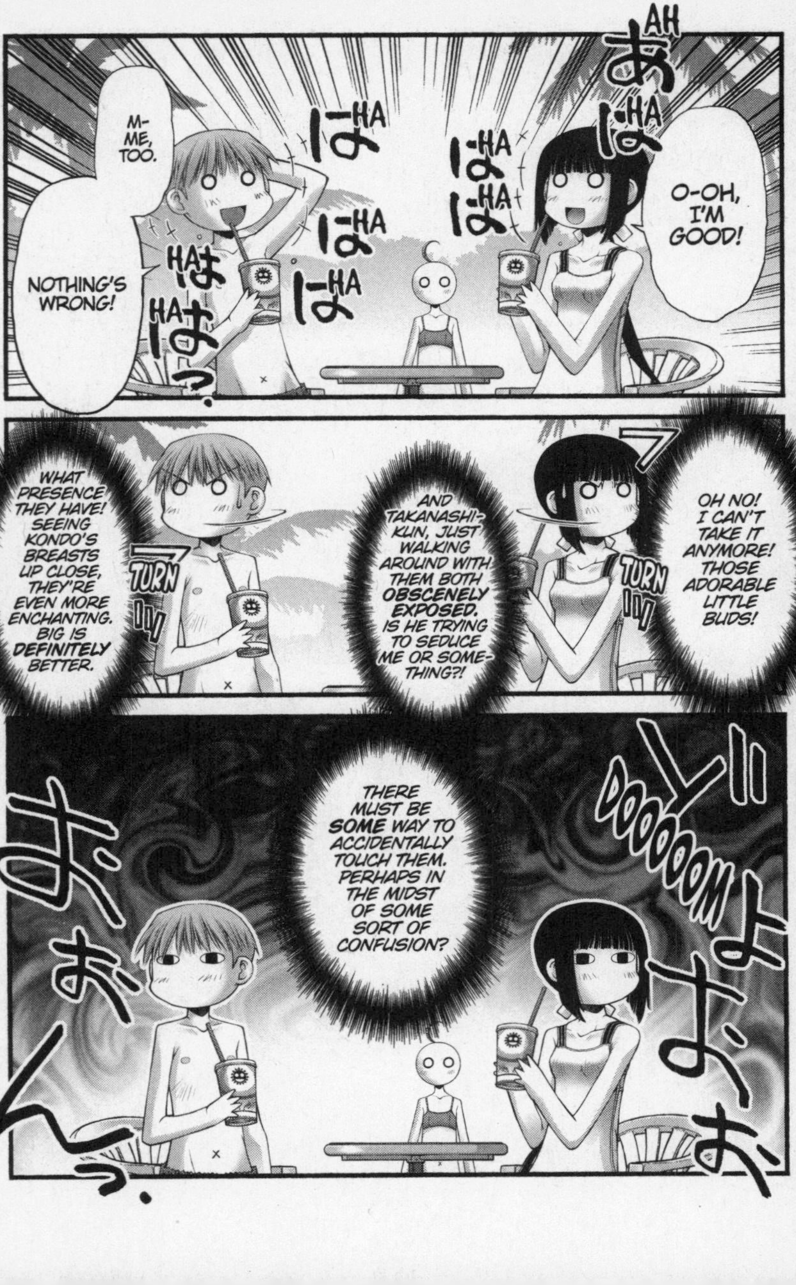
AH HA HA HA
O-OH, I'M GOOD!
HA HA HA HA HA
M-ME, TOO.
NOTHING'S WRONG!
OH NO! I CAN'T TAKE IT ANYMORE! THOSE ADORABLE LITTLE BUDS!
TURN
AND TAKANASHI-KUN, JUST WALKING AROUND WITH THEM BOTH **OBSCENELY EXPOSED.** IS HE TRYING TO SEDUCE ME OR SOMETHING?!
TURN
WHAT PRESENCE THEY HAVE! SEEING KONDO'S BREASTS UP CLOSE, THEY'RE EVEN MORE ENCHANTING. BIG IS **DEFINITELY** BETTER.
DOOOOOOM
THERE MUST BE **SOME** WAY TO ACCIDENTALLY TOUCH THEM. PERHAPS IN THE MIDST OF SOME SORT OF CONFUSION?

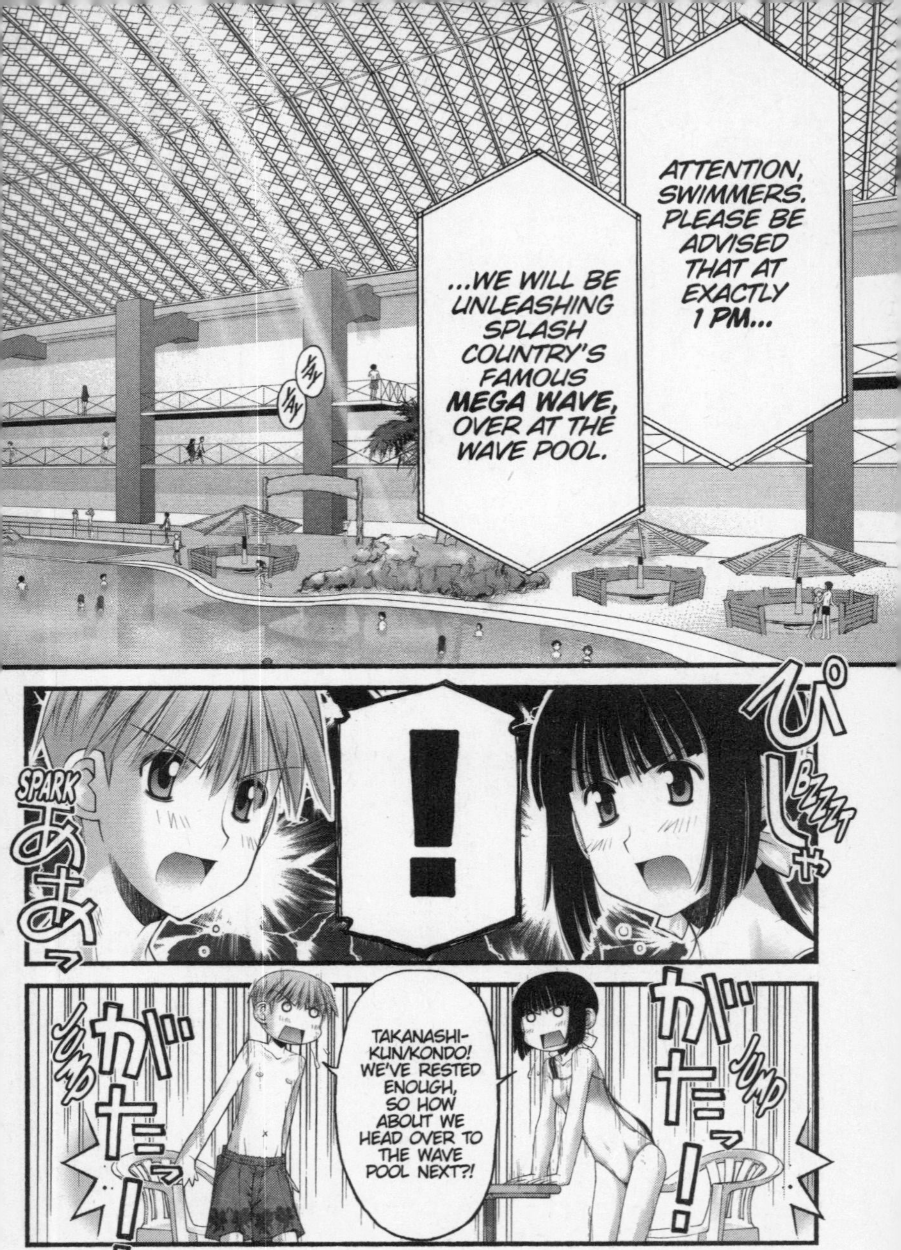
ATTENTION, SWIMMERS. PLEASE BE ADVISED THAT AT EXACTLY 1 PM...
...WE WILL BE UNLEASHING SPLASH COUNTRY'S FAMOUS **MEGA WAVE,** OVER AT THE WAVE POOL.
YAY
YAY
ぴしゃ
BZZZT
!
SPARK
あぁっ
がたーっ!
JUMP
TAKANASHI-KUN/KONDO! WE'VE RESTED ENOUGH, SO HOW ABOUT WE HEAD OVER TO THE WAVE POOL NEXT?!
がたーっ!
JUMP

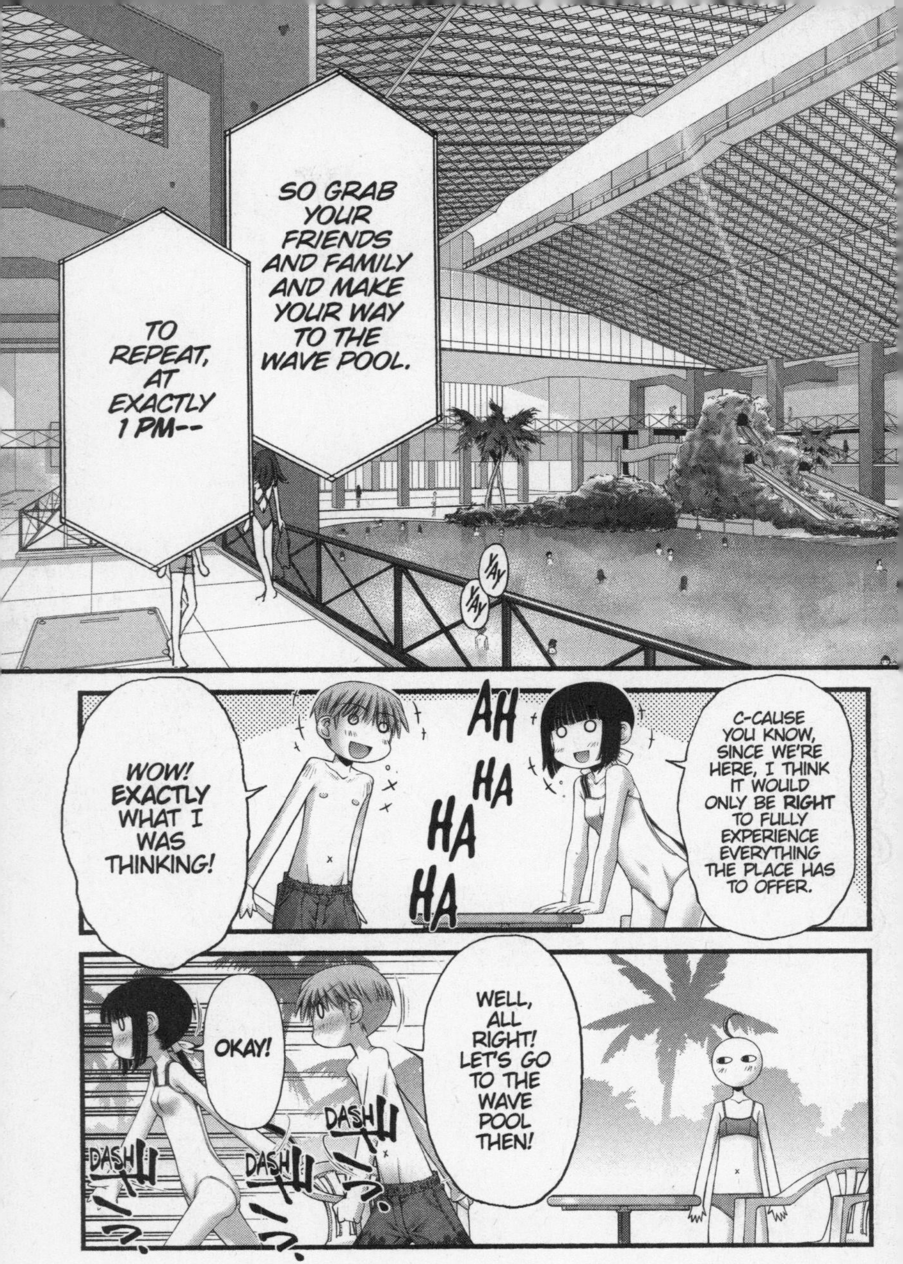
SO GRAB YOUR FRIENDS AND FAMILY AND MAKE YOUR WAY TO THE WAVE POOL.
TO REPEAT, AT EXACTLY 1 PM--
YAY
YAY
C-CAUSE YOU KNOW, SINCE WE'RE HERE, I THINK IT WOULD ONLY BE **RIGHT** TO FULLY EXPERIENCE EVERYTHING THE PLACE HAS TO OFFER.
AH HA HA HA HA
WOW! EXACTLY WHAT I WAS THINKING!
WELL, ALL RIGHT! LET'S GO TO THE WAVE POOL THEN!
OKAY!
DASH
DASH
DASH

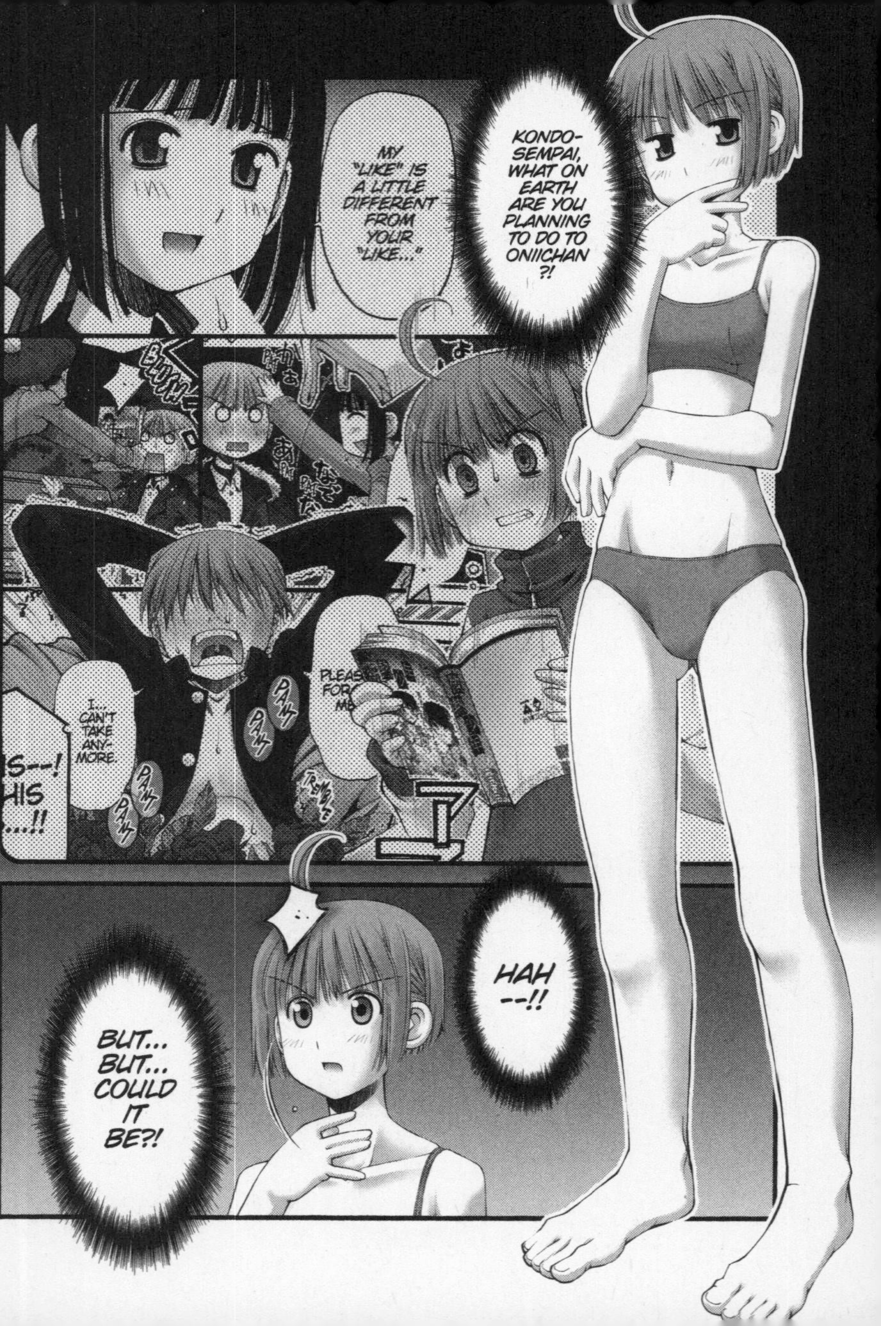
KONDO-SEMPAI, WHAT ON EARTH ARE YOU PLANNING TO DO TO ONIICHAN ?!
MY "LIKE" IS A LITTLE DIFFERENT FROM YOUR "LIKE..."
I... CAN'T TAKE ANY-MORE.
HAH --!!
BUT... BUT... COULD IT BE?!

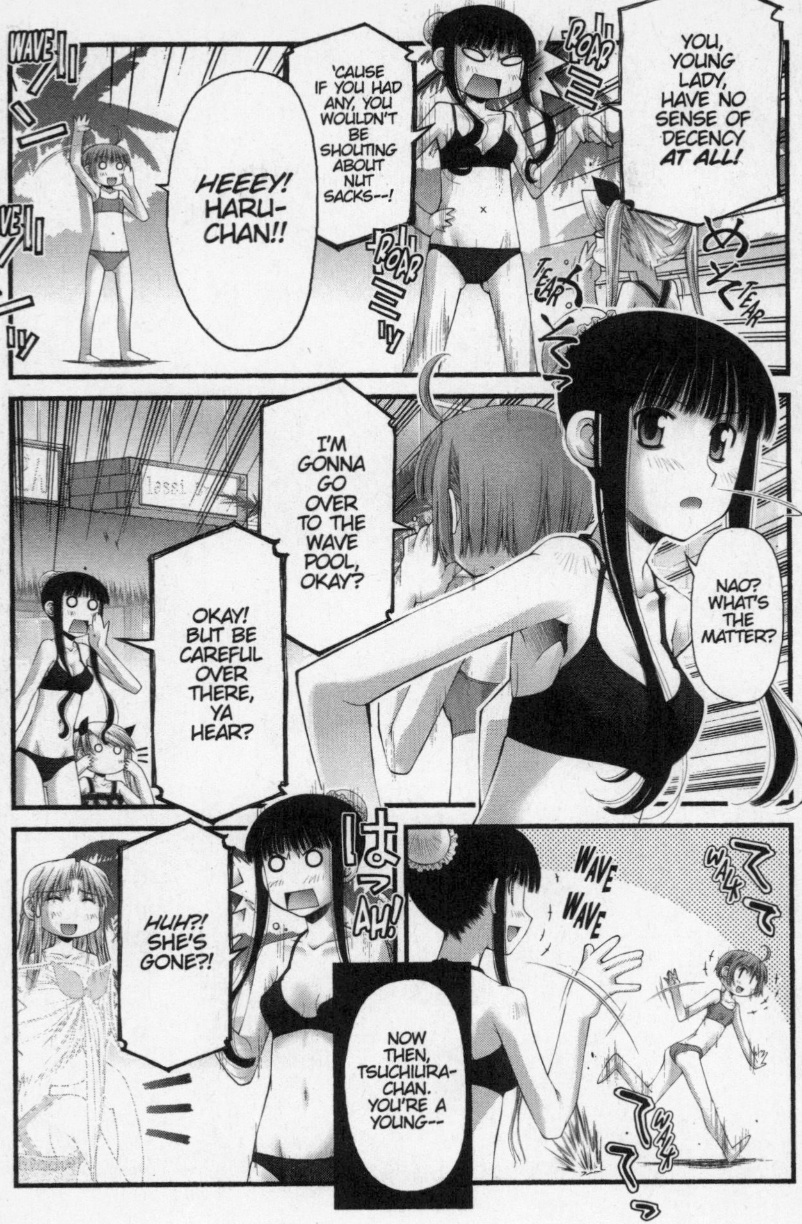
YOU, YOUNG LADY, HAVE NO SENSE OF DECENCY AT ALL!
ROAR
'CAUSE IF YOU HAD ANY, YOU WOULDN'T BE SHOUTING ABOUT NUT SACKS--!
ROAR
TEAR TEAR
HEEEY! HARU-CHAN!!
WAVE
WAVE
NAO? WHAT'S THE MATTER?
I'M GONNA GO OVER TO THE WAVE POOL, OKAY?
OKAY! BUT BE CAREFUL OVER THERE, YA HEAR?
WALK
WAVE WAVE
WALK
NOW THEN, TSUCHIURA-CHAN. YOU'RE A YOUNG--
AH!
HUH?! SHE'S GONE?!

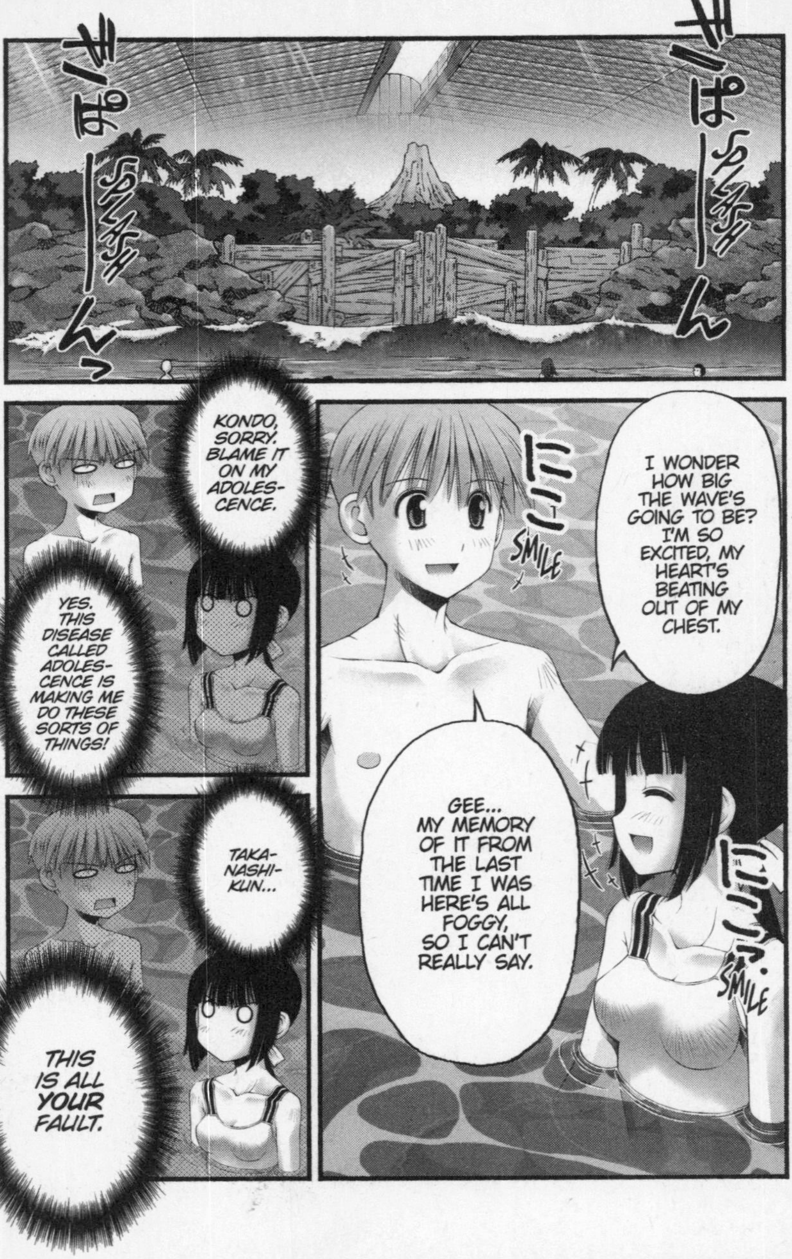
ざぱーん
SPLASH
ざぱーんっ
SPLASH
にこ
SMILE
I WONDER HOW BIG THE WAVE'S GOING TO BE? I'M SO EXCITED, MY HEART'S BEATING OUT OF MY CHEST.
GEE... MY MEMORY OF IT FROM THE LAST TIME I WAS HERE'S ALL FOGGY, SO I CAN'T REALLY SAY.
にこっ
SMILE
KONDO, SORRY. BLAME IT ON MY ADOLES-CENCE.
YES. THIS DISEASE CALLED ADOLES-CENCE IS MAKING ME DO THESE SORTS OF THINGS!
TAKA-NASHI-KUN...
THIS IS ALL YOUR FAULT.

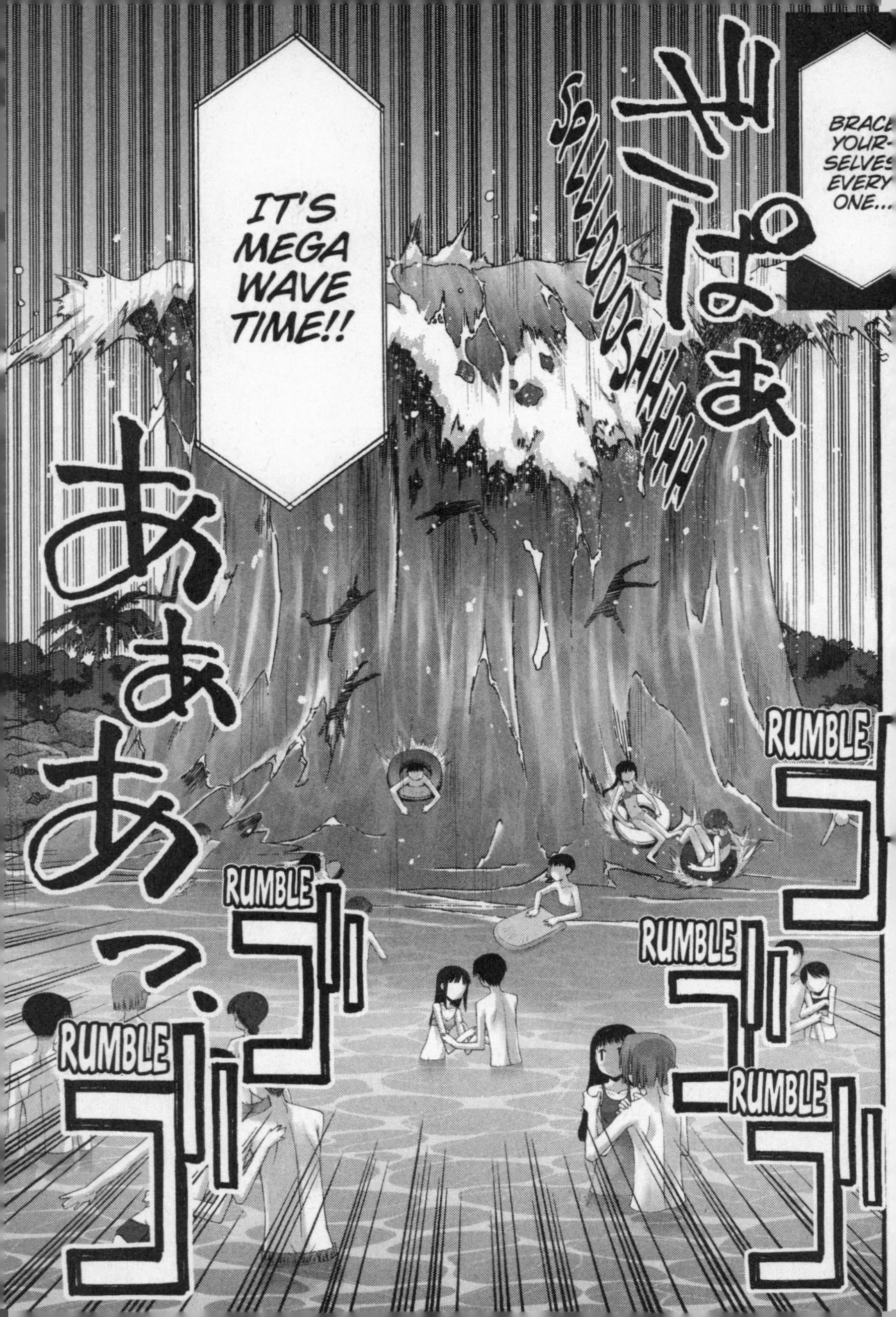
BRACE YOUR-SELVES EVERY ONE...
ざぱぁ
SPLLOOOSHHHHH
IT'S MEGA WAVE TIME!!
RUMBLE
RUMBLE
RUMBLE
RUMBLE
RUMBLE
あぁあっ

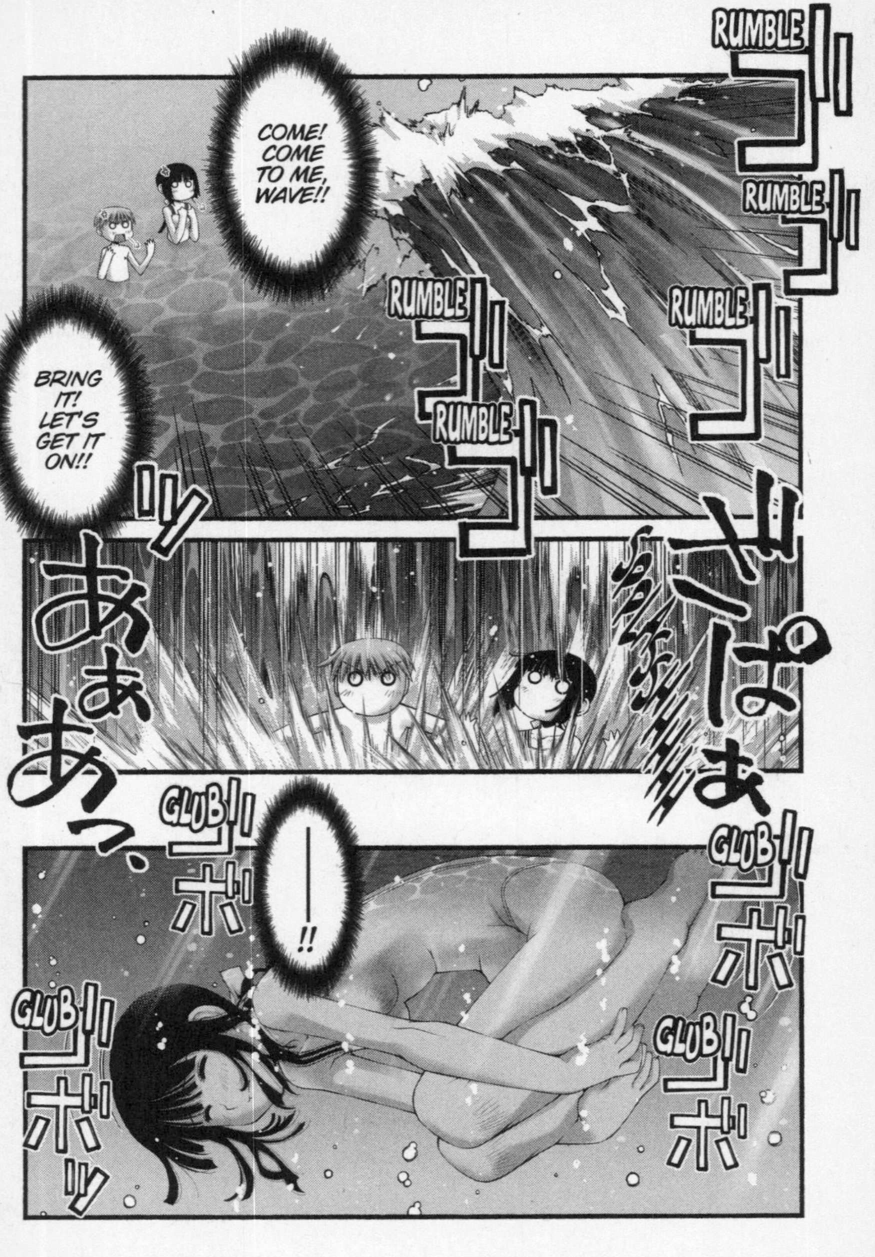

RUMBLE
ゴ
RUMBLE
ゴ
RUMBLE
ゴ
COME! COME TO ME, WAVE!!
RUMBLE
ゴ
RUMBLE
ゴ
BRING IT! LET'S GET IT ON!!
ざぱぁ
あぁあっ、
GLUB
ゴボ
GLUB
ゴボ
——!!
GLUB
ゴボ
GLUB
ゴボッ

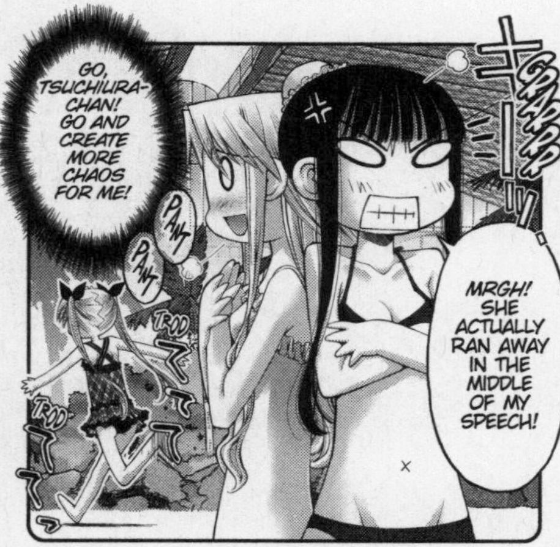
GRARRR
MRGH! SHE ACTUALLY RAN AWAY IN THE MIDDLE OF MY SPEECH!
GO, TSUCHIURA-CHAN! GO AND CREATE MORE CHAOS FOR ME!
PANT
PANT
TROD
TROD

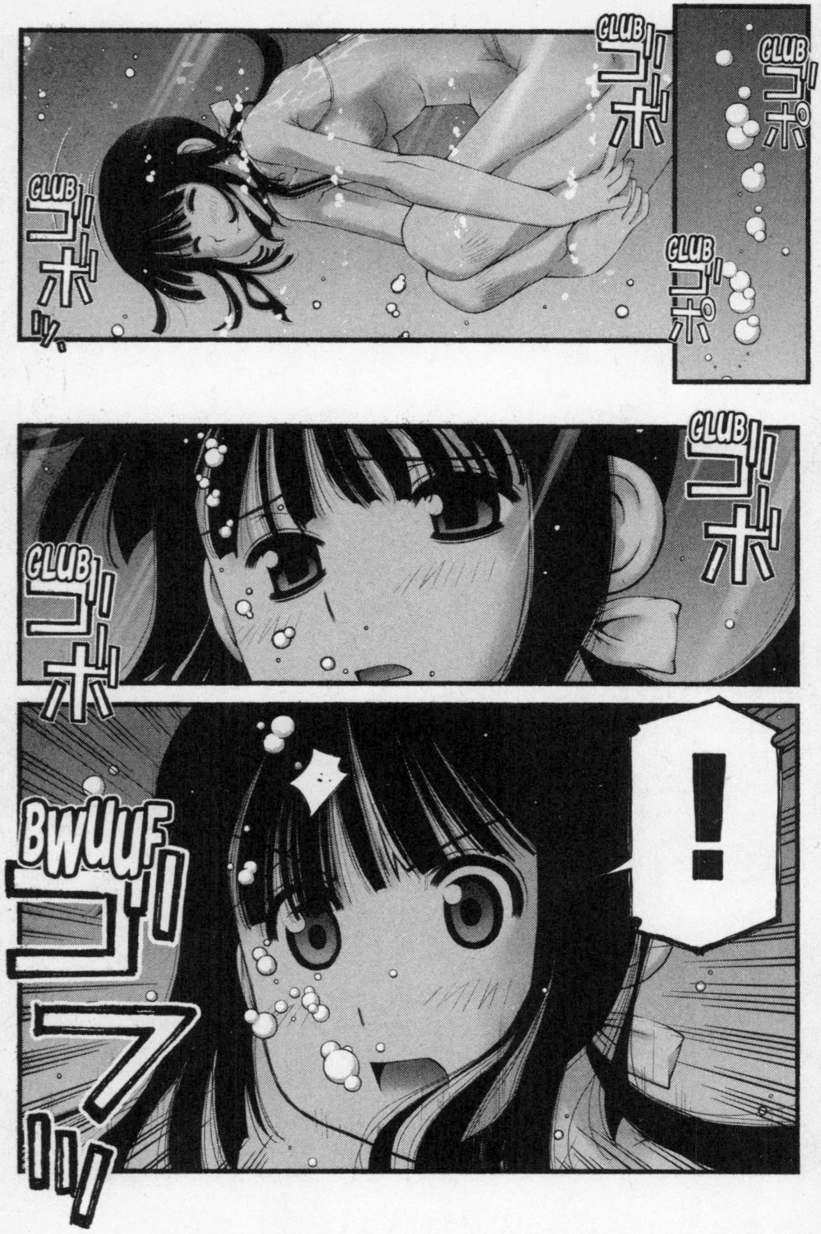
GLUB
ゴポ
GLUB
ゴポ
GLUB
ゴボ
GLUB
ゴボッ
GLUB
ゴボ
GLUB
ゴボ
!
BWUUF
ゴフッ

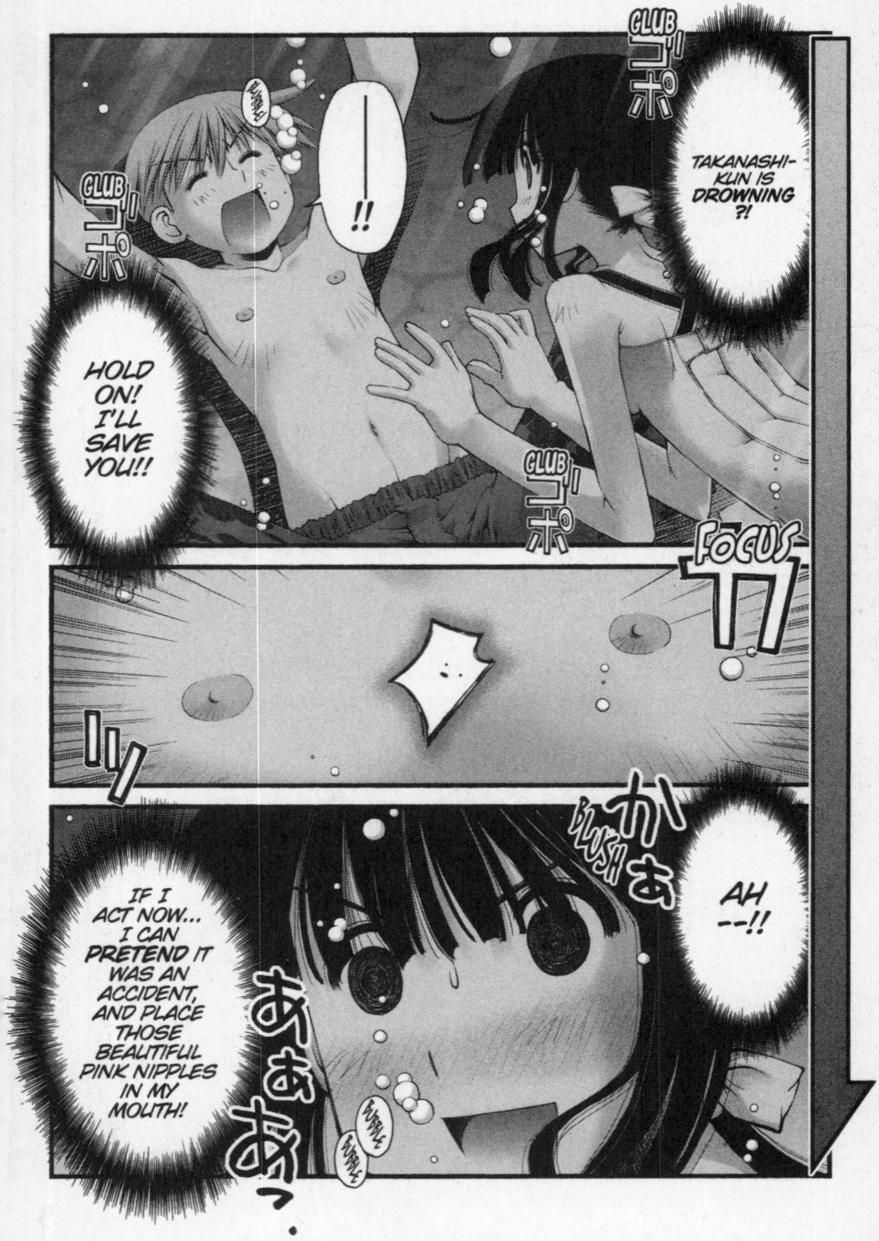
CLUB
TAKANASHI-KUN IS DROWNING ?!
——!!
CLUB
HOLD ON! I'LL SAVE YOU!!
CLUB
FOCUS
BLUSH
AH --!!
IF I ACT NOW... I CAN PRETEND IT WAS AN ACCIDENT, AND PLACE THOSE BEAUTIFUL PINK NIPPLES IN MY MOUTH!
BUBBLE
BUBBLE

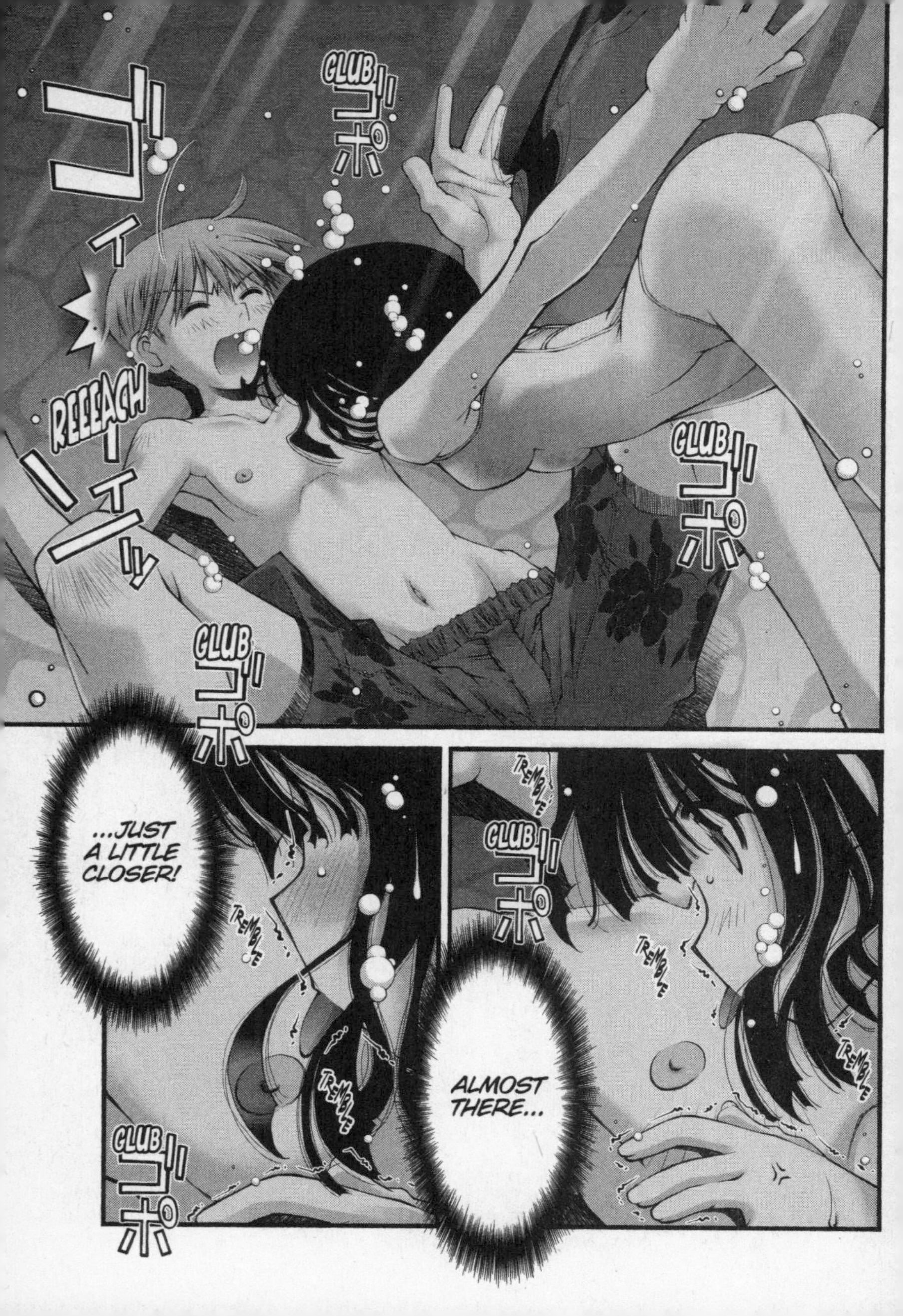

GLUB ゴポ
GLUB ゴポ
ゴイーーイーーッ
REEEACH
GLUB ゴポ
TREMBLE
GLUB ゴポ
TREMBLE
TREMBLE
ALMOST THERE...
...JUST A LITTLE CLOSER!
TREMBLE
TREMBLE
GLUB ゴポ

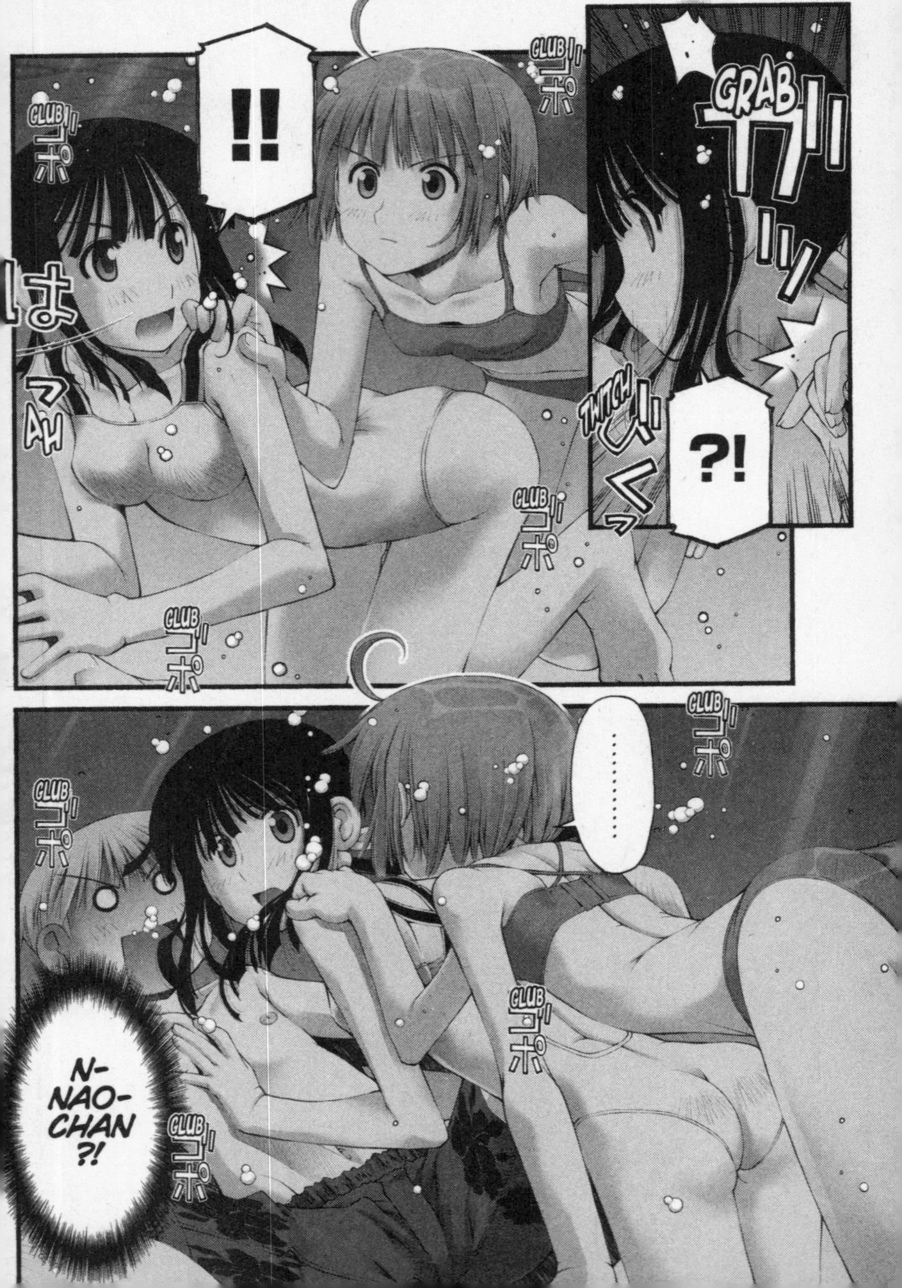
GRAB
?!
TWITCH
CLUB ゴポ
!!
CLUB ゴポ
AH
CLUB ゴポ
CLUB ゴポ
CLUB ゴポ
......
CLUB ゴポ
CLUB ゴポ
CLUB ゴポ
N-NAO-CHAN?!

CHAPTER 32 Caught Red-Handed and Under Arrest

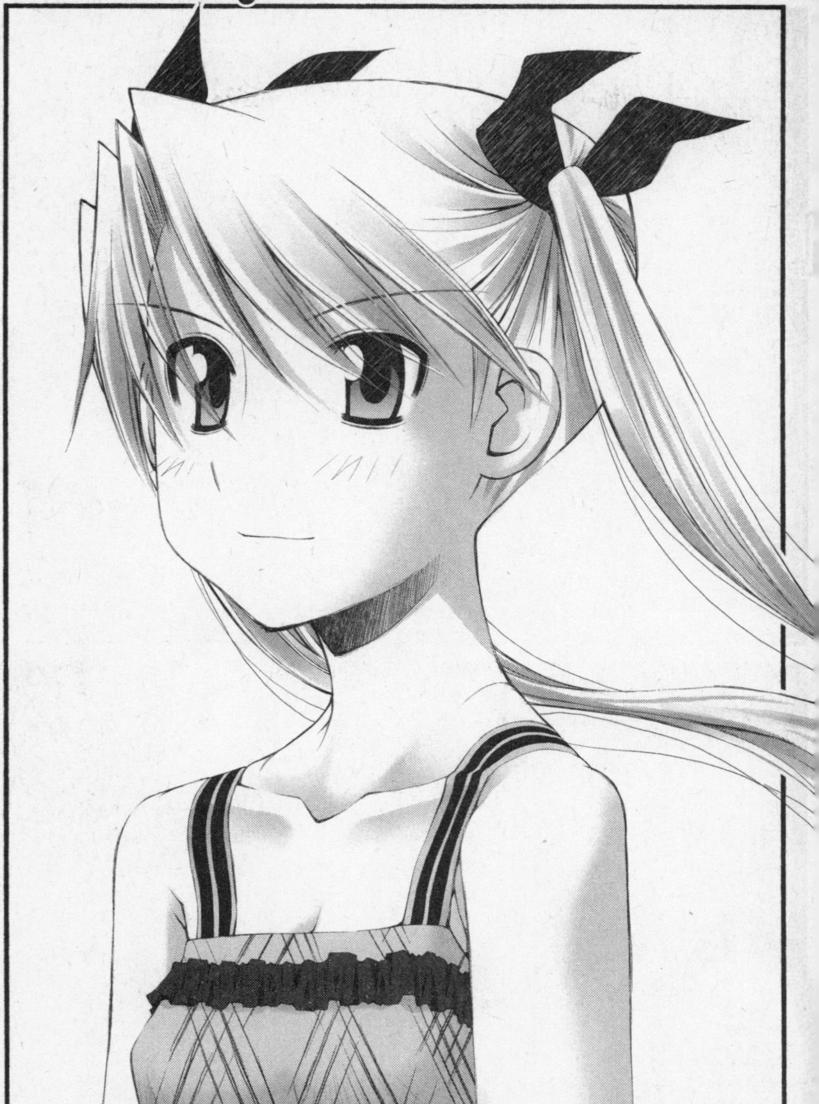

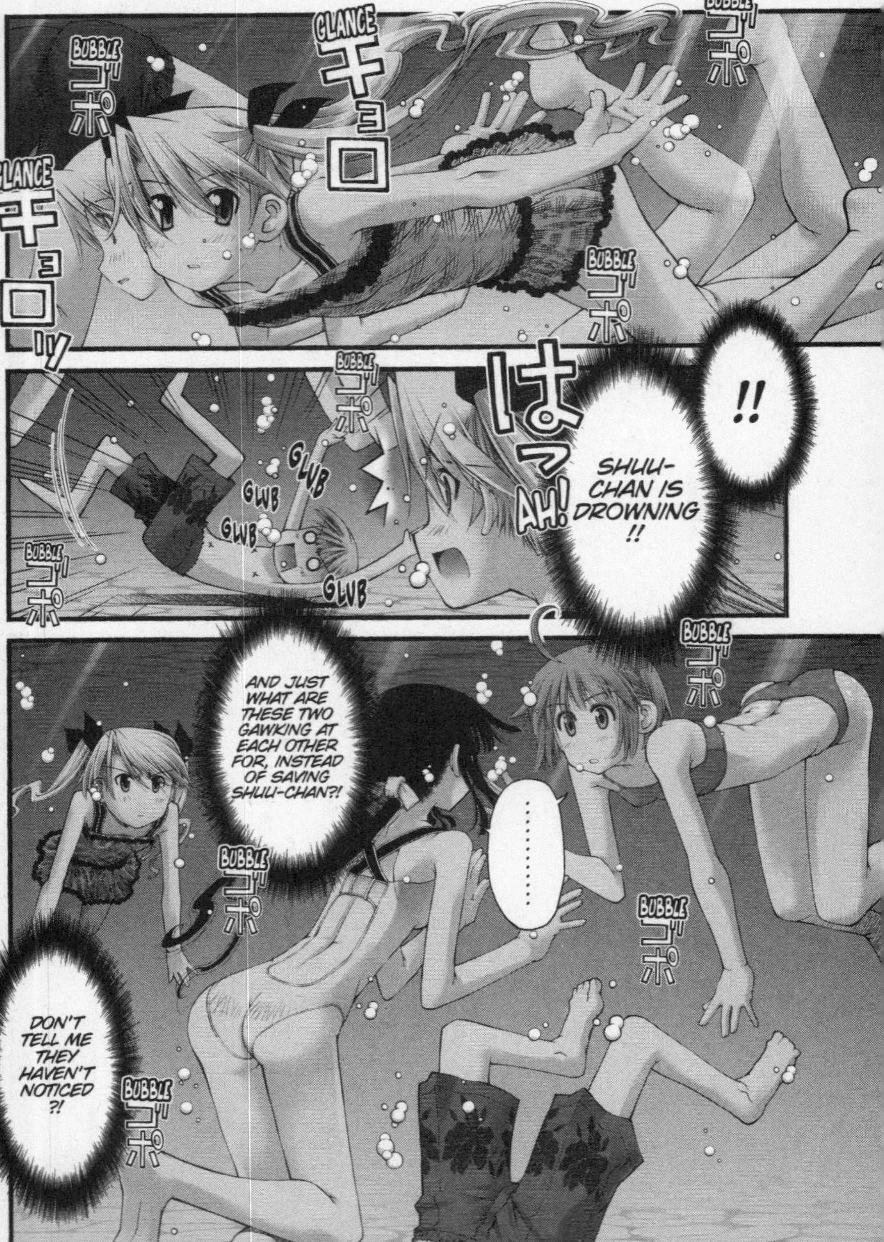
BUBBLE
ゴポ
GLANCE
キョロ
BUBBLE
ゴポ
GLANCE
キョロッ
BUBBLE
ゴポ
!!
SHUU-CHAN IS DROWNING !!
はっ
AH!
BUBBLE
ゴポ
GLUB
GLUB
GLUB
GLUB
BUBBLE
ゴポ
BUBBLE
ゴポ
AND JUST WHAT ARE THESE TWO GAWKING AT EACH OTHER FOR, INSTEAD OF SAVING SHUU-CHAN?!
....
BUBBLE
ゴポ
BUBBLE
ゴポ
DON'T TELL ME THEY HAVEN'T NOTICED ?!
BUBBLE
ゴポ

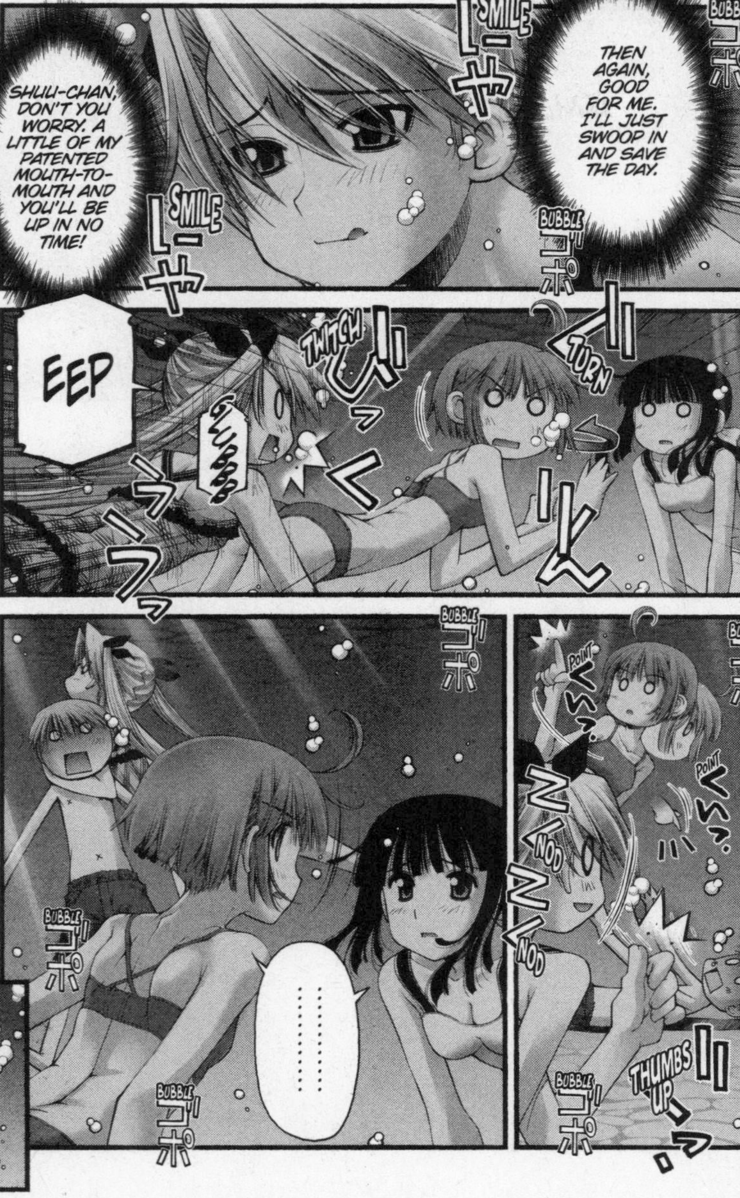
BUBBLE
THEN AGAIN, GOOD FOR ME. I'LL JUST SWOOP IN AND SAVE THE DAY.
SMILE
SHUU-CHAN, DON'T YOU WORRY. A LITTLE OF MY PATENTED MOUTH-TO-MOUTH AND YOU'LL BE UP IN NO TIME!
SMILE
BUBBLE
TURN
TWITCH
EEP
GLUBBBB
BUBBLE
POINT
POINT
NOD
NOD
THUMBS UP
BUBBLE
BUBBLE
BUBBLE
BUBBLE

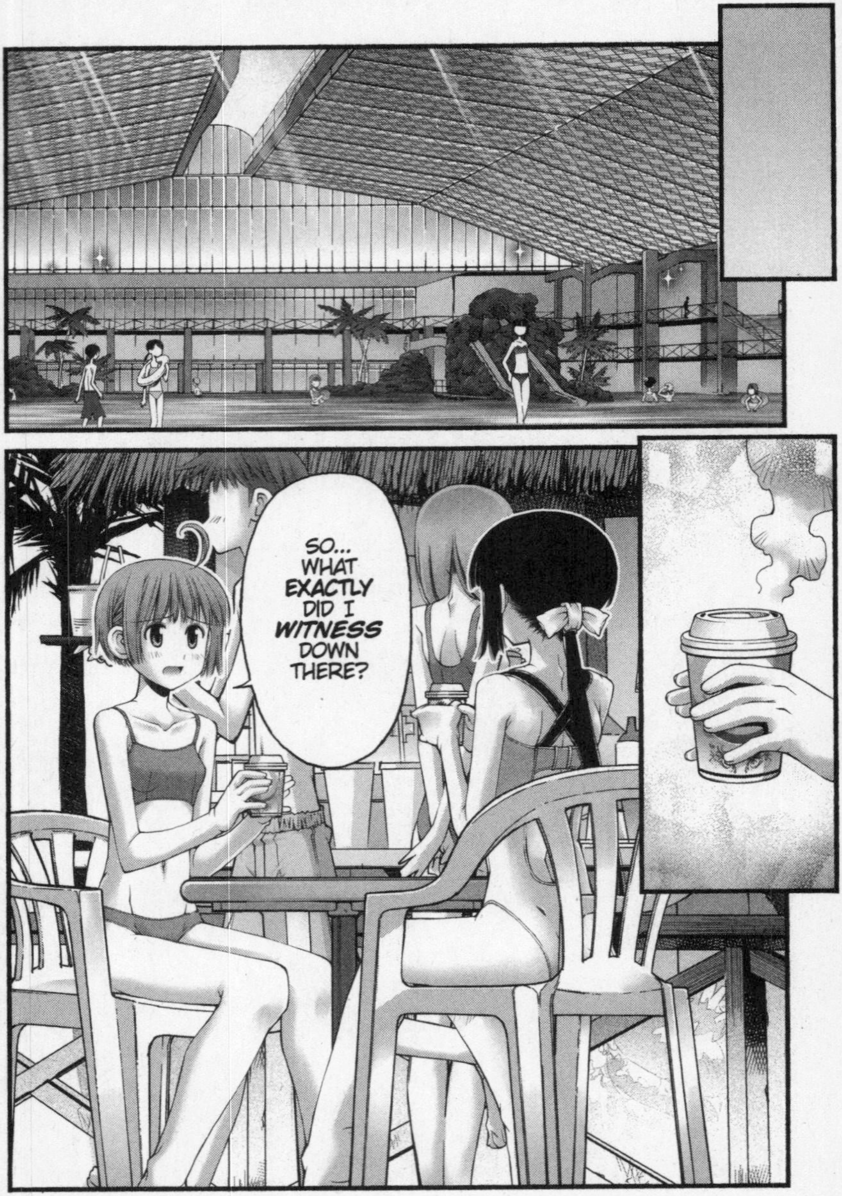
SO... WHAT EXACTLY DID I WITNESS DOWN THERE?

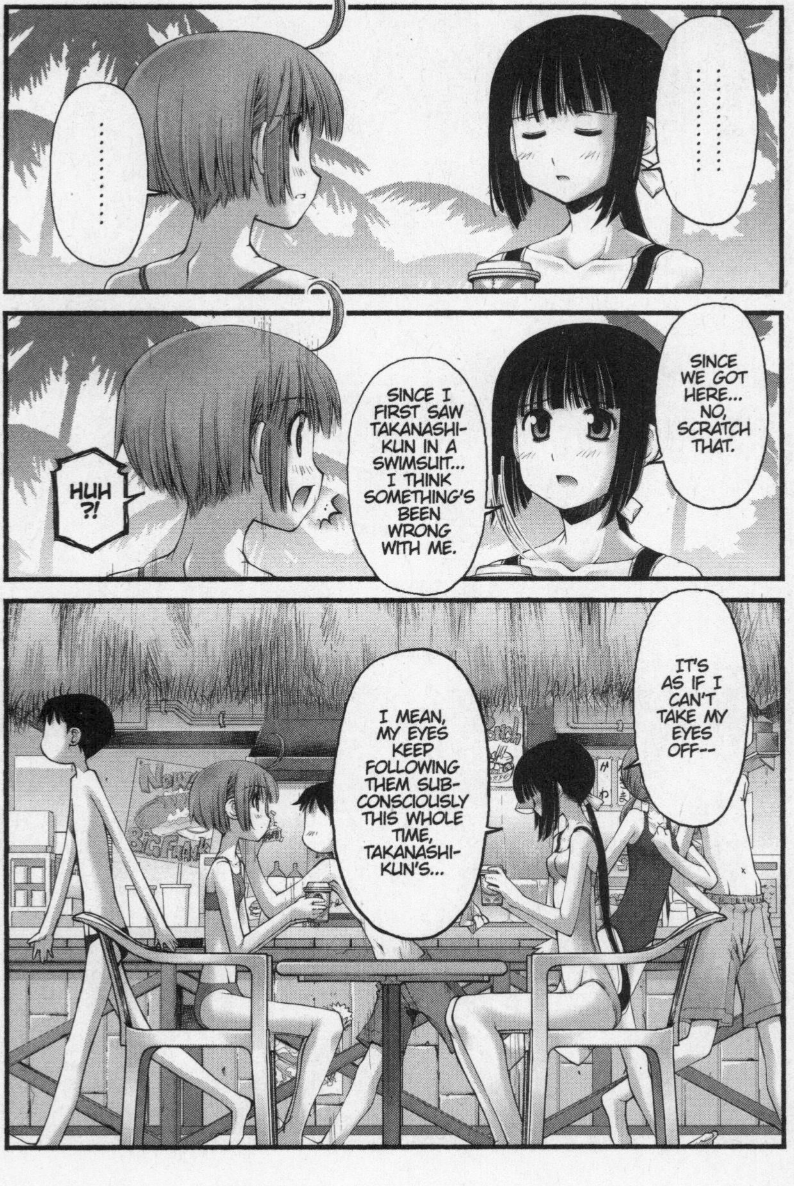
......
......
SINCE WE GOT HERE... NO, SCRATCH THAT.
SINCE I FIRST SAW TAKANASHI-KUN IN A SWIMSUIT... I THINK SOMETHING'S BEEN WRONG WITH ME.
HUH ?!
IT'S AS IF I CAN'T TAKE MY EYES OFF--
I MEAN, MY EYES KEEP FOLLOWING THEM SUB-CONSCIOUSLY THIS WHOLE TIME, TAKANASHI-KUN'S...

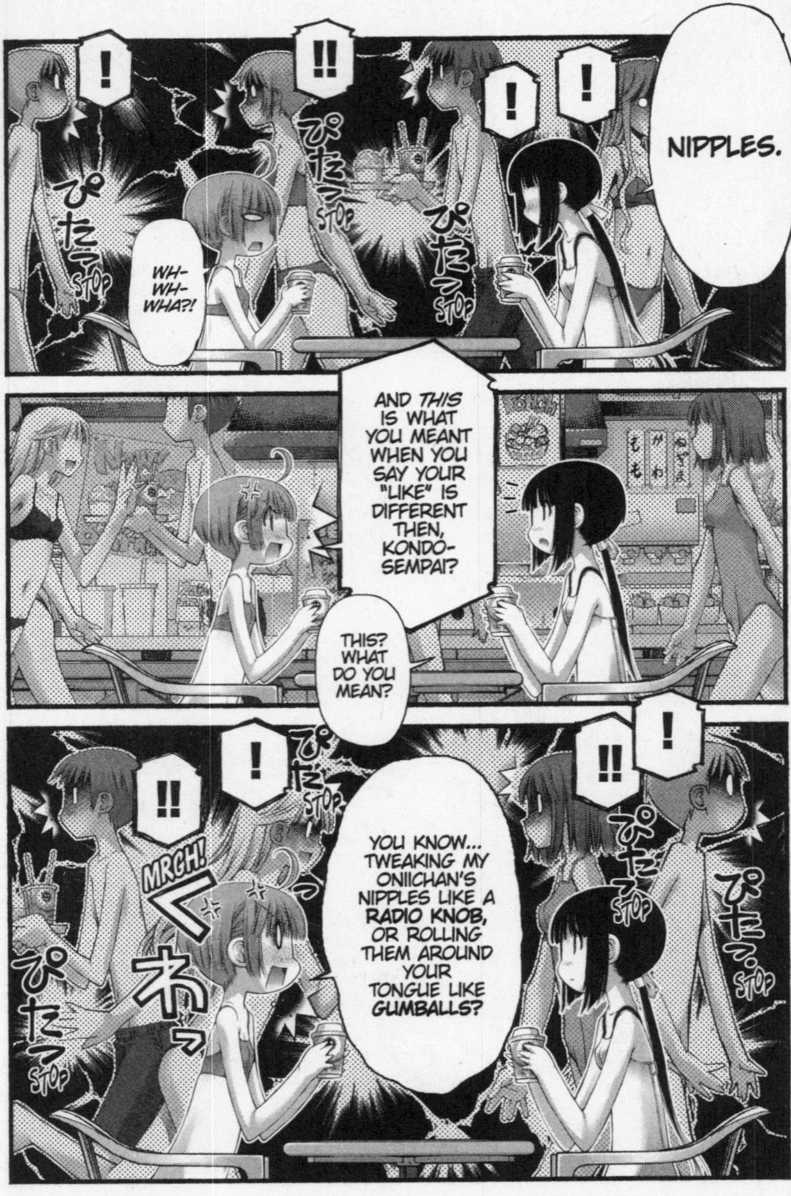
NIPPLES.
!
!
!!
!
ぴたっ STOP
ぴたっ STOP
ぴたっ STOP
WH-WH-WHA?!
AND THIS IS WHAT YOU MEANT WHEN YOU SAY YOUR "LIKE" IS DIFFERENT THEN, KONDO-SEMPAI?
THIS? WHAT DO YOU MEAN?
!
!!
ぴたっ STOP
ぴたっ STOP
YOU KNOW... TWEAKING MY ONIICHAN'S NIPPLES LIKE A RADIO KNOB, OR ROLLING THEM AROUND YOUR TONGUE LIKE GUMBALLS?
!
ぴたっ STOP
!!
MRGH! くわっ
ぴたっ STOP

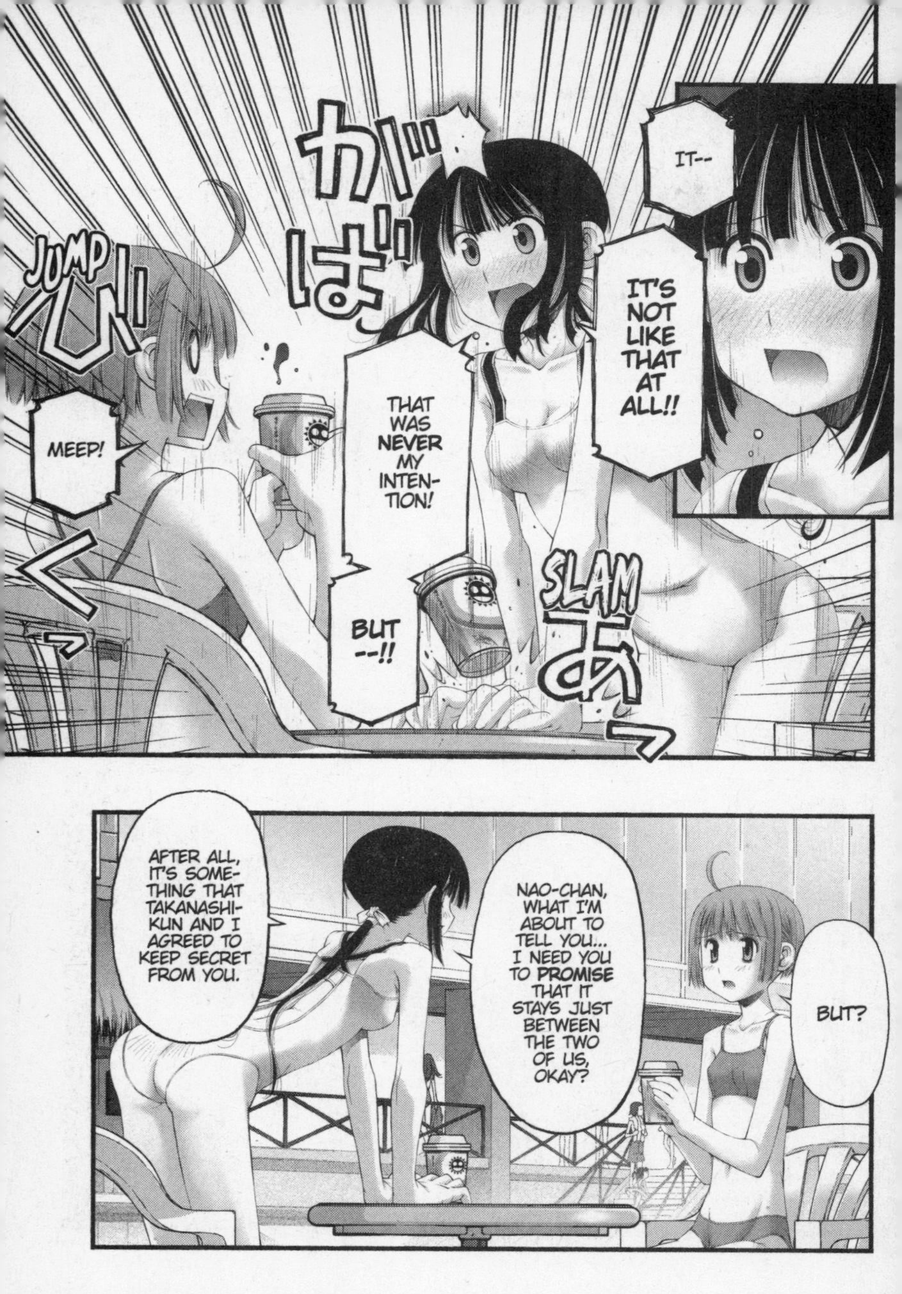
IT--
IT'S NOT LIKE THAT AT ALL!!
がば
THAT WAS NEVER MY INTENTION!
BUT --!!
SLAM
あ
JUMP
びく
MEEP!
BUT?
NAO-CHAN, WHAT I'M ABOUT TO TELL YOU... I NEED YOU TO PROMISE THAT IT STAYS JUST BETWEEN THE TWO OF US, OKAY?
AFTER ALL, IT'S SOMETHING THAT TAKANASHI-KUN AND I AGREED TO KEEP SECRET FROM YOU.

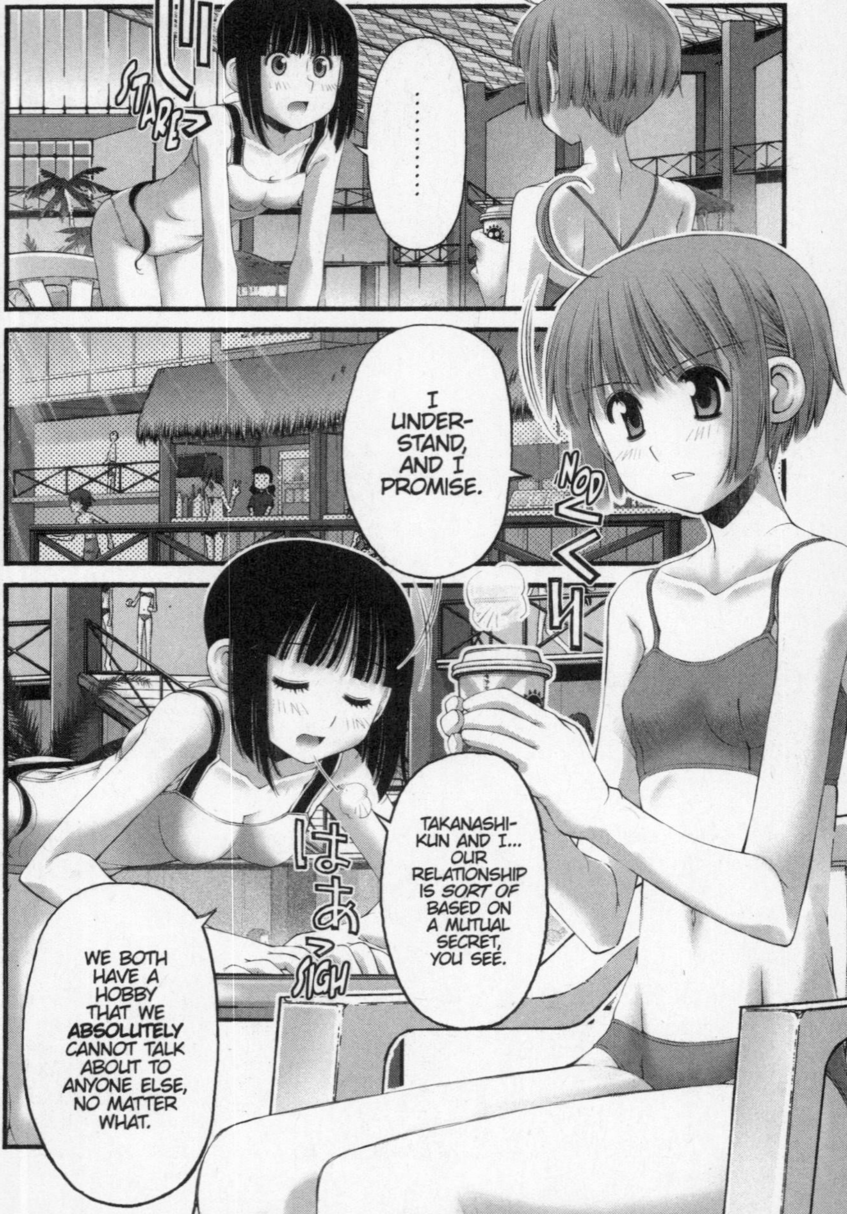
……
STARE
I UNDER-STAND, AND I PROMISE.
NOD
TAKANASHI-KUN AND I... OUR RELATIONSHIP IS *SORT OF* BASED ON A MUTUAL SECRET, YOU SEE.
SIGH
WE BOTH HAVE A HOBBY THAT WE **ABSOLUTELY** CANNOT TALK ABOUT TO ANYONE ELSE, NO MATTER WHAT.

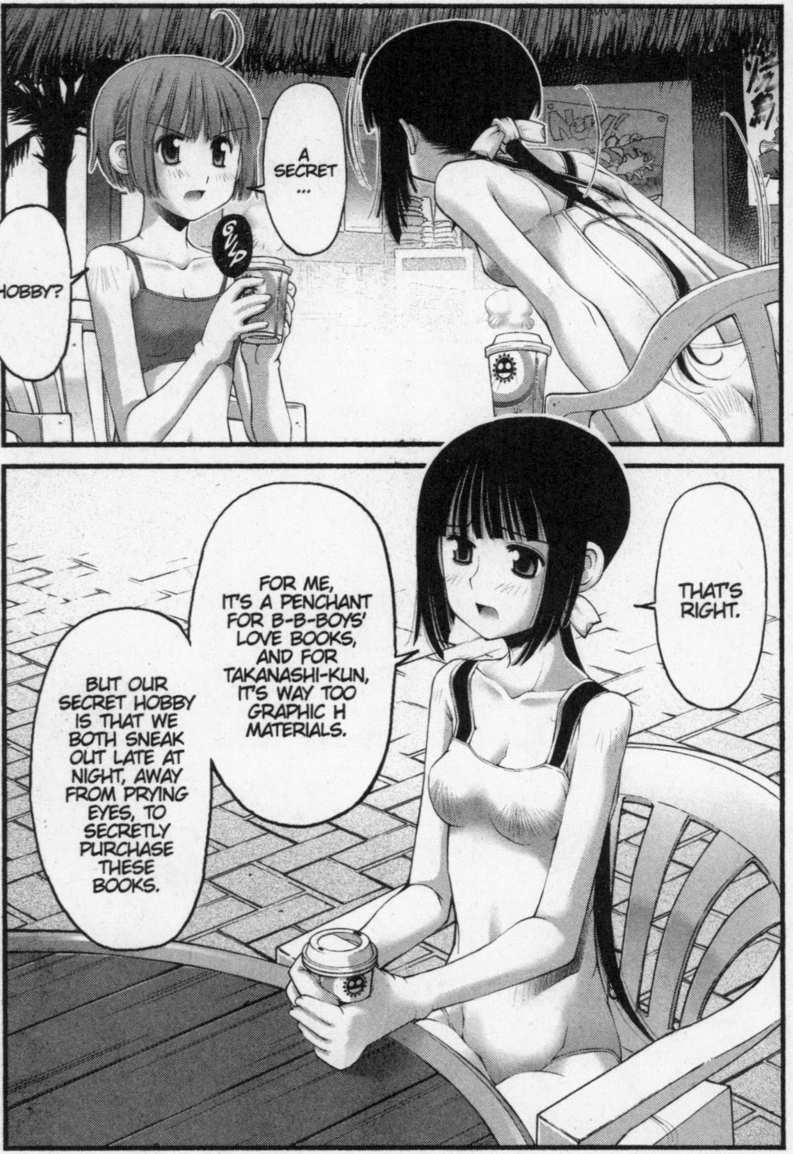
A SECRET ...
GULP
HOBBY?
THAT'S RIGHT.
FOR ME, IT'S A PENCHANT FOR B-B-BOYS' LOVE BOOKS, AND FOR TAKANASHI-KUN, IT'S WAY TOO GRAPHIC H MATERIALS.
BUT OUR SECRET HOBBY IS THAT WE BOTH SNEAK OUT LATE AT NIGHT, AWAY FROM PRYING EYES, TO SECRETLY PURCHASE THESE BOOKS.

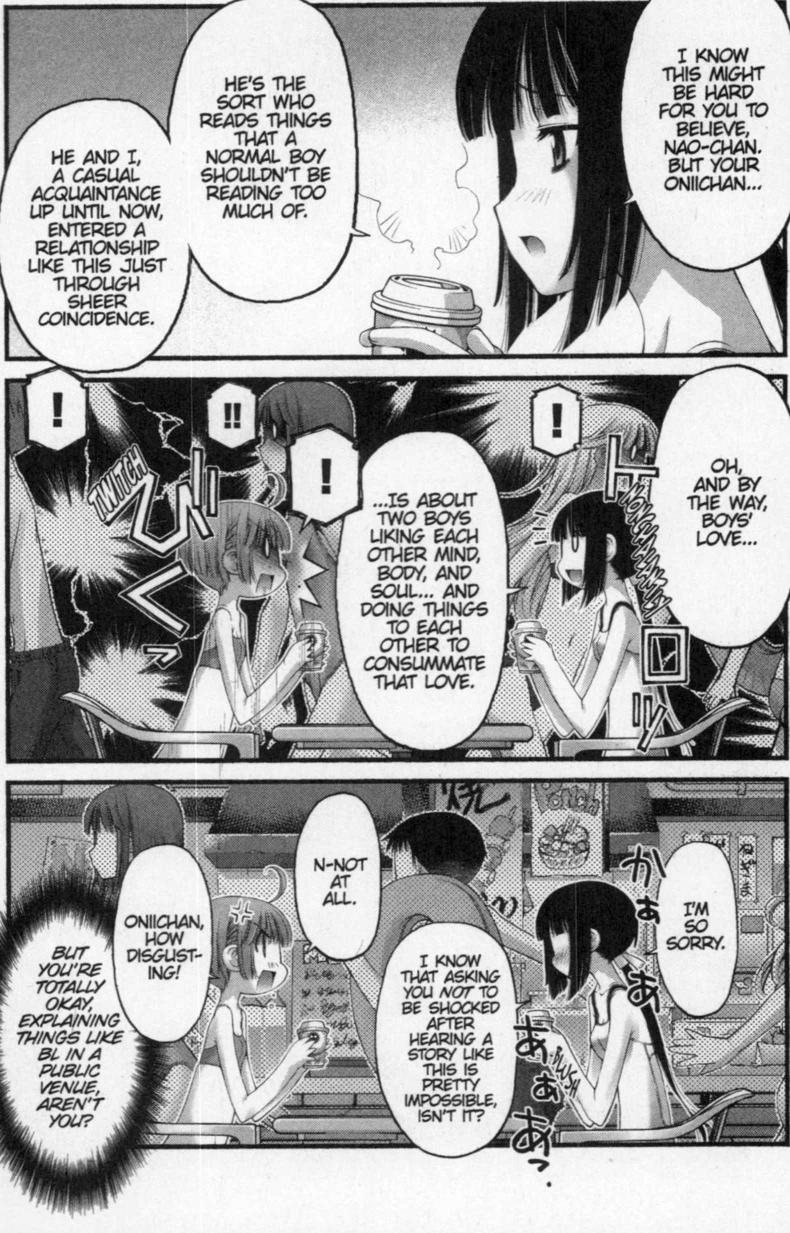

I KNOW THIS MIGHT BE HARD FOR YOU TO BELIEVE, NAO-CHAN. BUT YOUR ONIICHAN...
HE'S THE SORT WHO READS THINGS THAT A NORMAL BOY SHOULDN'T BE READING TOO MUCH OF.
HE AND I, A CASUAL ACQUAINTANCE UP UNTIL NOW, ENTERED A RELATIONSHIP LIKE THIS JUST THROUGH SHEER COINCIDENCE.
OH, AND BY THE WAY, BOYS' LOVE...
NONCHALANTLY
!
...IS ABOUT TWO BOYS LIKING EACH OTHER MIND, BODY, AND SOUL... AND DOING THINGS TO EACH OTHER TO CONSUMMATE THAT LOVE.
!
!!
!
TWITCH
I'M SO SORRY.
かあああああっ
BLUSH
I KNOW THAT ASKING YOU *NOT* TO BE SHOCKED AFTER HEARING A STORY LIKE THIS IS PRETTY IMPOSSIBLE, ISN'T IT?
N-NOT AT ALL.
ONIICHAN, HOW DISGUST-ING!
BUT YOU'RE TOTALLY OKAY, EXPLAINING THINGS LIKE BL IN A PUBLIC VENUE, AREN'T YOU?

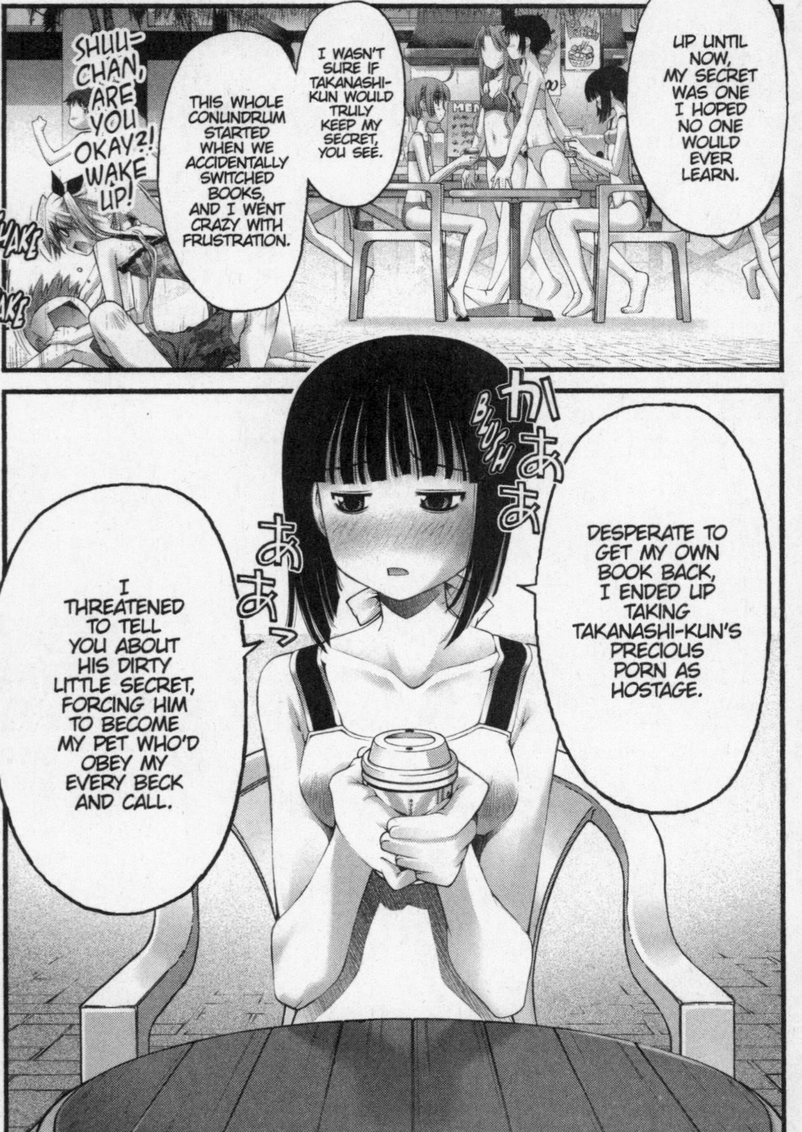
UP UNTIL NOW, MY SECRET WAS ONE I HOPED NO ONE WOULD EVER LEARN.
I WASN'T SURE IF TAKANASHI-KUN WOULD TRULY KEEP MY SECRET, YOU SEE.
THIS WHOLE CONUNDRUM STARTED WHEN WE ACCIDENTALLY SWITCHED BOOKS, AND I WENT CRAZY WITH FRUSTRATION.
SHUU-CHAN, ARE YOU OKAY?! WAKE UP!
SHAKE
SHAKE
DESPERATE TO GET MY OWN BOOK BACK, I ENDED UP TAKING TAKANASHI-KUN'S PRECIOUS PORN AS HOSTAGE.
かあああ
BLUSH
ああ
I THREATENED TO TELL YOU ABOUT HIS DIRTY LITTLE SECRET, FORCING HIM TO BECOME MY PET WHO'D OBEY MY EVERY BECK AND CALL.

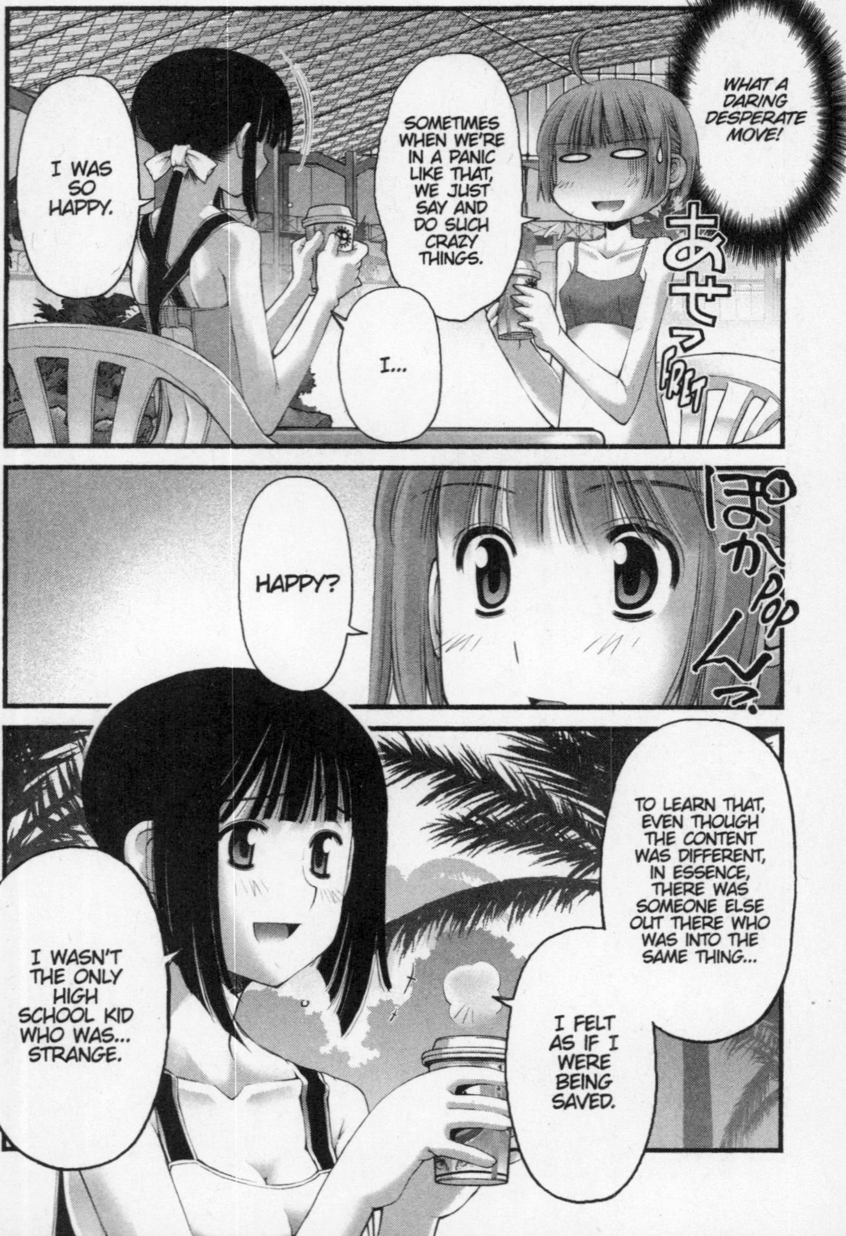
WHAT A DARING DESPERATE MOVE!
あせっ
FRET
SOMETIMES WHEN WE'RE IN A PANIC LIKE THAT, WE JUST SAY AND DO SUCH CRAZY THINGS.
I...
I WAS SO HAPPY.
ぽかんっ
POP
HAPPY?
TO LEARN THAT, EVEN THOUGH THE CONTENT WAS DIFFERENT, IN ESSENCE, THERE WAS SOMEONE ELSE OUT THERE WHO WAS INTO THE SAME THING...
I FELT AS IF I WERE BEING SAVED.
I WASN'T THE ONLY HIGH SCHOOL KID WHO WAS... STRANGE.

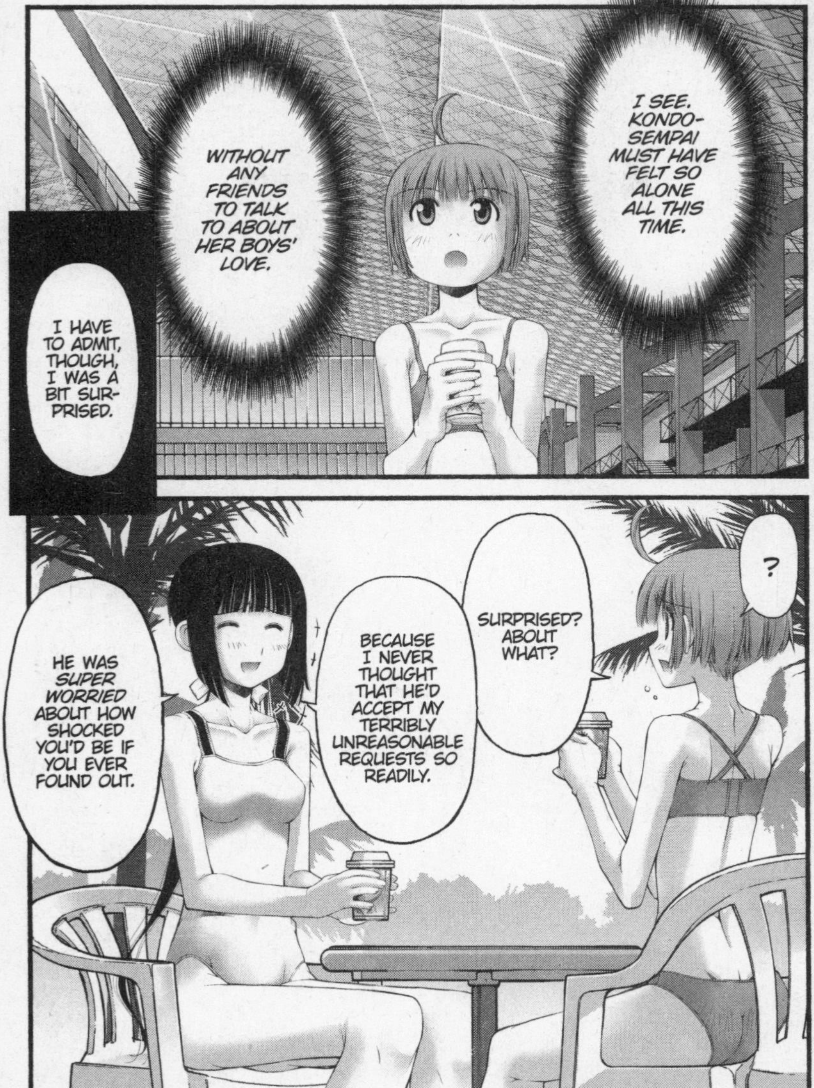
I SEE. KONDO-SEMPAI MUST HAVE FELT SO ALONE ALL THIS TIME.
WITHOUT ANY FRIENDS TO TALK TO ABOUT HER BOYS' LOVE.
I HAVE TO ADMIT, THOUGH, I WAS A BIT SURPRISED.
?
SURPRISED? ABOUT WHAT?
BECAUSE I NEVER THOUGHT THAT HE'D ACCEPT MY TERRIBLY UNREASONABLE REQUESTS SO READILY.
HE WAS SUPER WORRIED ABOUT HOW SHOCKED YOU'D BE IF YOU EVER FOUND OUT.

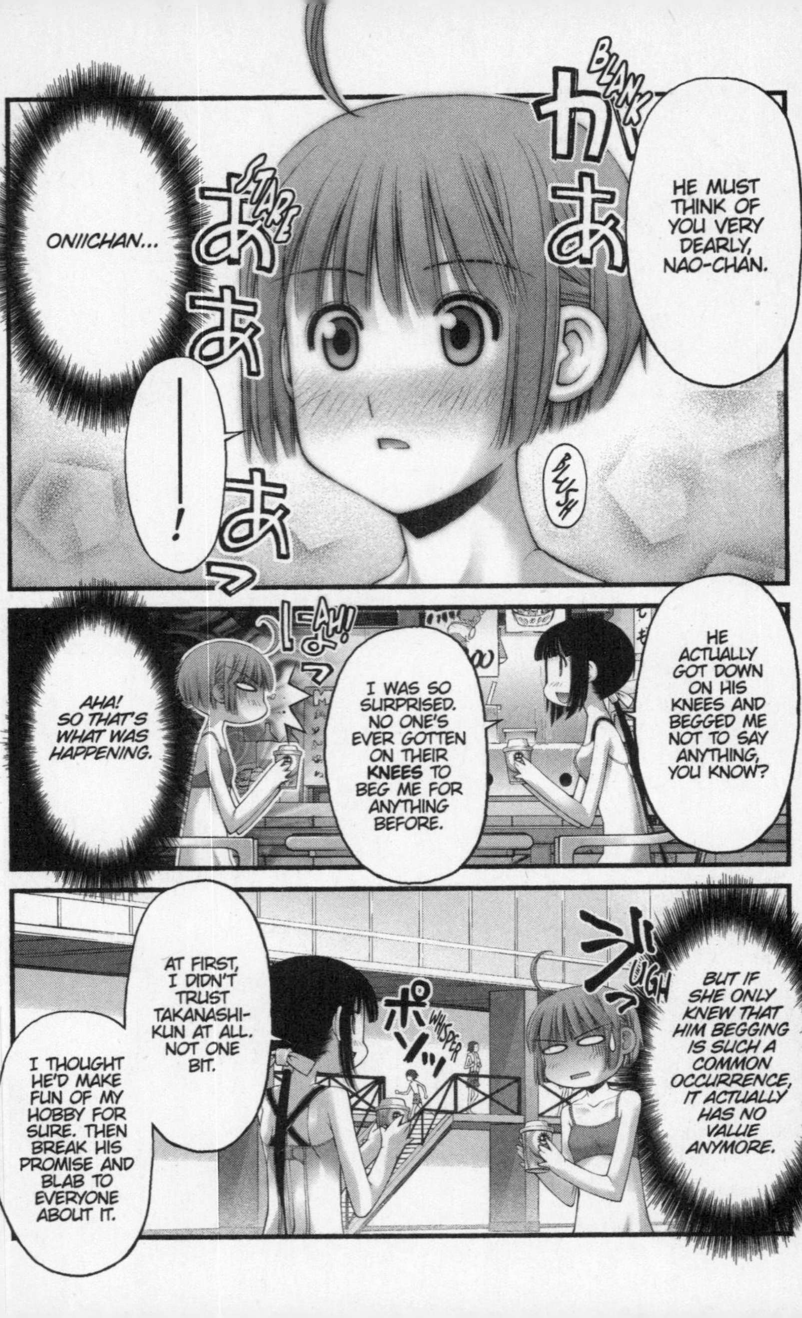
BLANK
HE MUST THINK OF YOU VERY DEARLY, NAO-CHAN.
STARE
BLUSH
ONIICHAN...
HE ACTUALLY GOT DOWN ON HIS KNEES AND BEGGED ME NOT TO SAY ANYTHING, YOU KNOW?
I WAS SO SURPRISED. NO ONE'S EVER GOTTEN ON THEIR **KNEES** TO BEG ME FOR ANYTHING BEFORE.
AH!
AHA! SO THAT'S WHAT WAS HAPPENING.
UGH
BUT IF SHE ONLY KNEW THAT HIM BEGGING IS SUCH A COMMON OCCURRENCE, IT ACTUALLY HAS NO VALUE ANYMORE.
WHISPER
AT FIRST, I DIDN'T TRUST TAKANASHI-KUN AT ALL. NOT ONE BIT.
I THOUGHT HE'D MAKE FUN OF MY HOBBY FOR SURE. THEN BREAK HIS PROMISE AND BLAB TO EVERYONE ABOUT IT.

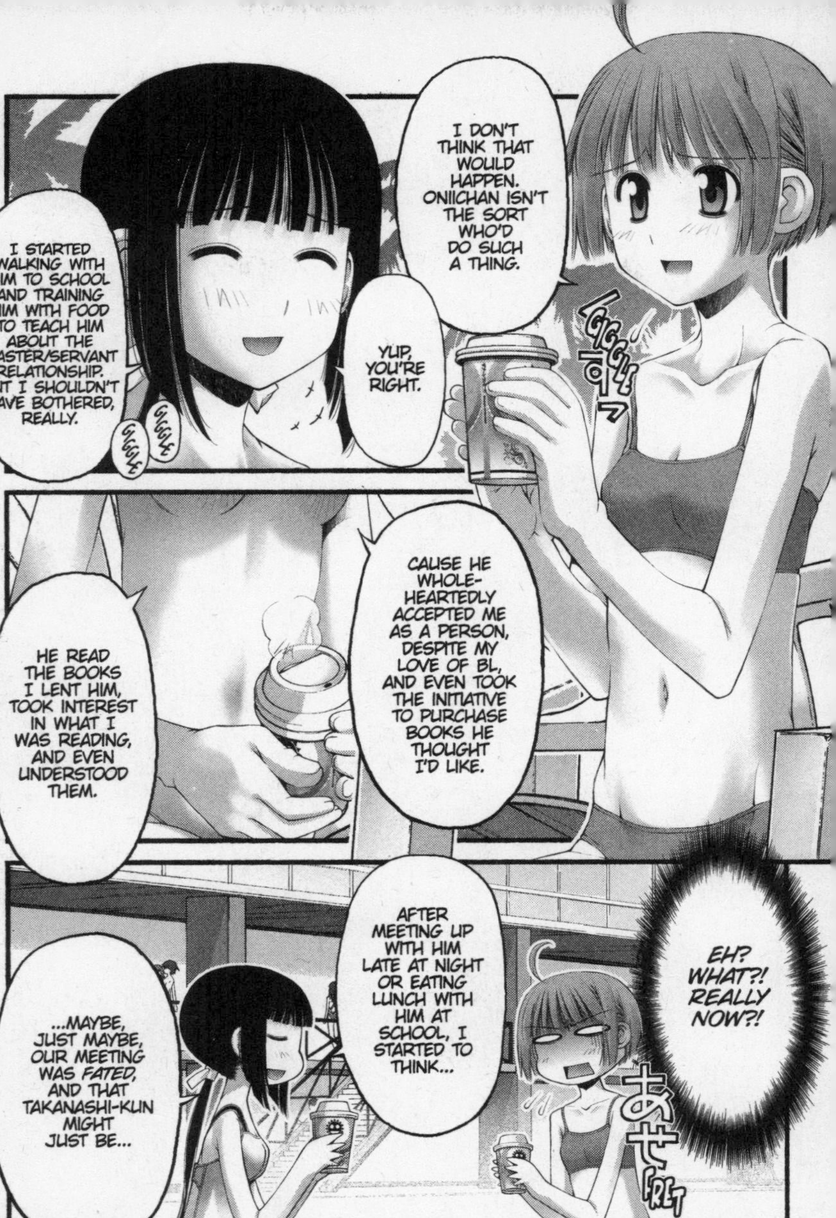
I DON'T THINK THAT WOULD HAPPEN. ONIICHAN ISN'T THE SORT WHO'D DO SUCH A THING.
GIGGLE
YUP, YOU'RE RIGHT.
I STARTED WALKING WITH HIM TO SCHOOL AND TRAINING HIM WITH FOOD TO TEACH HIM ABOUT THE MASTER/SERVANT RELATIONSHIP. BUT I SHOULDN'T HAVE BOTHERED, REALLY.
GIGGLE
GIGGLE
CAUSE HE WHOLE-HEARTEDLY ACCEPTED ME AS A PERSON, DESPITE MY LOVE OF BL, AND EVEN TOOK THE INITIATIVE TO PURCHASE BOOKS HE THOUGHT I'D LIKE.
HE READ THE BOOKS I LENT HIM, TOOK INTEREST IN WHAT I WAS READING, AND EVEN UNDERSTOOD THEM.
EH? WHAT?! REALLY NOW?!
AFTER MEETING UP WITH HIM LATE AT NIGHT OR EATING LUNCH WITH HIM AT SCHOOL, I STARTED TO THINK...
あせ
FRET
...MAYBE, JUST MAYBE, OUR MEETING WAS *FATED*, AND THAT TAKANASHI-KUN MIGHT JUST BE...

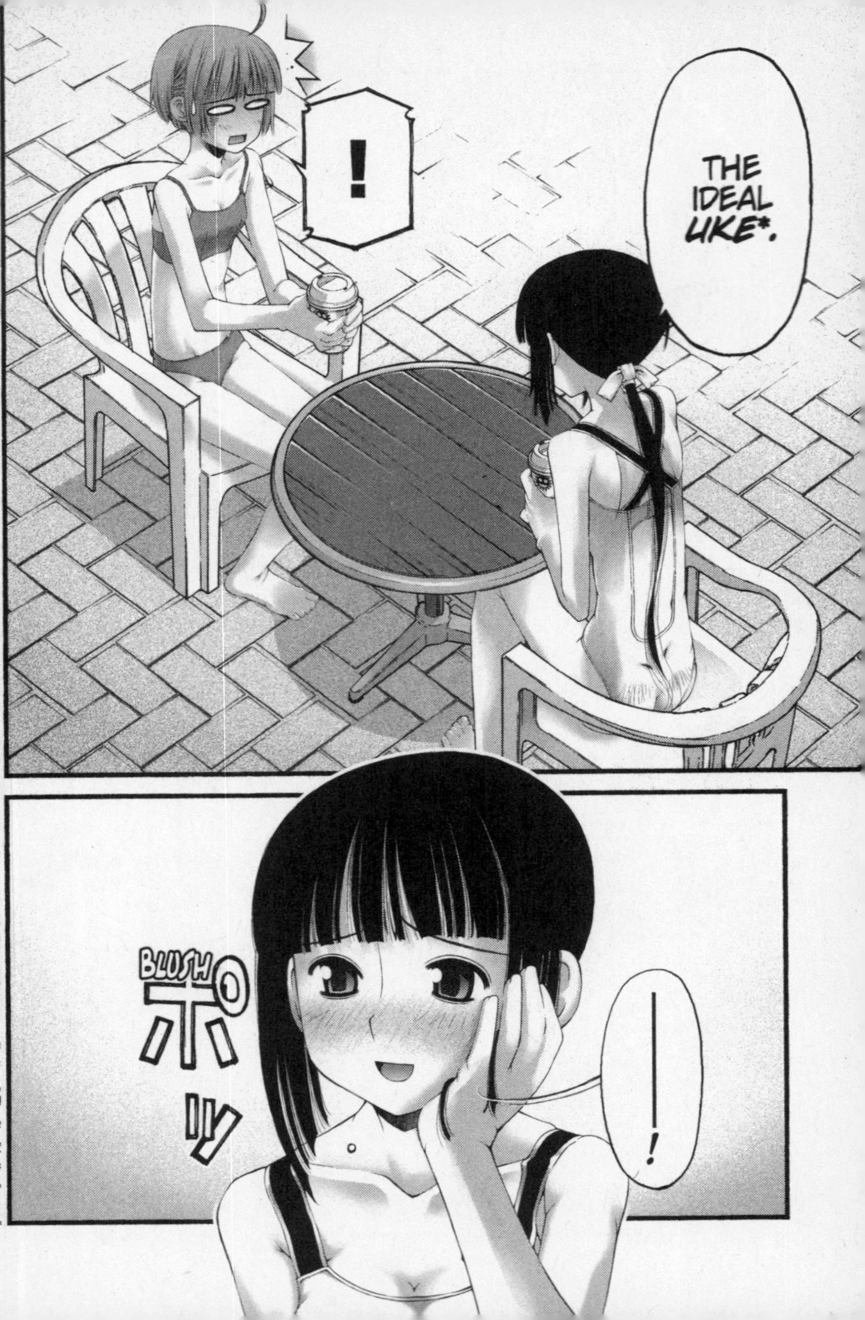
THE IDEAL UKE*.
!
BLUSH
ポッ
—!

*In a yaoi relationship, the "uke" (short for "ukeru," to receive) is the passive one or "bottom." The "top" is the "seme."

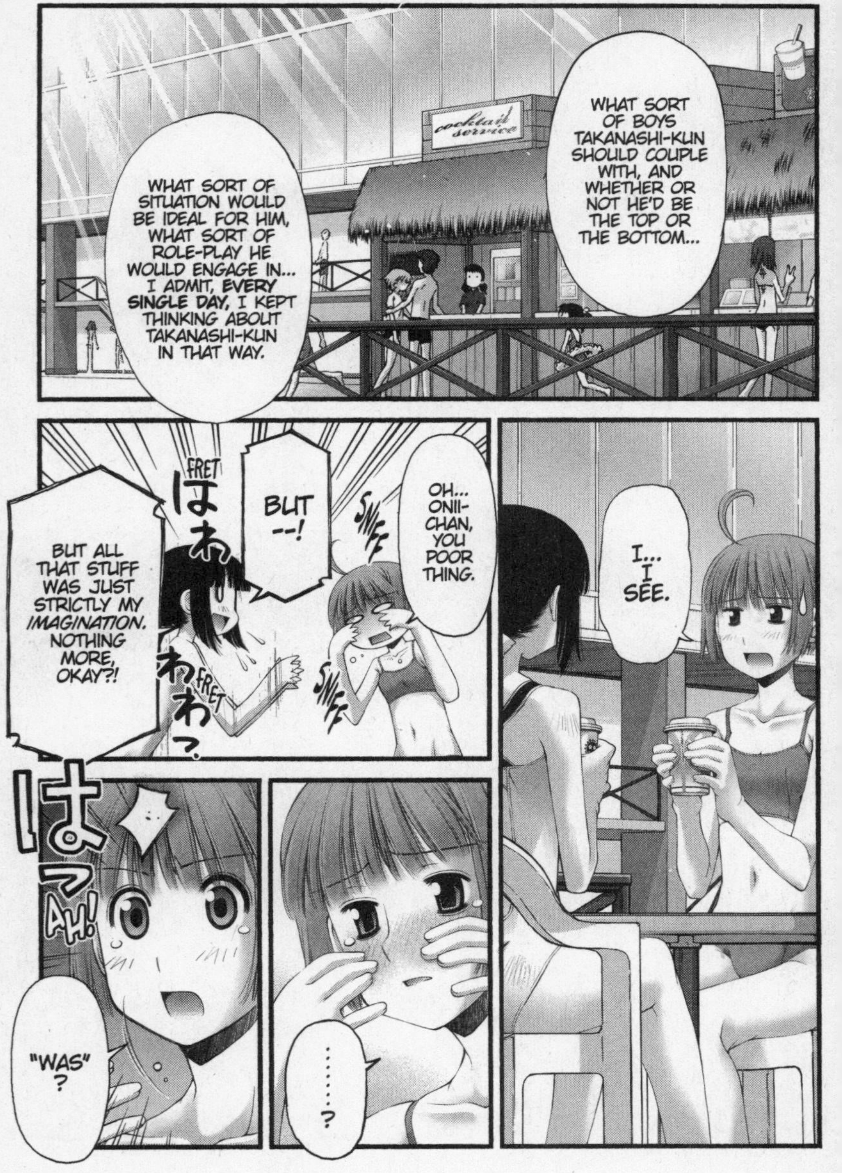

WHAT SORT OF BOYS TAKANASHI-KUN SHOULD COUPLE WITH, AND WHETHER OR NOT HE'D BE THE TOP OR THE BOTTOM...
cocktail service
WHAT SORT OF SITUATION WOULD BE IDEAL FOR HIM, WHAT SORT OF ROLE-PLAY HE WOULD ENGAGE IN... I ADMIT, EVERY SINGLE DAY, I KEPT THINKING ABOUT TAKANASHI-KUN IN THAT WAY.
I... I SEE.
OH... ONII-CHAN, YOU POOR THING.
SNIFF
BUT --!
FRET
はわ
BUT ALL THAT STUFF WAS JUST STRICTLY MY *IMAGINATION*. NOTHING MORE, OKAY?!
わわっ
FRET
SNIFF
......?
はっ
AH!
"WAS"?

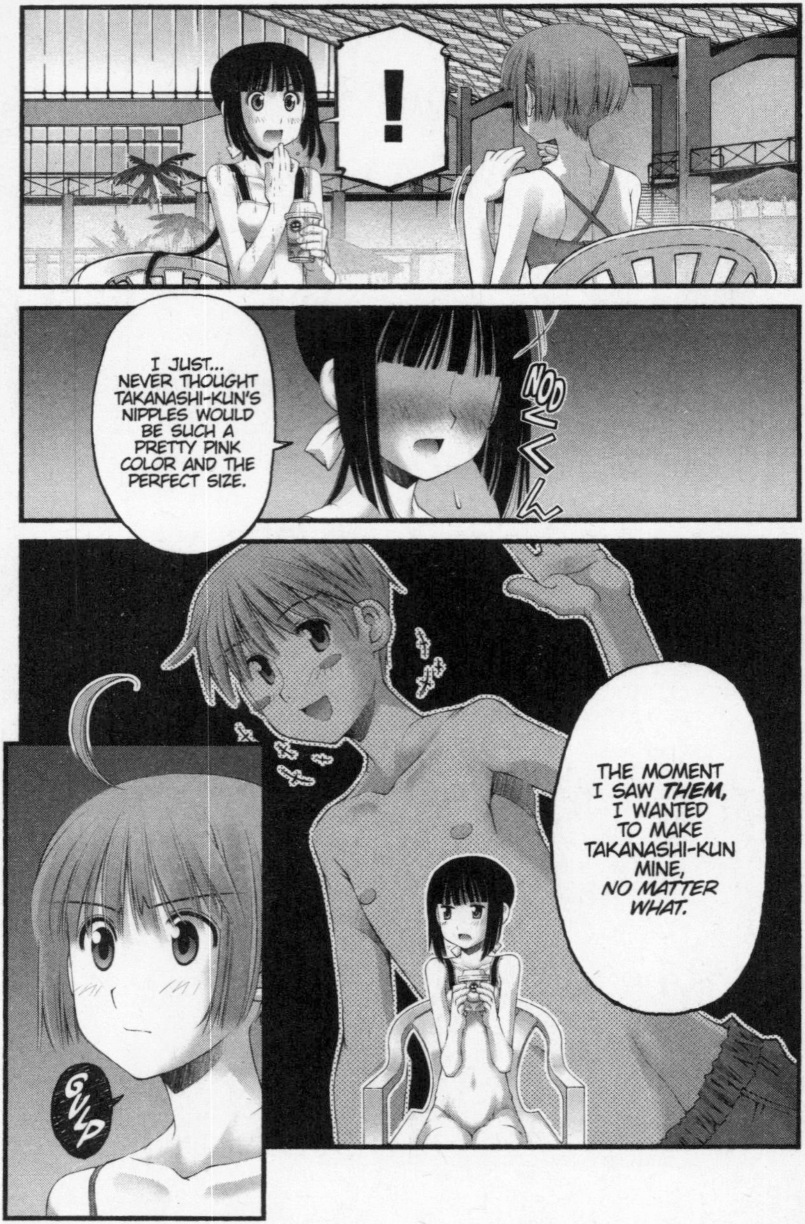
!
I JUST... NEVER THOUGHT TAKANASHI-KUN'S NIPPLES WOULD BE SUCH A PRETTY PINK COLOR AND THE PERFECT SIZE.
NOD
THE MOMENT I SAW *THEM,* I WANTED TO MAKE TAKANASHI-KUN MINE, *NO MATTER WHAT.*
GULP

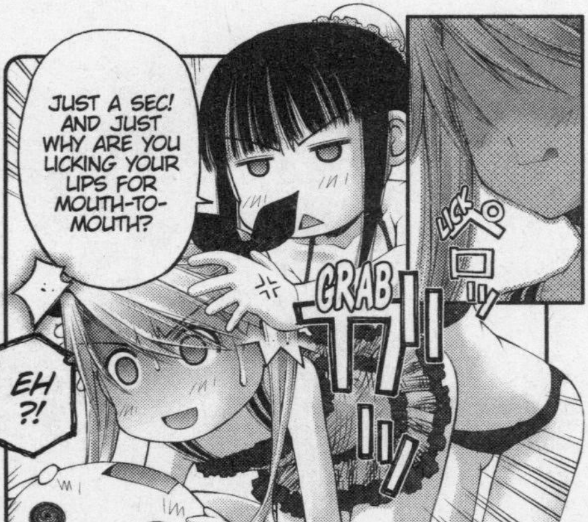
LICK
JUST A SEC! AND JUST WHY ARE YOU LICKING YOUR LIPS FOR MOUTH-TO-MOUTH?
GRAB
EH ?!

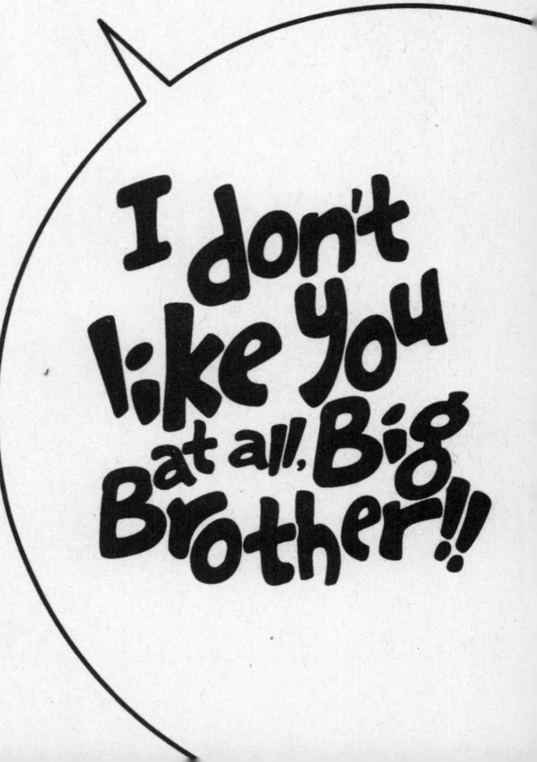
I don't like you at all, Big Brother!!

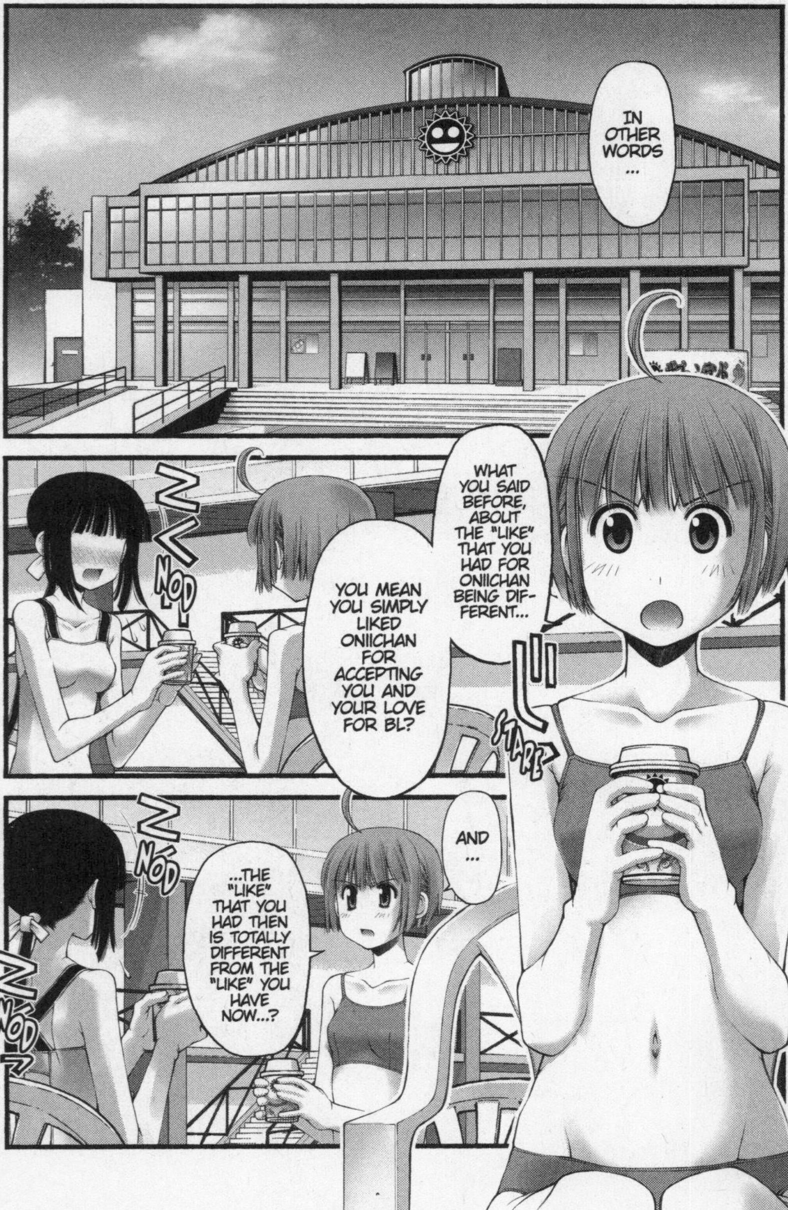
IN OTHER WORDS ...
WHAT YOU SAID BEFORE, ABOUT THE "LIKE" THAT YOU HAD FOR ONIICHAN BEING DIFFERENT...
STARE
YOU MEAN YOU SIMPLY LIKED ONIICHAN FOR ACCEPTING YOU AND YOUR LOVE FOR BL?
NOD
AND ...
...THE "LIKE" THAT YOU HAD THEN IS TOTALLY DIFFERENT FROM THE "LIKE" YOU HAVE NOW...?
NOD
NOD

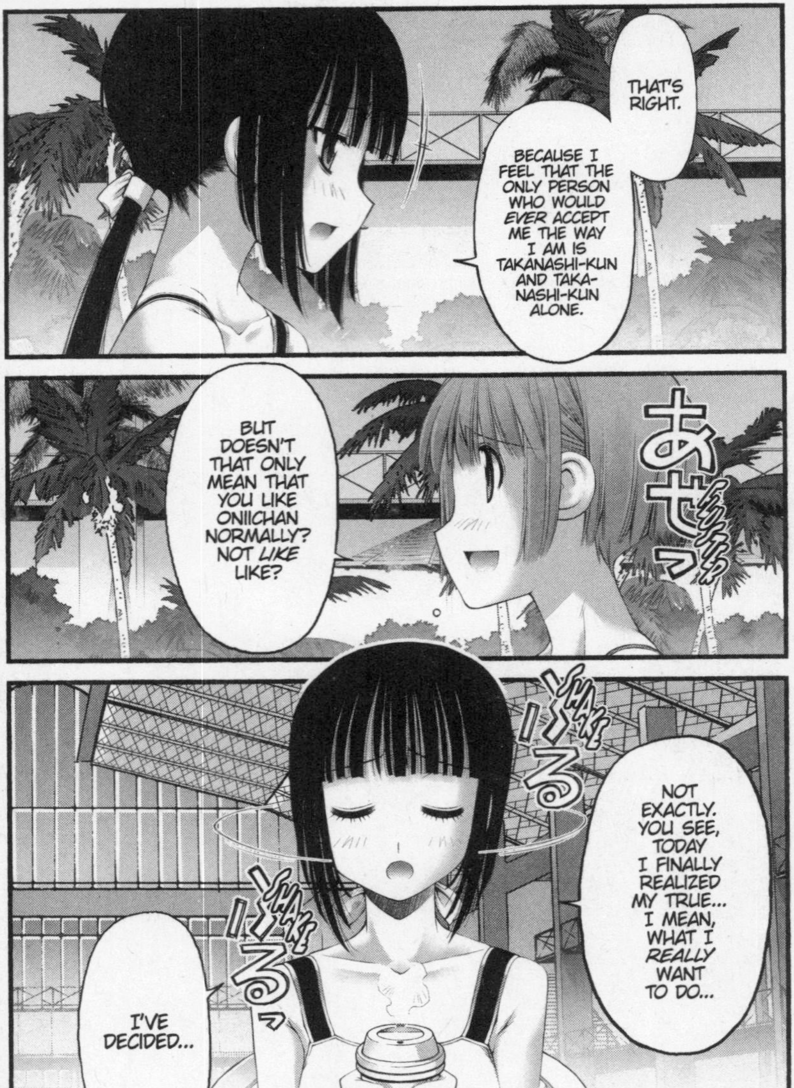
THAT'S RIGHT.
BECAUSE I FEEL THAT THE ONLY PERSON WHO WOULD *EVER* ACCEPT ME THE WAY I AM IS TAKANASHI-KUN AND TAKA-NASHI-KUN ALONE.
あせっ
BUT DOESN'T THAT ONLY MEAN THAT YOU LIKE ONIICHAN NORMALLY? NOT *LIKE* LIKE?
SHAKE
NOT EXACTLY. YOU SEE, TODAY I FINALLY REALIZED MY TRUE... I MEAN, WHAT I *REALLY* WANT TO DO...
SHAKE
I'VE DECIDED...

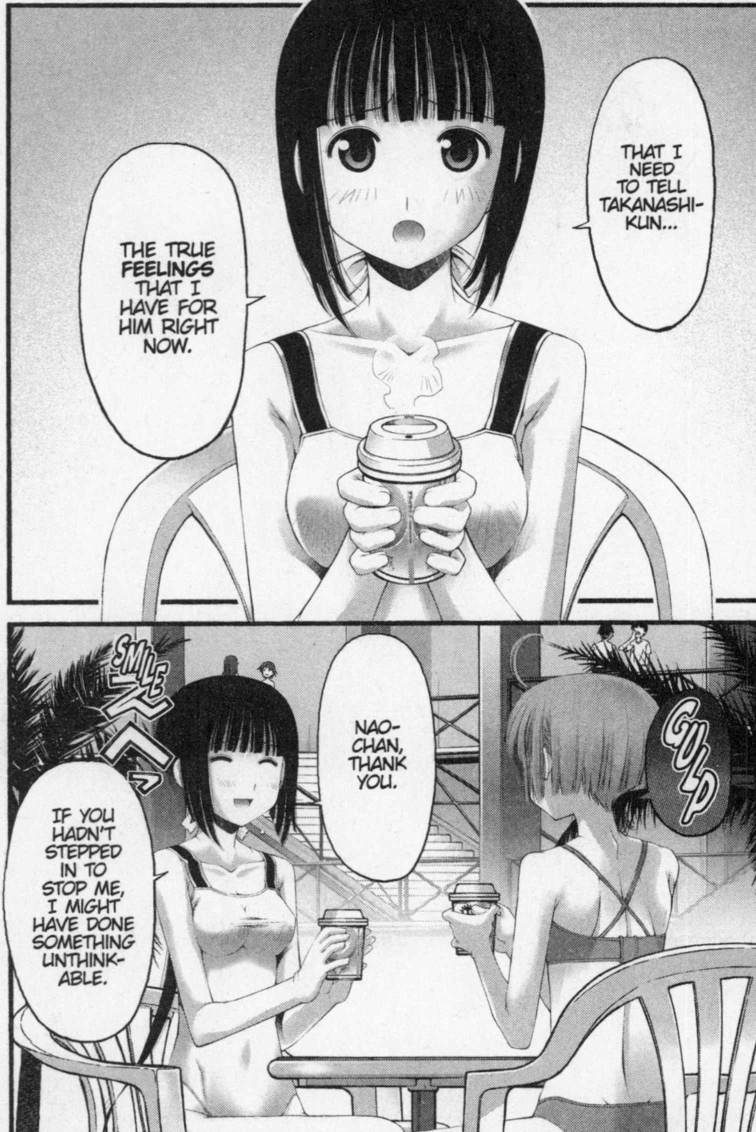
THAT I NEED TO TELL TAKANASHI-KUN...
THE TRUE FEELINGS THAT I HAVE FOR HIM RIGHT NOW.
GULP
NAO-CHAN, THANK YOU.
SMILE
IF YOU HADN'T STEPPED IN TO STOP ME, I MIGHT HAVE DONE SOMETHING UNTHINK-ABLE.

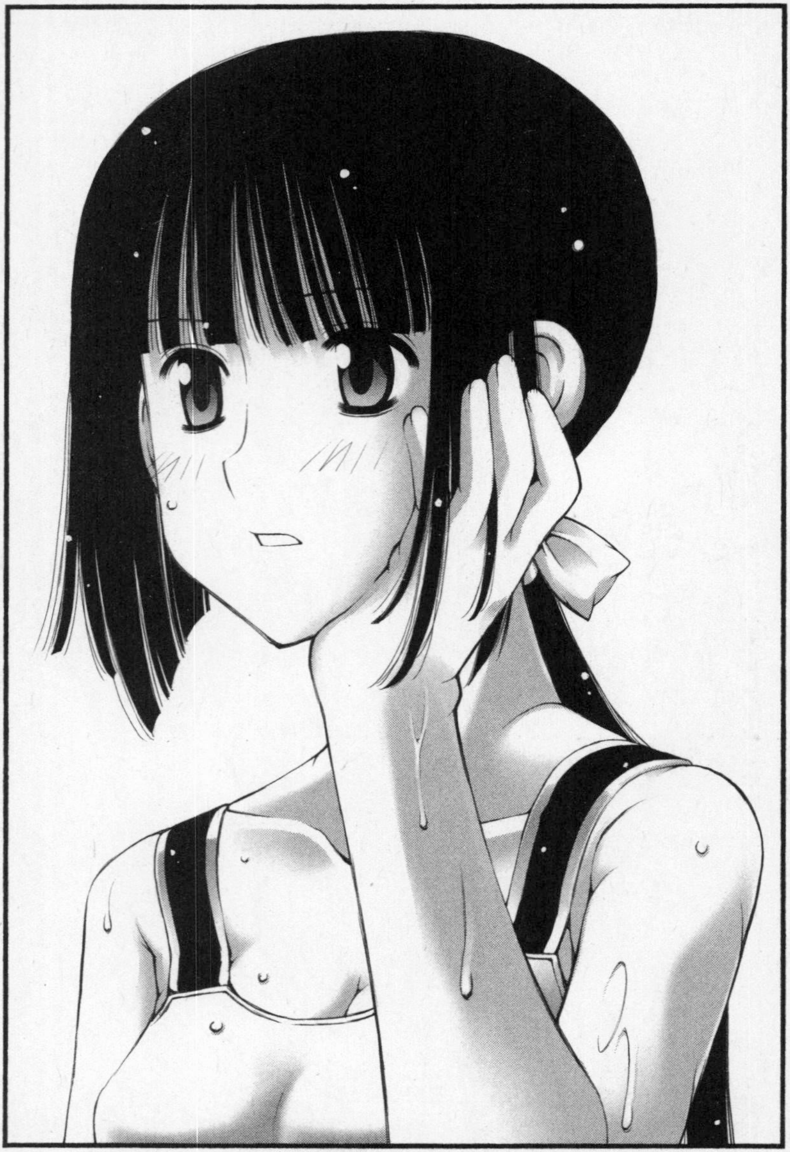

CHAPTER 33 Goodbye, Splash Country

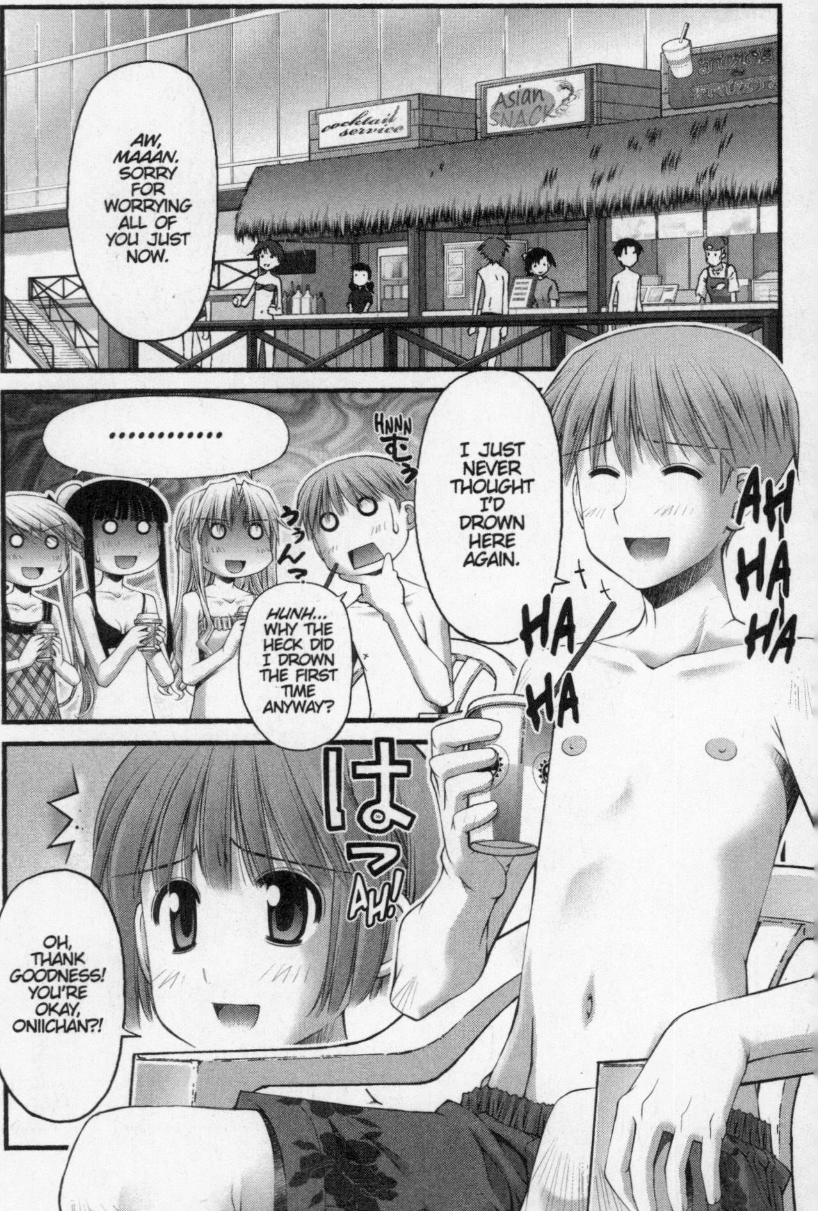
cocktail service
Asian SNACK
AW, MAAAN. SORRY FOR WORRYING ALL OF YOU JUST NOW.
I JUST NEVER THOUGHT I'D DROWN HERE AGAIN.
AH HA HA HA
HA HA HA
HNNN むっ
HUNH... WHY THE HECK DID I DROWN THE FIRST TIME ANYWAY?
....
はっ AH!
OH, THANK GOODNESS! YOU'RE OKAY, ONIICHAN?!

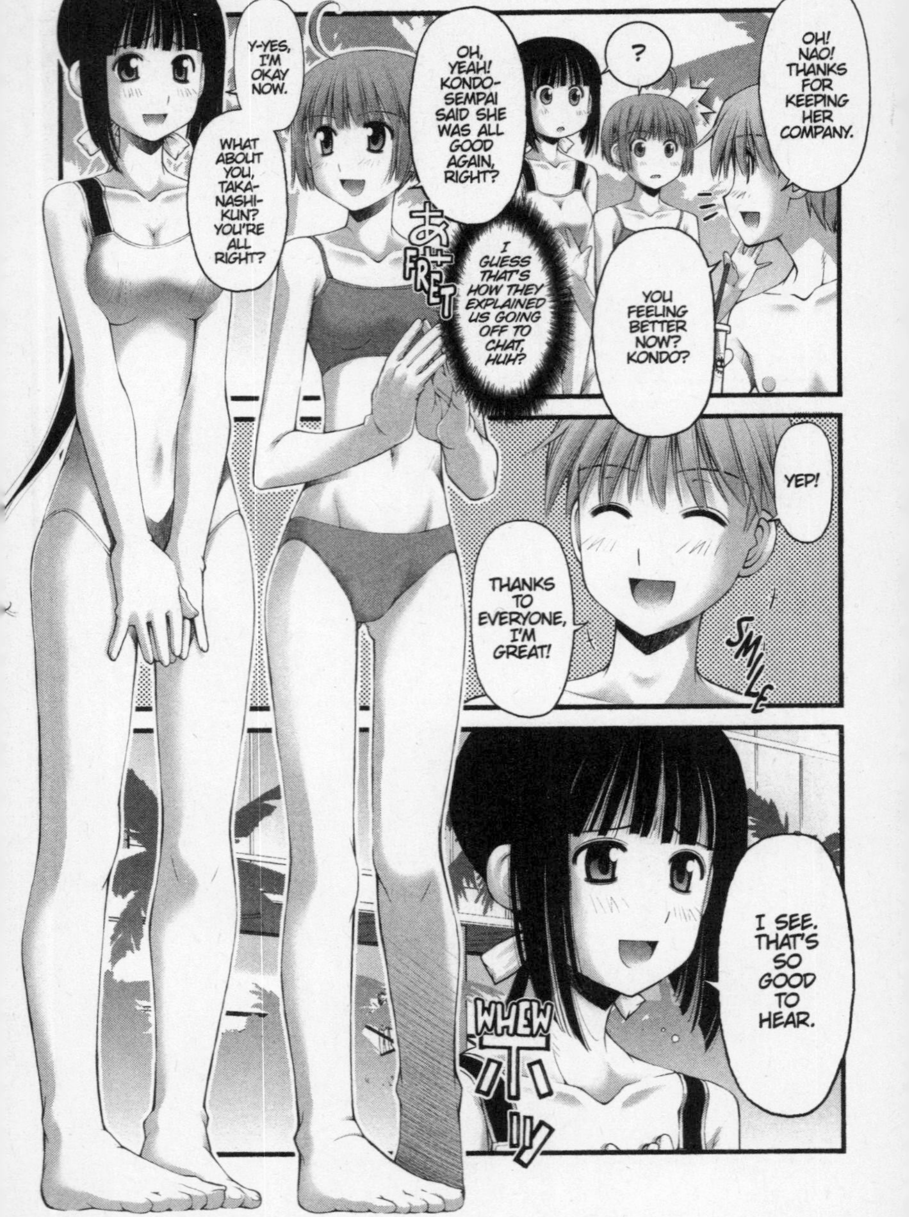
OH! NAO! THANKS FOR KEEPING HER COMPANY.
?
YOU FEELING BETTER NOW? KONDO?
YEP!
THANKS TO EVERYONE, I'M GREAT!
SMILE
I SEE. THAT'S SO GOOD TO HEAR.
WHEW
OH, YEAH! KONDO-SEMPAI SAID SHE WAS ALL GOOD AGAIN, RIGHT?
Y-YES, I'M OKAY NOW.
WHAT ABOUT YOU, TAKA-NASHI-KUN? YOU'RE ALL RIGHT?
I GUESS THAT'S HOW THEY EXPLAINED US GOING OFF TO CHAT, HUH?
FRET

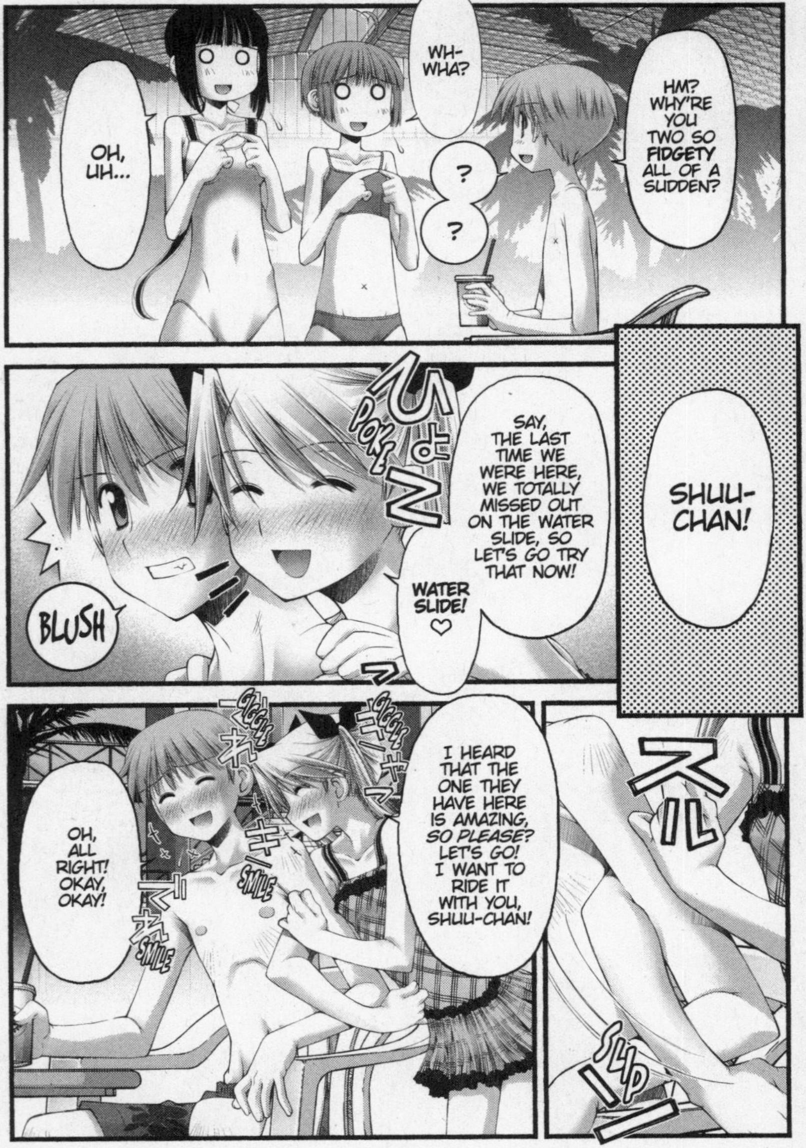
HM? WHY'RE YOU TWO SO FIDGETY ALL OF A SUDDEN?
? ?
WH- WHA?
OH, UH...
SHUU-CHAN!
POKE
SAY, THE LAST TIME WE WERE HERE, WE TOTALLY MISSED OUT ON THE WATER SLIDE, SO LET'S GO TRY THAT NOW!
WATER SLIDE! ♡
BLUSH
スル
SLIP
GIGGLE
GIGGLE
I HEARD THAT THE ONE THEY HAVE HERE IS AMAZING, *SO PLEASE?* LET'S GO! I WANT TO RIDE IT WITH YOU, SHUU-CHAN!
OH, ALL RIGHT! OKAY, OKAY!
SMILE
SMILE

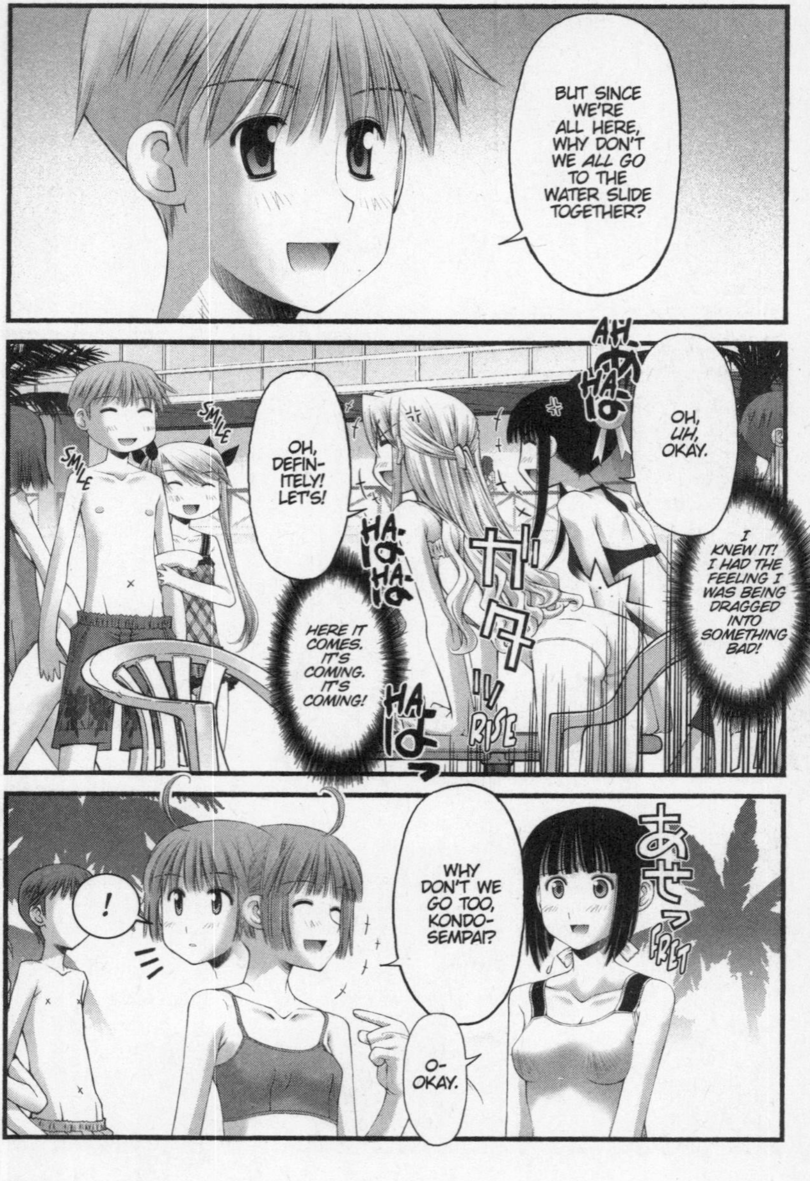
BUT SINCE WE'RE ALL HERE, WHY DON'T WE ALL GO TO THE WATER SLIDE TOGETHER?
AH あ HA は
OH, UH, OKAY.
I KNEW IT! I HAD THE FEELING I WAS BEING DRAGGED INTO SOMETHING BAD!
ガタ
RISE
OH, DEFINITELY! LET'S!
HA- は HA- は
HERE IT COMES. IT'S COMING. IT'S COMING!
HA- は
SMILE
SMILE
あせっ
FRET
WHY DON'T WE GO TOO, KONDO-SEMPAI?
O-OKAY.
!

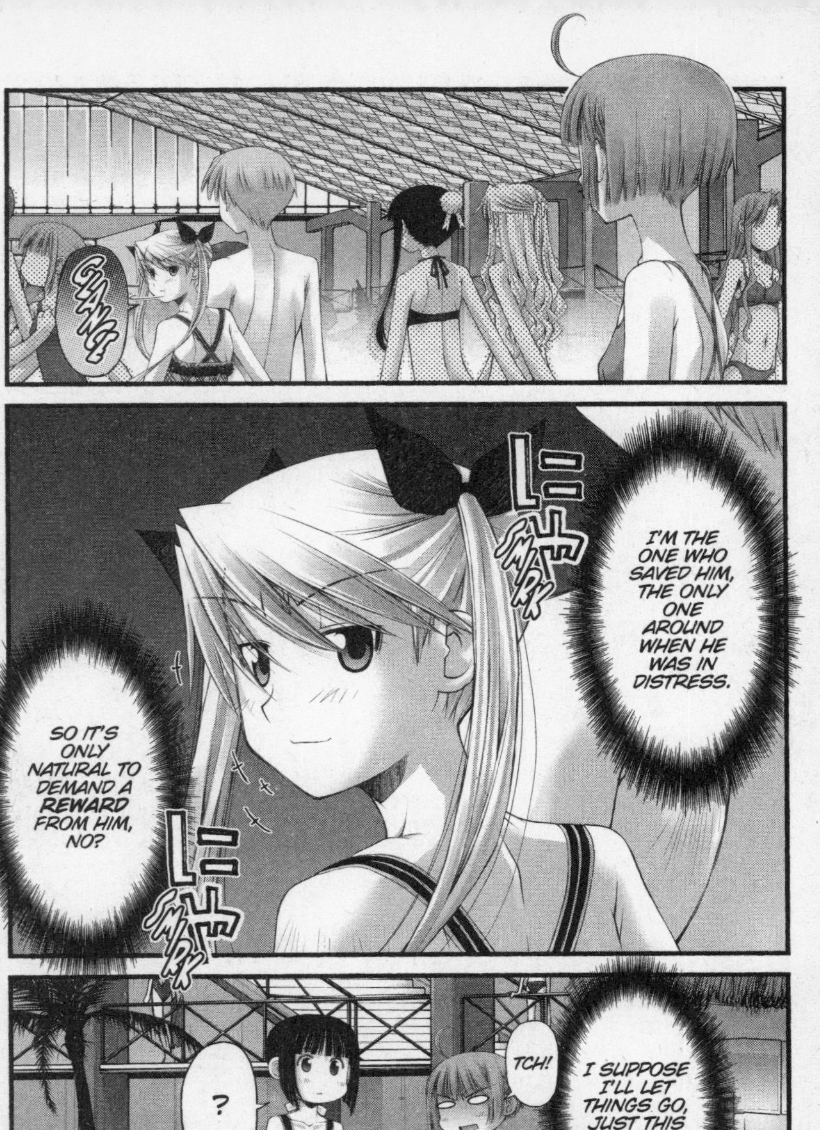
GLANCE
I'M THE ONE WHO SAVED HIM, THE ONLY ONE AROUND WHEN HE WAS IN DISTRESS.
SMIRK
SO IT'S ONLY NATURAL TO DEMAND A **REWARD** FROM HIM, NO?
SMIRK
I SUPPOSE I'LL LET THINGS GO, JUST THIS ONCE.
TCH!
?

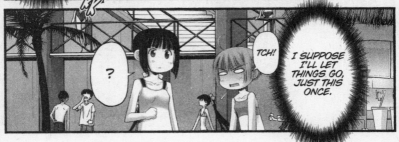

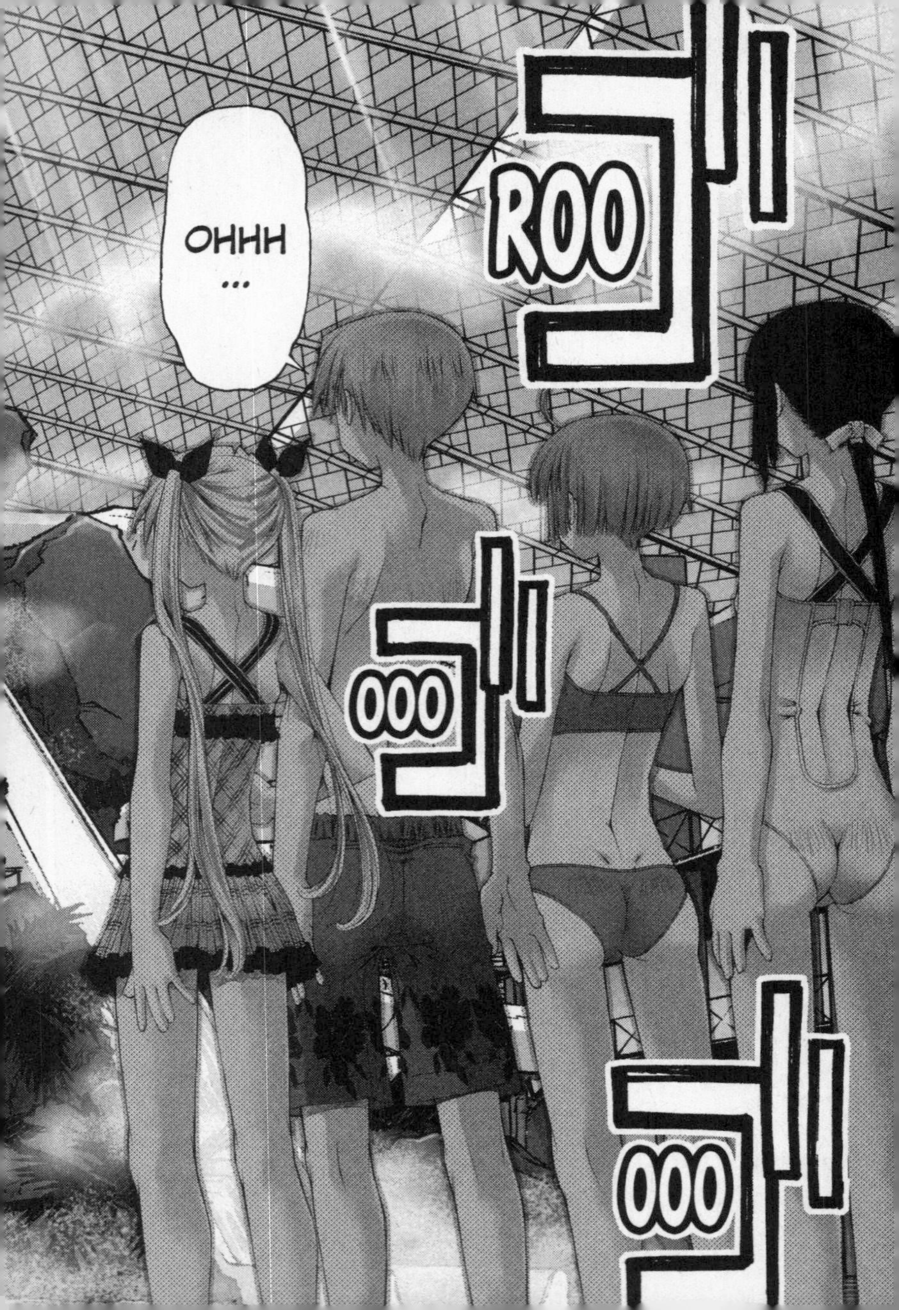
ROO
OHHH ...
OOO
OOO

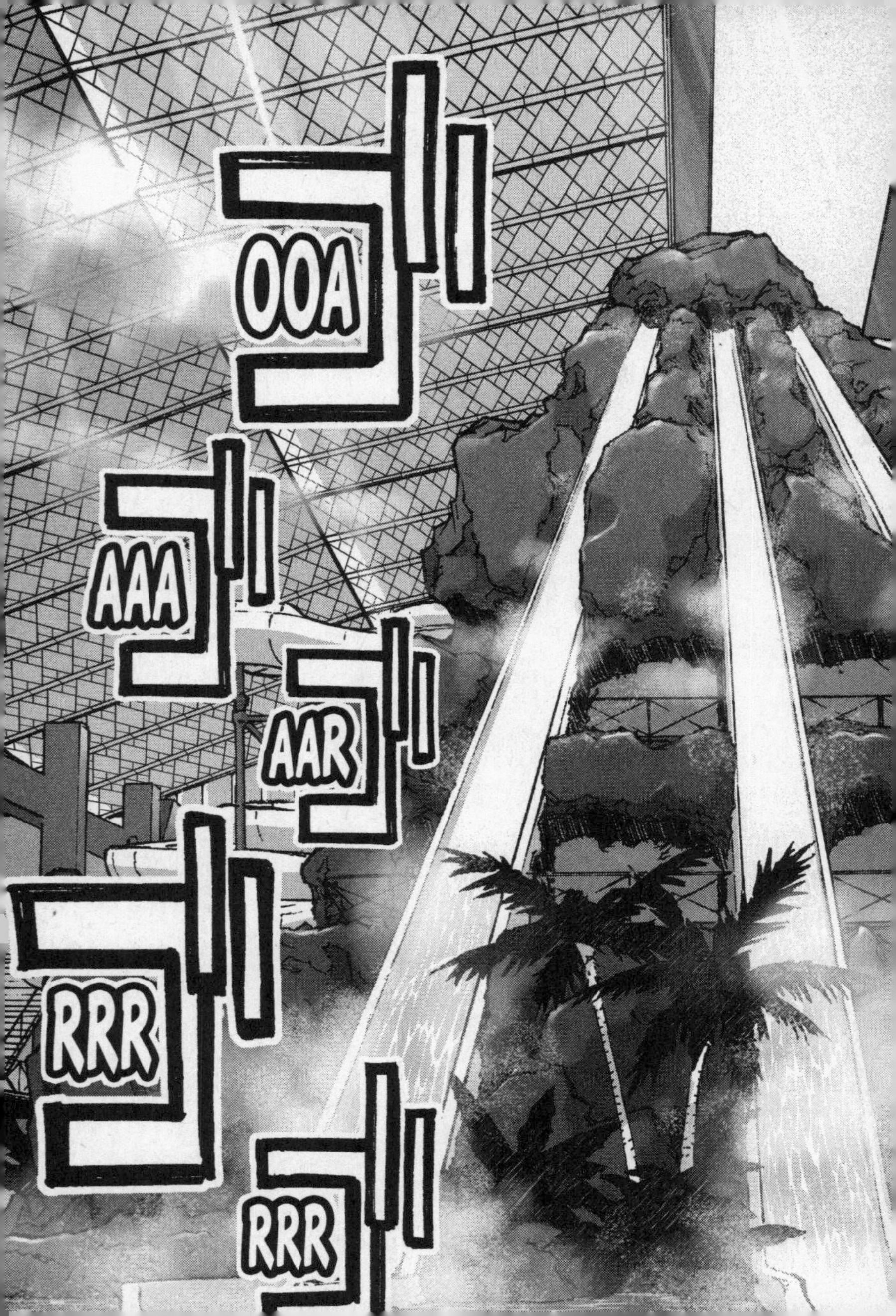
OOA
AAA
AAR
RRR
RRR

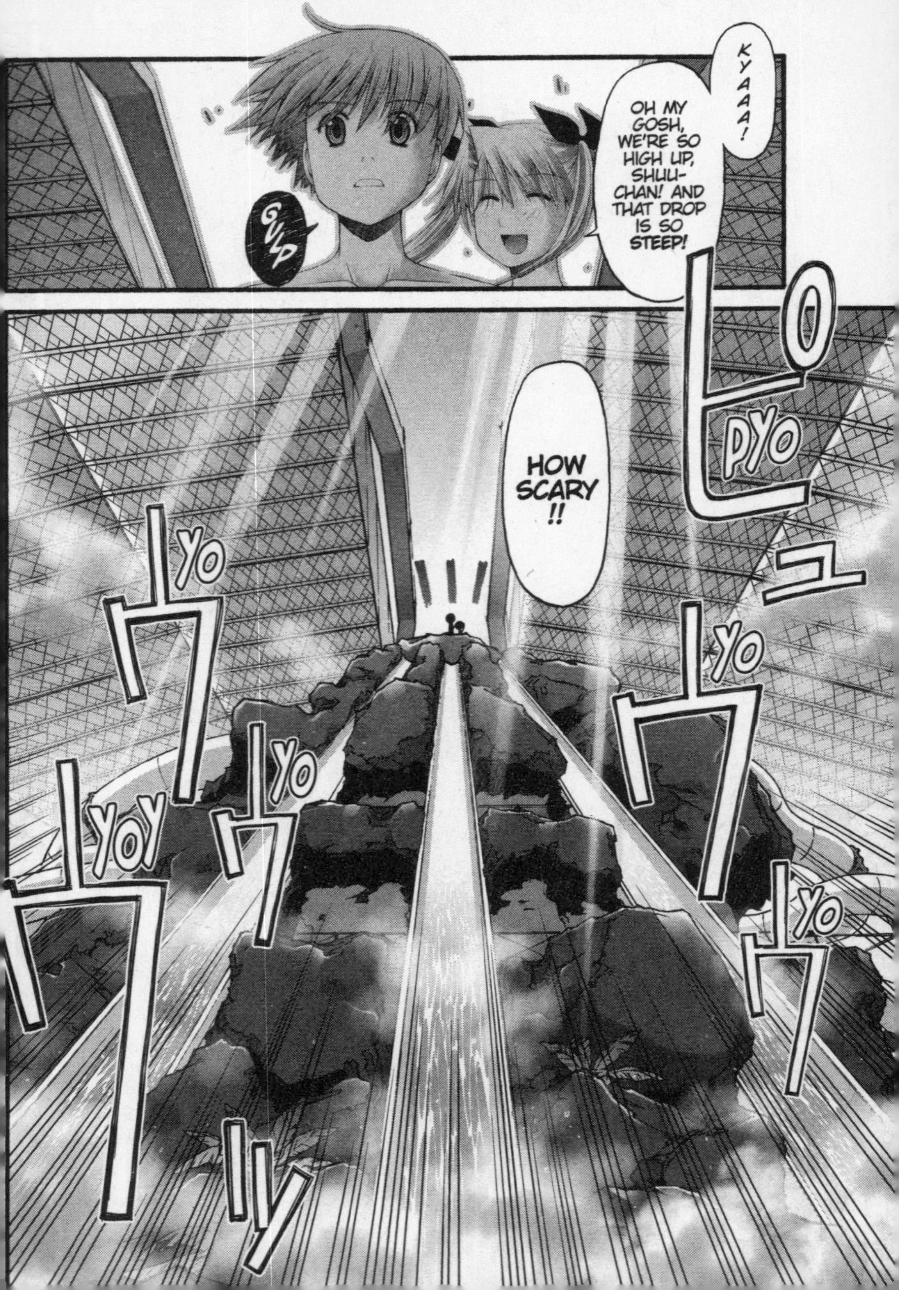
KYAAAA!
OH MY GOSH, WE'RE SO HIGH UP, SHUU-CHAN! AND THAT DROP IS SO STEEP!
GULP
PYO
HOW SCARY!!
YO
YO
YO
YO
YOY

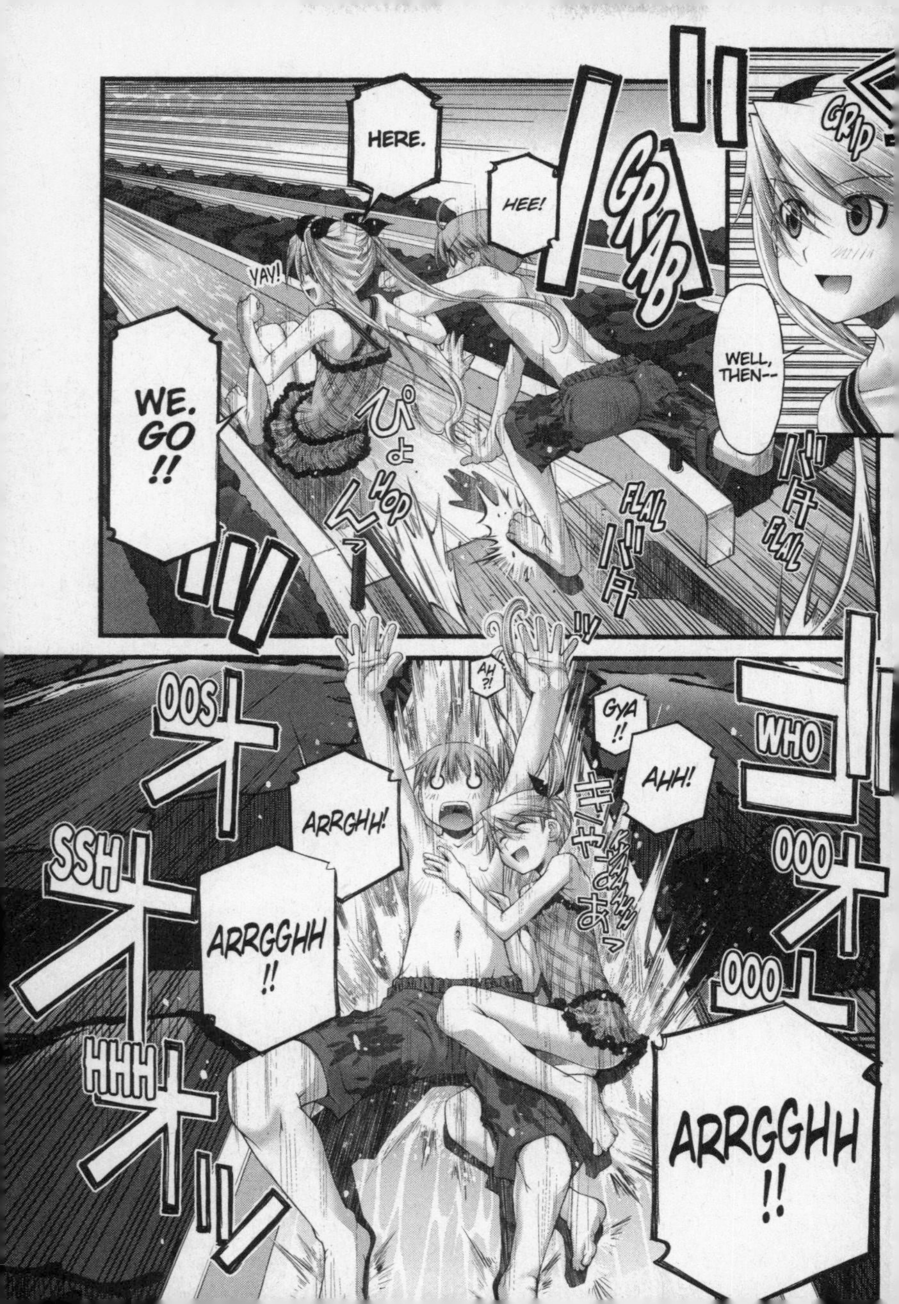
GRIP
WELL, THEN--
FLAL FLAL
GRAB
HEE!
HERE.
YAY!
WE. GO!!
ぴょん
HOP
WHO OOO OOO
GYA!!
AHH!
AH?!
ARRGHH!
ARRGGHH!!
ARRGGHH!!
OOS SSH HHH

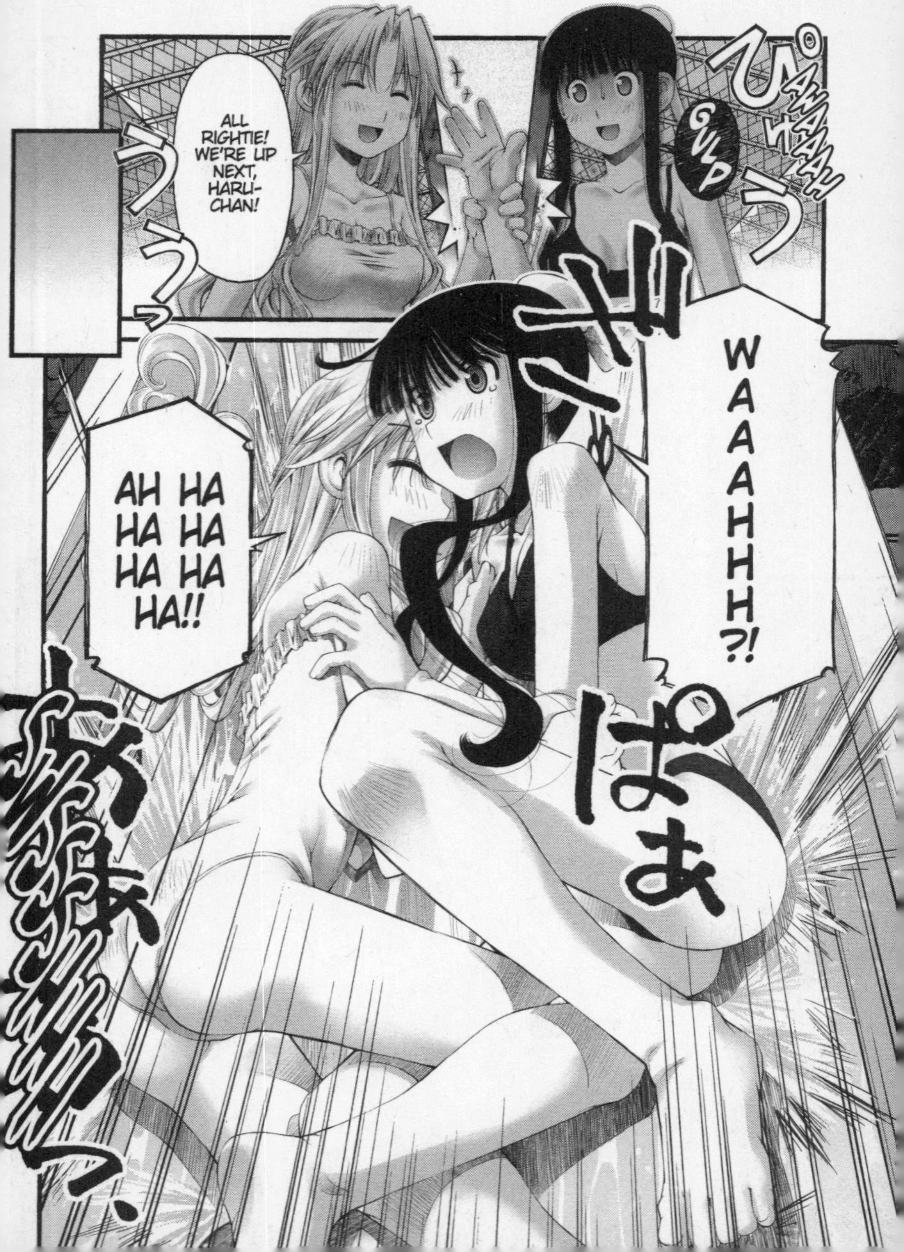
PWAWAAH
GULP
ALL RIGHTIE! WE'RE UP NEXT, HARU-CHAN!
WAAAAHHHH?!
AH HA HA HA HA HA HA!!
SWISHHHHH

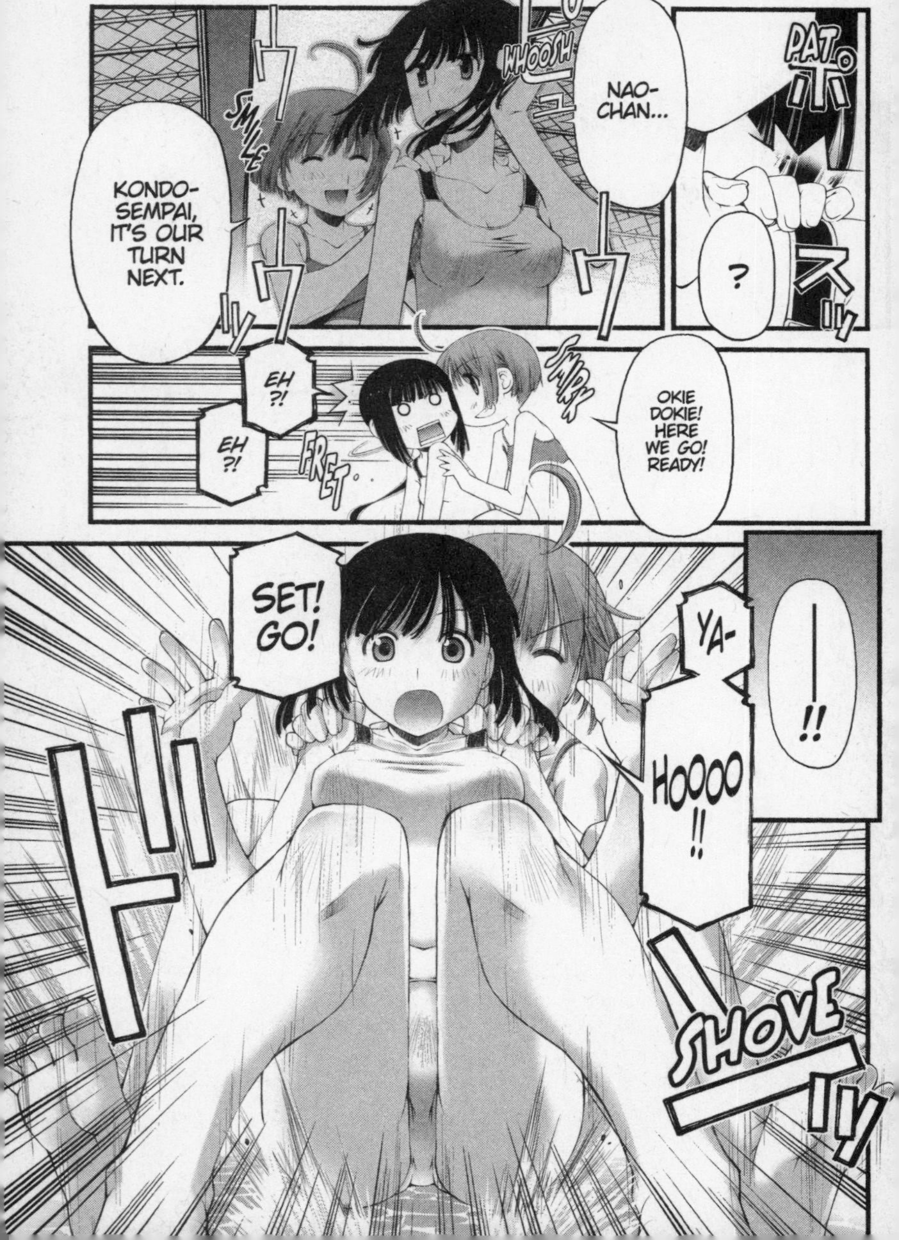
PAT
?
NAO-CHAN...
WHOOSH
SMILE
KONDO-SEMPAI, IT'S OUR TURN NEXT.
SMIRK
OKIE DOKIE! HERE WE GO! READY!
EH ?!
EH ?!
FRET
SET! GO!
YA-
—!!
HOOOO!!
SHOVE

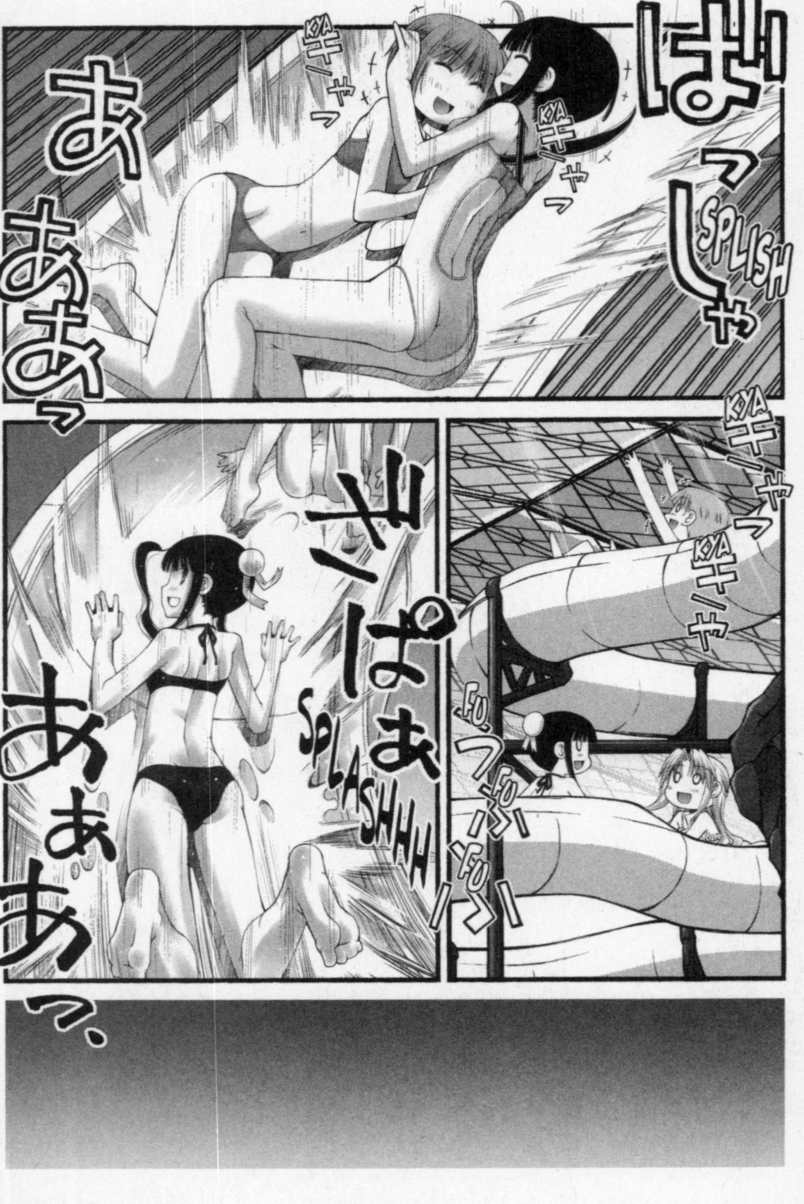
ぱっしゃ
SPLISH
KYA
キャーキャッ
KYA
キャーキャッ
あああっ
KYA
キャーキャッ
KYA
キャーキャ
FU
ふっ
FU
ふ〜ぃ
FU
ふ〜ぃ
ざぱぁ
SPLASHHH
あぁあっ、

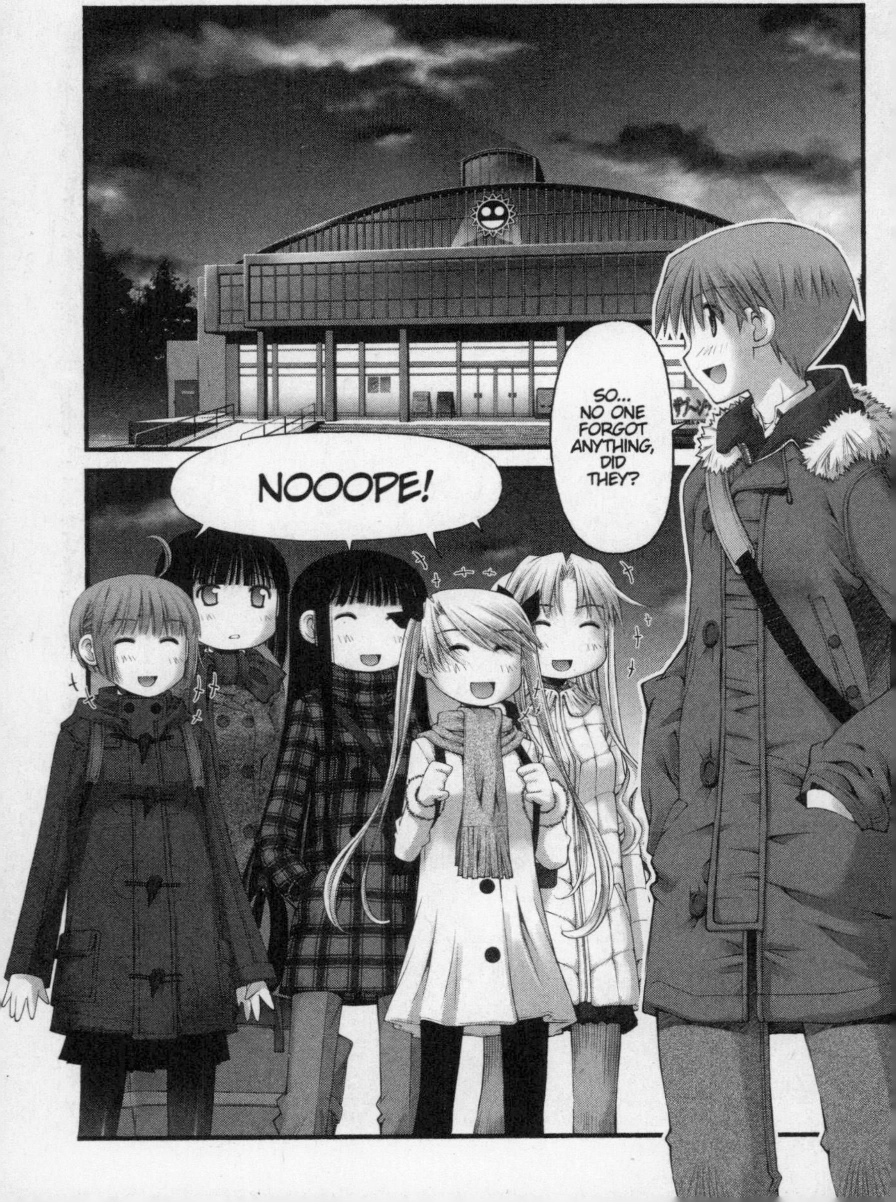
SO... NO ONE FORGOT ANYTHING, DID THEY?
NOOOPE!

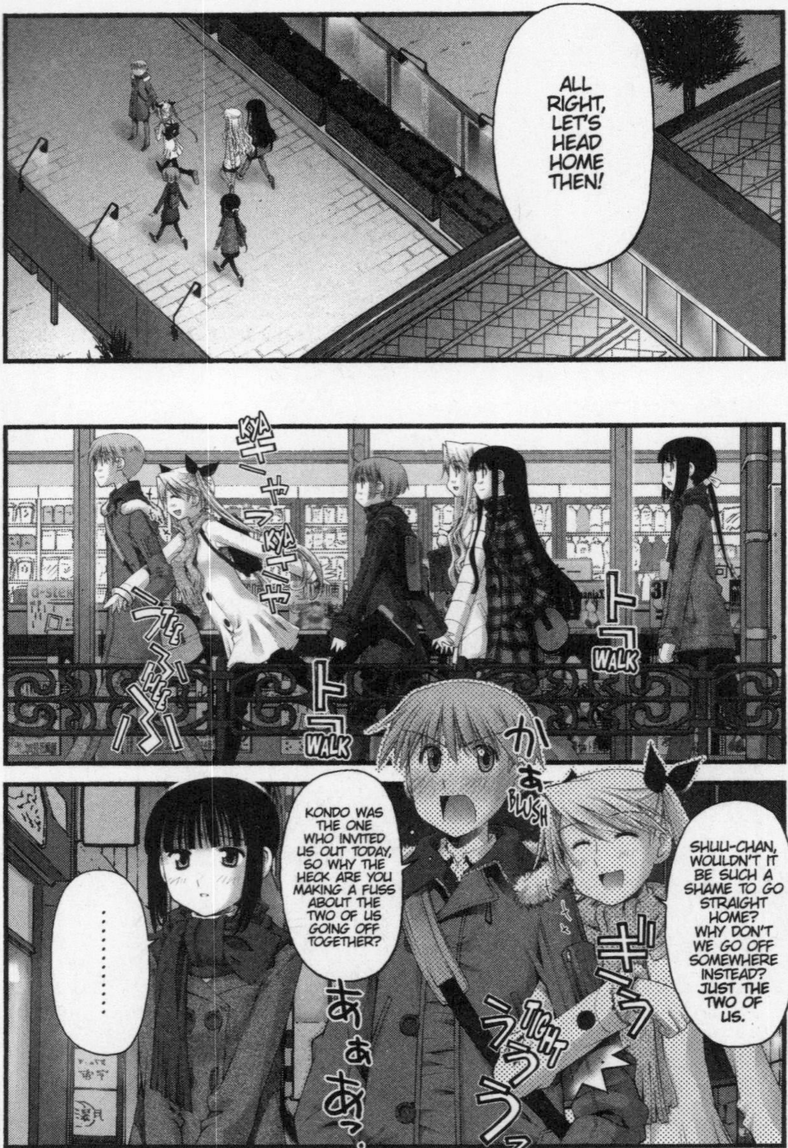
ALL RIGHT, LET'S HEAD HOME THEN!
トコ WALK
トコ WALK
ふふ TEE HEE
ふふ TEE HEE
KYA KYA
かぁ BLUSH
SHUU-CHAN, WOULDN'T IT BE SUCH A SHAME TO GO STRAIGHT HOME? WHY DON'T WE GO OFF SOMEWHERE INSTEAD? JUST THE TWO OF US.
ぎゅううう TIGHT
KONDO WAS THE ONE WHO INVITED US OUT TODAY, SO WHY THE HECK ARE YOU MAKING A FUSS ABOUT THE TWO OF US GOING OFF TOGETHER?
……

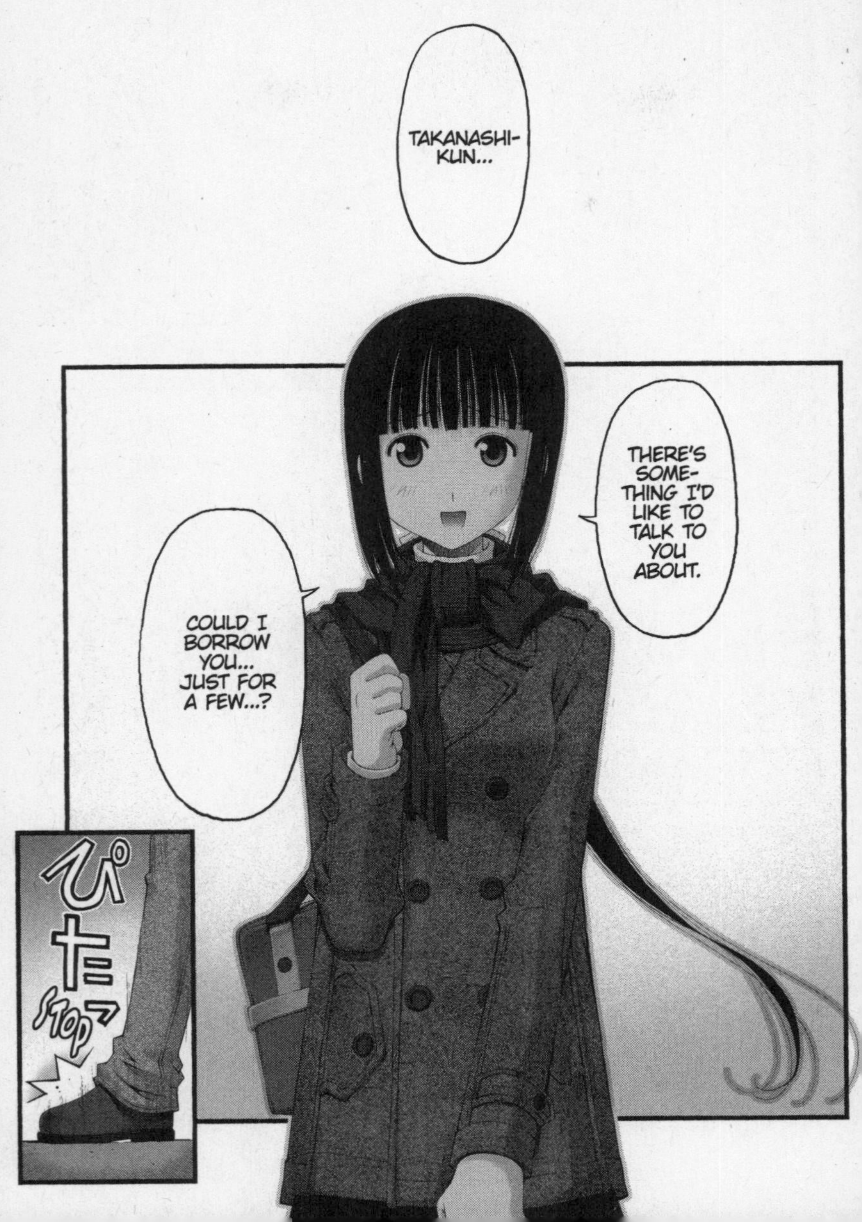
TAKANASHI-KUN...
THERE'S SOMETHING I'D LIKE TO TALK TO YOU ABOUT.
COULD I BORROW YOU... JUST FOR A FEW...?
ぴたっ
STOP

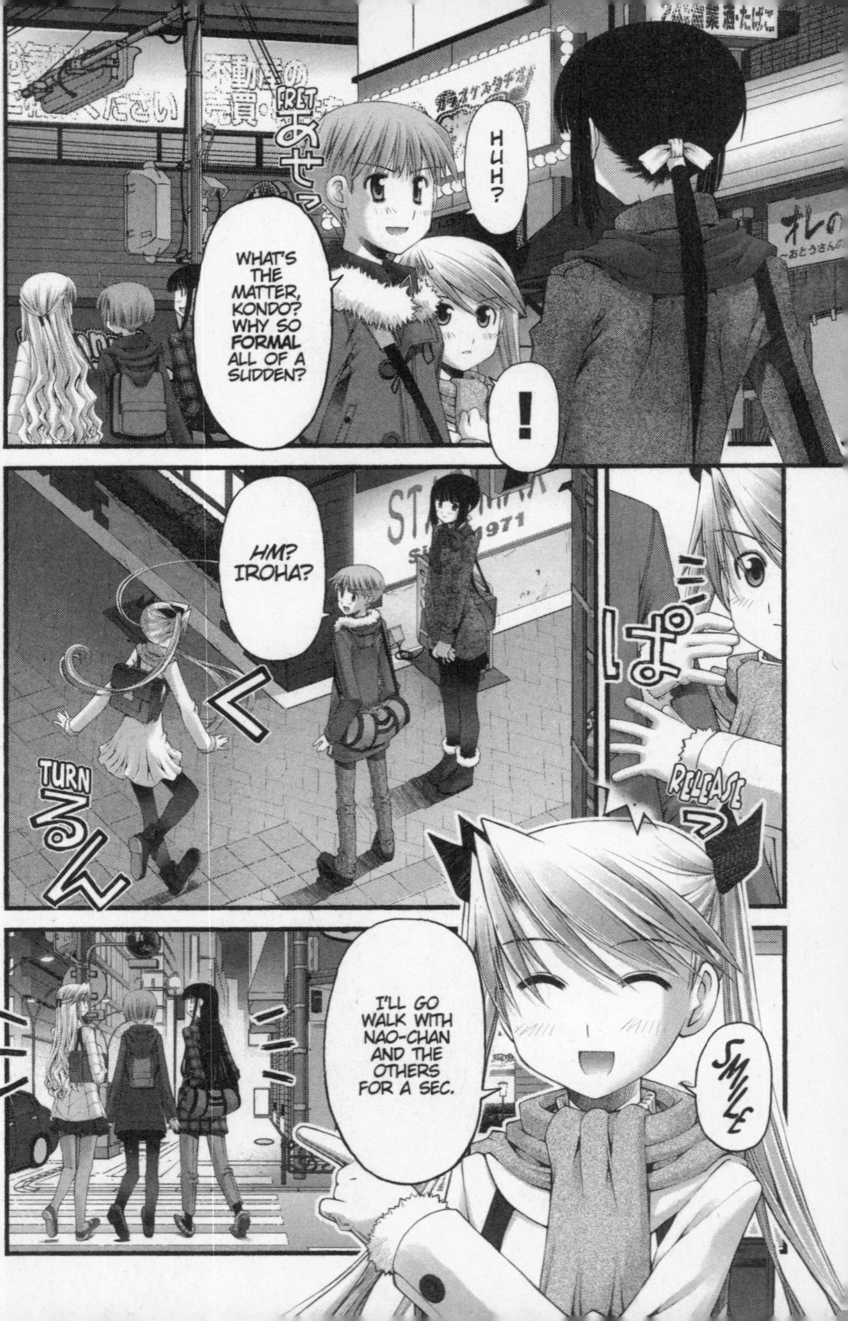
HUH?
!
FRET
あせっ
WHAT'S THE MATTER, KONDO? WHY SO FORMAL ALL OF A SUDDEN?
RELEASE
HM? IROHA?
く
TURN
るん
SMILE
I'LL GO WALK WITH NAO-CHAN AND THE OTHERS FOR A SEC.

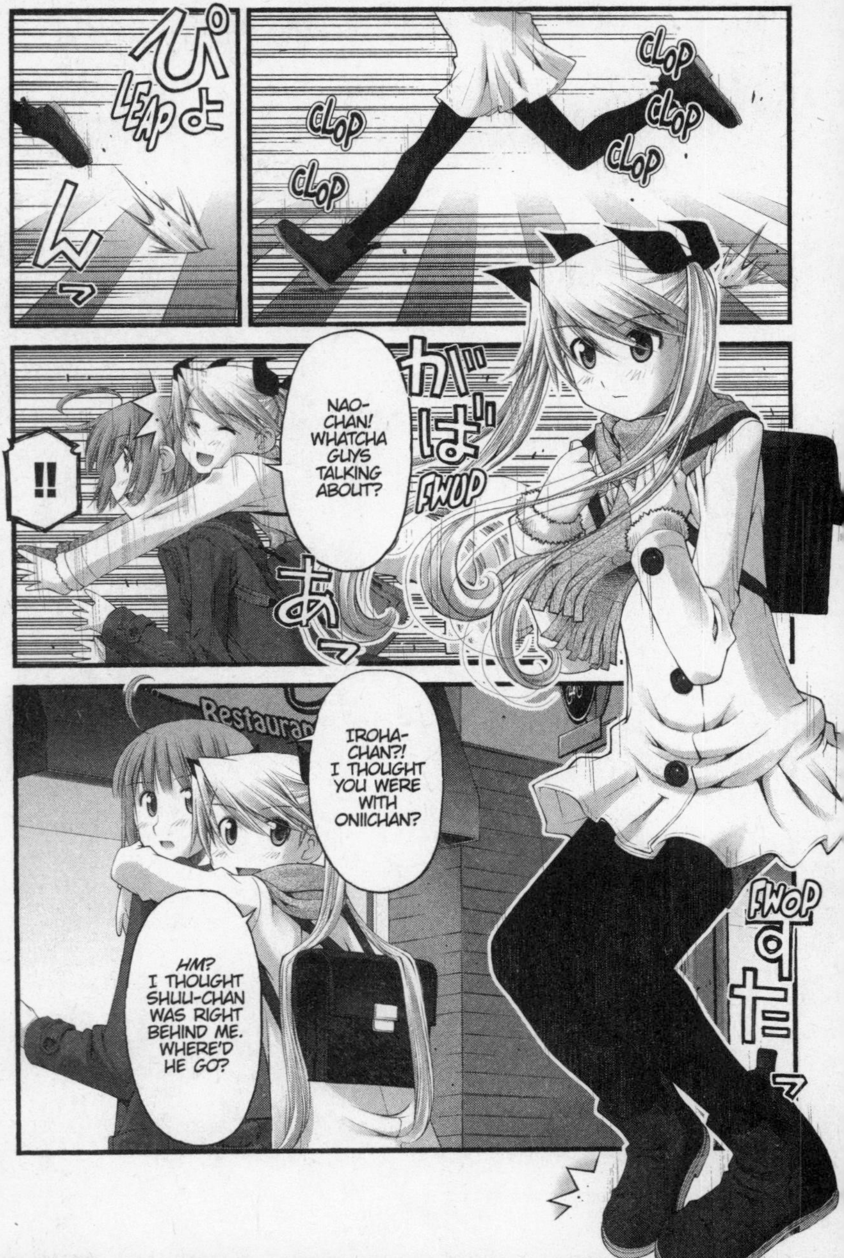

CLOP
CLOP
CLOP
CLOP
CLOP
ぴょんっ
LEAP
すたっ
FWOP
がばっ
FWOP
NAO-CHAN! WHATCHA GUYS TALKING ABOUT?
!!
あっ
IROHA-CHAN?! I THOUGHT YOU WERE WITH ONIICHAN?
HM? I THOUGHT SHUU-CHAN WAS RIGHT BEHIND ME. WHERE'D HE GO?
Restauran

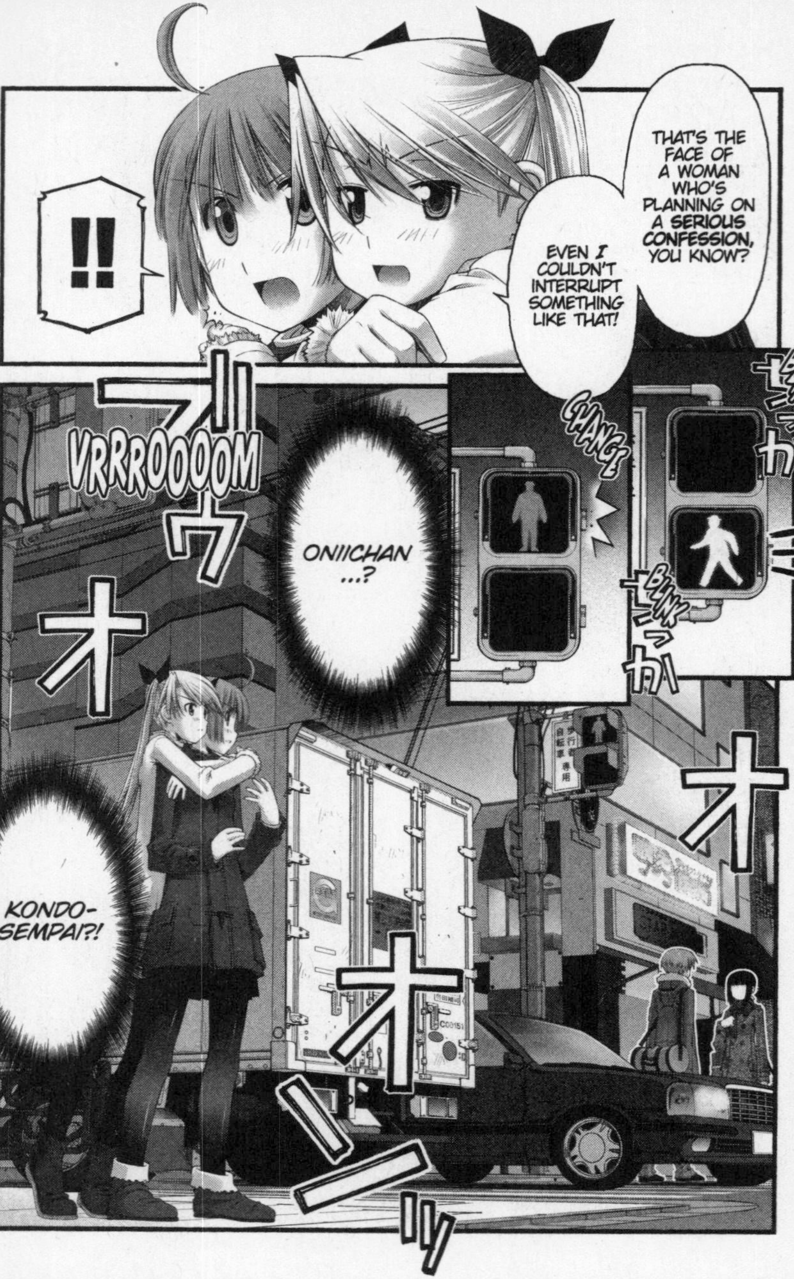
THAT'S THE FACE OF A WOMAN WHO'S PLANNING ON A SERIOUS CONFESSION, YOU KNOW?
EVEN I COULDN'T INTERRUPT SOMETHING LIKE THAT!
!!
BLINK
CHANGE
BLINK
VRRROOOOM
ONIICHAN ...?
KONDO-SEMPAI?!

CHAPTER 34

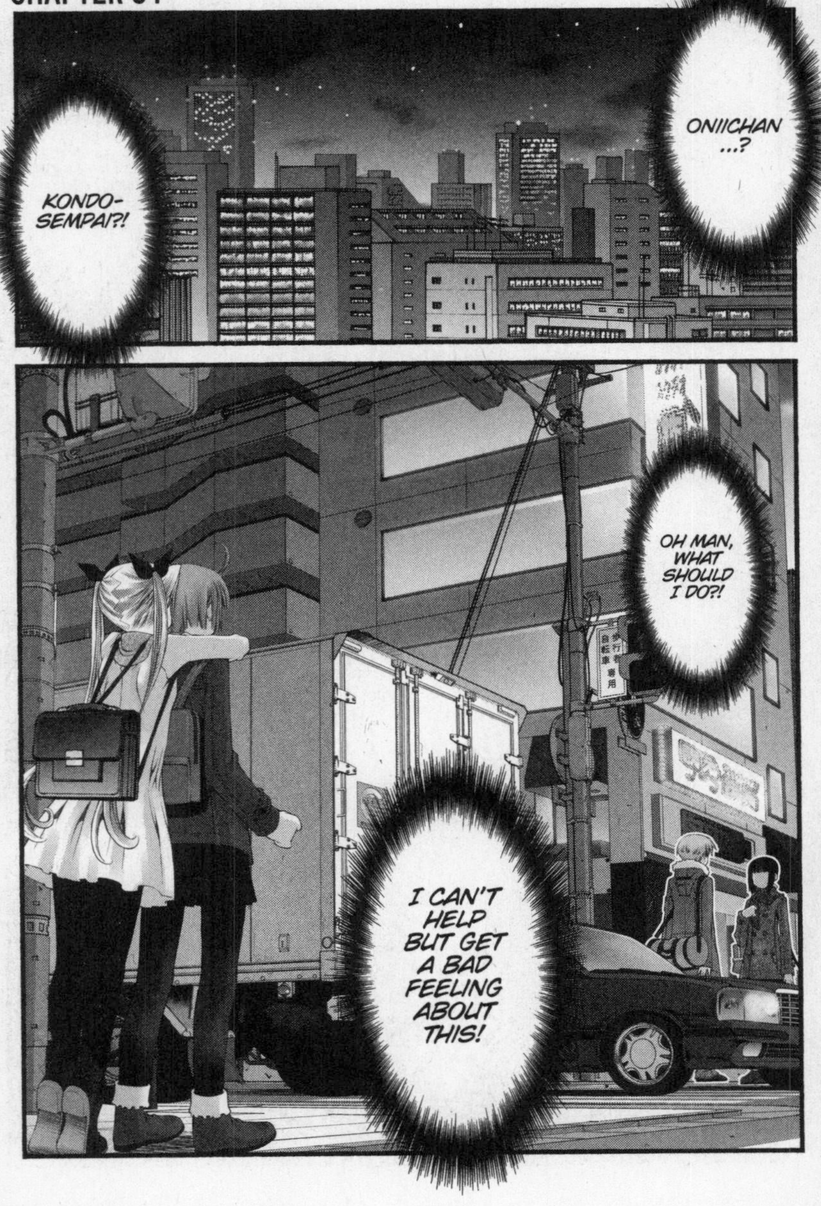
ONIICHAN ...?
KONDO-SEMPAI?!
OH MAN, WHAT SHOULD I DO?!
I CAN'T HELP BUT GET A BAD FEELING ABOUT THIS!

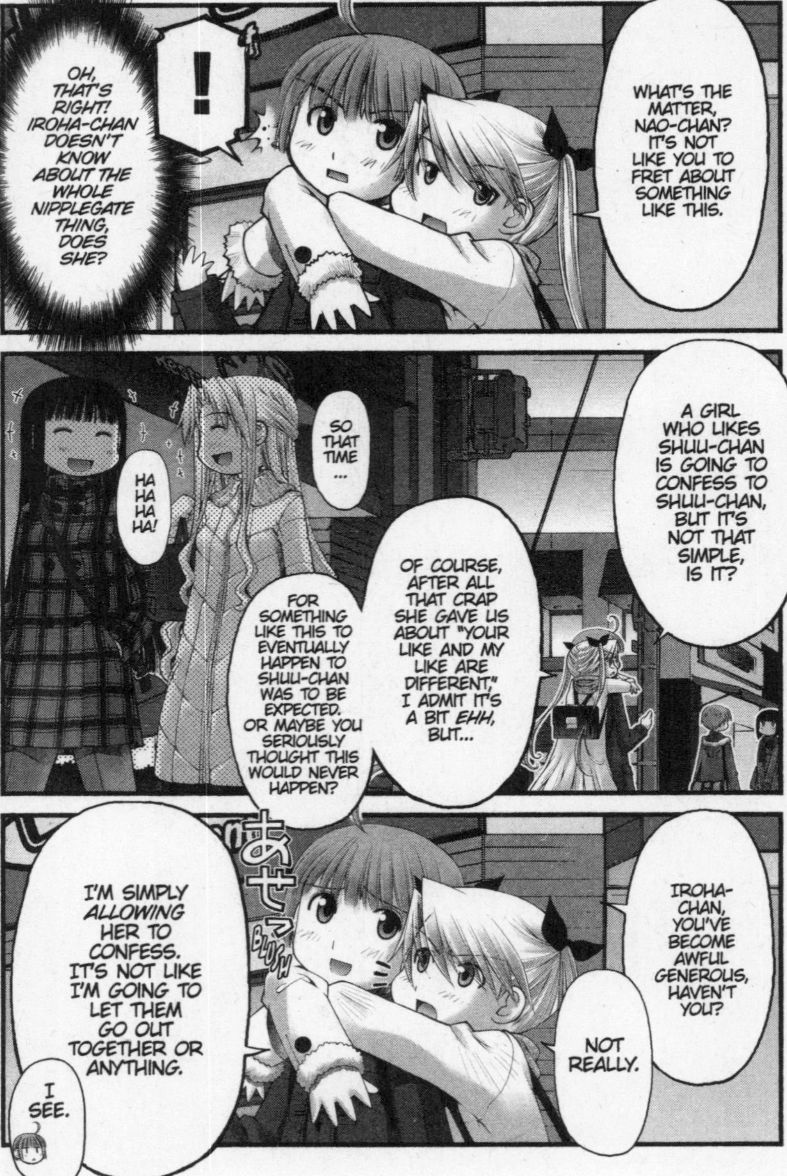
WHAT'S THE MATTER, NAO-CHAN? IT'S NOT LIKE YOU TO FRET ABOUT SOMETHING LIKE THIS.
!
OH, THAT'S RIGHT! IROHA-CHAN DOESN'T KNOW ABOUT THE WHOLE NIPPLEGATE THING, DOES SHE?
A GIRL WHO LIKES SHUU-CHAN IS GOING TO CONFESS TO SHUU-CHAN, BUT IT'S NOT THAT SIMPLE, IS IT?
OF COURSE, AFTER ALL THAT CRAP SHE GAVE US ABOUT "YOUR LIKE AND MY LIKE ARE DIFFERENT," I ADMIT IT'S A BIT *EHH*, BUT...
FOR SOMETHING LIKE THIS TO EVENTUALLY HAPPEN TO SHUU-CHAN WAS TO BE EXPECTED. OR MAYBE YOU SERIOUSLY THOUGHT THIS WOULD NEVER HAPPEN?
SO THAT TIME ...
HA HA HA HA!
IROHA-CHAN, YOU'VE BECOME AWFUL GENEROUS, HAVEN'T YOU?
NOT REALLY.
あせっ
BLUSH
I'M SIMPLY *ALLOWING* HER TO CONFESS. IT'S NOT LIKE I'M GOING TO LET THEM GO OUT TOGETHER OR ANYTHING.
I SEE.

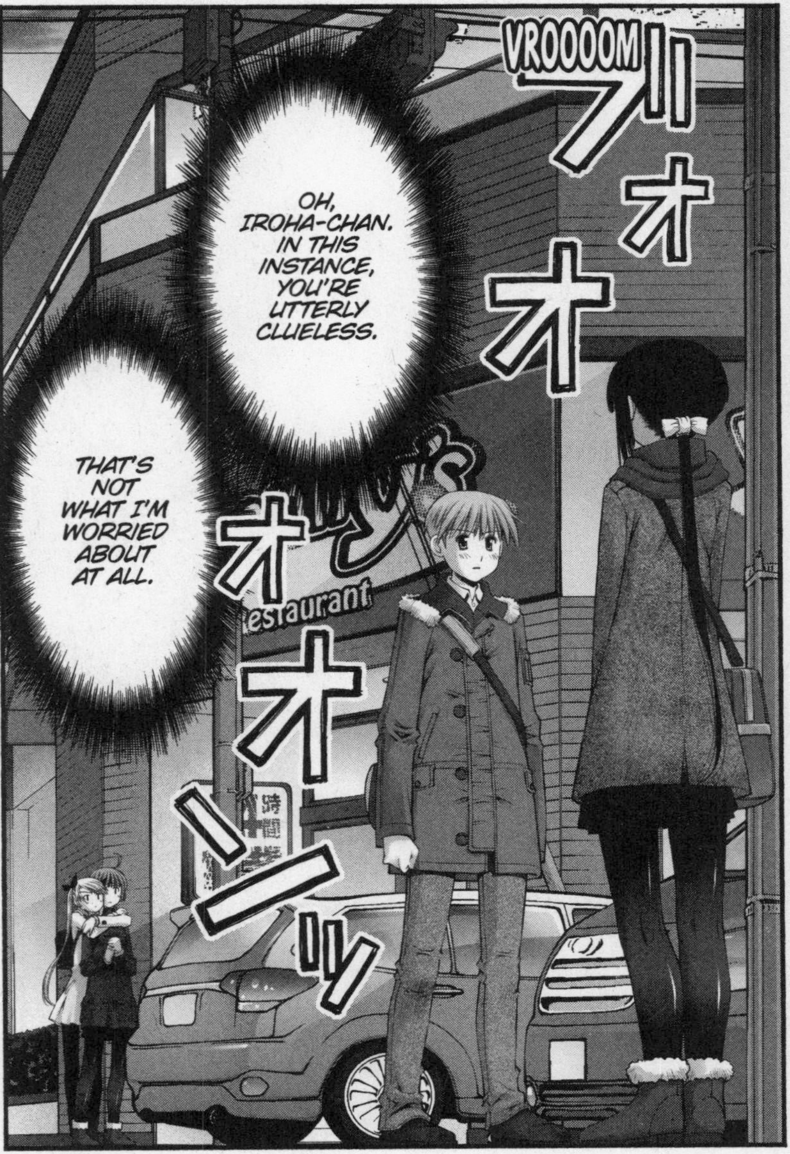
VROOOOM
ブォオオオオーンッ
OH, IROHA-CHAN. IN THIS INSTANCE, YOU'RE UTTERLY CLUELESS.
THAT'S NOT WHAT I'M WORRIED ABOUT AT ALL.
Restaurant

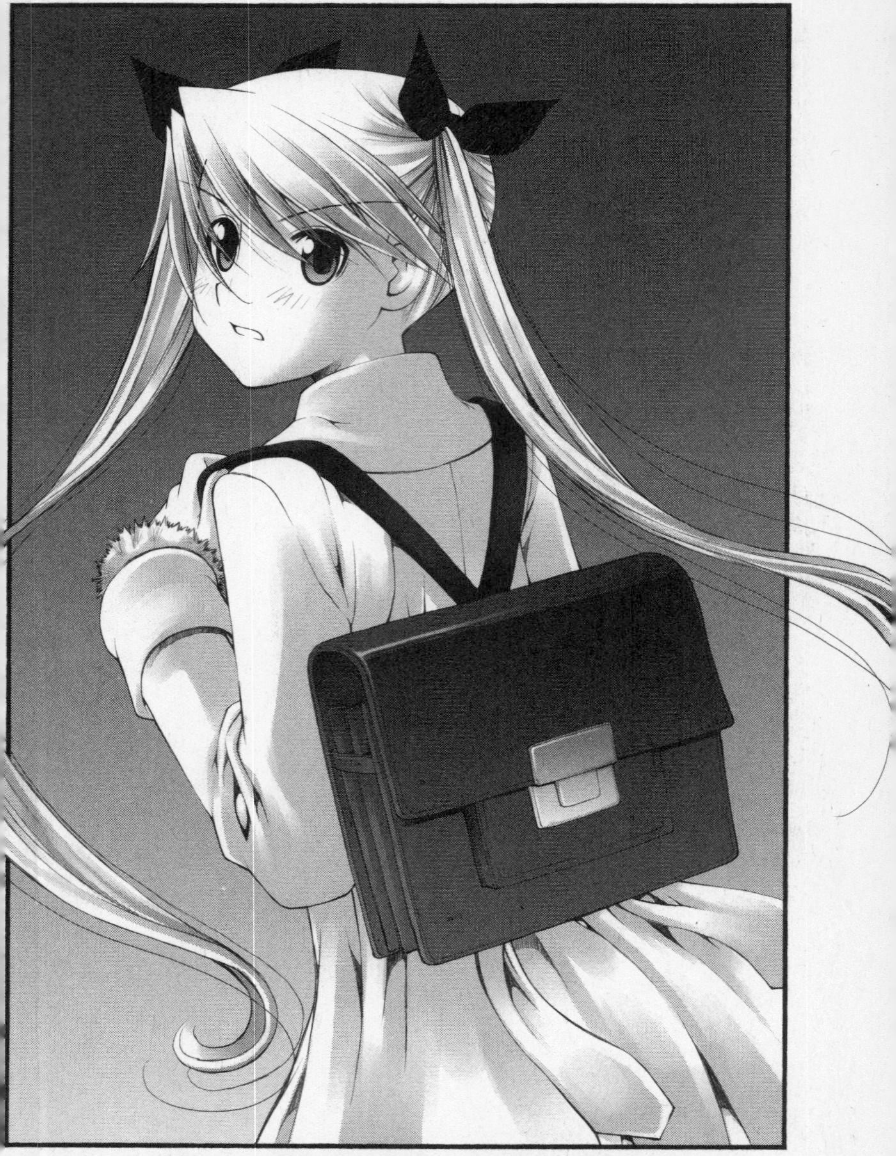

CHAPTER 34 That Which Approaches

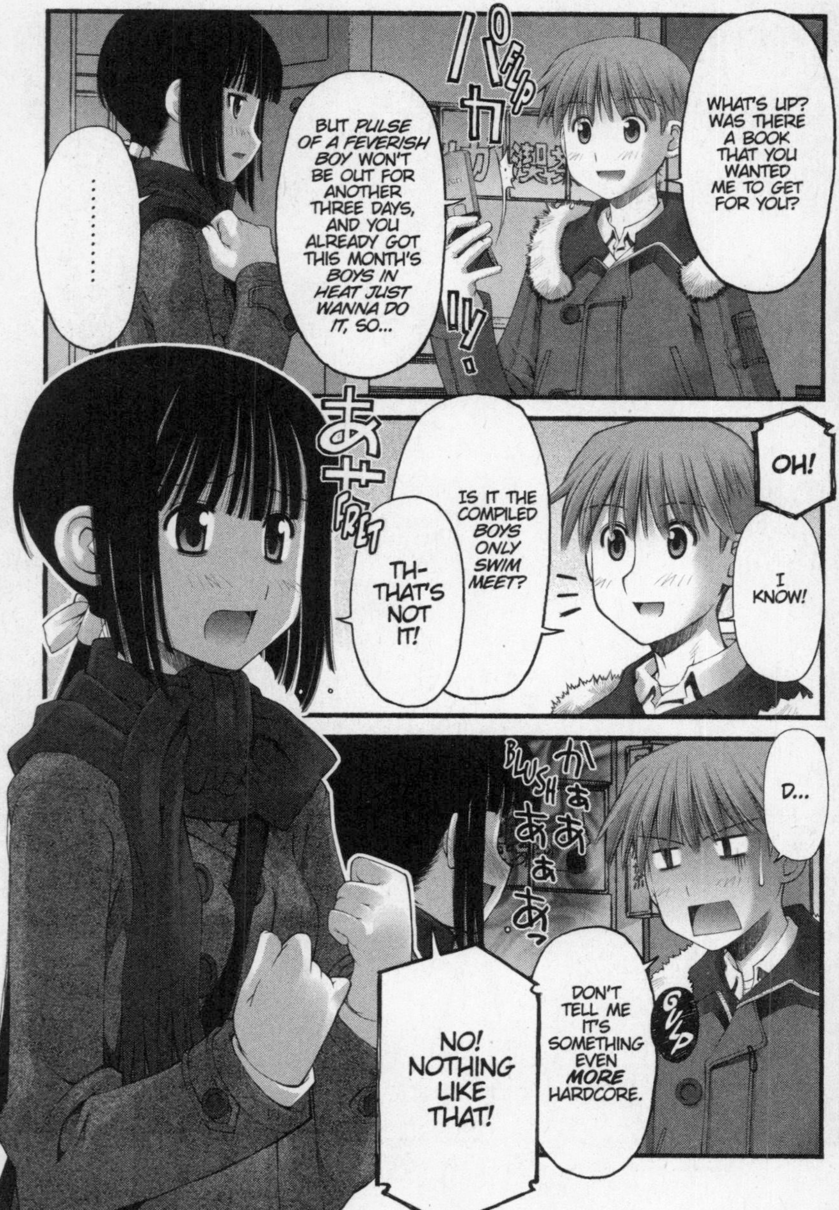
WHAT'S UP? WAS THERE A BOOK THAT YOU WANTED ME TO GET FOR YOU?
パカッ
FLIP
BUT *PULSE OF A FEVERISH BOY* WON'T BE OUT FOR ANOTHER THREE DAYS, AND YOU ALREADY GOT THIS MONTH'S *BOYS IN HEAT JUST WANNA DO IT*, SO...
......
OH!
I KNOW!
IS IT THE COMPILED *BOYS ONLY SWIM MEET*?
あせ
FRET
TH- THAT'S NOT IT!
D...
DON'T TELL ME IT'S SOMETHING EVEN *MORE* HARDCORE.
GULP
かぁぁぁ あぁぁぁっ
BLUSH
NO! NOTHING LIKE THAT!

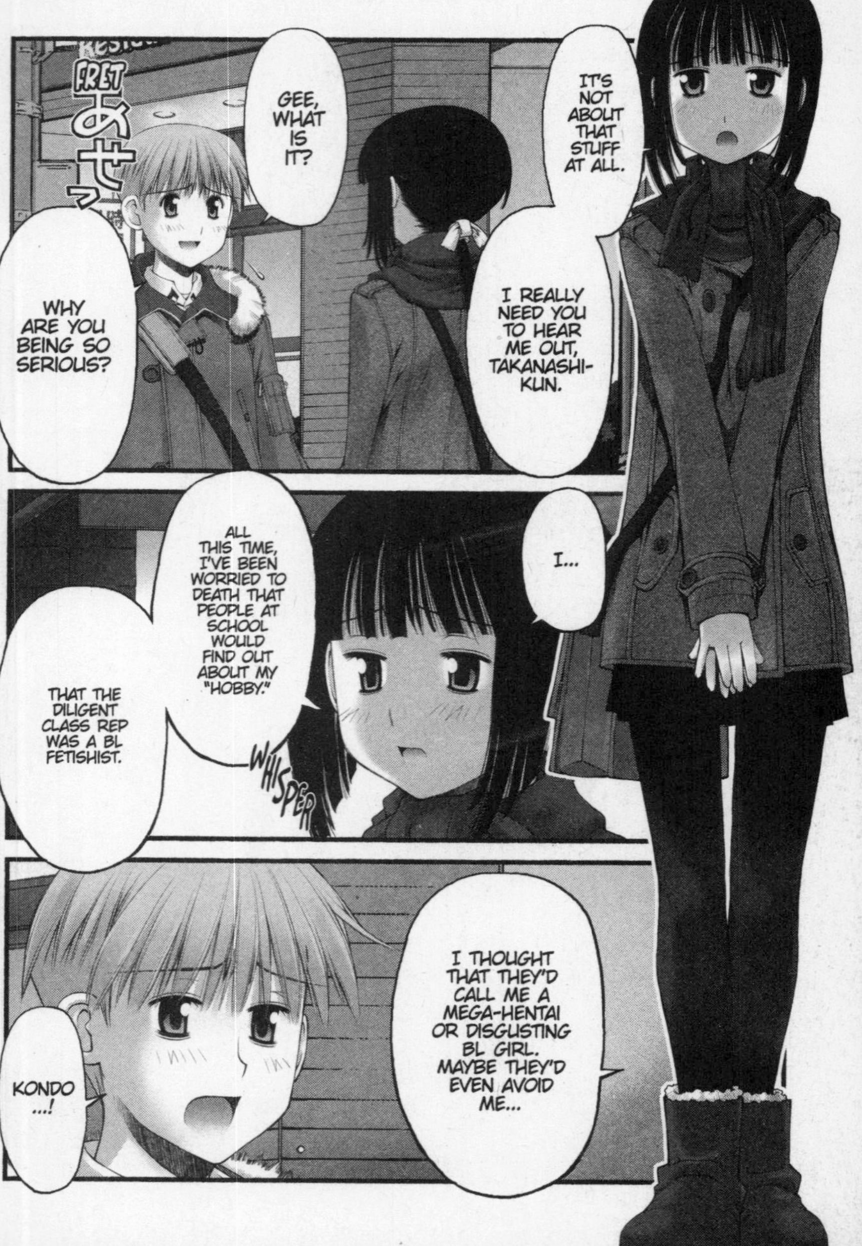
FRET
あせっ
GEE, WHAT IS IT?
WHY ARE YOU BEING SO SERIOUS?
IT'S NOT ABOUT THAT STUFF AT ALL.
I REALLY NEED YOU TO HEAR ME OUT, TAKANASHI-KUN.
I...
ALL THIS TIME, I'VE BEEN WORRIED TO DEATH THAT PEOPLE AT SCHOOL WOULD FIND OUT ABOUT MY "HOBBY."
THAT THE DILIGENT CLASS REP WAS A BL FETISHIST.
WHISPER
I THOUGHT THAT THEY'D CALL ME A MEGA-HENTAI OR DISGUSTING BL GIRL. MAYBE THEY'D EVEN AVOID ME...
KONDO ...!

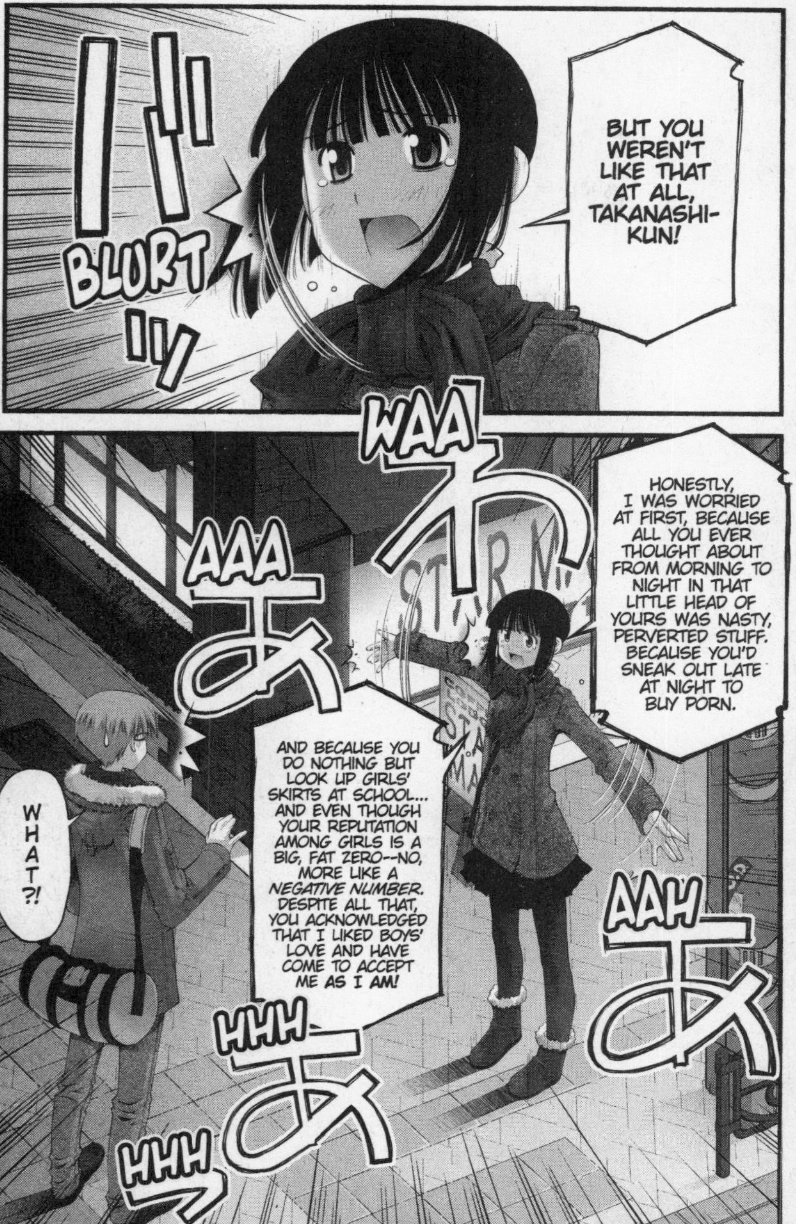
BUT YOU WEREN'T LIKE THAT AT ALL, TAKANASHI-KUN!
BLURT
WAA
HONESTLY, I WAS WORRIED AT FIRST, BECAUSE ALL YOU EVER THOUGHT ABOUT FROM MORNING TO NIGHT IN THAT LITTLE HEAD OF YOURS WAS NASTY, PERVERTED STUFF. BECAUSE YOU'D SNEAK OUT LATE AT NIGHT TO BUY PORN.
AAA
AND BECAUSE YOU DO NOTHING BUT LOOK UP GIRLS' SKIRTS AT SCHOOL... AND EVEN THOUGH YOUR REPUTATION AMONG GIRLS IS A BIG, FAT ZERO--NO, MORE LIKE A *NEGATIVE NUMBER*. DESPITE ALL THAT, YOU ACKNOWLEDGED THAT I LIKED BOYS' LOVE AND HAVE COME TO ACCEPT ME AS I AM!
AAH
WHAT?!
HHH
HHH

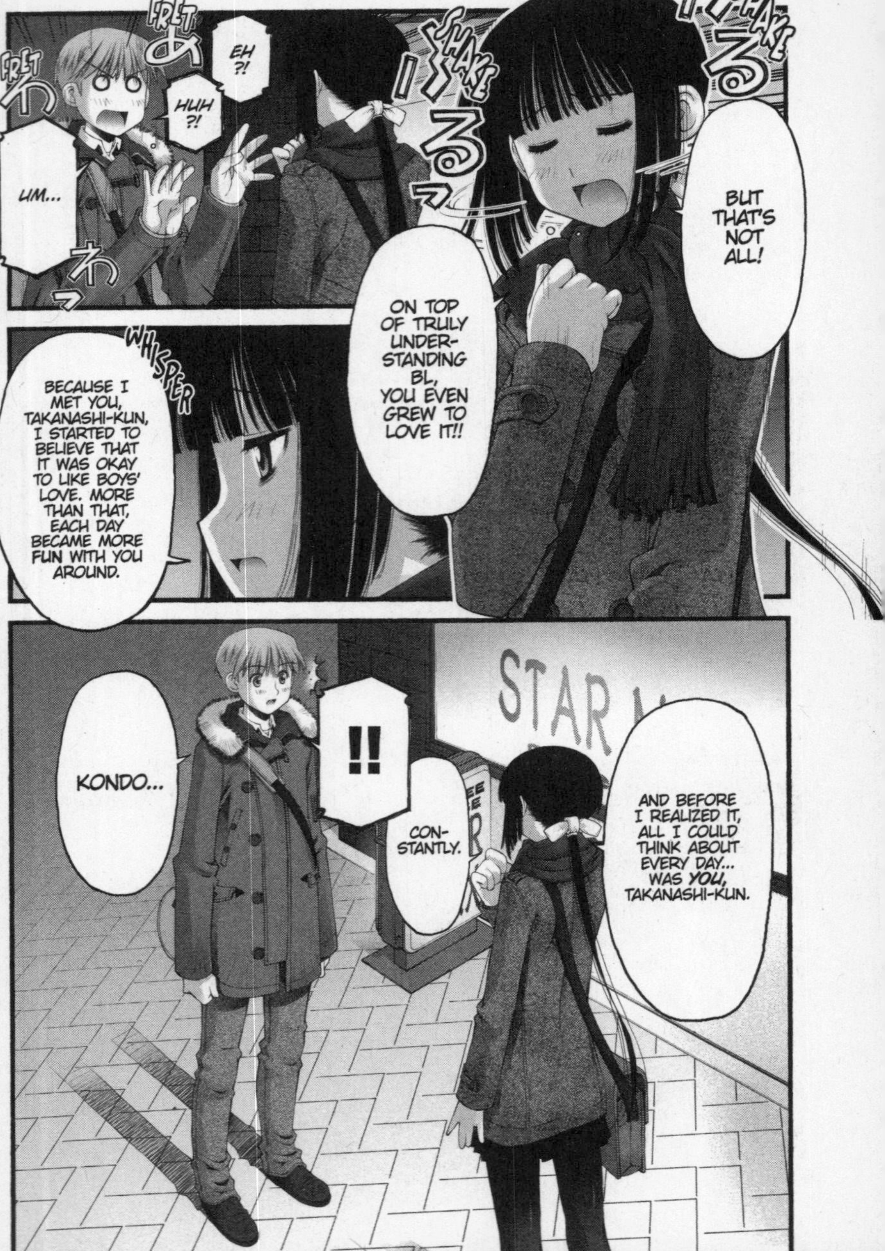
SHAKE る
SHAKE る
BUT THAT'S NOT ALL!
ON TOP OF TRULY UNDER-STANDING BL, YOU EVEN GREW TO LOVE IT!!
FRET あ
FRET わ
EH ?!
HUH ?!
UM...
わ
WHISPER
BECAUSE I MET YOU, TAKANASHI-KUN, I STARTED TO BELIEVE THAT IT WAS OKAY TO LIKE BOYS' LOVE. MORE THAN THAT, EACH DAY BECAME MORE FUN WITH YOU AROUND.
STAR
AND BEFORE I REALIZED IT, ALL I COULD THINK ABOUT EVERY DAY... WAS *YOU*, TAKANASHI-KUN.
CON-STANTLY.
!!
KONDO...

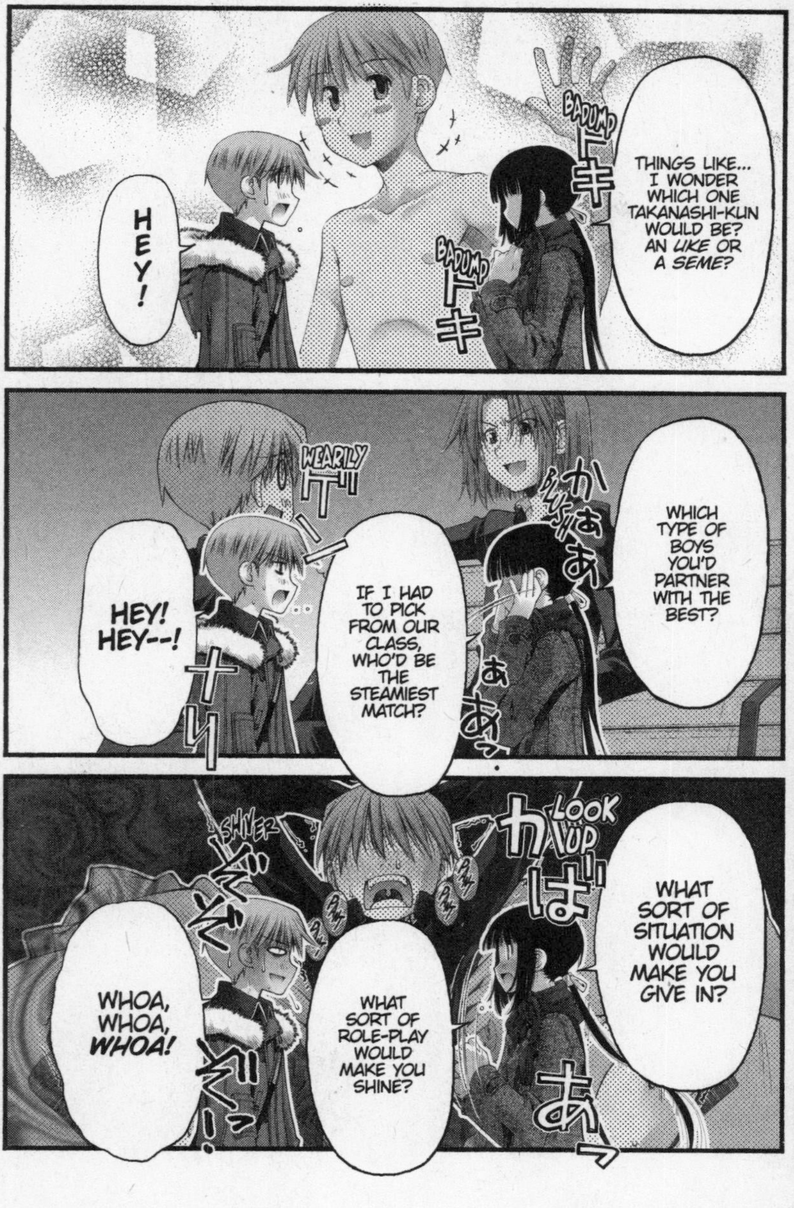
BADUMP
ドキ
THINGS LIKE... I WONDER WHICH ONE TAKANASHI-KUN WOULD BE? AN *UKE* OR A *SEME*?
BADUMP
ドキ
HEY!
WHICH TYPE OF BOYS YOU'D PARTNER WITH THE BEST?
BLUSH
かあああ
IF I HAD TO PICK FROM OUR CLASS, WHO'D BE THE STEAMIEST MATCH?
WEARILY
ゲンナリ
HEY! HEY--!
WHAT SORT OF SITUATION WOULD MAKE YOU GIVE IN?
LOOK UP
がばっ
あっ
WHAT SORT OF ROLE-PLAY WOULD MAKE YOU SHINE?
SHIVER
ぞぞぞっ
WHOA, WHOA, ***WHOA!***

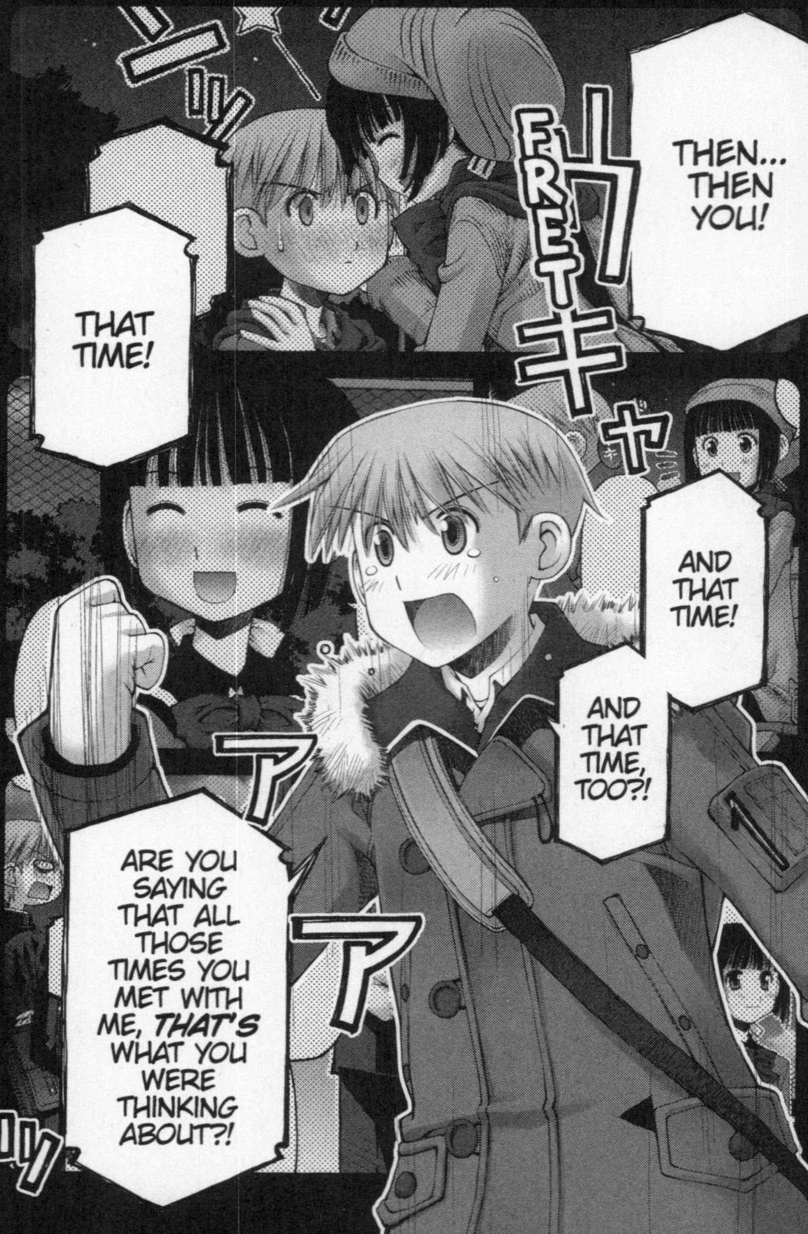

THEN... THEN YOU!
FRET
THAT TIME!
AND THAT TIME!
AND THAT TIME, TOO?!
ARE YOU SAYING THAT ALL THOSE TIMES YOU MET WITH ME, *THAT'S* WHAT YOU WERE THINKING ABOUT?!

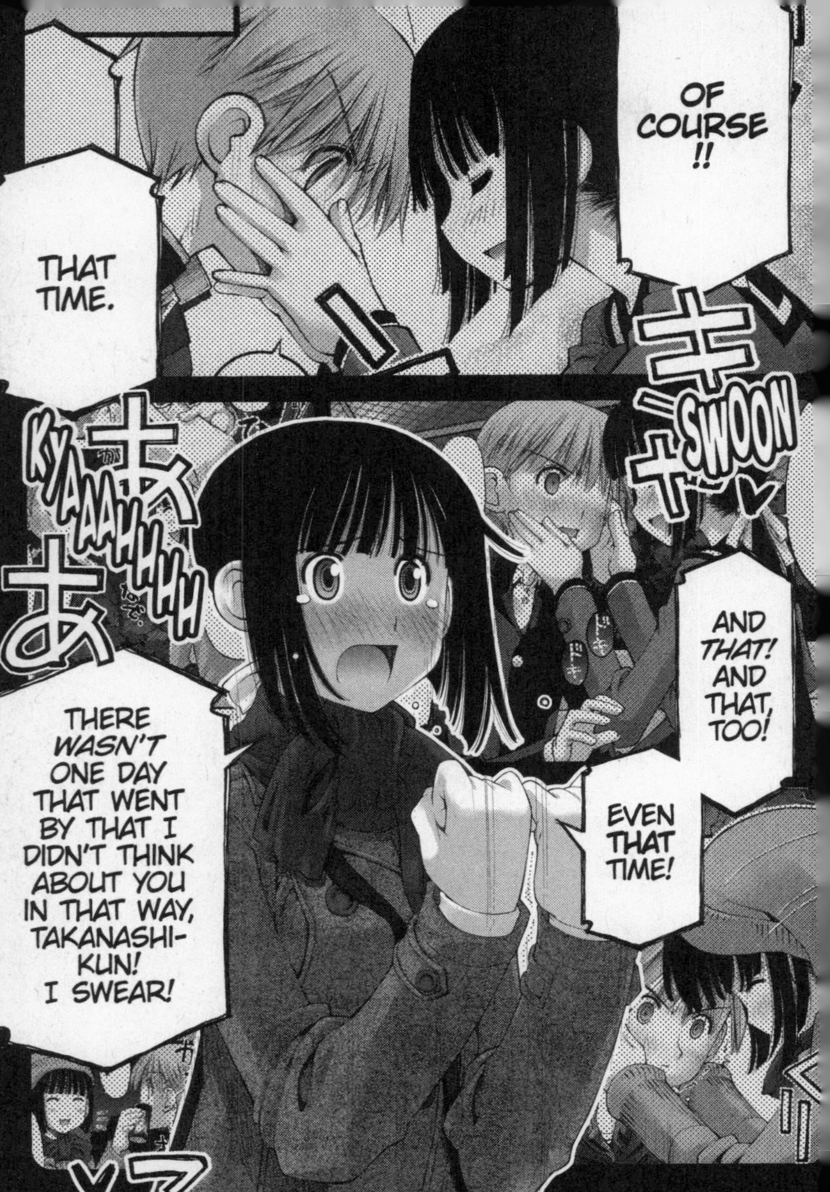
OF COURSE!!
THAT TIME.
SWOON
AND THAT! AND THAT, TOO!
EVEN THAT TIME!
KYAAAHHHHH
THERE WASN'T ONE DAY THAT WENT BY THAT I DIDN'T THINK ABOUT YOU IN THAT WAY, TAKANASHI-KUN! I SWEAR!

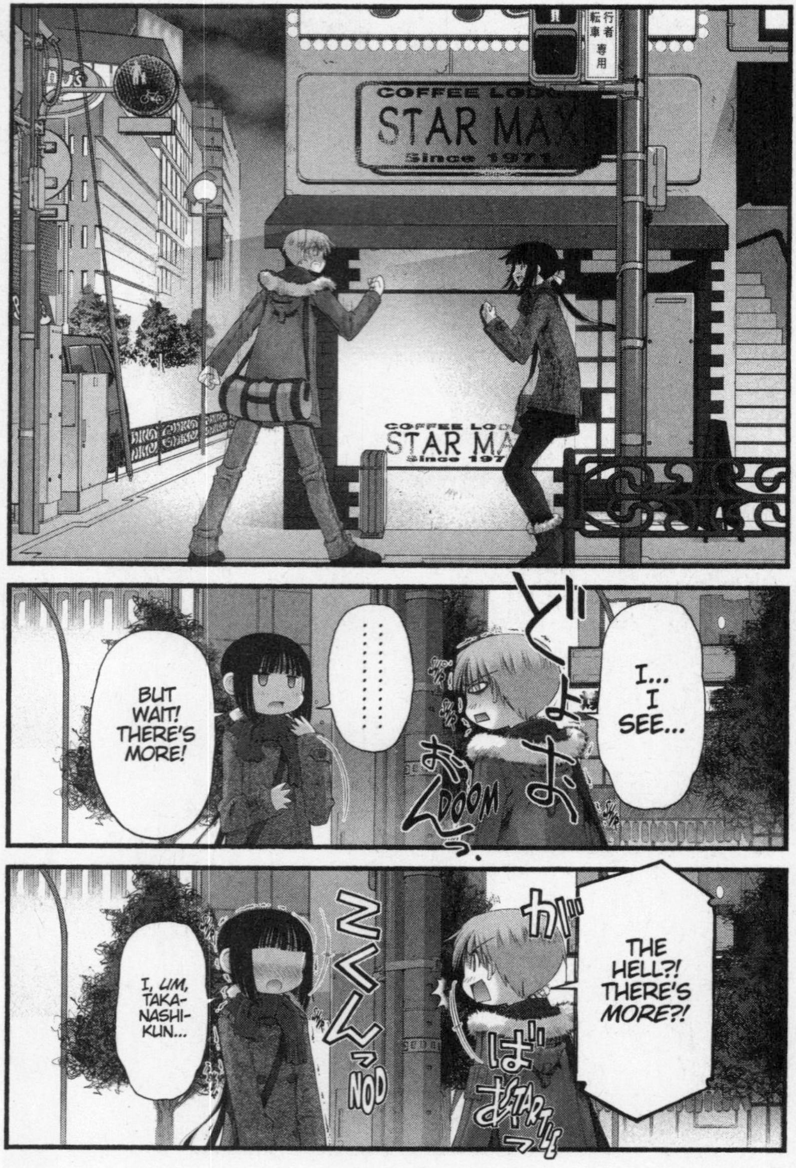

COFFEE LOD
STAR MAX
Since 1971
行者 転車 専用
COFFEE LOD
STAR MA
Since 197
どよよおんっ
DOOM
I... I SEE...
......
BUT WAIT! THERE'S MORE!
がばっ
STARTLE
THE HELL?! THERE'S MORE?!
こくんっ
NOD
I, UM, TAKA-NASHI-KUN...

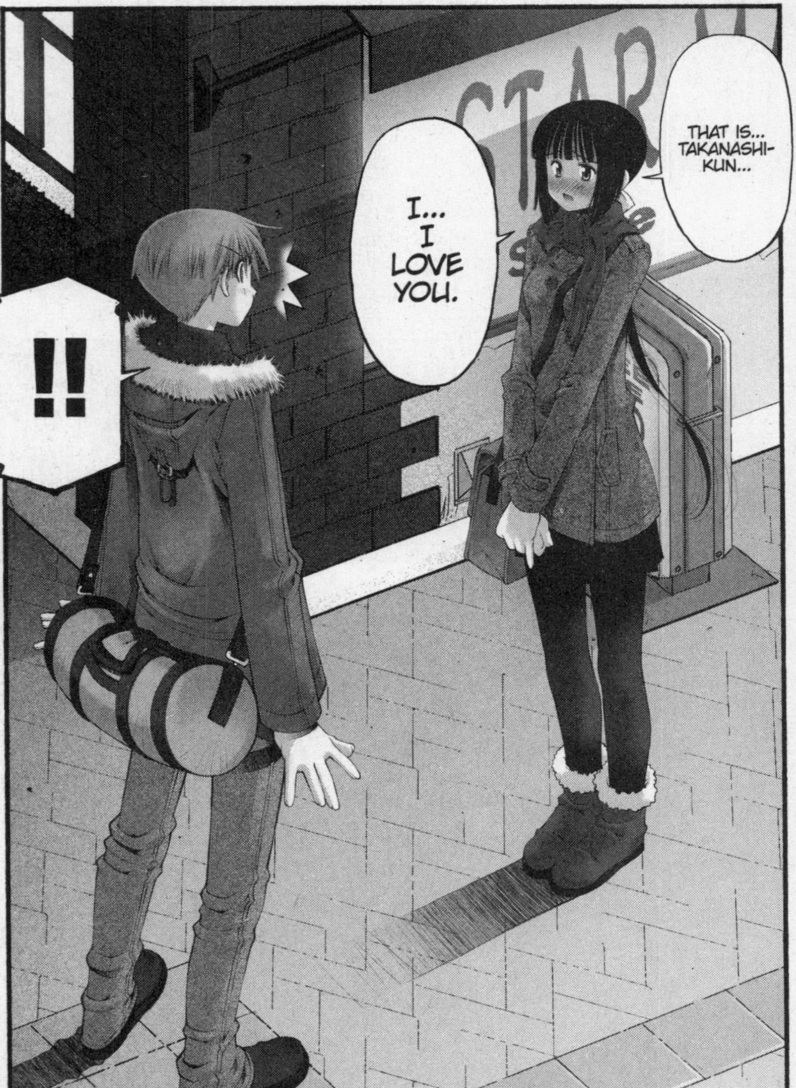
THAT IS... TAKANASHI-KUN...
I... I LOVE YOU.
!!

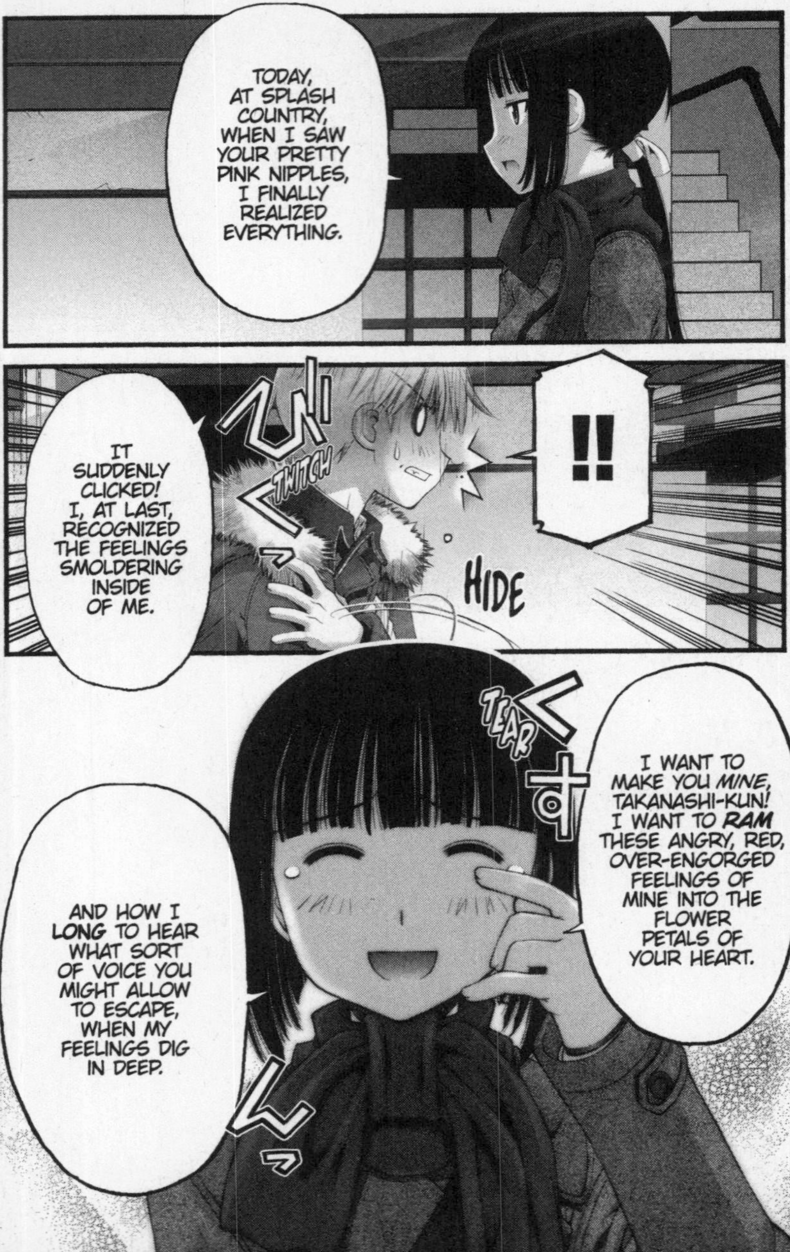
TODAY, AT SPLASH COUNTRY, WHEN I SAW YOUR PRETTY PINK NIPPLES, I FINALLY REALIZED EVERYTHING.
!!
TWITCH
HIDE
IT SUDDENLY CLICKED! I, AT LAST, RECOGNIZED THE FEELINGS SMOLDERING INSIDE OF ME.
TEAR
I WANT TO MAKE YOU *MINE*, TAKANASHI-KUN! I WANT TO ***RAM*** THESE ANGRY, RED, OVER-ENGORGED FEELINGS OF MINE INTO THE FLOWER PETALS OF YOUR HEART.
AND HOW I **LONG** TO HEAR WHAT SORT OF VOICE YOU MIGHT ALLOW TO ESCAPE, WHEN MY FEELINGS DIG IN DEEP.

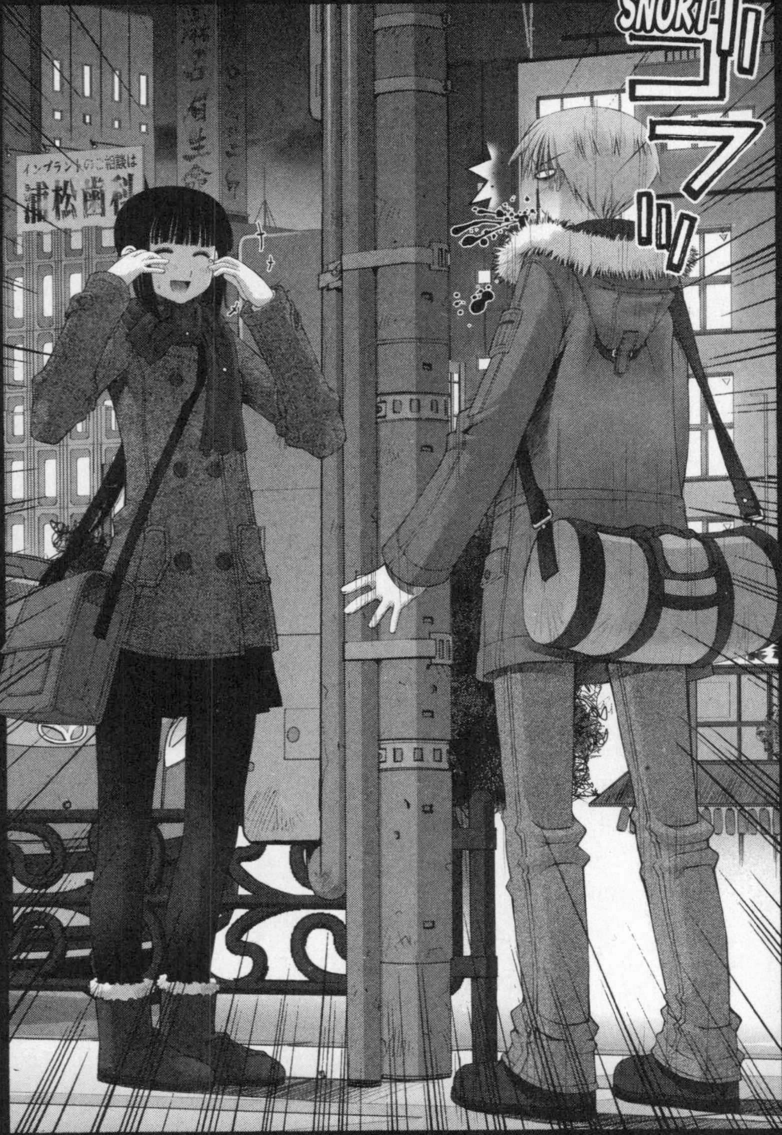
SNORT
ゴフッ
インプラントのご相談は
浦松歯科

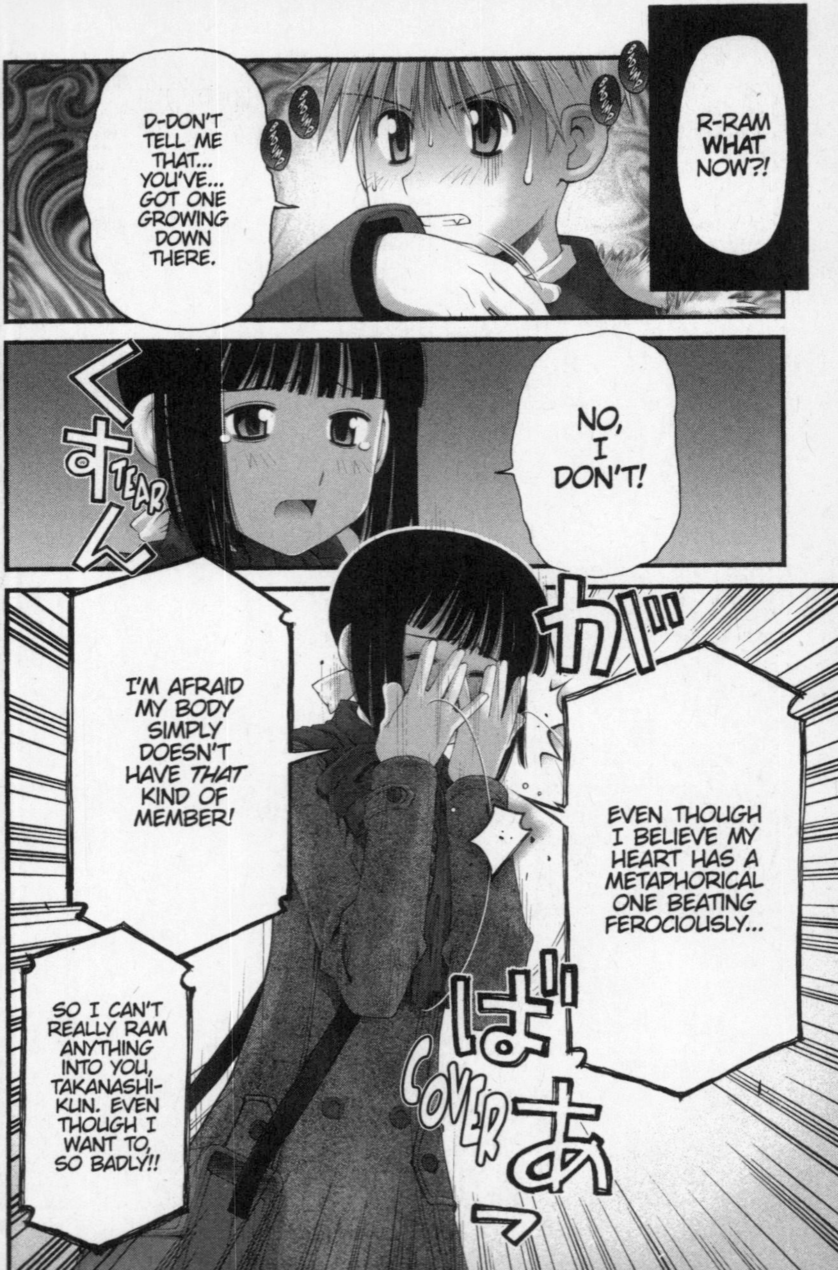
R-RAM WHAT NOW?!
BADUMP
BADUMP
BADUMP
BADUMP
D-DON'T TELL ME THAT... YOU'VE... GOT ONE GROWING DOWN THERE.
NO, I DON'T!
くすん
TEAR
ガバ
EVEN THOUGH I BELIEVE MY HEART HAS A METAPHORICAL ONE BEATING FEROCIOUSLY...
I'M AFRAID MY BODY SIMPLY DOESN'T HAVE *THAT* KIND OF MEMBER!
ばあっ
COVER
SO I CAN'T REALLY RAM ANYTHING INTO YOU, TAKANASHI-KUN. EVEN THOUGH I WANT TO, SO BADLY!!

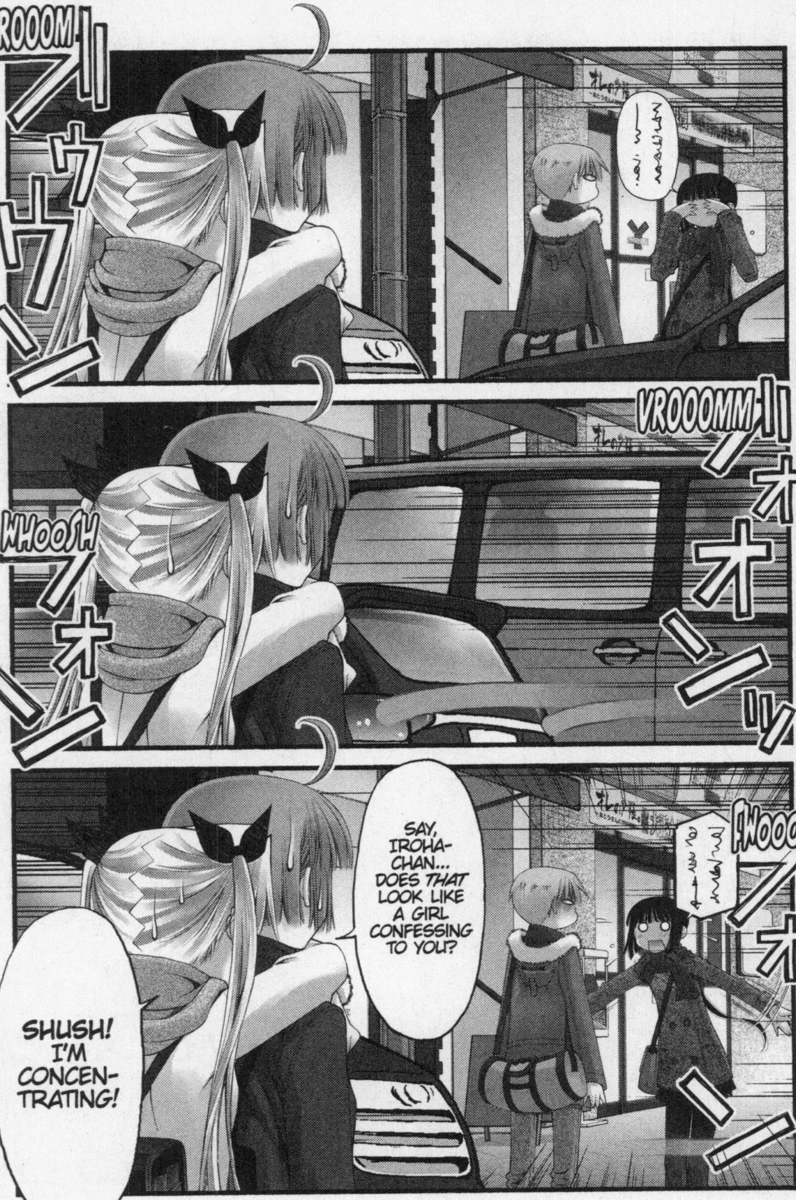
VROOOM
VROOOMM
WHOOSH
FWOOO!
SAY, IROHA-CHAN... DOES *THAT* LOOK LIKE A GIRL CONFESSING TO YOU?
SHUSH! I'M CONCEN-TRATING!

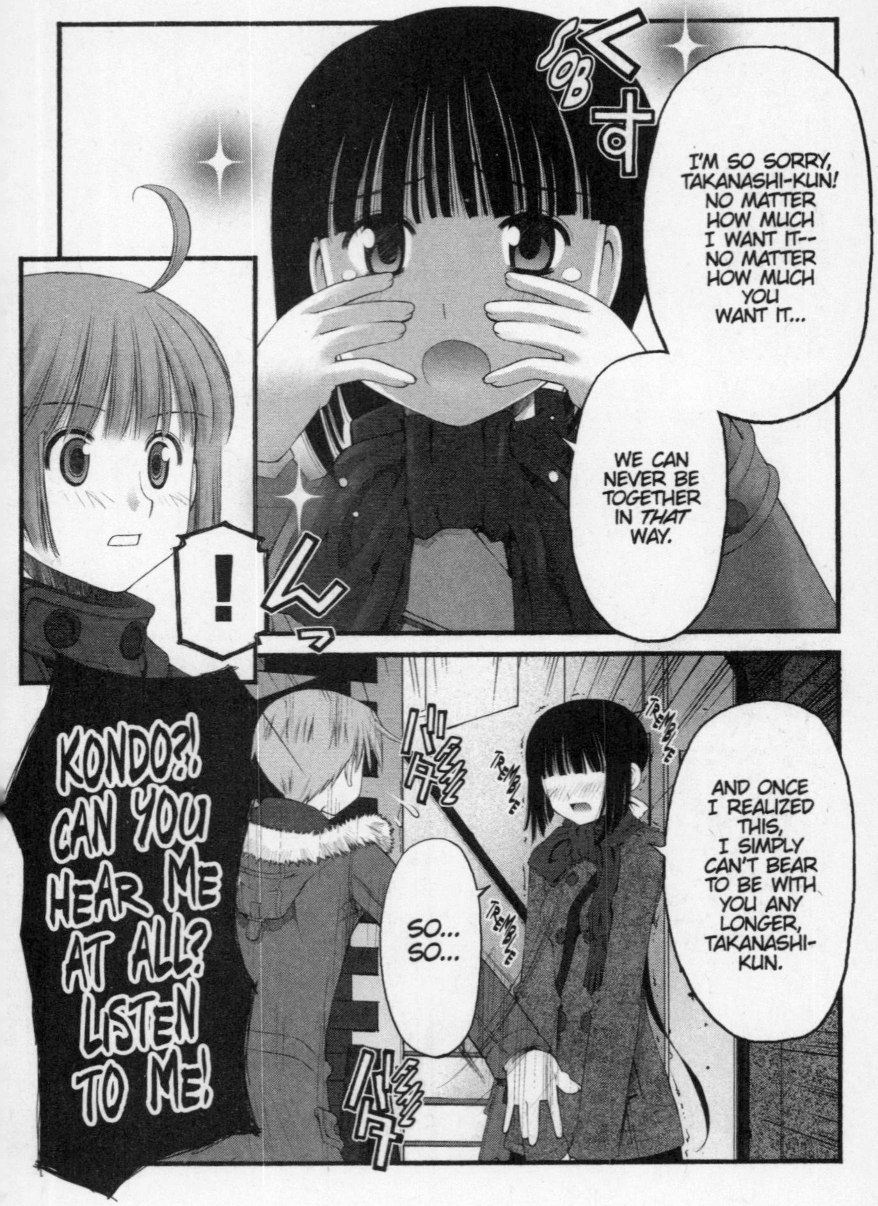
SOB
I'M SO SORRY, TAKANASHI-KUN! NO MATTER HOW MUCH I WANT IT-- NO MATTER HOW MUCH YOU WANT IT...
WE CAN NEVER BE TOGETHER IN *THAT* WAY.
!
AND ONCE I REALIZED THIS, I SIMPLY CAN'T BEAR TO BE WITH YOU ANY LONGER, TAKANASHI-KUN.
TREMBLE
TREMBLE
SO... SO...
TREMBLE
KONDO?! CAN YOU HEAR ME AT ALL? LISTEN TO ME!

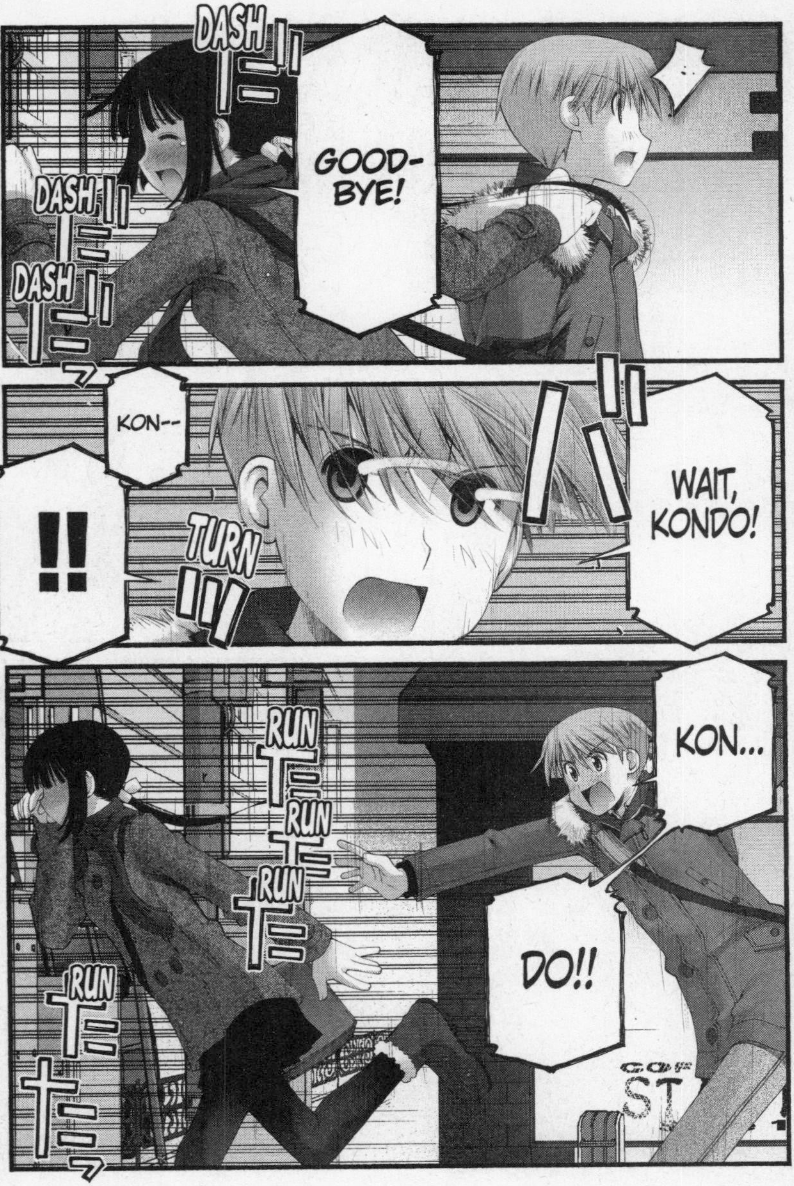
GOOD-BYE!
DASH
DASH
DASH
WAIT, KONDO!
KON--
TURN
!!
KON...
DO!!
RUN
RUN
RUN
RUN

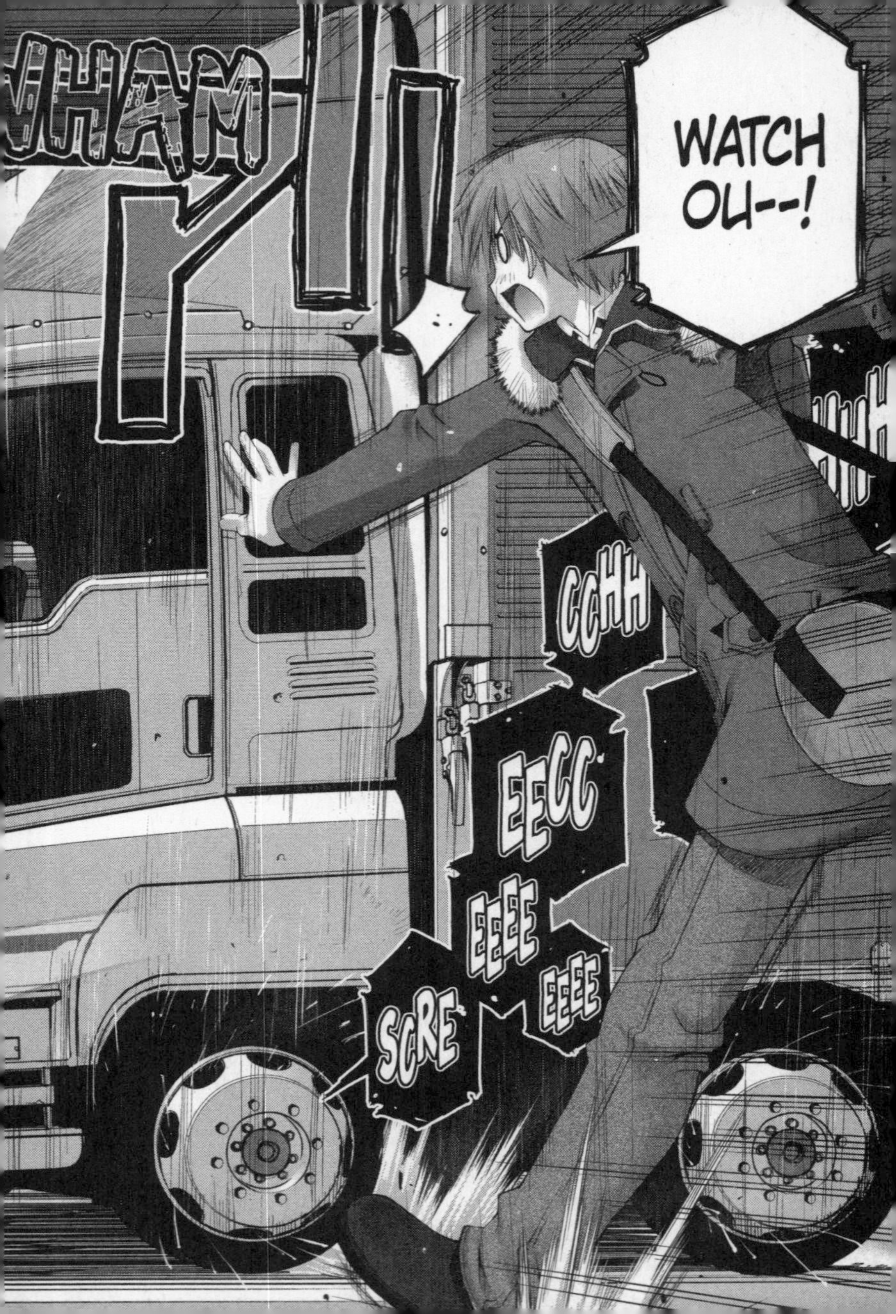
WATCH OU--!
WHAM
SCRE
EEEE
EEEE
EECC
CCHH

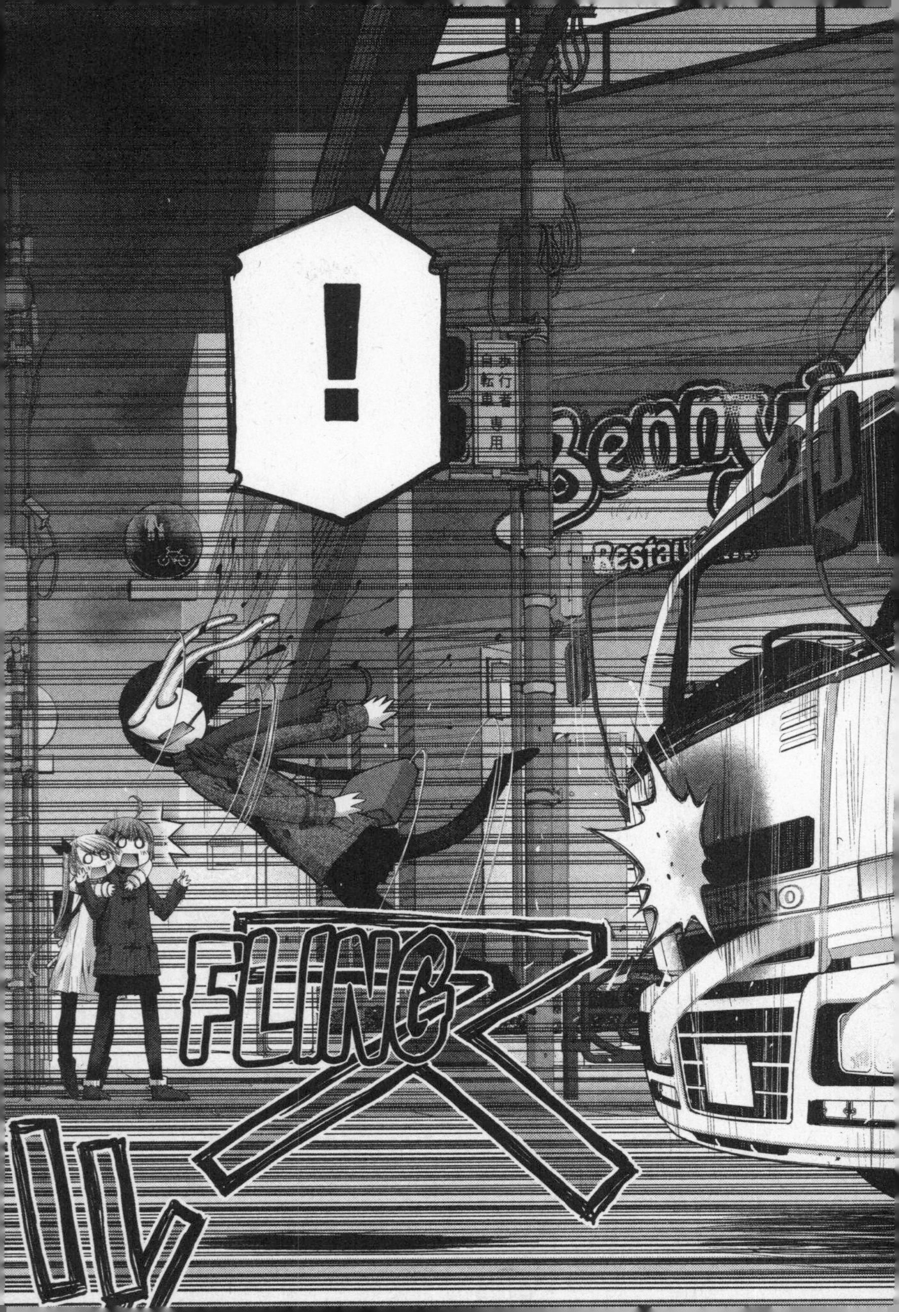
!
歩行者自転車専用
FLING

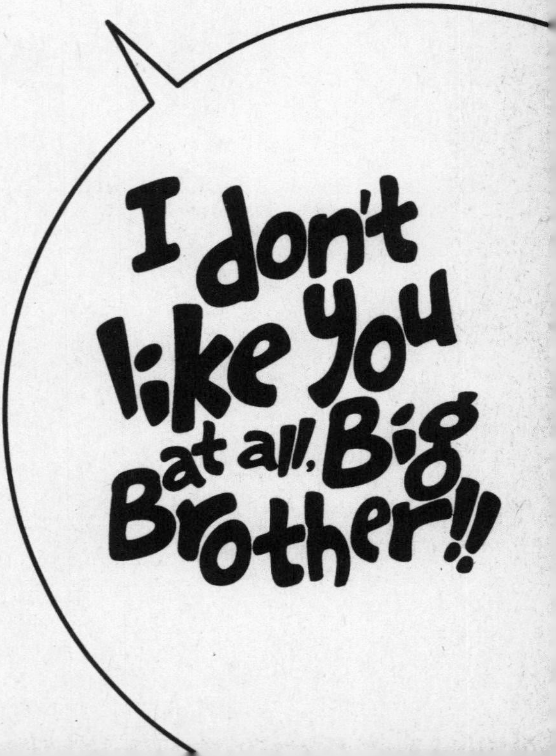
I don't like you at all, Big Brother!!

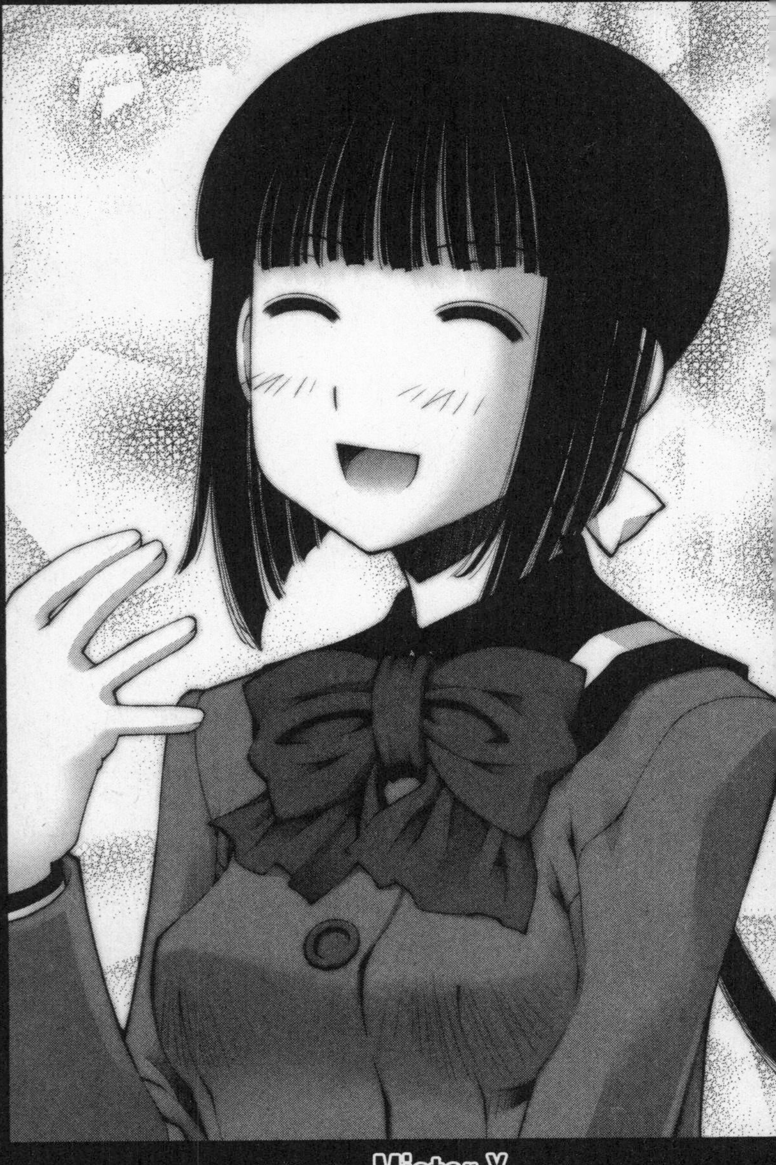

CHAPTER Mister X

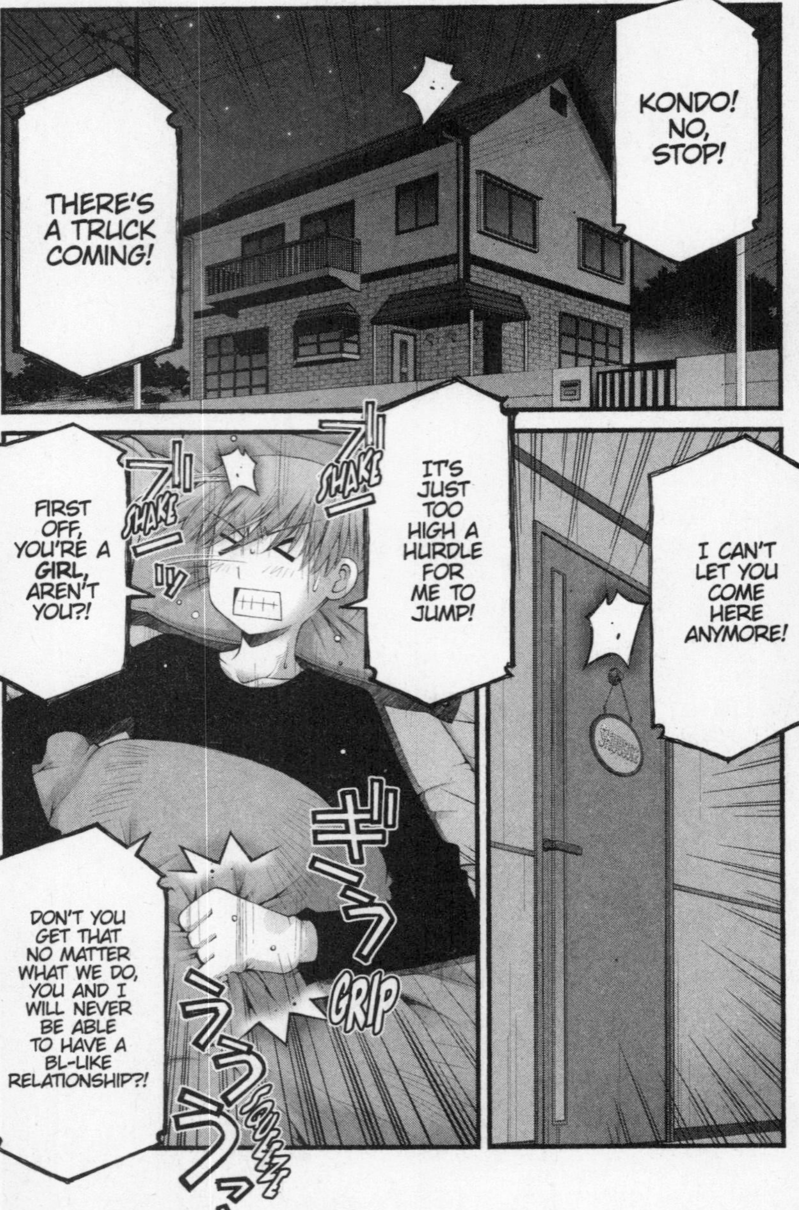
KONDO! NO, STOP!
THERE'S A TRUCK COMING!
I CAN'T LET YOU COME HERE ANYMORE!
IT'S JUST TOO HIGH A HURDLE FOR ME TO JUMP!
SHAKE
SHAKE
FIRST OFF, YOU'RE A GIRL, AREN'T YOU?!
GRIP
SQUEEZE
DON'T YOU GET THAT NO MATTER WHAT WE DO, YOU AND I WILL NEVER BE ABLE TO HAVE A BL-LIKE RELATIONSHIP?!

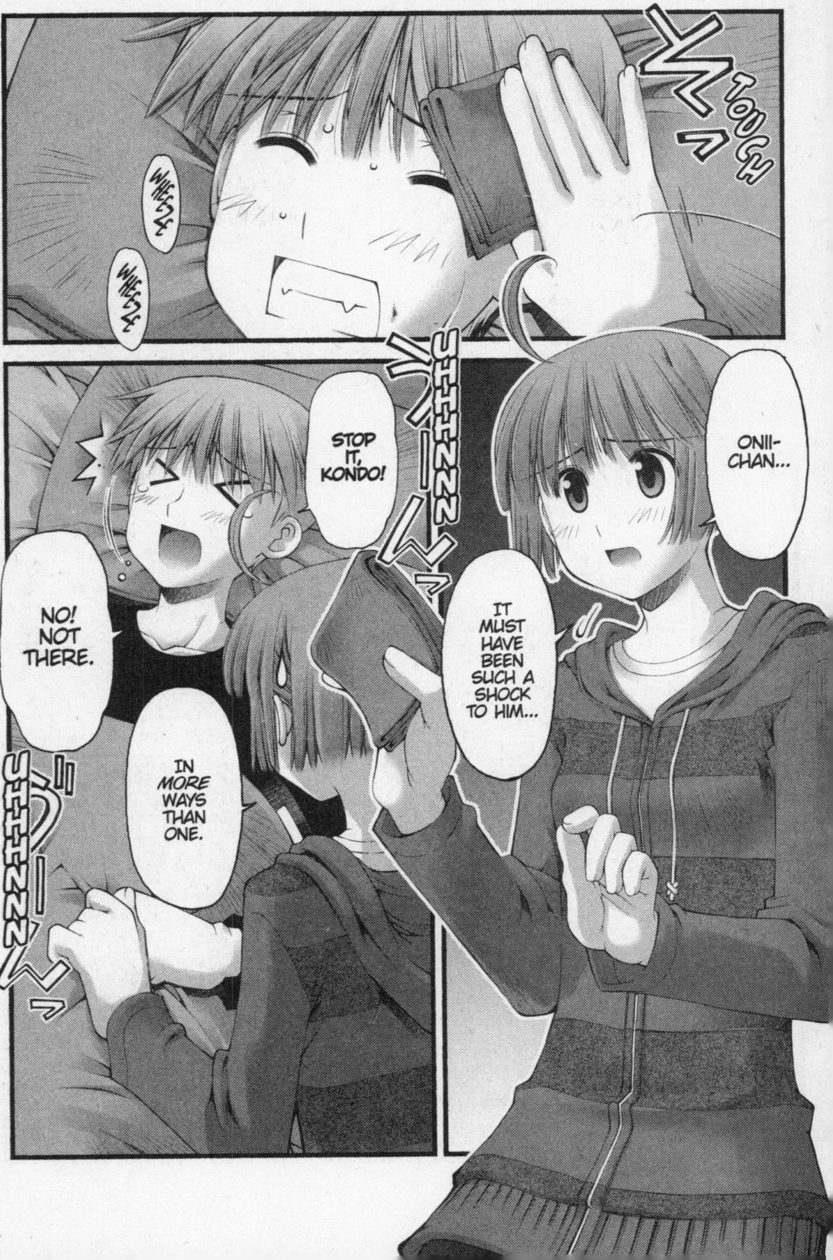
TOUCH
WHEEZE
WHEEZE
ONII-CHAN...
IT MUST HAVE BEEN SUCH A SHOCK TO HIM...
UHHHNNNN
STOP IT, KONDO!
NO! NOT THERE.
IN MORE WAYS THAN ONE.
UHHHNNNN

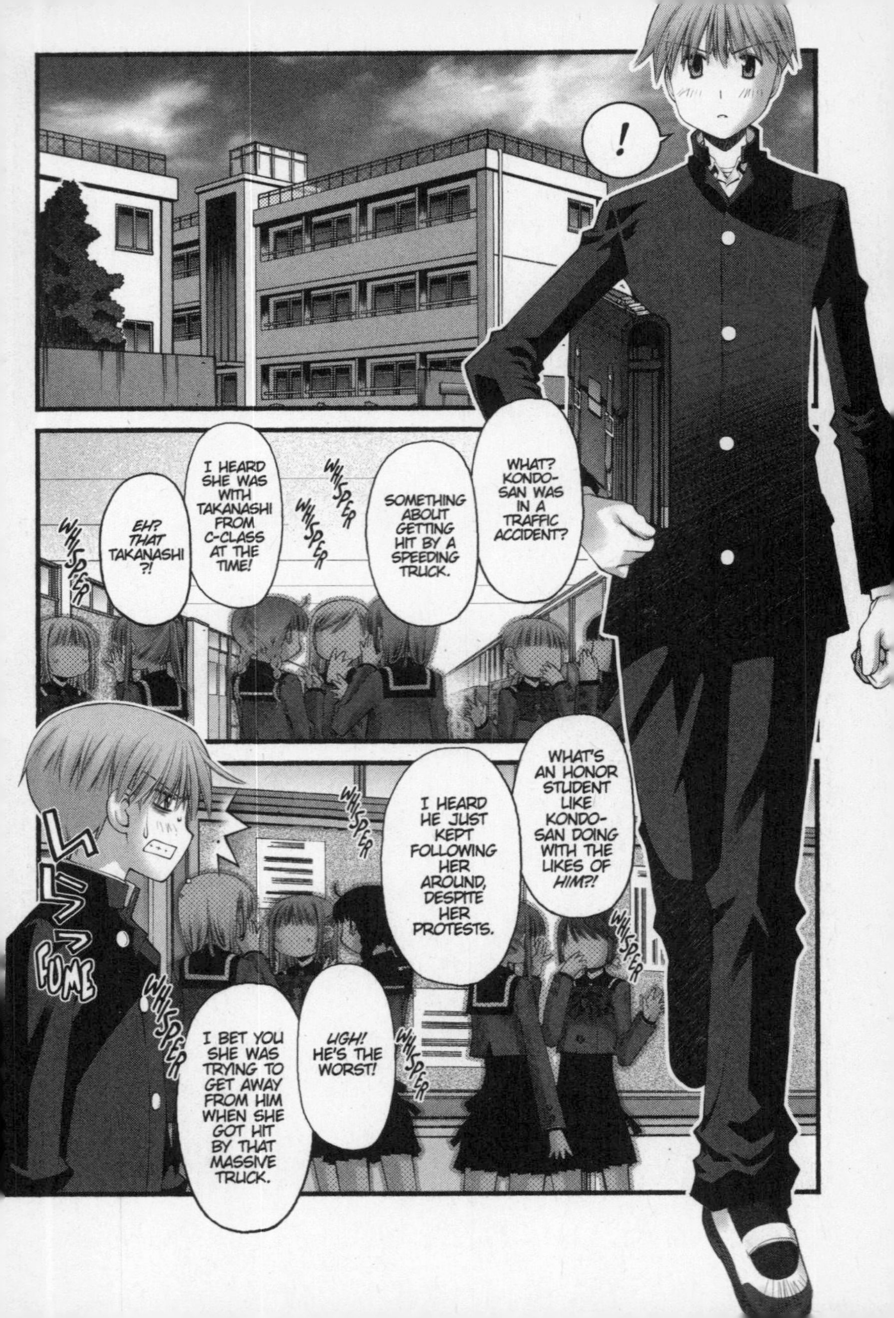
!
WHAT? KONDO-SAN WAS IN A TRAFFIC ACCIDENT?
SOMETHING ABOUT GETTING HIT BY A SPEEDING TRUCK.
WHISPER
WHISPER
I HEARD SHE WAS WITH TAKANASHI FROM C-CLASS AT THE TIME!
EH? THAT TAKANASHI ?!
WHISPER
WHAT'S AN HONOR STUDENT LIKE KONDO-SAN DOING WITH THE LIKES OF *HIM?!*
WHISPER
WHISPER
I HEARD HE JUST KEPT FOLLOWING HER AROUND, DESPITE HER PROTESTS.
WHISPER
UGH! HE'S THE WORST!
I BET YOU SHE WAS TRYING TO GET AWAY FROM HIM WHEN SHE GOT HIT BY THAT MASSIVE TRUCK.
WHISPER
FUME

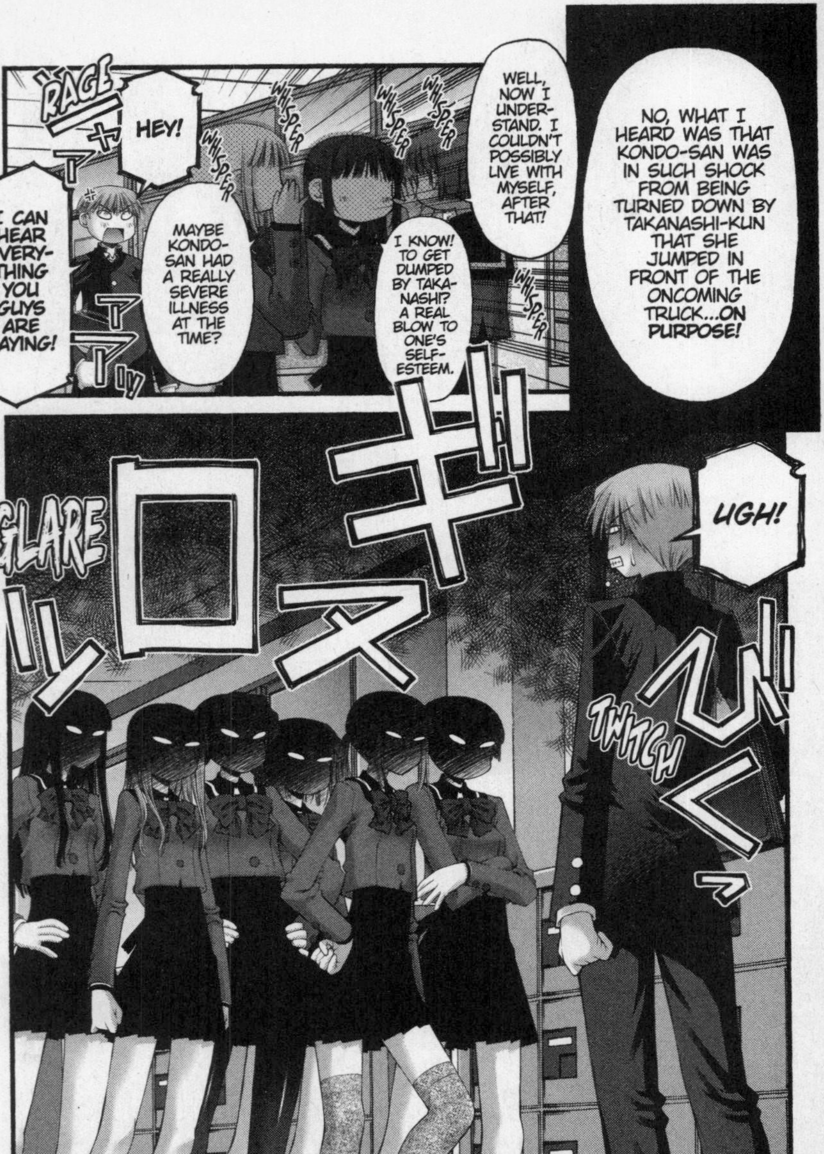
NO, WHAT I HEARD WAS THAT KONDO-SAN WAS IN SUCH SHOCK FROM BEING TURNED DOWN BY TAKANASHI-KUN THAT SHE JUMPED IN FRONT OF THE ONCOMING TRUCK...ON PURPOSE!
WHISPER
WHISPER
WELL, NOW I UNDER-STAND. I COULDN'T POSSIBLY LIVE WITH MYSELF, AFTER THAT!
WHISPER
I KNOW! TO GET DUMPED BY TAKA-NASHI? A REAL BLOW TO ONE'S SELF-ESTEEM.
WHISPER
WHISPER
MAYBE KONDO-SAN HAD A REALLY SEVERE ILLNESS AT THE TIME?
RAGE
HEY!
I CAN HEAR EVERY-THING YOU GUYS ARE SAYING!
UGH!
TWITCH
GLARE

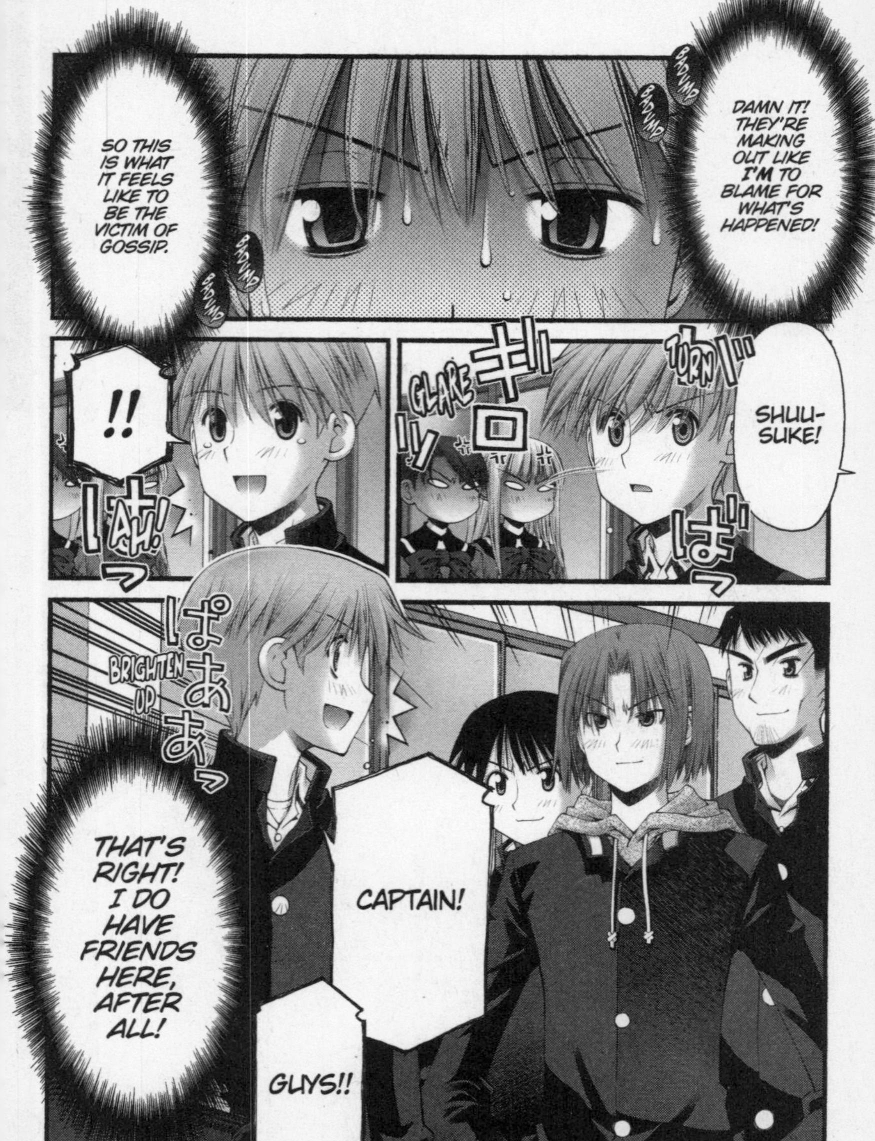

BADUMP
BADUMP
BADUMP
DAMN IT! THEY'RE MAKING OUT LIKE I'M TO BLAME FOR WHAT'S HAPPENED!
SO THIS IS WHAT IT FEELS LIKE TO BE THE VICTIM OF GOSSIP.
BADUMP
BADUMP
TURN
SHUU-SUKE!
GLARE
!!
AH!
BRIGHTEN UP
CAPTAIN!
THAT'S RIGHT! I DO HAVE FRIENDS HERE, AFTER ALL!
GUYS!!

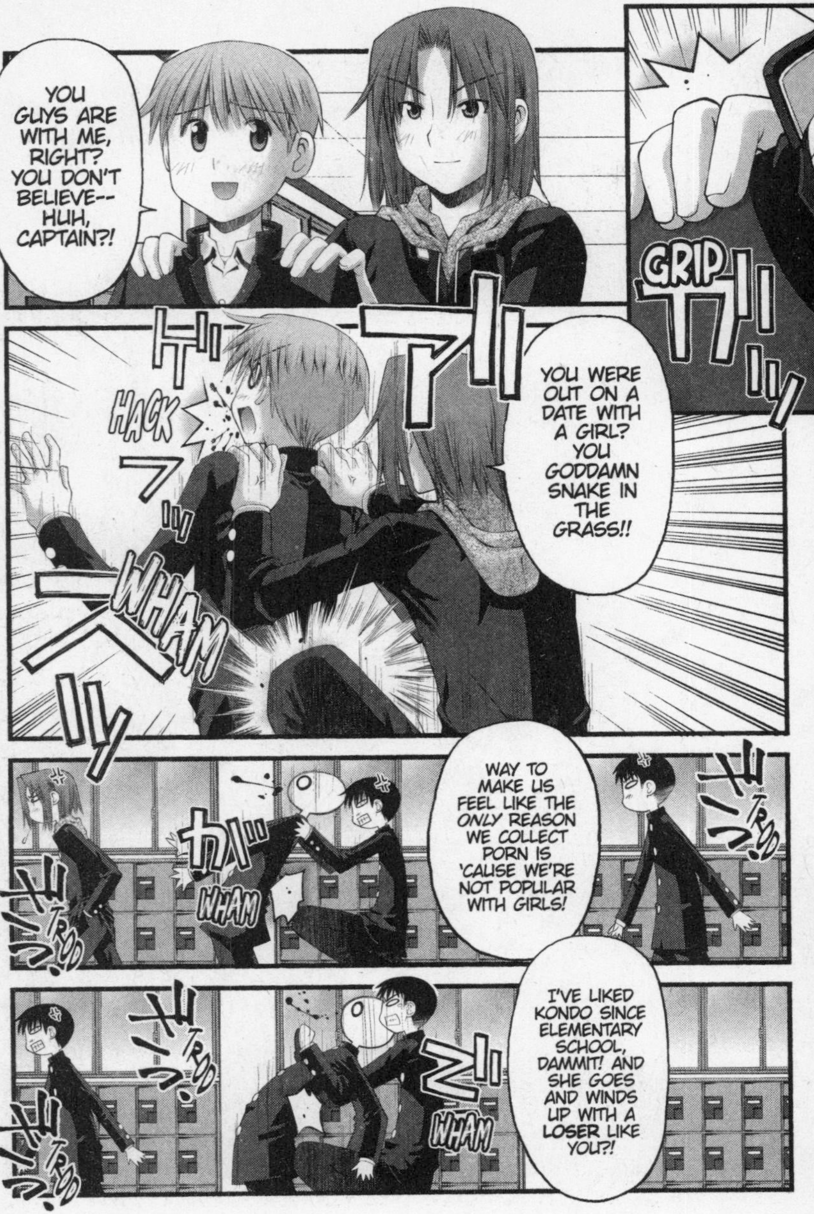
GRIP
YOU GUYS ARE WITH ME, RIGHT? YOU DON'T BELIEVE-- HUH, CAPTAIN?!
YOU WERE OUT ON A DATE WITH A GIRL? YOU GODDAMN SNAKE IN THE GRASS!!
HACK
WHAM
TROD
WAY TO MAKE US FEEL LIKE THE *ONLY* REASON WE COLLECT PORN IS 'CAUSE WE'RE NOT POPULAR WITH GIRLS!
WHAM
TROD
I'VE LIKED KONDO SINCE ELEMENTARY SCHOOL, DAMMIT! AND SHE GOES AND WINDS UP WITH A **LOSER** LIKE YOU?!
WHAM
TROD
TROD

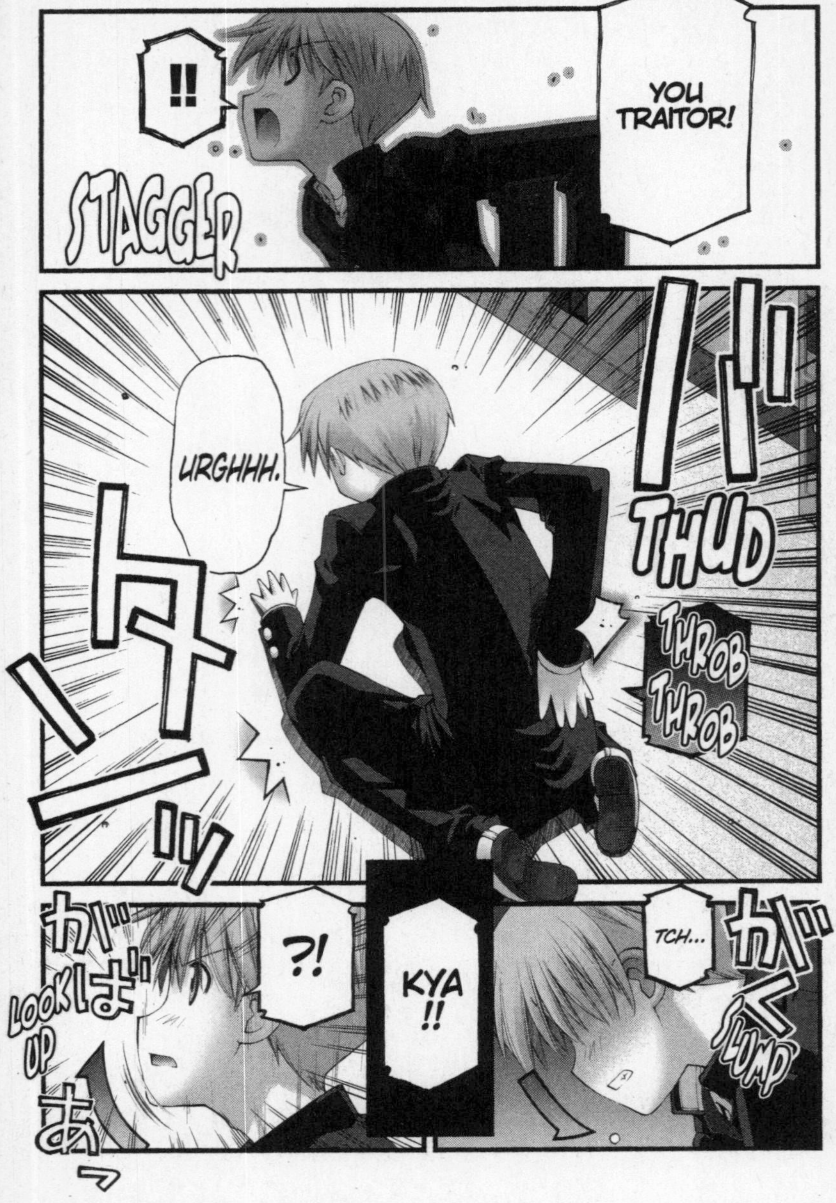
YOU TRAITOR!
!!
STAGGER
THUD
URGHHH.
THROB THROB
TCH...
SLUMP
KYA!!
?!
LOOK UP

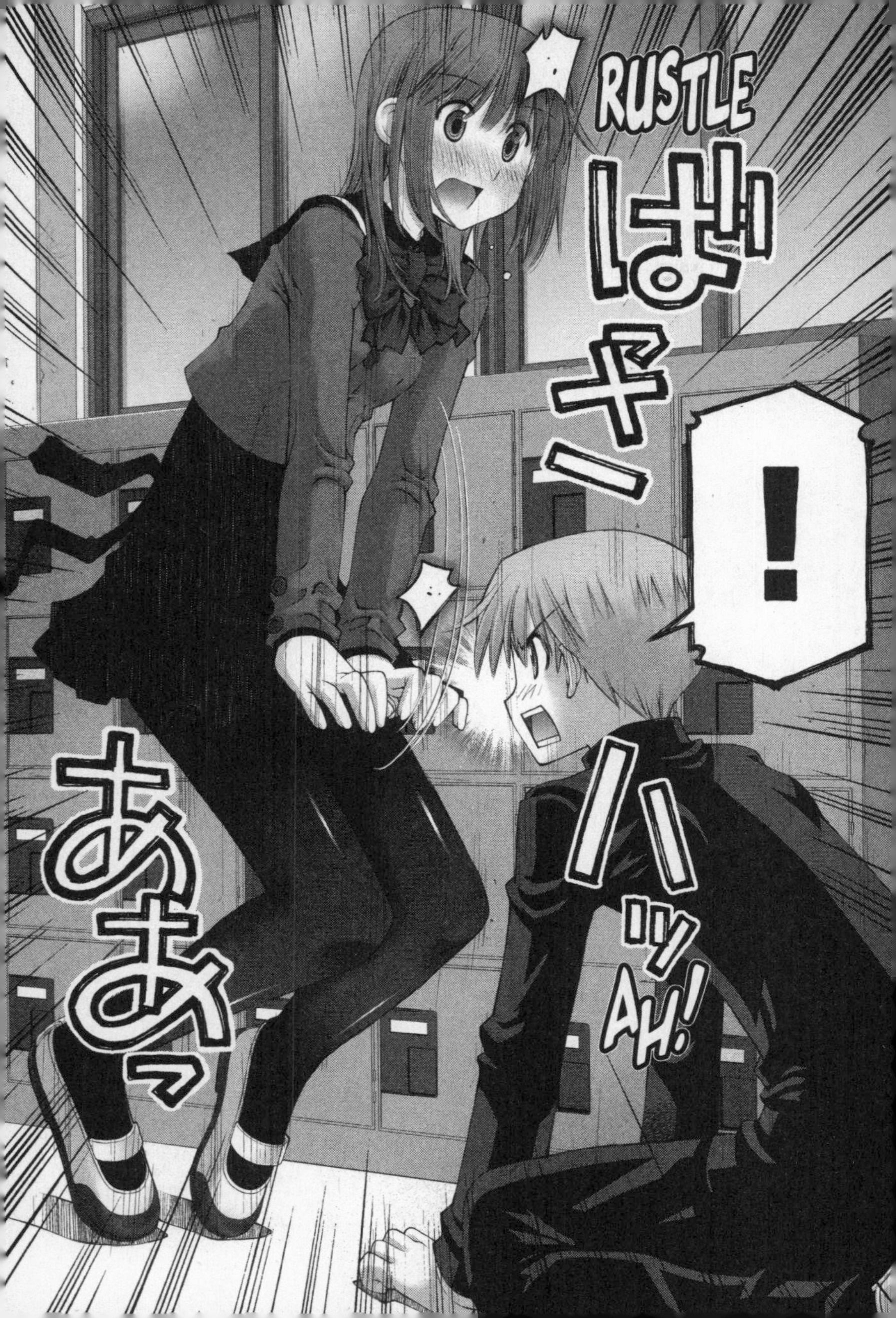
RUSTLE
ばさっ
!
あぁっ
ハッ
AH!

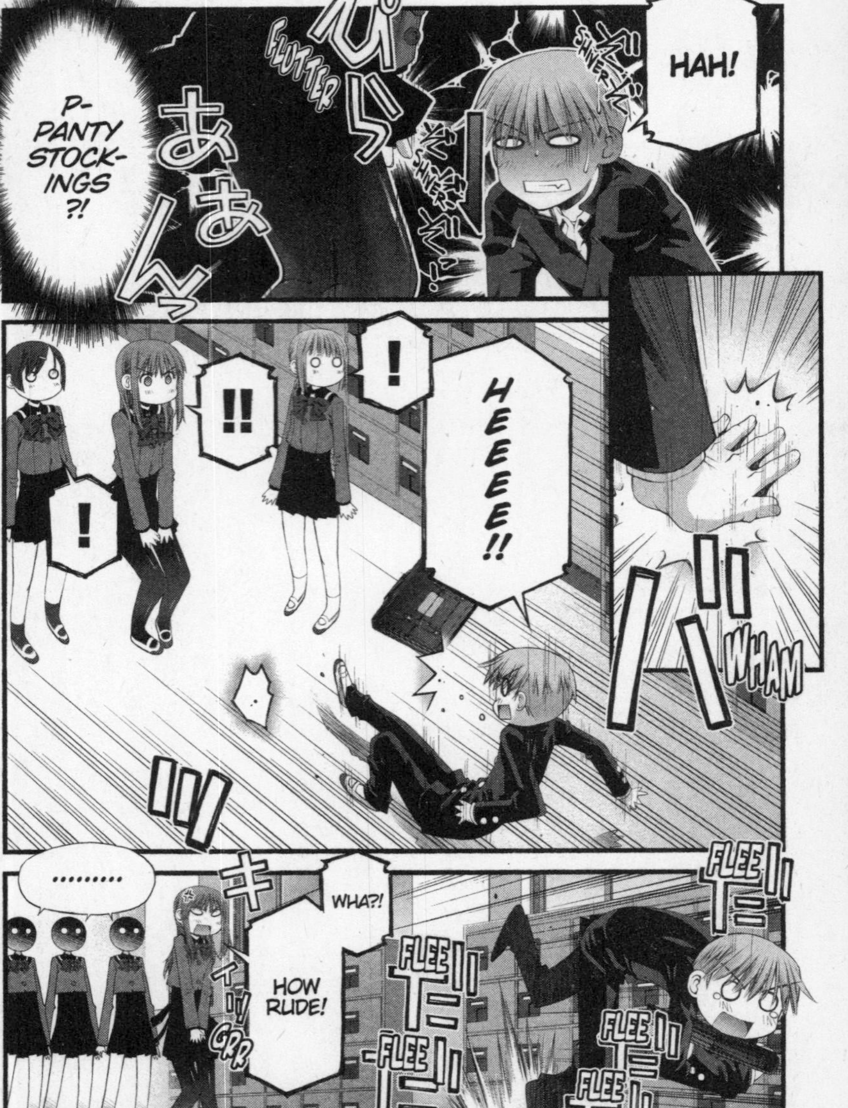
HAH!
SHIVER
SHIVER
ぴら
FLUTTER
ああんっ
P-PANTY STOCKINGS?!
WHAM
!
HEEEEE!!
!!
!
FLEE
FLEE
FLEE
FLEE
FLEE
WHA?!
HOW RUDE!
キィ!!
GRR
....

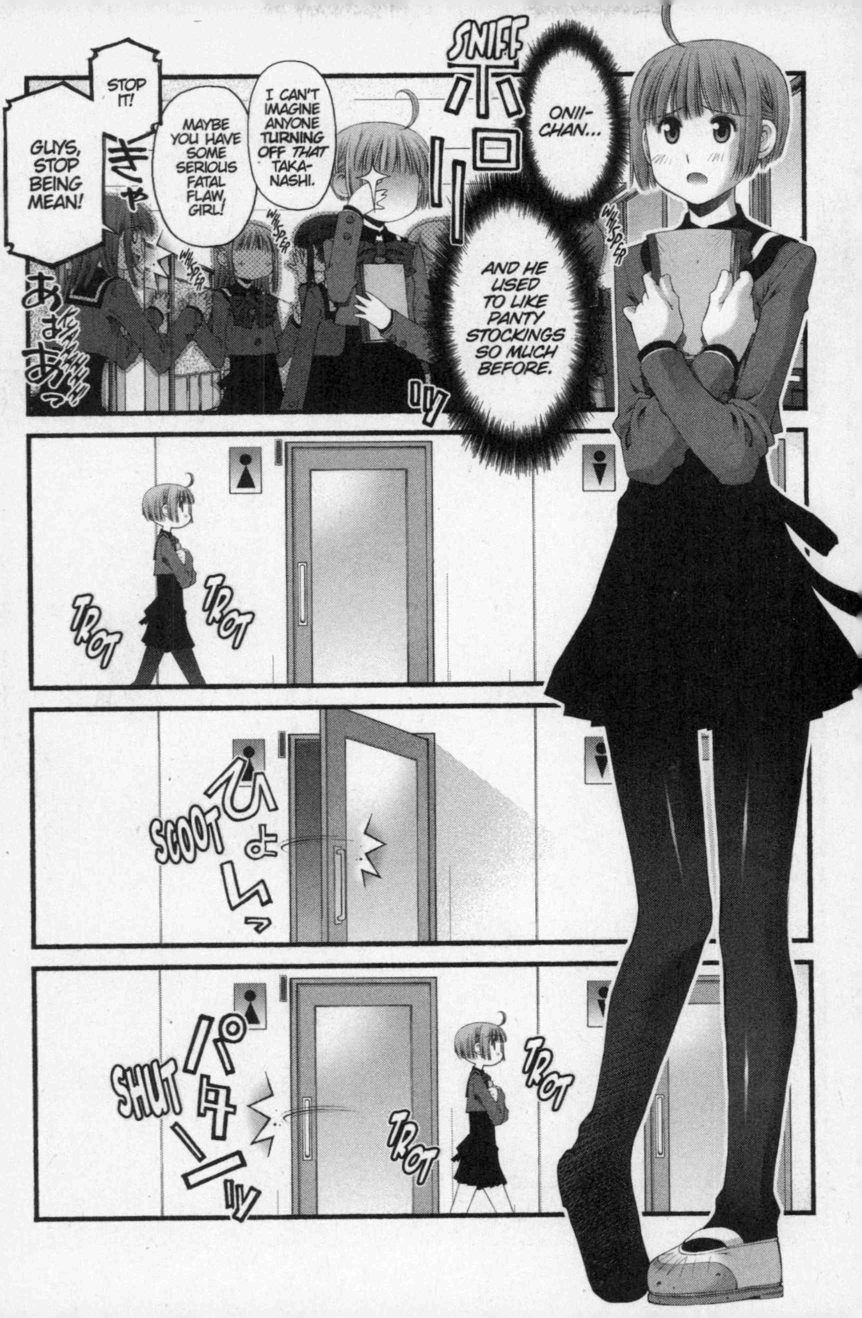
SNIFF
ONII-CHAN...
AND HE USED TO LIKE PANTY STOCKINGS SO MUCH BEFORE.
WHISPER
I CAN'T IMAGINE ANYONE TURNING OFF THAT TAKA-NASHI.
MAYBE YOU HAVE SOME SERIOUS FATAL FLAW, GIRL!
WHISPER
STOP IT!
WHISPER
GUYS, STOP BEING MEAN!
TROT
TROT
SCOOT
TROT
TROT
SHUT

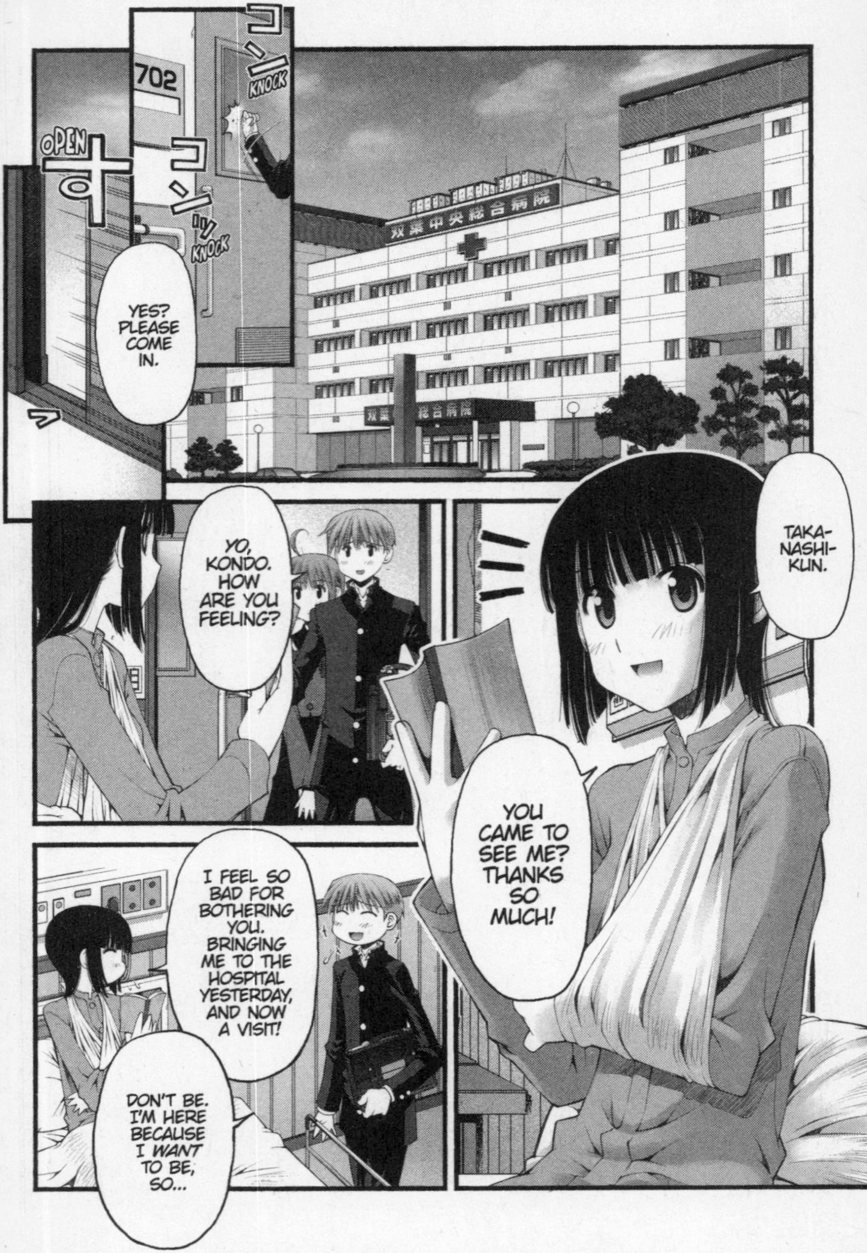

双葉中央総合病院
702
コン
KNOCK
コン
KNOCK
YES? PLEASE COME IN.
すっ
OPEN
TAKANASHI-KUN.
YOU CAME TO SEE ME? THANKS SO MUCH!
YO, KONDO. HOW ARE YOU FEELING?
I FEEL SO BAD FOR BOTHERING YOU. BRINGING ME TO THE HOSPITAL YESTERDAY, AND NOW A VISIT!
DON'T BE. I'M HERE BECAUSE I *WANT* TO BE, SO...

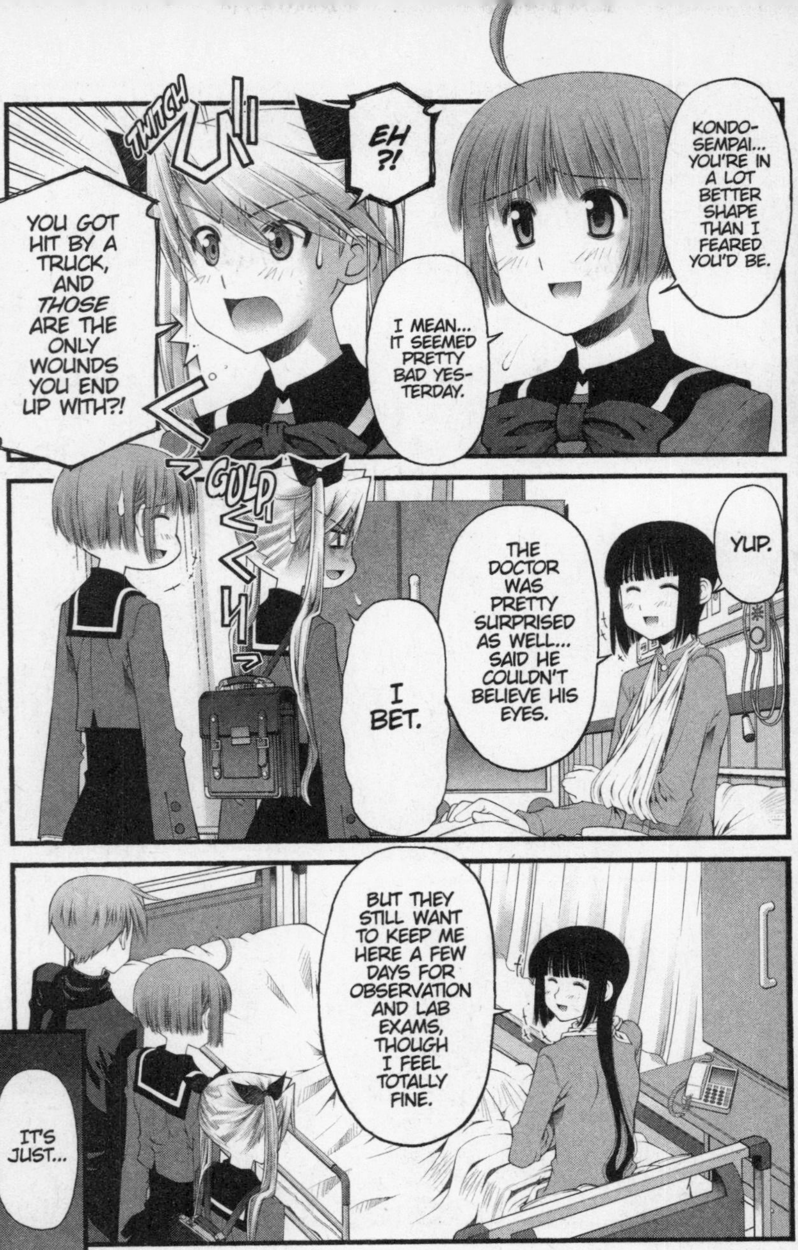
KONDO-SEMPAI... YOU'RE IN A LOT BETTER SHAPE THAN I FEARED YOU'D BE.
I MEAN... IT SEEMED PRETTY BAD YES-TERDAY.
EH ?!
TWITCH
YOU GOT HIT BY A TRUCK, AND *THOSE* ARE THE ONLY WOUNDS YOU END UP WITH?!
YUP.
THE DOCTOR WAS PRETTY SURPRISED AS WELL... SAID HE COULDN'T BELIEVE HIS EYES.
I BET.
GULP
BUT THEY STILL WANT TO KEEP ME HERE A FEW DAYS FOR OBSERVATION AND LAB EXAMS, THOUGH I FEEL TOTALLY FINE.
IT'S JUST...

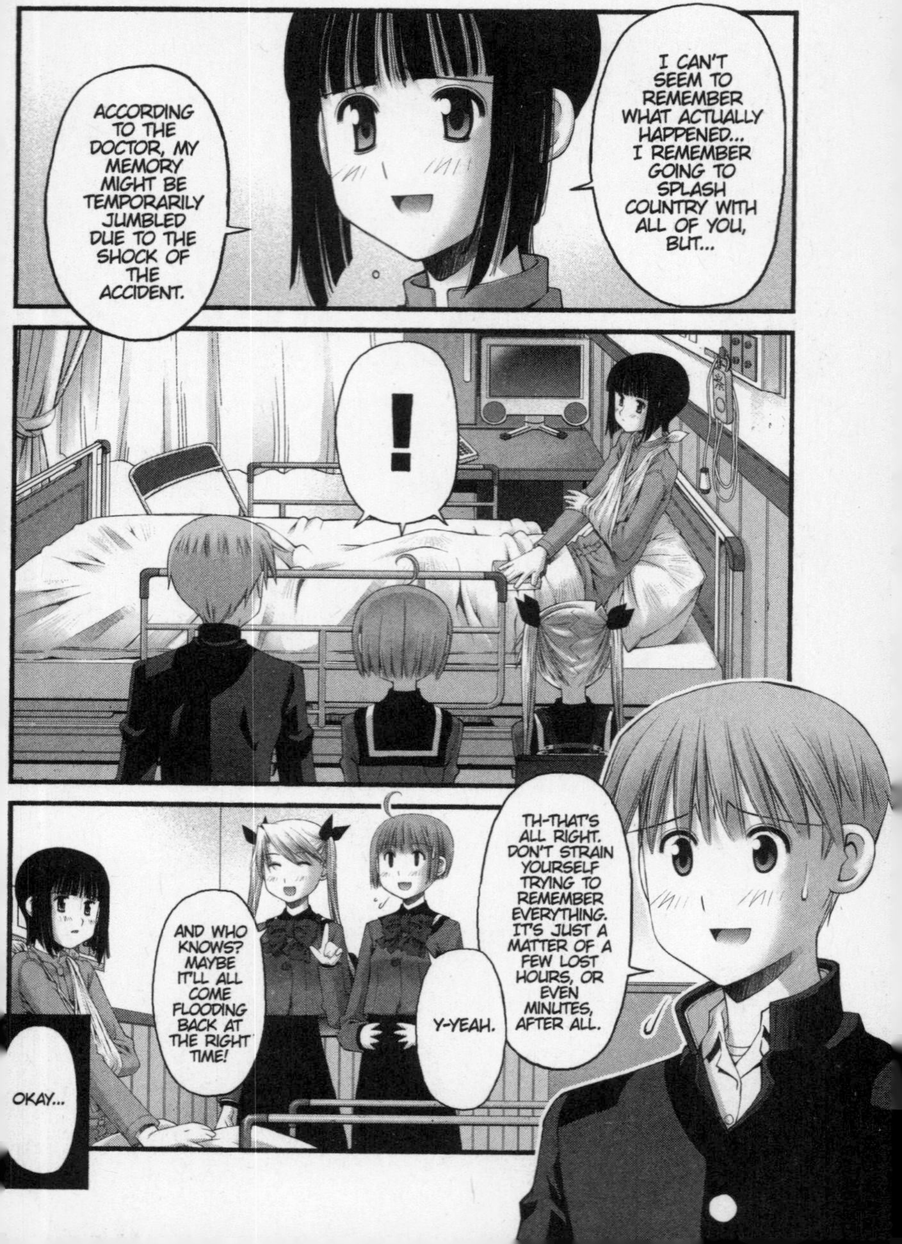
I CAN'T SEEM TO REMEMBER WHAT ACTUALLY HAPPENED... I REMEMBER GOING TO SPLASH COUNTRY WITH ALL OF YOU, BUT...
ACCORDING TO THE DOCTOR, MY MEMORY MIGHT BE TEMPORARILY JUMBLED DUE TO THE SHOCK OF THE ACCIDENT.
!
TH-THAT'S ALL RIGHT. DON'T STRAIN YOURSELF TRYING TO REMEMBER EVERYTHING. IT'S JUST A MATTER OF A FEW LOST HOURS, OR EVEN MINUTES, AFTER ALL.
Y-YEAH.
AND WHO KNOWS? MAYBE IT'LL ALL COME FLOODING BACK AT THE RIGHT TIME!
OKAY...

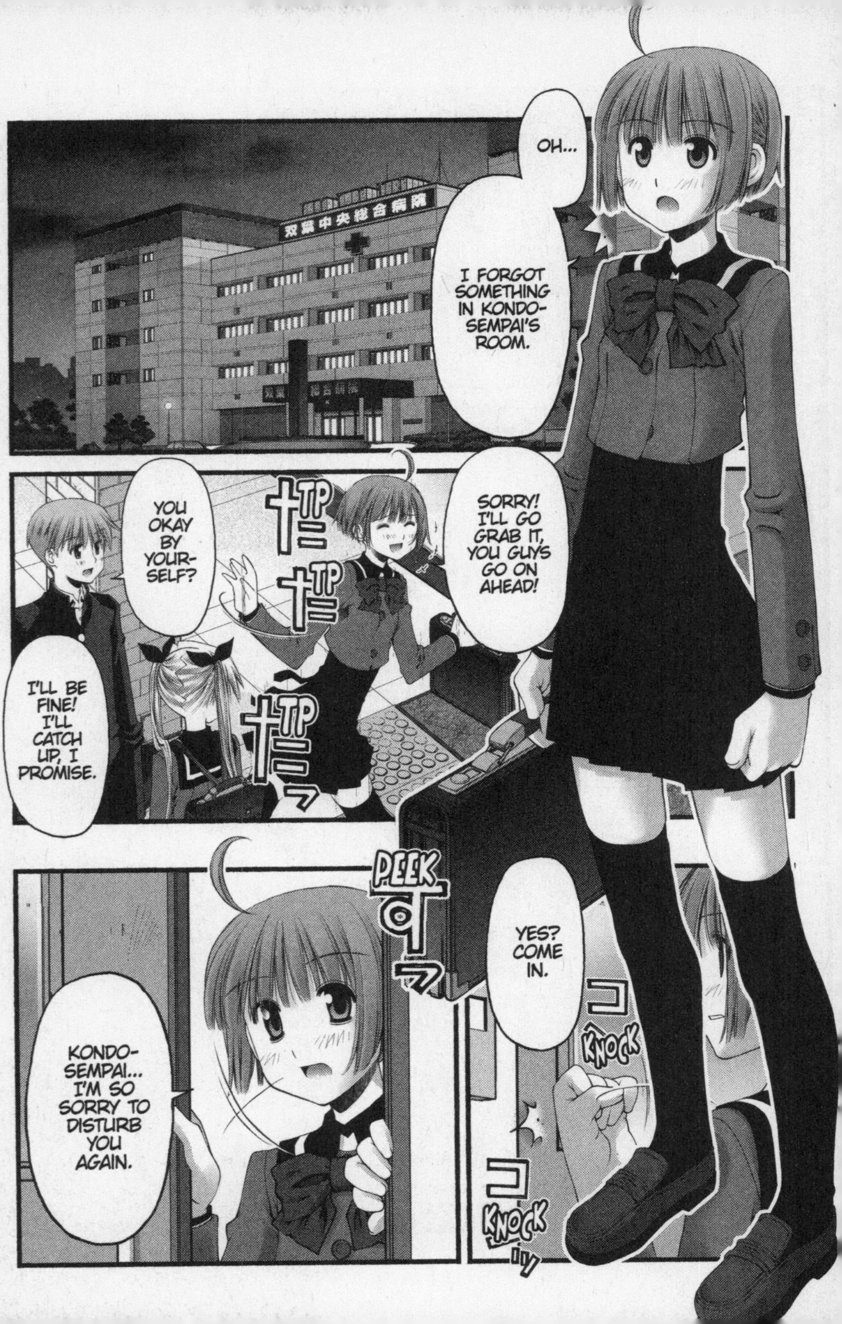
双葉中央総合病院
OH...
I FORGOT SOMETHING IN KONDO-SEMPAI'S ROOM.
SORRY! I'LL GO GRAB IT, YOU GUYS GO ON AHEAD!
TP TP TP
YOU OKAY BY YOUR-SELF?
I'LL BE FINE! I'LL CATCH UP, I PROMISE.
KNOCK KNOCK
YES? COME IN.
PEEK
KONDO-SEMPAI... I'M SO SORRY TO DISTURB YOU AGAIN.

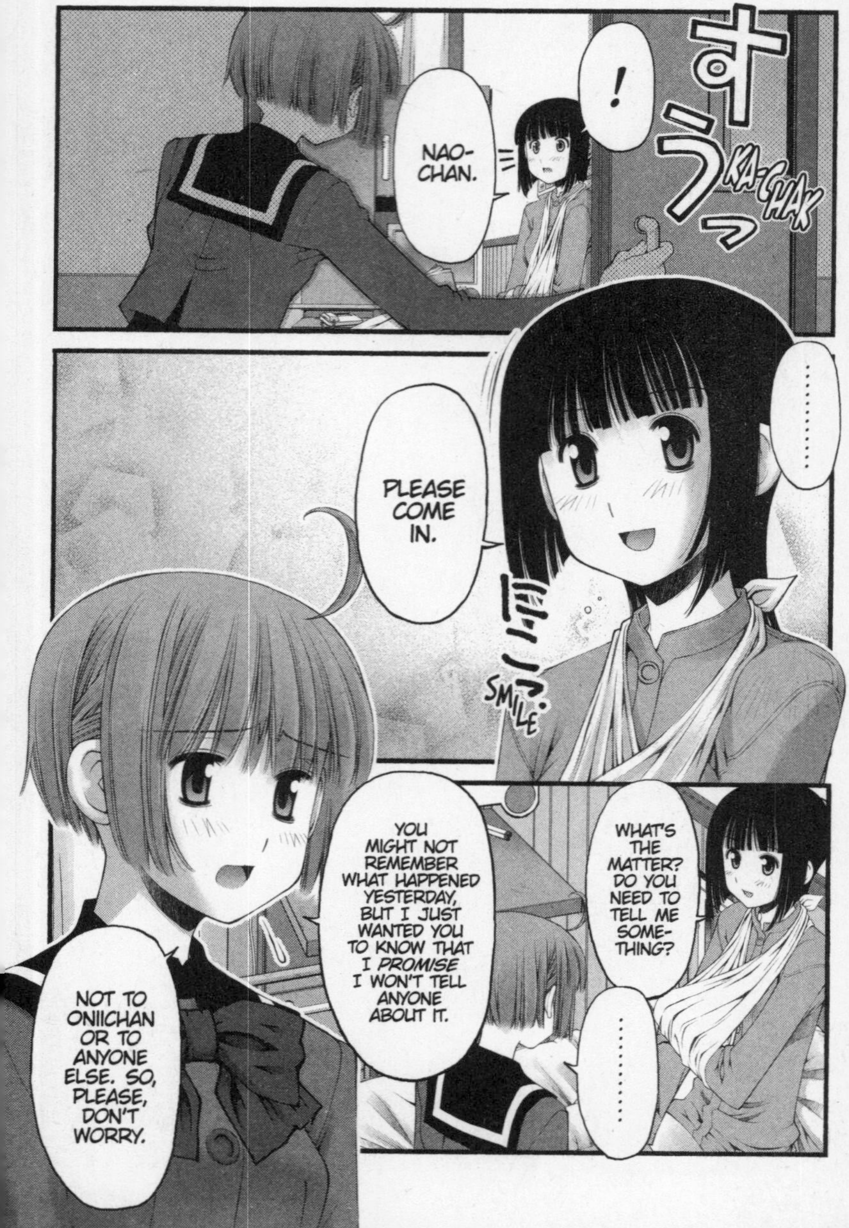

すうっ
KA-CHAK
!
NAO-CHAN.
......
PLEASE COME IN.
ニコッ
SMILE
WHAT'S THE MATTER? DO YOU NEED TO TELL ME SOMETHING?
......
YOU MIGHT NOT REMEMBER WHAT HAPPENED YESTERDAY, BUT I JUST WANTED YOU TO KNOW THAT I *PROMISE* I WON'T TELL ANYONE ABOUT IT.
NOT TO ONIICHAN OR TO ANYONE ELSE. SO, PLEASE, DON'T WORRY.

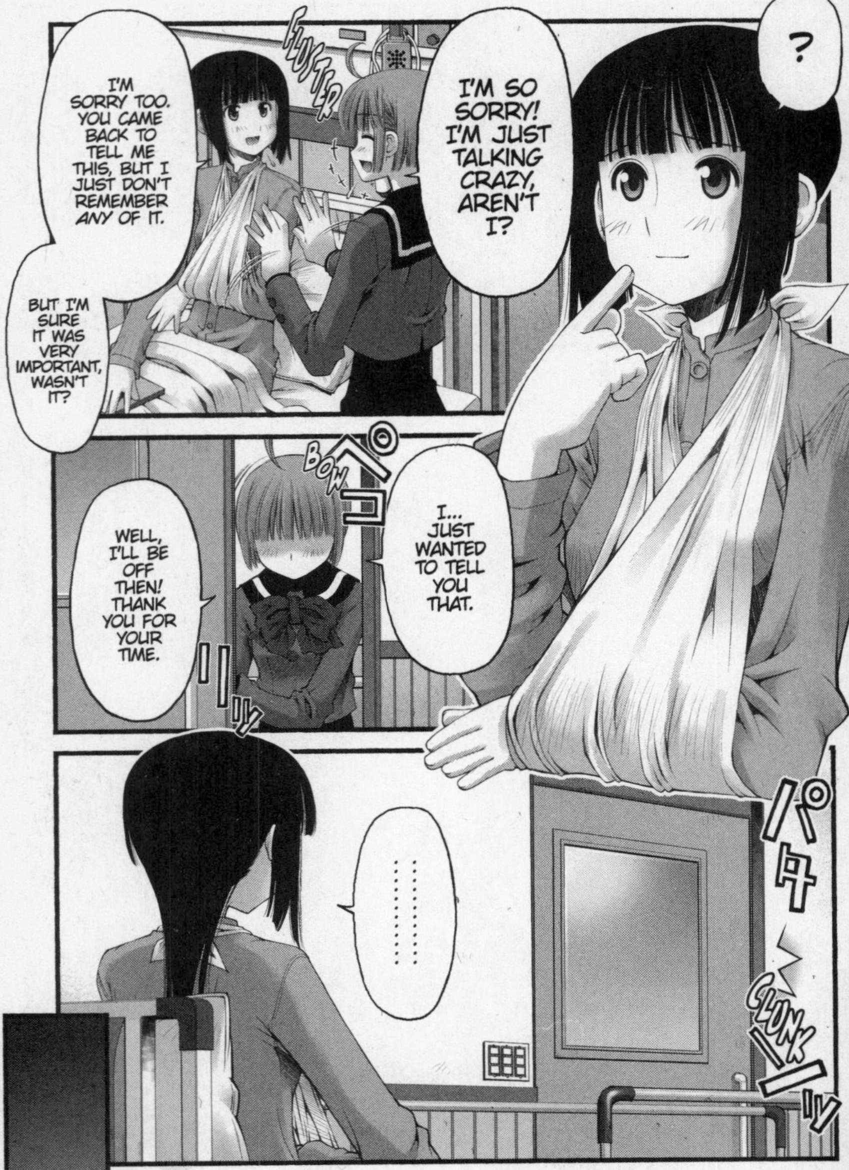
?
I'M SO SORRY! I'M JUST TALKING CRAZY, AREN'T I?
FLUSTER
I'M SORRY TOO. YOU CAME BACK TO TELL ME THIS, BUT I JUST DON'T REMEMBER ANY OF IT.
BUT I'M SURE IT WAS VERY IMPORTANT, WASN'T IT?
BOW
I... JUST WANTED TO TELL YOU THAT.
WELL, I'LL BE OFF THEN! THANK YOU FOR YOUR TIME.
CLONK
......

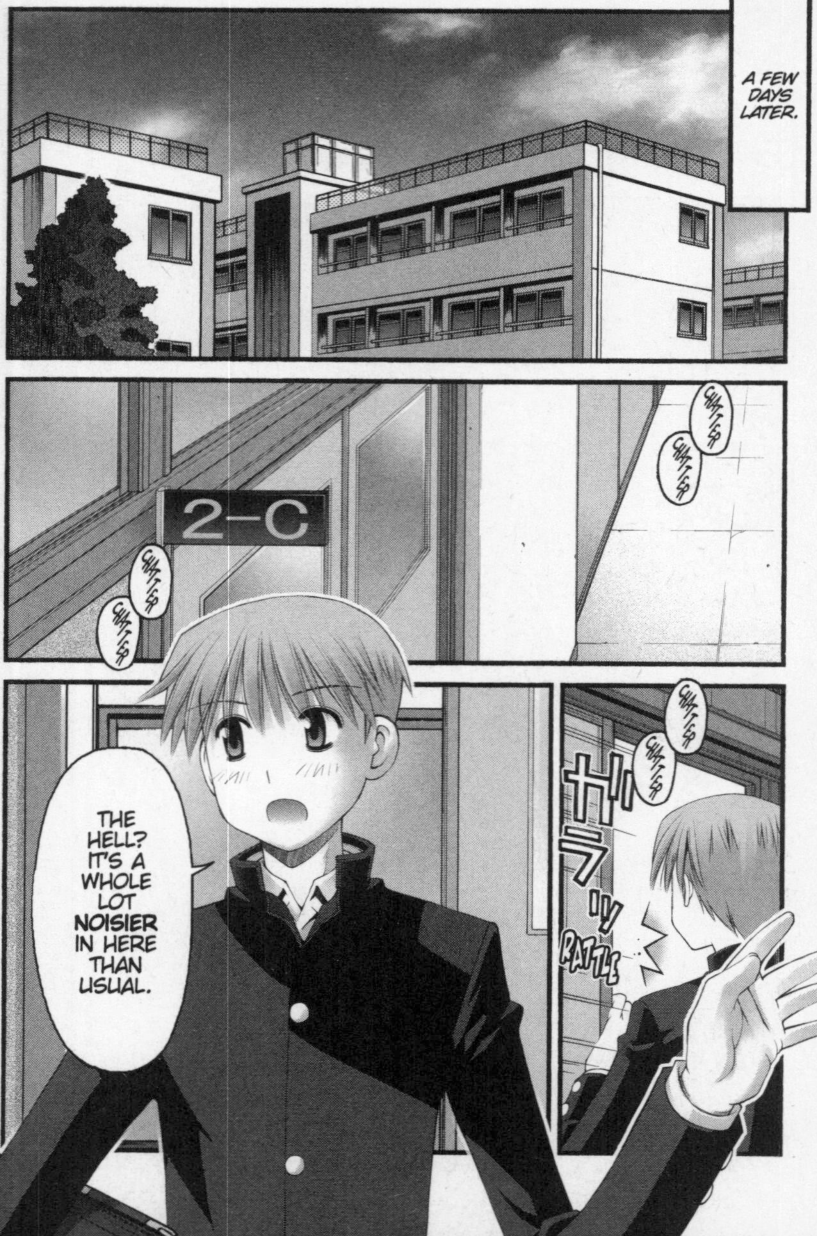
A FEW DAYS LATER.
CHATTER
CHATTER
CHATTER
CHATTER
CHATTER
CHATTER
ガラッ
RATTLE
THE HELL? IT'S A WHOLE LOT NOISIER IN HERE THAN USUAL.

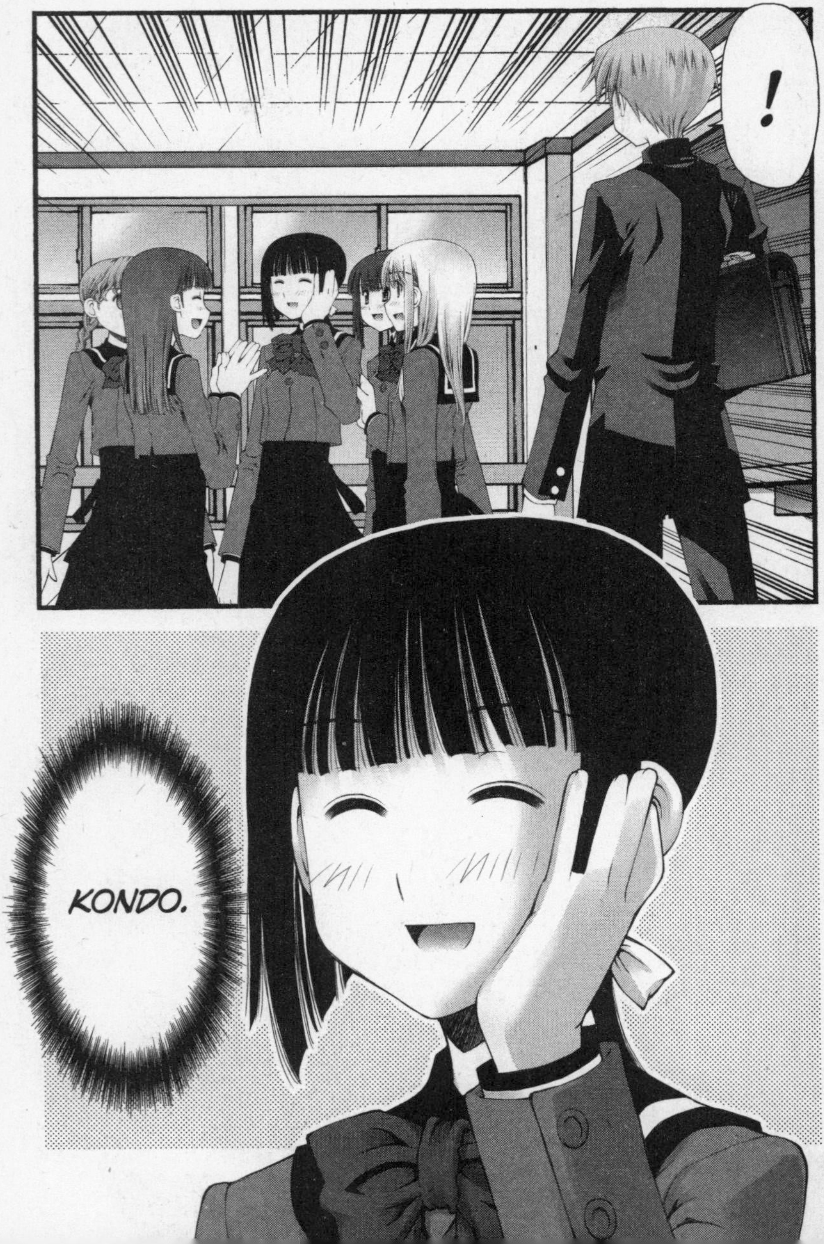
!
KONDO.

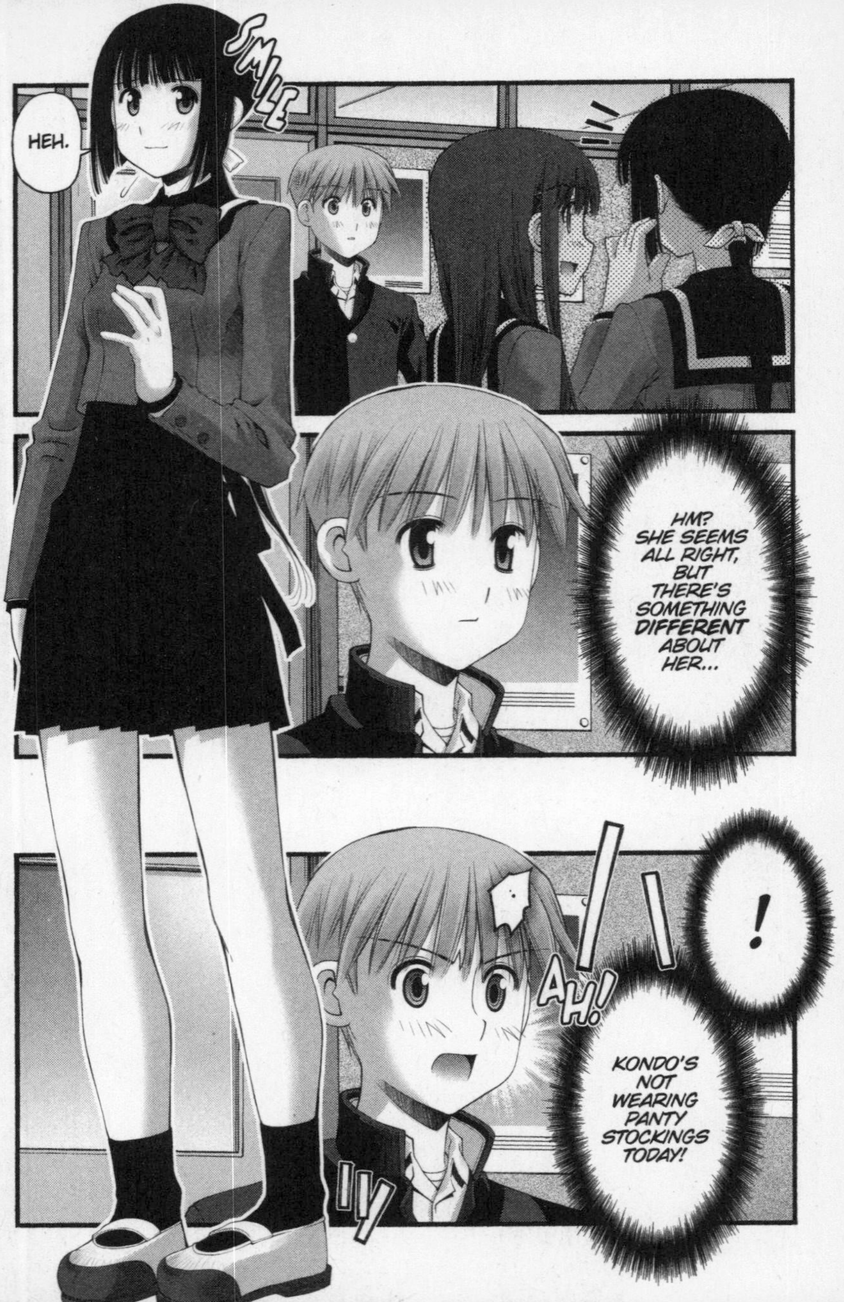
HM? SHE SEEMS ALL RIGHT, BUT THERE'S SOMETHING DIFFERENT ABOUT HER...
!
AH!
KONDO'S NOT WEARING PANTY STOCKINGS TODAY!
SMILE
HEH.

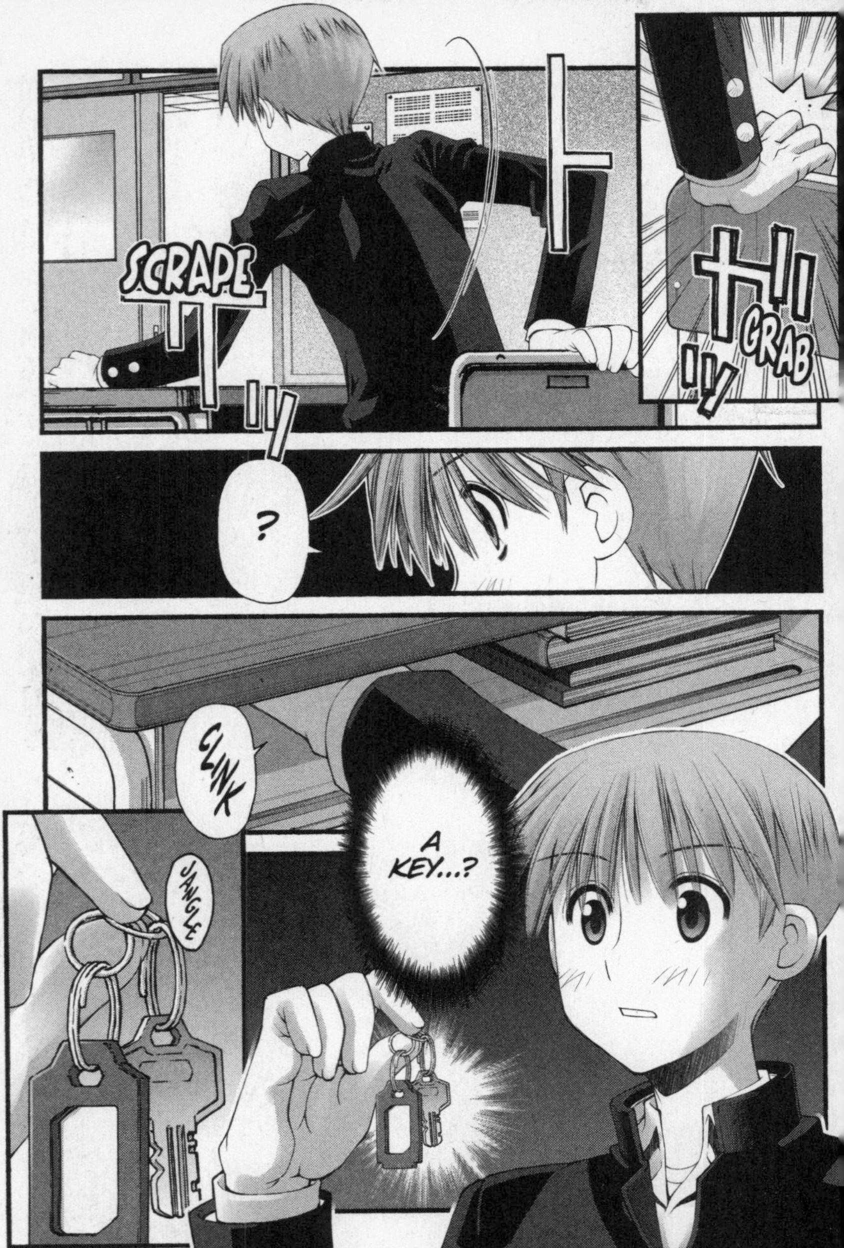
GRAB
SCRAPE
?
CLINK
A KEY...?
JANGLE

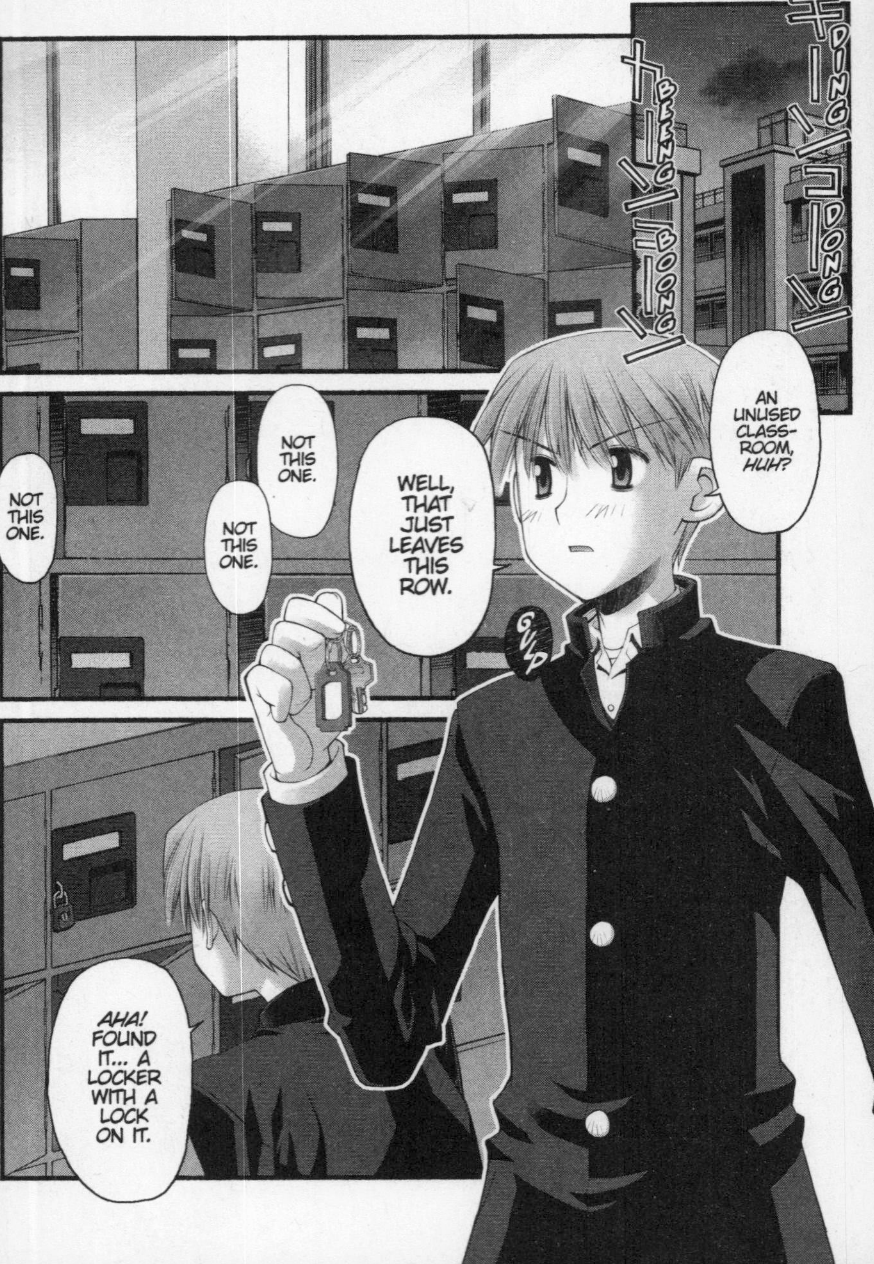
キーンコーン
DING DONG
カーンコーン
BEENG BOONG
AN UNUSED CLASSROOM, HUH?
NOT THIS ONE.
NOT THIS ONE.
NOT THIS ONE.
WELL, THAT JUST LEAVES THIS ROW.
GULP
AHA! FOUND IT... A LOCKER WITH A LOCK ON IT.

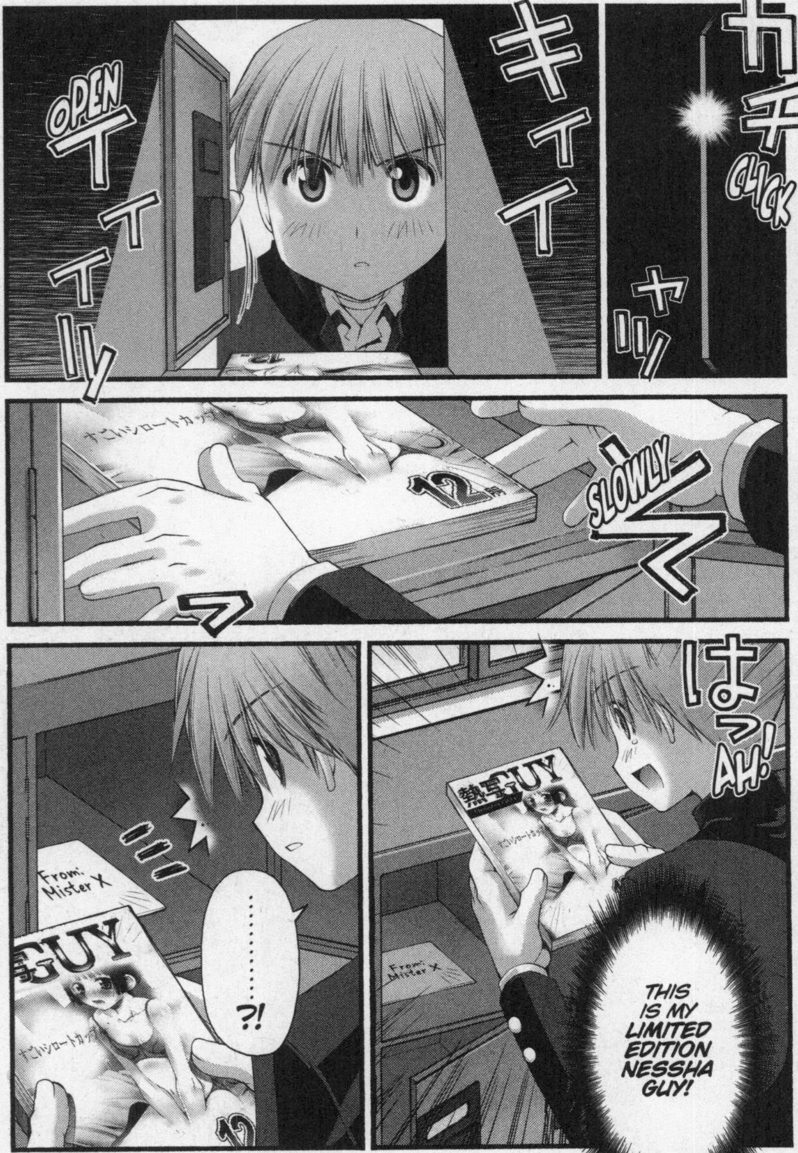
カチ
CLICK
ャッ
キイイ
OPEN
イイイーッ
SLOWLY
ス
っ
はっ!
AH!
熱写GUY
From: Mister X
THIS IS MY LIMITED EDITION NESSHA GUY!
From: Mister X
GUY
......?!

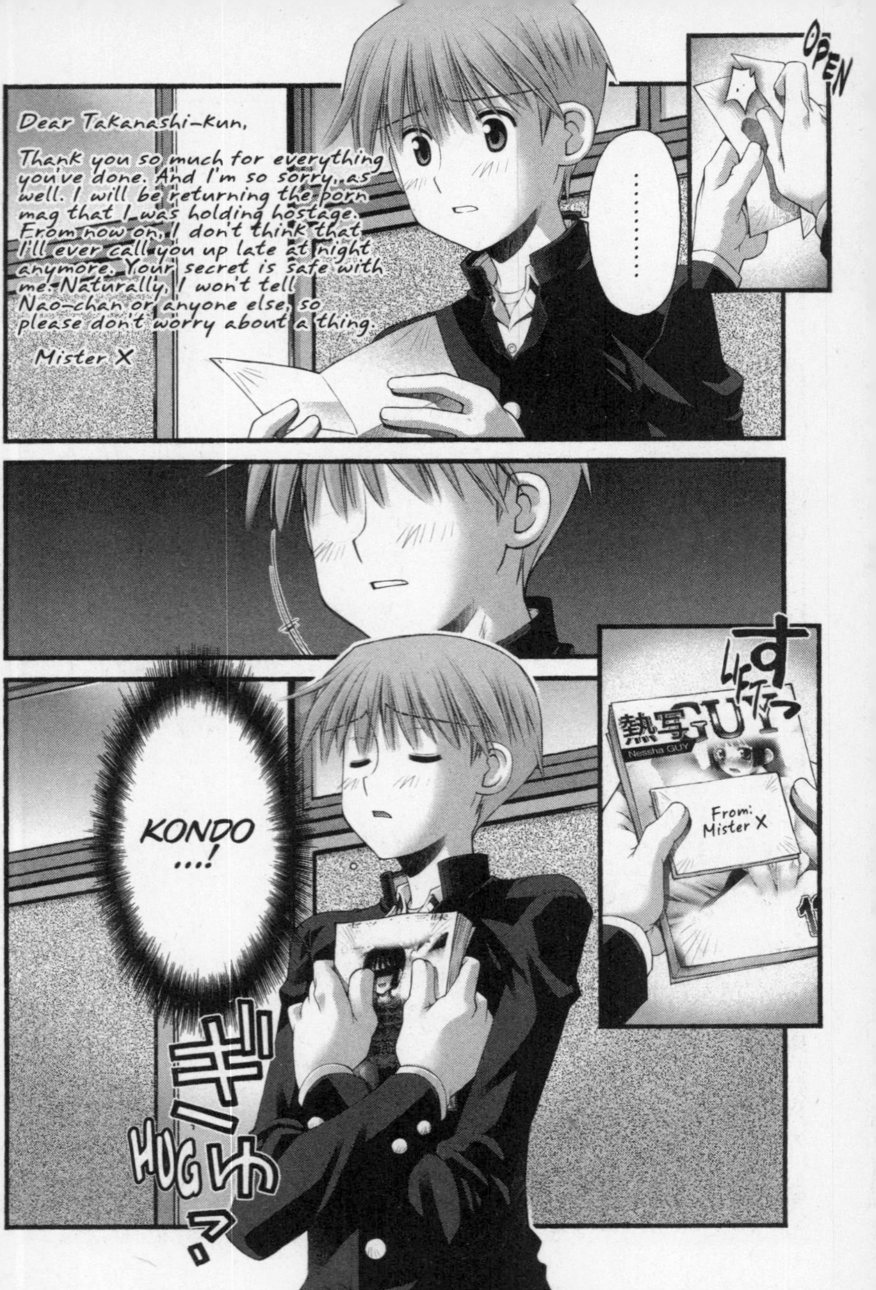
OPEN
Dear Takanashi-kun,
Thank you so much for everything you've done. And I'm so sorry, as well. I will be returning the porn mag that I was holding hostage. From now on, I don't think that I'll ever call you up late at night anymore. Your secret is safe with me. Naturally, I won't tell Nao-chan or anyone else, so please don't worry about a thing.
Mister X
......
LIFT
熱写GUY
Nessha GUY
From: Mister X
KONDO ...!
HUG

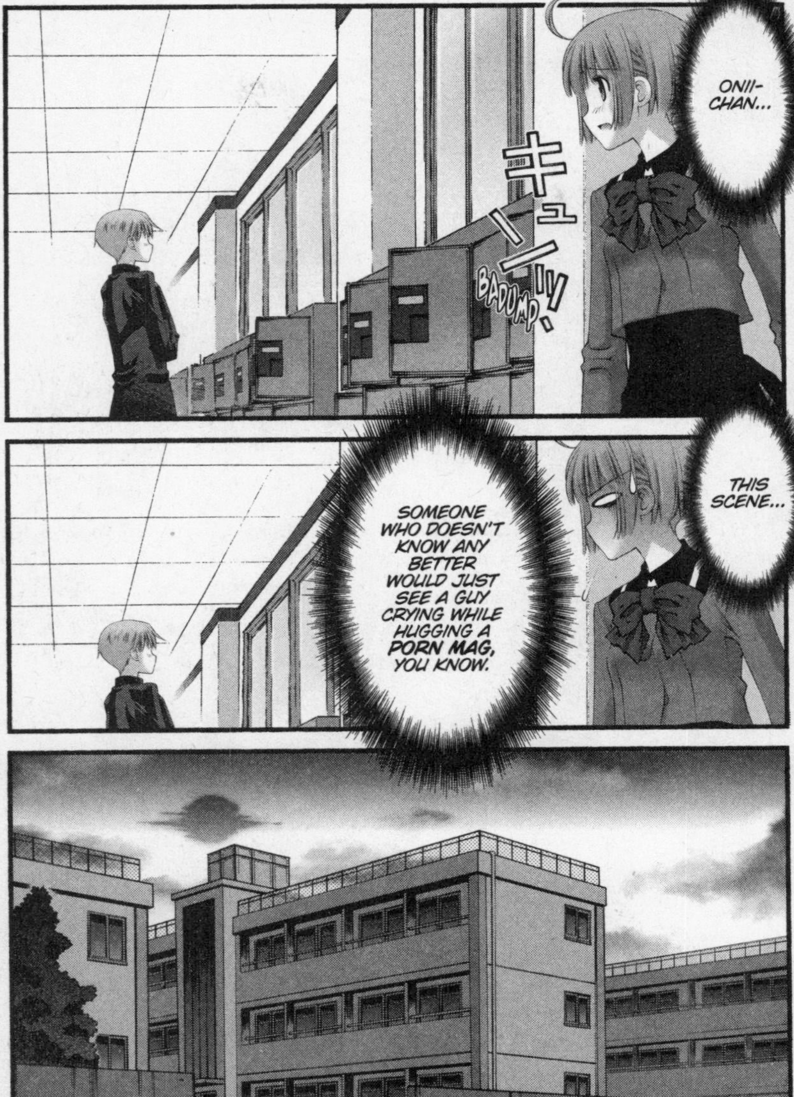
ONII-CHAN...
キューー!!
BADUMP!
THIS SCENE...
SOMEONE WHO DOESN'T KNOW ANY BETTER WOULD JUST SEE A GUY CRYING WHILE HUGGING A PORN MAG, YOU KNOW.

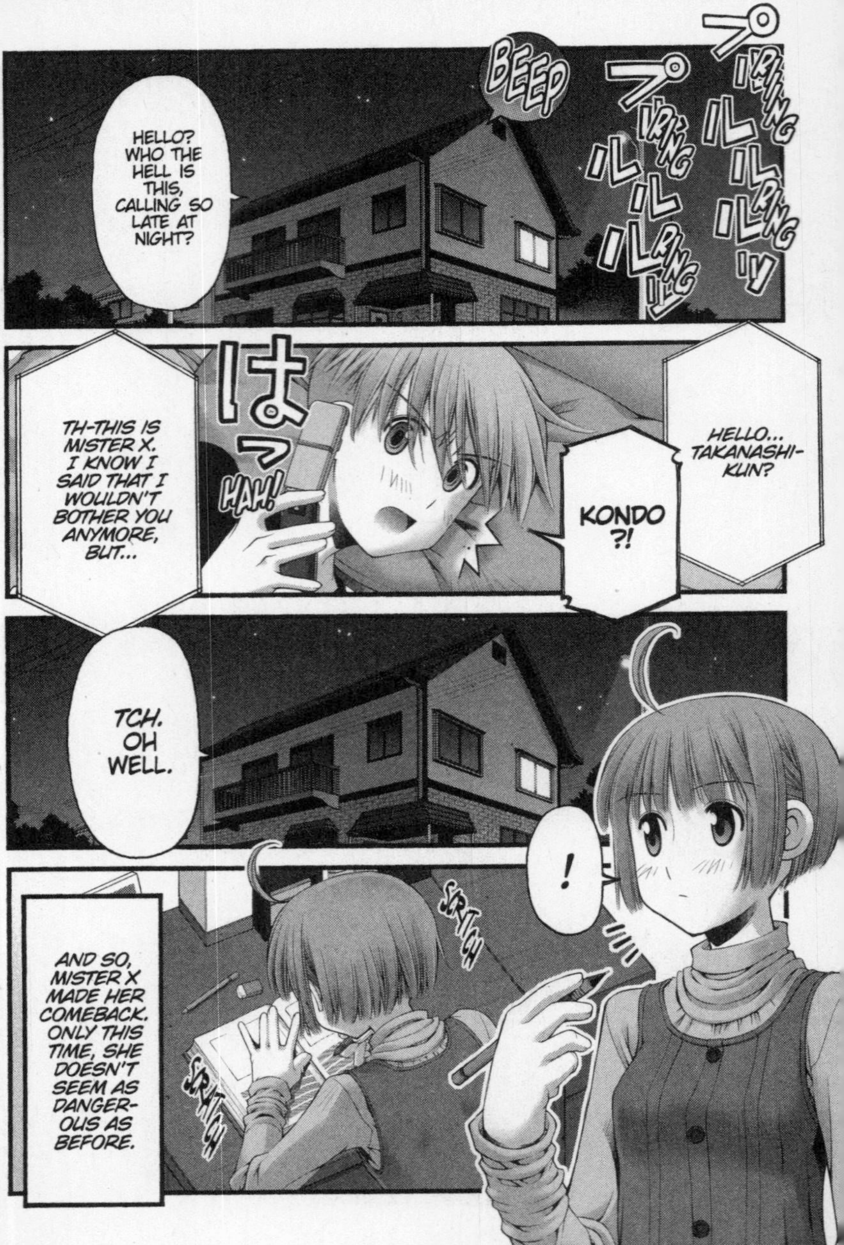
RING RING RING RING
BEEP
RING RING RING
HELLO? WHO THE HELL IS THIS, CALLING SO LATE AT NIGHT?
HELLO... TAKANASHI-KUN?
KONDO ?!
HAH!
TH-THIS IS MISTER X. I KNOW I SAID THAT I WOULDN'T BOTHER YOU ANYMORE, BUT...
TCH. OH WELL.
!
SCRATCH
SCRATCH
AND SO, MISTER X MADE HER COMEBACK. ONLY THIS TIME, SHE DOESN'T SEEM AS DANGER-OUS AS BEFORE.

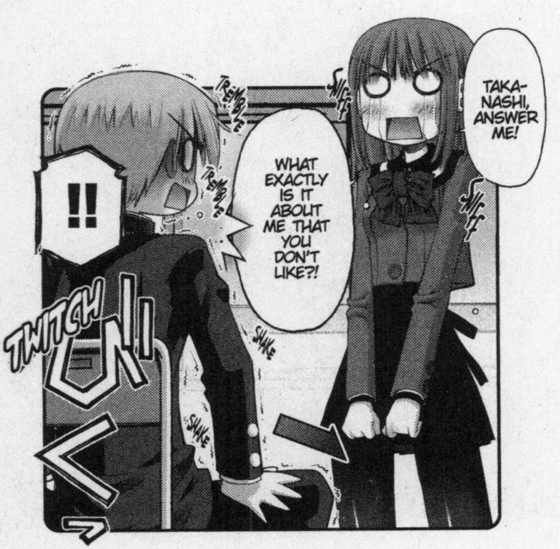
TAKA-NASHI, ANSWER ME!
SNIFF
SNIFF
WHAT EXACTLY IS IT ABOUT ME THAT YOU DON'T LIKE?!
TREMBLE
TREMBLE
!!
SHAKE
SHAKE
TWITCH

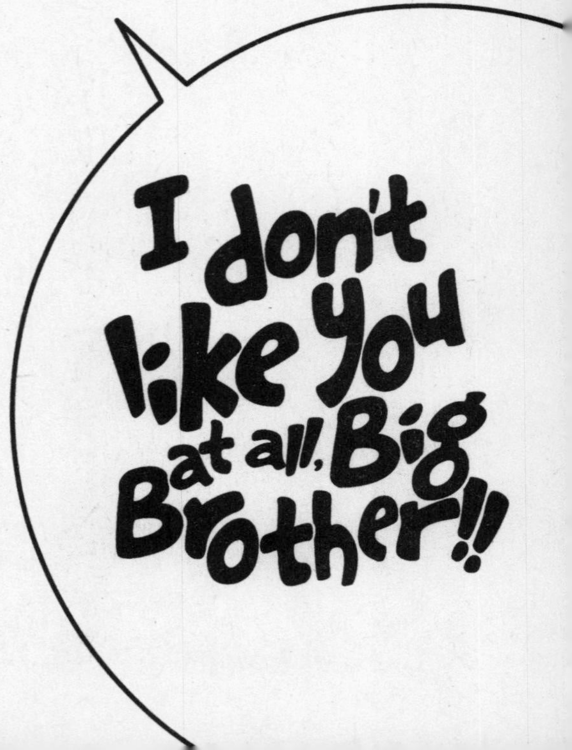
I don't like you at all, Big Brother!!

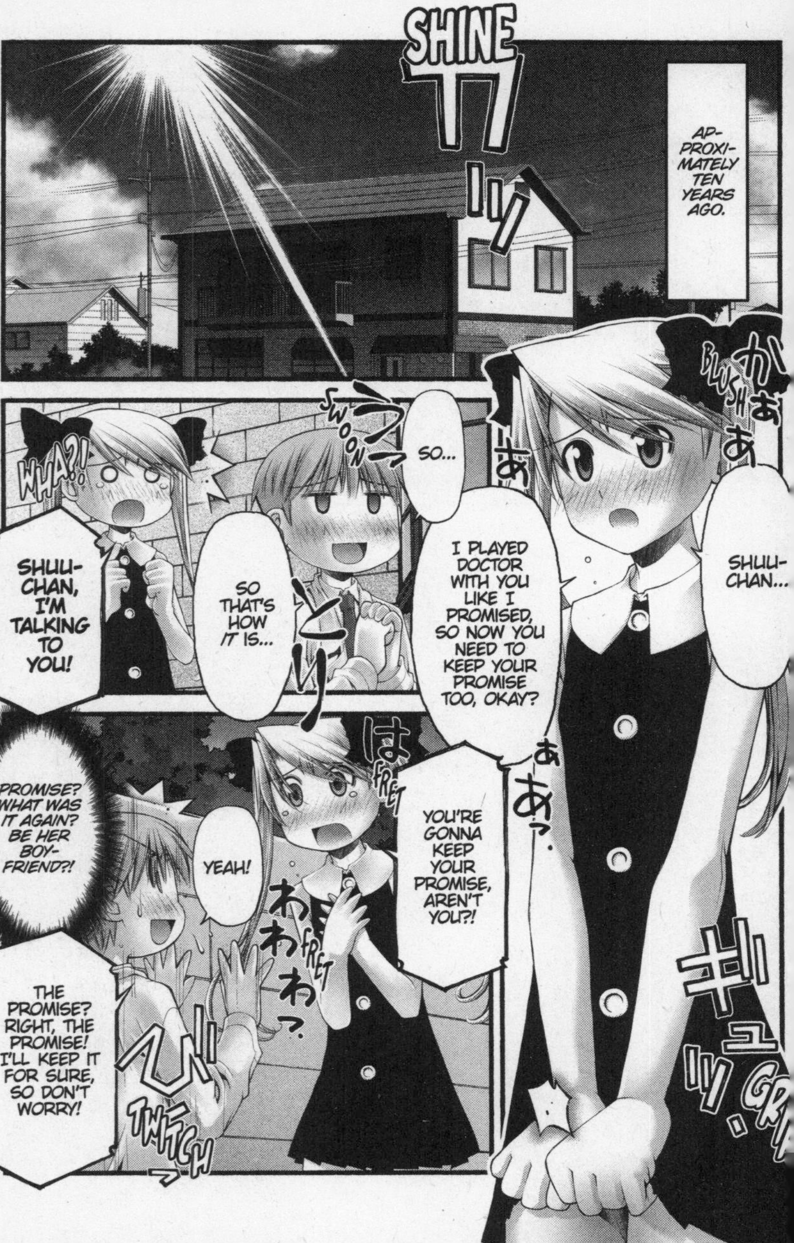
APPROXIMATELY TEN YEARS AGO.
BLUSH
SHUU-CHAN...
I PLAYED DOCTOR WITH YOU LIKE I PROMISED, SO NOW YOU NEED TO KEEP YOUR PROMISE TOO, OKAY?
YOU'RE GONNA KEEP YOUR PROMISE, AREN'T YOU?!
GRIP
SHINE
SWOON
SO...
SO THAT'S HOW IT IS...
WHA?!
SHUU-CHAN, I'M TALKING TO YOU!
FRET
YEAH!
PROMISE? WHAT WAS IT AGAIN? BE HER BOY-FRIEND?!
FRET
THE PROMISE? RIGHT, THE PROMISE! I'LL KEEP IT FOR SURE, SO DON'T WORRY!
TWITCH

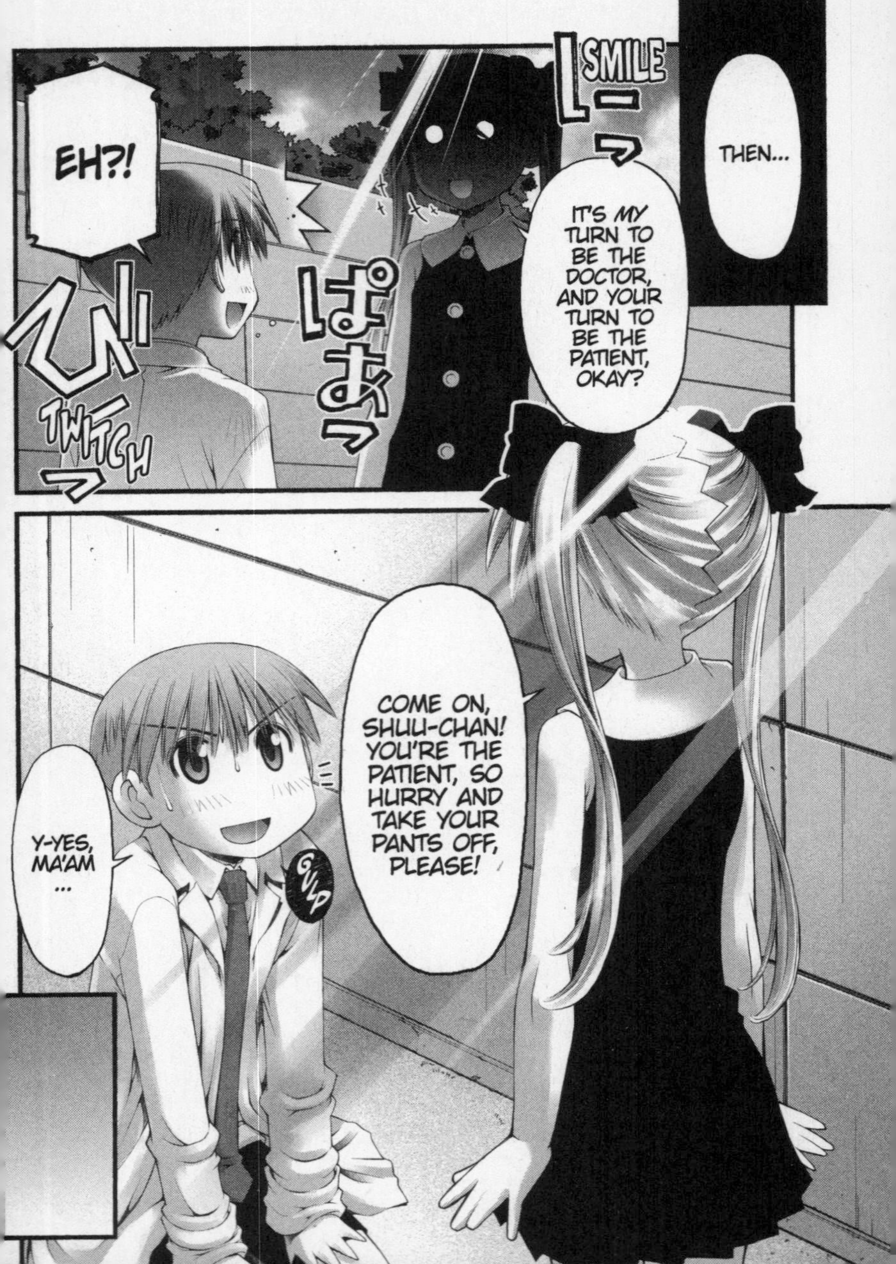
THEN...
SMILE
IT'S MY TURN TO BE THE DOCTOR, AND YOUR TURN TO BE THE PATIENT, OKAY?
ぱあっ
EH?!
TWITCH
COME ON, SHUU-CHAN! YOU'RE THE PATIENT, SO HURRY AND TAKE YOUR PANTS OFF, PLEASE!
GULP
Y-YES, MA'AM ...

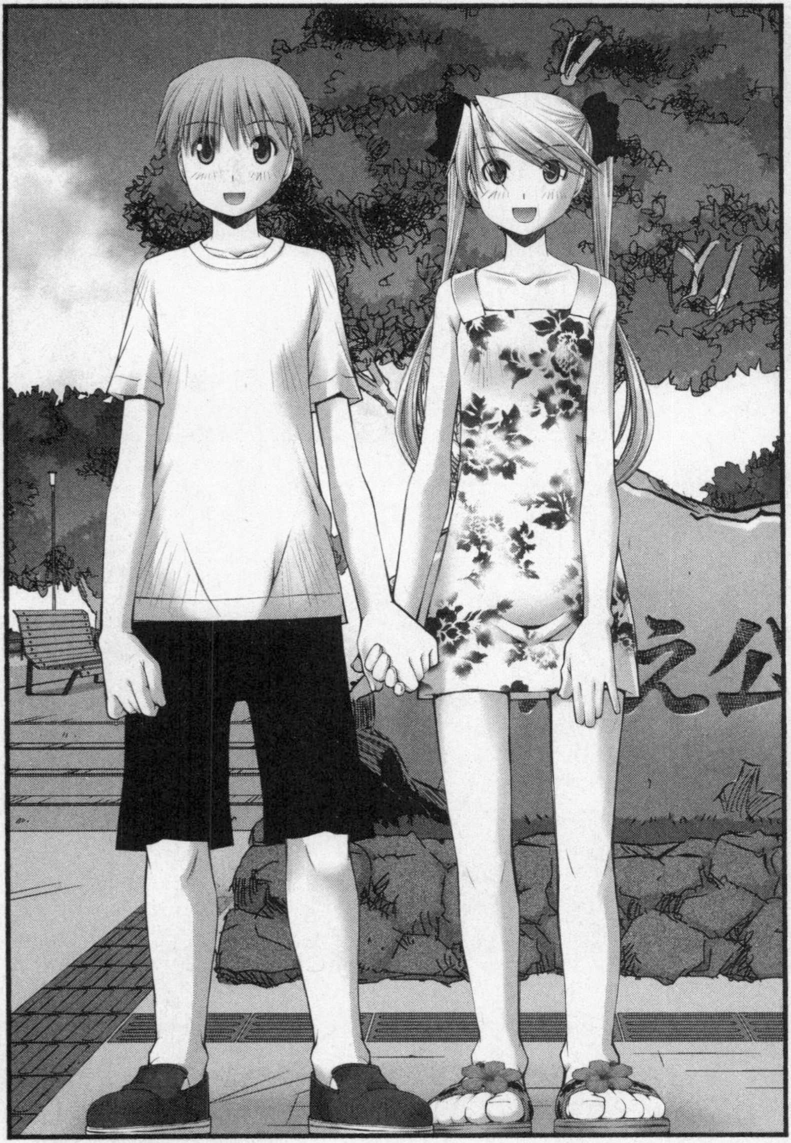

CHAPTER 36

Dr. Iroha's Truly Terrifying Family Practice

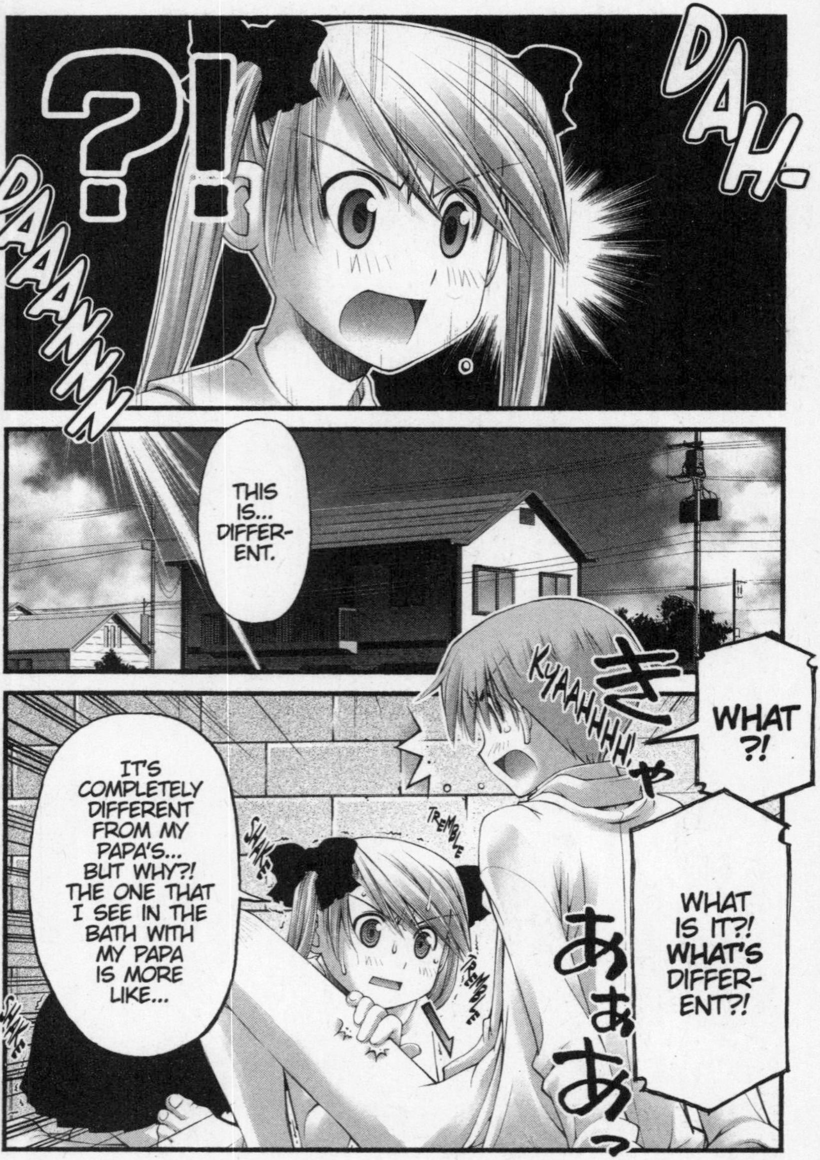

DAH-DAAANNN
?!
THIS IS... DIFFERENT.
WHAT?!
KYAAHHHH!
きゃああああっ
WHAT IS IT?! WHAT'S DIFFERENT?!
TREMBLE
TREMBLE
SHAKE
SHAKE
IT'S COMPLETELY DIFFERENT FROM MY PAPA'S... BUT WHY?! THE ONE THAT I SEE IN THE BATH WITH MY PAPA IS MORE LIKE...

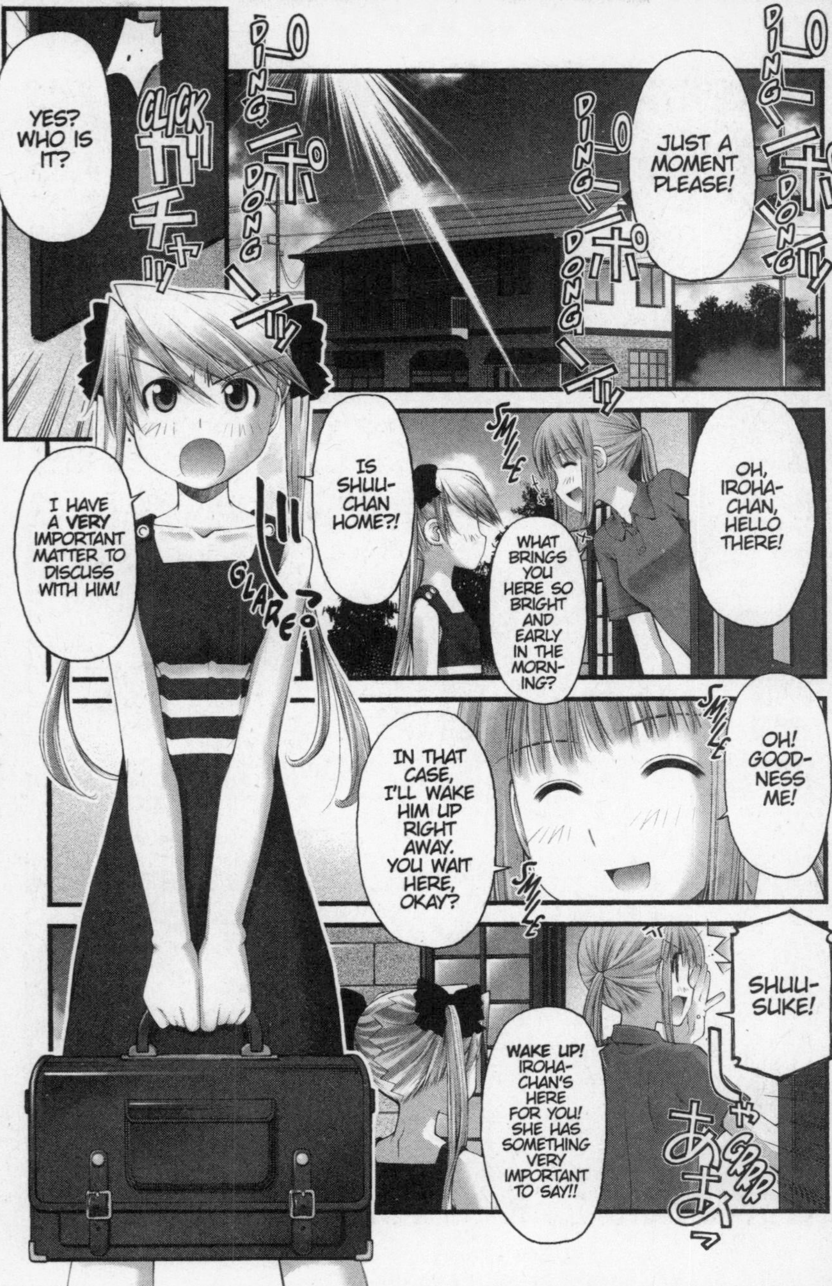
DING DONG
DING DONG
JUST A MOMENT PLEASE!
DING DONG
CLICK
YES? WHO IS IT?
OH, IROHA-CHAN, HELLO THERE!
SMILE
WHAT BRINGS YOU HERE SO BRIGHT AND EARLY IN THE MORNING?
SMILE
OH! GOODNESS ME!
IN THAT CASE, I'LL WAKE HIM UP RIGHT AWAY. YOU WAIT HERE, OKAY?
SMILE
SHUU-SUKE!
WAKE UP! IROHA-CHAN'S HERE FOR YOU! SHE HAS SOMETHING VERY IMPORTANT TO SAY!!
GRRR
IS SHUU-CHAN HOME?!
GLARE
I HAVE A VERY IMPORTANT MATTER TO DISCUSS WITH HIM!

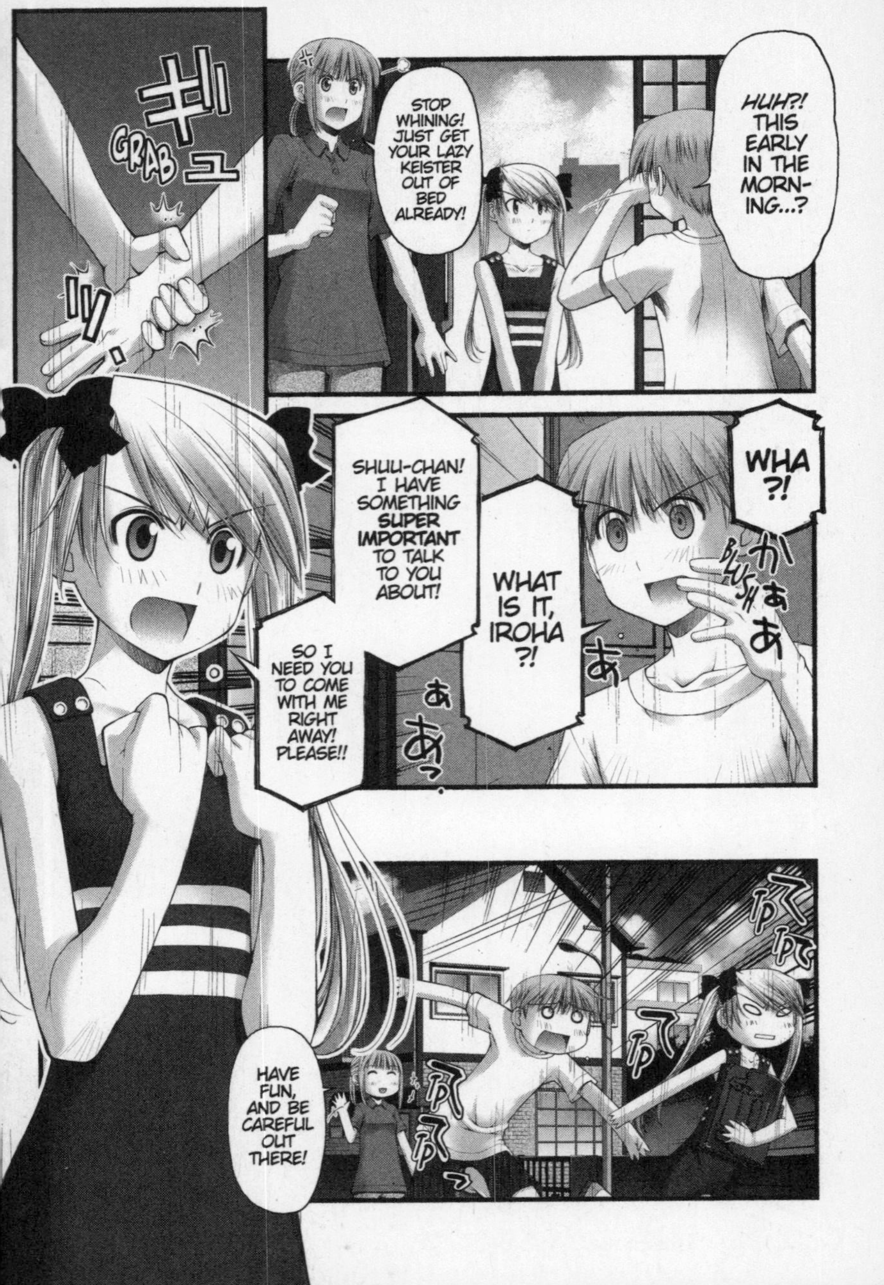
HUH?! THIS EARLY IN THE MORNING-...?
STOP WHINING! JUST GET YOUR LAZY KEISTER OUT OF BED ALREADY!
ギュ
GRAB
WHA ?!
かぁぁ
BLUSH
WHAT IS IT, IROHA ?!
SHUU-CHAN! I HAVE SOMETHING **SUPER IMPORTANT** TO TALK TO YOU ABOUT!
SO I NEED YOU TO COME WITH ME RIGHT AWAY! PLEASE!!
HAVE FUN, AND BE CAREFUL OUT THERE!

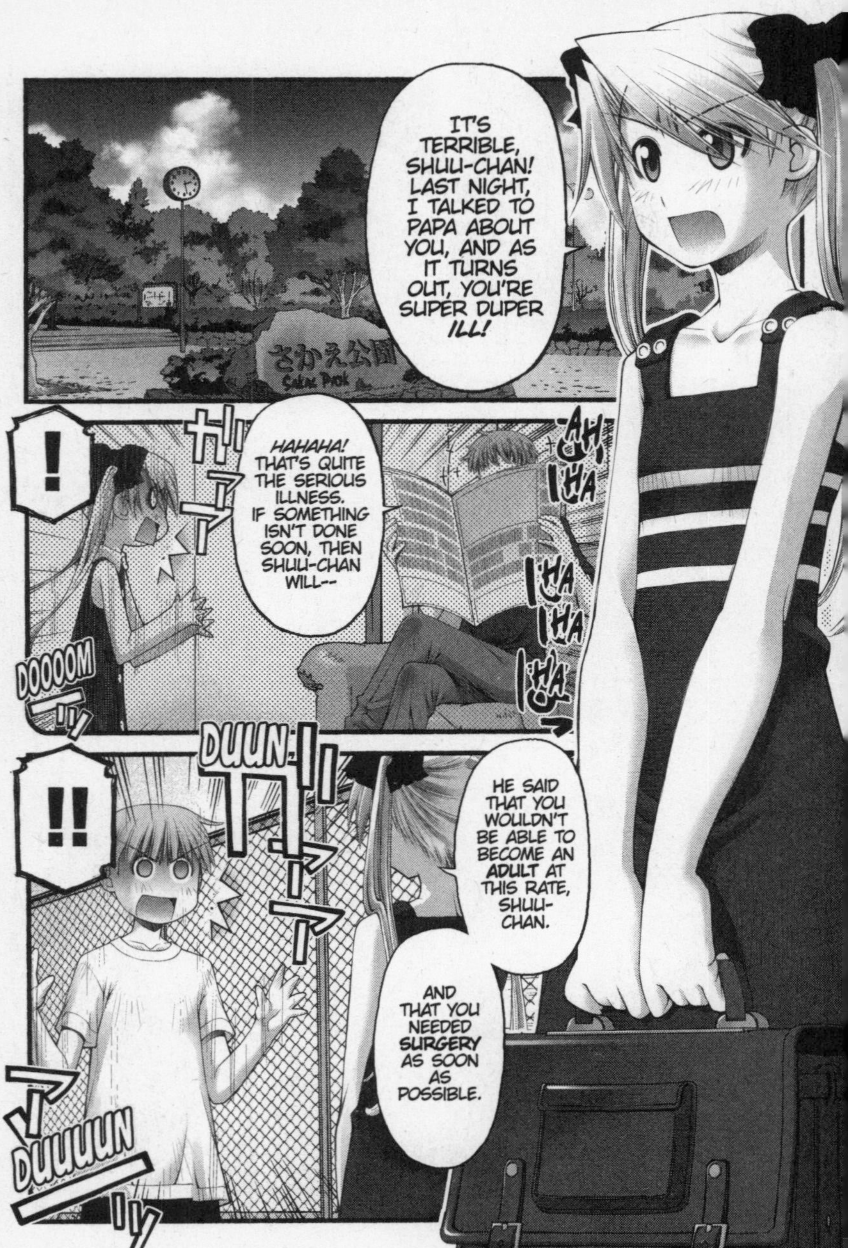
IT'S TERRIBLE, SHUU-CHAN! LAST NIGHT, I TALKED TO PAPA ABOUT YOU, AND AS IT TURNS OUT, YOU'RE SUPER DUPER *ILL!*
さかえ公園
AH HA HA HA HA HA
HAHAHA! THAT'S QUITE THE SERIOUS ILLNESS. IF SOMETHING ISN'T DONE SOON, THEN SHUU-CHAN WILL--
!
DOOOOM
HE SAID THAT YOU WOULDN'T BE ABLE TO BECOME AN **ADULT** AT THIS RATE, SHUU-CHAN.
AND THAT YOU NEEDED **SURGERY** AS SOON AS POSSIBLE.
DUUN
!!
DUUUUN

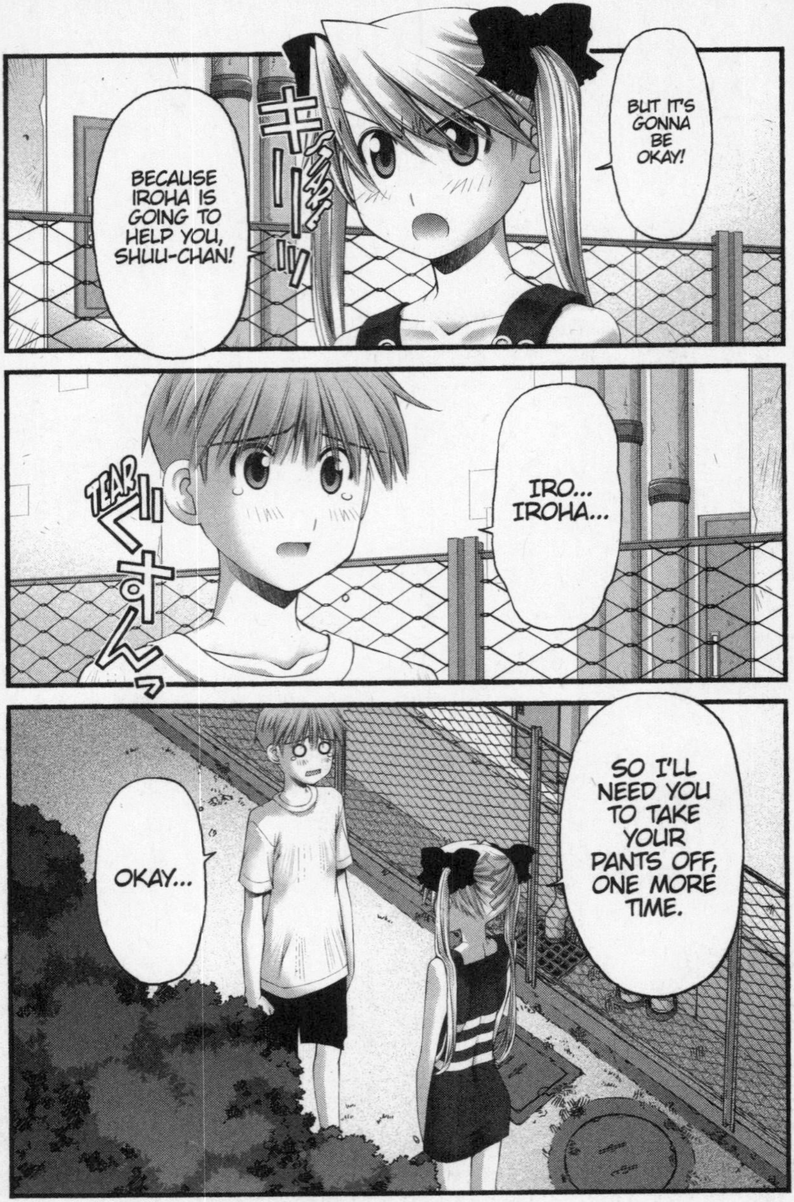
BUT IT'S GONNA BE OKAY!
BECAUSE IROHA IS GOING TO HELP YOU, SHUU-CHAN!
キーッ
IRO... IROHA...
TEAR
ぐすんっ
SO I'LL NEED YOU TO TAKE YOUR PANTS OFF, ONE MORE TIME.
OKAY...

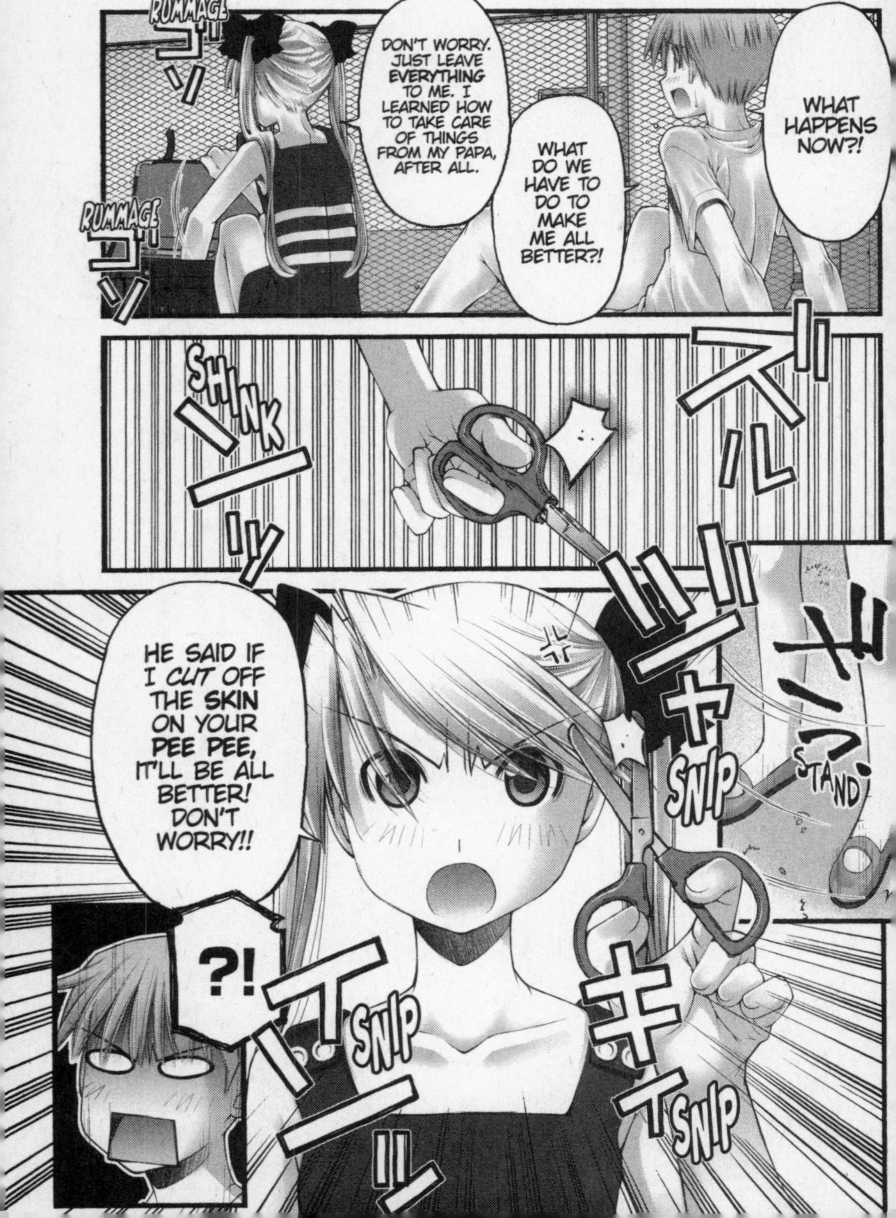
WHAT HAPPENS NOW?!
WHAT DO WE HAVE TO DO TO MAKE ME ALL BETTER?!
DON'T WORRY. JUST LEAVE EVERYTHING TO ME. I LEARNED HOW TO TAKE CARE OF THINGS FROM MY PAPA, AFTER ALL.
RUMMAGE
RUMMAGE
SHINK
STAND
SNIP
HE SAID IF I CUT OFF THE SKIN ON YOUR PEE PEE, IT'LL BE ALL BETTER! DON'T WORRY!!
SNIP
SNIP
?!

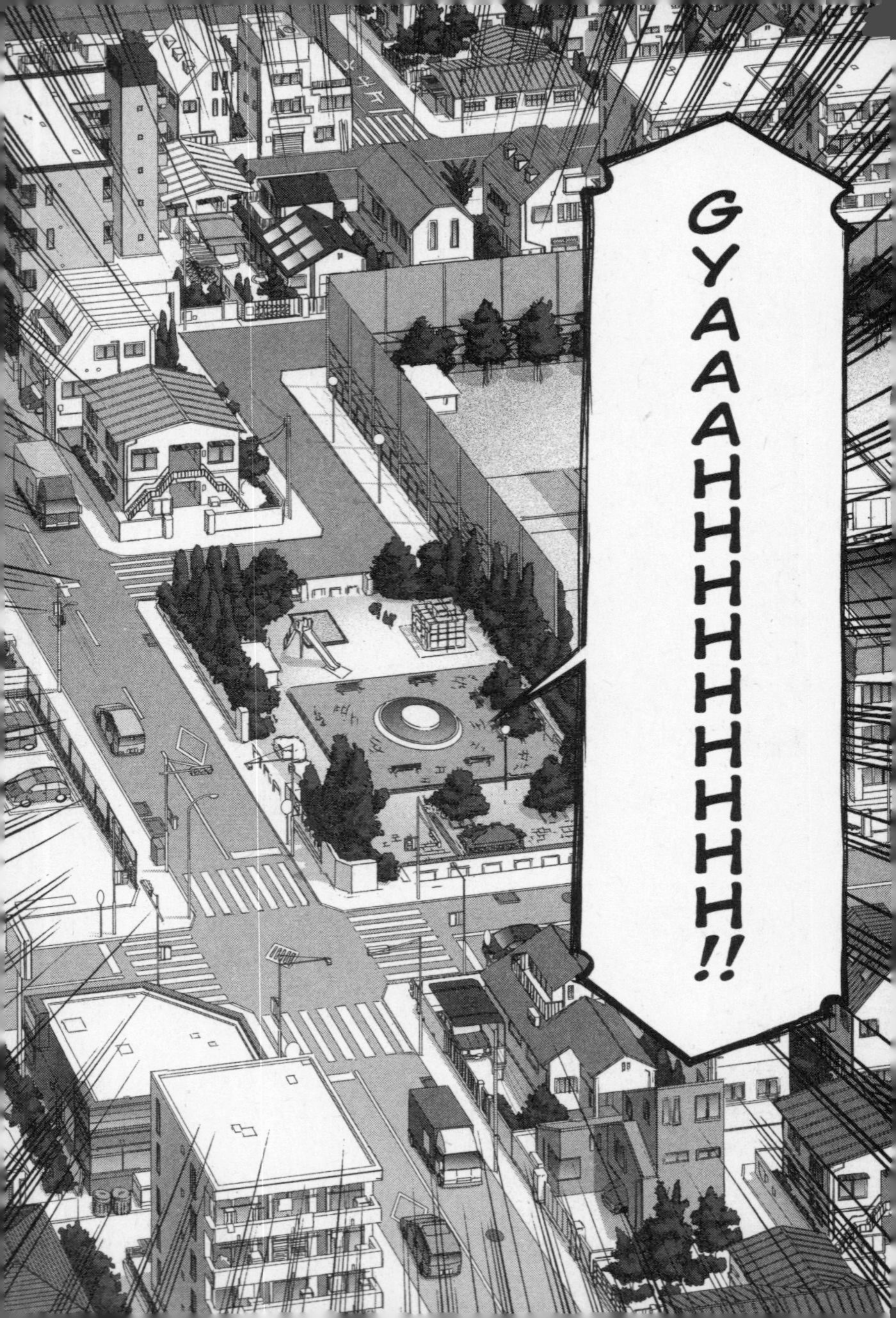
GYAAAHHHHHHHHH!!

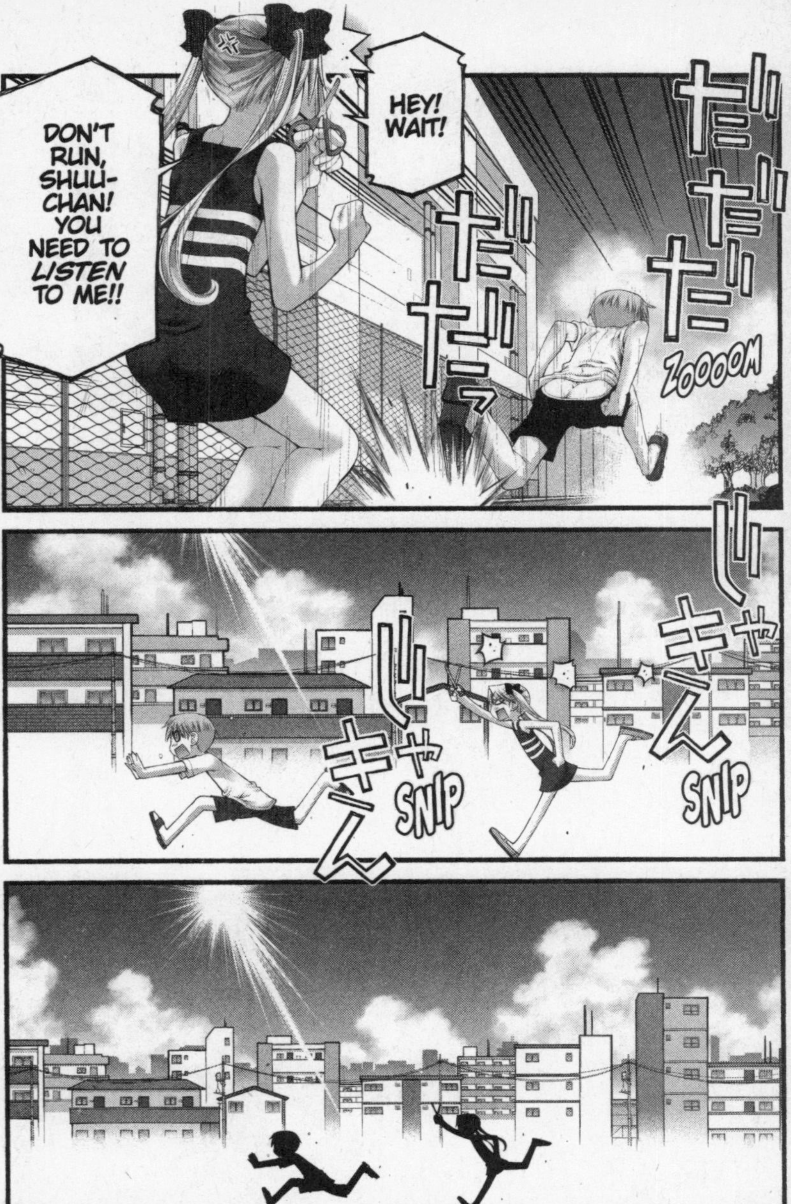
ZOOOOM
HEY! WAIT!
DON'T RUN, SHUU-CHAN! YOU NEED TO LISTEN TO ME!!
SNIP
SNIP

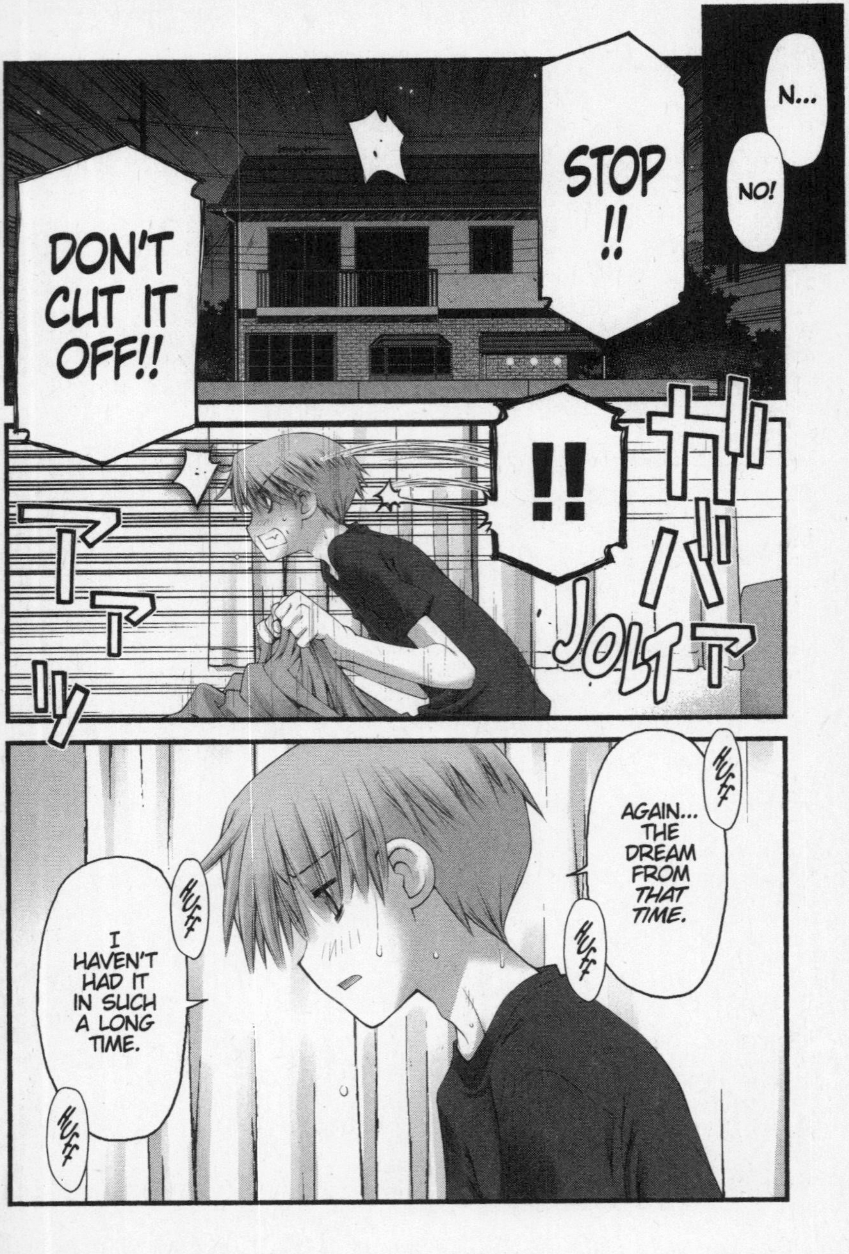
N...
NO!
STOP!!
DON'T CUT IT OFF!!
!!
JOLT
HUFF
AGAIN... THE DREAM FROM THAT TIME.
HUFF
HUFF
I HAVEN'T HAD IT IN SUCH A LONG TIME.
HUFF

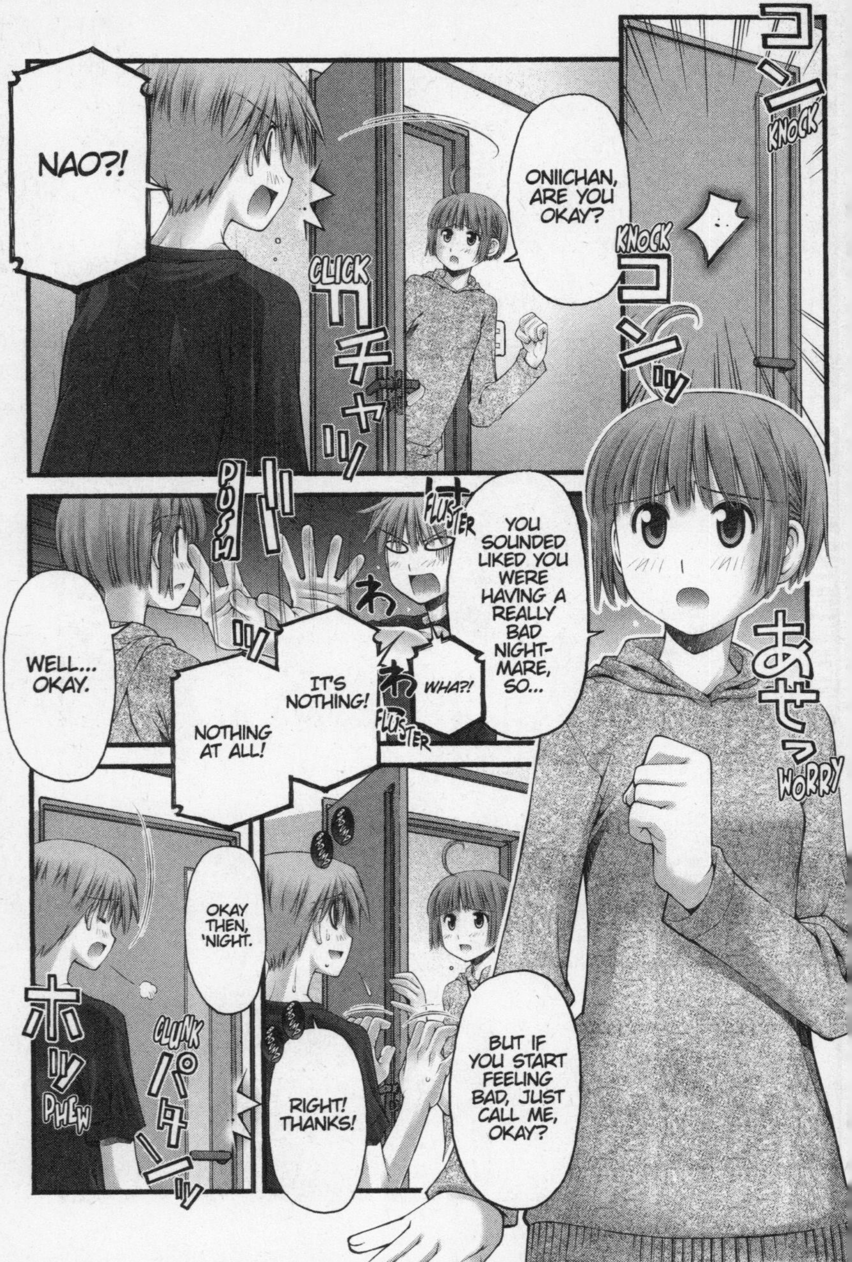
KNOCK
KNOCK
ONIICHAN, ARE YOU OKAY?
CLICK
NAO?!
YOU SOUNDED LIKED YOU WERE HAVING A REALLY BAD NIGHTMARE, SO...
WORRY
FLUSTER
WHA?!
FLUSTER
PUSH
IT'S NOTHING!
NOTHING AT ALL!
WELL... OKAY.
BUT IF YOU START FEELING BAD, JUST CALL ME, OKAY?
RIGHT! THANKS!
OKAY THEN, 'NIGHT.
CLUNK
PHEW

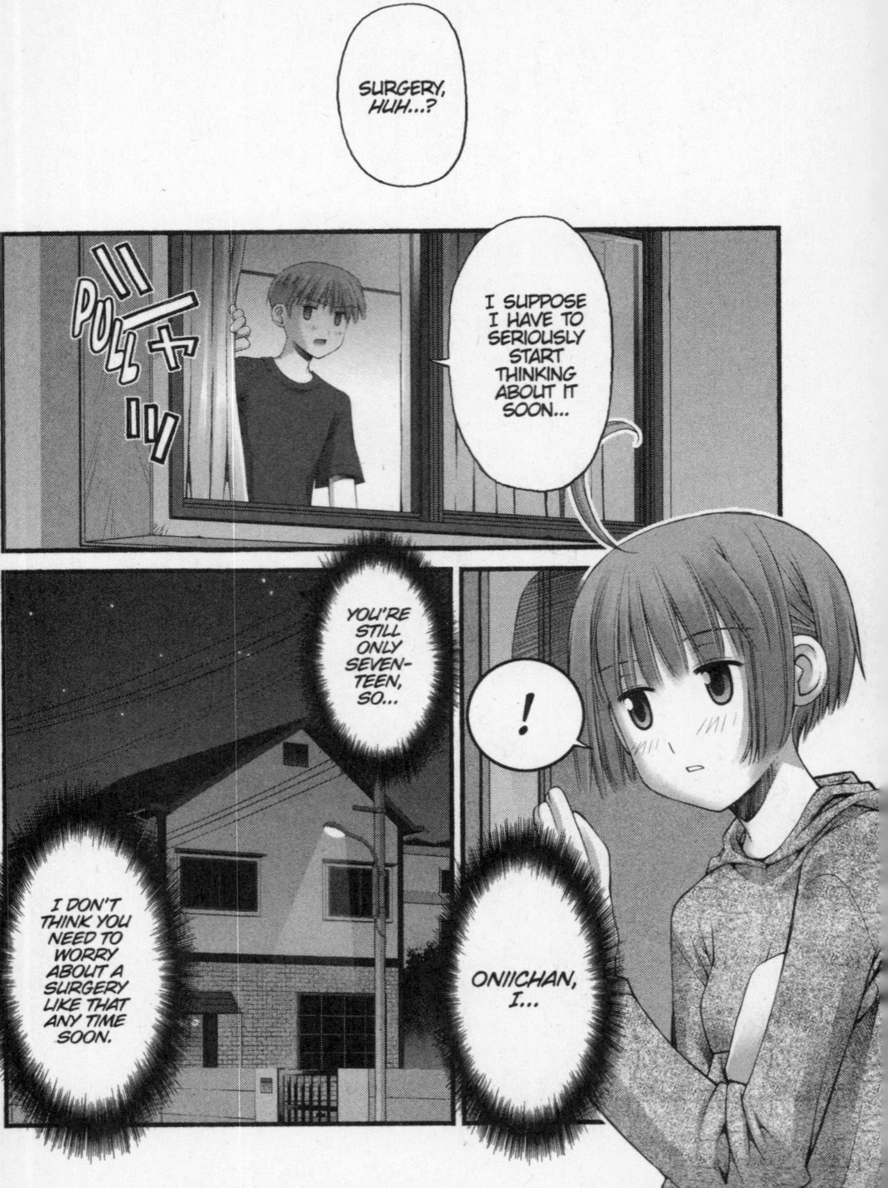
SURGERY, HUH...?
PULL
I SUPPOSE I HAVE TO SERIOUSLY START THINKING ABOUT IT SOON...
!
YOU'RE STILL ONLY SEVENTEEN, SO...
I DON'T THINK YOU NEED TO WORRY ABOUT A SURGERY LIKE THAT ANY TIME SOON.
ONIICHAN, I...

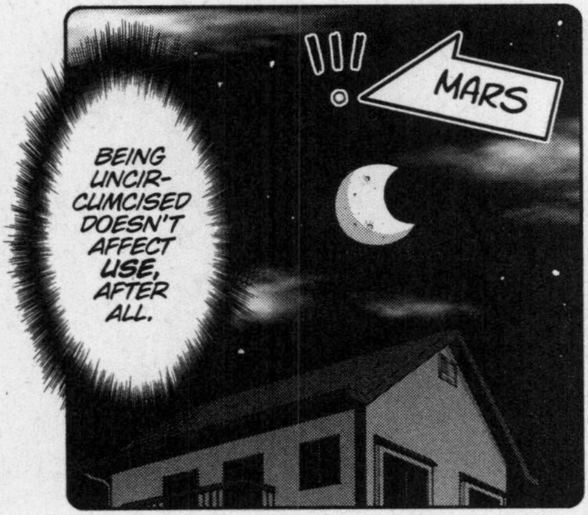

MARS
BEING UNCIR-CUMCISED DOESN'T AFFECT USE, AFTER ALL.

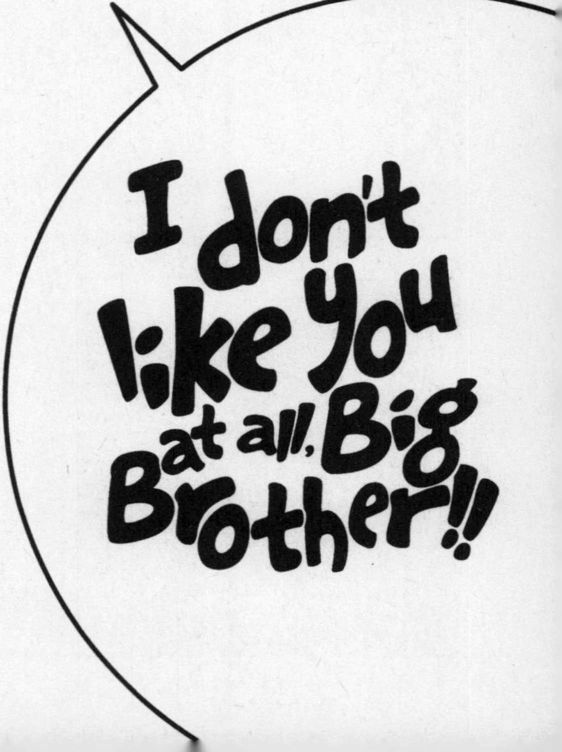
I don't like you at all, Big Brother!!

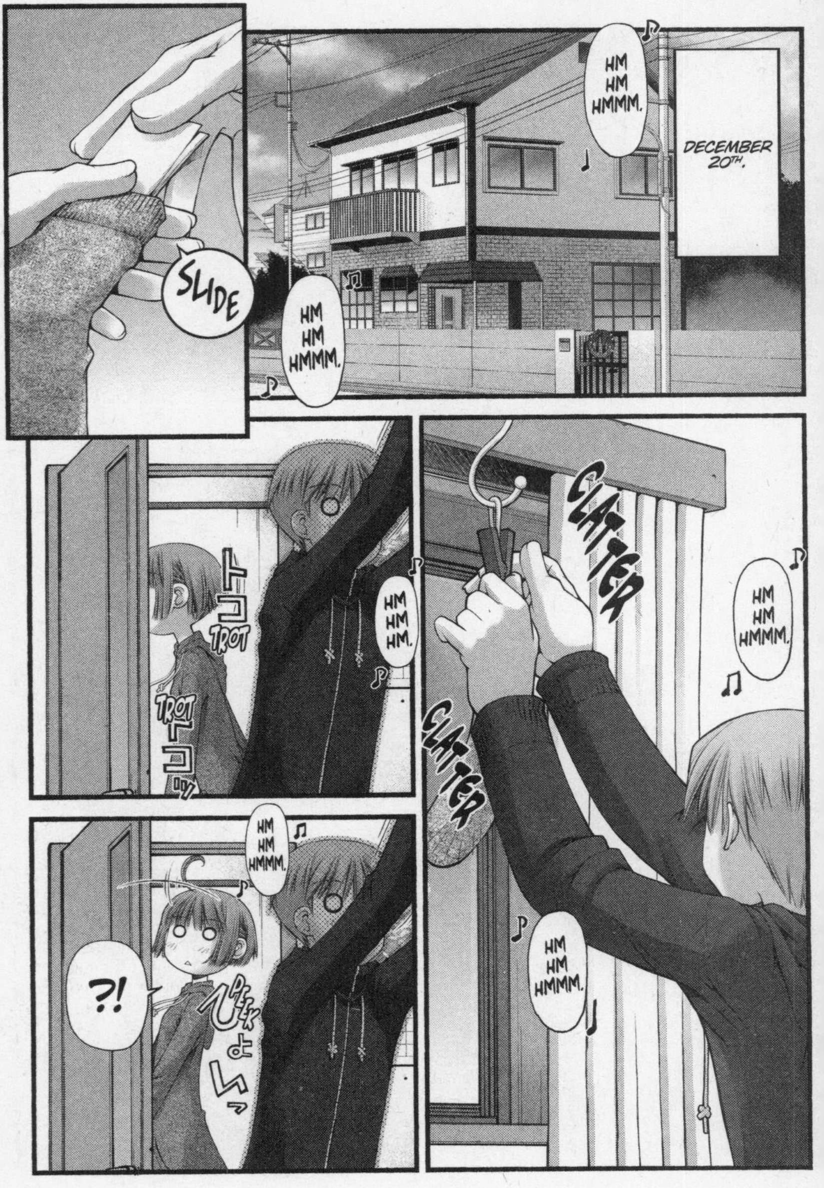
DECEMBER 20TH.
HM HM HMMM.
HM HM HMMM.
SLIDE
CLATTER
HM HM HMMM.
CLATTER
HM HM HMMM.
HM HM HM.
TROT
TROT
HM HM HMMM.
?!
PEEK

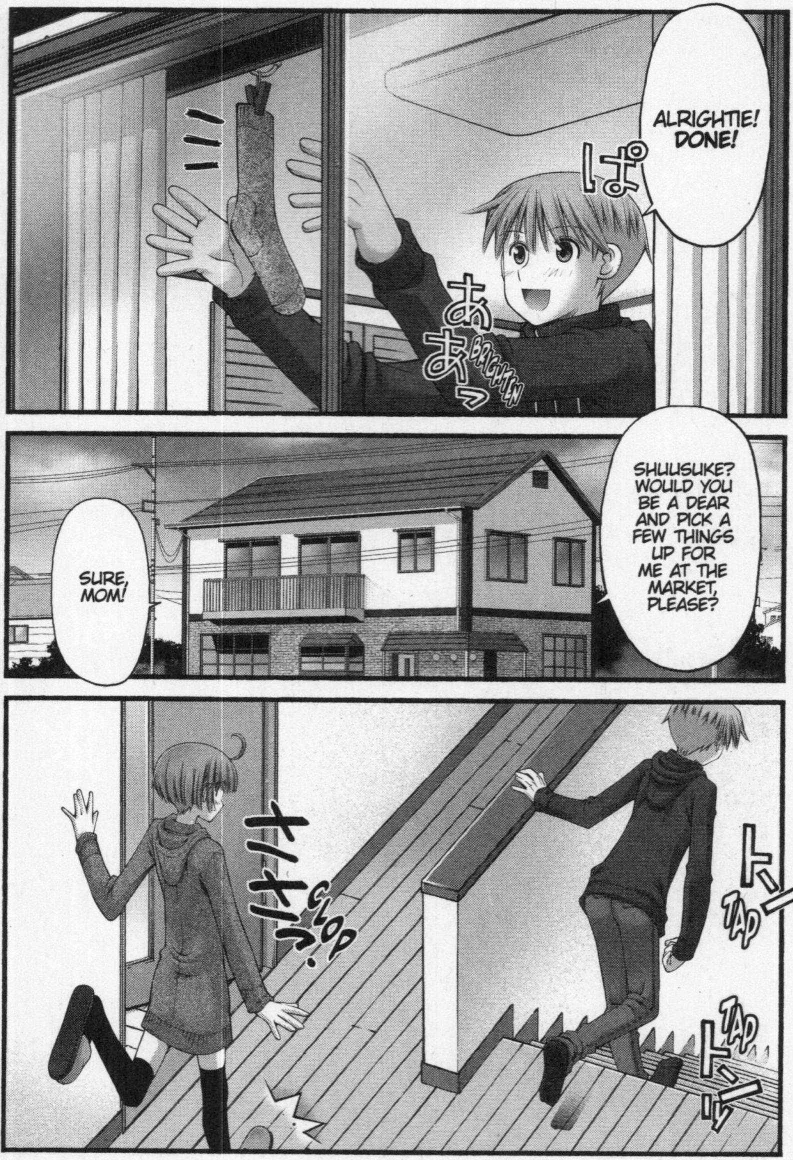
ALRIGHTIE! DONE!
ぱ
ああっ
BRIGHTEN
SHUUSUKE? WOULD YOU BE A DEAR AND PICK A FEW THINGS UP FOR ME AT THE MARKET, PLEASE?
SURE, MOM!
TAP
TAP
CLOP

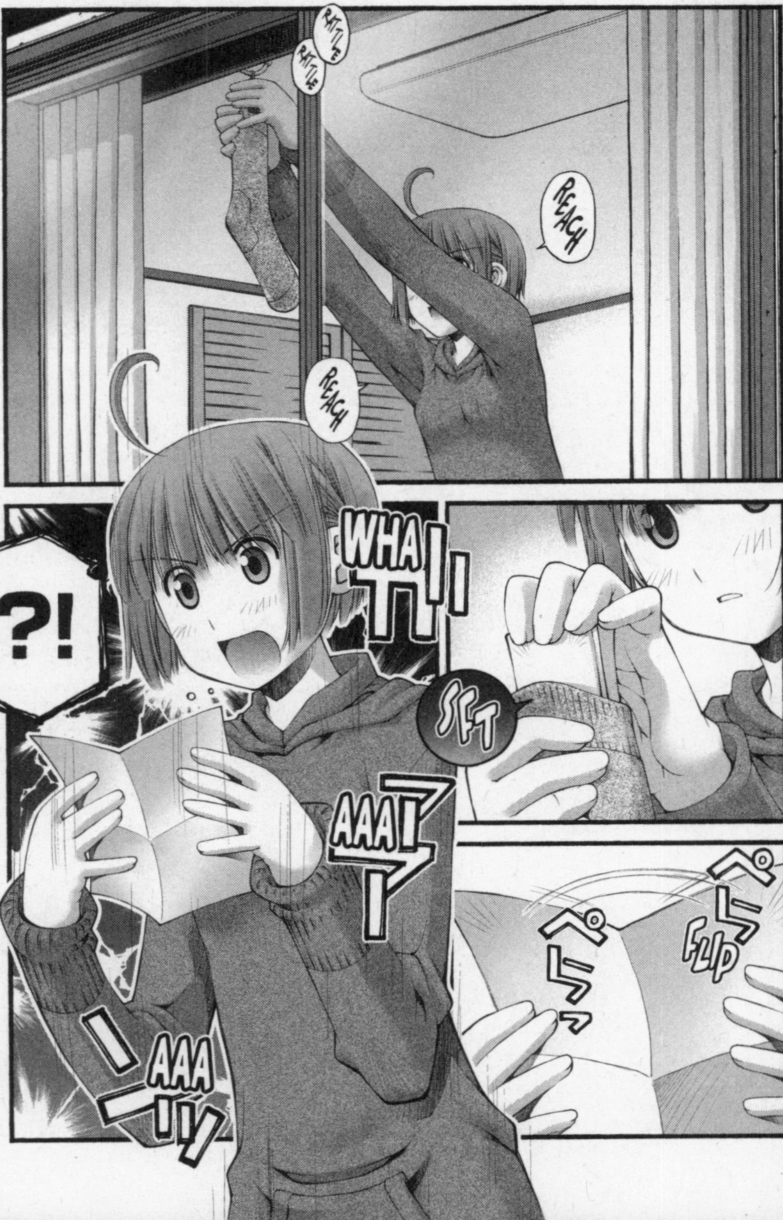
RATTLE
RATTLE
REACH
REACH
SFT
ぺら〜
FLIP
ぺらっ
?!
WHAT
AAA
AAA

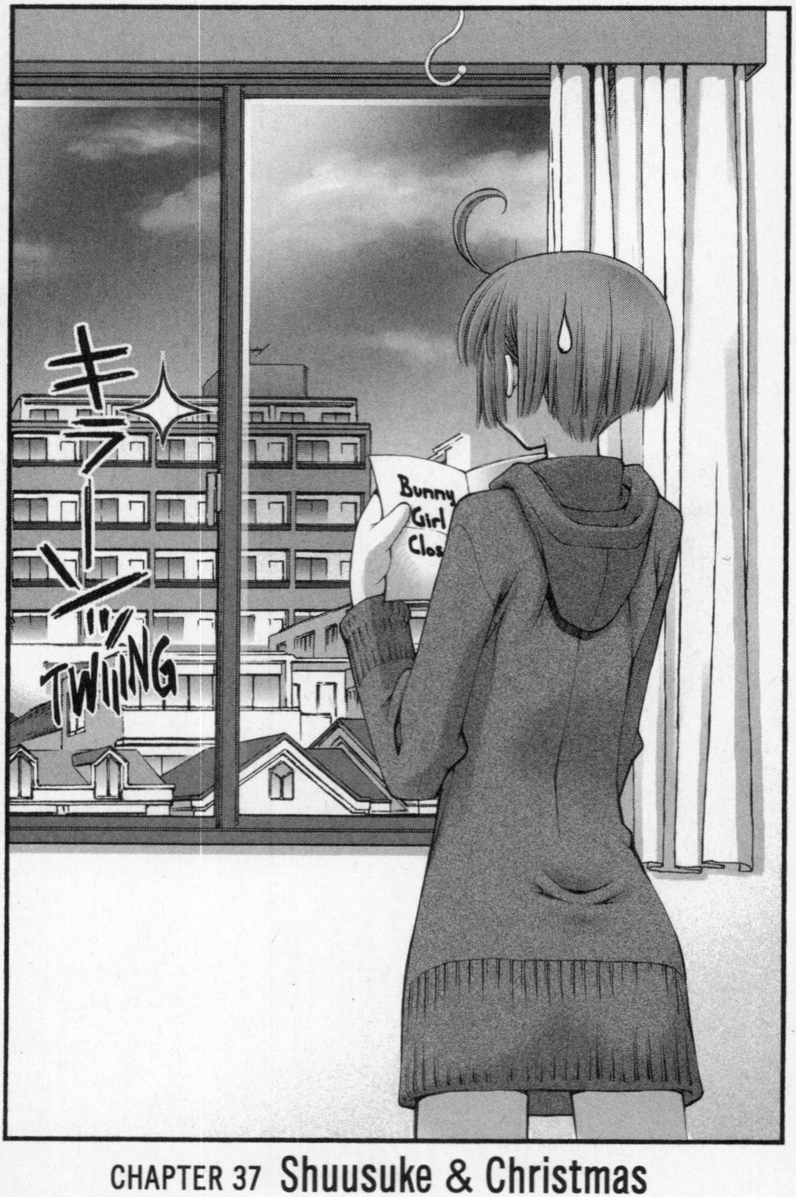
キラーン
TWIIING
Bunny Girl Clos

CHAPTER 37 Shuusuke & Christmas

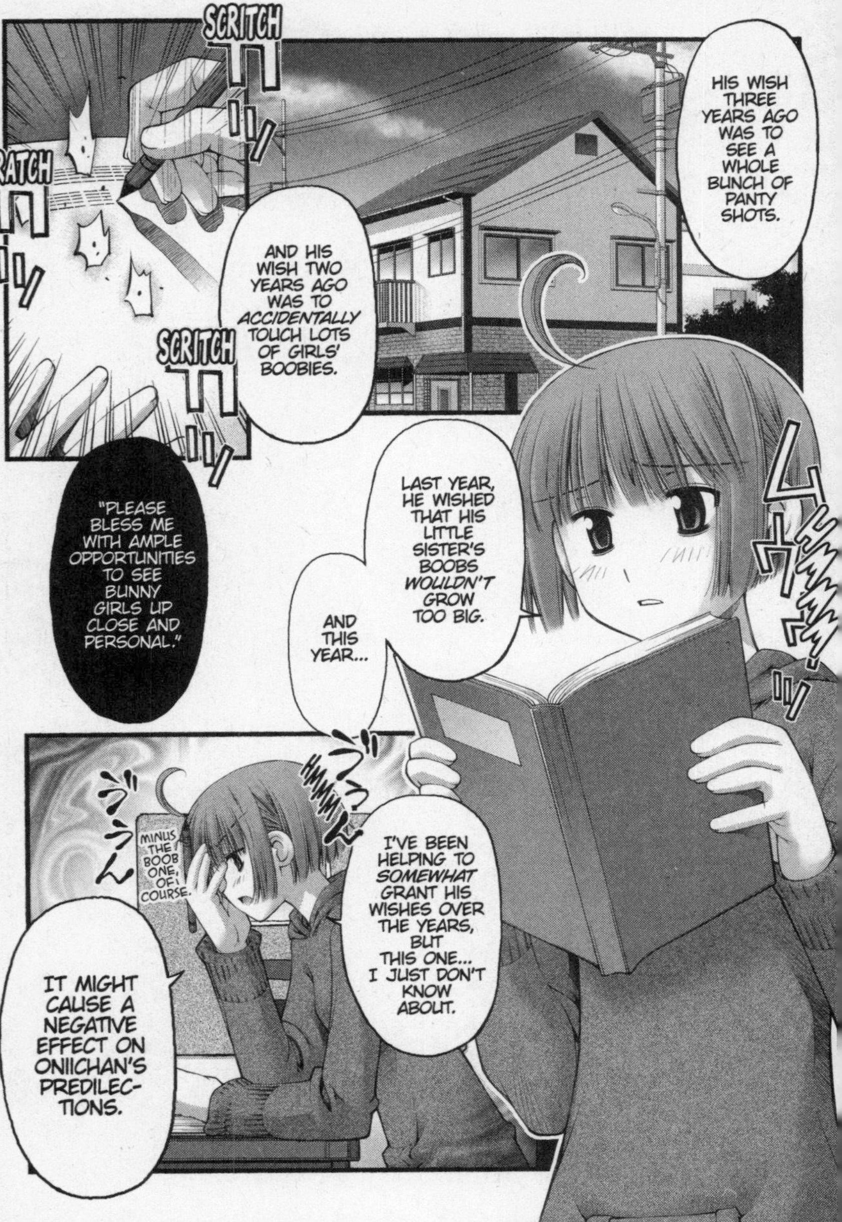
HIS WISH THREE YEARS AGO WAS TO SEE A WHOLE BUNCH OF PANTY SHOTS.
AND HIS WISH TWO YEARS AGO WAS TO *ACCIDENTALLY* TOUCH LOTS OF GIRLS' BOOBIES.
SCRITCH
SCRATCH
SCRITCH
HMMMM!
LAST YEAR, HE WISHED THAT HIS LITTLE SISTER'S BOOBS *WOULDN'T* GROW TOO BIG.
AND THIS YEAR...
"PLEASE BLESS ME WITH AMPLE OPPORTUNITIES TO SEE BUNNY GIRLS UP CLOSE AND PERSONAL."
HMMMM
I'VE BEEN HELPING TO *SOMEWHAT* GRANT HIS WISHES OVER THE YEARS, BUT THIS ONE... I JUST DON'T KNOW ABOUT.
MINUS THE BOOB ONE, OF COURSE.
IT MIGHT CAUSE A NEGATIVE EFFECT ON ONIICHAN'S PREDILEC-TIONS.

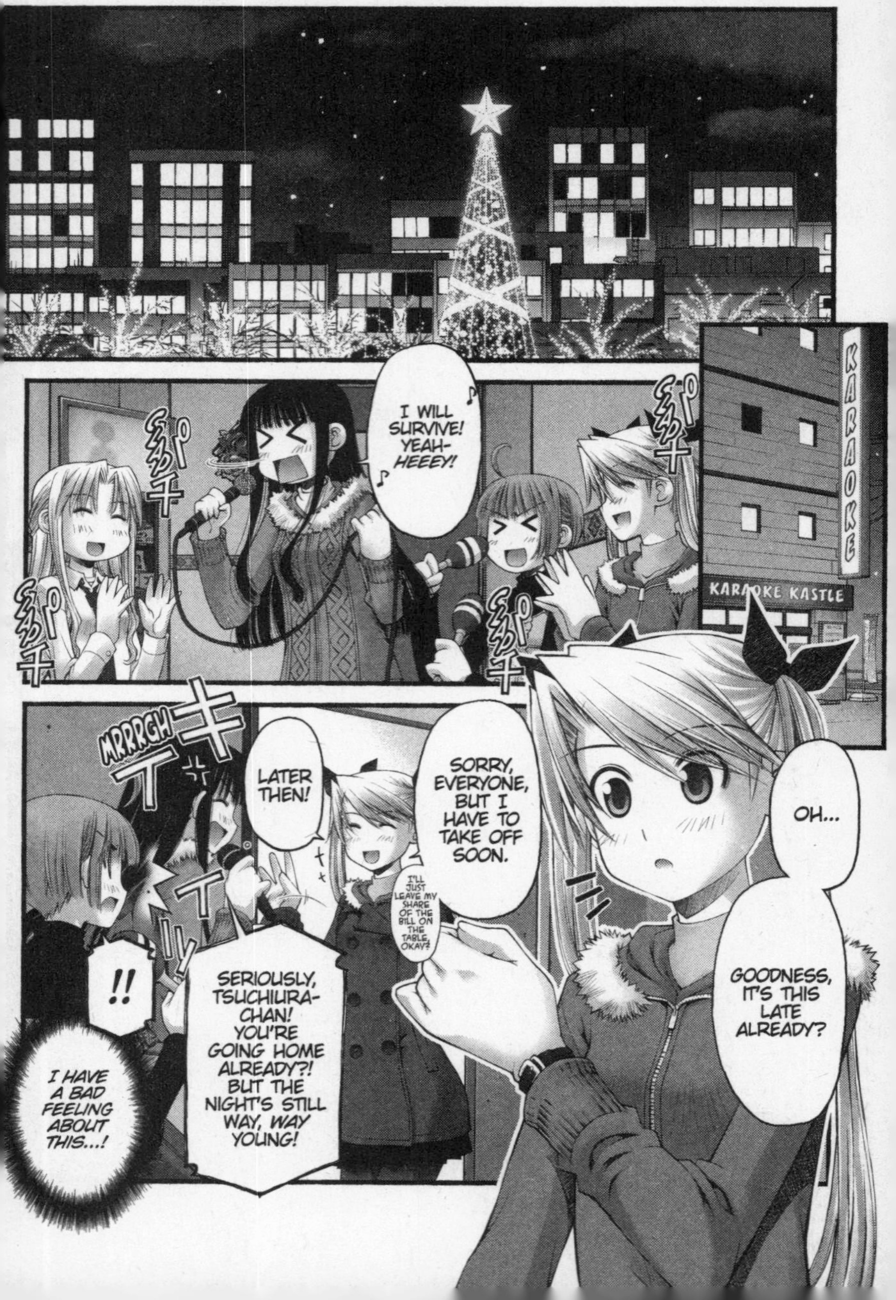
KARAOKE
KARAOKE KASTLE
I WILL SURVIVE! YEAH-HEEEY!
OH...
GOODNESS, IT'S THIS LATE ALREADY?
SORRY, EVERYONE, BUT I HAVE TO TAKE OFF SOON.
I'LL JUST LEAVE MY SHARE OF THE BILL ON THE TABLE, OKAY?
LATER THEN!
MRRRGH
SERIOUSLY, TSUCHIURA-CHAN! YOU'RE GOING HOME ALREADY?! BUT THE NIGHT'S STILL WAY, WAY YOUNG!
!!
I HAVE A BAD FEELING ABOUT THIS...!

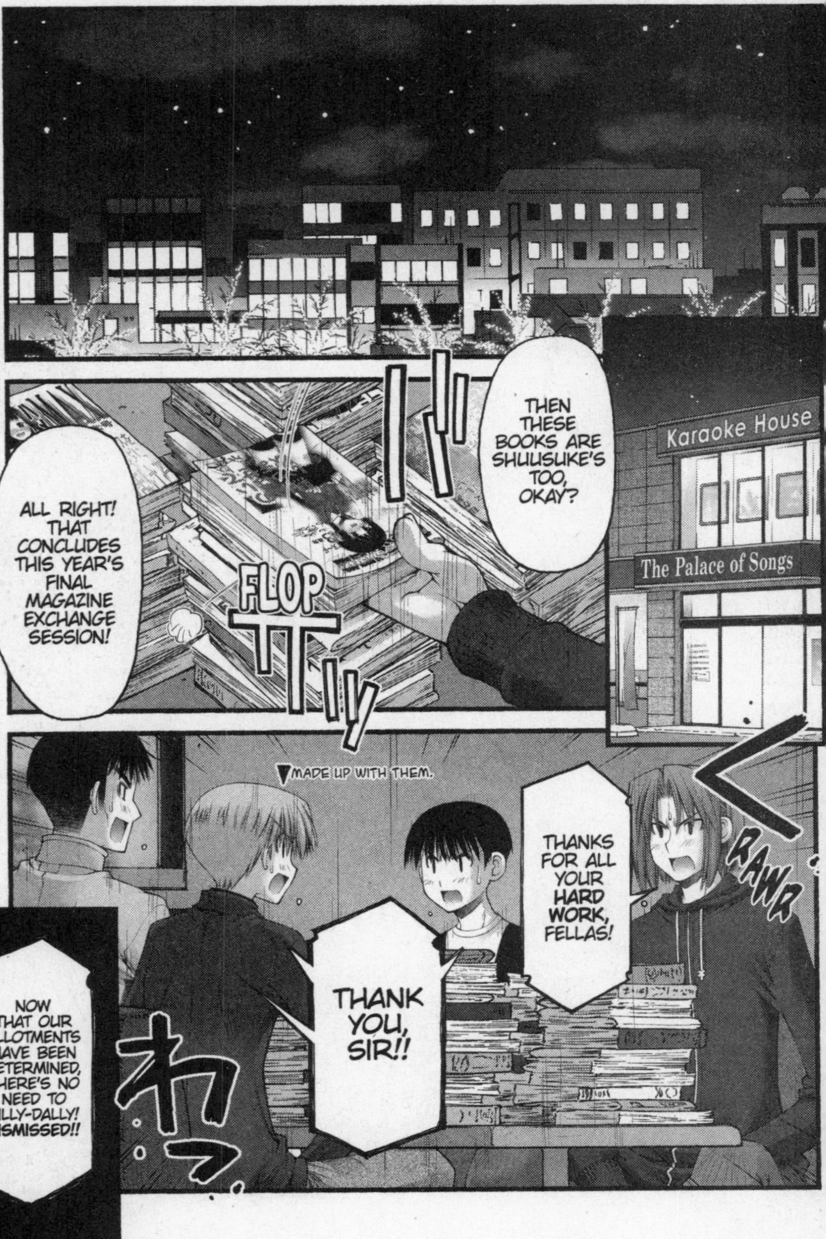
Karaoke House
The Palace of Songs
THEN THESE BOOKS ARE SHUUSUKE'S TOO, OKAY?
ALL RIGHT! THAT CONCLUDES THIS YEAR'S FINAL MAGAZINE EXCHANGE SESSION!
FLOP
RAWR
THANKS FOR ALL YOUR HARD WORK, FELLAS!
MADE UP WITH THEM.
THANK YOU, SIR!!
わっ
NOW THAT OUR ALLOTMENTS HAVE BEEN DETERMINED, THERE'S NO NEED TO DILLY-DALLY! DISMISSED!!

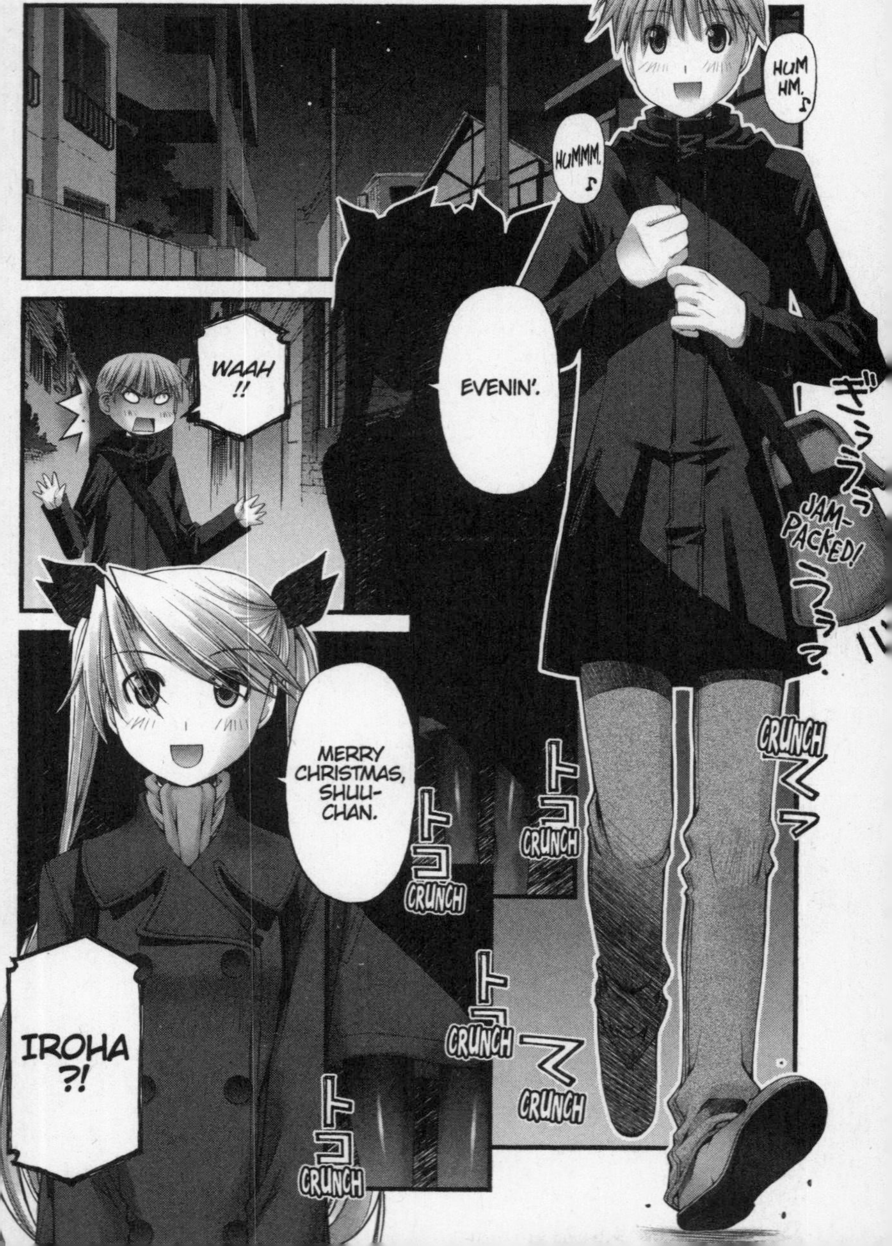
HUM HM. ♪
HUMMM. ♪
EVENIN'.
JAM-PACKED!
CRUNCH
CRUNCH
CRUNCH
WAAH!!
MERRY CHRISTMAS, SHUU-CHAN.
CRUNCH
CRUNCH
CRUNCH
IROHA?!

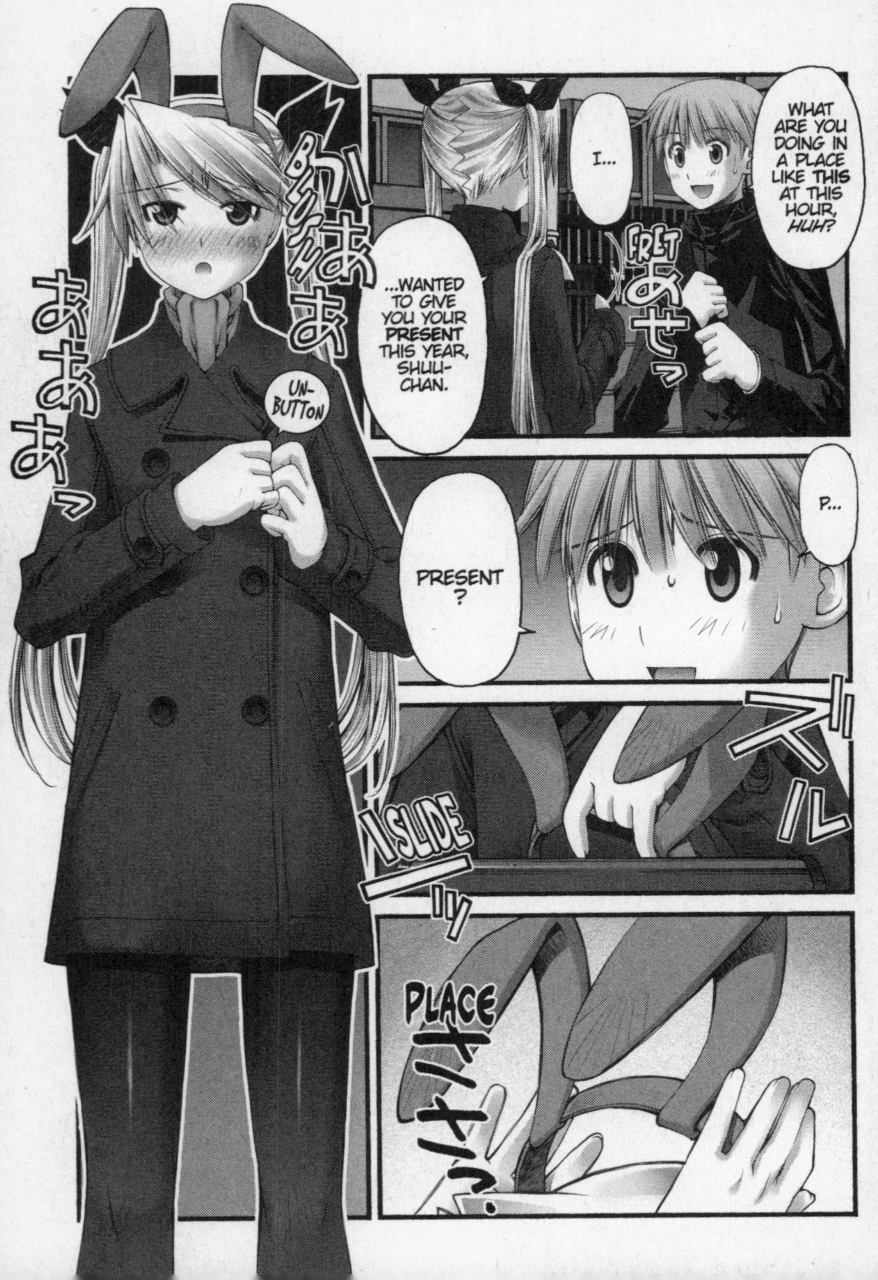
WHAT ARE YOU DOING IN A PLACE LIKE THIS AT THIS HOUR, HUH?
FRET あせっ
I...
...WANTED TO GIVE YOU YOUR PRESENT THIS YEAR, SHUU-CHAN.
P...
PRESENT?
SLIDE
PLACE
UN-BUTTON
BLUSH かあああああっ

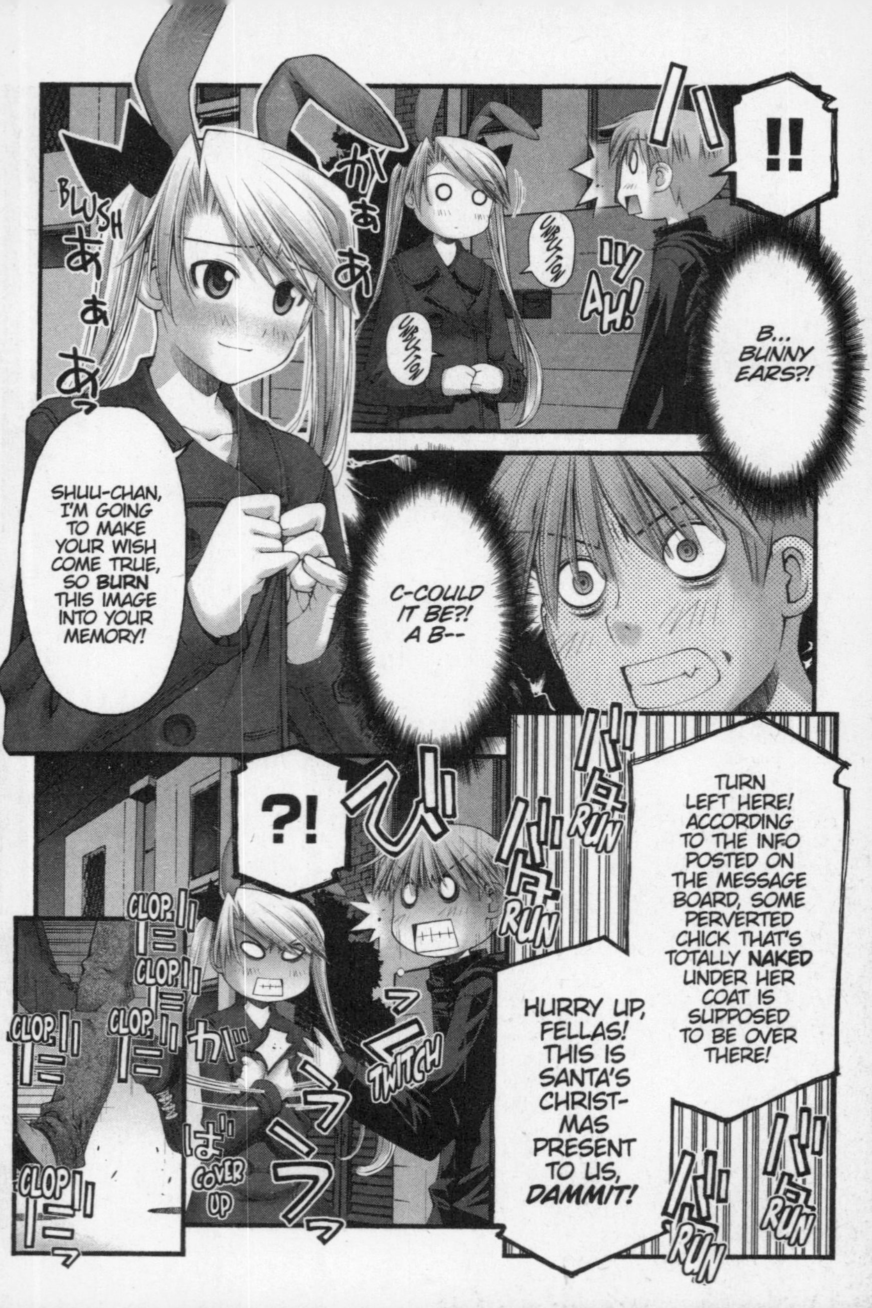
!!
IIY AH!
UNBUTTON
UNBUTTON
B... BUNNY EARS?!
C-COULD IT BE?! A B--
BLUSH
SHUU-CHAN, I'M GOING TO MAKE YOUR WISH COME TRUE, SO BURN THIS IMAGE INTO YOUR MEMORY!
RUN
RUN
TURN LEFT HERE! ACCORDING TO THE INFO POSTED ON THE MESSAGE BOARD, SOME PERVERTED CHICK THAT'S TOTALLY NAKED UNDER HER COAT IS SUPPOSED TO BE OVER THERE!
RUN
RUN
HURRY UP, FELLAS! THIS IS SANTA'S CHRIST-MAS PRESENT TO US, DAMMIT!
?!
TWITCH
COVER UP
CLOP
CLOP
CLOP
CLOP
CLOP

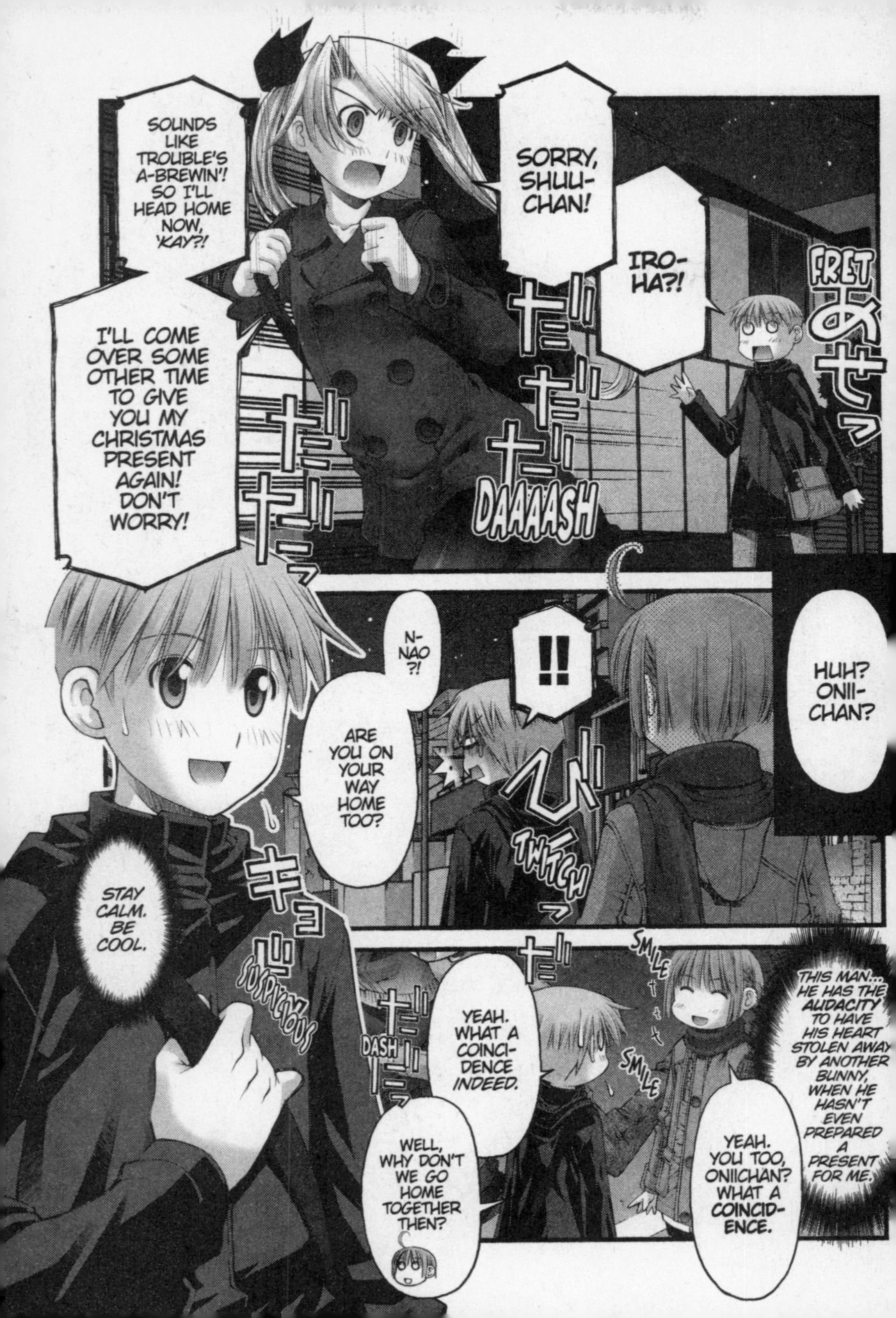
FRET
あせっ
IRO-HA?!
SORRY, SHUU-CHAN!
SOUNDS LIKE TROUBLE'S A-BREWIN'! SO I'LL HEAD HOME NOW, 'KAY?!
I'LL COME OVER SOME OTHER TIME TO GIVE YOU MY CHRISTMAS PRESENT AGAIN! DON'T WORRY!
DAAAASH
HUH? ONII-CHAN?
!!
TWITCH
N-NAO?!
ARE YOU ON YOUR WAY HOME TOO?
STAY CALM. BE COOL.
SUSPICIOUS
THIS MAN... HE HAS THE AUDACITY TO HAVE HIS HEART STOLEN AWAY BY ANOTHER BUNNY, WHEN HE HASN'T EVEN PREPARED A PRESENT FOR ME.
SMILE
SMILE
YEAH. YOU TOO, ONIICHAN? WHAT A COINCID-ENCE.
YEAH. WHAT A COINCI-DENCE INDEED.
DASH
WELL, WHY DON'T WE GO HOME TOGETHER THEN?

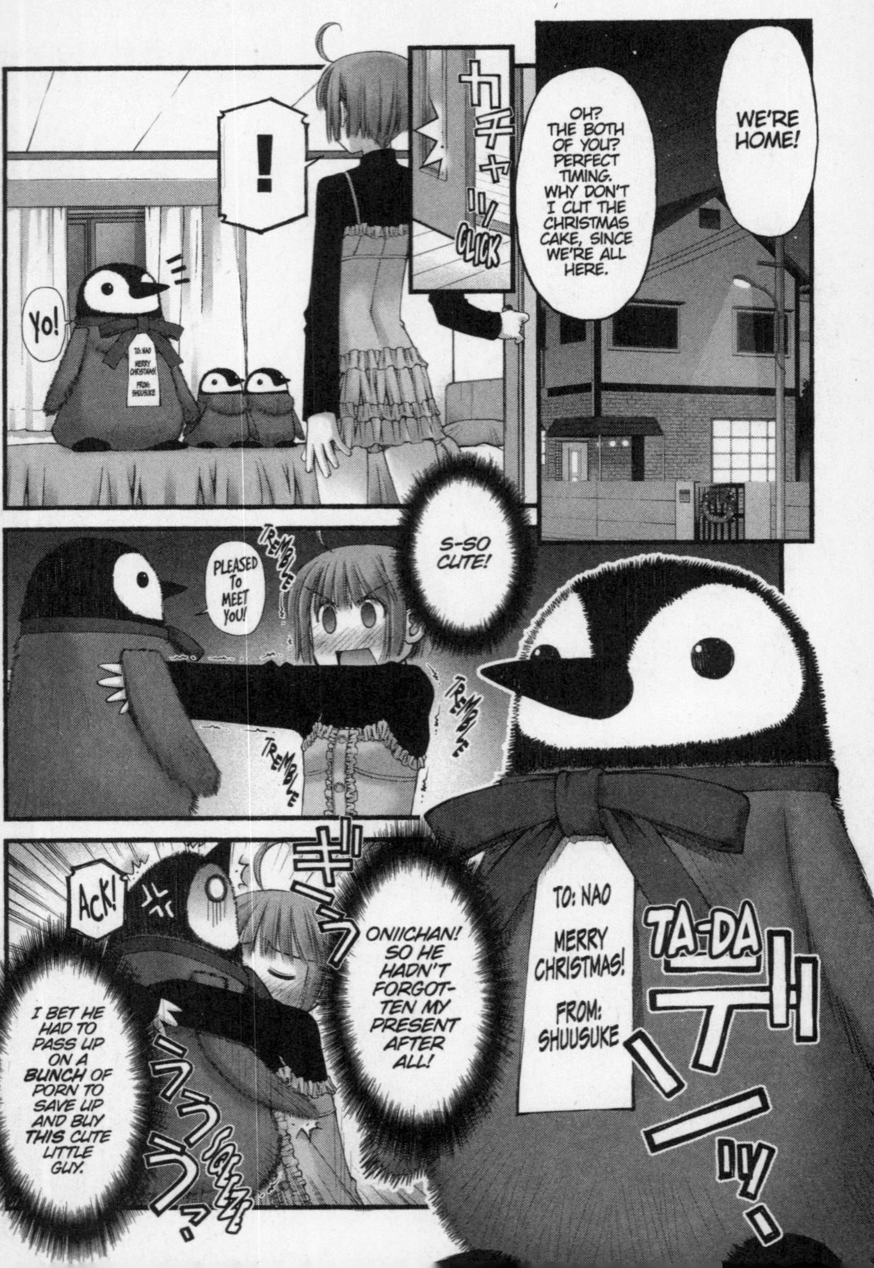
WE'RE HOME!
OH? THE BOTH OF YOU? PERFECT TIMING. WHY DON'T I CUT THE CHRISTMAS CAKE, SINCE WE'RE ALL HERE.
CLICK
!
YO!
TO: NAO MERRY CHRISTMAS! FROM: SHUUSUKE
TO: NAO
MERRY CHRISTMAS!
FROM: SHUUSUKE
TA-DA
S-SO CUTE!
TREMBLE
PLEASED TO MEET YOU!
TREMBLE
TREMBLE
ONIICHAN! SO HE HADN'T FORGOT-TEN MY PRESENT AFTER ALL!
ACK!
I BET HE HAD TO PASS UP ON A BUNCH OF PORN TO SAVE UP AND BUY THIS CUTE LITTLE GUY.
SQUEEZE

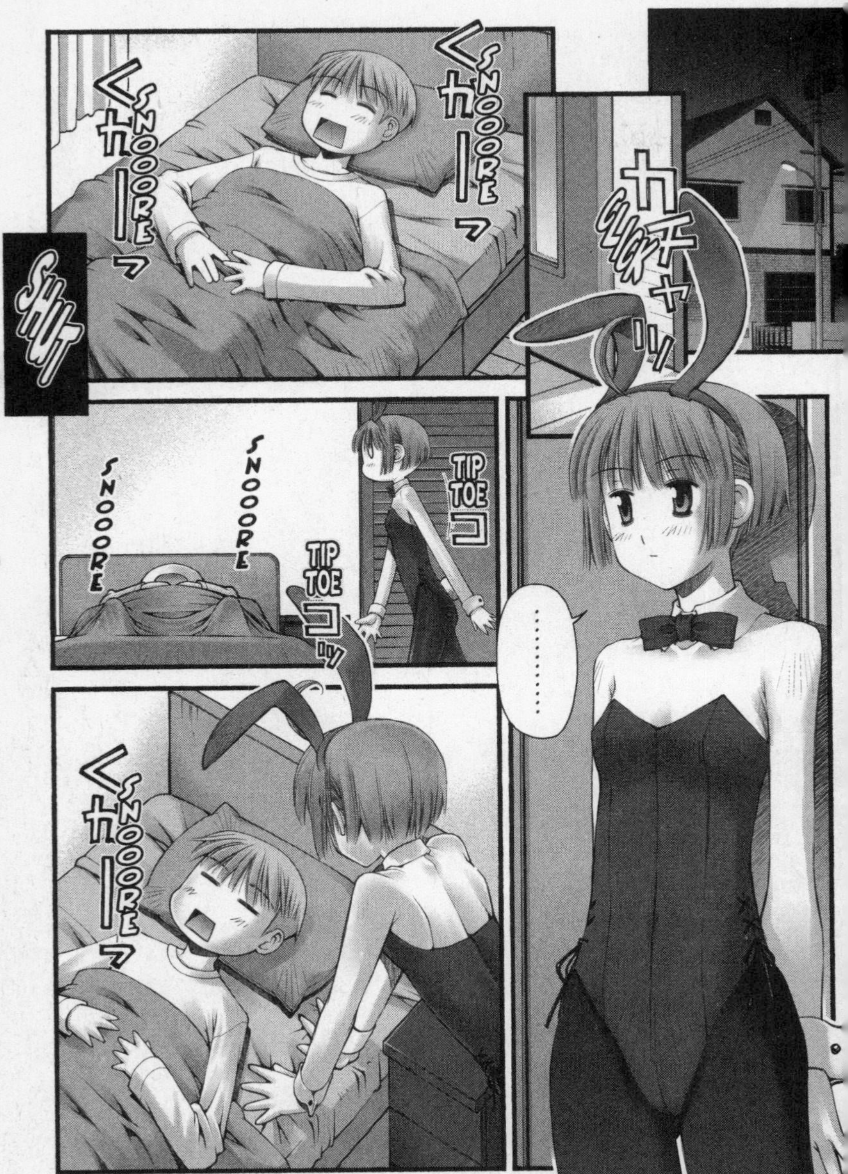
カチャッ
CLICK
くかーっ
SNOOORE
くかーっ
SNOOORE
SHUT
……
TIP TOE
コ
TIP TOE
コッ
SNOOORE
SNOOORE
くかーっ
SNOOORE

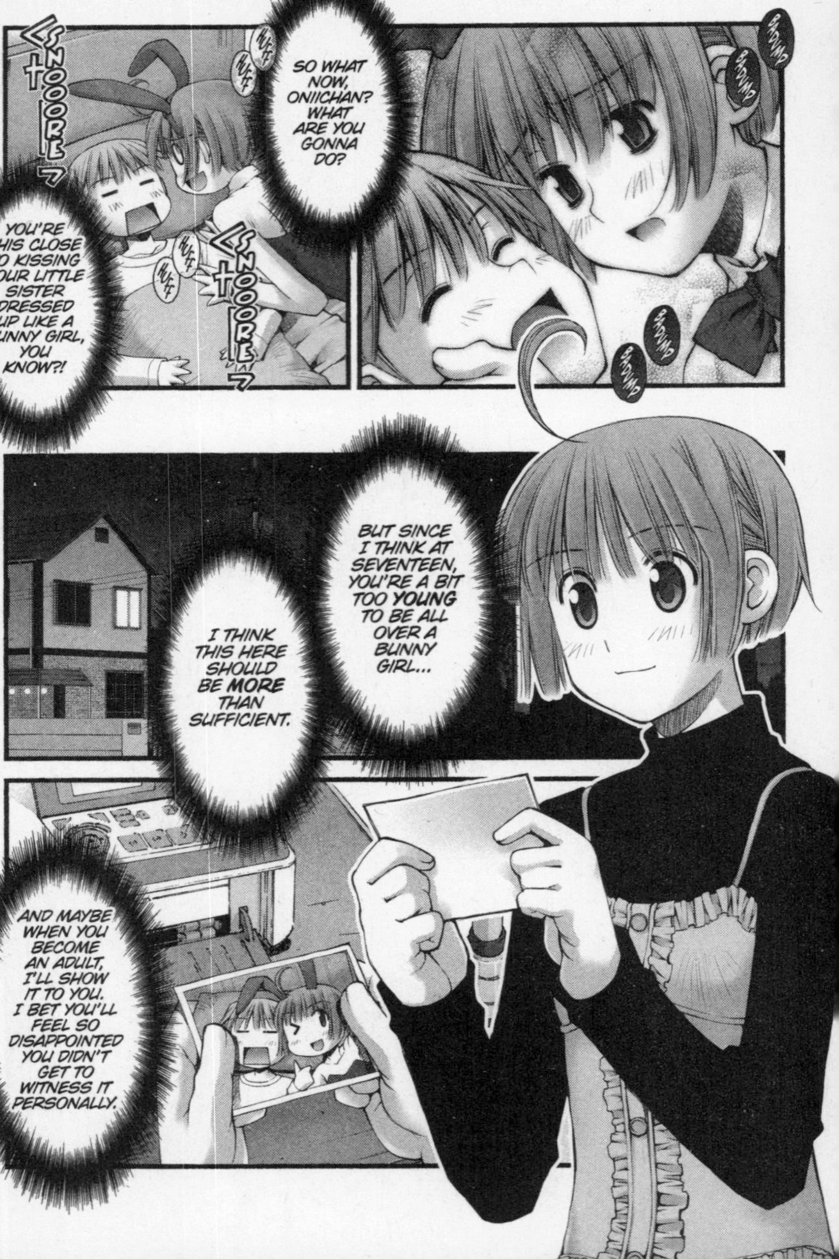
BADUMP
BADUMP
BADUMP
BADUMP
BADUMP
SO WHAT NOW, ONIICHAN? WHAT ARE YOU GONNA DO?
HUFF
HUFF
SNOOORE
HUFF
HUFF
SNOOORE
YOU'RE THIS CLOSE TO KISSING YOUR LITTLE SISTER DRESSED UP LIKE A BUNNY GIRL, YOU KNOW?!
BUT SINCE I THINK AT SEVENTEEN, YOU'RE A BIT TOO YOUNG TO BE ALL OVER A BUNNY GIRL...
I THINK THIS HERE SHOULD BE MORE THAN SUFFICIENT.
AND MAYBE WHEN YOU BECOME AN ADULT, I'LL SHOW IT TO YOU. I BET YOU'LL FEEL SO DISAPPOINTED YOU DIDN'T GET TO WITNESS IT PERSONALLY.

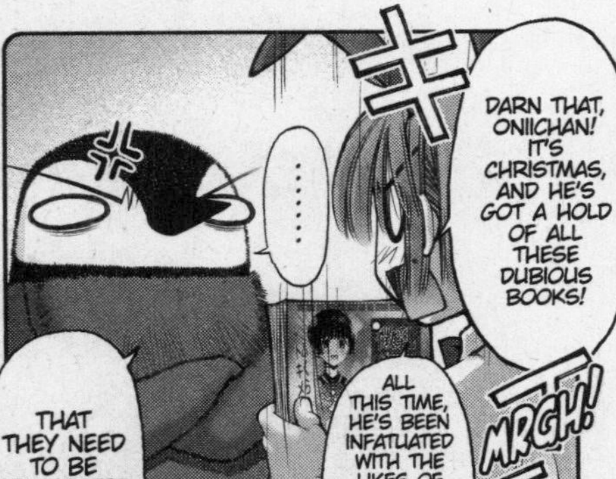
DARN THAT, ONIICHAN! IT'S CHRISTMAS, AND HE'S GOT A HOLD OF ALL THESE DUBIOUS BOOKS!
....
MRGH!
ALL THIS TIME, HE'S BEEN INFATUATED WITH THE LIKES OF THESE TWIN TAILED BUNNY GIRLS! WHAT DO YOU THINK?!
THAT THEY NEED TO BE ERADICATED, BABE!

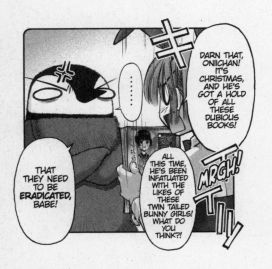

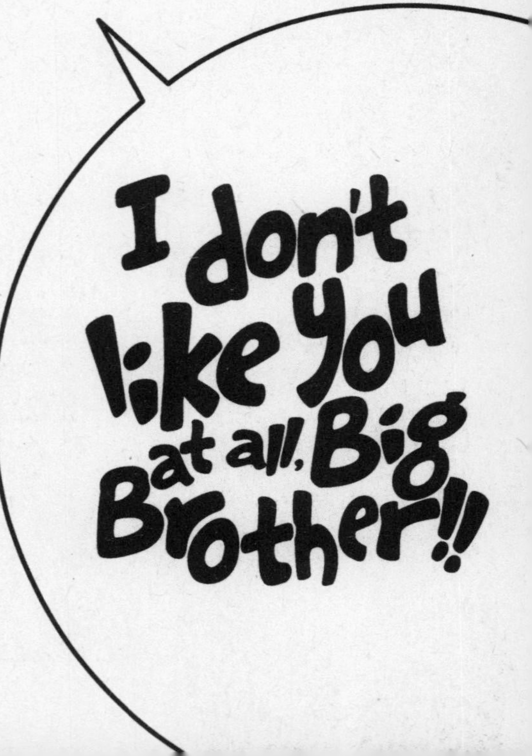
I don't like you at all, Big Brother!!

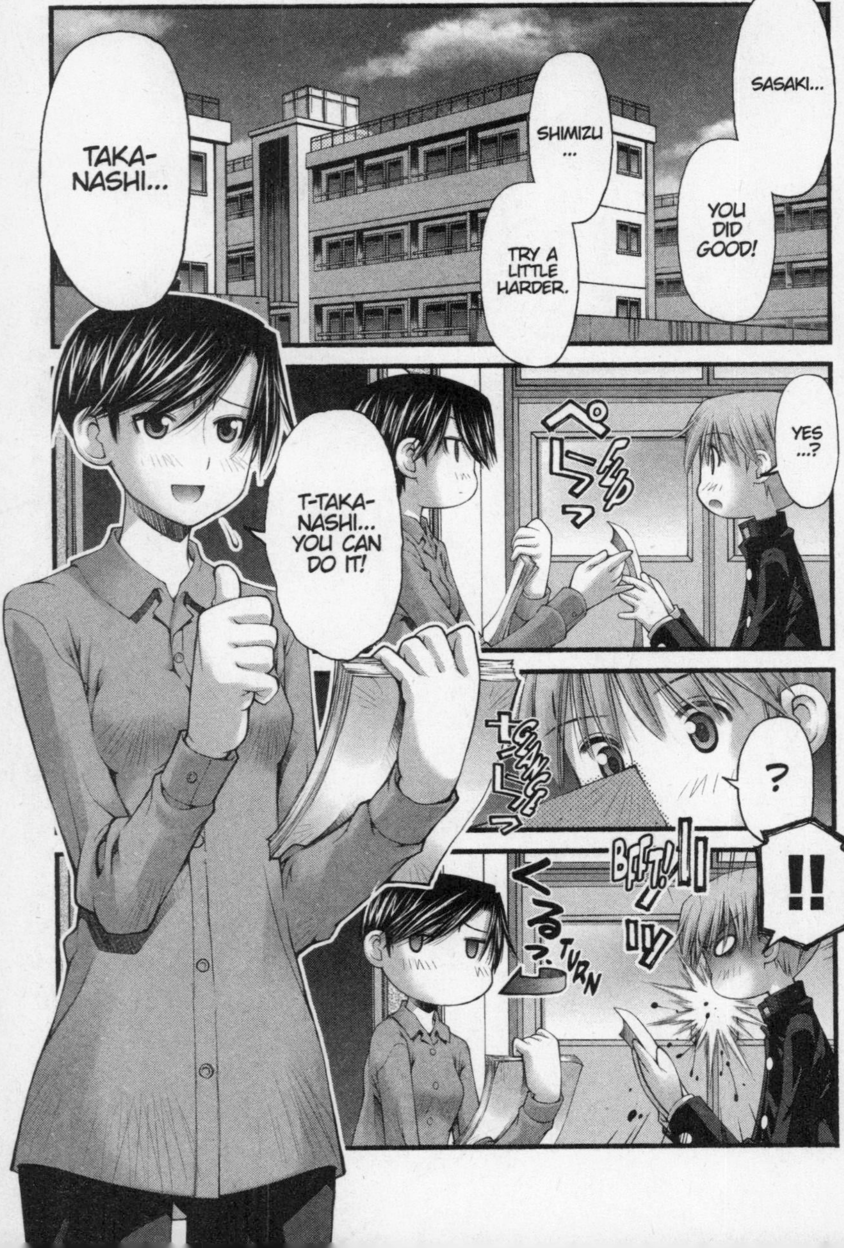
SASAKI...
YOU DID GOOD!
SHIMIZU...
TRY A LITTLE HARDER.
TAKA-NASHI...
YES...?
ぺらっ
FLIP
ちらっ
GLANCE
?
!!
BFFT!
くるっ
TURN
T-TAKA-NASHI... YOU CAN DO IT!

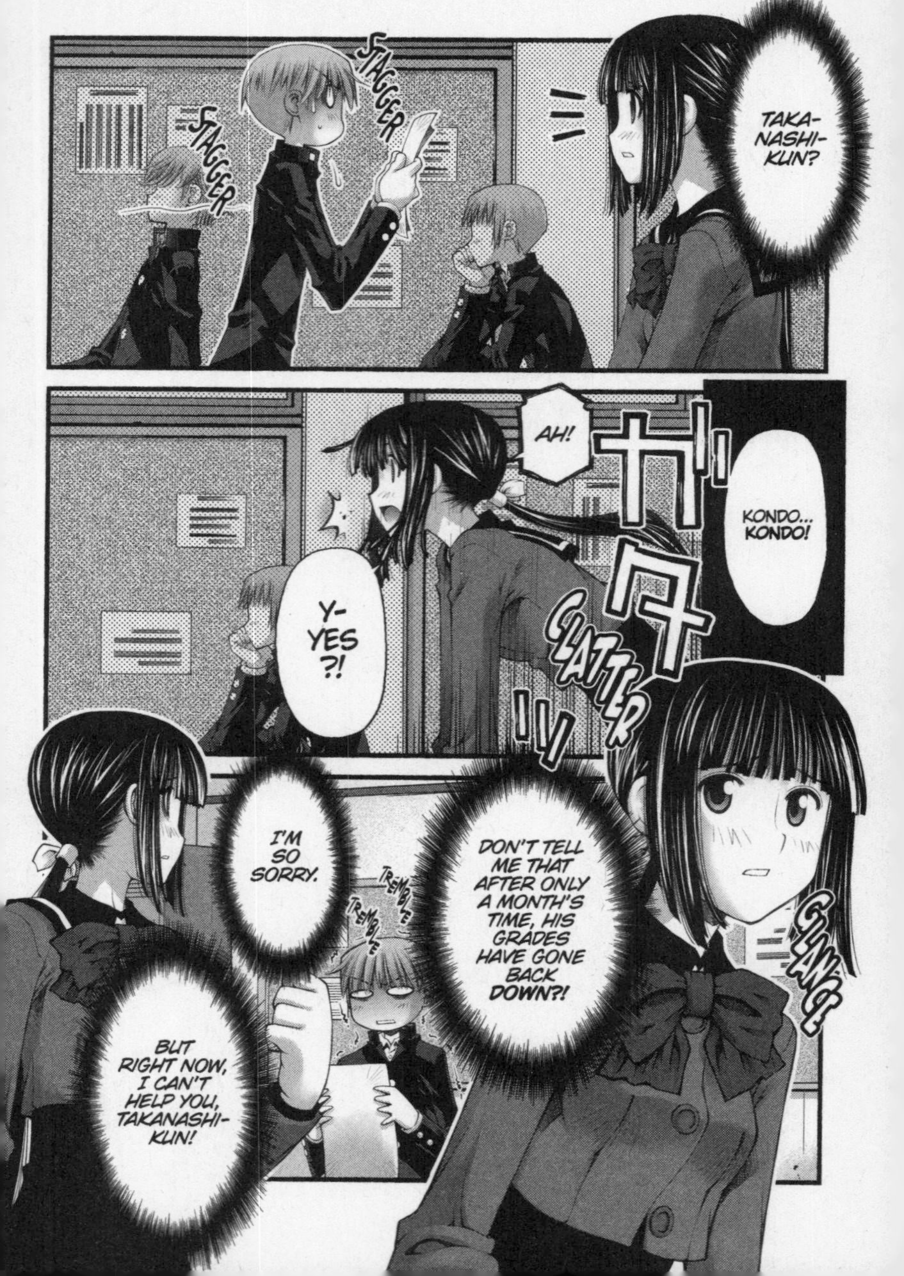

TAKA-NASHI-KUN?
STAGGER
STAGGER
KONDO... KONDO!
ガタ
CLATTER
AH!
Y-YES?!
GLANCE
DON'T TELL ME THAT AFTER ONLY A MONTH'S TIME, HIS GRADES HAVE GONE BACK DOWN?!
TREMBLE
TREMBLE
I'M SO SORRY.
BUT RIGHT NOW, I CAN'T HELP YOU, TAKANASHI-KUN!

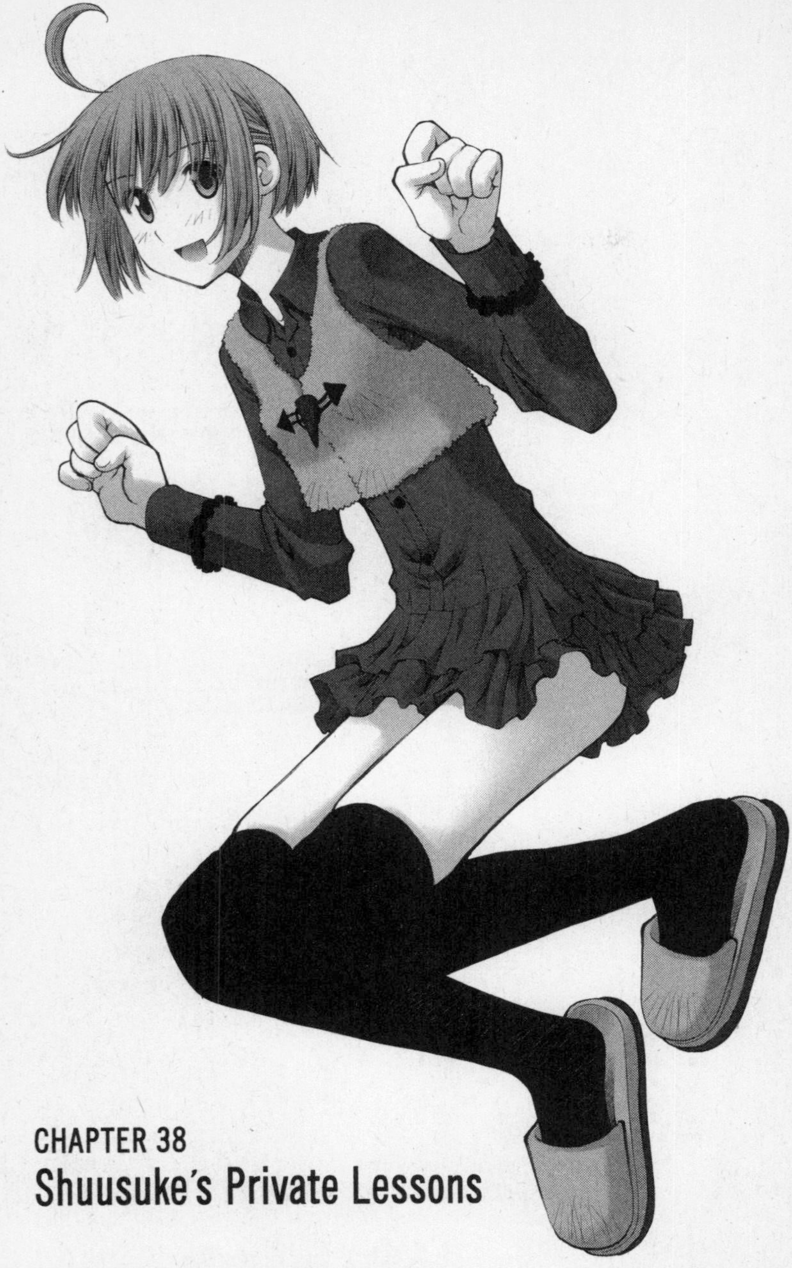

CHAPTER 38

Shuusuke's Private Lessons

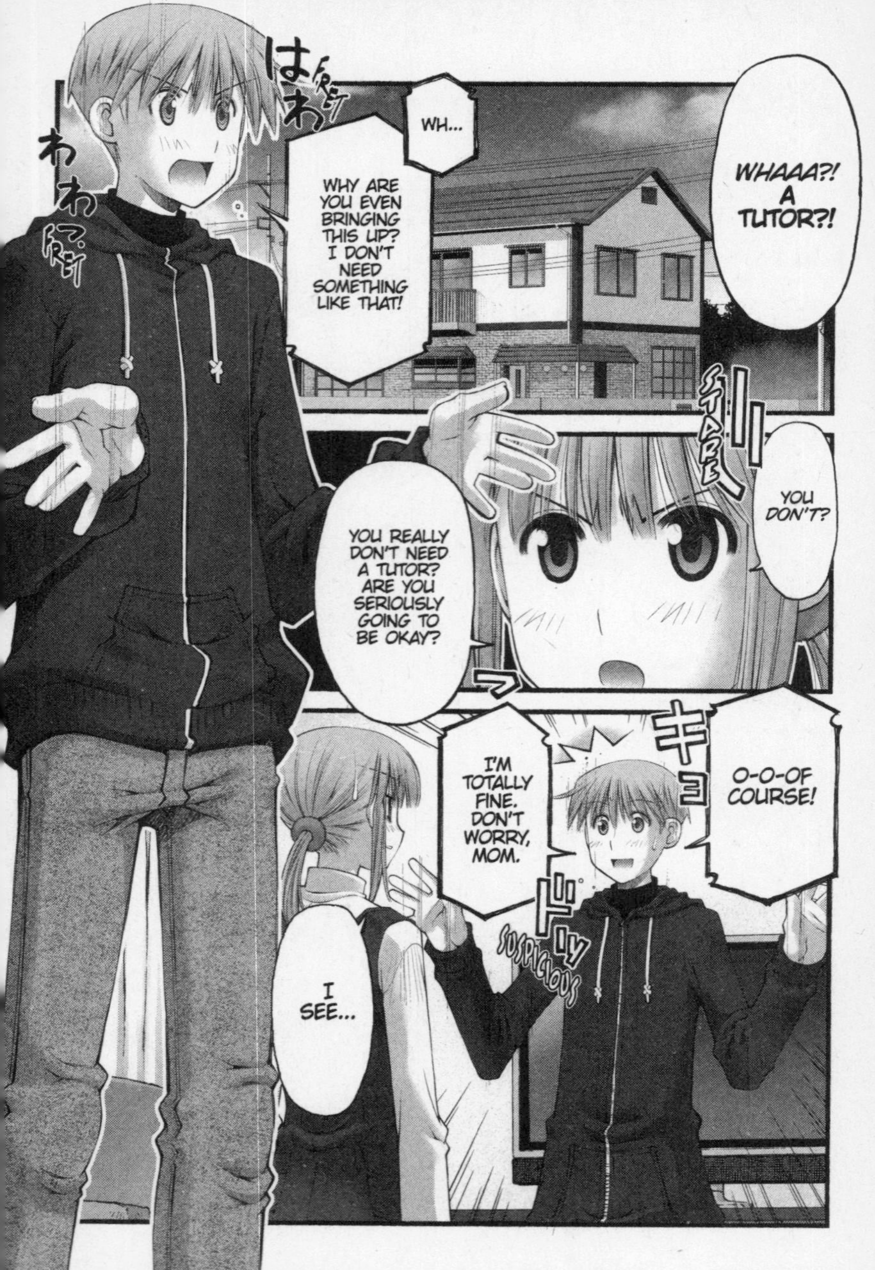
WHAAA?! A TUTOR?!
WH...
WHY ARE YOU EVEN BRINGING THIS UP? I DON'T NEED SOMETHING LIKE THAT!
FRET
FRET
STARE
YOU DON'T?
YOU REALLY DON'T NEED A TUTOR? ARE YOU SERIOUSLY GOING TO BE OKAY?
O-O-O-OF COURSE!
I'M TOTALLY FINE. DON'T WORRY, MOM.
SUSPICIOUS
I SEE...

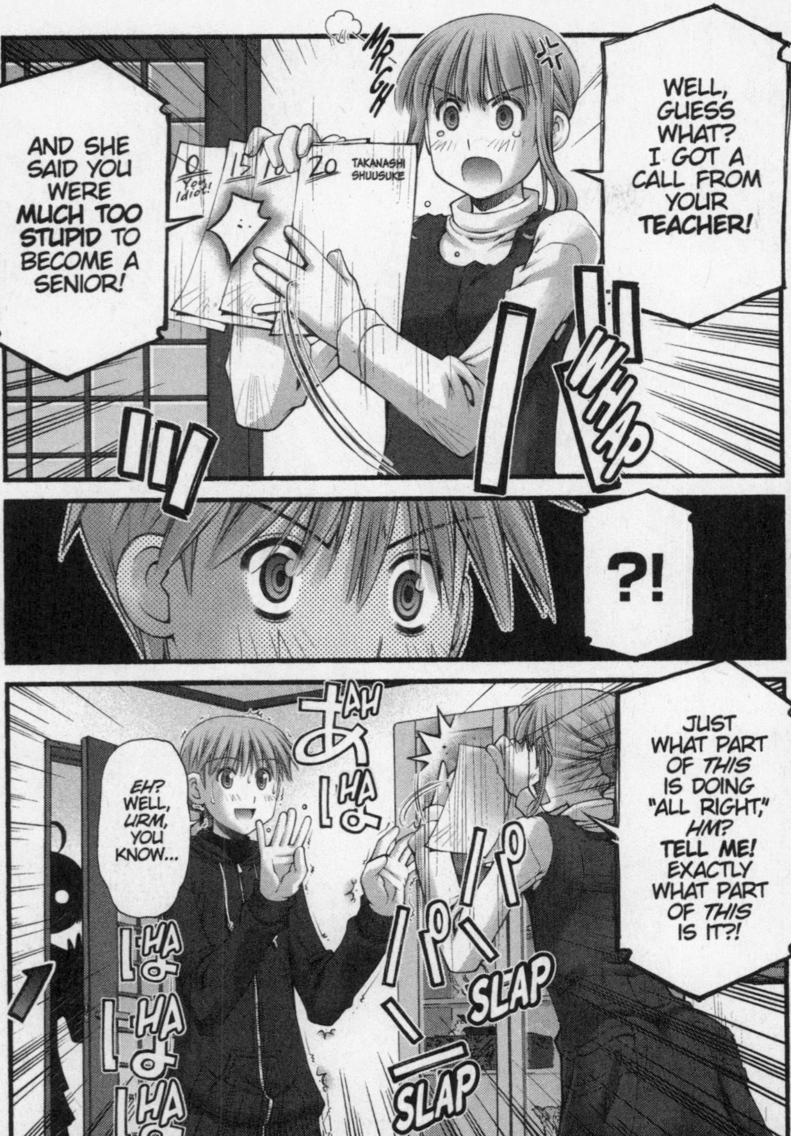

WELL, GUESS WHAT? I GOT A CALL FROM YOUR TEACHER!
MRGH
AND SHE SAID YOU WERE MUCH TOO STUPID TO BECOME A SENIOR!
TAKANASHI SHUUSUKE
20
10
15
0
You Idiot!
WHAP
?!
JUST WHAT PART OF *THIS* IS DOING "ALL RIGHT," *HM?* TELL ME! EXACTLY WHAT PART OF *THIS* IS IT?!
SLAP
SLAP
AH
HA
EH? WELL, URM, YOU KNOW...
HA
HA
HA

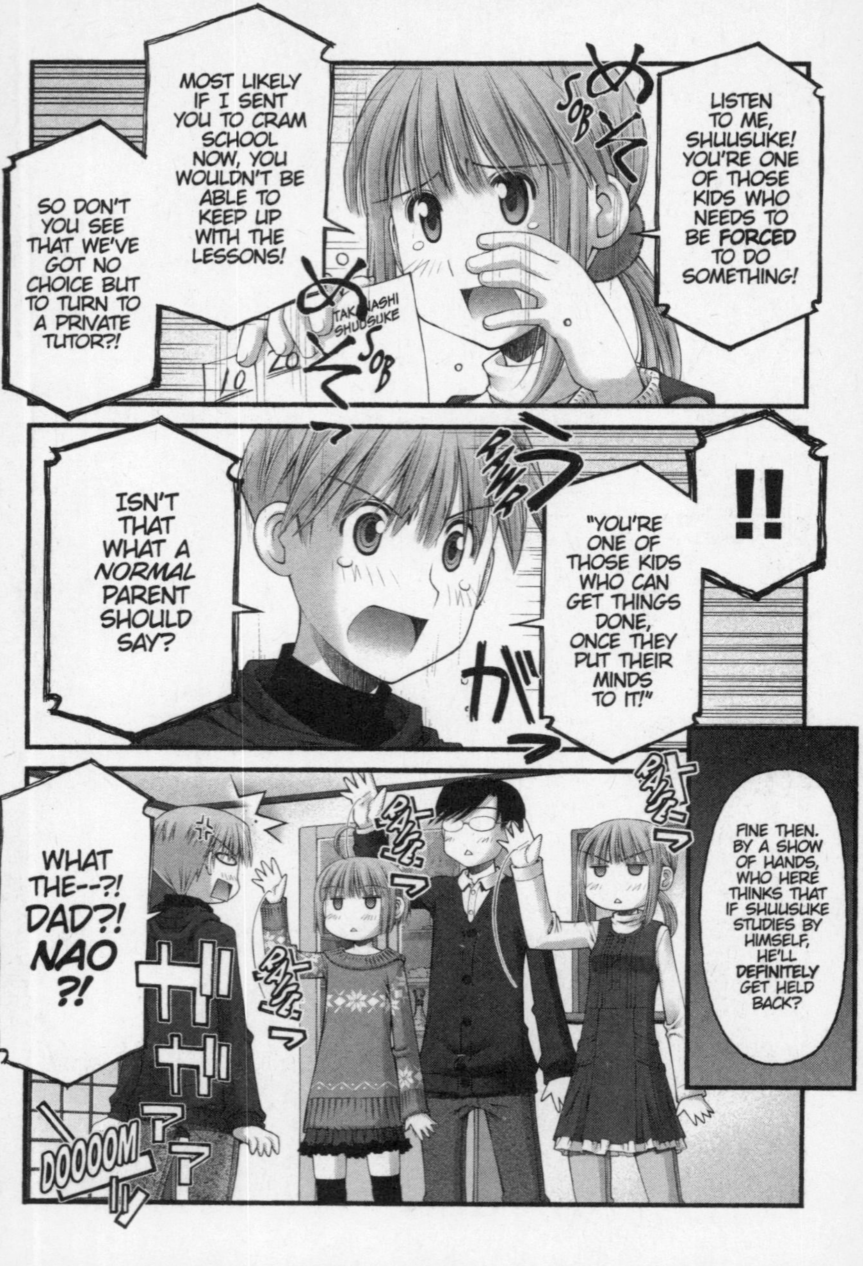
LISTEN TO ME, SHUUSUKE! YOU'RE ONE OF THOSE KIDS WHO NEEDS TO BE **FORCED** TO DO SOMETHING!
SOB
MOST LIKELY IF I SENT YOU TO CRAM SCHOOL NOW, YOU WOULDN'T BE ABLE TO KEEP UP WITH THE LESSONS!
SOB
SO DON'T YOU SEE THAT WE'VE GOT NO CHOICE BUT TO TURN TO A PRIVATE TUTOR?!
!!
RAWR
"YOU'RE ONE OF THOSE KIDS WHO CAN GET THINGS DONE, ONCE THEY PUT THEIR MINDS TO IT!"
ISN'T THAT WHAT A *NORMAL* PARENT SHOULD SAY?
FINE THEN. BY A SHOW OF HANDS, WHO HERE THINKS THAT IF SHUUSUKE STUDIES BY HIMSELF, HE'LL **DEFINITELY** GET HELD BACK?
RAYSE
RAYSE
RAYSE
WHAT THE--?! **DAD?! *NAO*?!**
DOOOOM

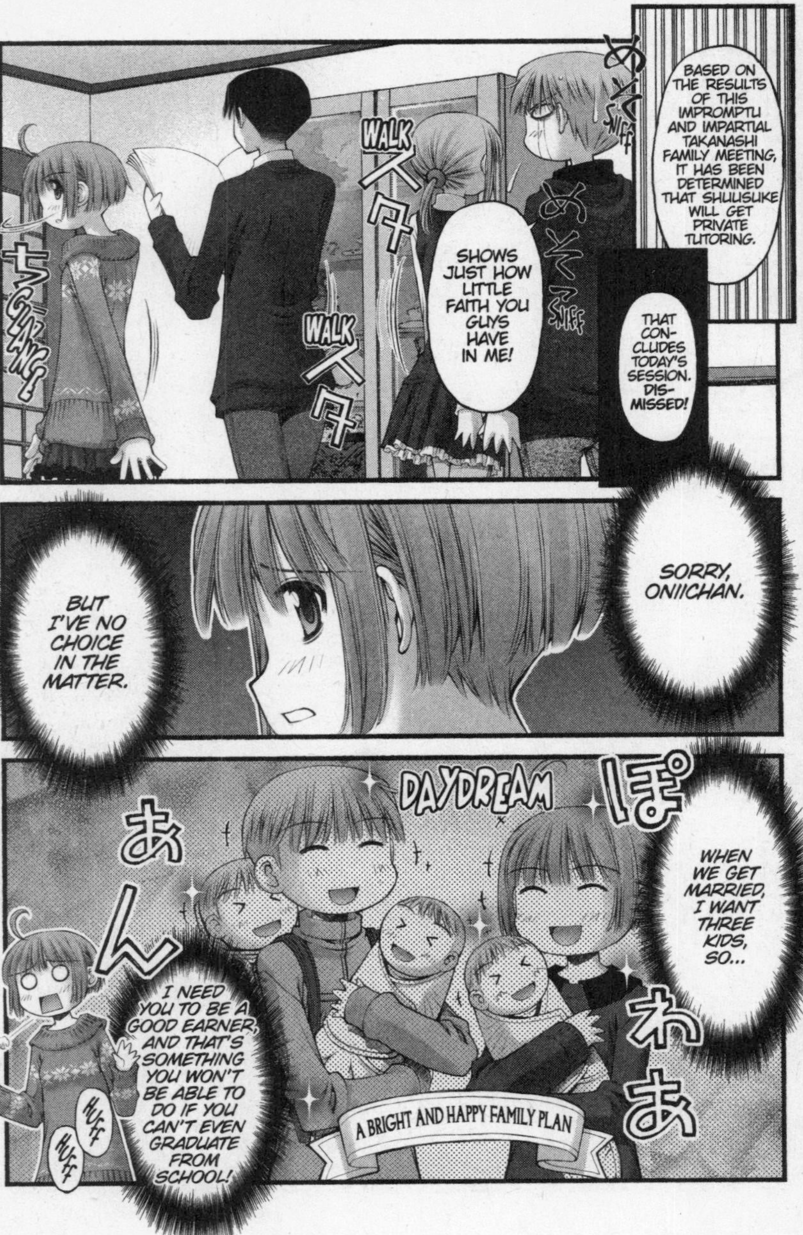

BASED ON THE RESULTS OF THIS IMPROMPTU AND IMPARTIAL TAKANASHI FAMILY MEETING, IT HAS BEEN DETERMINED THAT SHUUSUKE WILL GET PRIVATE TUTORING.
めそ SNIFF
THAT CON-CLUDES TODAY'S SESSION. DIS-MISSED!
めそ SNIFF
SHOWS JUST HOW LITTLE FAITH YOU GUYS HAVE IN ME!
WALK スタ
WALK スタ
GLANCE
SORRY, ONIICHAN.
BUT I'VE NO CHOICE IN THE MATTER.
ぽ
DAYDREAM
WHEN WE GET MARRIED, I WANT THREE KIDS, SO...
わあ
あん
I NEED YOU TO BE A GOOD EARNER, AND THAT'S SOMETHING YOU WON'T BE ABLE TO DO IF YOU CAN'T EVEN GRADUATE FROM SCHOOL!
HUFF
HUFF
A BRIGHT AND HAPPY FAMILY PLAN

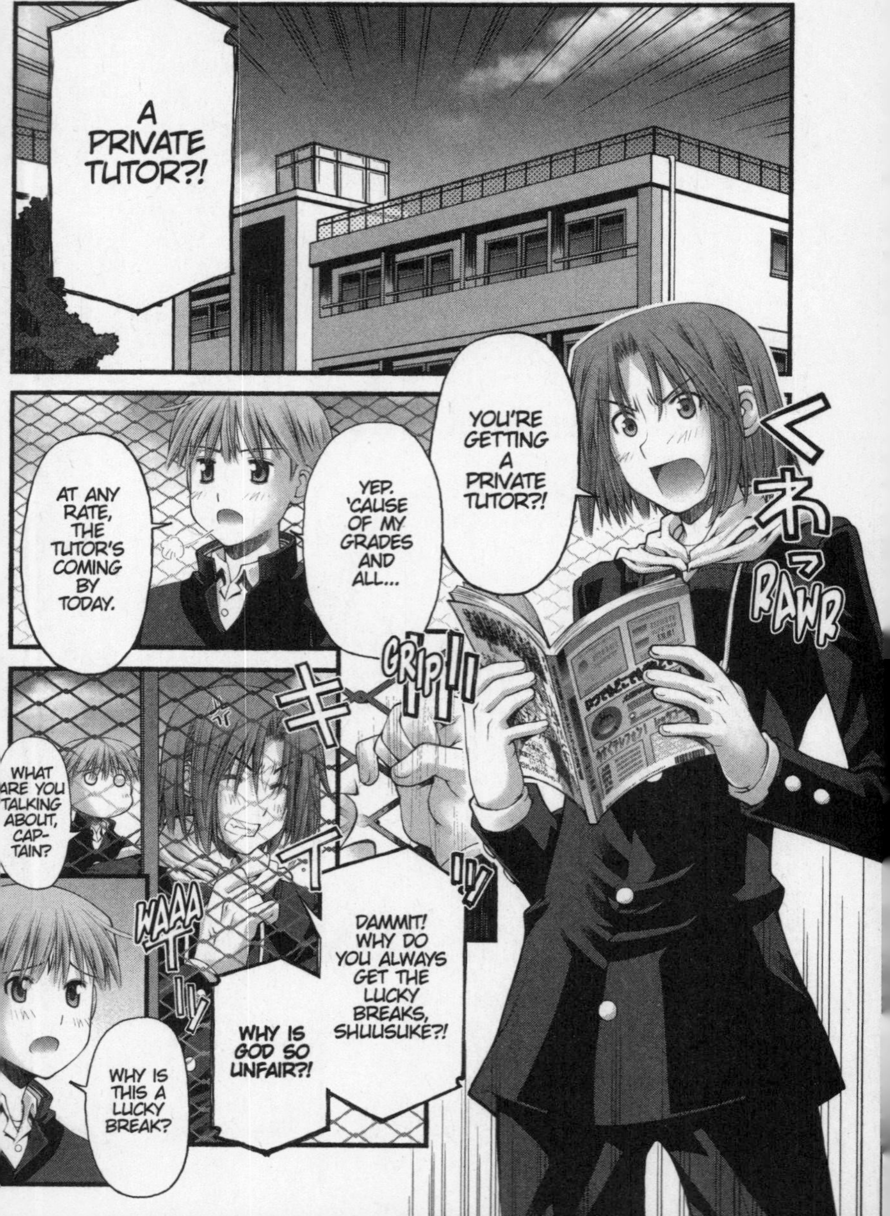
A PRIVATE TUTOR?!
YOU'RE GETTING A PRIVATE TUTOR?!
くわっ
RAWR
YEP. 'CAUSE OF MY GRADES AND ALL...
AT ANY RATE, THE TUTOR'S COMING BY TODAY.
GRIP
DAMMIT! WHY DO YOU ALWAYS GET THE LUCKY BREAKS, SHUUSUKE?!
WHY IS GOD SO UNFAIR?!
WAAA
WHAT ARE YOU TALKING ABOUT, CAPTAIN?
WHY IS THIS A LUCKY BREAK?

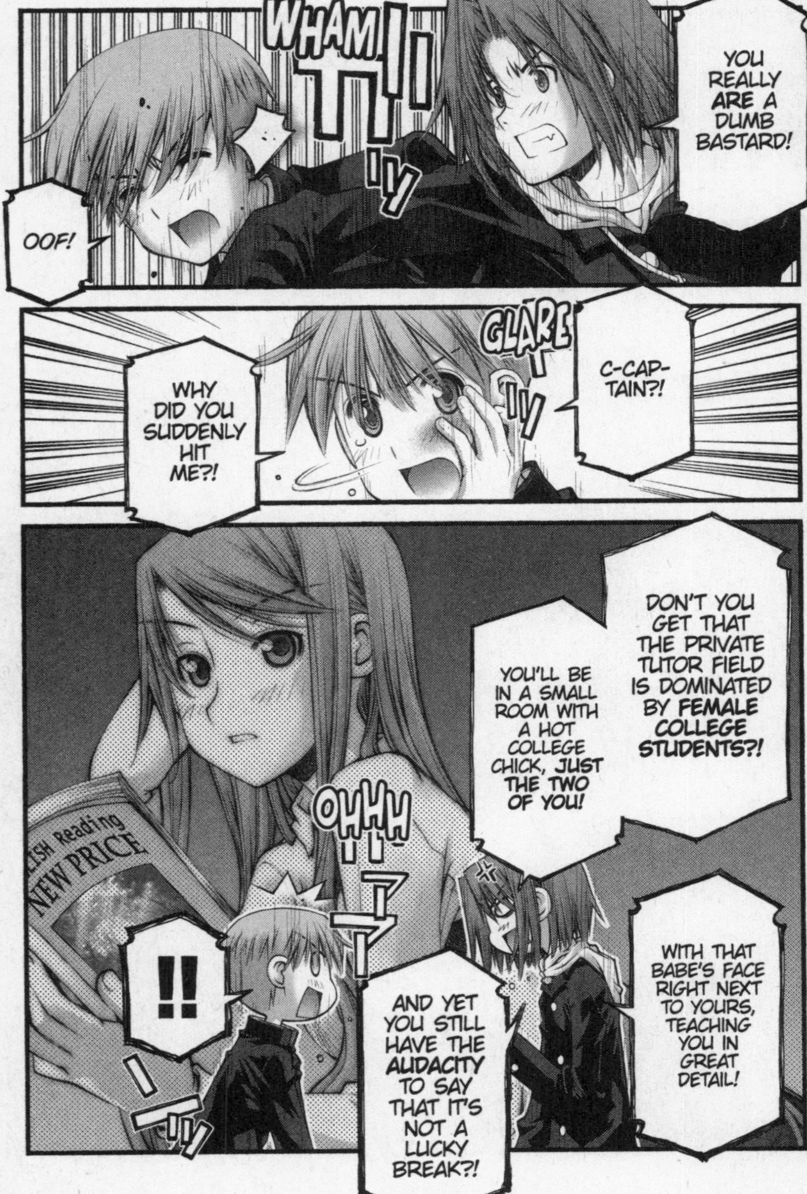
YOU REALLY ARE A DUMB BASTARD!
WHAM!!
OOF!
C-CAP-TAIN?!
GLARE
WHY DID YOU SUDDENLY HIT ME?!
DON'T YOU GET THAT THE PRIVATE TUTOR FIELD IS DOMINATED BY FEMALE COLLEGE STUDENTS?!
YOU'LL BE IN A SMALL ROOM WITH A HOT COLLEGE CHICK, JUST THE TWO OF YOU!
OHHH
Reading
NEW PRICE
WITH THAT BABE'S FACE RIGHT NEXT TO YOURS, TEACHING YOU IN GREAT DETAIL!
AND YET YOU STILL HAVE THE AUDACITY TO SAY THAT IT'S NOT A LUCKY BREAK?!
!!

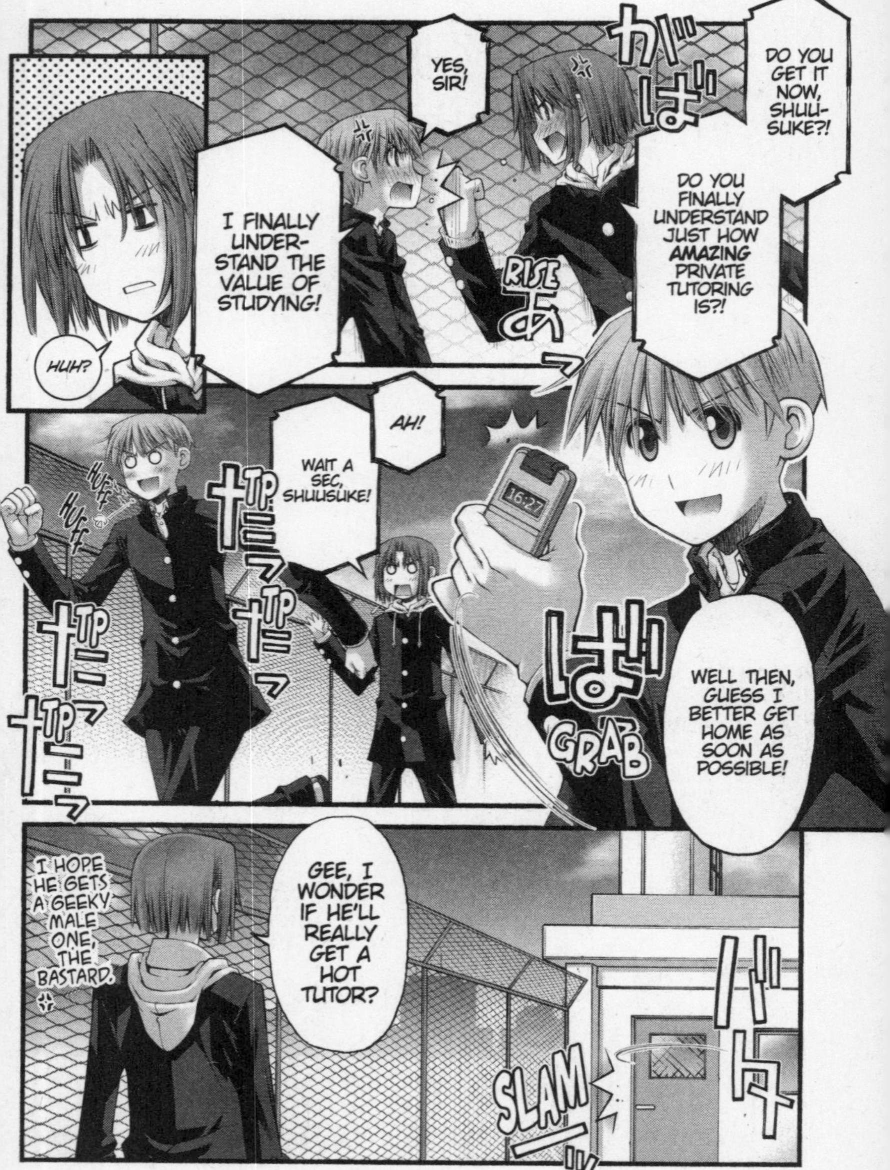
DO YOU GET IT NOW, SHUU-SUKE?!
DO YOU FINALLY UNDERSTAND JUST HOW AMAZING PRIVATE TUTORING IS?!
YES, SIR!
I FINALLY UNDER-STAND THE VALUE OF STUDYING!
RISE
HUH?
GRAB
WELL THEN, GUESS I BETTER GET HOME AS SOON AS POSSIBLE!
AH!
WAIT A SEC, SHUUSUKE!
HUFF
HUFF
TP
TP
TP
TP
16:27
SLAM
GEE, I WONDER IF HE'LL REALLY GET A HOT TUTOR?
I HOPE HE GETS A GEEKY MALE ONE, THE BASTARD.

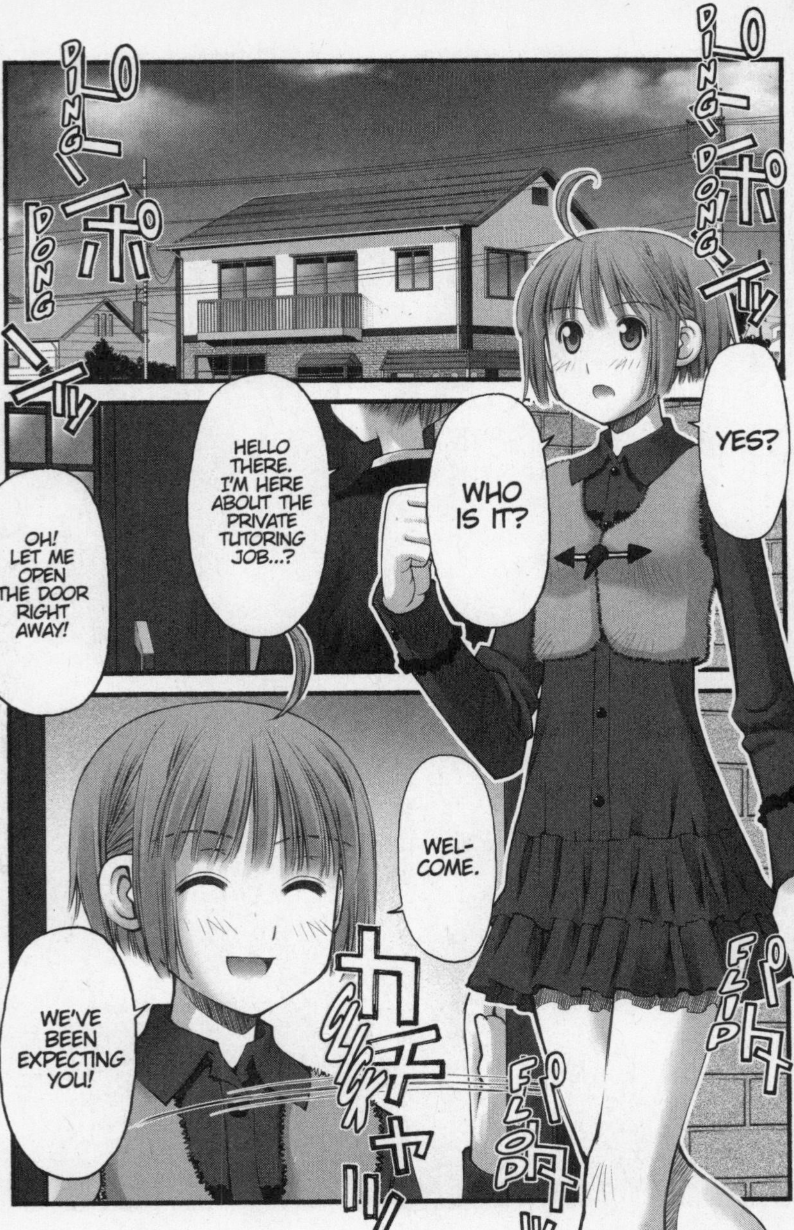
DING DONG
DING DONG
YES?
WHO IS IT?
HELLO THERE. I'M HERE ABOUT THE PRIVATE TUTORING JOB...?
OH! LET ME OPEN THE DOOR RIGHT AWAY!
FLIP
FLIP
WEL-COME.
CLICK
WE'VE BEEN EXPECTING YOU!

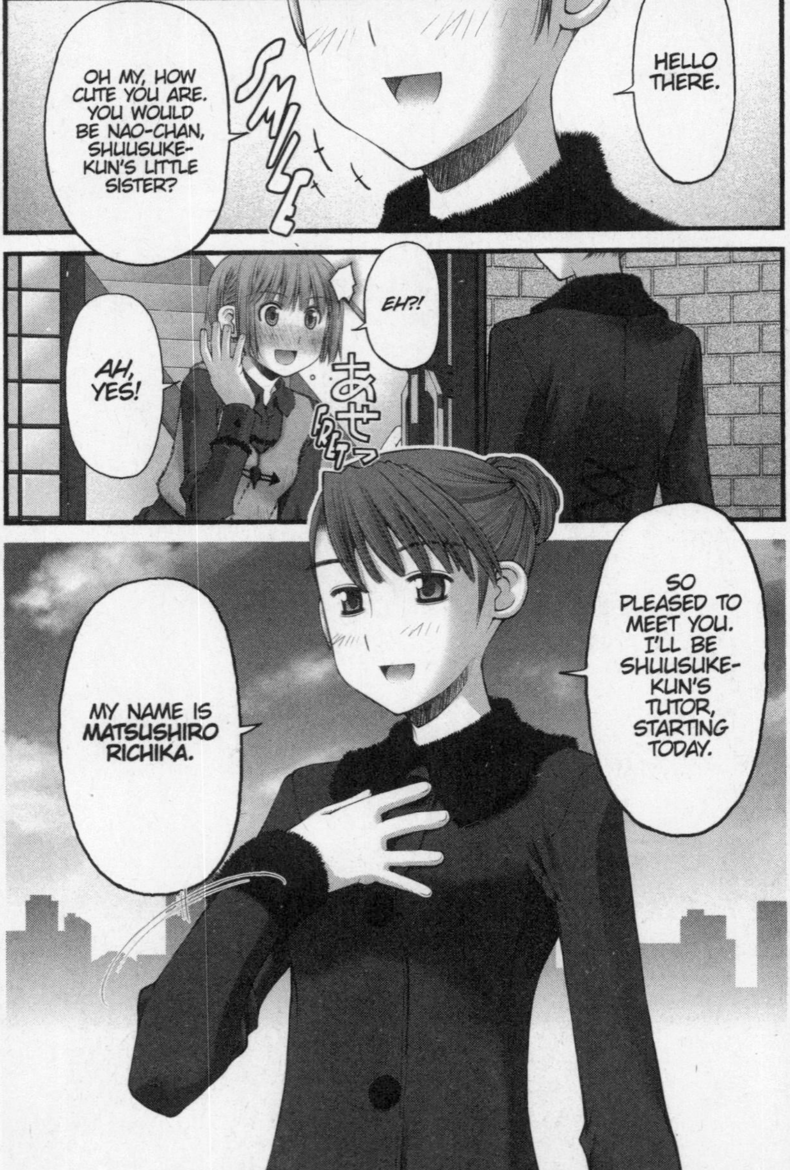
HELLO THERE.
SMILE
OH MY, HOW CUTE YOU ARE. YOU WOULD BE NAO-CHAN, SHUUSUKE-KUN'S LITTLE SISTER?
EH?!
あせっ
FRET
AH, YES!
SO PLEASED TO MEET YOU. I'LL BE SHUUSUKE-KUN'S TUTOR, STARTING TODAY.
MY NAME IS MATSUSHIRO RICHIKA.

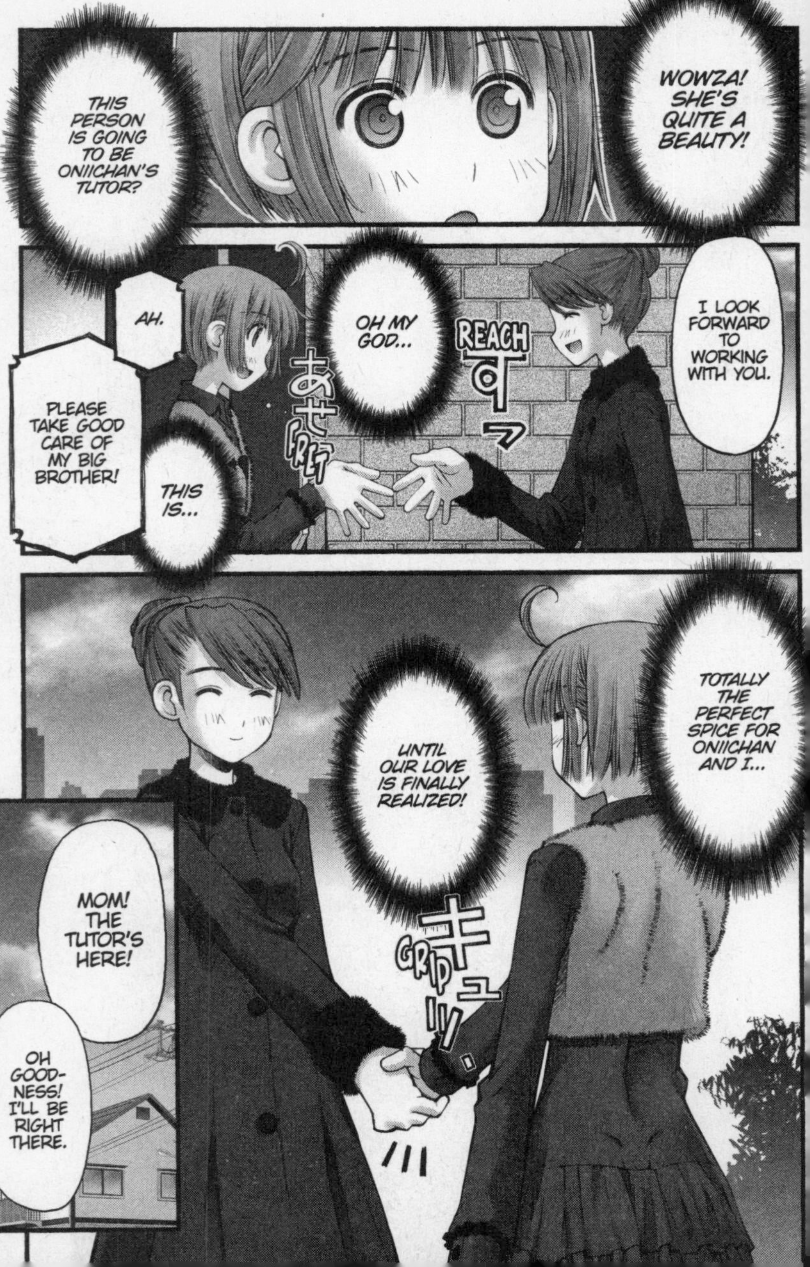
WOWZA! SHE'S QUITE A BEAUTY!
THIS PERSON IS GOING TO BE ONIICHAN'S TUTOR?
I LOOK FORWARD TO WORKING WITH YOU.
すっ REACH
OH MY GOD...
あせ FRET
THIS IS...
AH.
PLEASE TAKE GOOD CARE OF MY BIG BROTHER!
TOTALLY THE PERFECT SPICE FOR ONIICHAN AND I...
UNTIL OUR LOVE IS FINALLY REALIZED!
キュッ GRIP
MOM! THE TUTOR'S HERE!
OH GOODNESS! I'LL BE RIGHT THERE.

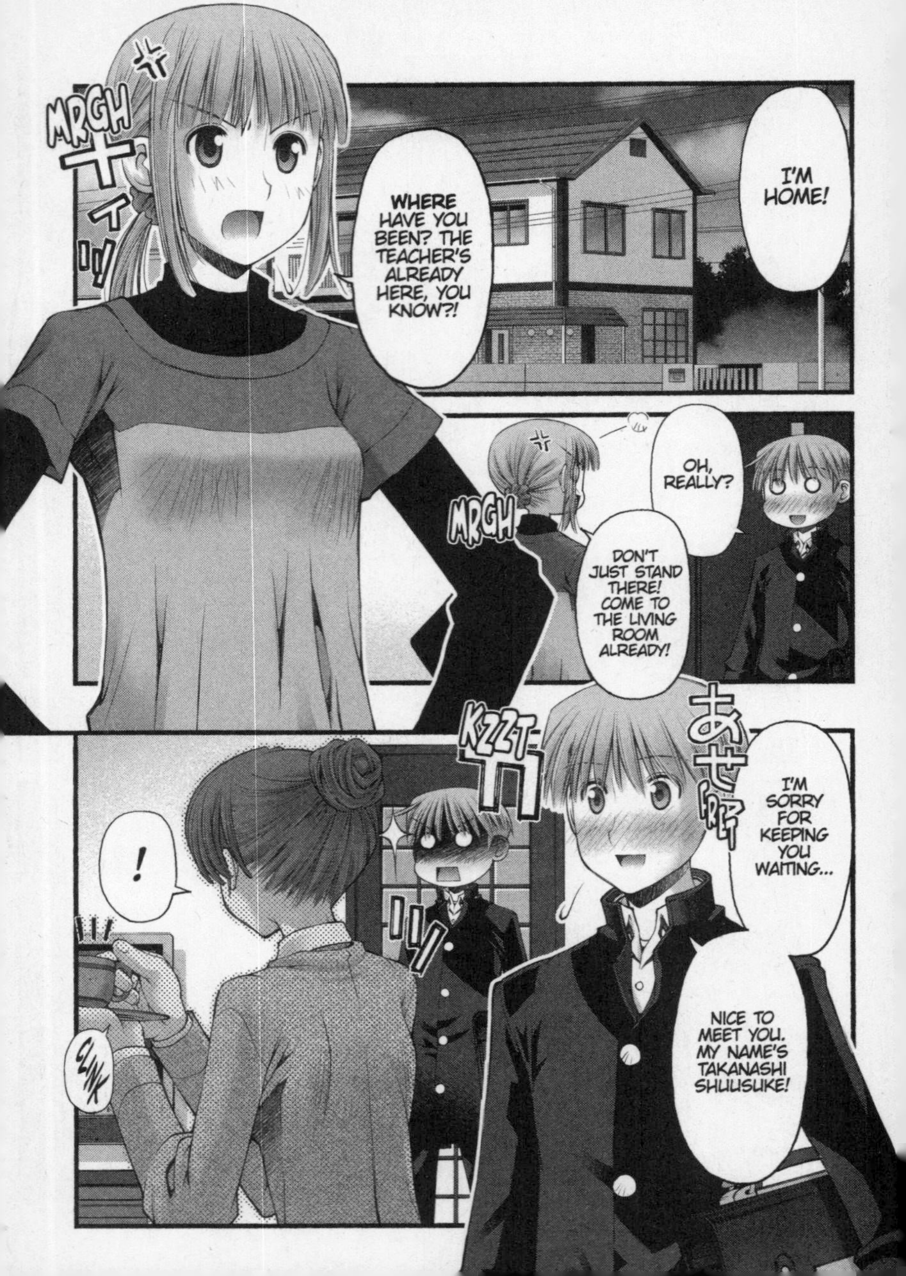
I'M HOME!
MRGH
WHERE HAVE YOU BEEN? THE TEACHER'S ALREADY HERE, YOU KNOW?!
OH, REALLY?
MRGH
DON'T JUST STAND THERE! COME TO THE LIVING ROOM ALREADY!
あせ
FRET
I'M SORRY FOR KEEPING YOU WAITING...
NICE TO MEET YOU. MY NAME'S TAKANASHI SHUUSUKE!
KZZT
!
CLINK

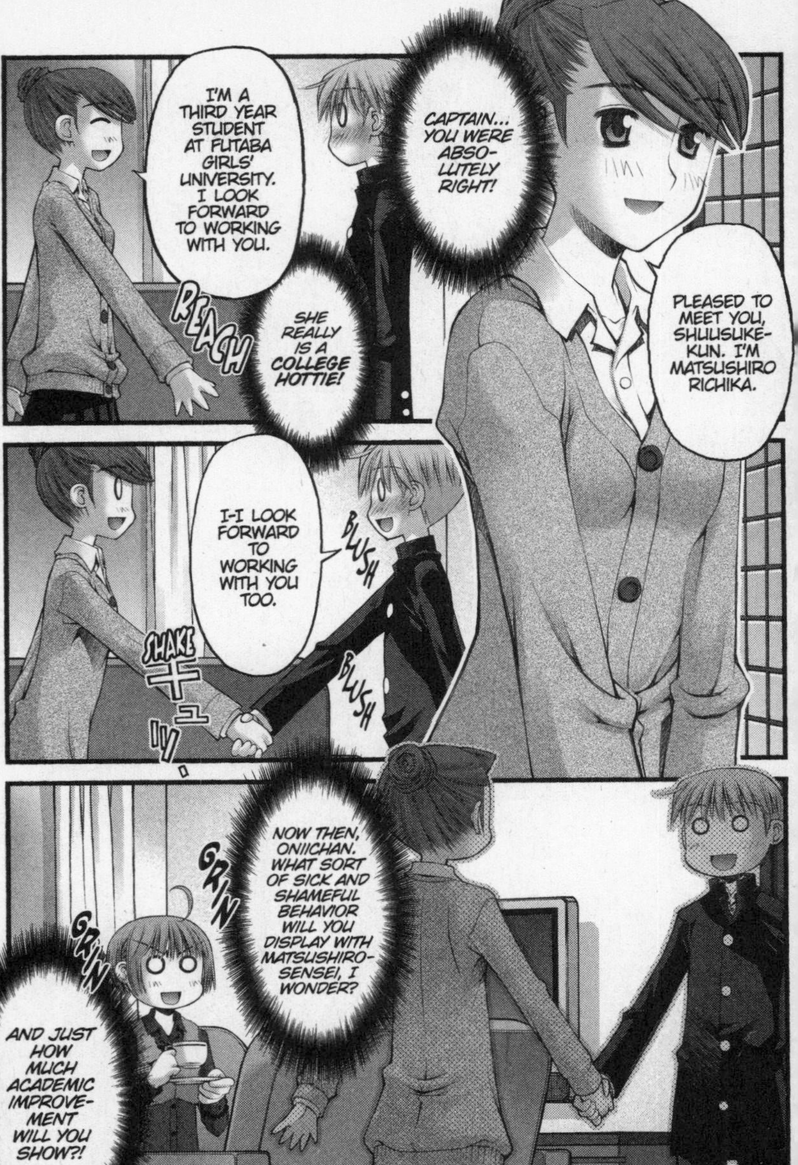
PLEASED TO MEET YOU, SHUUSUKE-KUN. I'M MATSUSHIRO RICHIKA.
CAPTAIN... YOU WERE ABSO-LUTELY RIGHT!
I'M A THIRD YEAR STUDENT AT FUTABA GIRLS' UNIVERSITY. I LOOK FORWARD TO WORKING WITH YOU.
SHE REALLY IS A COLLEGE HOTTIE!
REACH
I-I LOOK FORWARD TO WORKING WITH YOU TOO.
BLUSH
BLUSH
SHAKE
NOW THEN, ONIICHAN. WHAT SORT OF SICK AND SHAMEFUL BEHAVIOR WILL YOU DISPLAY WITH MATSUSHIRO-SENSEI, I WONDER?
GRIN
GRIN
AND JUST HOW MUCH ACADEMIC IMPROVE-MENT WILL YOU SHOW?!

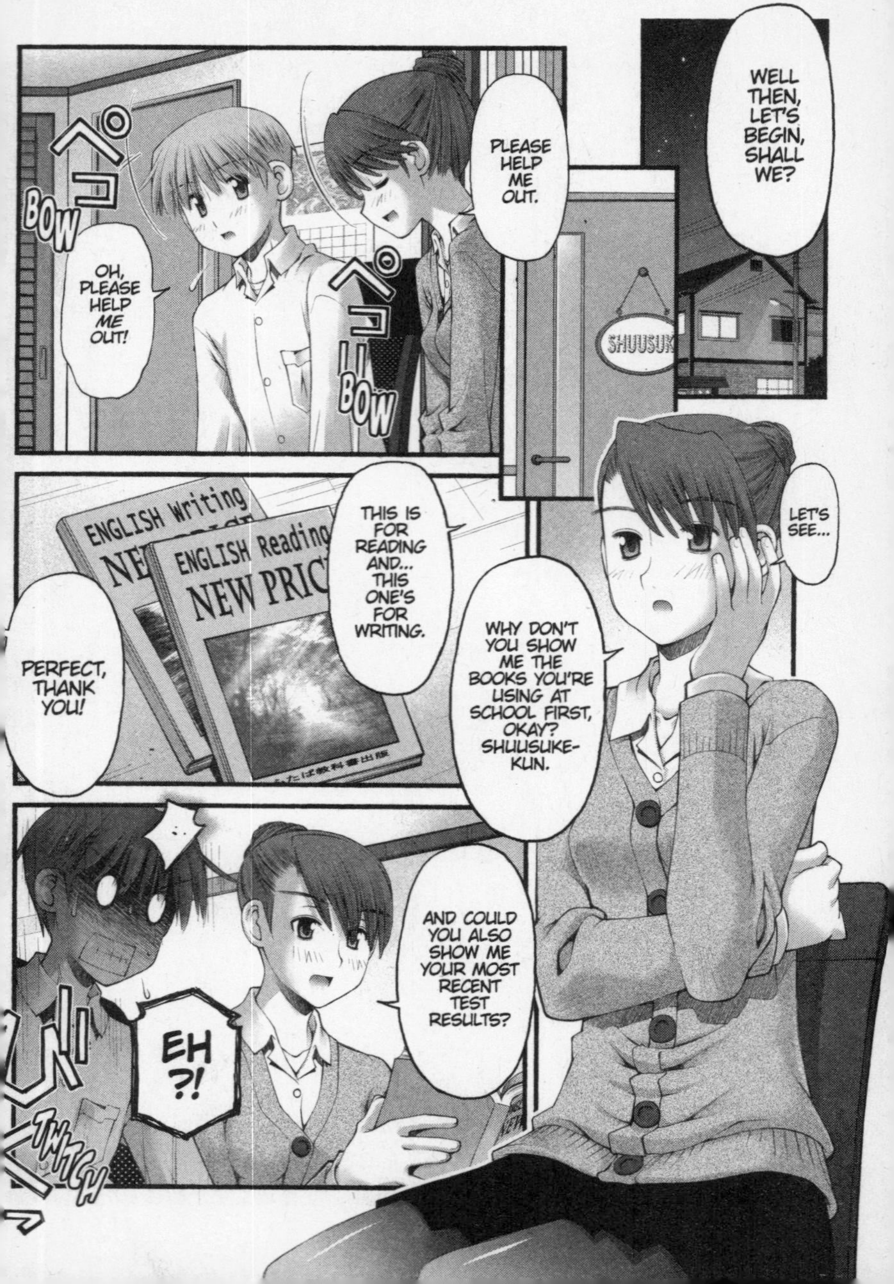
WELL THEN, LET'S BEGIN, SHALL WE?
SHUUSUK
PLEASE HELP ME OUT.
ペコ
BOW
OH, PLEASE HELP ME OUT!
ペコ
BOW
LET'S SEE...
WHY DON'T YOU SHOW ME THE BOOKS YOU'RE USING AT SCHOOL FIRST, OKAY? SHUUSUKE-KUN.
ENGLISH Writing
ENGLISH Reading
THIS IS FOR READING AND... THIS ONE'S FOR WRITING.
PERFECT, THANK YOU!
AND COULD YOU ALSO SHOW ME YOUR MOST RECENT TEST RESULTS?
EH ?!
TWITCH

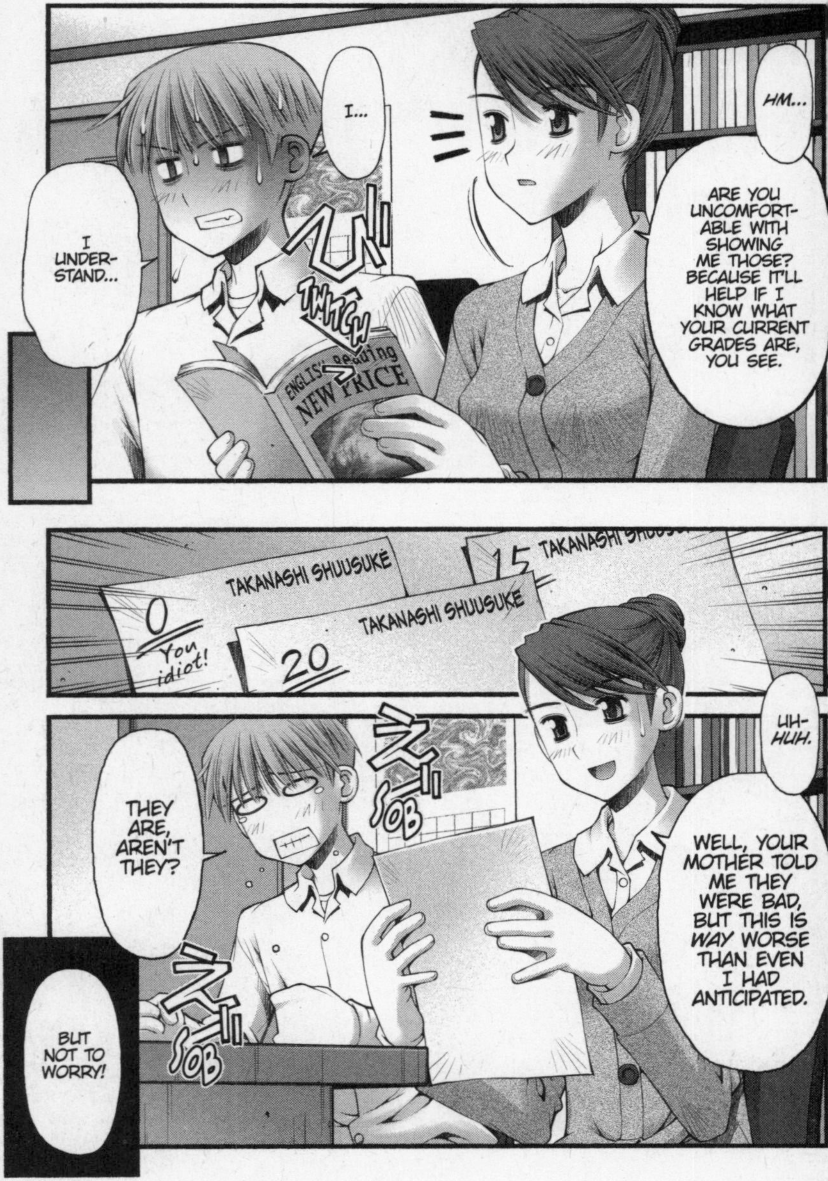
HM...
ARE YOU UNCOMFORTABLE WITH SHOWING ME THOSE? BECAUSE IT'LL HELP IF I KNOW WHAT YOUR CURRENT GRADES ARE, YOU SEE.
I...
TWITCH
ENGLISH Reading NEW PRICE
I UNDERSTAND...
TAKANASHI SHUUSUKE
15
TAKANASHI SHUUSUKE
0
You idiot!
TAKANASHI SHUUSUKE
20
UH-HUH.
WELL, YOUR MOTHER TOLD ME THEY WERE BAD, BUT THIS IS WAY WORSE THAN EVEN I HAD ANTICIPATED.
SOB
THEY ARE, AREN'T THEY?
SOB
BUT NOT TO WORRY!

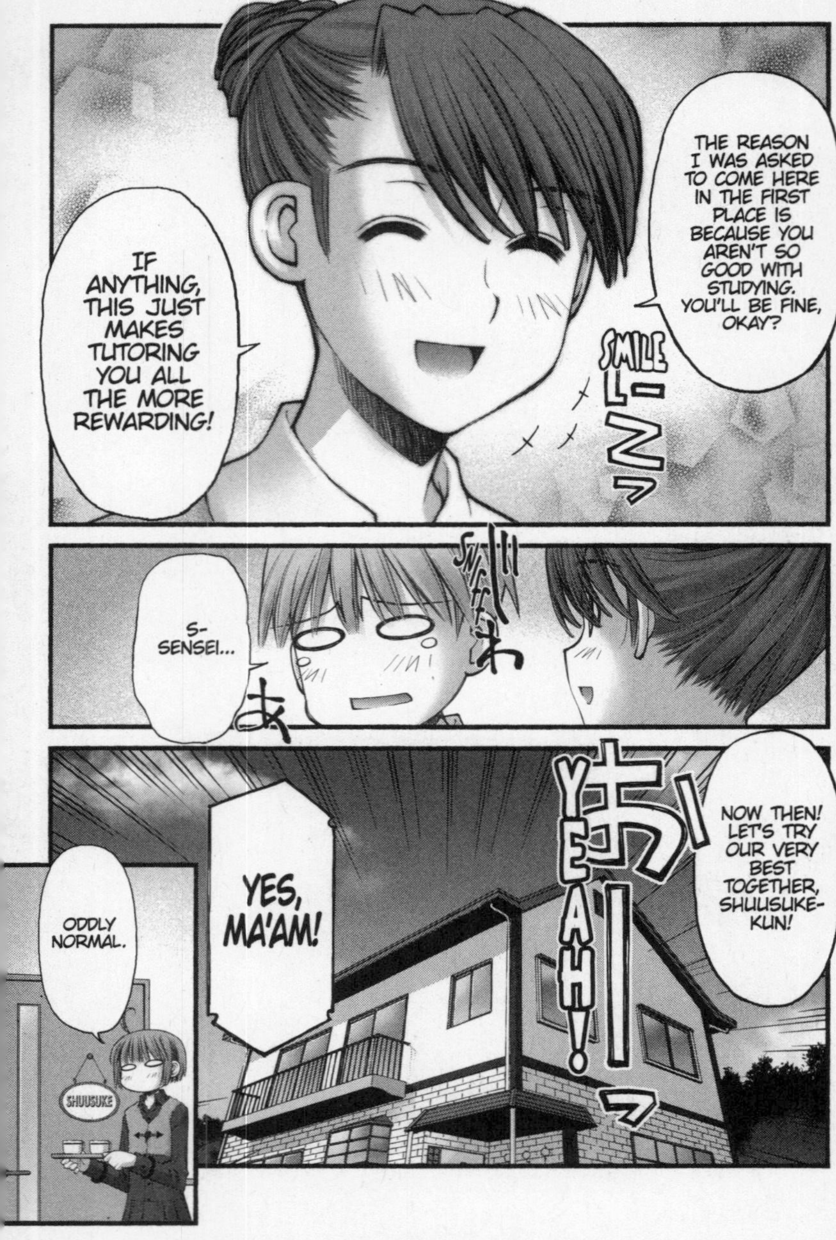
THE REASON I WAS ASKED TO COME HERE IN THE FIRST PLACE IS BECAUSE YOU AREN'T SO GOOD WITH STUDYING. YOU'LL BE FINE, OKAY?
SMILE
IF ANYTHING, THIS JUST MAKES TUTORING YOU ALL THE MORE REWARDING!
SNIFF
じわ
S-SENSEI...
あ
NOW THEN! LET'S TRY OUR VERY BEST TOGETHER, SHUUSUKE-KUN!
おー
YEAH!
YES, MA'AM!
ODDLY NORMAL.
SHUUSUKE

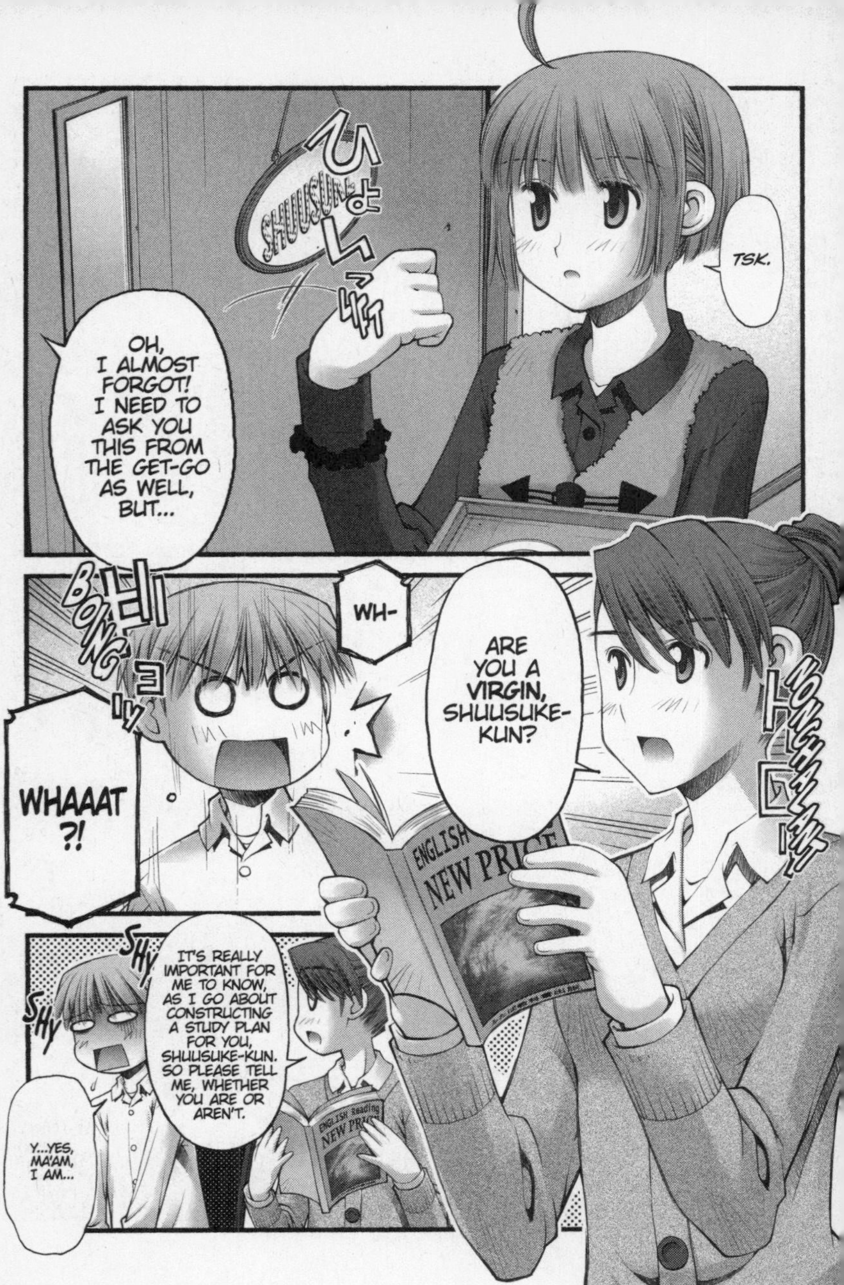
TSK.
SHUUSUN
OH, I ALMOST FORGOT! I NEED TO ASK YOU THIS FROM THE GET-GO AS WELL, BUT...
NONCHALANT
ARE YOU A VIRGIN, SHUUSUKE-KUN?
WH-
BONG
WHAAAT ?!
ENGLISH
NEW PRICE
IT'S REALLY IMPORTANT FOR ME TO KNOW, AS I GO ABOUT CONSTRUCTING A STUDY PLAN FOR YOU, SHUUSUKE-KUN. SO PLEASE TELL ME, WHETHER YOU ARE OR AREN'T.
SHY
SHY
Y...YES, MA'AM, I AM...

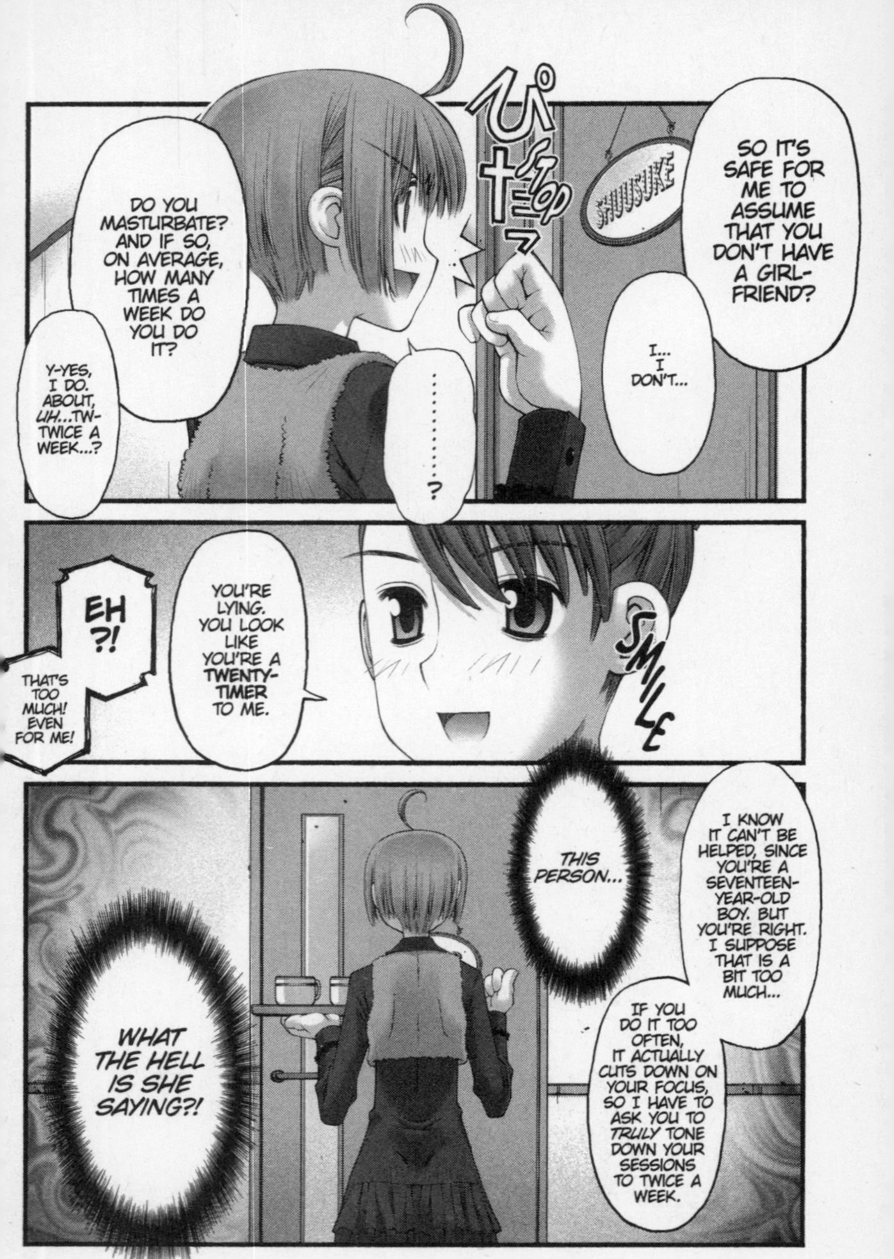
SO IT'S SAFE FOR ME TO ASSUME THAT YOU DON'T HAVE A GIRL-FRIEND?
I... I DON'T...
SHUUSUKE
STOP
......?
DO YOU MASTURBATE? AND IF SO, ON AVERAGE, HOW MANY TIMES A WEEK DO YOU DO IT?
Y-YES, I DO. ABOUT, *UH*...TW-TWICE A WEEK...?
SMILE
YOU'RE LYING. YOU LOOK LIKE YOU'RE A **TWENTY-TIMER** TO ME.
EH?!
THAT'S TOO MUCH! EVEN FOR ME!
I KNOW IT CAN'T BE HELPED, SINCE YOU'RE A SEVENTEEN-YEAR-OLD BOY. BUT YOU'RE RIGHT. I SUPPOSE THAT IS A BIT TOO MUCH...
IF YOU DO IT TOO OFTEN, IT ACTUALLY CUTS DOWN ON YOUR FOCUS, SO I HAVE TO ASK YOU TO *TRULY* TONE DOWN YOUR SESSIONS TO TWICE A WEEK.
THIS PERSON...
WHAT THE HELL IS SHE SAYING?!

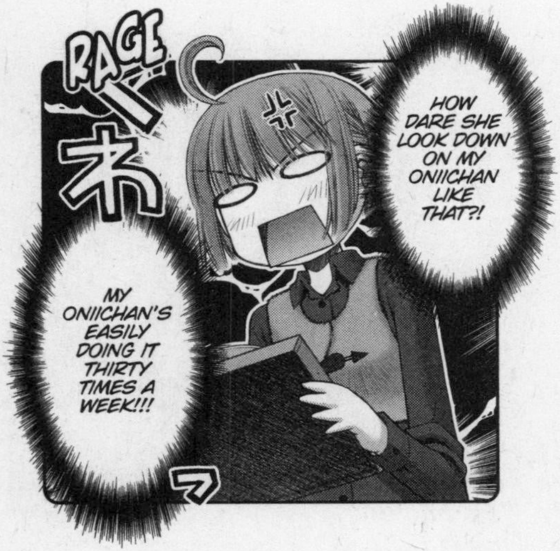
RAGE
HOW DARE SHE LOOK DOWN ON MY ONIICHAN LIKE THAT?!
MY ONIICHAN'S EASILY DOING IT THIRTY TIMES A WEEK!!!

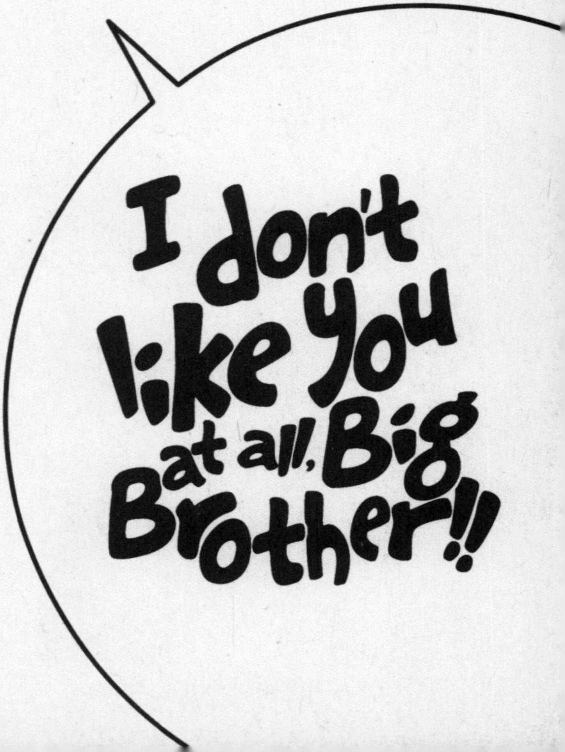
I don't like you at all, Big Brother!!

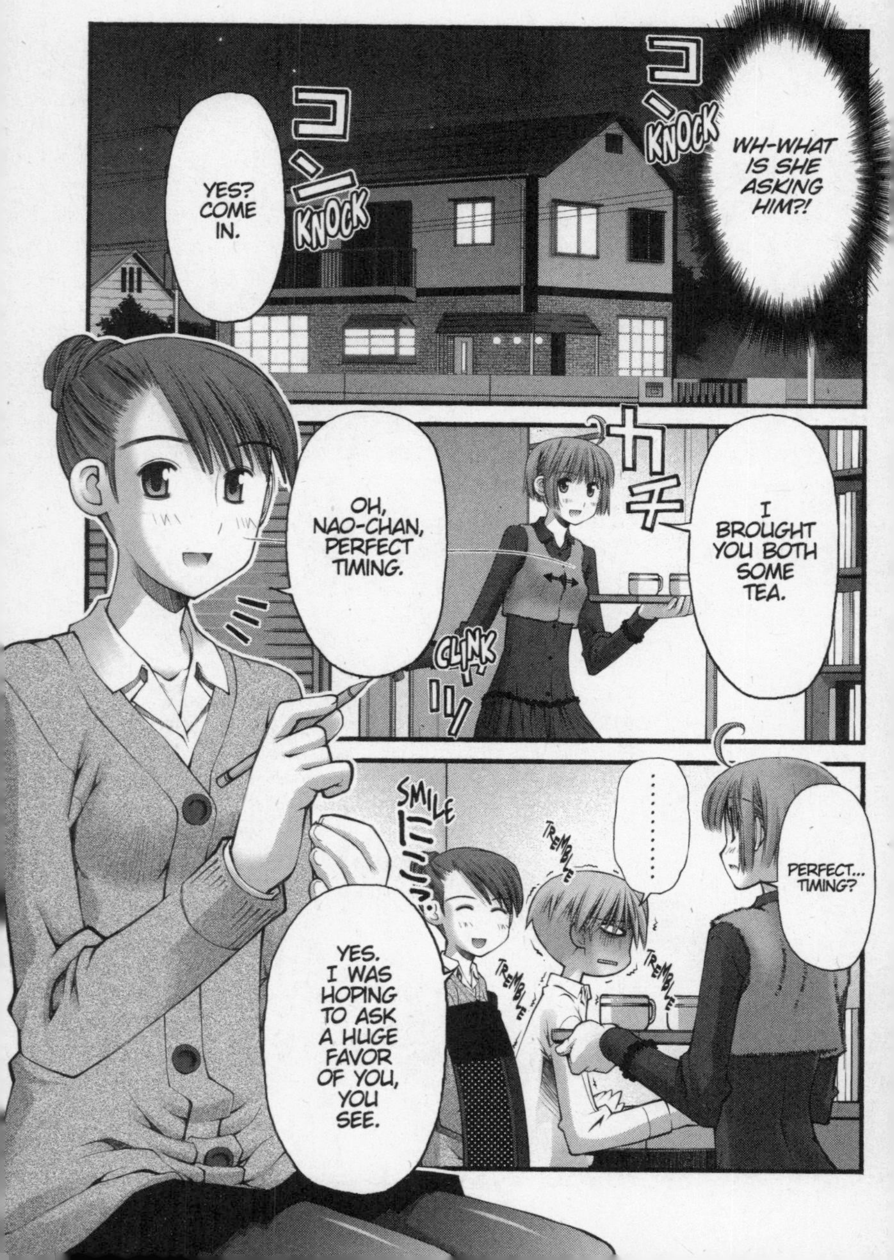

コン
KNOCK
WH-WHAT IS SHE ASKING HIM?!
コン
KNOCK
YES? COME IN.
I BROUGHT YOU BOTH SOME TEA.
カチ
OH, NAO-CHAN, PERFECT TIMING.
CLINK
PERFECT... TIMING?
......
TREMBLE
TREMBLE
TREMBLE
SMILE
YES. I WAS HOPING TO ASK A HUGE FAVOR OF YOU, YOU SEE.

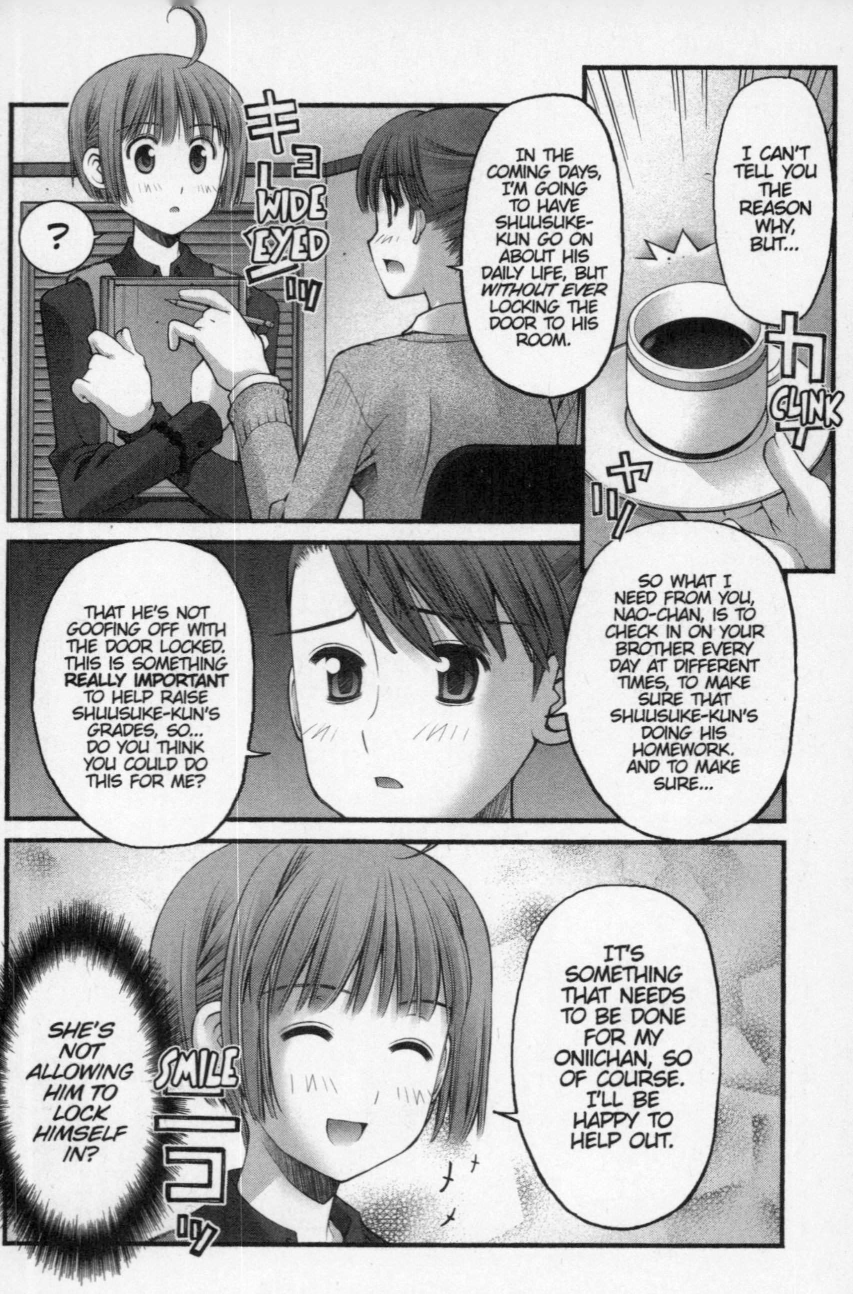

I CAN'T TELL YOU THE REASON WHY, BUT...
CLINK
IN THE COMING DAYS, I'M GOING TO HAVE SHUUSUKE-KUN GO ON ABOUT HIS DAILY LIFE, BUT *WITHOUT EVER* LOCKING THE DOOR TO HIS ROOM.
WIDE EYED
?
SO WHAT I NEED FROM YOU, NAO-CHAN, IS TO CHECK IN ON YOUR BROTHER EVERY DAY AT DIFFERENT TIMES, TO MAKE SURE THAT SHUUSUKE-KUN'S DOING HIS HOMEWORK. AND TO MAKE SURE...
THAT HE'S NOT GOOFING OFF WITH THE DOOR LOCKED. THIS IS SOMETHING **REALLY IMPORTANT** TO HELP RAISE SHUUSUKE-KUN'S GRADES, SO... DO YOU THINK YOU COULD DO THIS FOR ME?
IT'S SOMETHING THAT NEEDS TO BE DONE FOR MY ONIICHAN, SO OF COURSE. I'LL BE HAPPY TO HELP OUT.
SMILE
SHE'S NOT ALLOWING HIM TO LOCK HIMSELF IN?

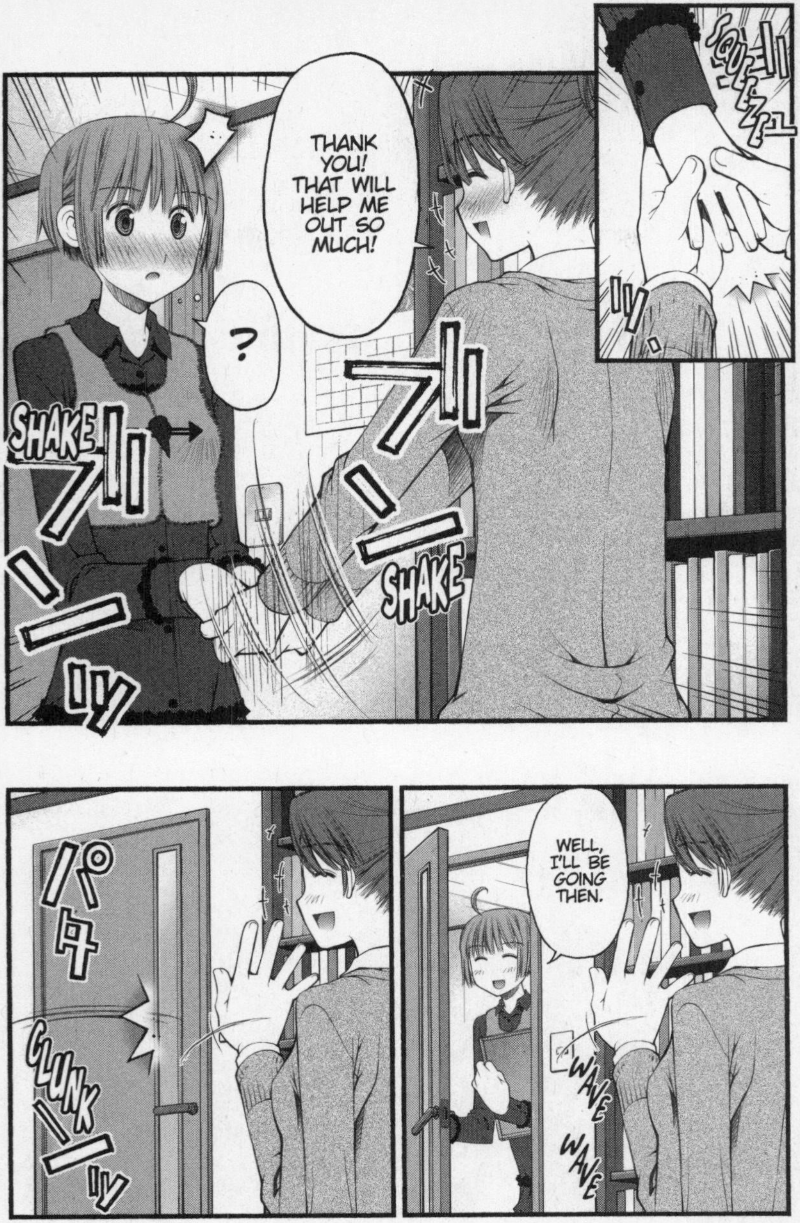
SQUEEZE
THANK YOU! THAT WILL HELP ME OUT SO MUCH!
?
SHAKE
SHAKE
WELL, I'LL BE GOING THEN.
WAVE
WAVE
CLUNK

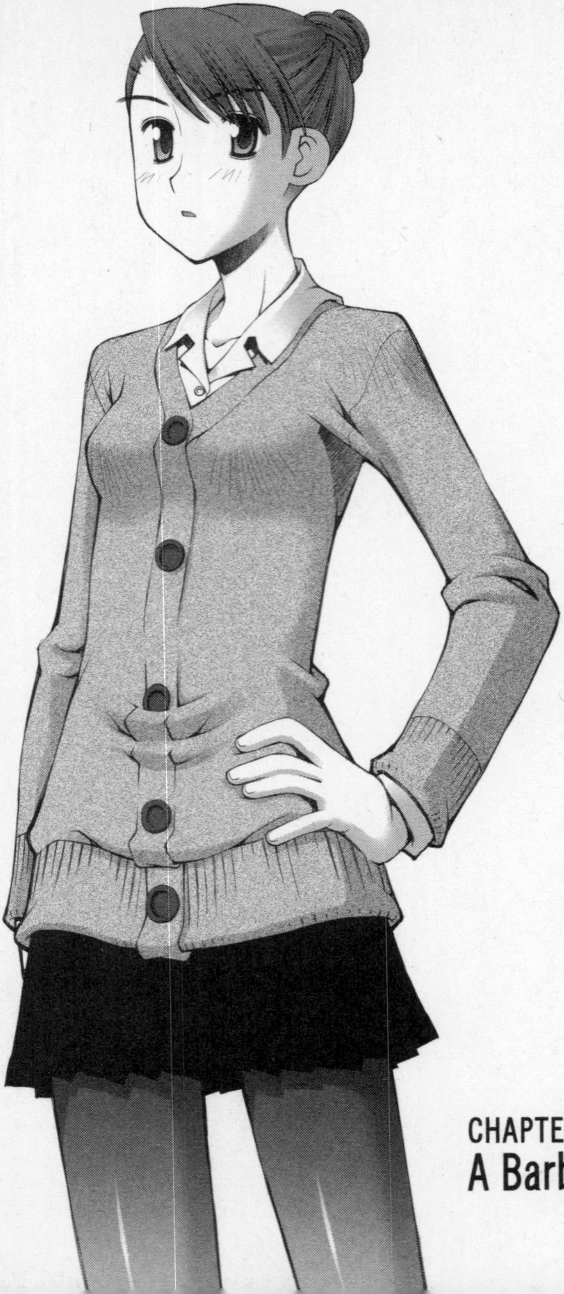

CHAPTER 39
A Barbaric Tutor

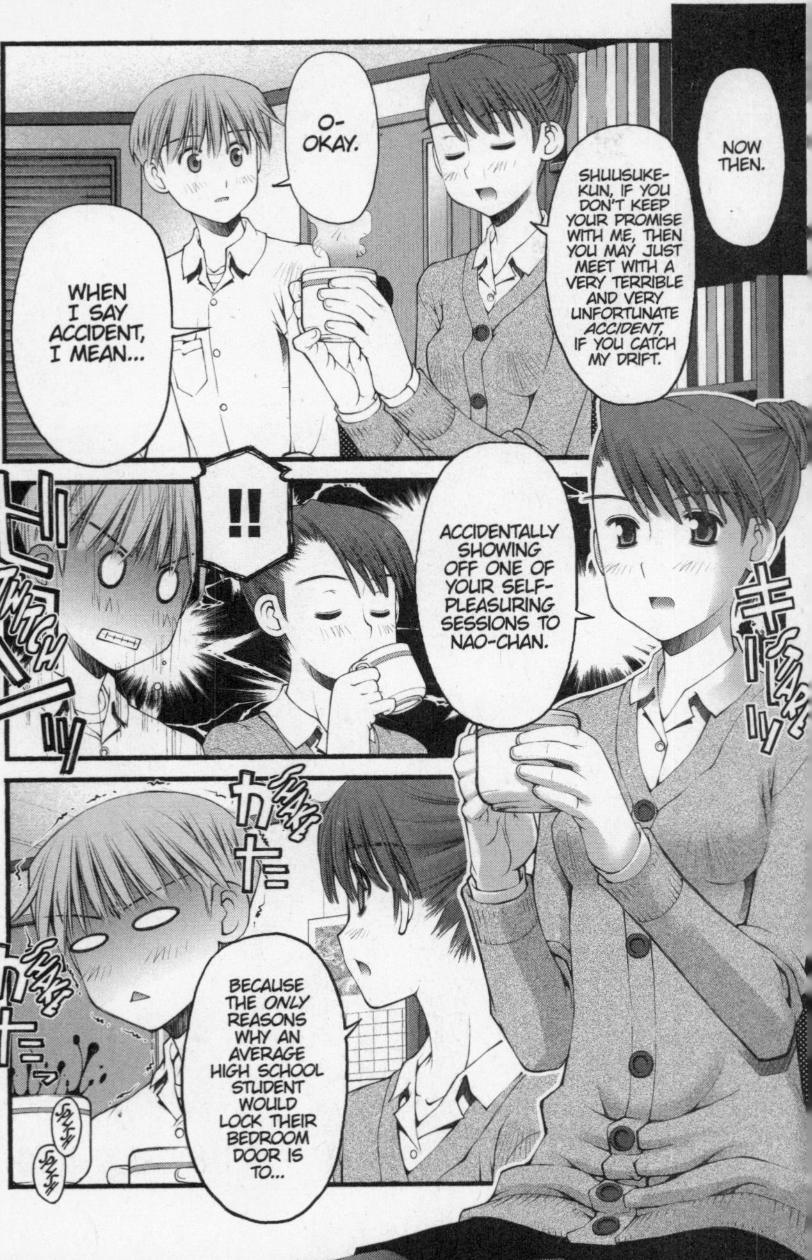
NOW THEN.
SHUUSUKE-KUN, IF YOU DON'T KEEP YOUR PROMISE WITH ME, THEN YOU MAY JUST MEET WITH A VERY TERRIBLE AND VERY UNFORTUNATE *ACCIDENT,* IF YOU CATCH MY DRIFT.
O-OKAY.
WHEN I SAY ACCIDENT, I MEAN...
ACCIDENTALLY SHOWING OFF ONE OF YOUR SELF-PLEASURING SESSIONS TO NAO-CHAN.
SCARE
!!
TWITCH
SHAKE
SHAKE
BECAUSE THE *ONLY* REASONS WHY AN AVERAGE HIGH SCHOOL STUDENT WOULD LOCK THEIR BEDROOM DOOR IS TO...

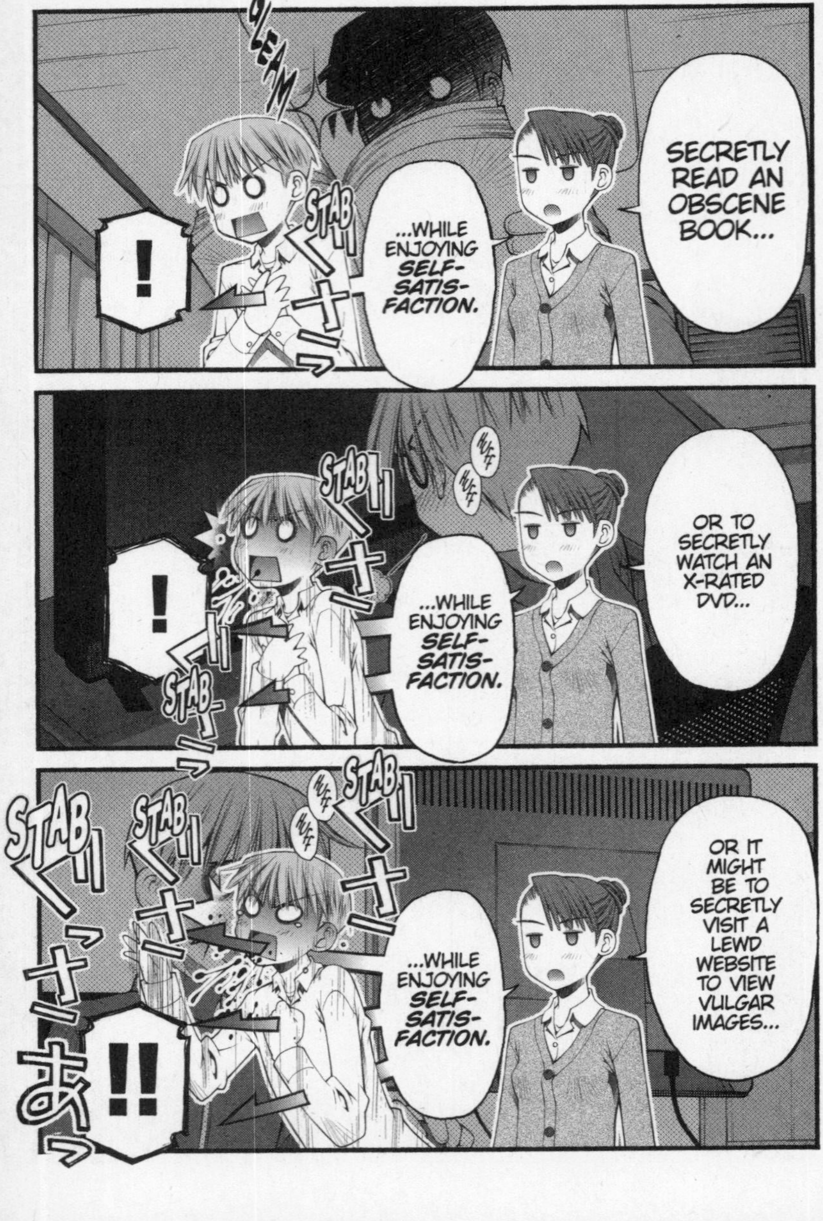

SECRETLY READ AN OBSCENE BOOK...
...WHILE ENJOYING SELF-SATIS-FACTION.
GLEAM
STAB
!
OR TO SECRETLY WATCH AN X-RATED DVD...
...WHILE ENJOYING SELF-SATIS-FACTION.
HUFF HUFF
STAB
STAB
!
OR IT MIGHT BE TO SECRETLY VISIT A LEWD WEBSITE TO VIEW VULGAR IMAGES...
...WHILE ENJOYING SELF-SATIS-FACTION.
HUFF HUFF HUFF
STAB
STAB
STAB
!!

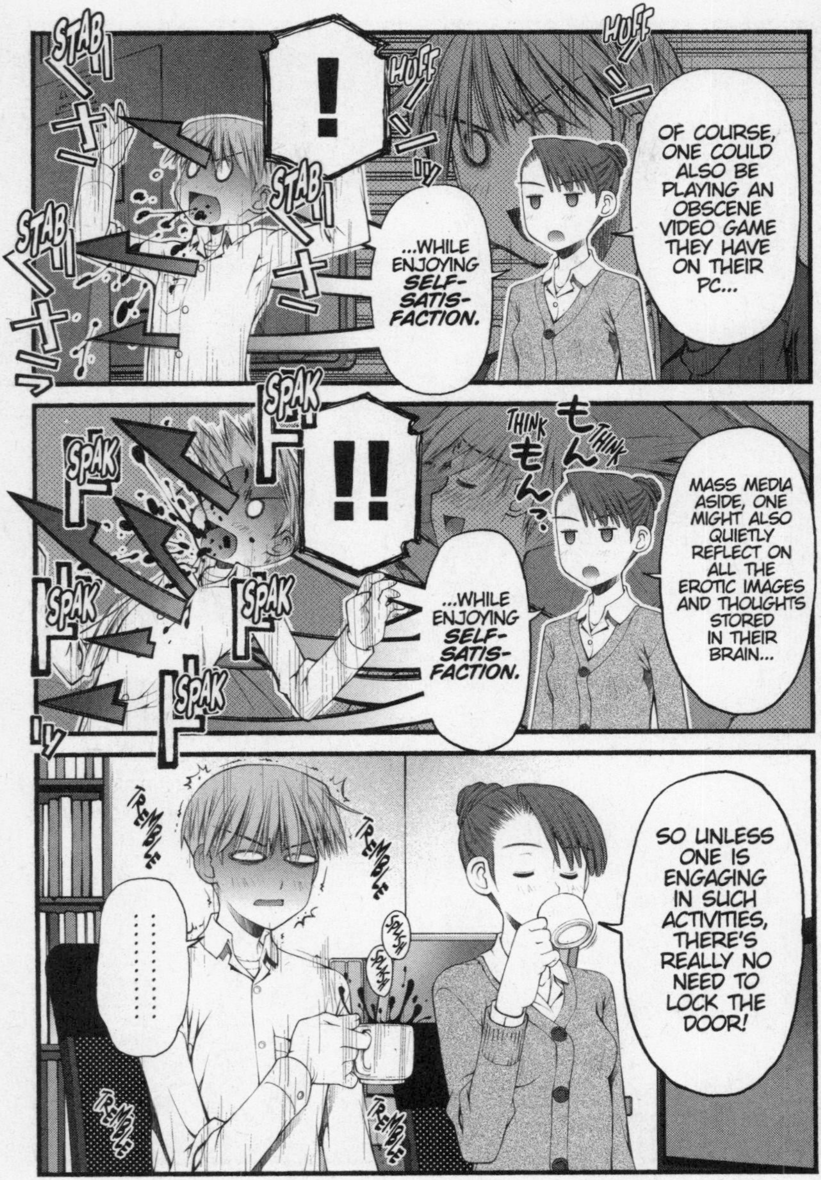
HUFF
OF COURSE, ONE COULD ALSO BE PLAYING AN OBSCENE VIDEO GAME THEY HAVE ON THEIR PC...
HUFF
...WHILE ENJOYING SELF-SATIS-FACTION.
!
STAB
STAB
STAB
THINK もん
THINK もんっ
MASS MEDIA ASIDE, ONE MIGHT ALSO QUIETLY REFLECT ON ALL THE EROTIC IMAGES AND THOUGHTS STORED IN THEIR BRAIN...
...WHILE ENJOYING SELF-SATIS-FACTION.
!!
SPAK
SPAK
SPAK
SPAK
SPAK
SO UNLESS ONE IS ENGAGING IN SUCH ACTIVITIES, THERE'S REALLY NO NEED TO LOCK THE DOOR!
TREMBLE
TREMBLE
SPLISH
SPLISH
......
TREMBLE
TREMBLE

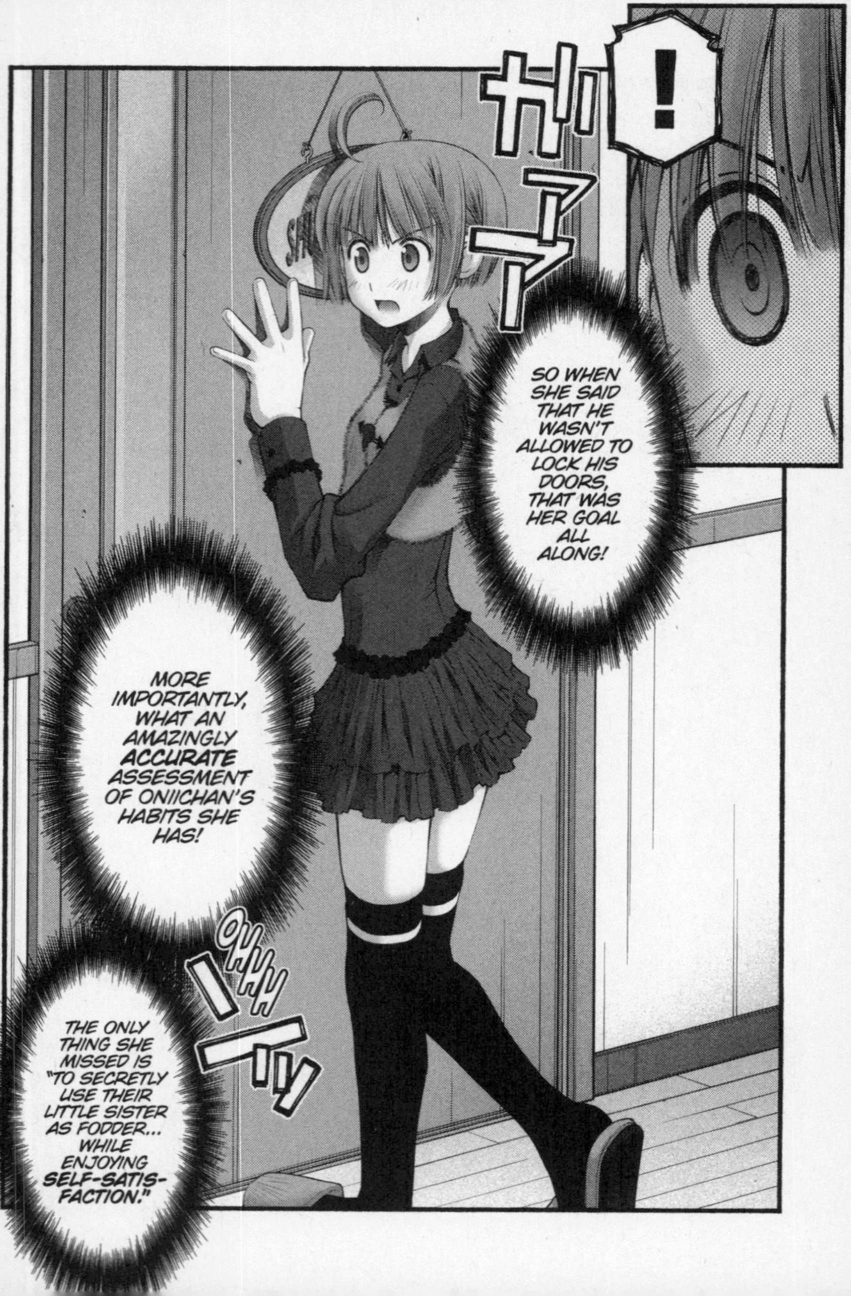
!
SO WHEN SHE SAID THAT HE WASN'T ALLOWED TO LOCK HIS DOORS, THAT WAS HER GOAL ALL ALONG!
MORE IMPORTANTLY, WHAT AN AMAZINGLY **ACCURATE** ASSESSMENT OF ONIICHAN'S HABITS SHE HAS!
OHHH
THE ONLY THING SHE MISSED IS "TO SECRETLY USE THEIR LITTLE SISTER AS FODDER... WHILE ENJOYING **SELF-SATIS-FACTION.**"

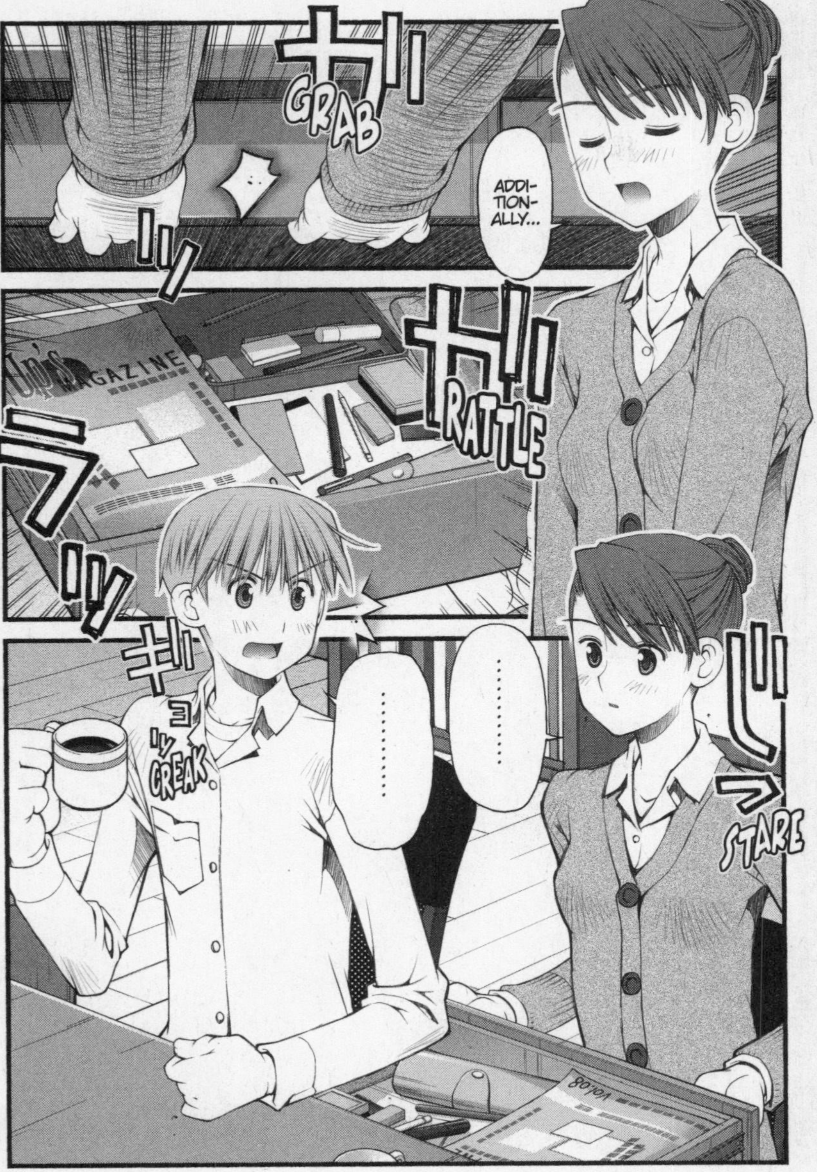
ADDI-TION-ALLY...
GRAB
MAGAZINE
RATTLE
STARE
......
......
CREAK

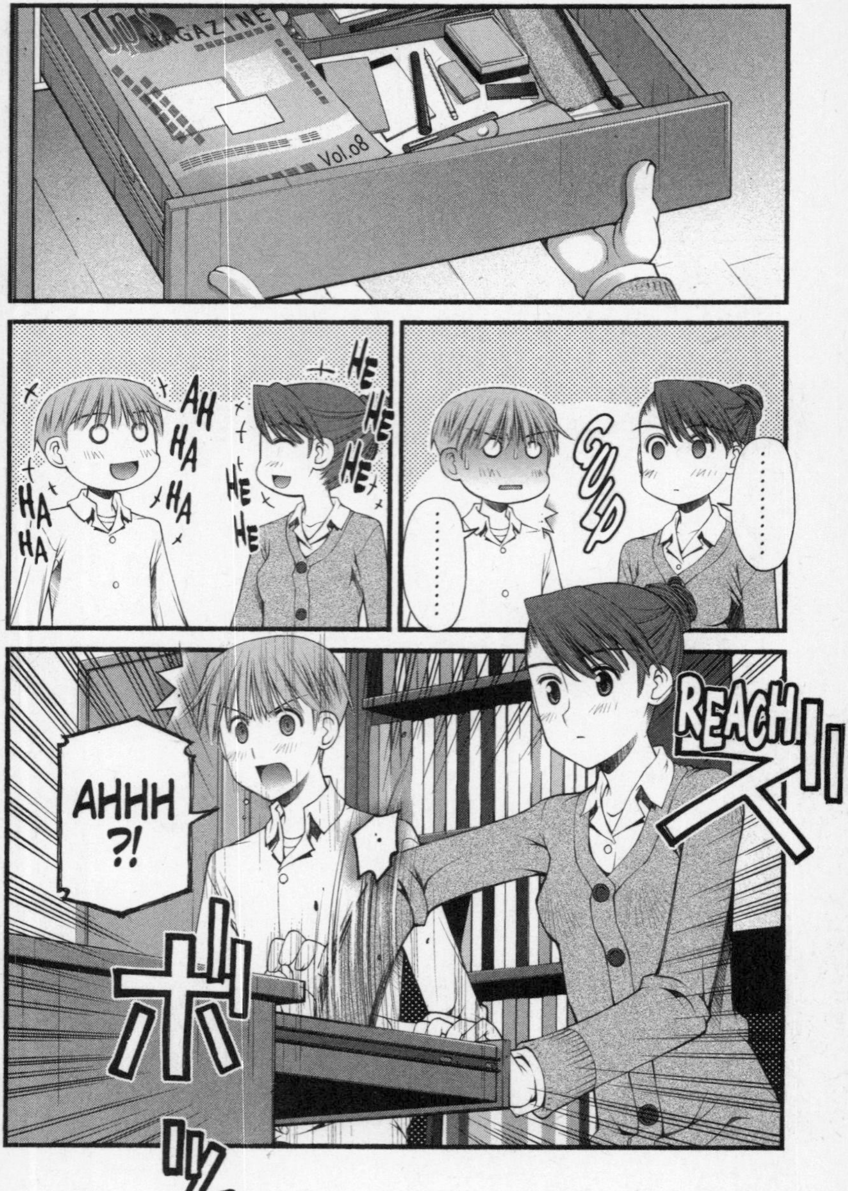
MAGAZINE
Vol.08
GULP
......
......
HE HE HE
HE HE
AH HA HA HA
HA HA
REACH
AHHH ?!

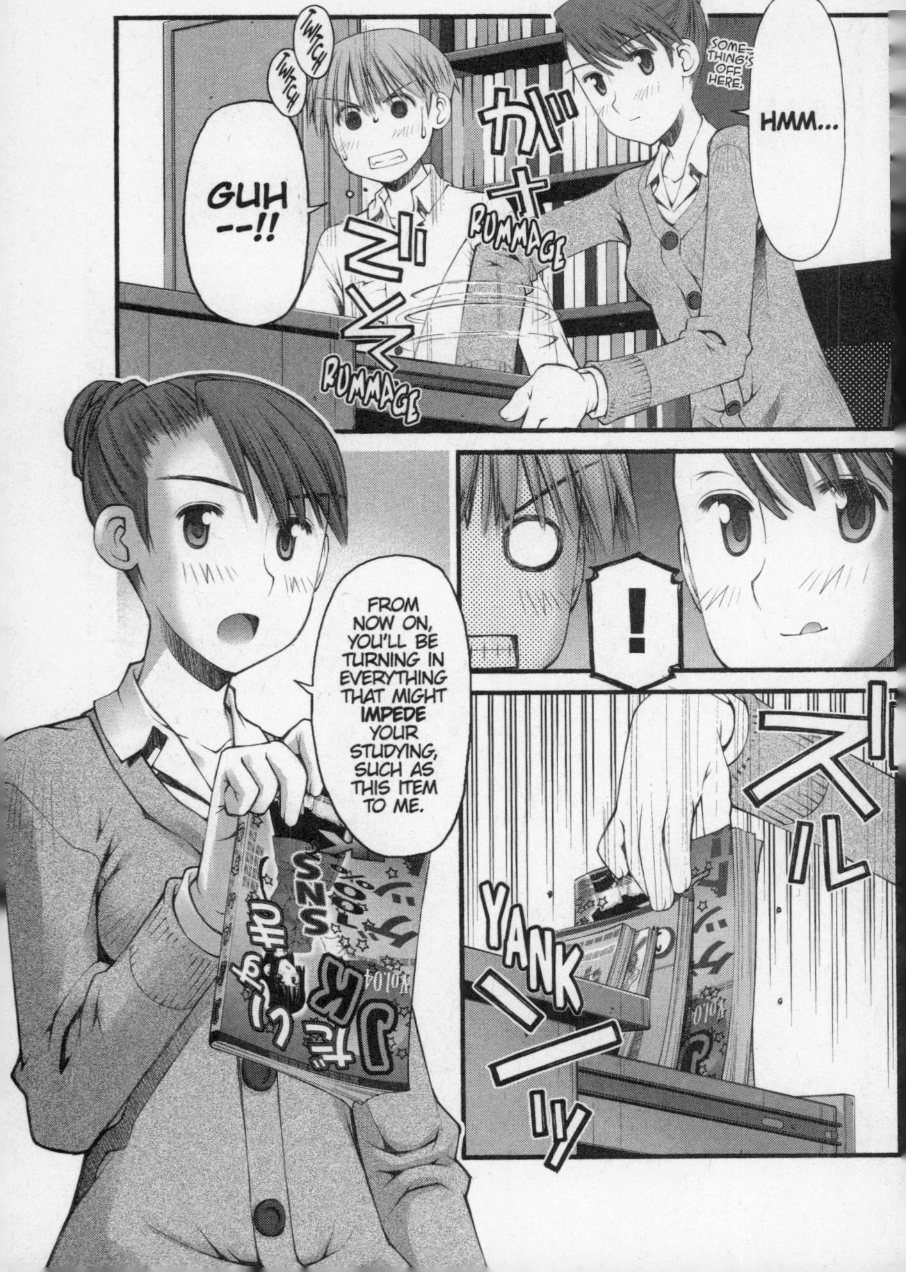

HMM...
SOME-THING'S OFF HERE.
RUMMAGE
TWITCH
TWITCH
GUH--!!
RUMMAGE
!
YANK
FROM NOW ON, YOU'LL BE TURNING IN EVERYTHING THAT MIGHT IMPEDE YOUR STUDYING, SUCH AS THIS ITEM TO ME.

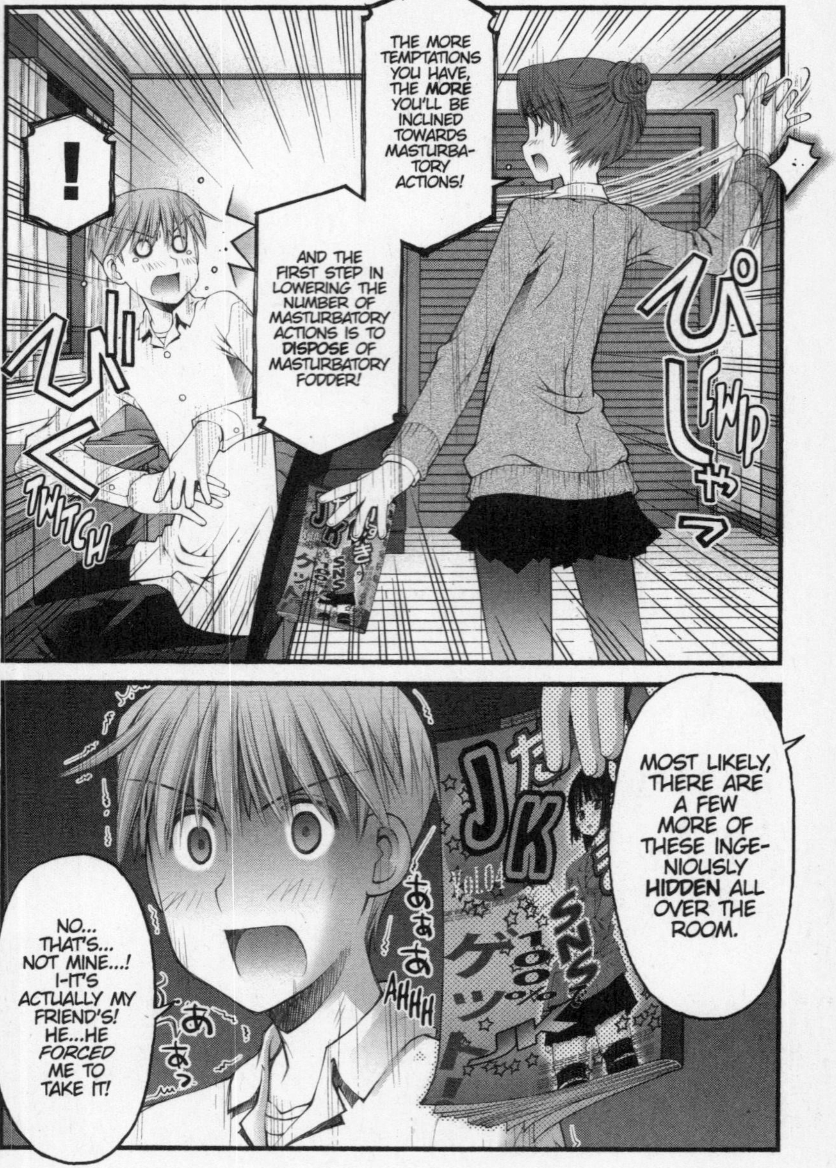
ぴしゃっ
FWIP
THE MORE TEMPTATIONS YOU HAVE, THE MORE YOU'LL BE INCLINED TOWARDS MASTURBATORY ACTIONS!
AND THE FIRST STEP IN LOWERING THE NUMBER OF MASTURBATORY ACTIONS IS TO DISPOSE OF MASTURBATORY FODDER!
!
TWITCH
MOST LIKELY, THERE ARE A FEW MORE OF THESE INGENIOUSLY HIDDEN ALL OVER THE ROOM.
JK
Vol.04
SNS
100%
あぁあ
AHHH
NO... THAT'S... NOT MINE...! I-IT'S ACTUALLY MY FRIEND'S! HE...HE FORCED ME TO TAKE IT!

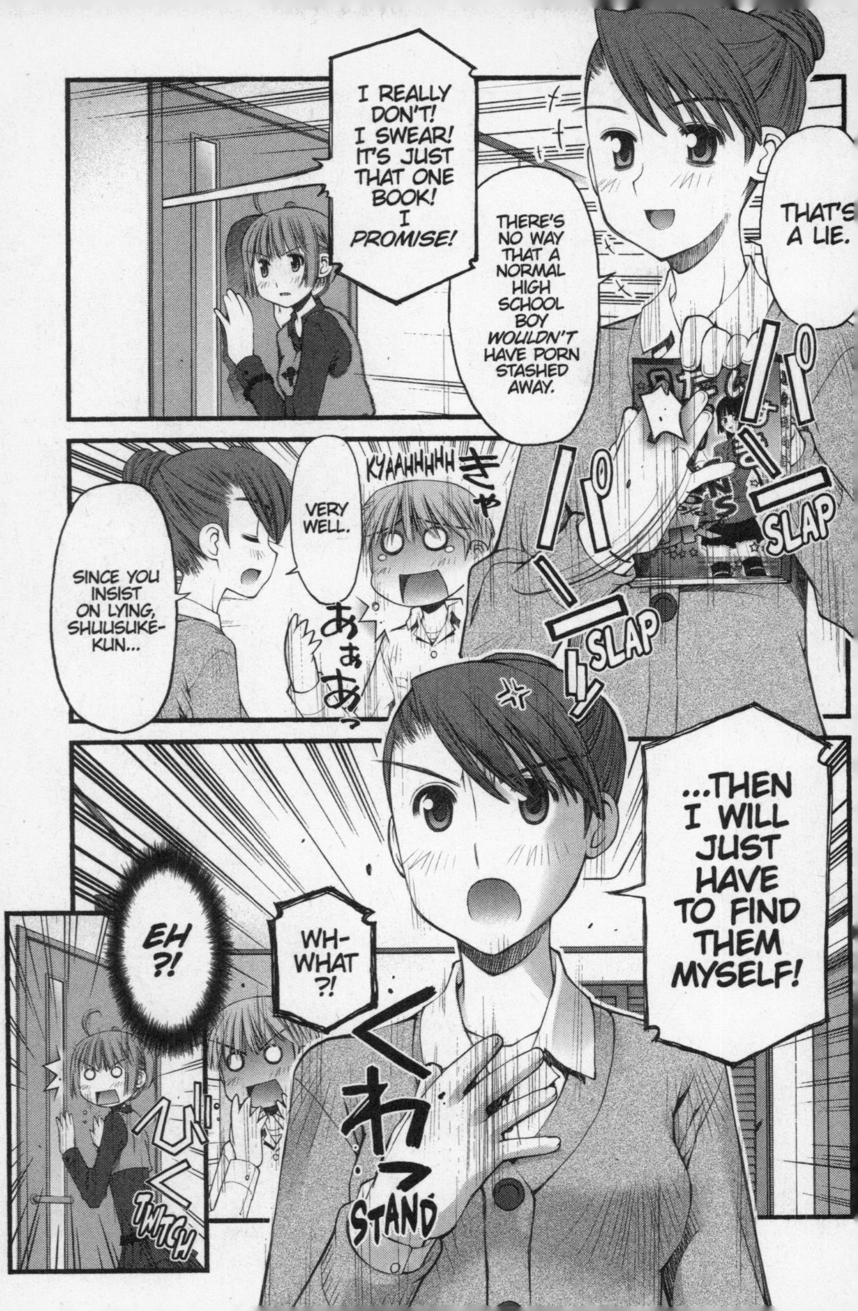
THAT'S A LIE.
THERE'S NO WAY THAT A NORMAL HIGH SCHOOL BOY *WOULDN'T* HAVE PORN STASHED AWAY.
SLAP
SLAP
I REALLY DON'T! I SWEAR! IT'S JUST THAT ONE BOOK! I *PROMISE!*
KYAAHHHHH きゃ
VERY WELL.
SINCE YOU INSIST ON LYING, SHUUSUKE-KUN...
あぁあっ
...THEN I WILL JUST HAVE TO FIND THEM MYSELF!
くわっ
STAND
WH-WHAT?!
EH?!
TWITCH

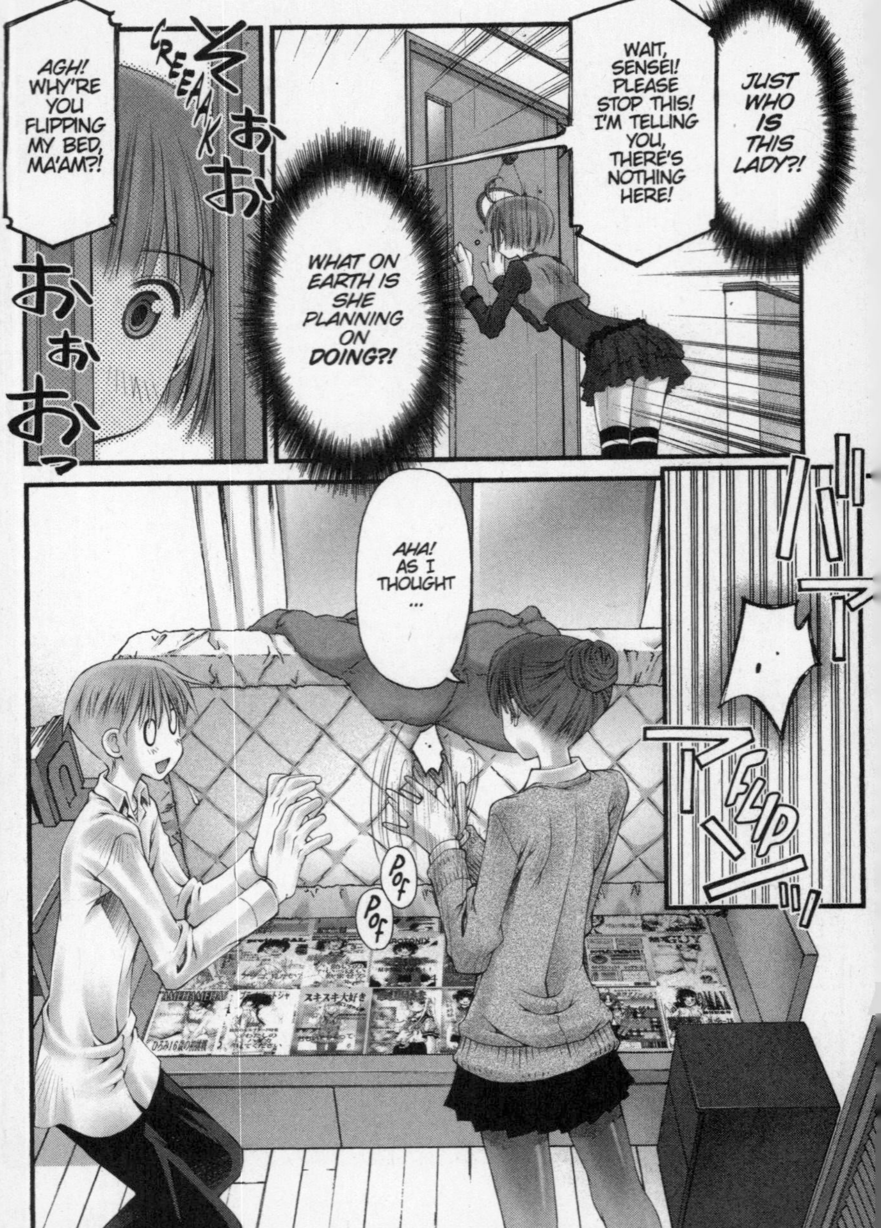
JUST WHO IS THIS LADY?!
WAIT, SENSEI! PLEASE STOP THIS! I'M TELLING YOU, THERE'S NOTHING HERE!
WHAT ON EARTH IS SHE PLANNING ON DOING?!
CREEAAK
AGH! WHY'RE YOU FLIPPING MY BED, MA'AM?!
FLIP
AHA! AS I THOUGHT ...
Pof
Pof

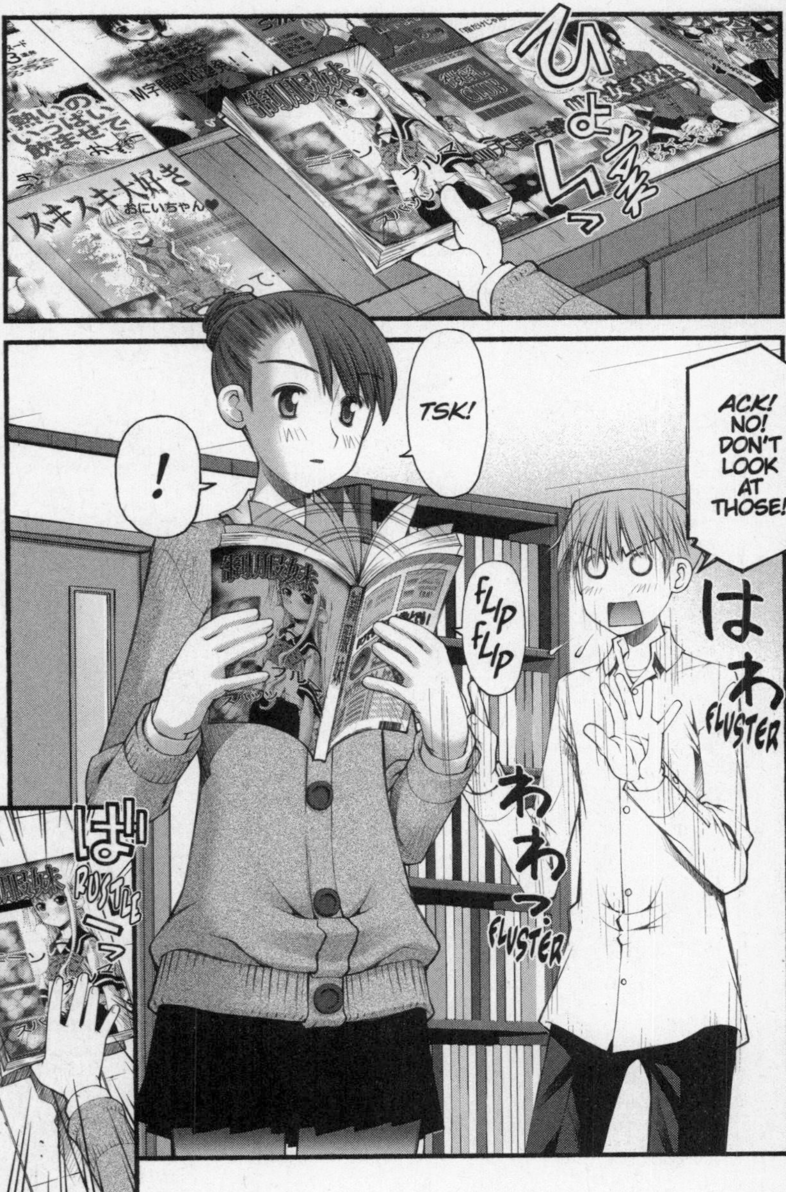
ひょいっ
YANK
スキスキ大好き
おにいちゃん
ACK! NO! DON'T LOOK AT THOSE!
TSK!
!
FLIP FLIP
はわ
FLUSTER
わわっ
FLUSTER
ばっ
RUSTLE

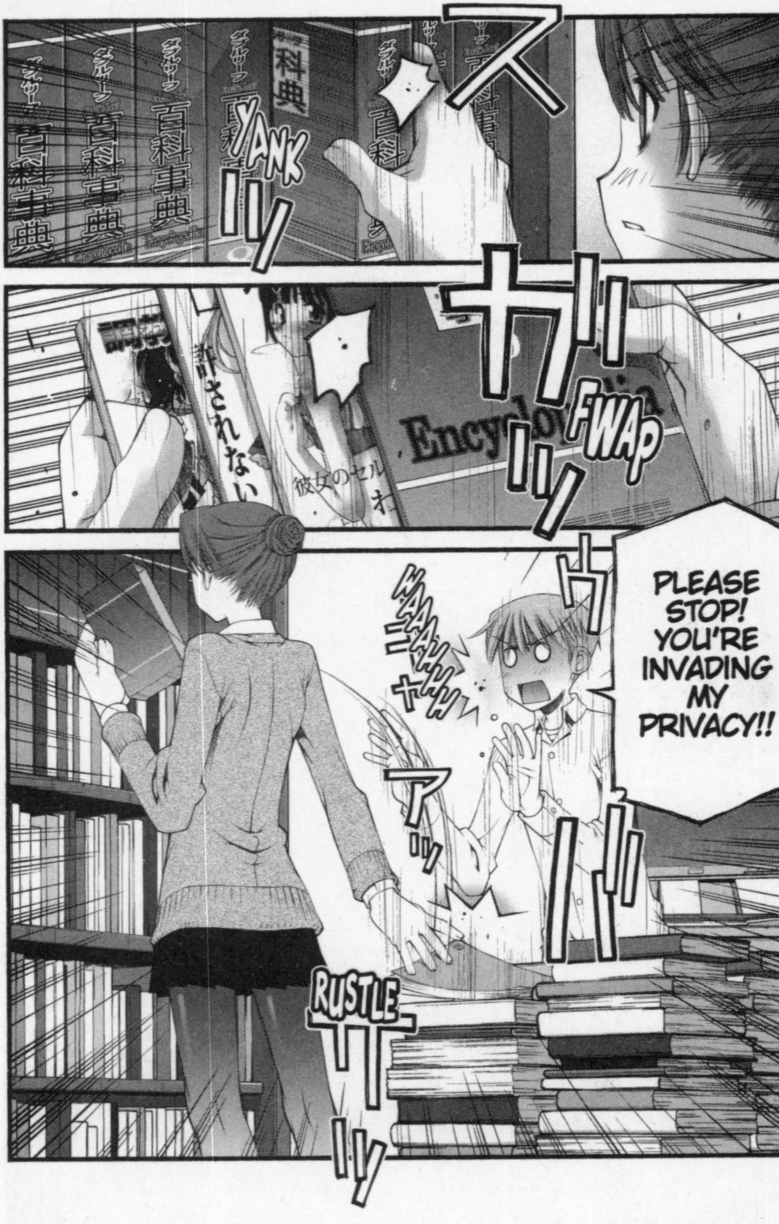
YANK
百科事典
Encyclopedia
FWAP
Encyclopedia
許されない
彼女のセル
PLEASE STOP! YOU'RE INVADING MY PRIVACY!!
WAAAHHH
RUSTLE

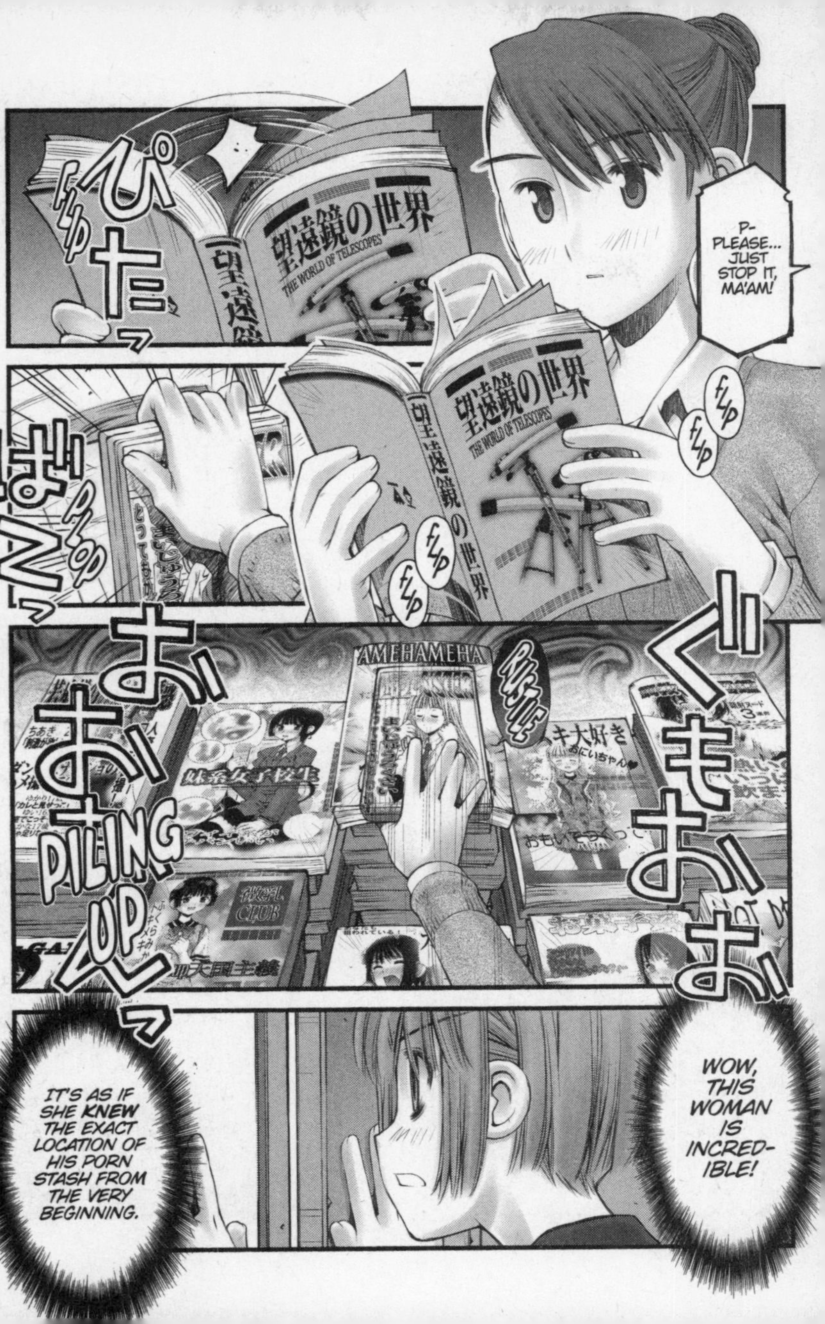

P-PLEASE... JUST STOP IT, MA'AM!
ぴたっ
FLIP
FLIP
FLIP
FLIP
FLIP
ぱっ
PLOP
ぐもおおお
RUSTLE
おおん
PILING UP
WOW, THIS WOMAN IS INCREDIBLE!
IT'S AS IF SHE KNEW THE EXACT LOCATION OF HIS PORN STASH FROM THE VERY BEGINNING.

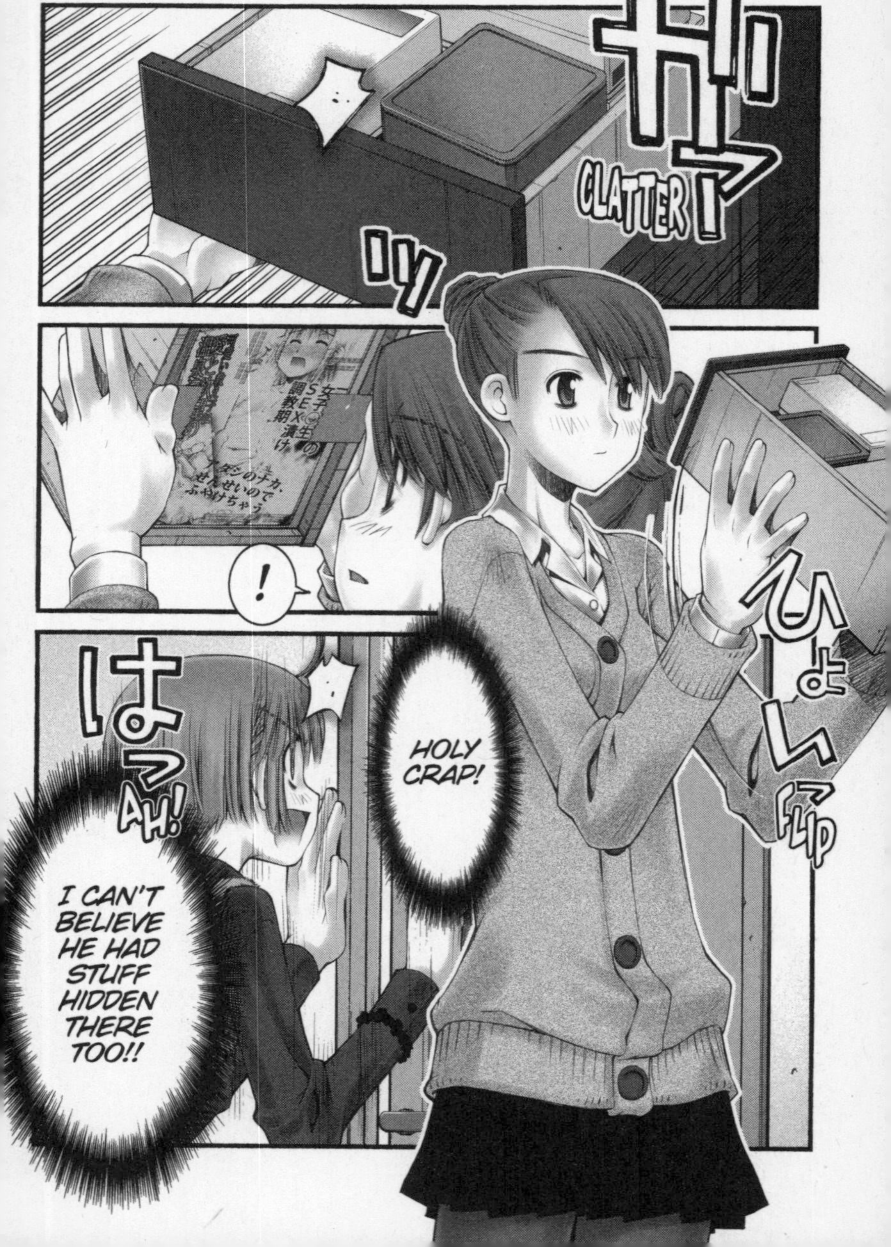
ガシャ
CLATTER
ひょいっ
FLIP
女子◯生のSEX調教朝漬け
アタシのナカ、せんせいのでふやけちゃう
!
はっ
AH!
HOLY CRAP!
I CAN'T BELIEVE HE HAD STUFF HIDDEN THERE TOO!!

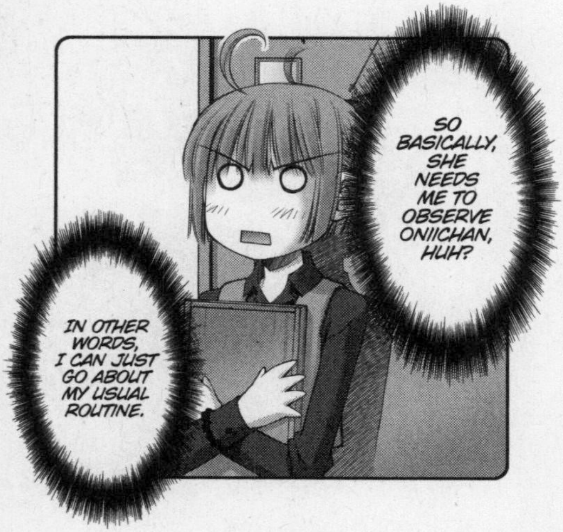
SO BASICALLY, SHE NEEDS ME TO OBSERVE ONIICHAN, HUH?
IN OTHER WORDS, I CAN JUST GO ABOUT MY USUAL ROUTINE.

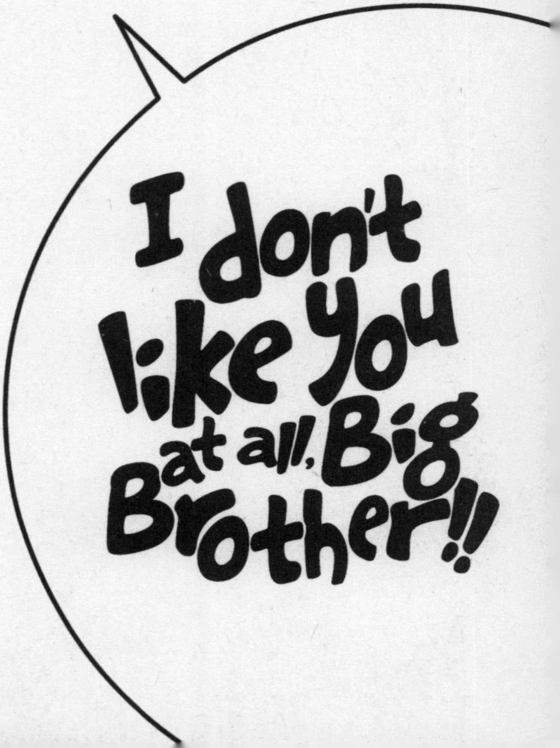
I don't like you at all, Big Brother!!

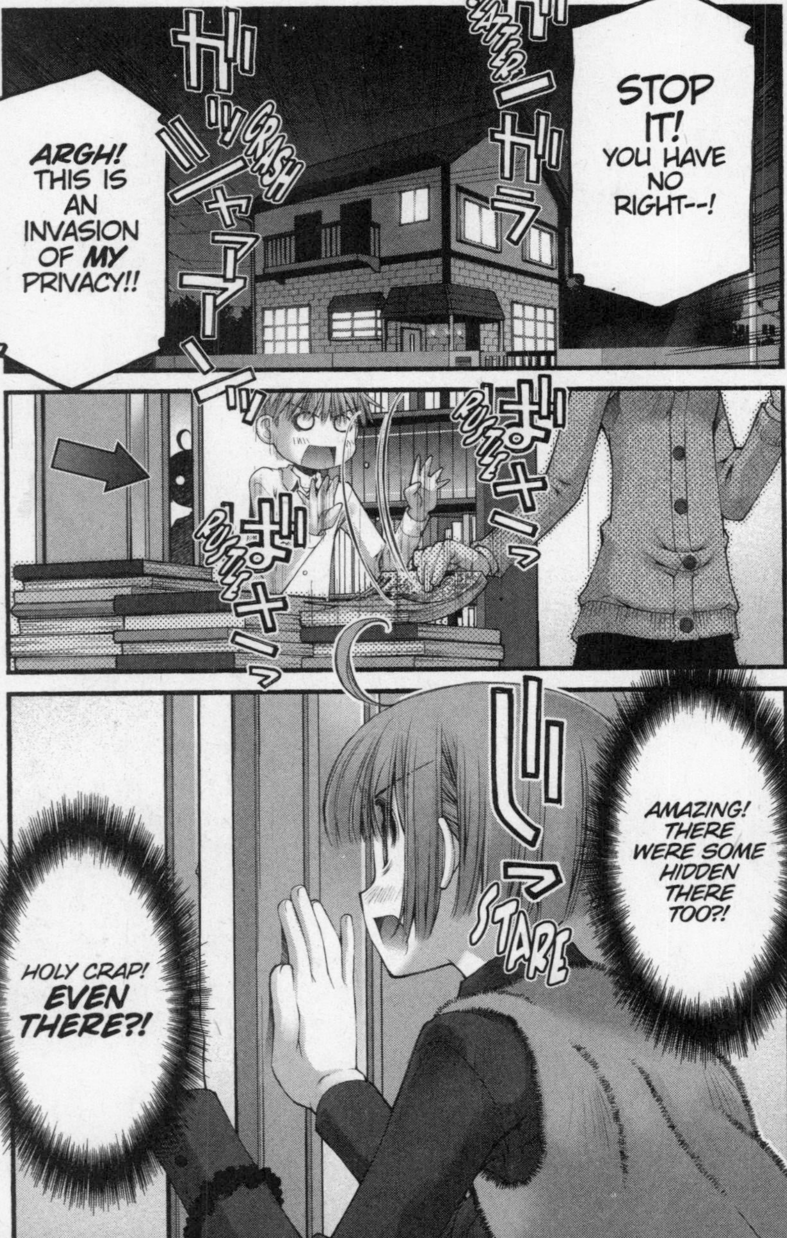
STOP IT! YOU HAVE NO RIGHT--!
CLATTER
CRASH
ARGH! THIS IS AN INVASION OF MY PRIVACY!!
RUSTLE
RUSTLE
STARE
AMAZING! THERE WERE SOME HIDDEN THERE TOO?!
HOLY CRAP! EVEN THERE?!

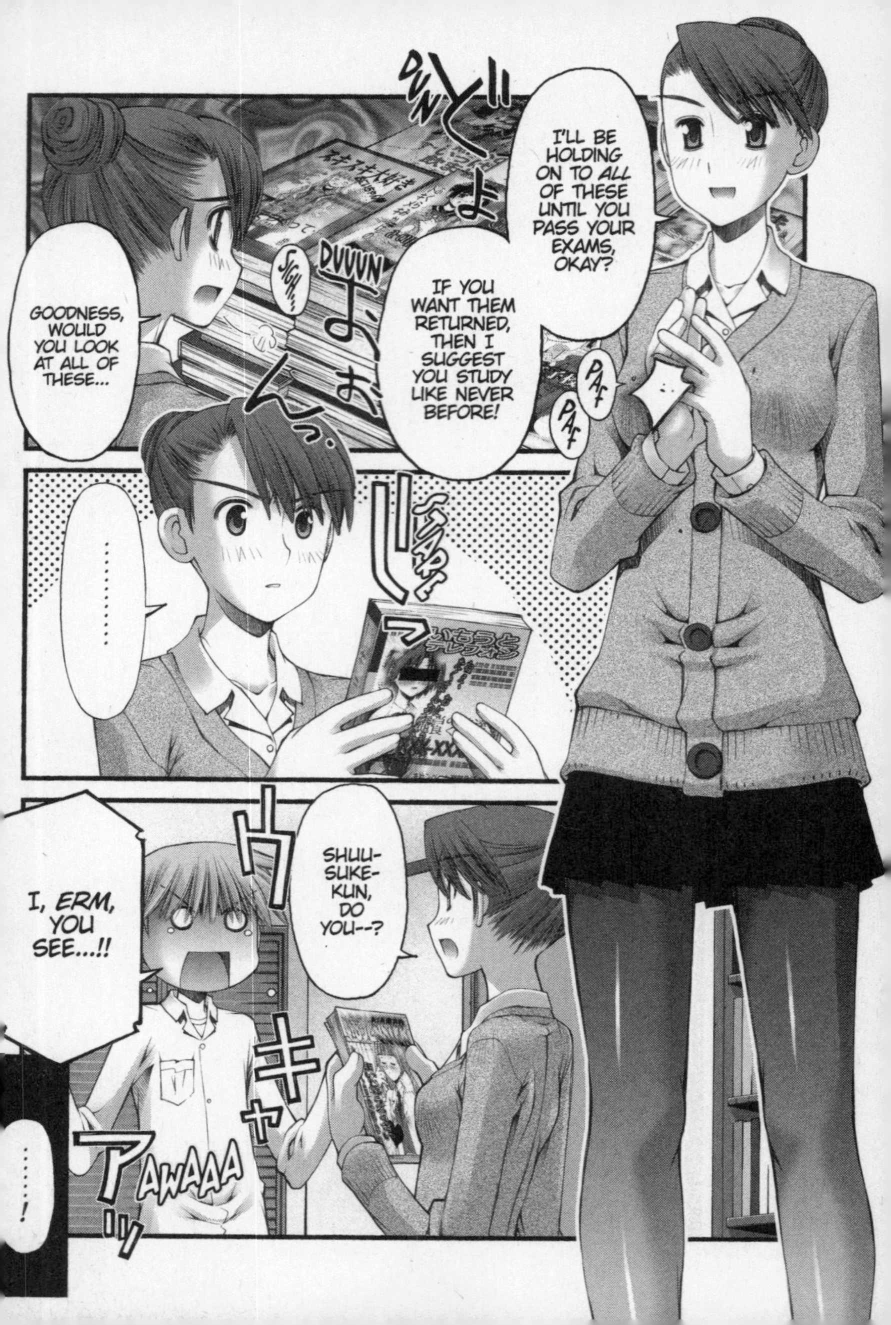
I'LL BE HOLDING ON TO ALL OF THESE UNTIL YOU PASS YOUR EXAMS, OKAY?
DUN
IF YOU WANT THEM RETURNED, THEN I SUGGEST YOU STUDY LIKE NEVER BEFORE!
PAF
PAF
DUUUN
SIGH...
GOODNESS, WOULD YOU LOOK AT ALL OF THESE...
STARE
......
SHUU-SUKE-KUN, DO YOU--?
I, ERM, YOU SEE...!!
AWAAA
......!

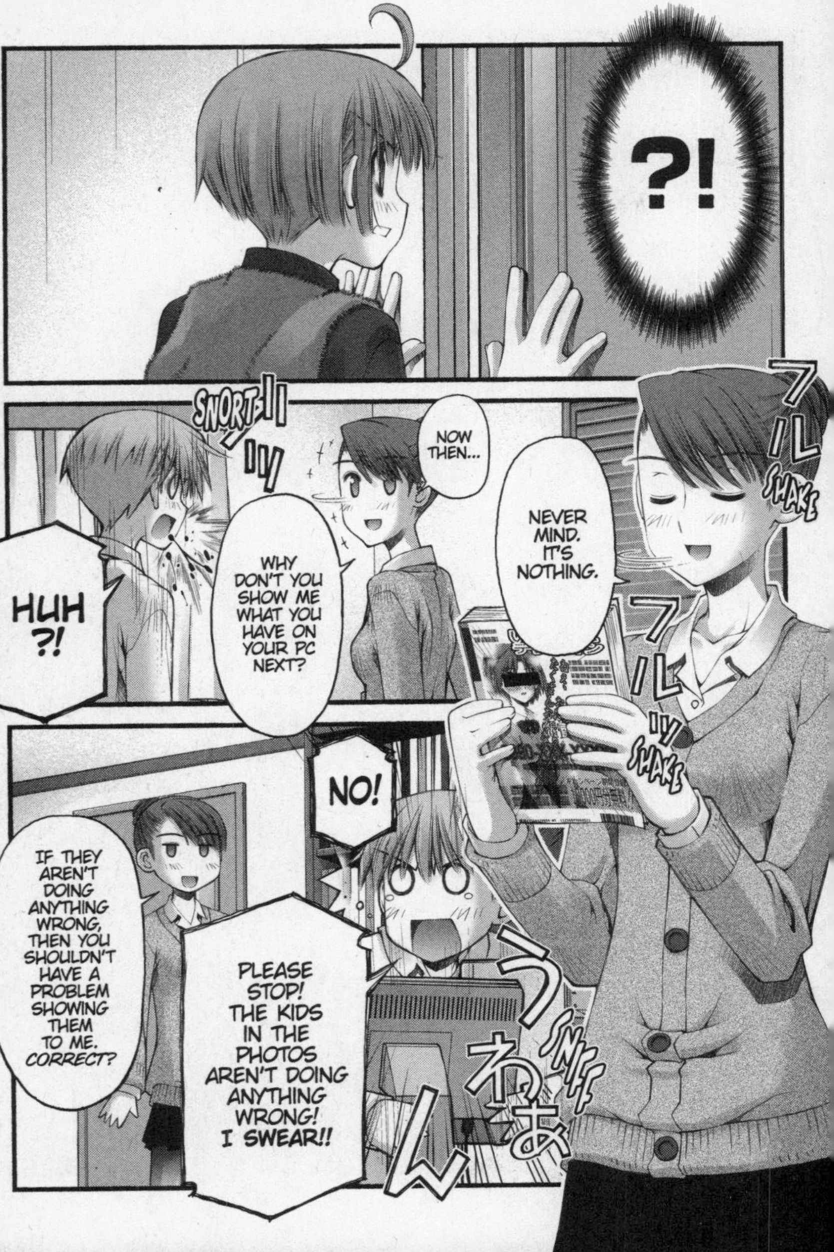
?!
フル
SHAKE
フル
SHAKE
NEVER MIND. IT'S NOTHING.
NOW THEN...
WHY DON'T YOU SHOW ME WHAT YOU HAVE ON YOUR PC NEXT?
SNORT
HUH?!
うわあん
SNIFF
NO!
PLEASE STOP! THE KIDS IN THE PHOTOS AREN'T DOING ANYTHING WRONG! I SWEAR!!
IF THEY AREN'T DOING ANYTHING WRONG, THEN YOU SHOULDN'T HAVE A PROBLEM SHOWING THEM TO ME. CORRECT?

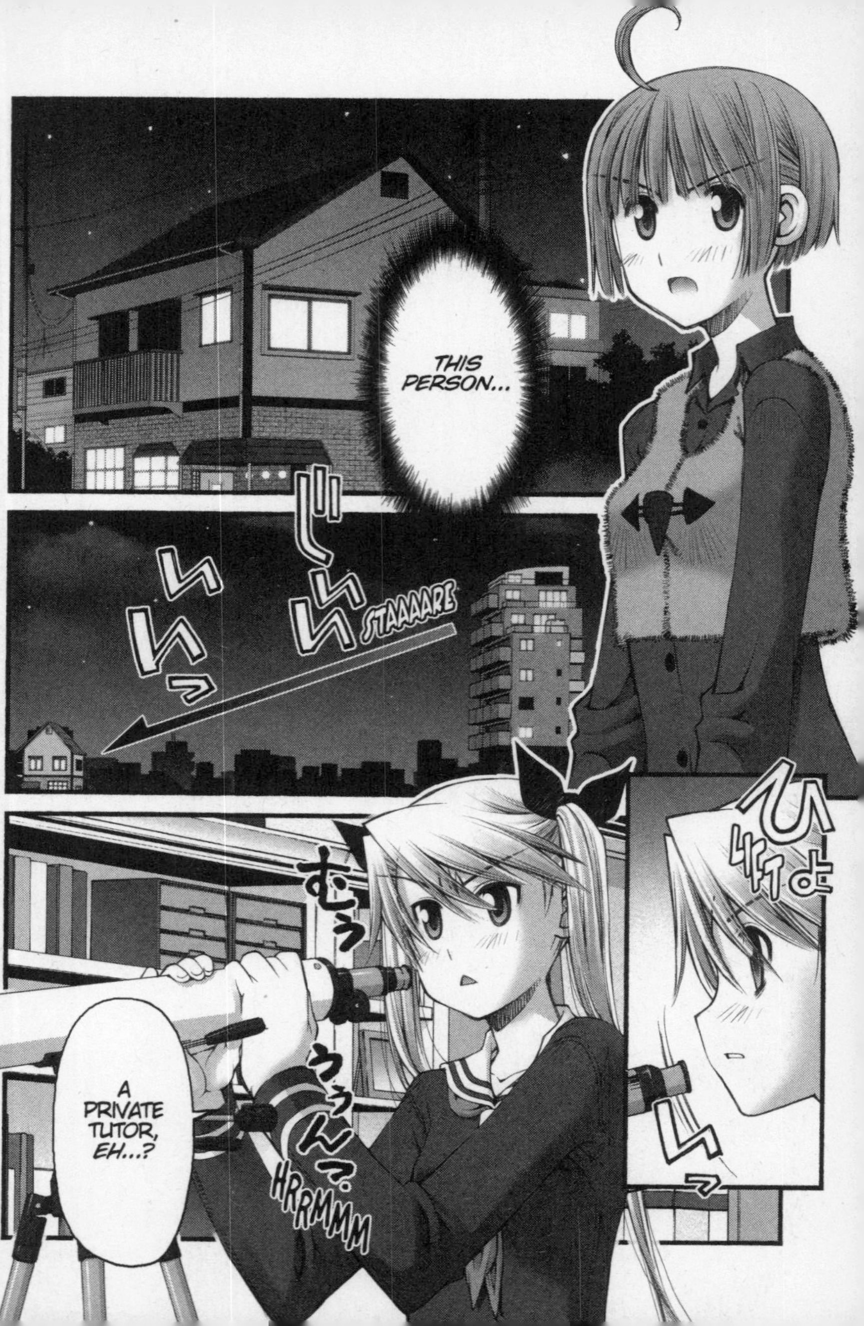
THIS PERSON...
じいいいいっ
STAAAARE
ひょいっ
むぅううんっ
HRRMMM
A PRIVATE TUTOR, EH...?

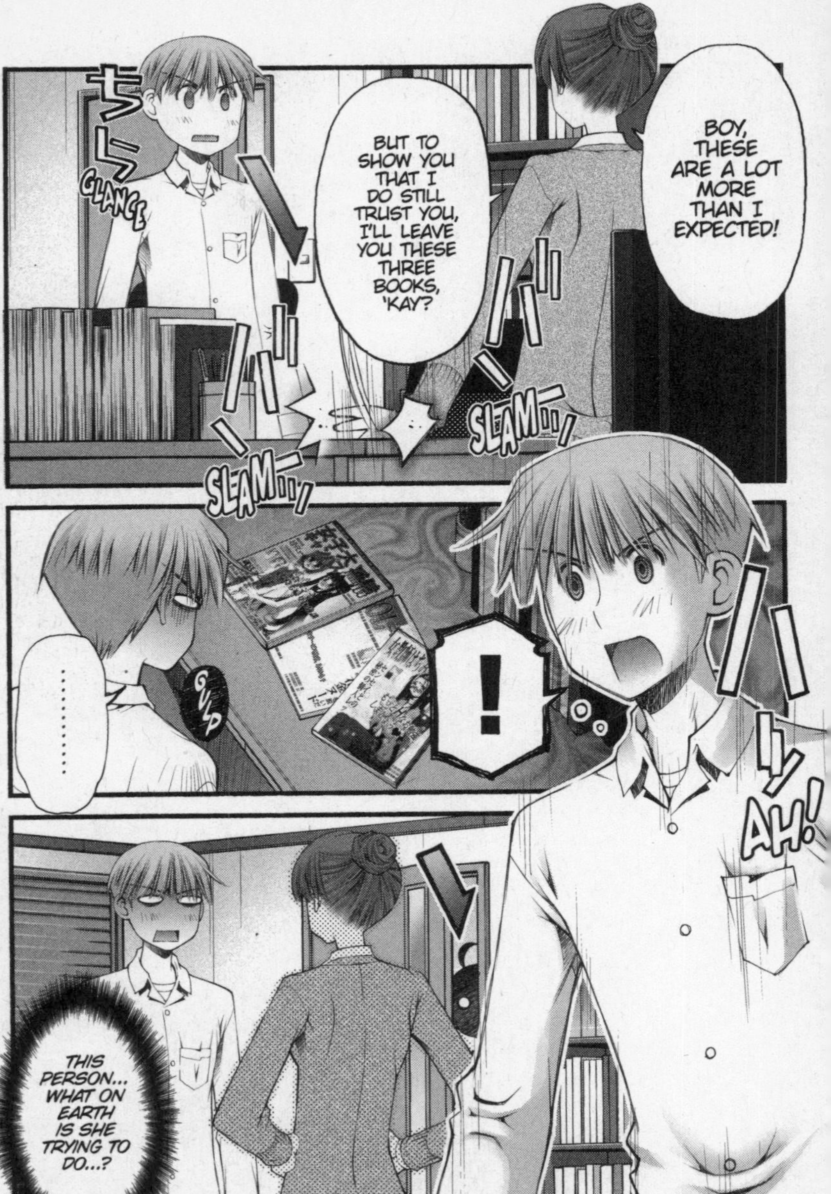
BOY, THESE ARE A LOT MORE THAN I EXPECTED!
BUT TO SHOW YOU THAT I DO STILL TRUST YOU, I'LL LEAVE YOU THESE THREE BOOKS, 'KAY?
SLAM
SLAM
GLANCE
!
AH!
GULP
......
THIS PERSON... WHAT ON EARTH IS SHE TRYING TO DO...?

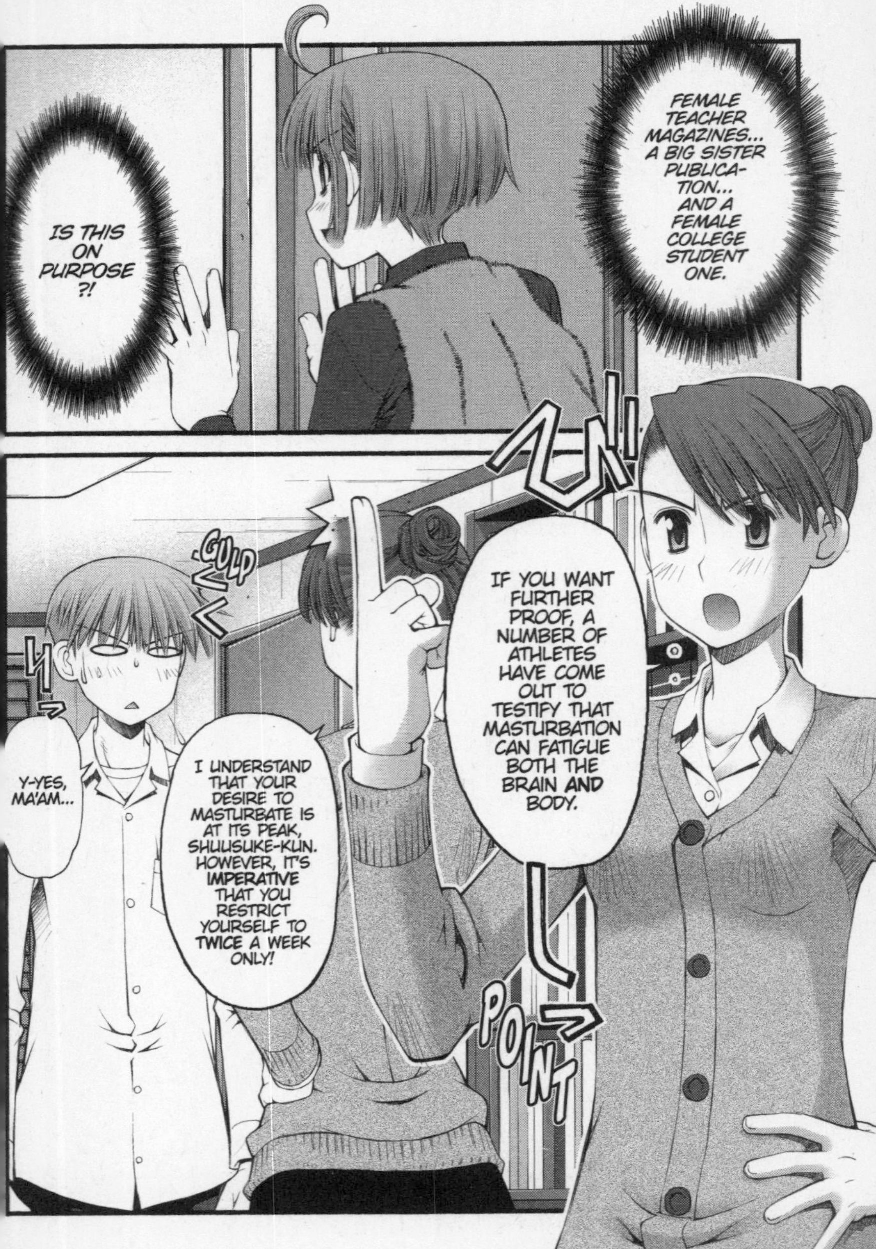
FEMALE TEACHER MAGAZINES... A BIG SISTER PUBLICATION... AND A FEMALE COLLEGE STUDENT ONE.
IS THIS ON PURPOSE?!
UN
IF YOU WANT FURTHER PROOF, A NUMBER OF ATHLETES HAVE COME OUT TO TESTIFY THAT MASTURBATION CAN FATIGUE BOTH THE BRAIN AND BODY.
POINT
I UNDERSTAND THAT YOUR DESIRE TO MASTURBATE IS AT ITS PEAK, SHUUSUKE-KUN. HOWEVER, IT'S IMPERATIVE THAT YOU RESTRICT YOURSELF TO TWICE A WEEK ONLY!
GULP
Y-YES, MA'AM...

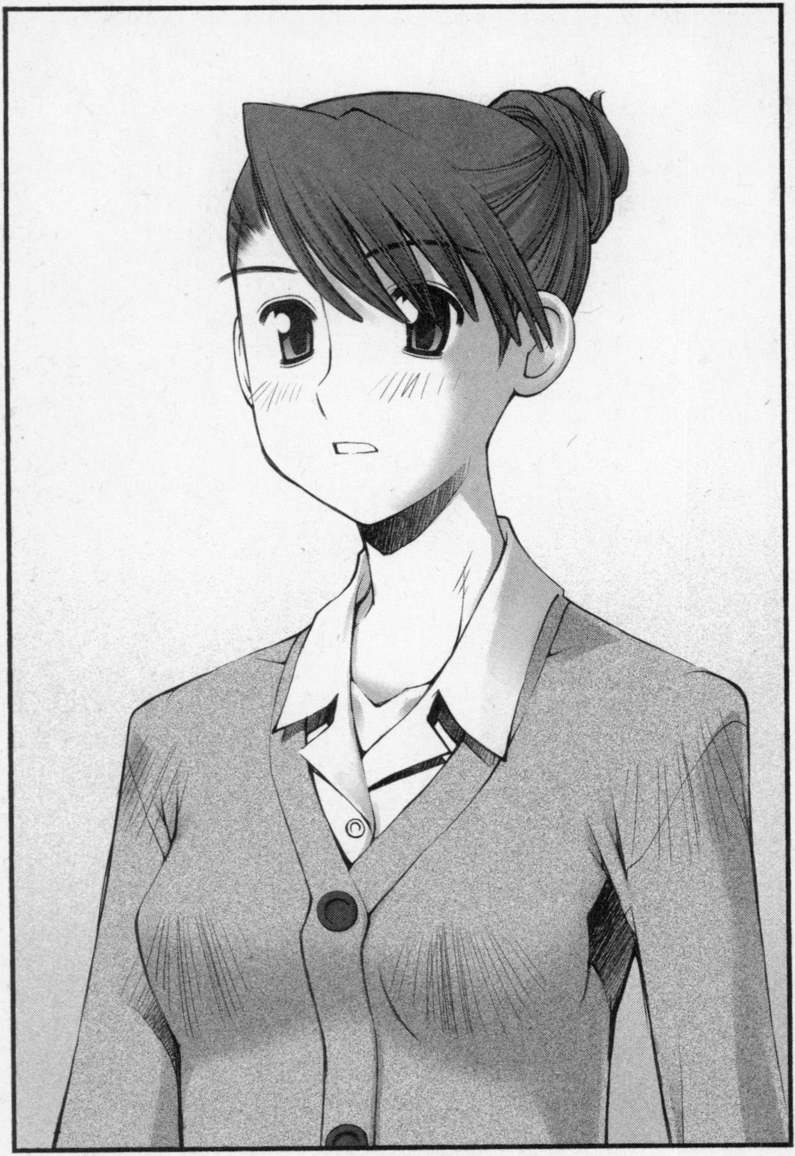

CHAPTER 40 Richika's Aim

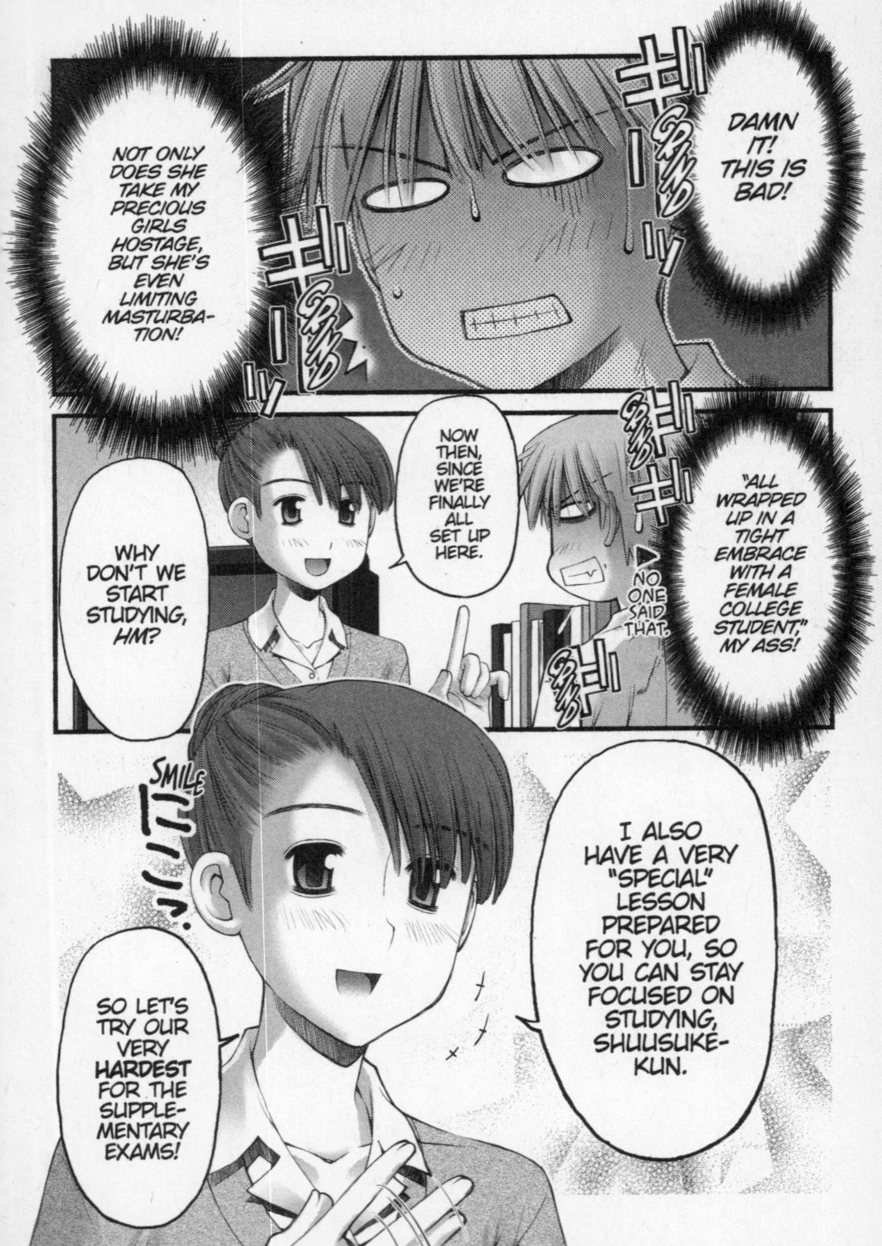

DAMN IT! THIS IS BAD!
GRIND
GRIND
NOT ONLY DOES SHE TAKE MY PRECIOUS GIRLS HOSTAGE, BUT SHE'S EVEN LIMITING MASTURBA-TION!
"ALL WRAPPED UP IN A TIGHT EMBRACE WITH A FEMALE COLLEGE STUDENT," MY ASS!
GRIND
GRIND
NO ONE SAID THAT.
NOW THEN, SINCE WE'RE FINALLY ALL SET UP HERE.
WHY DON'T WE START STUDYING, HM?
SMILE
I ALSO HAVE A VERY "SPECIAL" LESSON PREPARED FOR YOU, SO YOU CAN STAY FOCUSED ON STUDYING, SHUUSUKE-KUN.
SO LET'S TRY OUR VERY HARDEST FOR THE SUPPLE-MENTARY EXAMS!

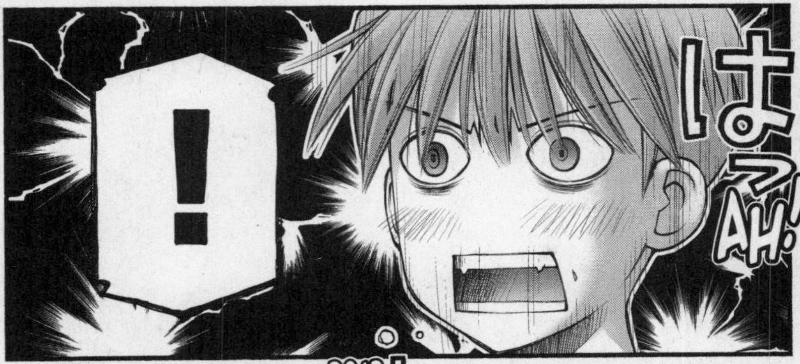
はっ
AH!
!

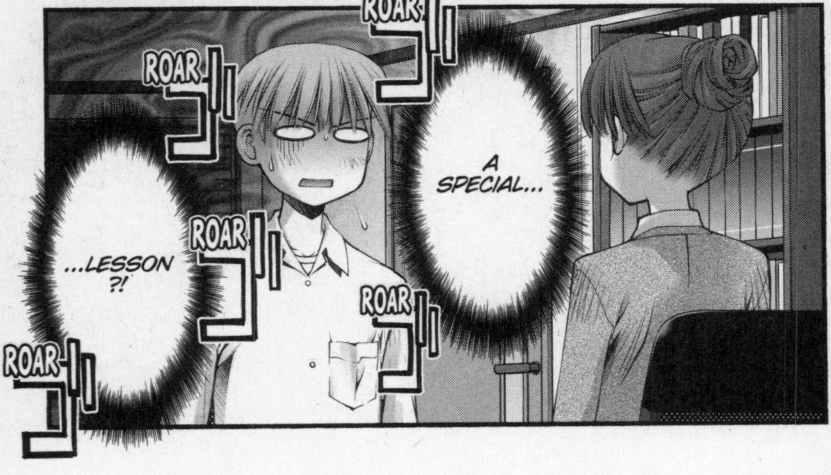
ROAR
A SPECIAL...
ROAR
ROAR
ROAR
...LESSON ?!
ROAR

BY "SPECIAL LESSON"...

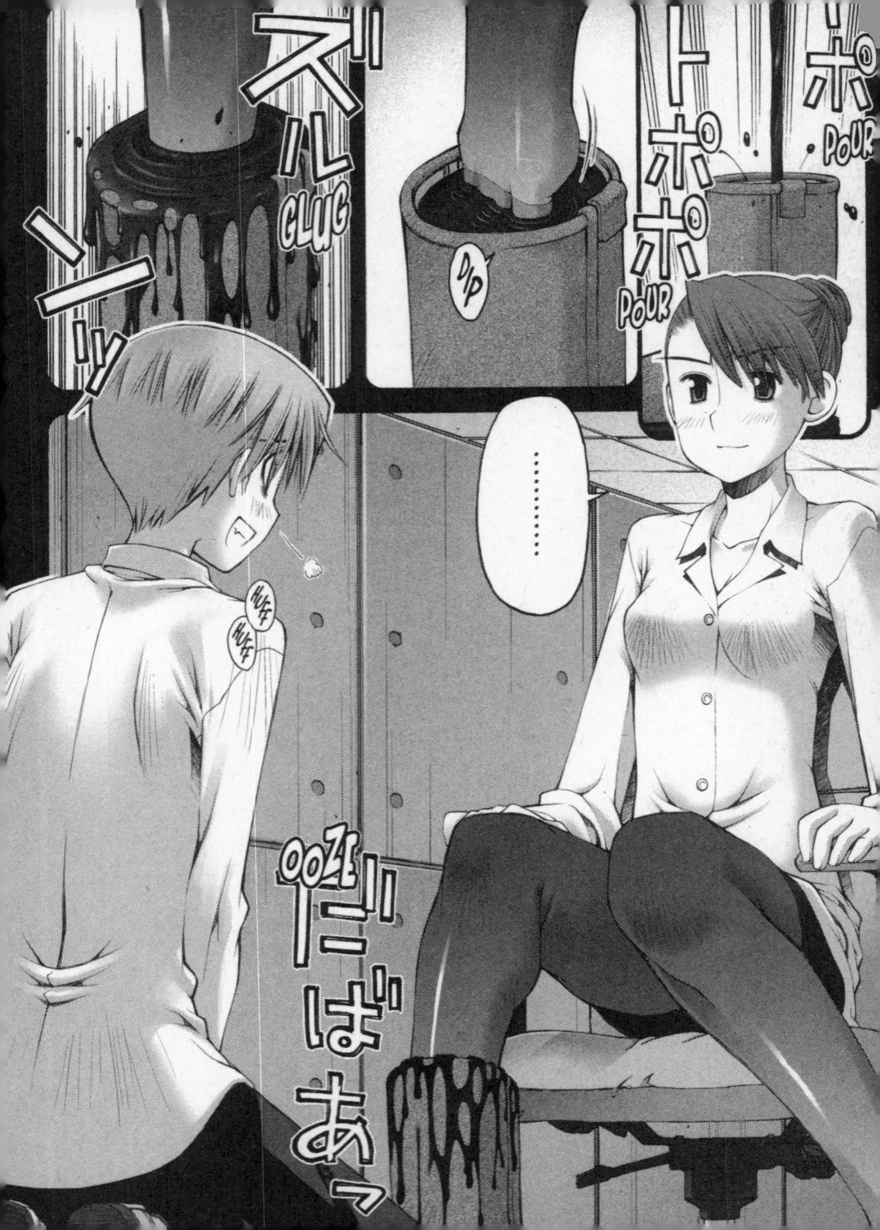
ポ
POUR
トポポポ
POUR
DIP
ズルンッ
GLUG
……
HUFF
HUFF
にばあっ
OOZE

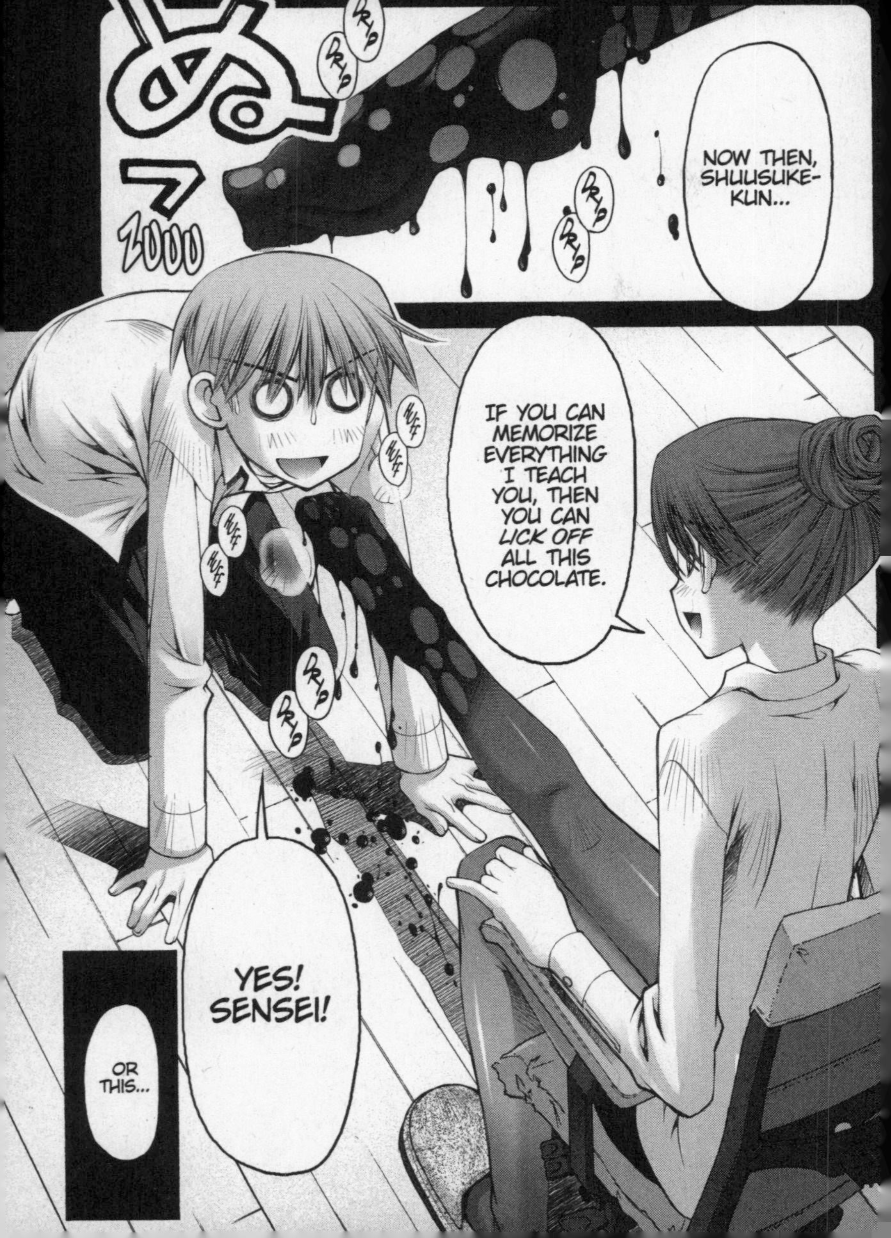
NOW THEN, SHUUSUKE-KUN...
ぬ～
ZUUU
DRIP DRIP
DRIP DRIP
IF YOU CAN MEMORIZE EVERYTHING I TEACH YOU, THEN YOU CAN *LICK OFF* ALL THIS CHOCOLATE.
HUFF HUFF
HUFF HUFF
DRIP DRIP
YES! SENSEI!
OR THIS...

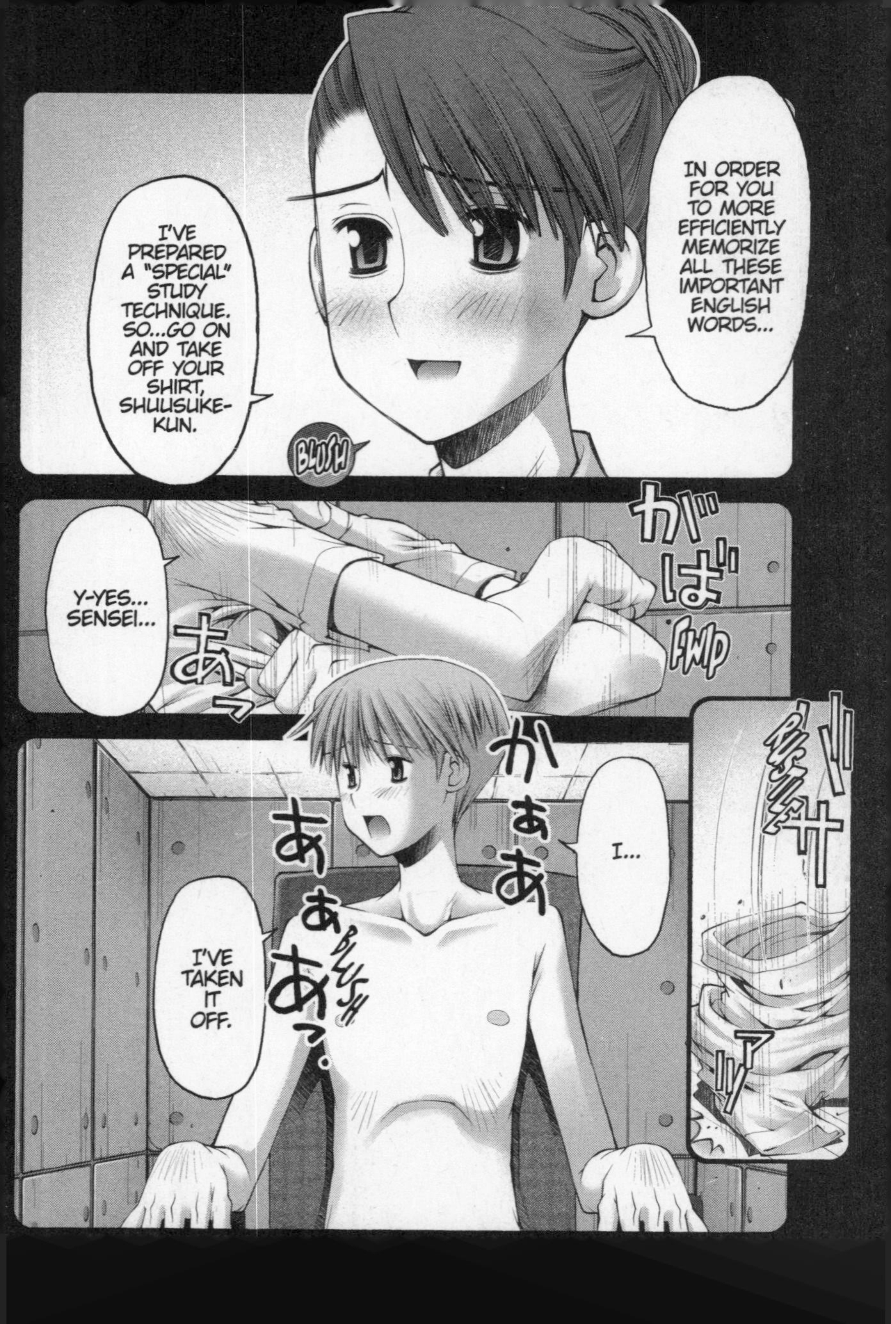
IN ORDER FOR YOU TO MORE EFFICIENTLY MEMORIZE ALL THESE IMPORTANT ENGLISH WORDS...
I'VE PREPARED A "SPECIAL" STUDY TECHNIQUE. SO...GO ON AND TAKE OFF YOUR SHIRT, SHUUSUKE-KUN.
BLUSH
がばっ
FWIP
Y-YES... SENSEI...
あっ
I...
I'VE TAKEN IT OFF.
かぁぁぁぁあっ
BLUSH

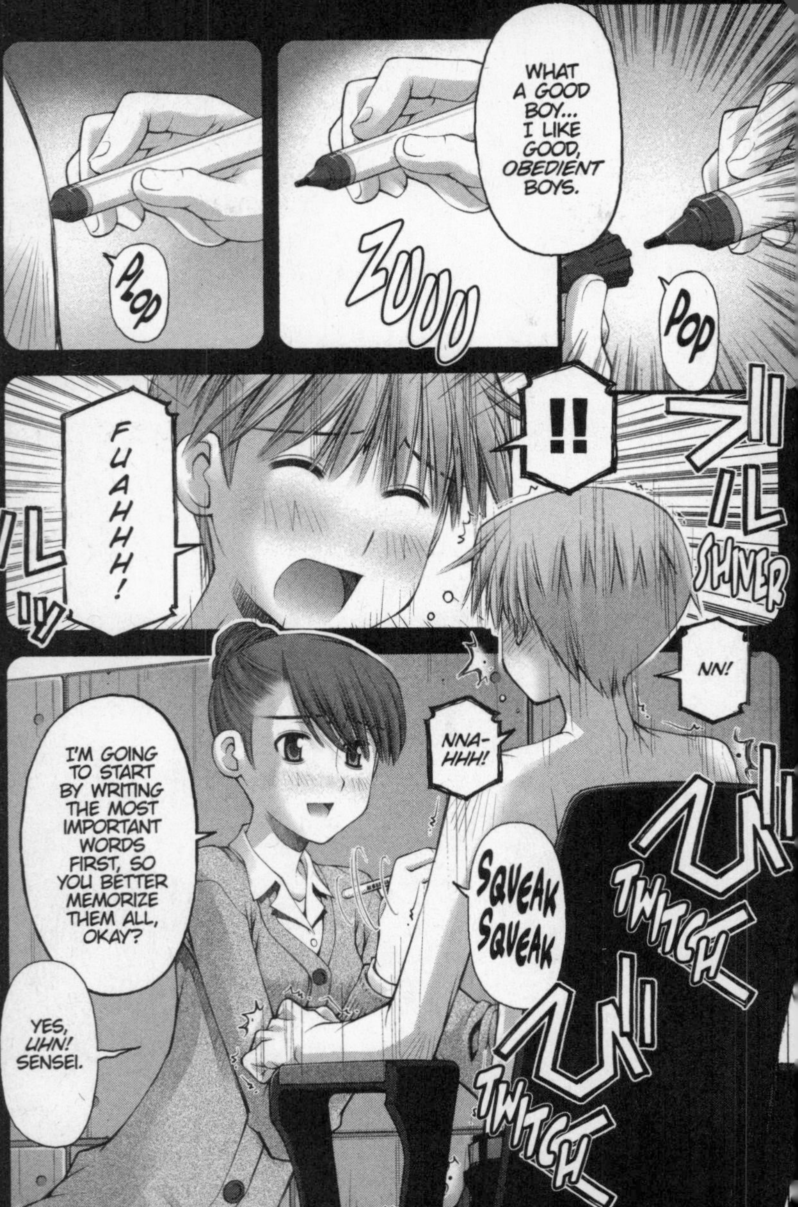
POP
WHAT A GOOD BOY... I LIKE GOOD, OBEDIENT BOYS.
ZUUU
PLOP
!!
SHIVER
FUAHHHH!
NN!
NNA-HHH!
TWITCH
TWITCH
SQUEAK SQUEAK
I'M GOING TO START BY WRITING THE MOST IMPORTANT WORDS FIRST, SO YOU BETTER MEMORIZE THEM ALL, OKAY?
YES, UHN! SENSEI.

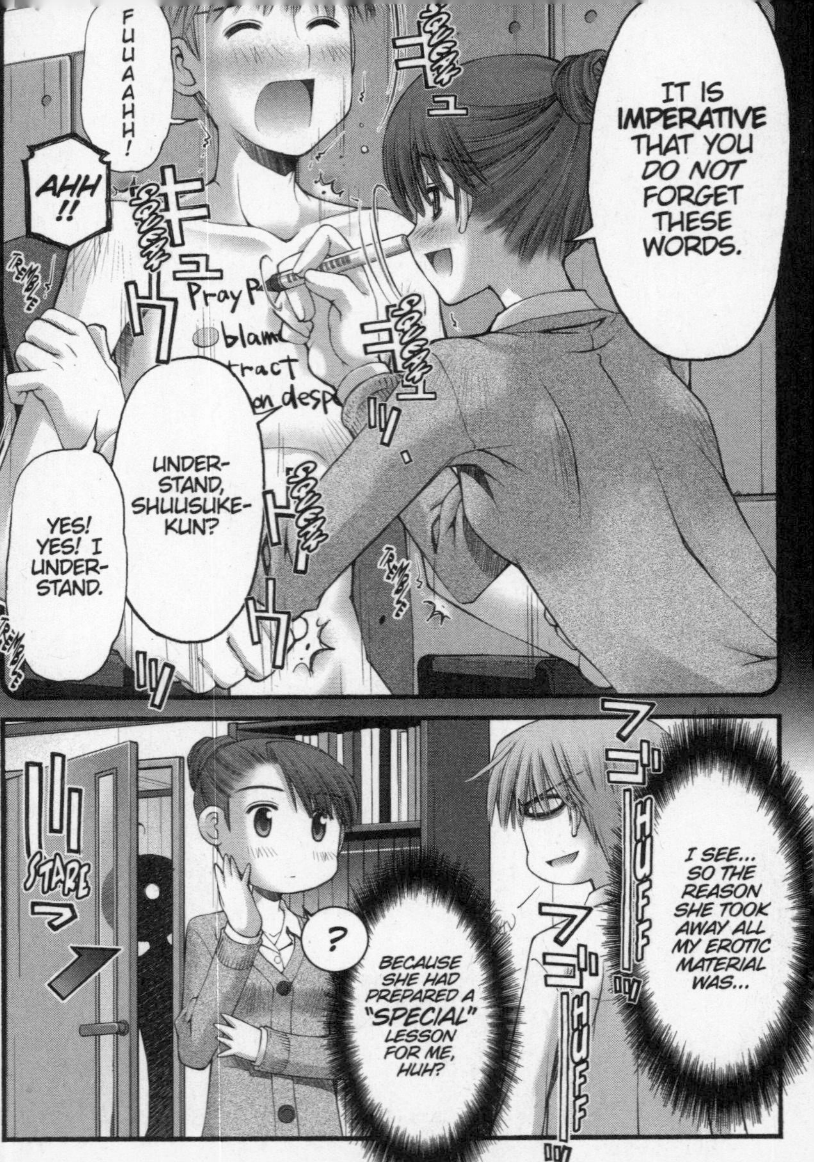
IT IS IMPERATIVE THAT YOU DO NOT FORGET THESE WORDS.
FUUAAHH!
AHH!!
TREMBLE
UNDERSTAND, SHUUSUKE-KUN?
YES! YES! I UNDERSTAND.
TREMBLE
TREMBLE
I SEE... SO THE REASON SHE TOOK AWAY ALL MY EROTIC MATERIAL WAS...
HUFF
HUFF
BECAUSE SHE HAD PREPARED A "SPECIAL" LESSON FOR ME, HUH?
?
STARE

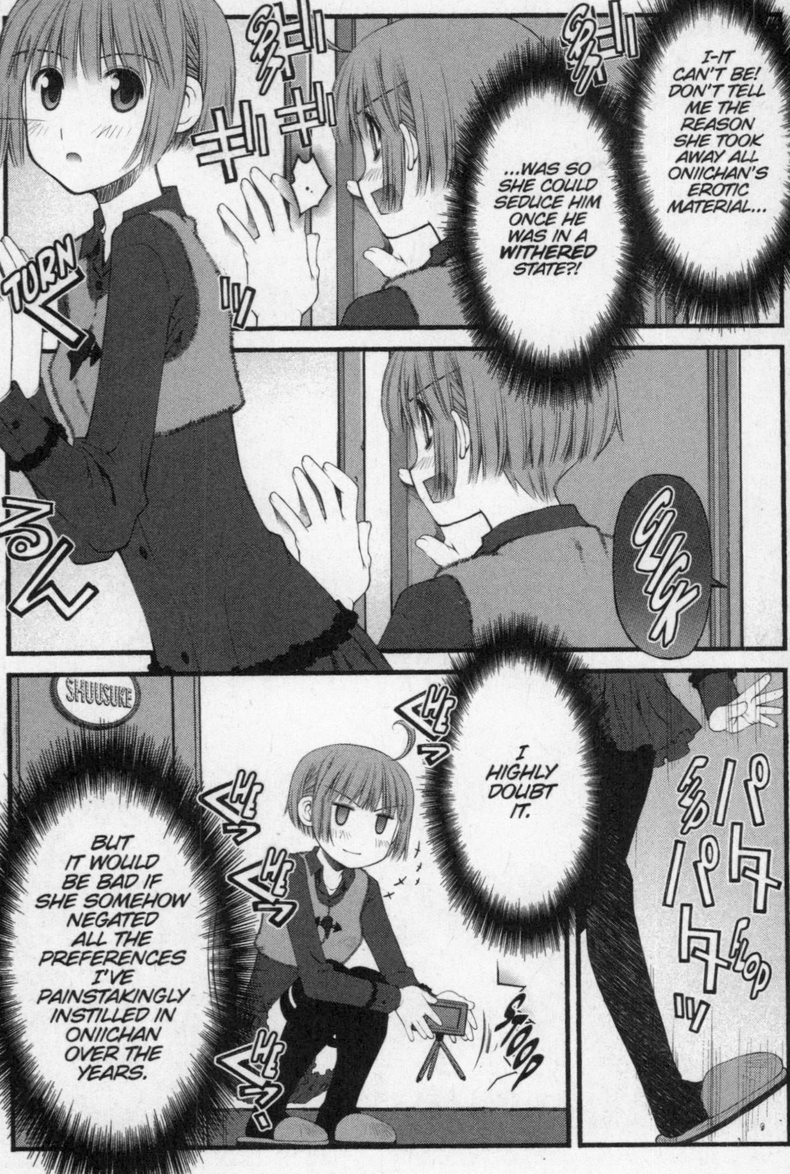
GRIT
I-IT CAN'T BE! DON'T TELL ME THE REASON SHE TOOK AWAY ALL ONIICHAN'S EROTIC MATERIAL...
...WAS SO SHE COULD SEDUCE HIM ONCE HE WAS IN A WITHERED STATE?!
GRIT
CLICK
TURN
るん
パタパタ
FLOP
I HIGHLY DOUBT IT.
HE
HE
HE
HE
STOOP
BUT IT WOULD BE BAD IF SHE SOMEHOW NEGATED ALL THE PREFERENCES I'VE PAINSTAKINGLY INSTILLED IN ONIICHAN OVER THE YEARS.
SHUUSUKE

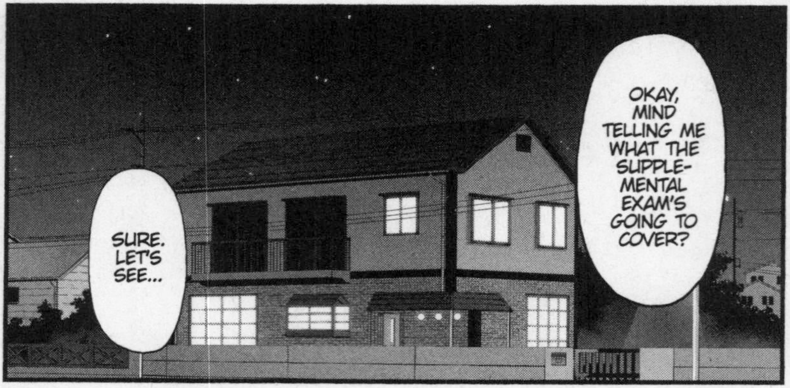
OKAY, MIND TELLING ME WHAT THE SUPPLE-MENTAL EXAM'S GOING TO COVER?
SURE. LET'S SEE...

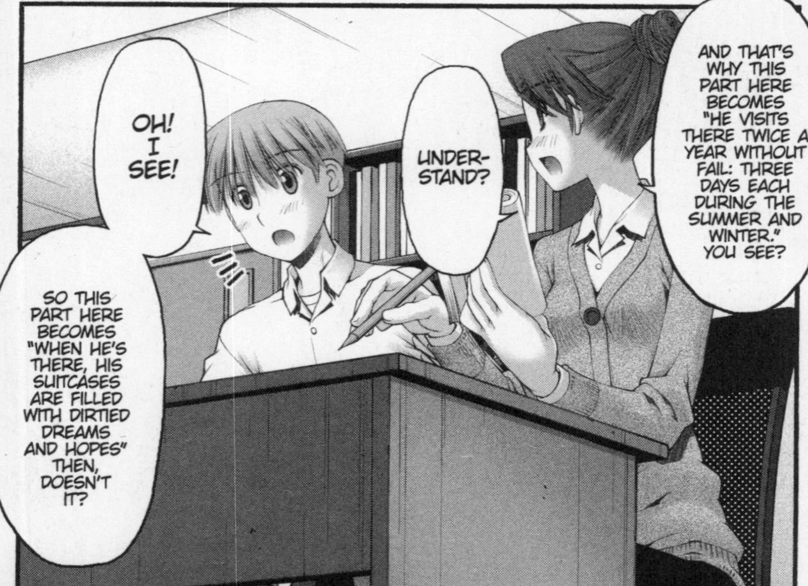
AND THAT'S WHY THIS PART HERE BECOMES "HE VISITS THERE TWICE A YEAR WITHOUT FAIL: THREE DAYS EACH DURING THE SUMMER AND WINTER." YOU SEE?
UNDER-STAND?
OH! I SEE!
SO THIS PART HERE BECOMES "WHEN HE'S THERE, HIS SUITCASES ARE FILLED WITH DIRTIED DREAMS AND HOPES" THEN, DOESN'T IT?

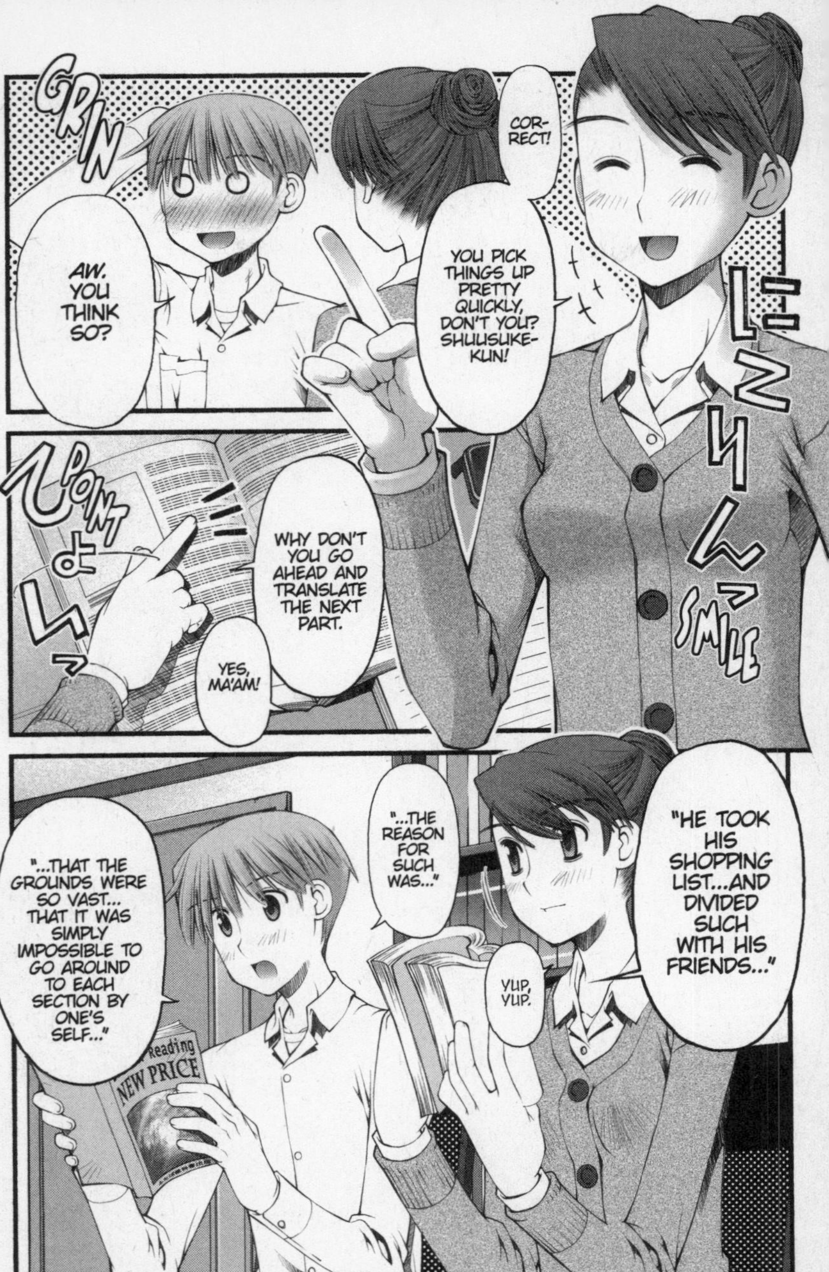
CORRECT!
YOU PICK THINGS UP PRETTY QUICKLY, DON'T YOU? SHUUSUKE-KUN!
SMILE
GRIN
AW. YOU THINK SO?
POINT
WHY DON'T YOU GO AHEAD AND TRANSLATE THE NEXT PART.
YES, MA'AM!
"HE TOOK HIS SHOPPING LIST...AND DIVIDED SUCH WITH HIS FRIENDS..."
"...THE REASON FOR SUCH WAS..."
YUP, YUP.
"...THAT THE GROUNDS WERE SO VAST... THAT IT WAS SIMPLY IMPOSSIBLE TO GO AROUND TO EACH SECTION BY ONE'S SELF..."
Reading
NEW PRICE

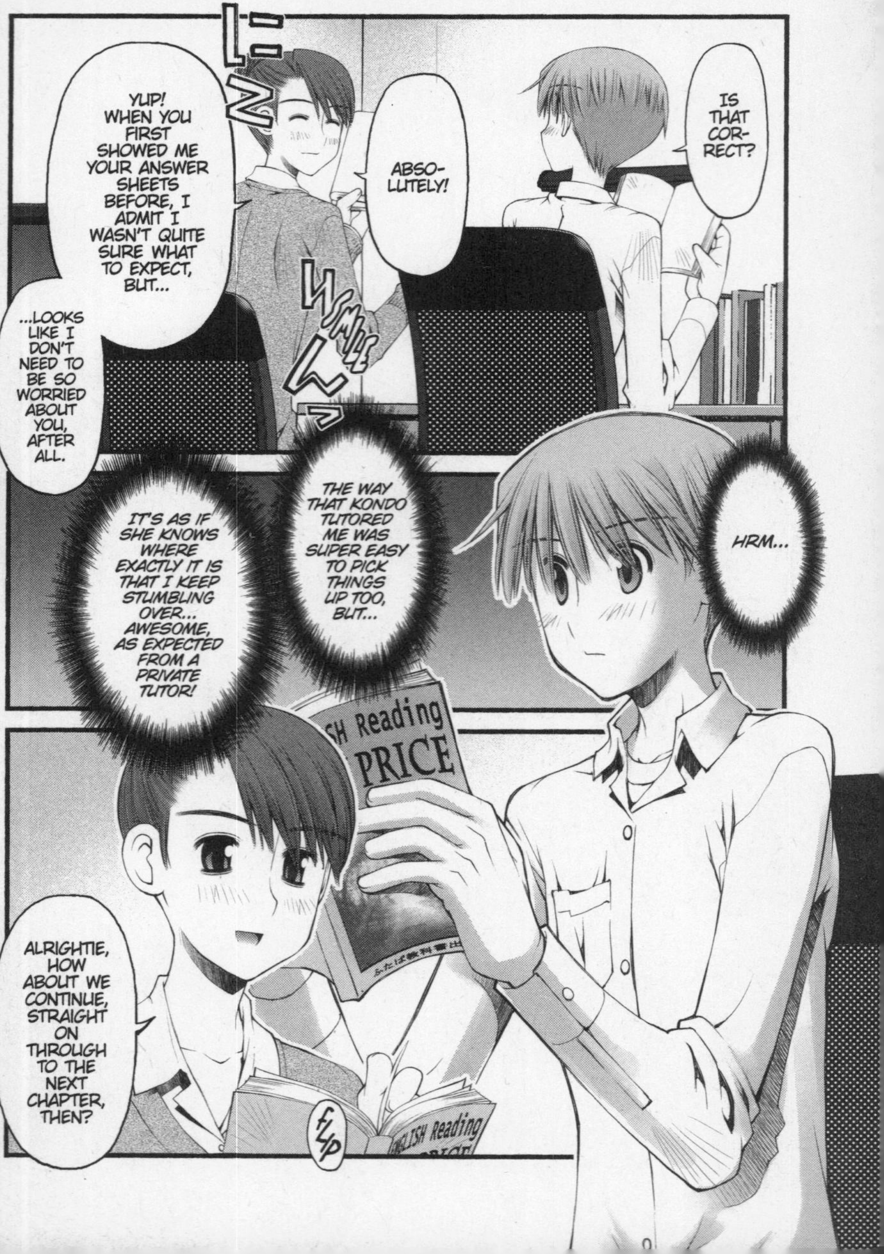
IS THAT COR-RECT?
ABSO-LUTELY!
YUP! WHEN YOU FIRST SHOWED ME YOUR ANSWER SHEETS BEFORE, I ADMIT I WASN'T QUITE SURE WHAT TO EXPECT, BUT...
SMILE
...LOOKS LIKE I DON'T NEED TO BE SO WORRIED ABOUT YOU, AFTER ALL.
HRM...
THE WAY THAT KONDO TUTORED ME WAS SUPER EASY TO PICK THINGS UP TOO, BUT...
IT'S AS IF SHE KNOWS WHERE EXACTLY IT IS THAT I KEEP STUMBLING OVER... AWESOME, AS EXPECTED FROM A PRIVATE TUTOR!
ALRIGHTIE, HOW ABOUT WE CONTINUE, STRAIGHT ON THROUGH TO THE NEXT CHAPTER, THEN?
FLIP

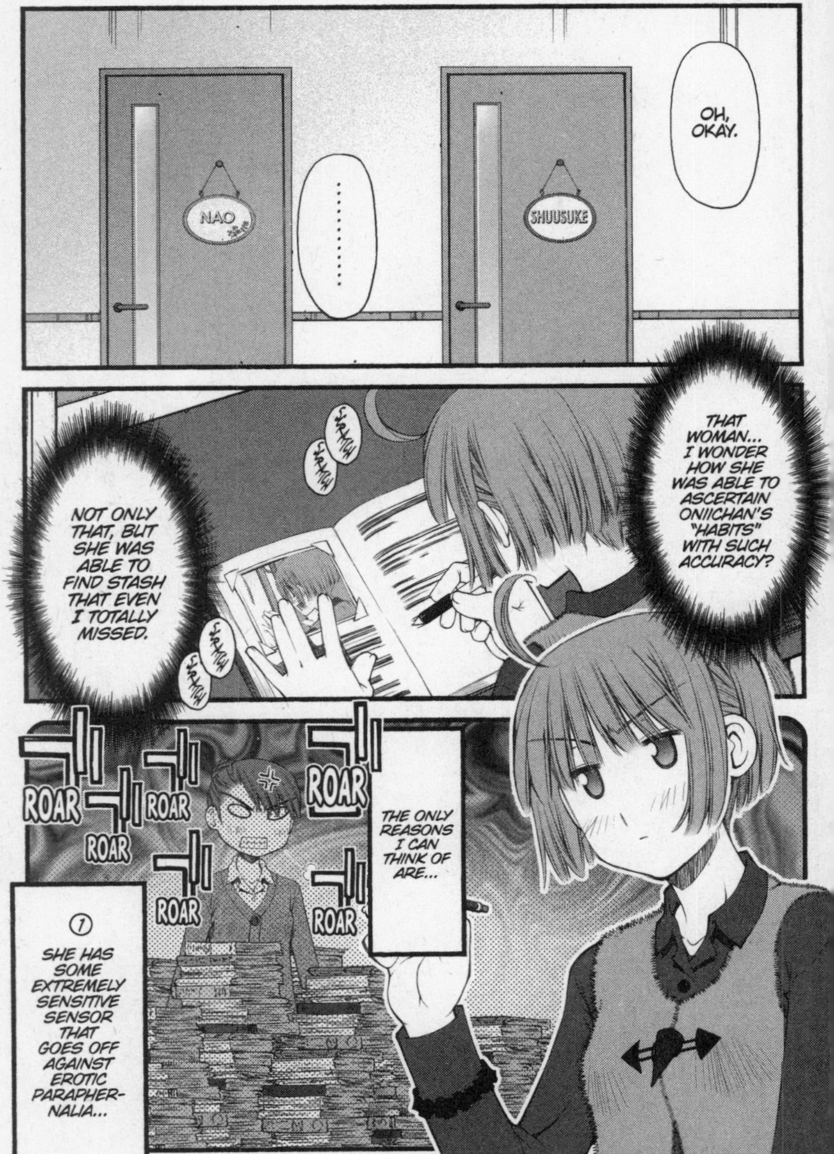

OH, OKAY.
SHUUSUKE
......
NAO
THAT WOMAN... I WONDER HOW SHE WAS ABLE TO ASCERTAIN ONIICHAN'S "HABITS" WITH SUCH ACCURACY?
NOT ONLY THAT, BUT SHE WAS ABLE TO FIND STASH THAT EVEN I TOTALLY MISSED.
THE ONLY REASONS I CAN THINK OF ARE...
ROAR
ROAR
ROAR
ROAR
ROAR
ROAR
ROAR
1
SHE HAS SOME EXTREMELY SENSITIVE SENSOR THAT GOES OFF AGAINST EROTIC PARAPHER-NALIA...

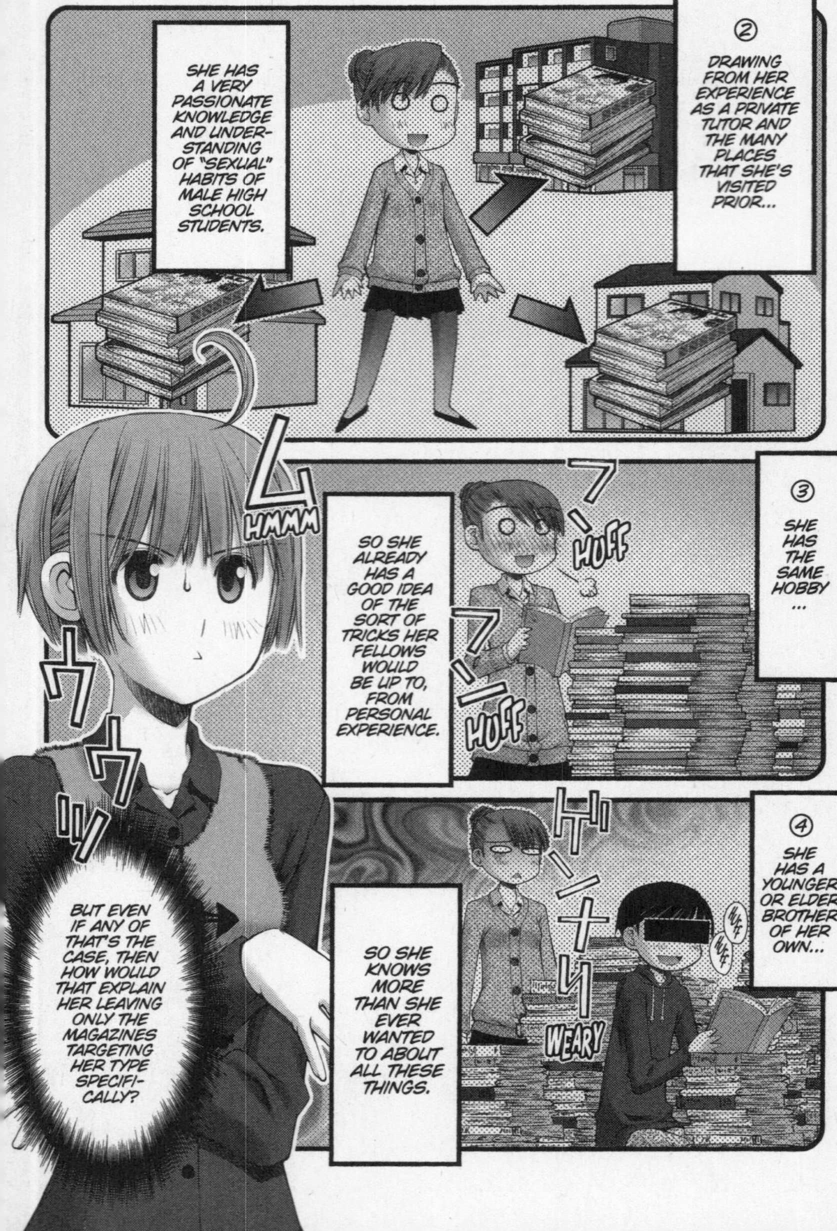
② DRAWING FROM HER EXPERIENCE AS A PRIVATE TUTOR AND THE MANY PLACES THAT SHE'S VISITED PRIOR...
SHE HAS A VERY PASSIONATE KNOWLEDGE AND UNDER-STANDING OF "SEXUAL" HABITS OF MALE HIGH SCHOOL STUDENTS.
③ SHE HAS THE SAME HOBBY ...
HUFF
SO SHE ALREADY HAS A GOOD IDEA OF THE SORT OF TRICKS HER FELLOWS WOULD BE UP TO, FROM PERSONAL EXPERIENCE.
HUFF
④ SHE HAS A YOUNGER OR ELDER BROTHER OF HER OWN...
HUFF
HUFF
WEARY
SO SHE KNOWS MORE THAN SHE EVER WANTED TO ABOUT ALL THESE THINGS.
HMMM
BUT EVEN IF ANY OF THAT'S THE CASE, THEN HOW WOULD THAT EXPLAIN HER LEAVING ONLY THE MAGAZINES TARGETING HER TYPE SPECIFI-CALLY?

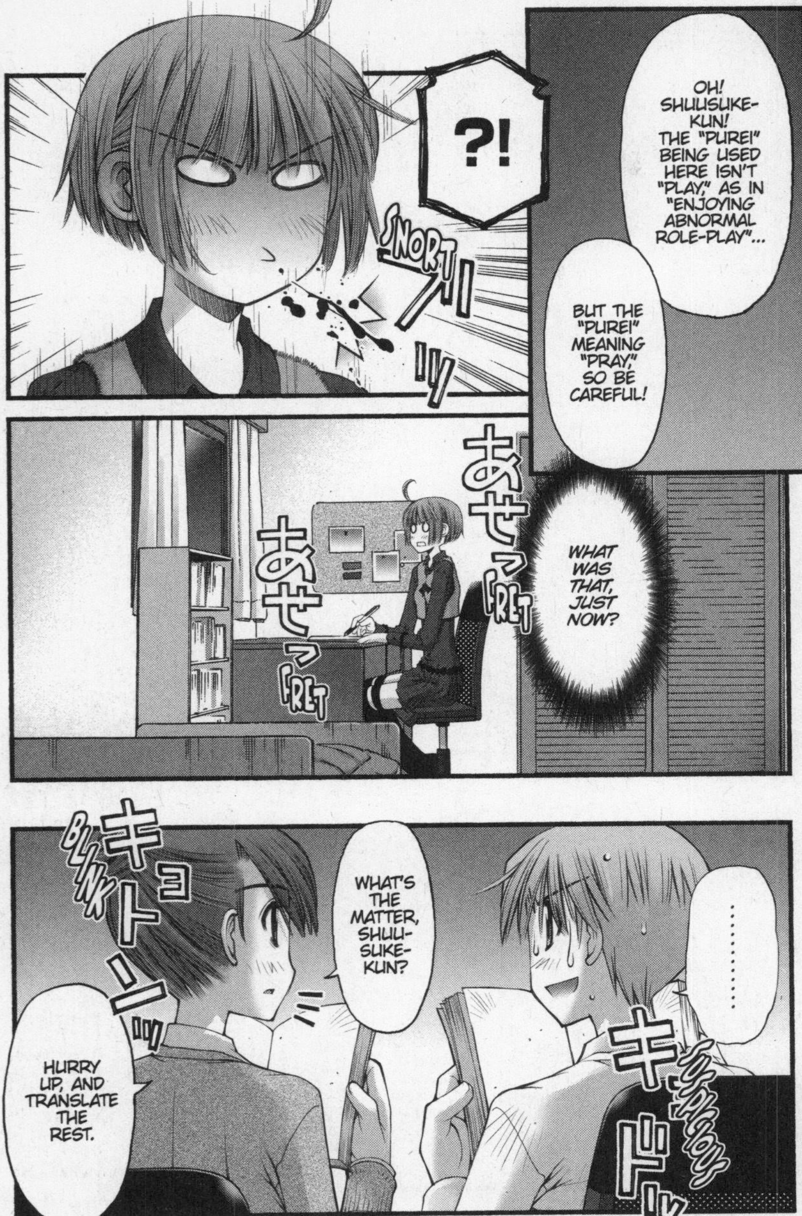
OH! SHUUSUKE-KUN! THE "PUREI" BEING USED HERE ISN'T "PLAY," AS IN "ENJOYING ABNORMAL ROLE-PLAY"...
BUT THE "PUREI" MEANING "PRAY," SO BE CAREFUL!
?!
SNORT
WHAT WAS THAT, JUST NOW?
あせっ
FRET
あせっ
FRET
....
キョトン
BLINK
WHAT'S THE MATTER, SHUU-SUKE-KUN?
HURRY UP, AND TRANSLATE THE REST.
ギクッ
SUSPICIOUS

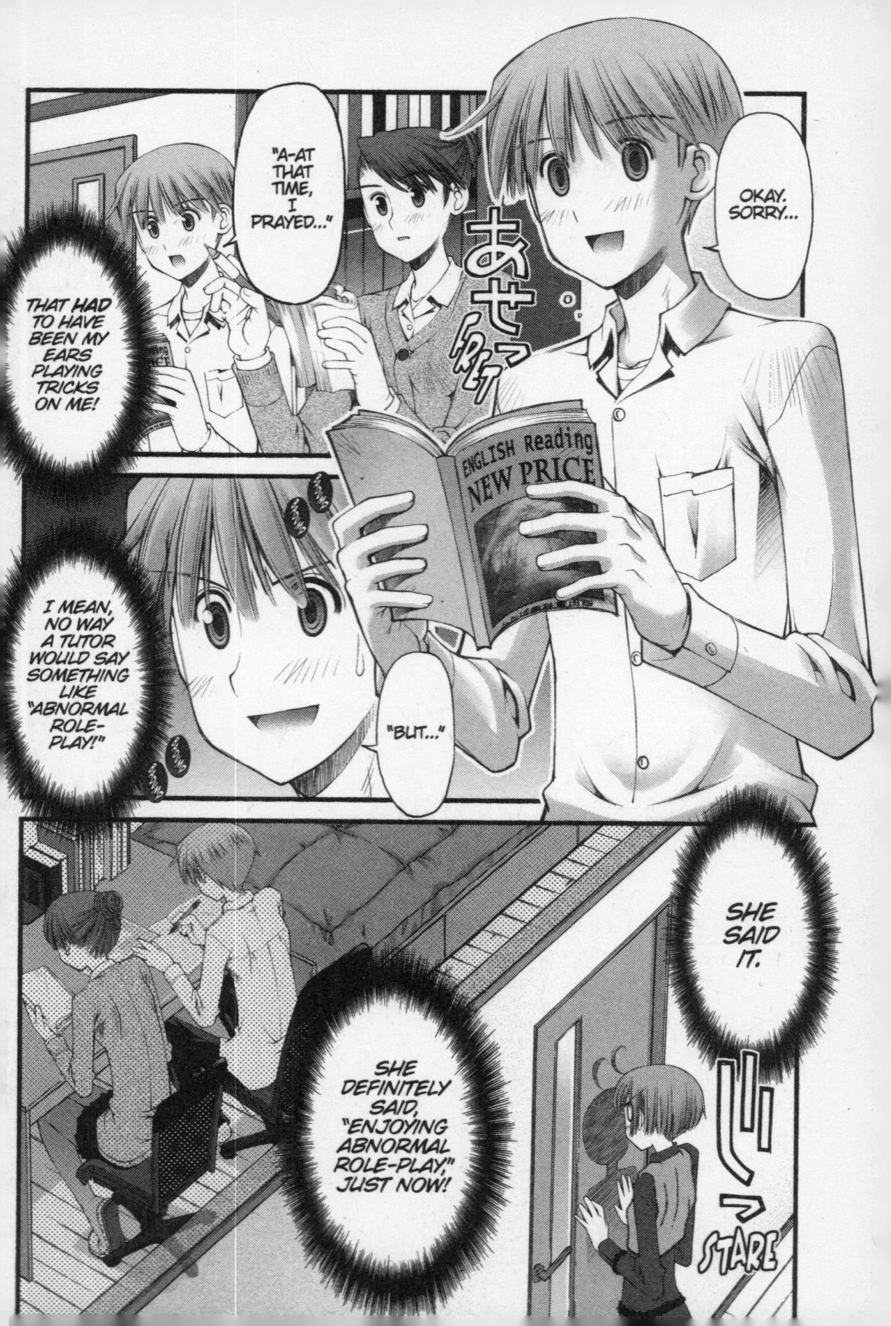
OKAY. SORRY...
あせっ
FRET
"A-AT THAT TIME, I PRAYED..."
THAT HAD TO HAVE BEEN MY EARS PLAYING TRICKS ON ME!
ENGLISH Reading NEW PRICE
"BUT..."
I MEAN, NO WAY A TUTOR WOULD SAY SOMETHING LIKE "ABNORMAL ROLE-PLAY!"
SHE SAID IT.
じー
STARE
SHE DEFINITELY SAID, "ENJOYING ABNORMAL ROLE-PLAY," JUST NOW!

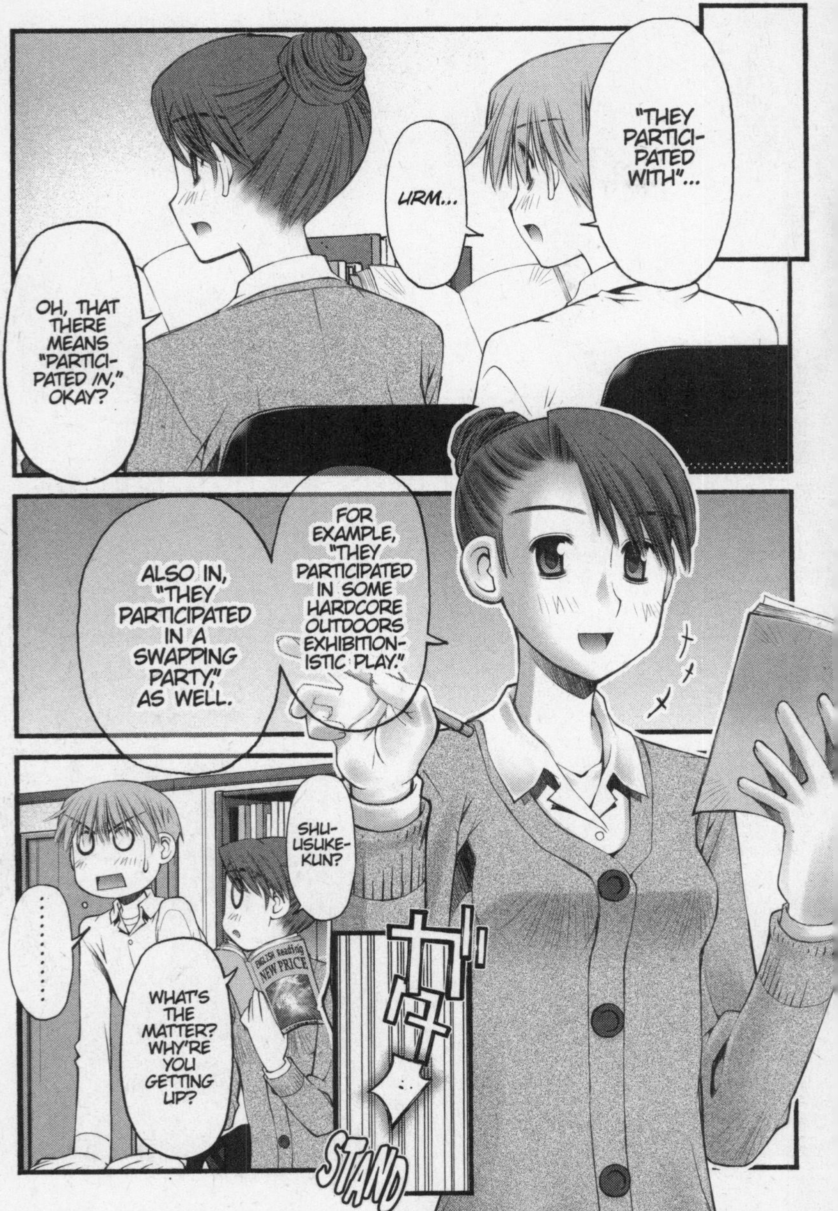
"THEY PARTICIPATED WITH"...
URM...
OH, THAT THERE MEANS "PARTICIPATED IN," OKAY?
FOR EXAMPLE, "THEY PARTICIPATED IN SOME HARDCORE OUTDOORS EXHIBITIONISTIC PLAY."
ALSO IN, "THEY PARTICIPATED IN A SWAPPING PARTY," AS WELL.
SHU-USUKE-KUN?
......
WHAT'S THE MATTER? WHY'RE YOU GETTING UP?
STAND

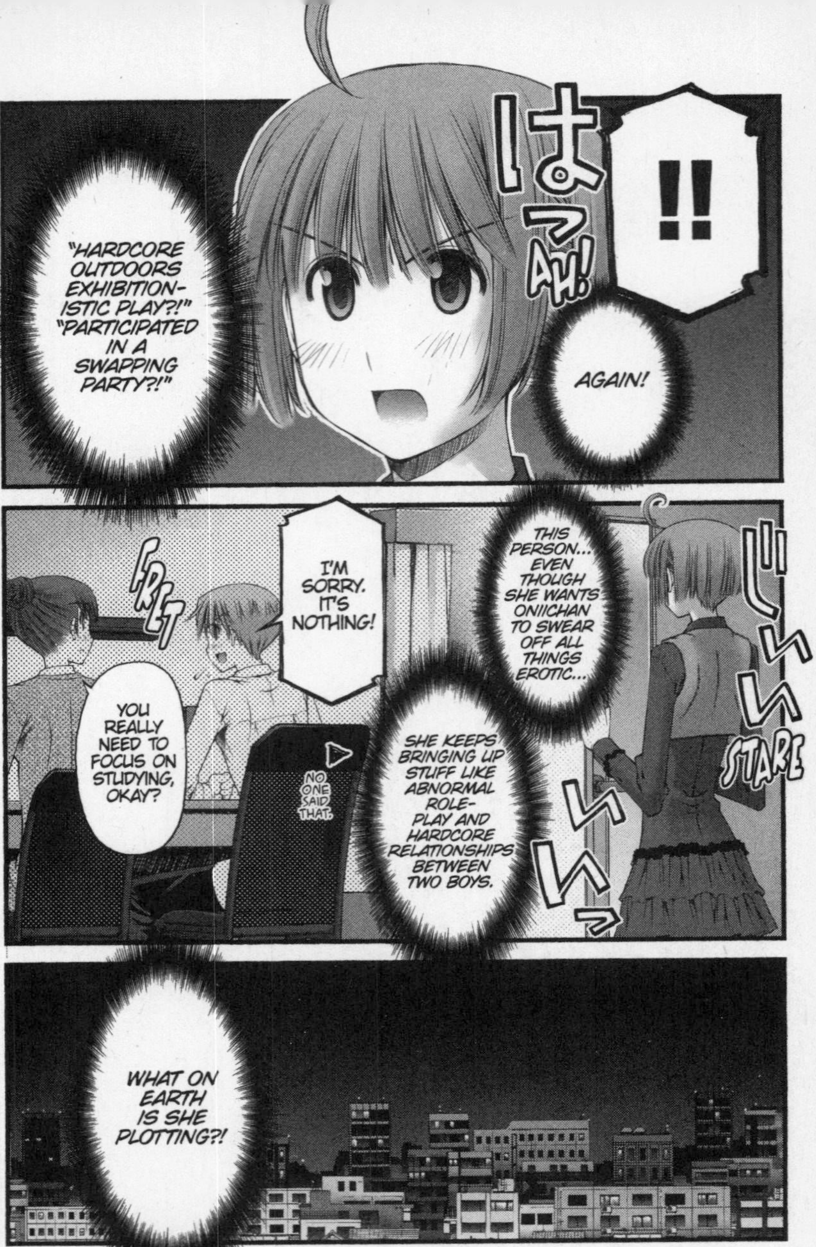
!!
はっ
AH!
AGAIN!
"HARDCORE OUTDOORS EXHIBITION-ISTIC PLAY?!" "PARTICIPATED IN A SWAPPING PARTY?!"
じぃぃぃっ
STARE
THIS PERSON... EVEN THOUGH SHE WANTS ONIICHAN TO SWEAR OFF ALL THINGS EROTIC...
SHE KEEPS BRINGING UP STUFF LIKE ABNORMAL ROLE-PLAY AND HARDCORE RELATIONSHIPS BETWEEN TWO BOYS.
I'M SORRY. IT'S NOTHING!
NO ONE SAID THAT.
FRET
YOU REALLY NEED TO FOCUS ON STUDYING, OKAY?
WHAT ON EARTH IS SHE PLOTTING?!

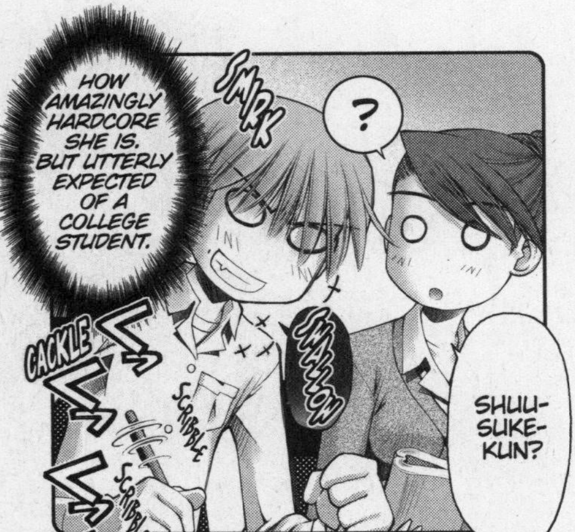
?
SHUU-SUKE-KUN?
SMIRK
HOW AMAZINGLY HARDCORE SHE IS. BUT UTTERLY EXPECTED OF A COLLEGE STUDENT.
SWALLOW
CACKLE
SCRIBBLE
SCRIBBLE

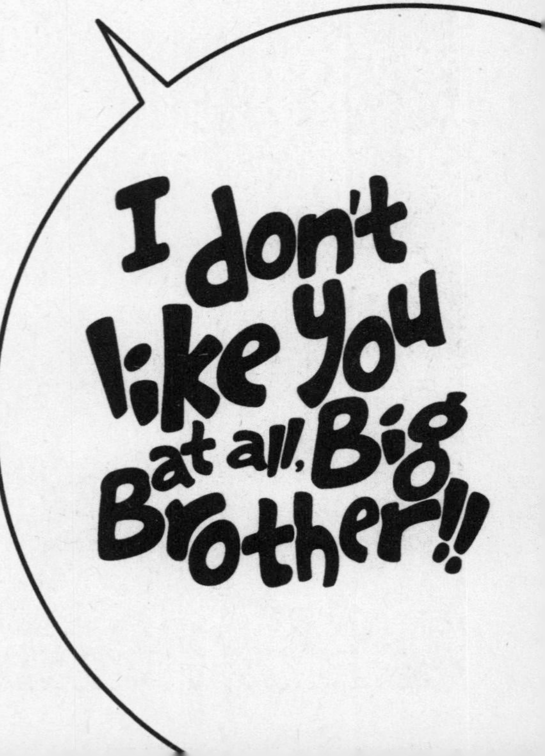
I don't like you at all, Big Brother!!

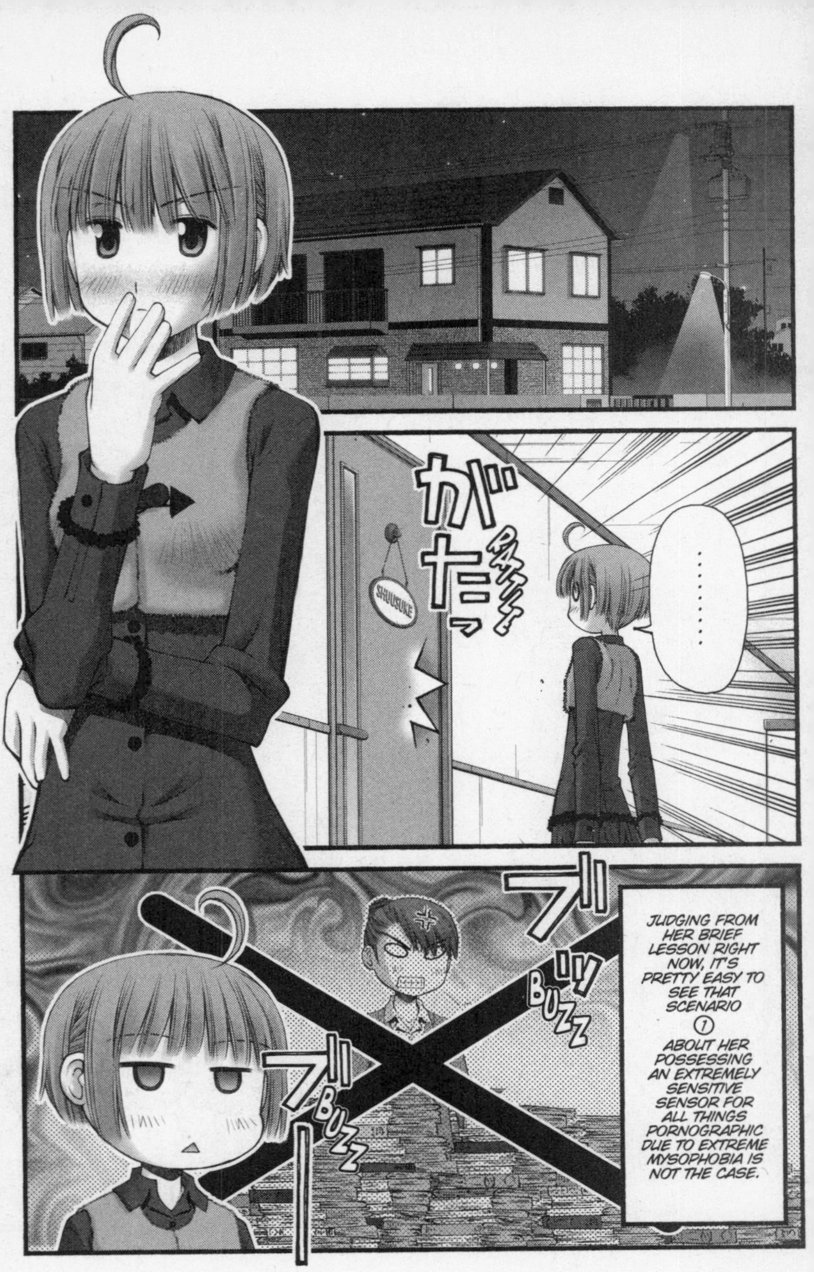
SHUUSUKE
ガたーっ
RATTLE
……
ブー
BUZZ
JUDGING FROM HER BRIEF LESSON RIGHT NOW, IT'S PRETTY EASY TO SEE THAT SCENARIO ① ABOUT HER POSSESSING AN EXTREMELY SENSITIVE SENSOR FOR ALL THINGS PORNOGRAPHIC DUE TO EXTREME MYSOPHOBIA IS NOT THE CASE.
ブー
BUZZ

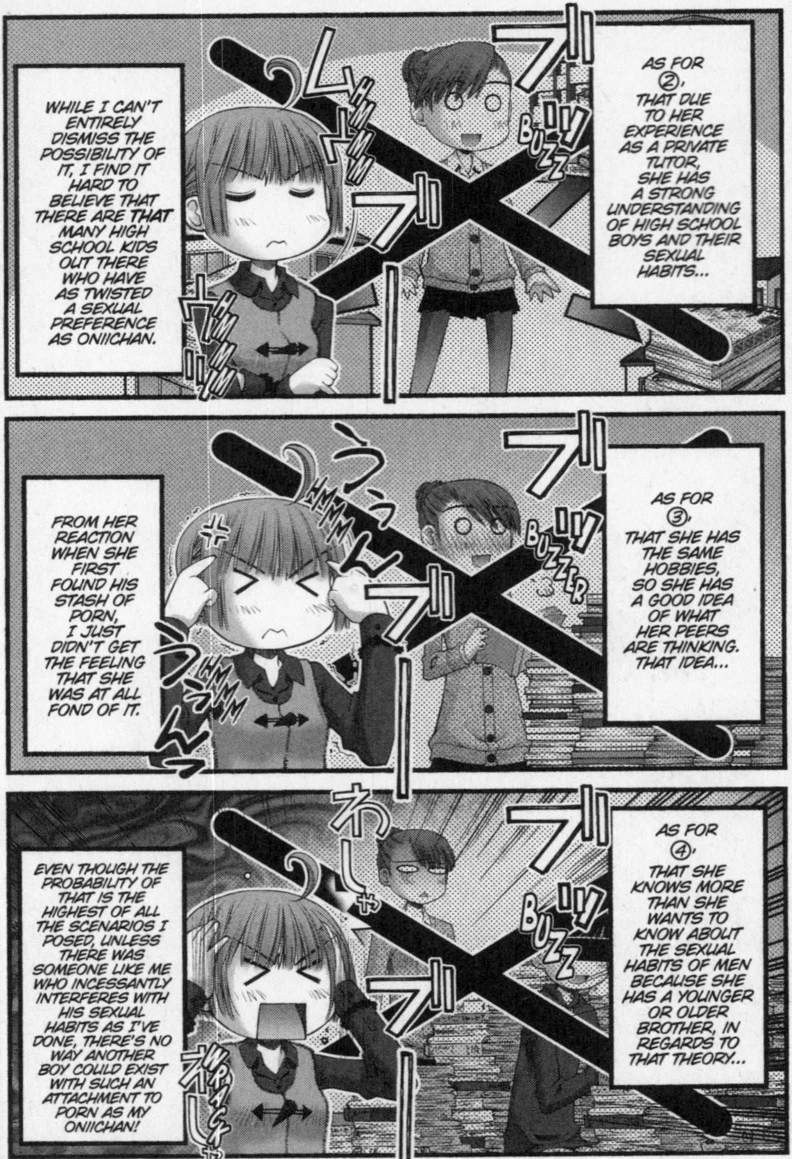
AS FOR ②, THAT DUE TO HER EXPERIENCE AS A PRIVATE TUTOR, SHE HAS A STRONG UNDERSTANDING OF HIGH SCHOOL BOYS AND THEIR SEXUAL HABITS...
BUZZ
HMMMM
WHILE I CAN'T ENTIRELY DISMISS THE POSSIBILITY OF IT, I FIND IT HARD TO BELIEVE THAT THERE ARE THAT MANY HIGH SCHOOL KIDS OUT THERE WHO HAVE AS TWISTED A SEXUAL PREFERENCE AS ONIICHAN.
HMMMM
AS FOR ③, THAT SHE HAS THE SAME HOBBIES, SO SHE HAS A GOOD IDEA OF WHAT HER PEERS ARE THINKING. THAT IDEA...
BUZZER
HMMMM
FROM HER REACTION WHEN SHE FIRST FOUND HIS STASH OF PORN, I JUST DIDN'T GET THE FEELING THAT SHE WAS AT ALL FOND OF IT.
HMMM
AS FOR ④, THAT SHE KNOWS MORE THAN SHE WANTS TO KNOW ABOUT THE SEXUAL HABITS OF MEN BECAUSE SHE HAS A YOUNGER OR OLDER BROTHER, IN REGARDS TO THAT THEORY...
BUZZ
EVEN THOUGH THE PROBABILITY OF THAT IS THE HIGHEST OF ALL THE SCENARIOS I POSED, UNLESS THERE WAS SOMEONE LIKE ME WHO INCESSANTLY INTERFERES WITH HIS SEXUAL HABITS AS I'VE DONE, THERE'S NO WAY ANOTHER BOY COULD EXIST WITH SUCH AN ATTACHMENT TO PORN AS MY ONIICHAN!
WRACK

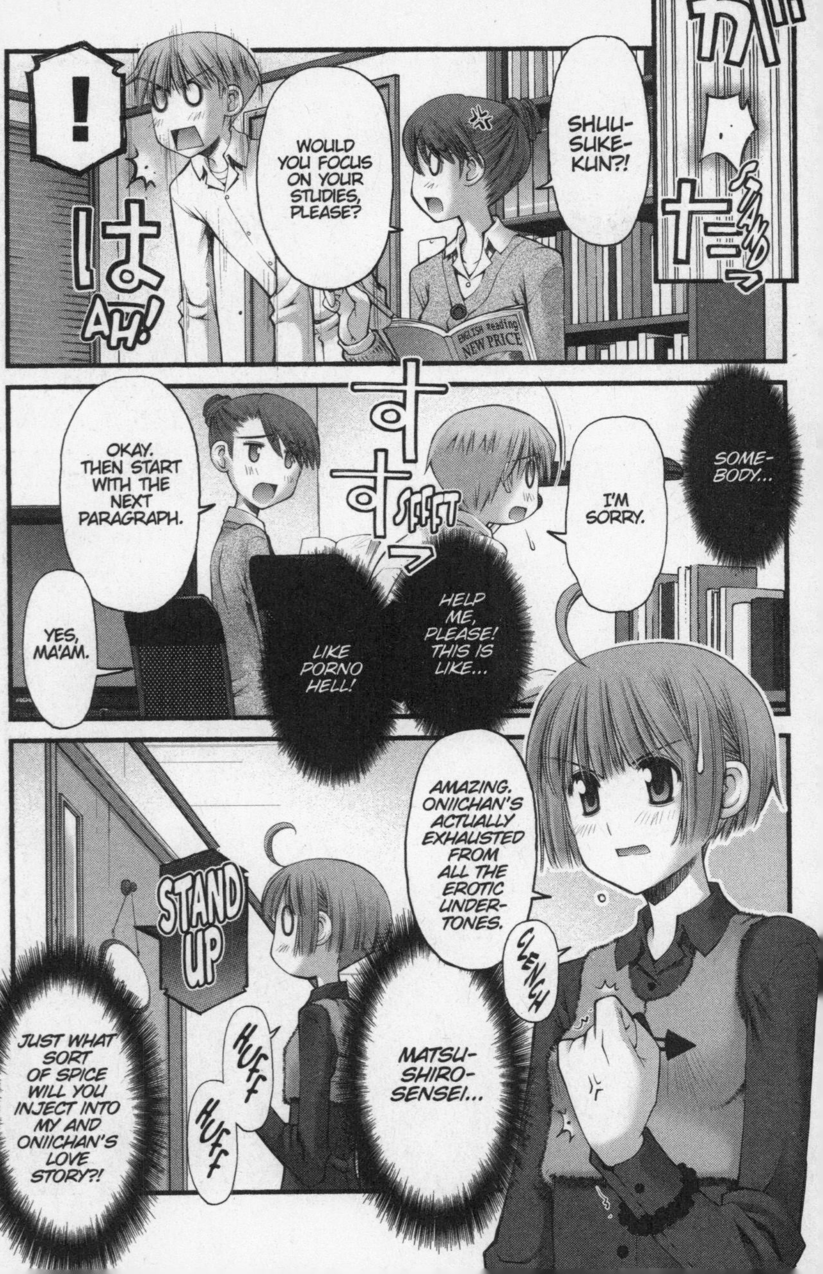
STAND
SHUU-SUKE-KUN?!
WOULD YOU FOCUS ON YOUR STUDIES, PLEASE?
ENGLISH reading NEW PRICE
!
は
AH!
SOME-BODY...
I'M SORRY.
HELP ME, PLEASE! THIS IS LIKE...
LIKE PORNO HELL!
すす
SFFFT
OKAY. THEN START WITH THE NEXT PARAGRAPH.
YES, MA'AM.
AMAZING. ONIICHAN'S ACTUALLY EXHAUSTED FROM ALL THE EROTIC UNDER-TONES.
CLENCH
MATSU-SHIRO-SENSEI...
HUFF HUFF
STAND UP
JUST WHAT SORT OF SPICE WILL YOU INJECT INTO MY AND ONIICHAN'S LOVE STORY?!

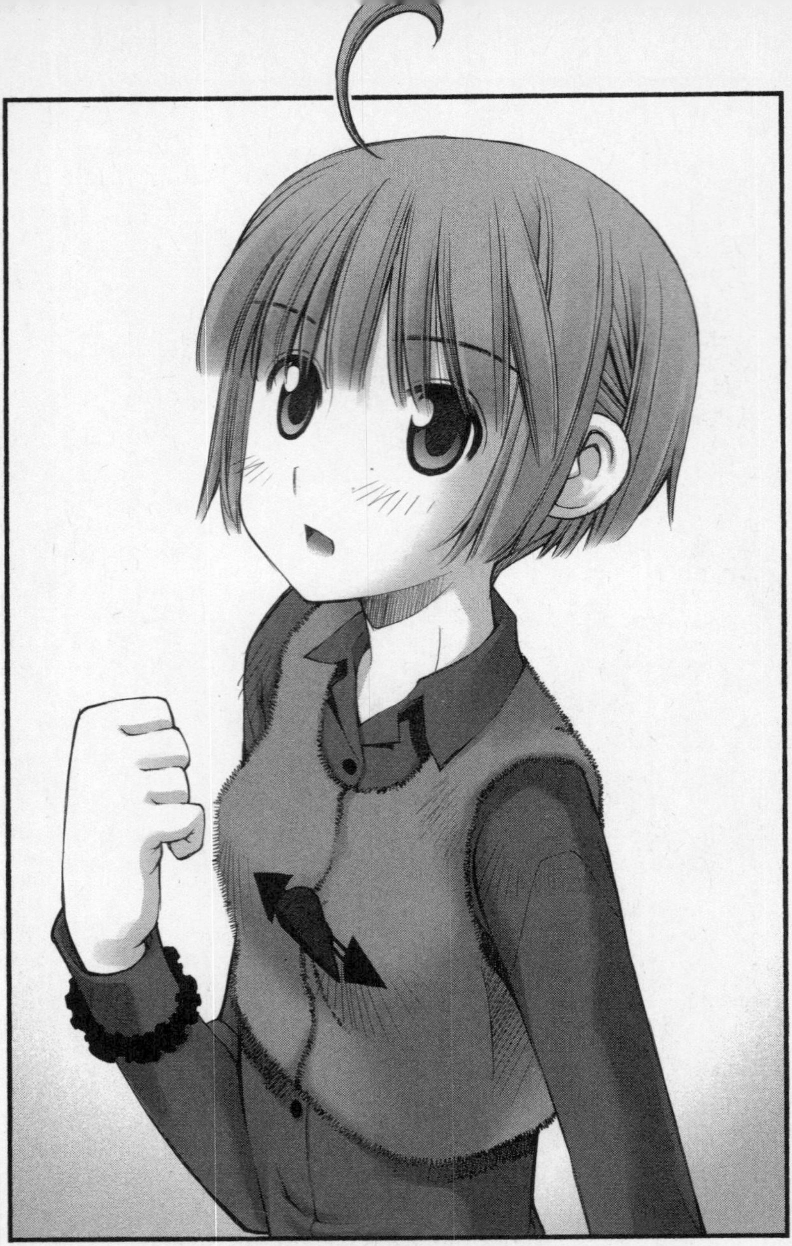

CHAPTER 41 A Special Lesson

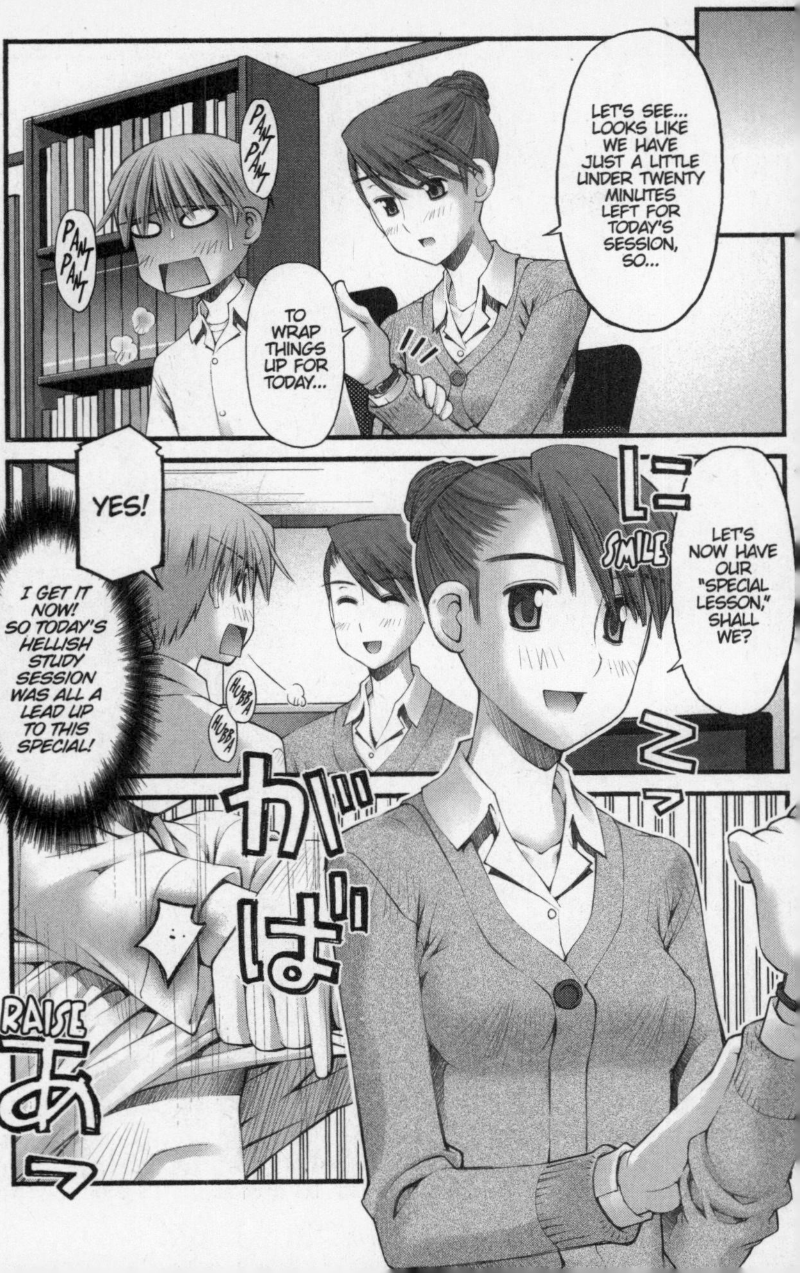
LET'S SEE... LOOKS LIKE WE HAVE JUST A LITTLE UNDER TWENTY MINUTES LEFT FOR TODAY'S SESSION, SO...
TO WRAP THINGS UP FOR TODAY...
PANT PANT
PANT PANT
SMILE
LET'S NOW HAVE OUR "SPECIAL LESSON," SHALL WE?
YES!
I GET IT NOW! SO TODAY'S HELLISH STUDY SESSION WAS ALL A LEAD UP TO THIS SPECIAL!
HUBBA HUBBA
がば
RAISE
あっ

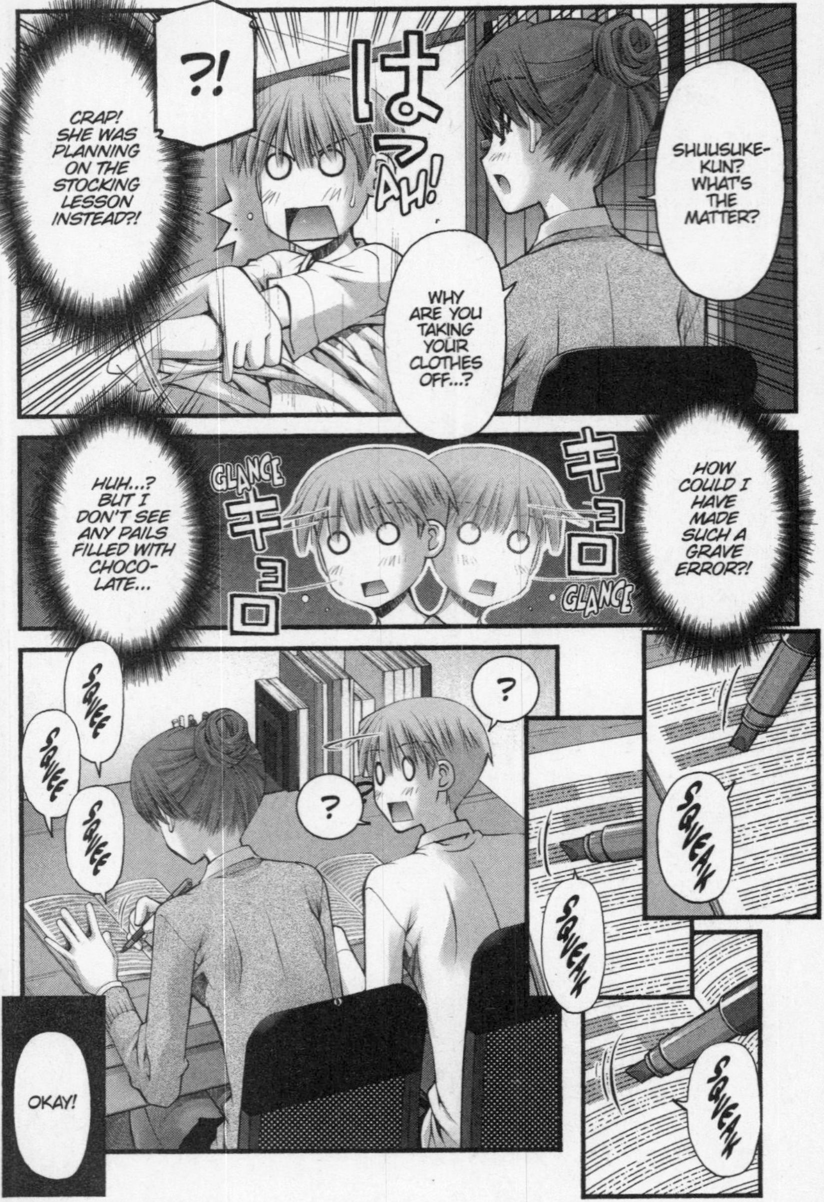
SHUUSUKE-KUN? WHAT'S THE MATTER?
WHY ARE YOU TAKING YOUR CLOTHES OFF...?
はっ
AH!
?!
CRAP! SHE WAS PLANNING ON THE STOCKING LESSON INSTEAD?!
HOW COULD I HAVE MADE SUCH A GRAVE ERROR?!
キョロ
GLANCE
キョロ
GLANCE
HUH...? BUT I DON'T SEE ANY PAILS FILLED WITH CHOCO-LATE...
SQUEAK
SQUEAK
SQUEAK
?
?
SQUEE
SQUEE
SQUEE
OKAY!

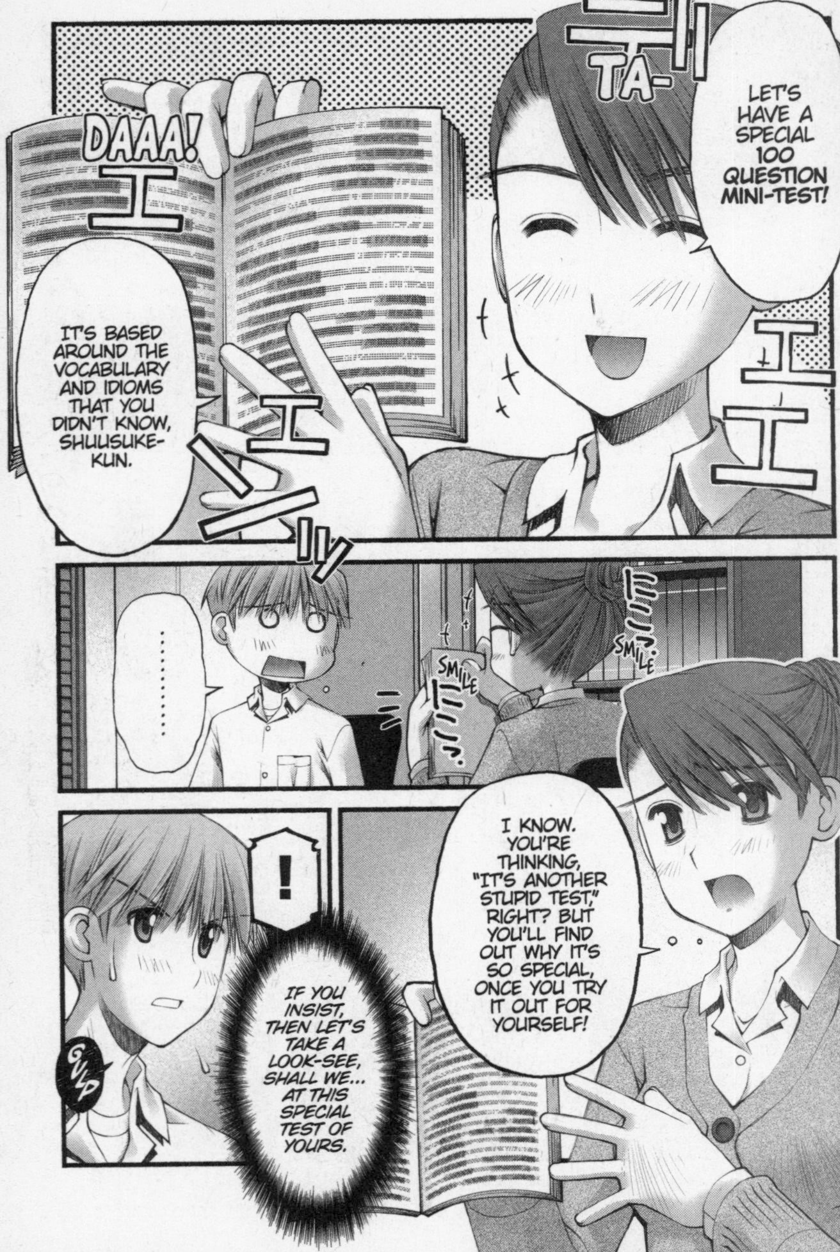
TA-
LET'S HAVE A SPECIAL 100 QUESTION MINI-TEST!
DAAA!
IT'S BASED AROUND THE VOCABULARY AND IDIOMS THAT YOU DIDN'T KNOW, SHUUSUKE-KUN.
SMILE
SMILE
......
I KNOW. YOU'RE THINKING, "IT'S ANOTHER STUPID TEST," RIGHT? BUT YOU'LL FIND OUT WHY IT'S SO SPECIAL, ONCE YOU TRY IT OUT FOR YOURSELF!
!
IF YOU INSIST, THEN LET'S TAKE A LOOK-SEE, SHALL WE... AT THIS SPECIAL TEST OF YOURS.
GULP

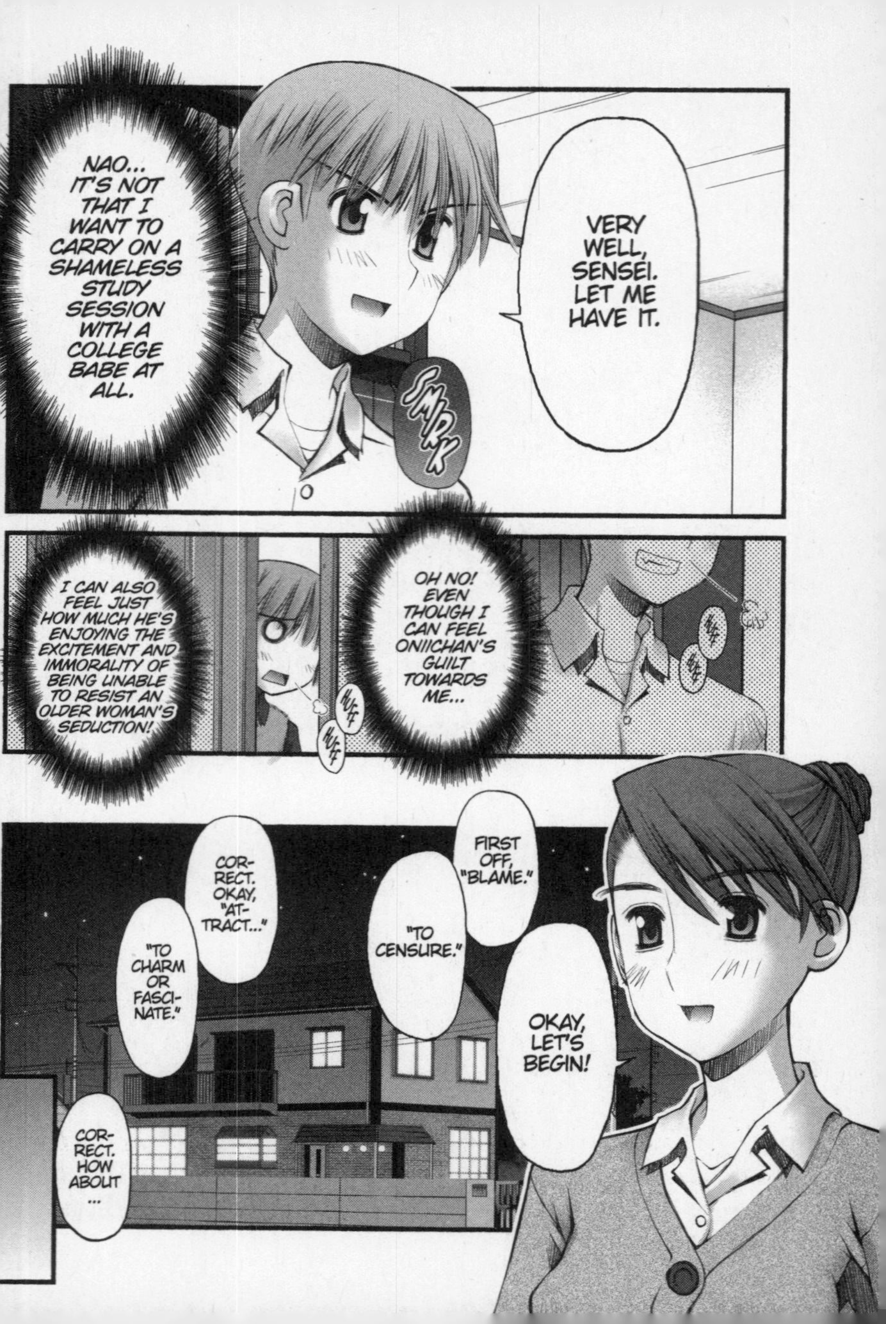
VERY WELL, SENSEI. LET ME HAVE IT.
SMIRK
NAO... IT'S NOT THAT I WANT TO CARRY ON A SHAMELESS STUDY SESSION WITH A COLLEGE BABE AT ALL.
HUFF
HUFF
OH NO! EVEN THOUGH I CAN FEEL ONIICHAN'S GUILT TOWARDS ME...
I CAN ALSO FEEL JUST HOW MUCH HE'S ENJOYING THE EXCITEMENT AND IMMORALITY OF BEING UNABLE TO RESIST AN OLDER WOMAN'S SEDUCTION!
HUFF
HUFF
OKAY, LET'S BEGIN!
FIRST OFF, "BLAME."
"TO CENSURE."
COR-RECT. OKAY, "AT-TRACT..."
"TO CHARM OR FASCI-NATE."
COR-RECT. HOW ABOUT ...

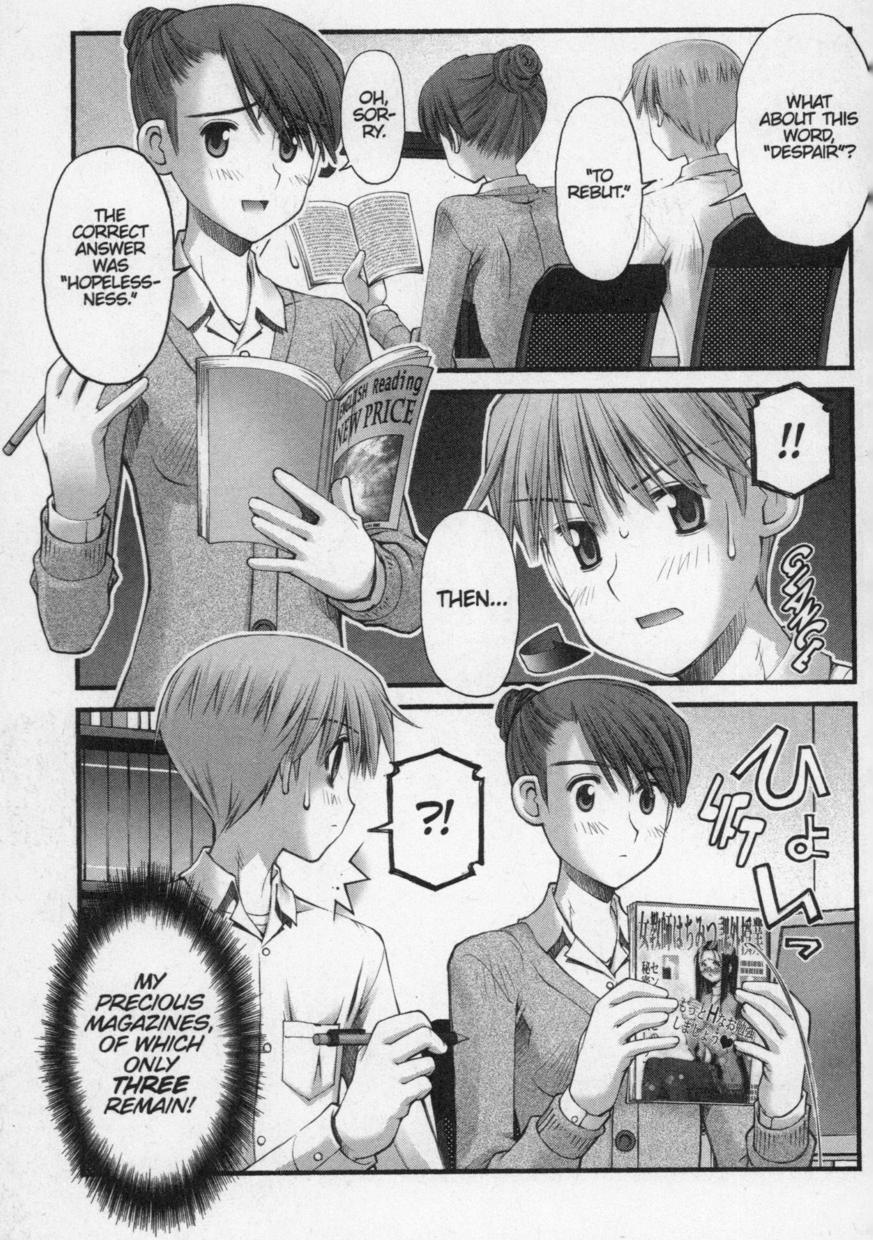
WHAT ABOUT THIS WORD, "DESPAIR"?
"TO REBUT."
OH, SORRY.
THE CORRECT ANSWER WAS "HOPELESSNESS."
ENGLISH Reading
NEW PRICE
!!
GLANCE
THEN...
ひょんっ
LIFT
?!
もっとHなお勉強しましょう♥
MY PRECIOUS MAGAZINES, OF WHICH ONLY THREE REMAIN!

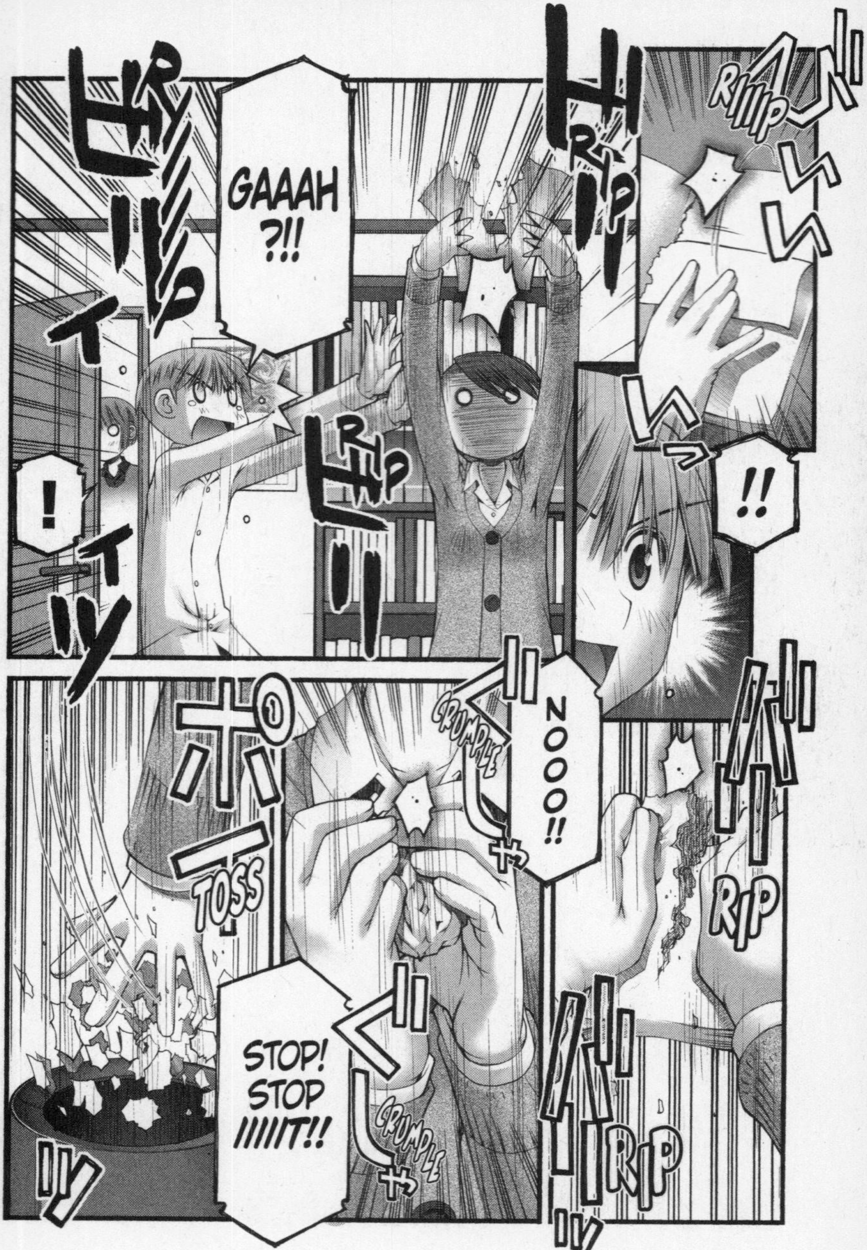
RIIIP
!!
RIP
RIP
GAAAH ?!!
RIP
!
RIP
RIP
NOOOO!!
CRUMPLE
STOP! STOP !!!!!!T!!
CRUMPLE
TOSS

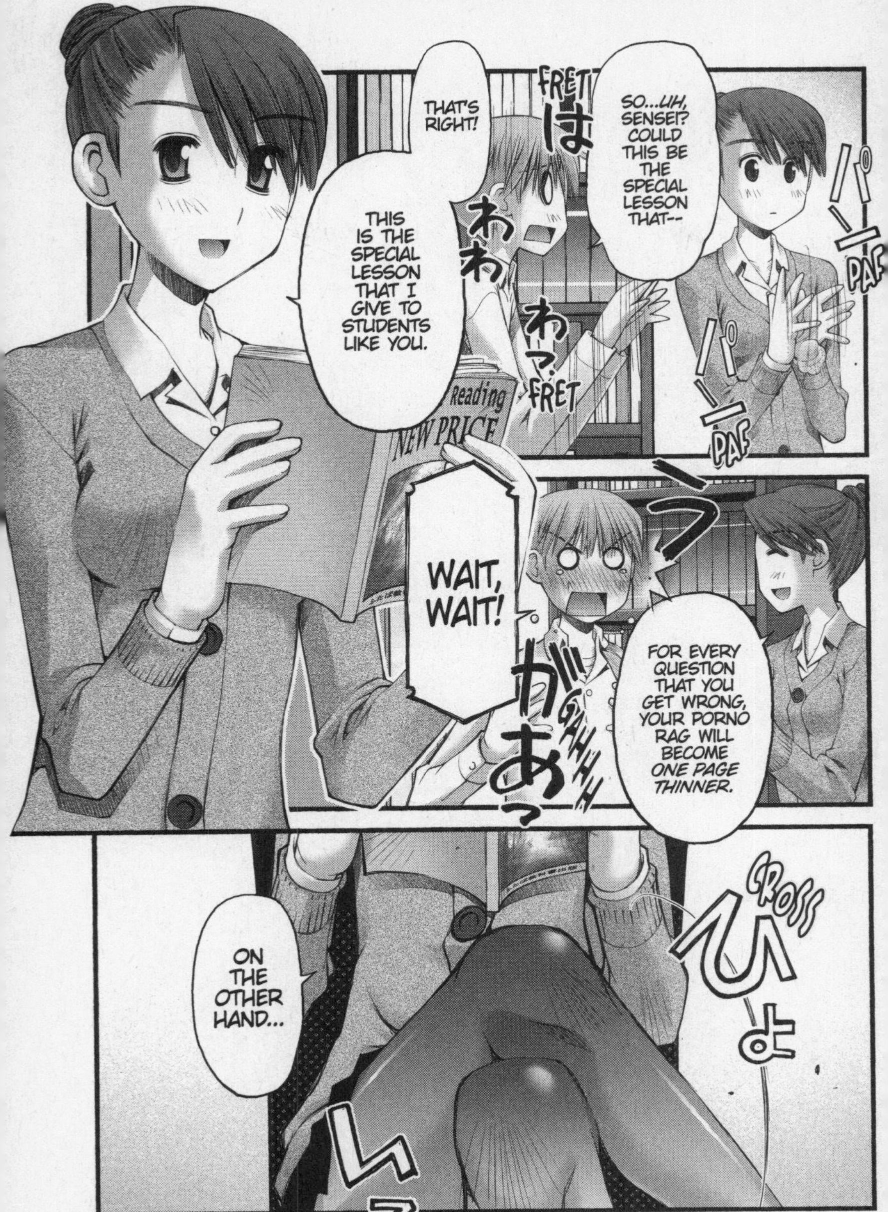
パーー
PAF
パーー
PAF
SO...UH, SENSEI? COULD THIS BE THE SPECIAL LESSON THAT--
FRET
はわわわっ
FRET
THAT'S RIGHT!
THIS IS THE SPECIAL LESSON THAT I GIVE TO STUDENTS LIKE YOU.
Reading
NEW PRICE
う
FOR EVERY QUESTION THAT YOU GET WRONG, YOUR PORNO RAG WILL BECOME ONE PAGE THINNER.
WAIT, WAIT!
があっ
GAHHH
CROSS
ひょ
ON THE OTHER HAND...
んっ

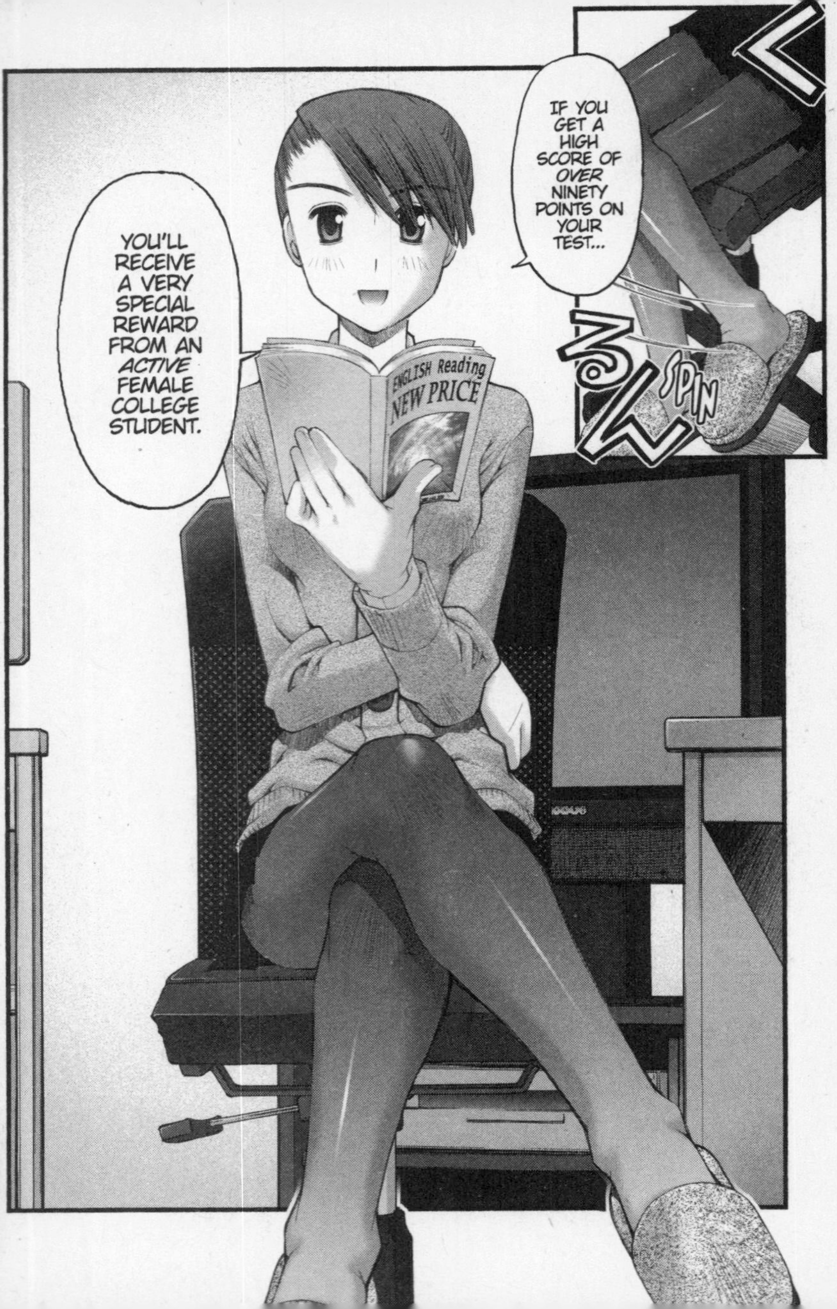
IF YOU GET A HIGH SCORE OF OVER NINETY POINTS ON YOUR TEST...
SPIN
YOU'LL RECEIVE A VERY SPECIAL REWARD FROM AN ACTIVE FEMALE COLLEGE STUDENT.
ENGLISH Reading
NEW PRICE

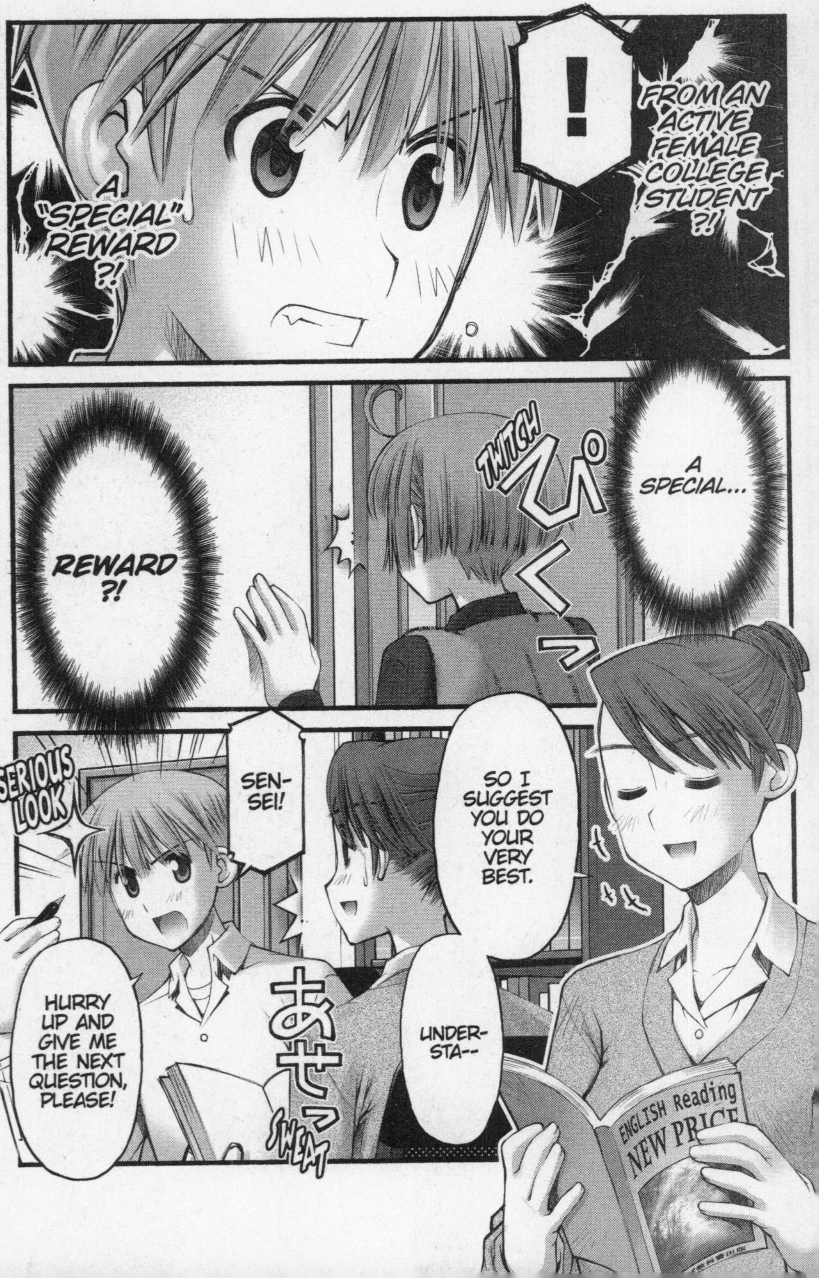
!
FROM AN ACTIVE FEMALE COLLEGE STUDENT ?!
A "SPECIAL" REWARD ?!
A SPECIAL...
ぴくっ
TWITCH
REWARD ?!
SO I SUGGEST YOU DO YOUR VERY BEST.
SEN-SEI!
SERIOUS LOOK
UNDER-STA--
あせっ
SWEAT
HURRY UP AND GIVE ME THE NEXT QUESTION, PLEASE!
ENGLISH Reading
NEW PRICE

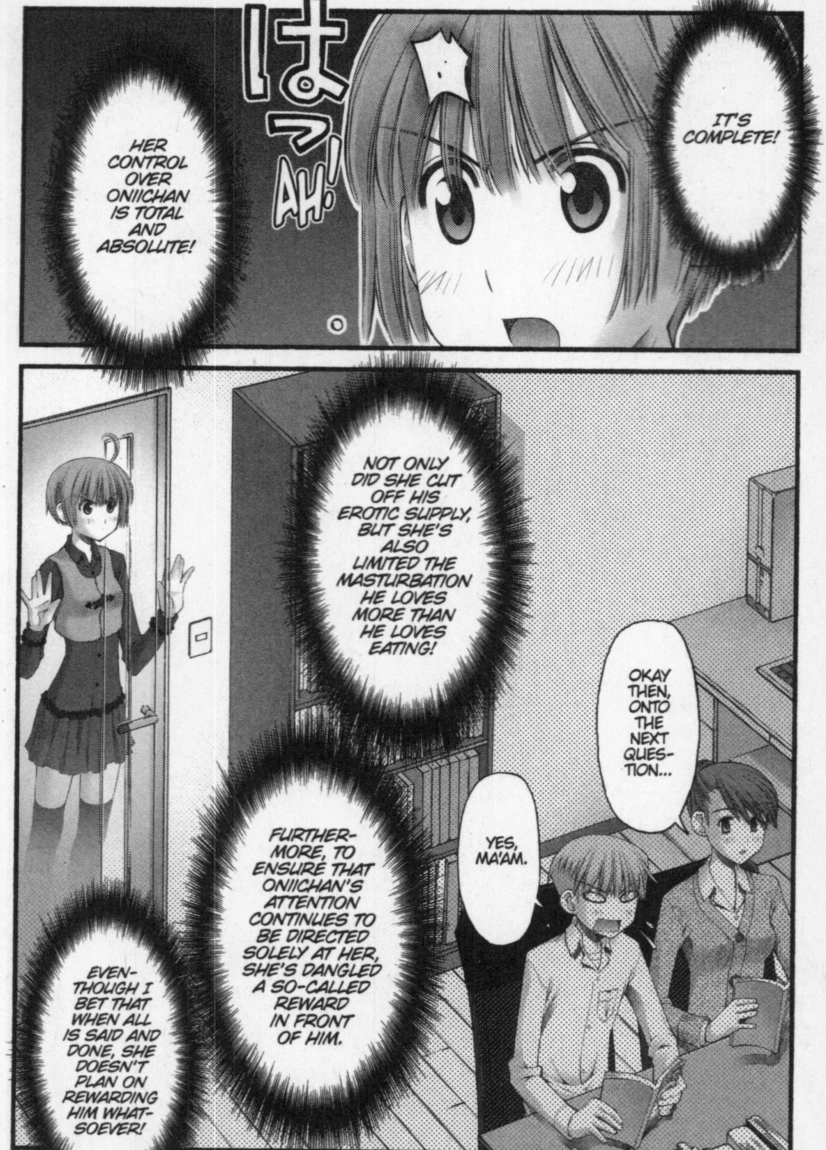

IT'S COMPLETE!
はっ
AH!
HER CONTROL OVER ONIICHAN IS TOTAL AND ABSOLUTE!
NOT ONLY DID SHE CUT OFF HIS EROTIC SUPPLY, BUT SHE'S ALSO LIMITED THE MASTURBATION HE LOVES MORE THAN HE LOVES EATING!
OKAY THEN, ONTO THE NEXT QUES-TION...
YES, MA'AM.
FURTHER-MORE, TO ENSURE THAT ONIICHAN'S ATTENTION CONTINUES TO BE DIRECTED SOLELY AT HER, SHE'S DANGLED A SO-CALLED REWARD IN FRONT OF HIM.
EVEN-THOUGH I BET THAT WHEN ALL IS SAID AND DONE, SHE DOESN'T PLAN ON REWARDING HIM WHAT-SOEVER!

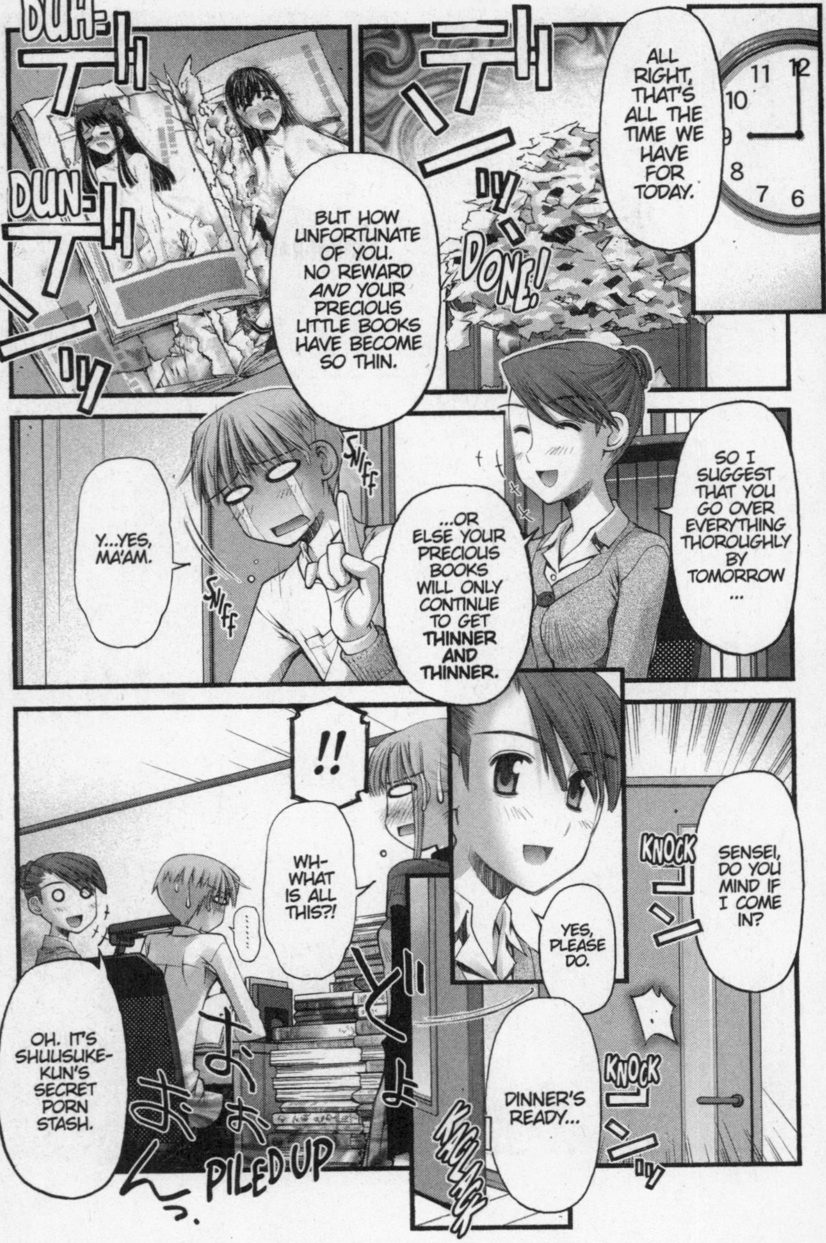
ALL RIGHT, THAT'S ALL THE TIME WE HAVE FOR TODAY.
DONE!
BUT HOW UNFORTUNATE OF YOU. NO REWARD AND YOUR PRECIOUS LITTLE BOOKS HAVE BECOME SO THIN.
DUH-
DUN-
SO I SUGGEST THAT YOU GO OVER EVERYTHING THOROUGHLY BY TOMORROW ...
...OR ELSE YOUR PRECIOUS BOOKS WILL ONLY CONTINUE TO GET THINNER AND THINNER.
SNIFF
Y...YES, MA'AM.
SNIFF
KNOCK
SENSEI, DO YOU MIND IF I COME IN?
KNOCK
YES, PLEASE DO.
DINNER'S READY...
!!
WH- WHAT IS ALL THIS?!
......
OH. IT'S SHUUSUKE-KUN'S SECRET PORN STASH.
PILED UP

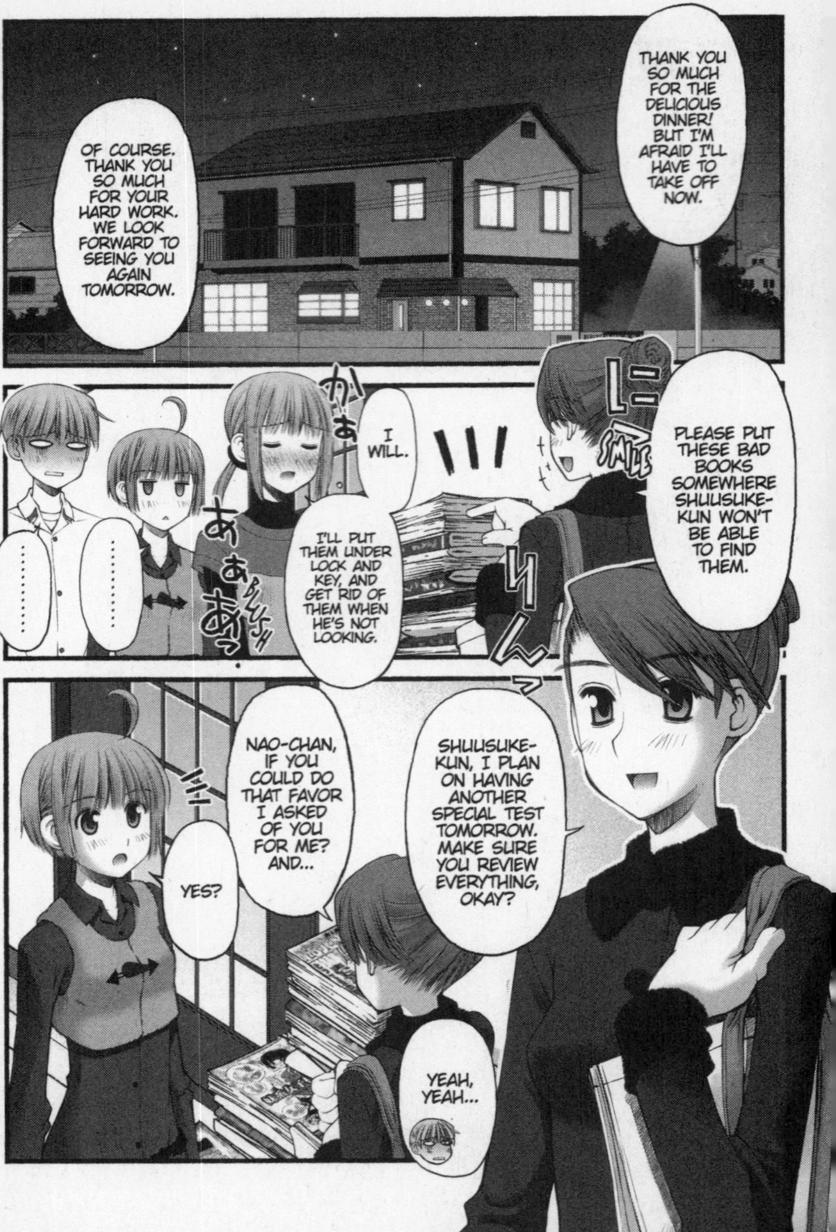
THANK YOU SO MUCH FOR THE DELICIOUS DINNER! BUT I'M AFRAID I'LL HAVE TO TAKE OFF NOW.
OF COURSE. THANK YOU SO MUCH FOR YOUR HARD WORK. WE LOOK FORWARD TO SEEING YOU AGAIN TOMORROW.
SMILE
PLEASE PUT THESE BAD BOOKS SOMEWHERE SHUUSUKE-KUN WON'T BE ABLE TO FIND THEM.
I WILL.
I'LL PUT THEM UNDER LOCK AND KEY, AND GET RID OF THEM WHEN HE'S NOT LOOKING.
BLUSH
……
……
SHUUSUKE-KUN, I PLAN ON HAVING ANOTHER SPECIAL TEST TOMORROW. MAKE SURE YOU REVIEW EVERYTHING, OKAY?
NAO-CHAN, IF YOU COULD DO THAT FAVOR I ASKED OF YOU FOR ME? AND...
YES?
YEAH, YEAH...

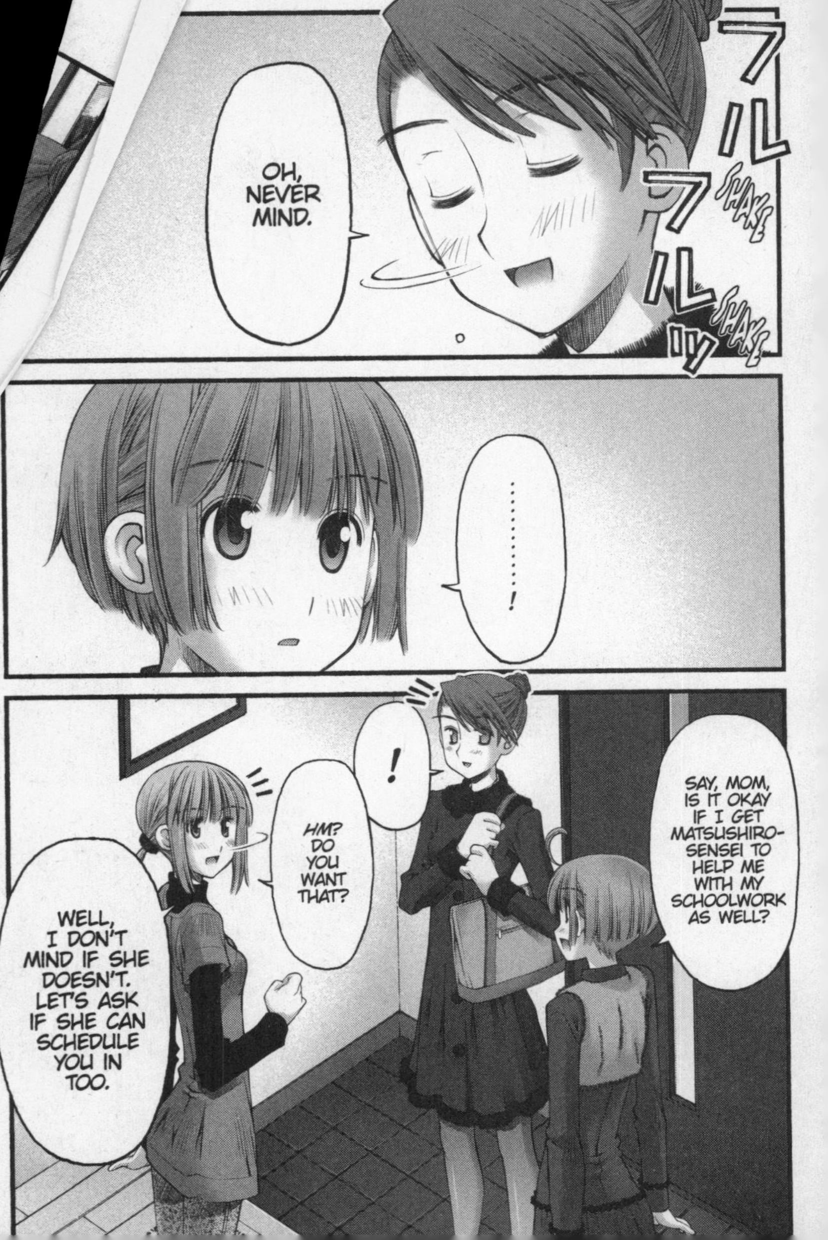
フルフルッ
SHAKE SHAKE
OH, NEVER MIND.
......!
SAY, MOM, IS IT OKAY IF I GET MATSUSHIRO-SENSEI TO HELP ME WITH MY SCHOOLWORK AS WELL?
!
HM? DO YOU WANT THAT?
WELL, I DON'T MIND IF SHE DOESN'T. LET'S ASK IF SHE CAN SCHEDULE YOU IN TOO.

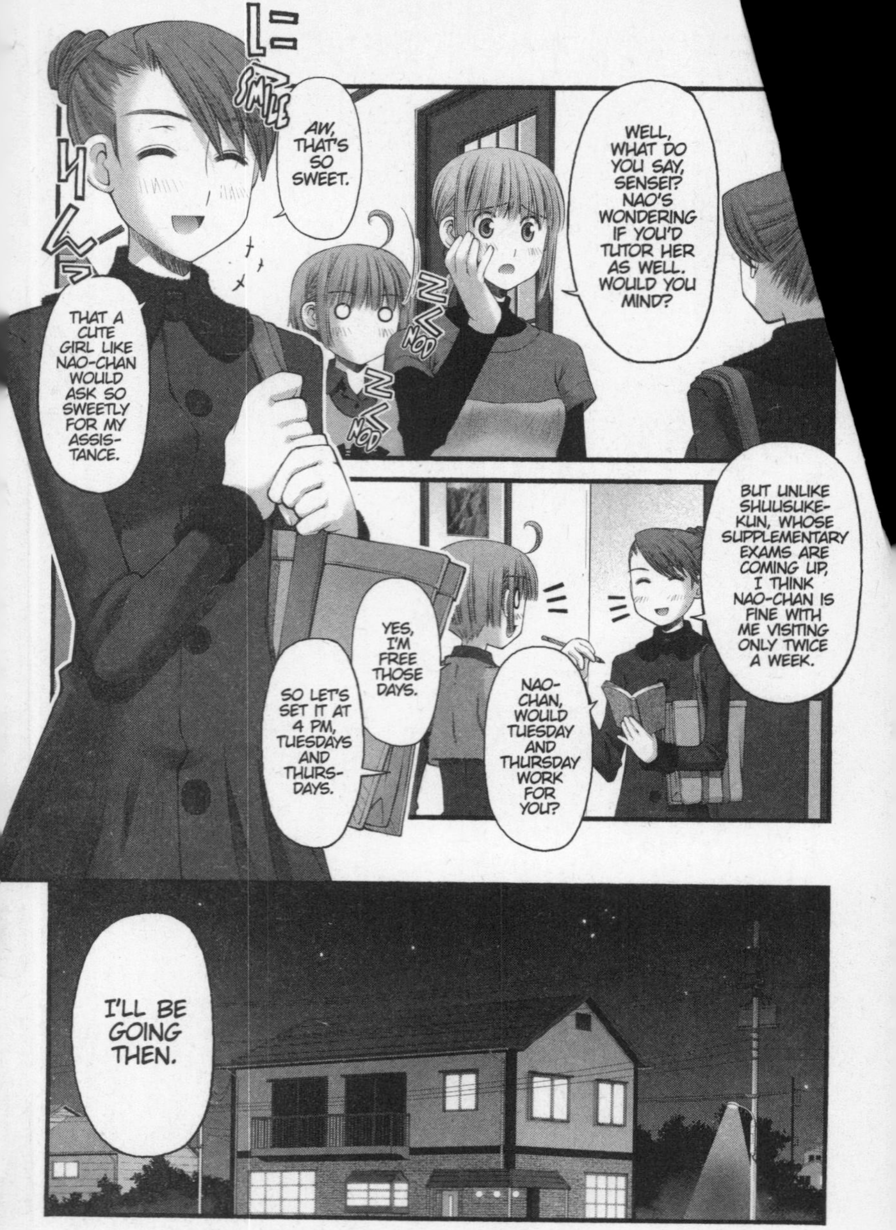
WELL, WHAT DO YOU SAY, SENSEI? NAO'S WONDERING IF YOU'D TUTOR HER AS WELL. WOULD YOU MIND?
NOD
NOD
BUT UNLIKE SHUUSUKE-KUN, WHOSE SUPPLEMENTARY EXAMS ARE COMING UP, I THINK NAO-CHAN IS FINE WITH ME VISITING ONLY TWICE A WEEK.
NAO-CHAN, WOULD TUESDAY AND THURSDAY WORK FOR YOU?
YES, I'M FREE THOSE DAYS.
SO LET'S SET IT AT 4 PM, TUESDAYS AND THURSDAYS.
SMILE
AW, THAT'S SO SWEET.
THAT A CUTE GIRL LIKE NAO-CHAN WOULD ASK SO SWEETLY FOR MY ASSISTANCE.
I'LL BE GOING THEN.

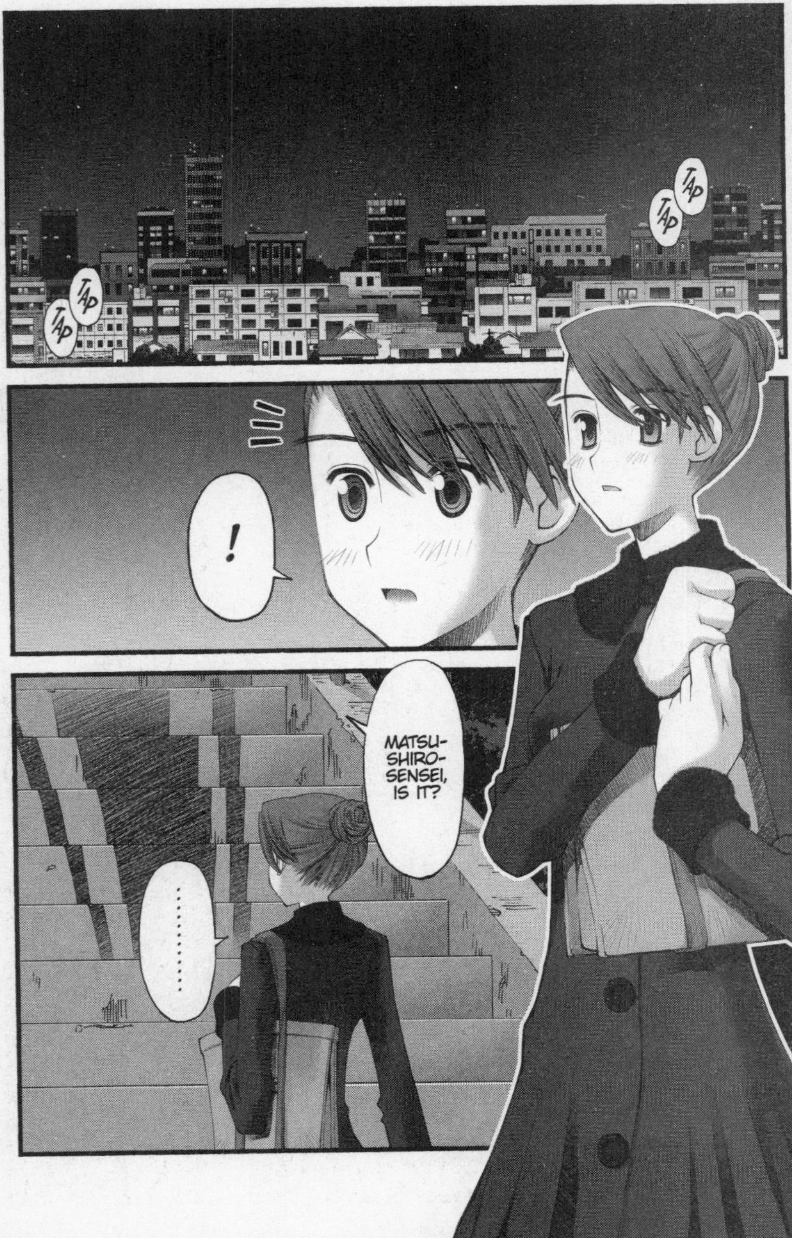
TAP TAP
TAP TAP
!
MATSU-SHIRO-SENSEI, IS IT?
....

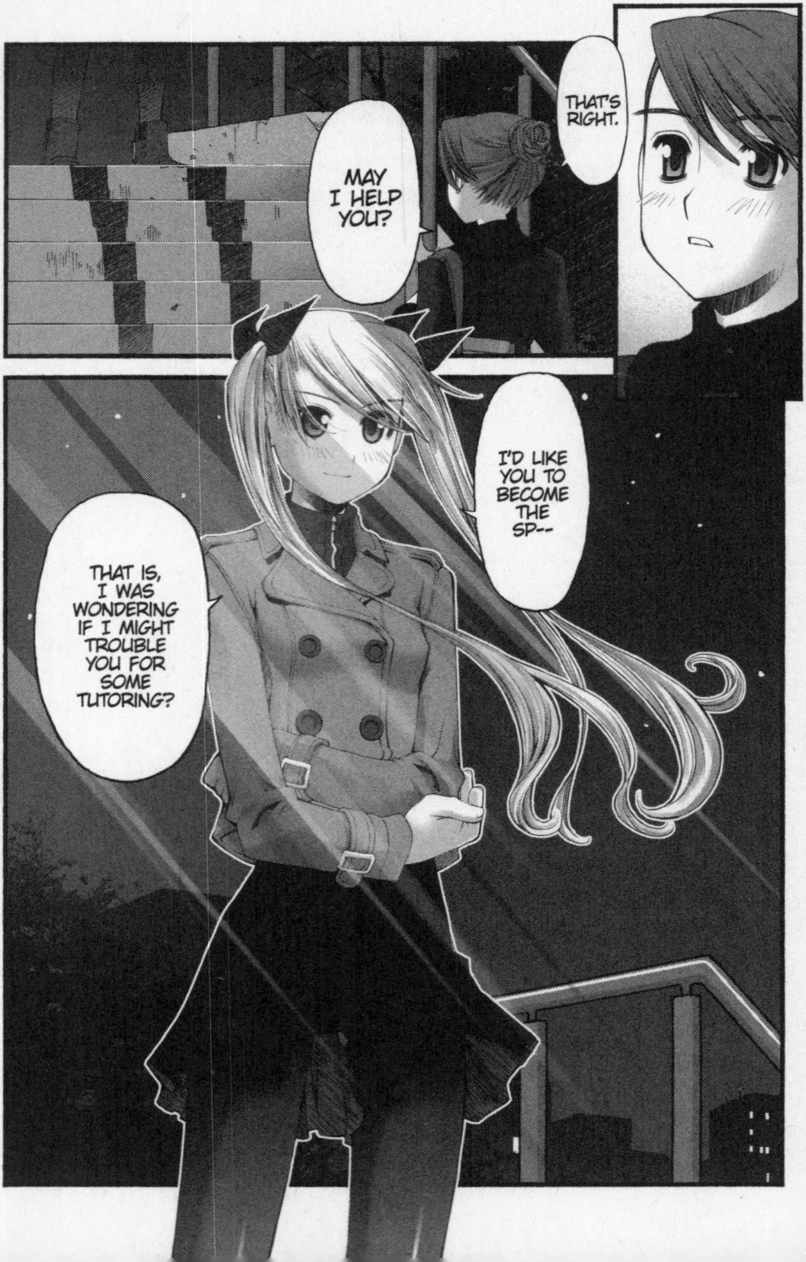
THAT'S RIGHT.
MAY I HELP YOU?
I'D LIKE YOU TO BECOME THE SP--
THAT IS, I WAS WONDERING IF I MIGHT TROUBLE YOU FOR SOME TUTORING?

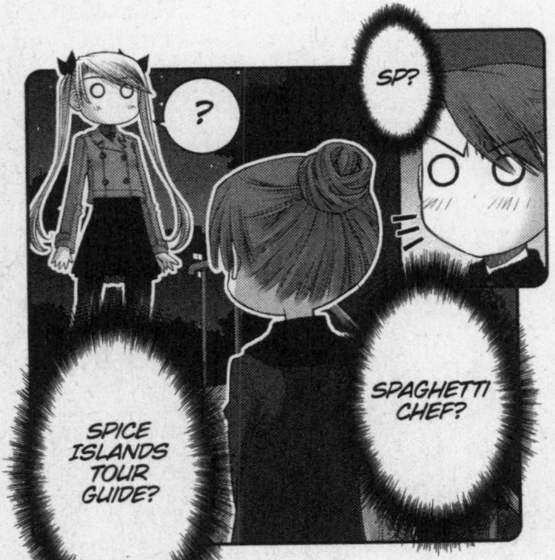
SP?
?
SPAGHETTI CHEF?
SPICE ISLANDS TOUR GUIDE?

★Special Comic★

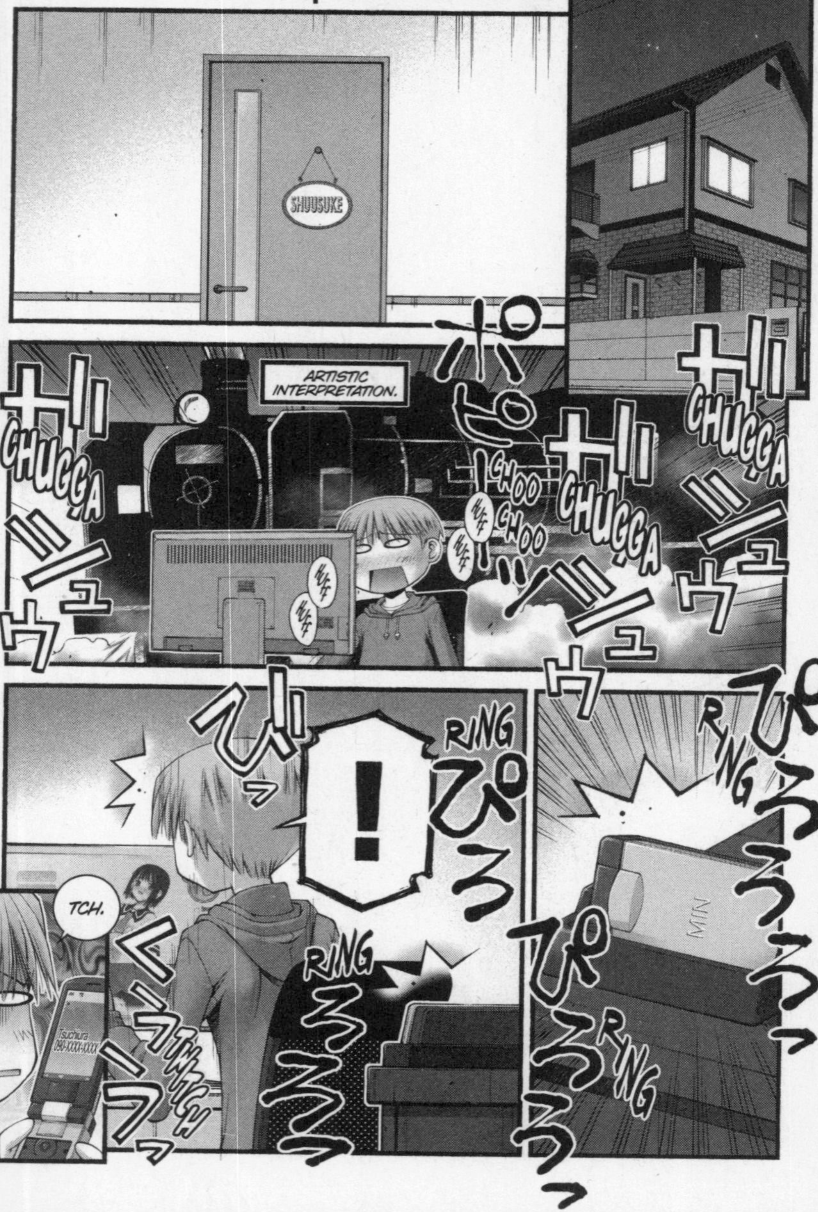
SHUUSUKE
CHUGGA
CHUGGA
ARTISTIC INTERPRETATION.
CHOO CHOO
HUFF HUFF
HUFF HUFF
CHUGGA
RING RING
RING
RING
RING
TCH.
TWITCH
Tsuchiura
090-XXXX-XXXX

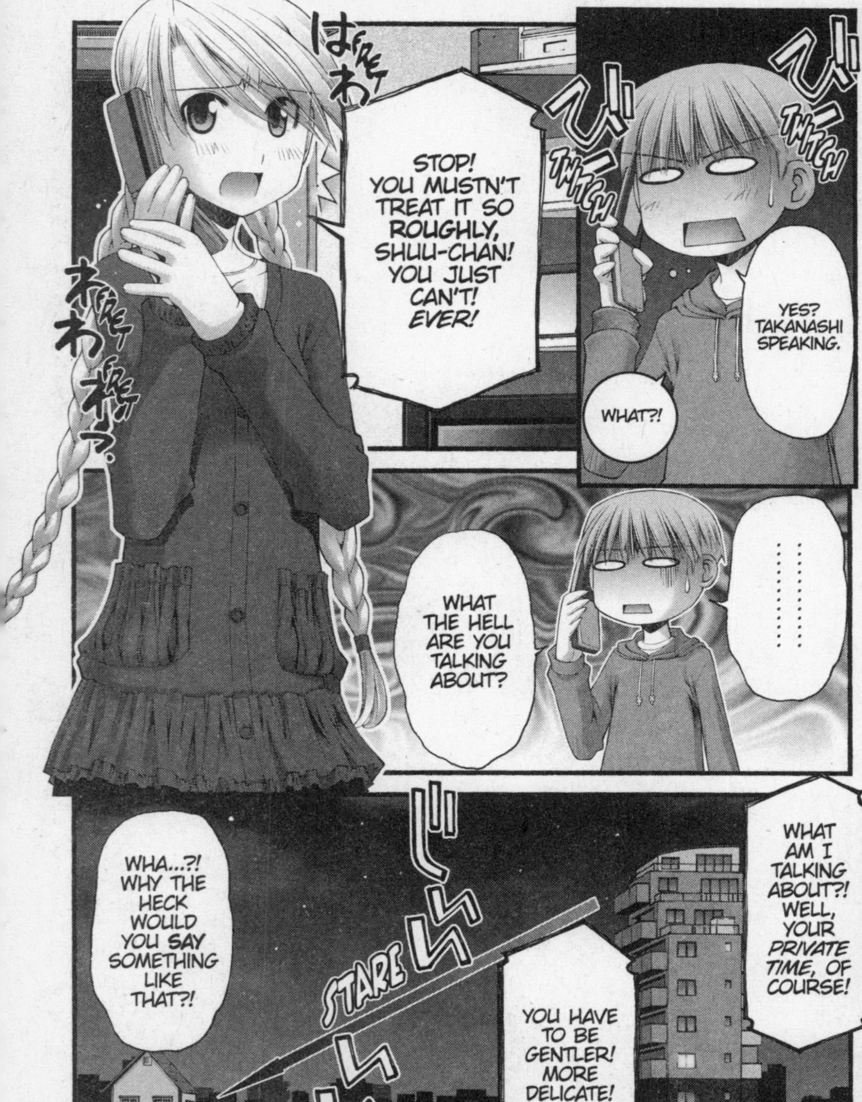
TWITCH
TWITCH
YES? TAKANASHI SPEAKING.
WHAT?!
FRET
STOP! YOU MUSTN'T TREAT IT SO ROUGHLY, SHUU-CHAN! YOU JUST CAN'T! EVER!
FRET FRET
......
WHAT THE HELL ARE YOU TALKING ABOUT?
WHAT AM I TALKING ABOUT?! WELL, YOUR PRIVATE TIME, OF COURSE!
YOU HAVE TO BE GENTLER! MORE DELICATE!
STARE
WHA...?! WHY THE HECK WOULD YOU SAY SOMETHING LIKE THAT?!

THE END

★~White Sister~★

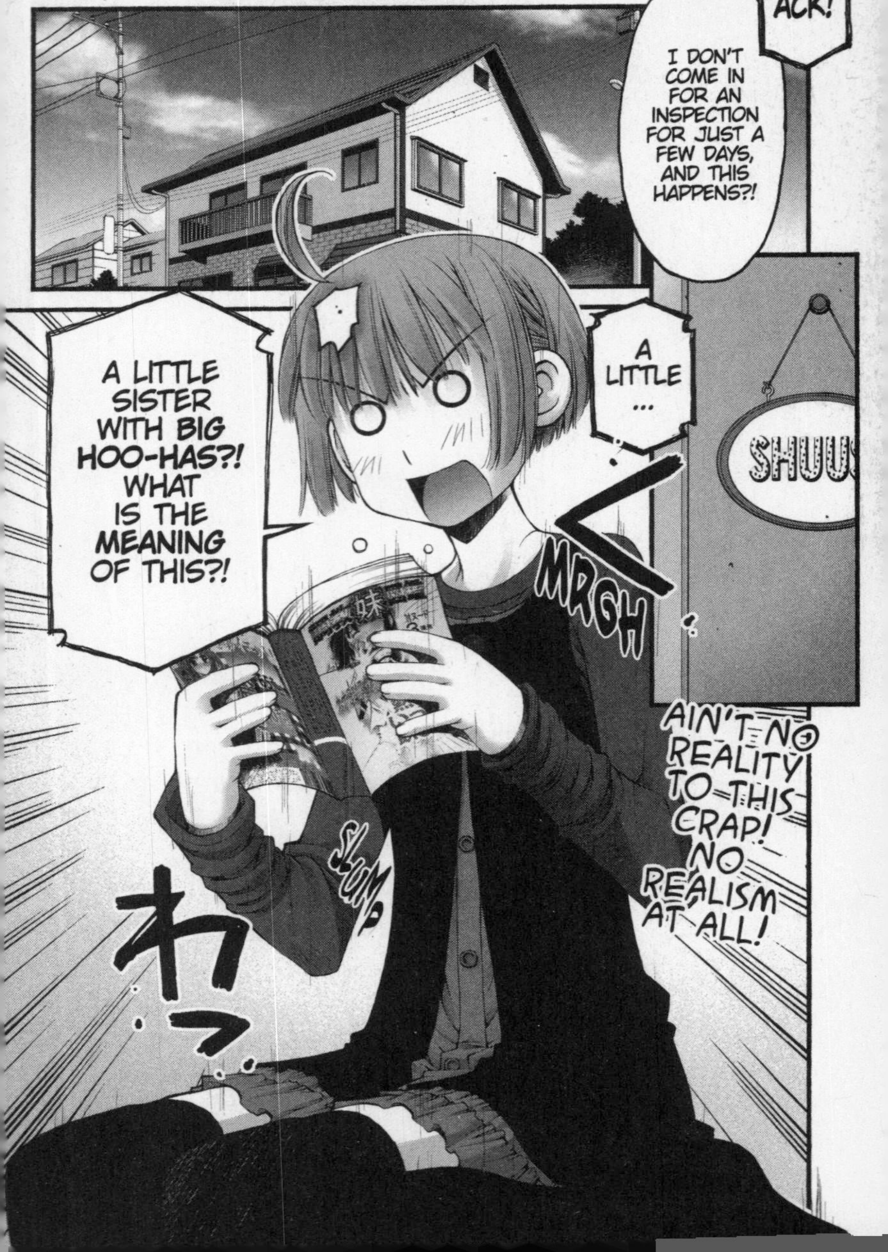
ACK!
I DON'T COME IN FOR AN INSPECTION FOR JUST A FEW DAYS, AND THIS HAPPENS?!
A LITTLE ...
A LITTLE SISTER WITH BIG HOO-HAS?! WHAT IS THE MEANING OF THIS?!
SHUUS
MRGH
AIN'T NO REALITY TO THIS CRAP! NO REALISM AT ALL!
SLUMP
わっ

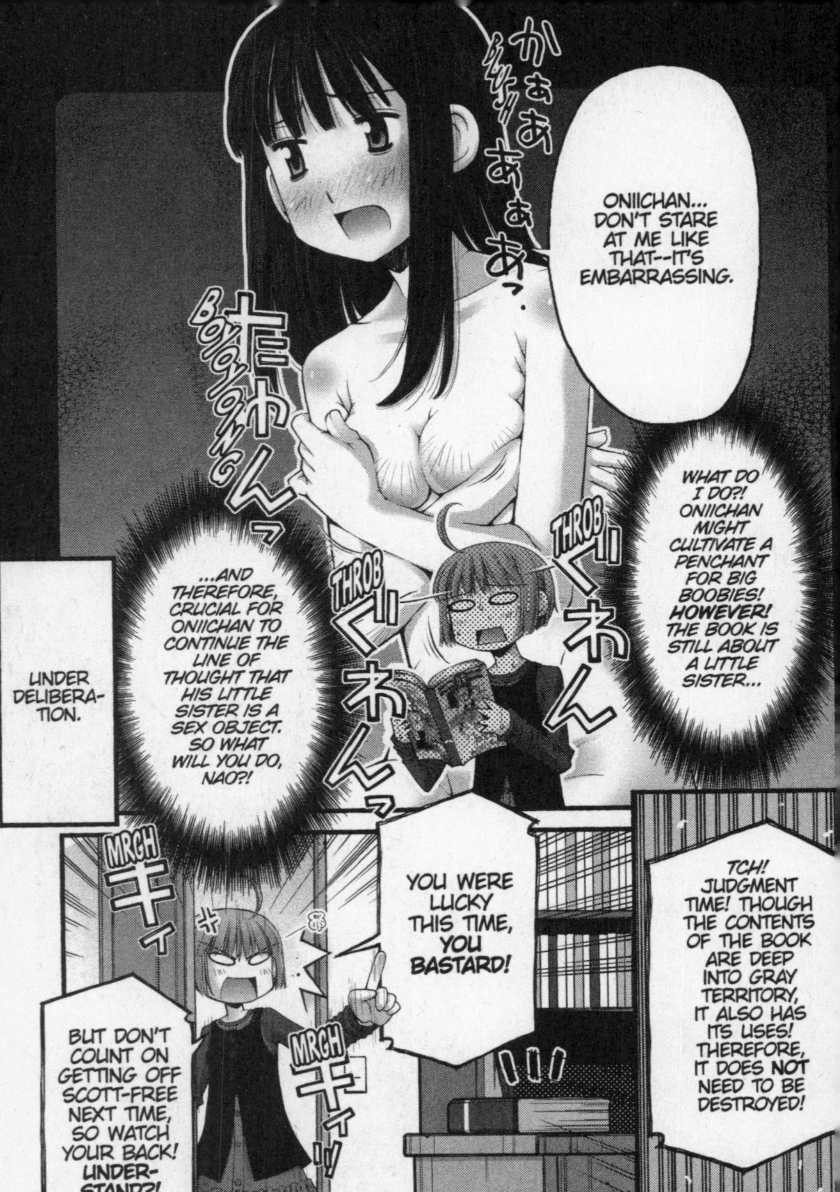
ONIICHAN... DON'T STARE AT ME LIKE THAT--IT'S EMBARRASSING.
BOYOYONG
たゆんっ
WHAT DO I DO?! ONIICHAN MIGHT CULTIVATE A PENCHANT FOR BIG BOOBIES! HOWEVER! THE BOOK IS STILL ABOUT A LITTLE SISTER...
THROB ぐれん
THROB ぐれんっ
...AND THEREFORE, CRUCIAL FOR ONIICHAN TO CONTINUE THE LINE OF THOUGHT THAT HIS LITTLE SISTER IS A SEX OBJECT. SO WHAT WILL YOU DO, NAO?!
UNDER DELIBERATION.
TCH! JUDGMENT TIME! THOUGH THE CONTENTS OF THE BOOK ARE DEEP INTO GRAY TERRITORY, IT ALSO HAS ITS USES! THEREFORE, IT DOES NOT NEED TO BE DESTROYED!
YOU WERE LUCKY THIS TIME, YOU BASTARD!
MRCH キィ
MRCH キィ
BUT DON'T COUNT ON GETTING OFF SCOTT-FREE NEXT TIME, SO WATCH YOUR BACK! UNDERSTAND?!

THE END

★~Black Sister~★

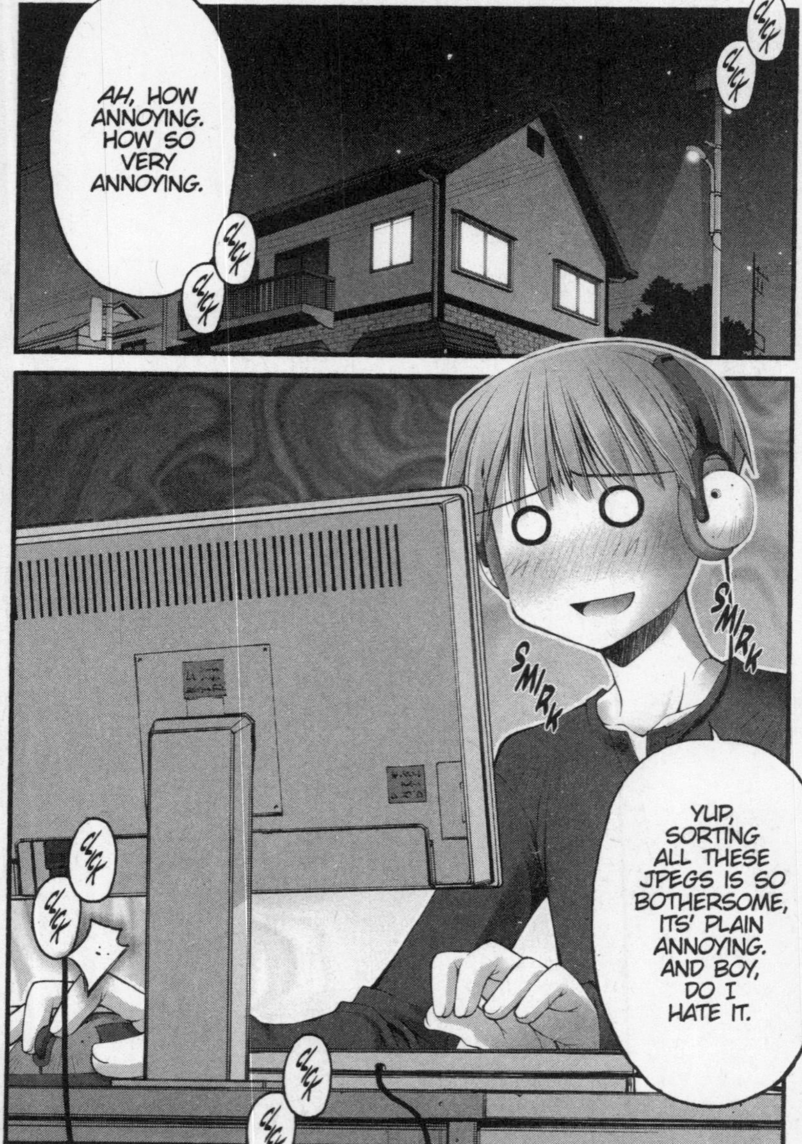
CLICK
CLICK
AH, HOW ANNOYING. HOW SO VERY ANNOYING.
CLICK
CLICK
SMIRK
SMIRK
YUP, SORTING ALL THESE JPEGS IS SO BOTHERSOME, ITS' PLAIN ANNOYING. AND BOY, DO I HATE IT.
CLICK
CLICK
CLICK
CLICK

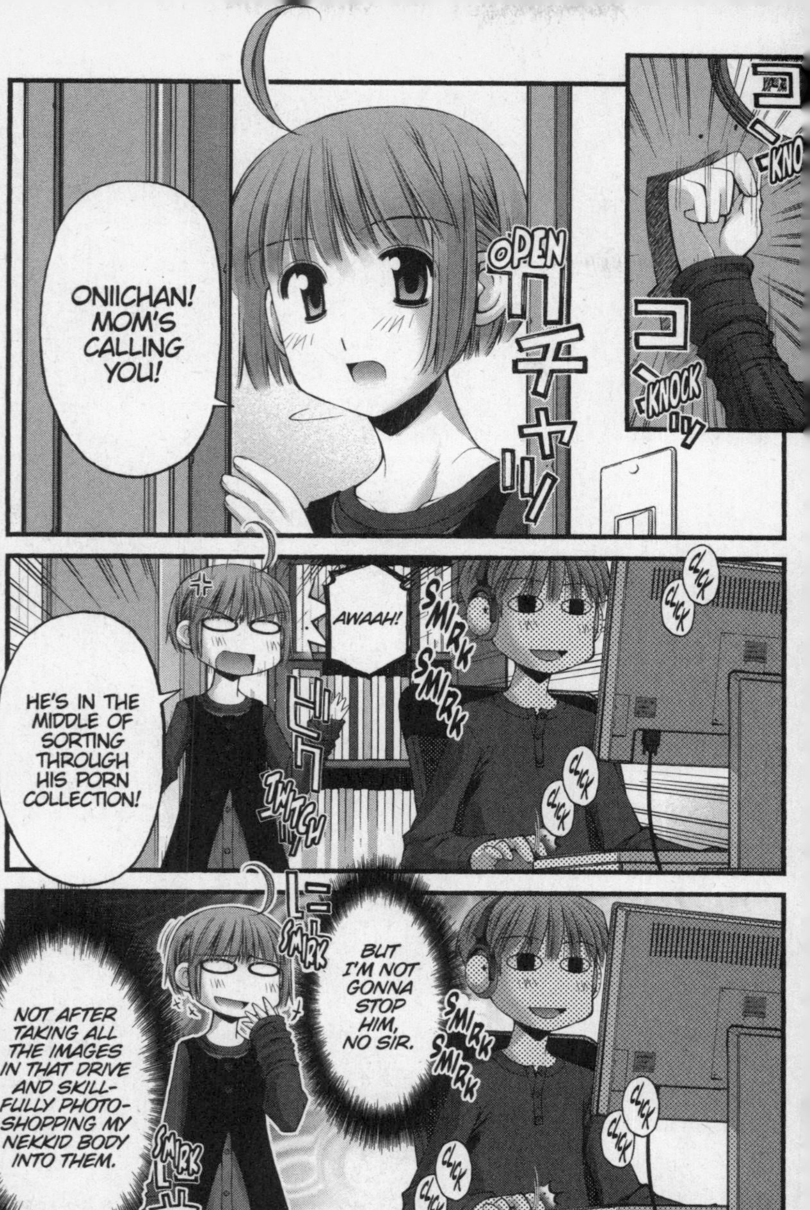

KNO
KNOCK
OPEN
ONIICHAN! MOM'S CALLING YOU!
CLICK CLICK
SMIRK SMIRK
AWAAH!
CLICK CLICK
TWITCH
HE'S IN THE MIDDLE OF SORTING THROUGH HIS PORN COLLECTION!
SMIRK
BUT I'M NOT GONNA STOP HIM, NO SIR.
SMIRK SMIRK
CLICK CLICK
CLICK CLICK
NOT AFTER TAKING ALL THE IMAGES IN THAT DRIVE AND SKILL-FULLY PHOTO-SHOPPING MY NEKKID BODY INTO THEM.
SMIRK

THE END

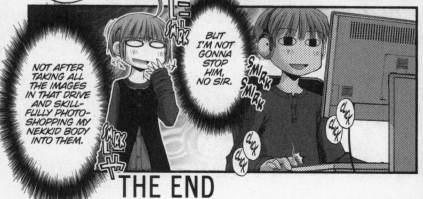

★A Girl's Day★ (Nao's Side)

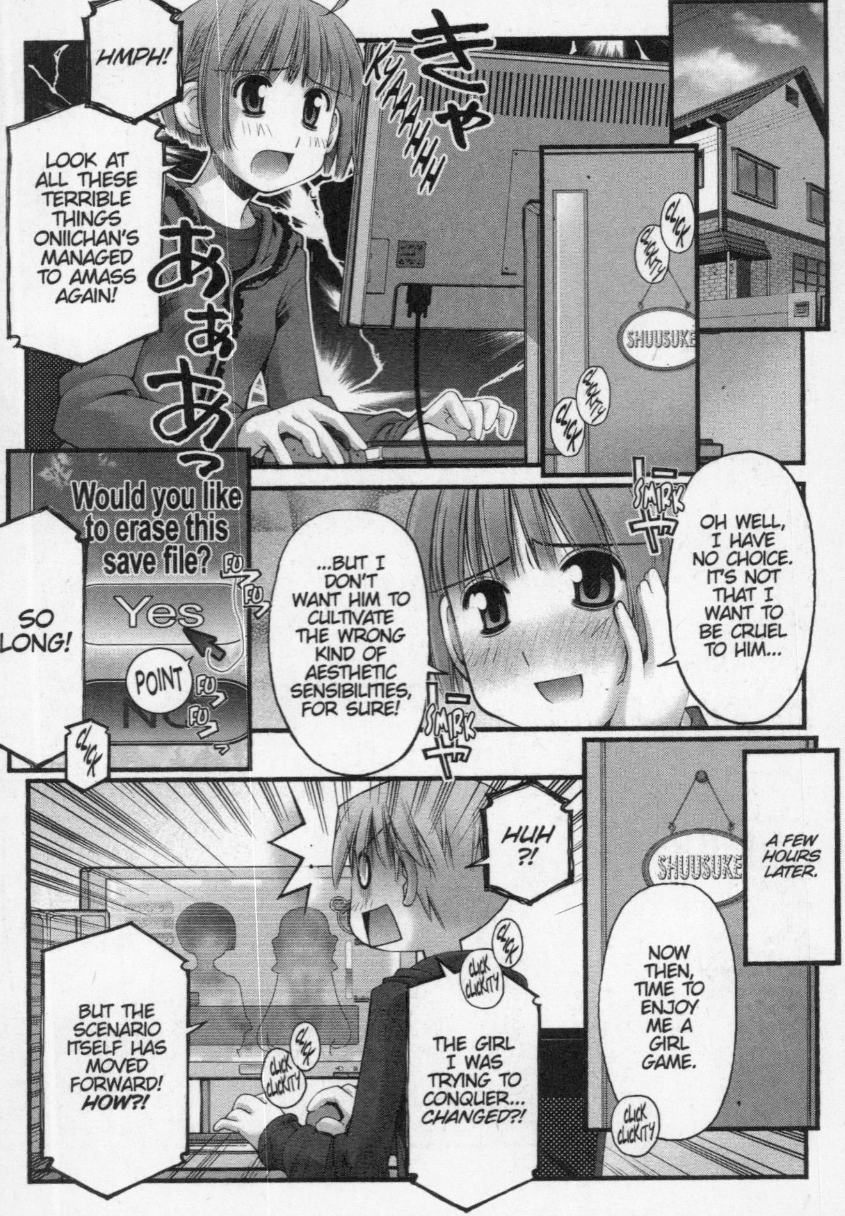
CLICK
CLICKITY
SHUUSUKE
CLICKITY
CLICK
きゃ
KYAAAAHHHH
HMPH!
LOOK AT ALL THESE TERRIBLE THINGS ONIICHAN'S MANAGED TO AMASS AGAIN!
あぁあっ
OH WELL, I HAVE NO CHOICE. IT'S NOT THAT I WANT TO BE CRUEL TO HIM...
SMIRK
...BUT I DON'T WANT HIM TO CULTIVATE THE WRONG KIND OF AESTHETIC SENSIBILITIES, FOR SURE!
SMIRK
Would you like to erase this save file?
Yes
FU FU
POINT
FU FU
SO LONG!
CLICK
A FEW HOURS LATER.
SHUUSUKE
NOW THEN, TIME TO ENJOY ME A GIRL GAME.
CLICK CLICKITY
HUH?!
CLICK
CLICK CLICKITY
THE GIRL I WAS TRYING TO CONQUER... CHANGED?!
CLICK
CLICK CLICKITY
BUT THE SCENARIO ITSELF HAS MOVED FORWARD! HOW?!

(Iroha's Side)

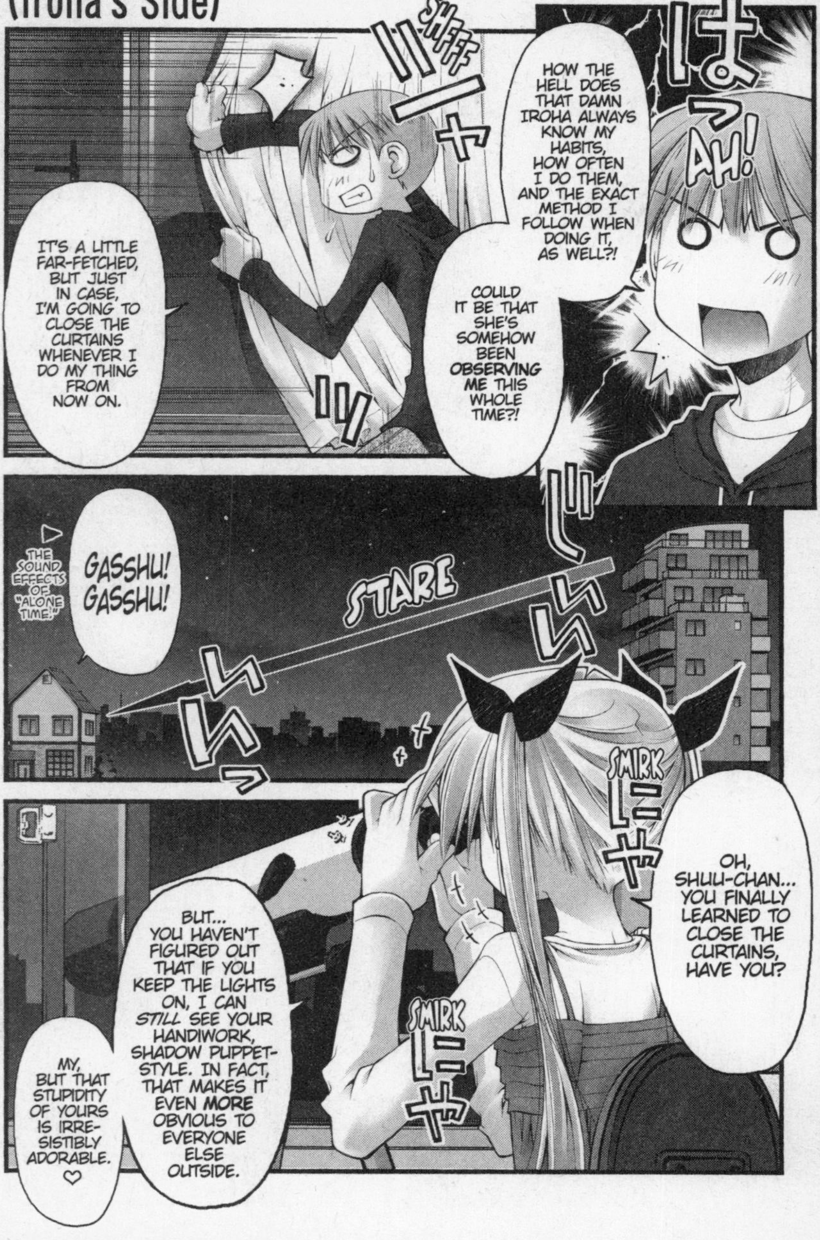
AH!
HOW THE HELL DOES THAT DAMN IROHA ALWAYS KNOW MY HABITS, HOW OFTEN I DO THEM, AND THE EXACT METHOD I FOLLOW WHEN DOING IT, AS WELL?!
COULD IT BE THAT SHE'S SOMEHOW BEEN **OBSERVING** ME THIS WHOLE TIME?!
SHFFF
IT'S A LITTLE FAR-FETCHED, BUT JUST IN CASE, I'M GOING TO CLOSE THE CURTAINS WHENEVER I DO MY THING FROM NOW ON.
STARE
GASSHU! GASSHU!
THE SOUND EFFECTS OF "ALONE TIME."
SMIRK
OH, SHUU-CHAN... YOU FINALLY LEARNED TO CLOSE THE CURTAINS, HAVE YOU?
SMIRK
BUT... YOU HAVEN'T FIGURED OUT THAT IF YOU KEEP THE LIGHTS ON, I CAN *STILL* SEE YOUR HANDIWORK, SHADOW PUPPET-STYLE. IN FACT, THAT MAKES IT EVEN **MORE** OBVIOUS TO EVERYONE ELSE OUTSIDE.
MY, BUT THAT STUPIDITY OF YOURS IS IRRESISTIBLY ADORABLE. ♡

(Mayuka's Side)

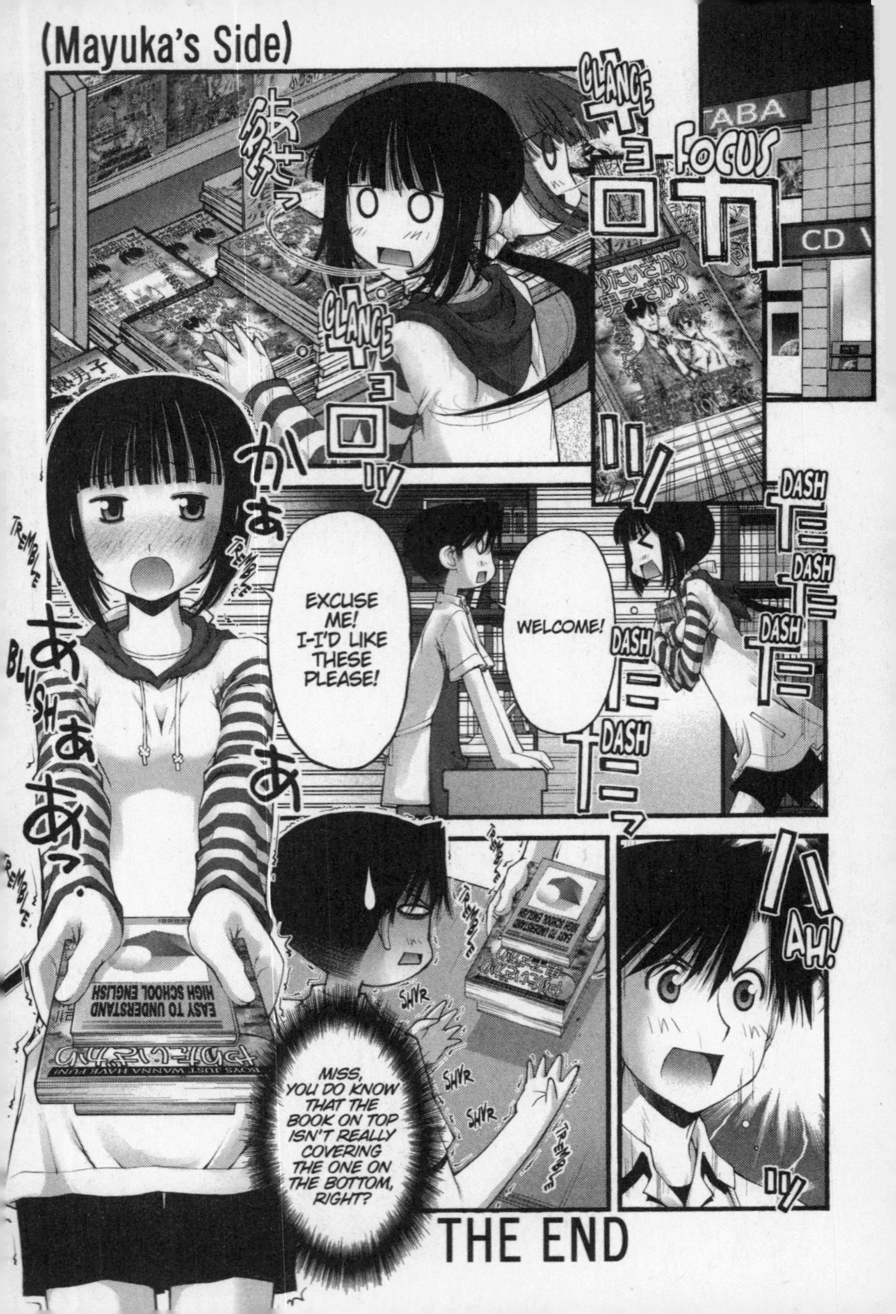
TABA
CD
FOCUS
GLANCE
GLANCE
DASH
DASH
DASH
DASH
DASH
WELCOME!
EXCUSE ME! I-I'D LIKE THESE PLEASE!
AH!
TREMBLE
SHVR
SHVR
SHVR
EASY TO UNDERSTAND HIGH SCHOOL ENGLISH
MISS, YOU DO KNOW THAT THE BOOK ON TOP ISN'T REALLY COVERING THE ONE ON THE BOTTOM, RIGHT?
TREMBLE
BLUSH
EASY TO UNDERSTAND HIGH SCHOOL ENGLISH
BOYS JUST WANNA HAVE FUN!

THE END

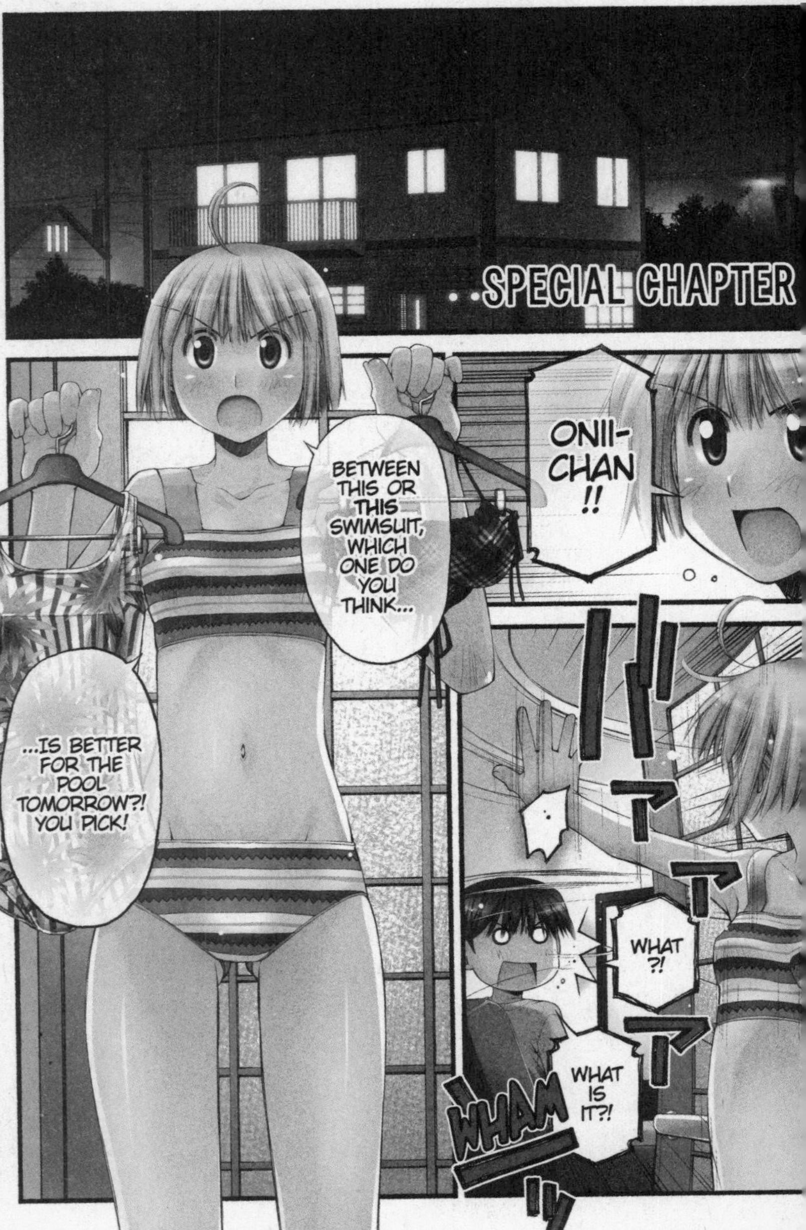
SPECIAL CHAPTER
ONII-CHAN!!
WHAT?!
WHAT IS IT?!
WHAM
BETWEEN THIS OR THIS SWIMSUIT, WHICH ONE DO YOU THINK...
...IS BETTER FOR THE POOL TOMORROW?! YOU PICK!

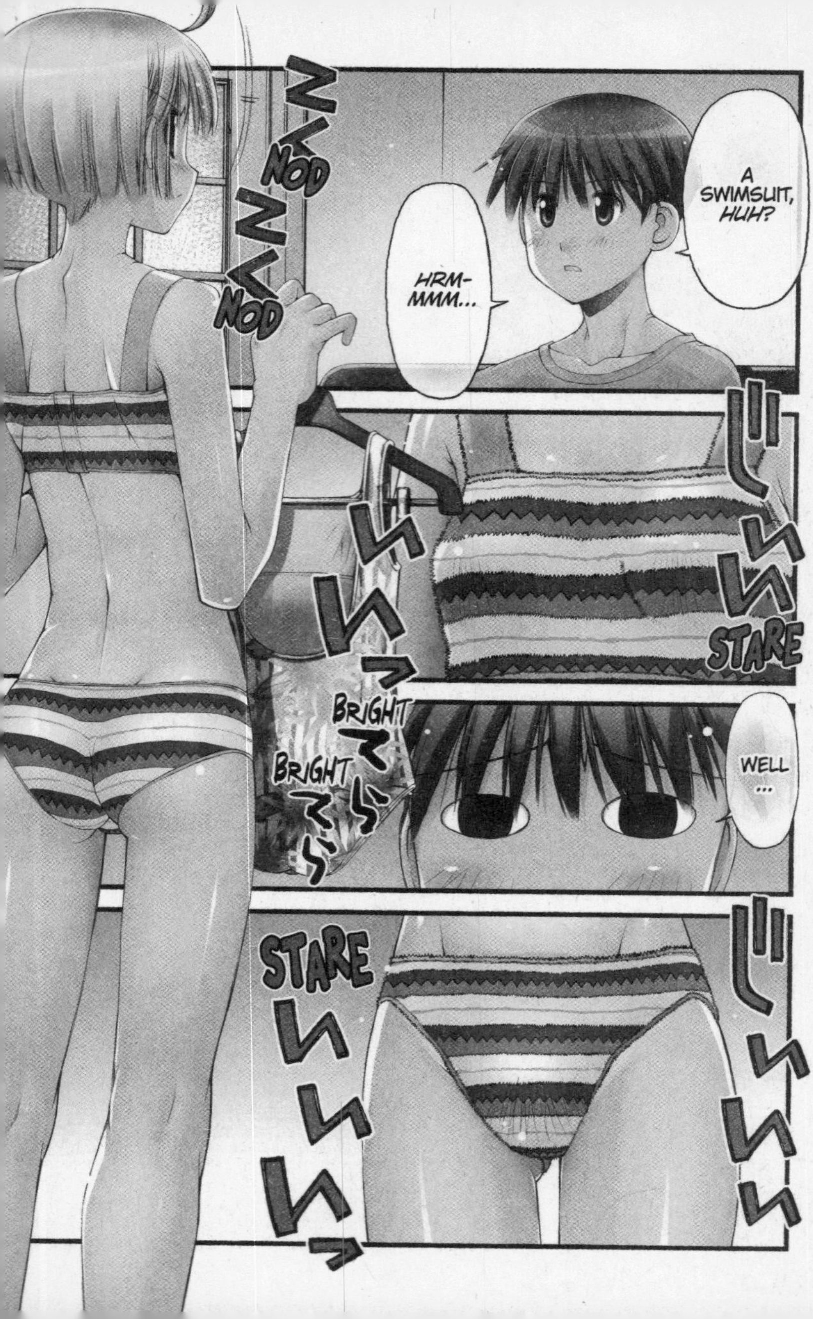
A SWIMSUIT, HUH?
HRM-MMM...
STARE
BRIGHT
BRIGHT
WELL ...
STARE
NOD
NOD

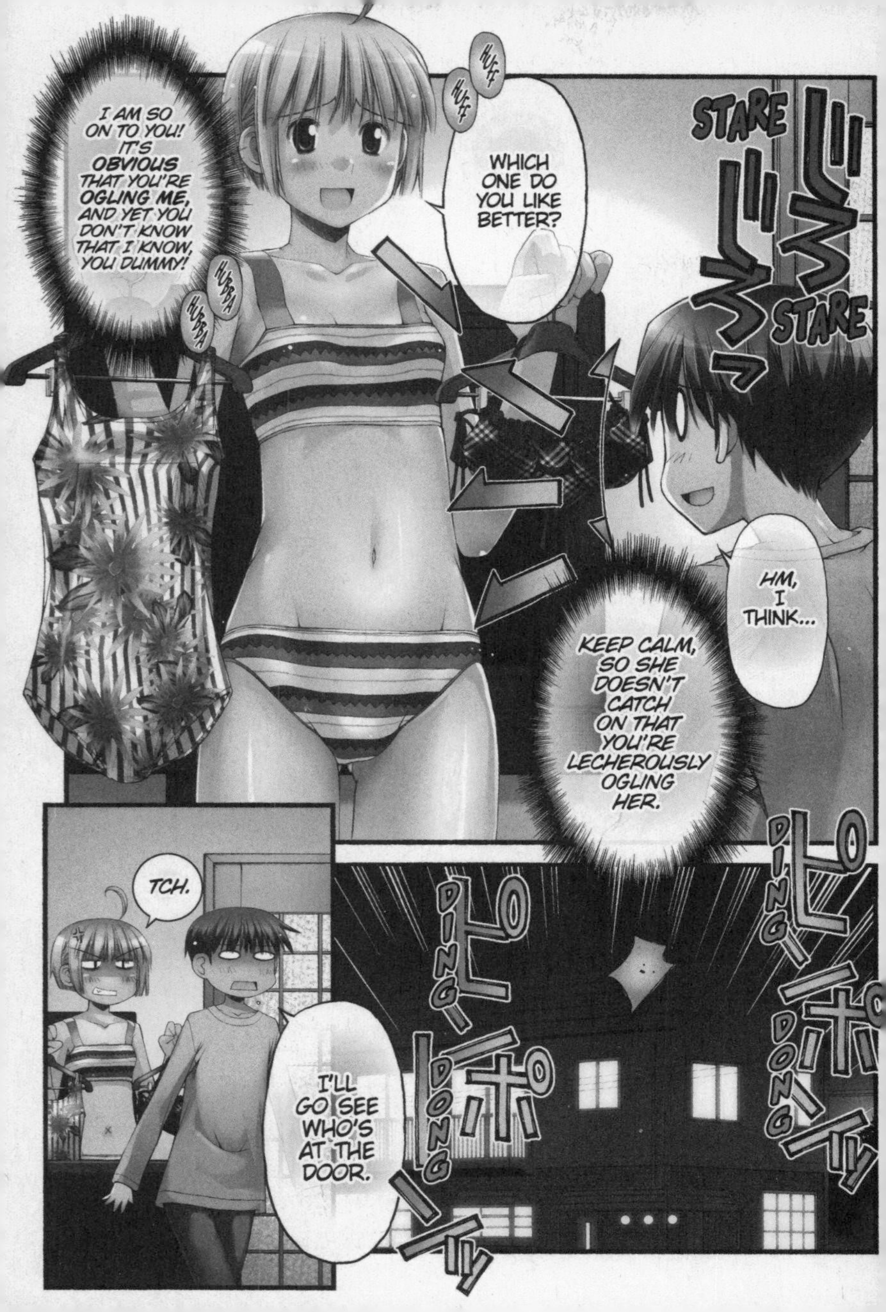
STARE
STARE
HUFF
HUFF
WHICH ONE DO YOU LIKE BETTER?
I AM SO ON TO YOU! IT'S OBVIOUS THAT YOU'RE OGLING ME, AND YET YOU DON'T KNOW THAT I KNOW, YOU DUMMY!
HUBBA
HUBBA
HM, I THINK...
KEEP CALM, SO SHE DOESN'T CATCH ON THAT YOU'RE LECHEROUSLY OGLING HER.
ピンポーン
DING DONG
ピンポーン
DING DONG
TCH.
I'LL GO SEE WHO'S AT THE DOOR.

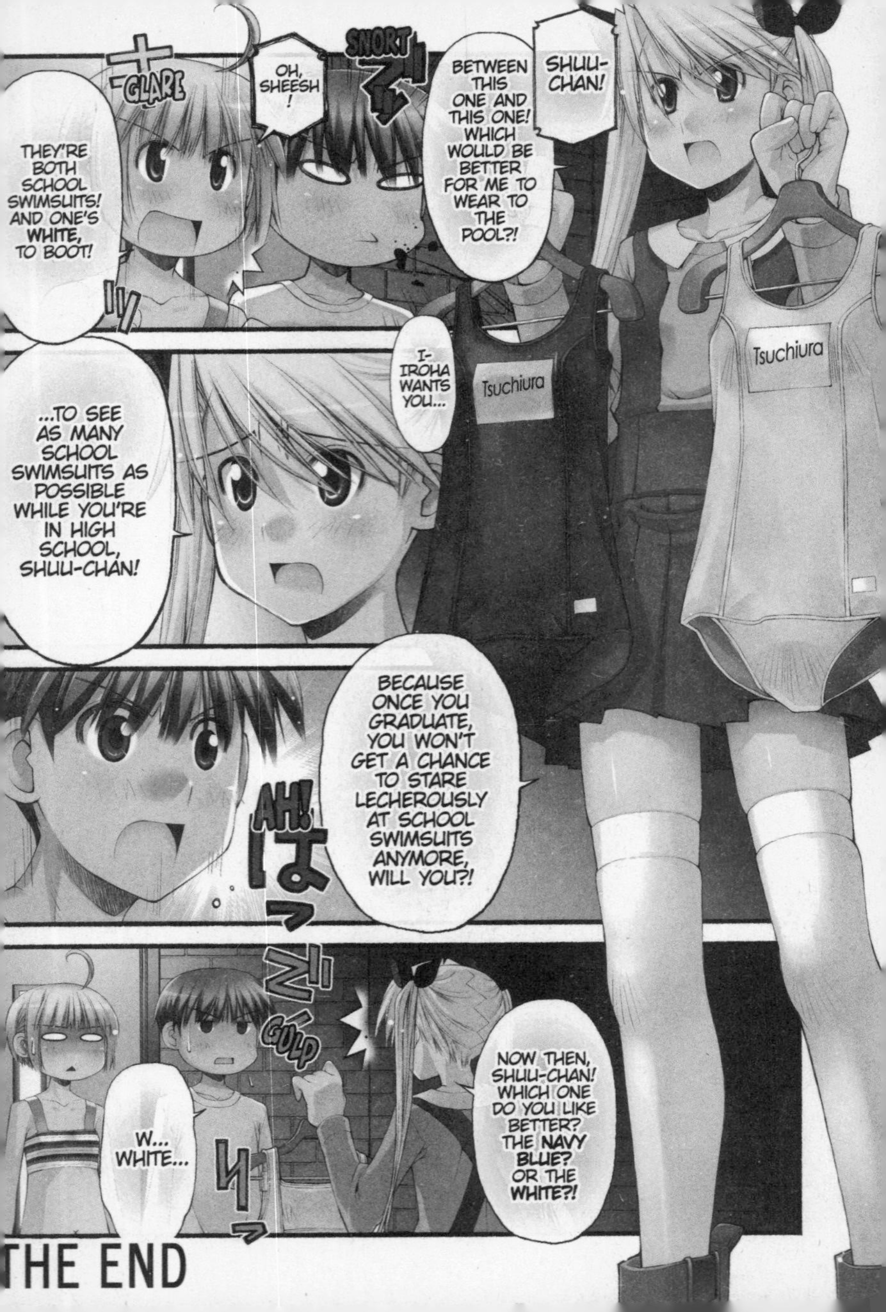
SHUU-CHAN!
BETWEEN THIS ONE AND THIS ONE! WHICH WOULD BE BETTER FOR ME TO WEAR TO THE POOL?!
Tsuchiura
Tsuchiura
SNORT
OH, SHEESH!
GLARE
THEY'RE BOTH SCHOOL SWIMSUITS! AND ONE'S WHITE, TO BOOT!
I-IROHA WANTS YOU...
...TO SEE AS MANY SCHOOL SWIMSUITS AS POSSIBLE WHILE YOU'RE IN HIGH SCHOOL, SHUU-CHAN!
BECAUSE ONCE YOU GRADUATE, YOU WON'T GET A CHANCE TO STARE LECHEROUSLY AT SCHOOL SWIMSUITS ANYMORE, WILL YOU?!
AH! はっ
GULP
NOW THEN, SHUU-CHAN! WHICH ONE DO YOU LIKE BETTER? THE NAVY BLUE? OR THE WHITE?!
W... WHITE...
THE END

AFTERWORD

HELLO, EVERYONE WHO PICKED UP *I DON'T LIKE YOU AT ALL, BIG BROTHER!!*
IT'S ME, KOUICHI KUSANO!
I HOPE YOU ALL ENJOYED *I DON'T LIKE YOU AT ALL, BIG BROTHER!!* VOL. 5!
THANKS TO EVERYONE'S SUPPORT, *BIG BROTHER* HAS FINALLY MADE IT TO THE 5TH COMPILED COMIC! AND I AM SO VERY THANKFUL FOR THAT!
STARTING WITH THE BROADCAST OF THE ANIME, THE PUBLICATION OF VOL. 4, AND NOW THIS, THE RELEASE OF VOL. 5 OF THE COMPILED COMICS, 2011 HAS BEEN JAM-PACKED WITH EVENTS—THE YEAR HAS TRULY BEEN LIKE A DREAM TO ME AND HAS GONE BY SO QUICKLY.
AND THE VERY LONG KONDO MAYUKA ARC HAS FINALLY REACHED ITS CLIMAX. IT'S BEEN ALMOST A YEAR AND A HALF SINCE I FIRST CAME UP WITH THIS STORY ARC, AND I MUST ADMIT THAT IT TOOK MUCH LONGER THAN I HAD EVEN ANTICIPATED TO COMPLETE. (SWEAT.)
MEANWHILE, THE ANIME BROADCAST HAS ENDED. HOWEVER, THE ORIGINAL MANGA SHOULD CONTINUE FOR QUITE SOME TIME, SO IF YOU WOULD ALL CONTINUE TO SUPPORT *BIG BROTHER* FROM HERE ON, I WOULD VERY, VERY MUCH APPRECIATE IT!
I LOOK VERY MUCH FORWARD TO SEEING YOU ALL AGAIN IN VOL. 6. UNTIL THEN.

A CERTAIN DAY IN MAY,
KOUICHI KUSANO

AND BEFORE I GO, I'D LIKE TO THANK EVERYONE WHO HELPED MAKE GETTING THIS BOOK PUBLISHED POSSIBLE. TO MY REGULAR ASSISTANT, KINBARA 1099-SAMA, I THANK YOU FOR STICKING IT OUT WITH ME ALL THIS TIME. AND THANK YOU TO UMASHIKA-SAMA, WHO DESPITE BEING BUSY WITH THEIR OWN WORK, STILL HAD TIME TO ASSIST ME. TO OKUDA TAKESHI-SAMA, WHO COMPLETED SOME TERRIBLY HARD AND COMPLICATED BACKGROUNDS WITH SUCH HIGH QUALITY. TO MIMI MIMIZU-SAMA, WHO CAME TO MY RESCUE SO MANY TIMES WHEN I WAS IN TROUBLE. TO MATSUAKI-SAMA, WHO NEVER ONCE PUT ON A SOUR FACE, DESPITE ALL THE TIMES I BROUGHT OVER MY NAMES TO DISCUSS WITH HIM, ALL THOSE LATE NIGHTS. TO MY VERY FIRST HANDLER, N-MURA-SAMA, WHO GAVE *BIG BROTHER* ITS FIRST CHANCE AND FIRST PUBLICATION RUN. TO MY SECOND HANDLER, N-I-SAMA, WHO EVER SO PATIENTLY AWAITS MY MANUSCRIPT. AND TO EVERYONE ELSE WHO HAS WORKED TO MAKE THIS BOOK A POSSIBILITY, THANK YOU SO VERY MUCH!

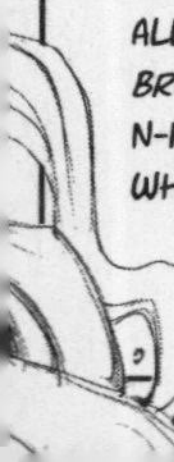

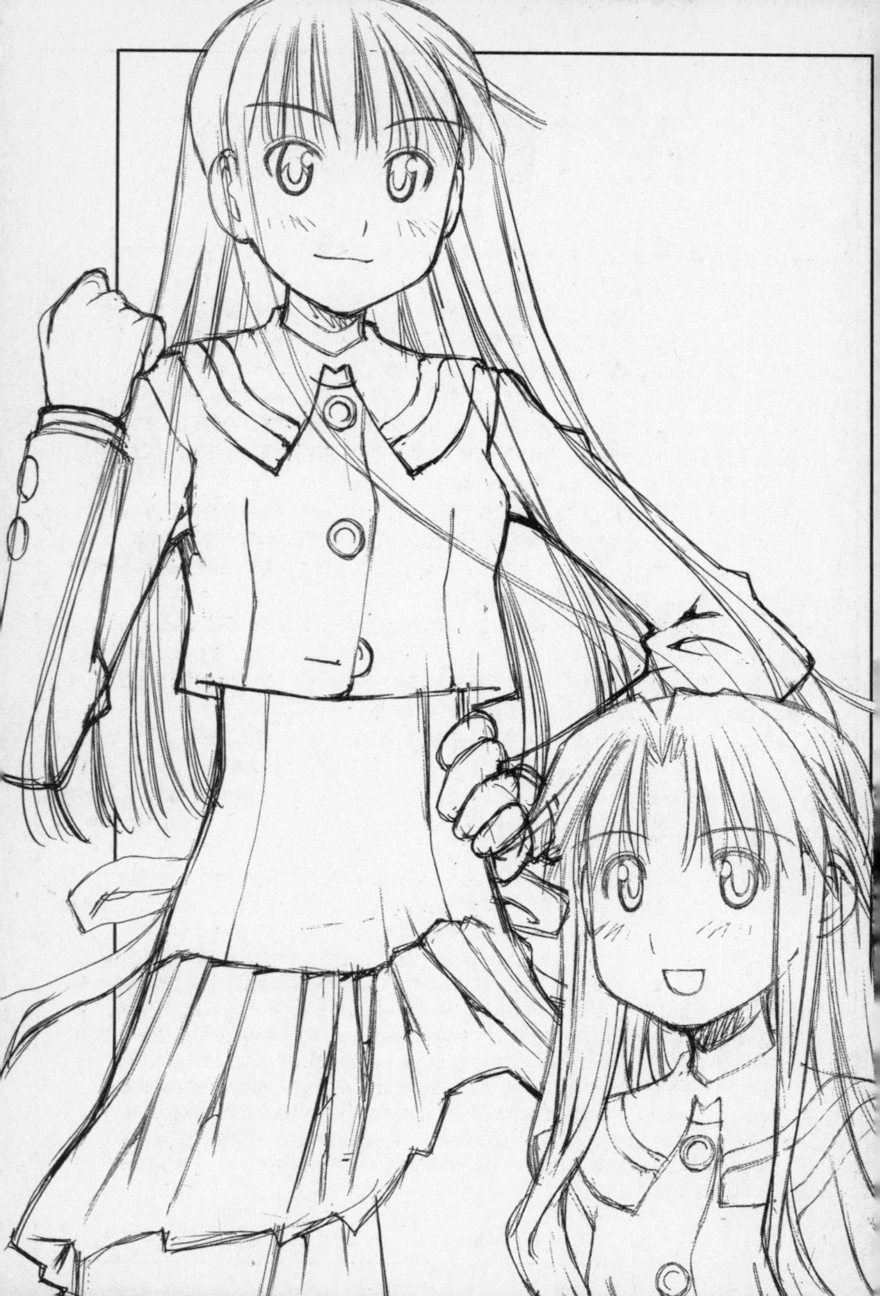

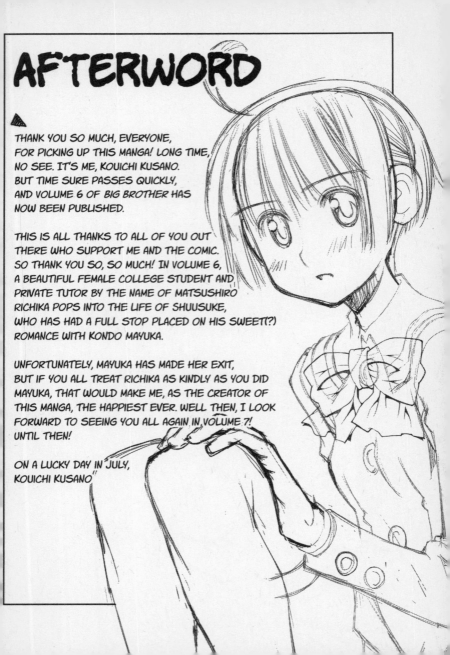

AFTERWORD

THANK YOU SO MUCH, EVERYONE, FOR PICKING UP THIS MANGA! LONG TIME, NO SEE. IT'S ME, KOUICHI KUSANO. BUT TIME SURE PASSES QUICKLY, AND VOLUME 6 OF BIG BROTHER HAS NOW BEEN PUBLISHED.

THIS IS ALL THANKS TO ALL OF YOU OUT THERE WHO SUPPORT ME AND THE COMIC. SO THANK YOU SO, SO MUCH! IN VOLUME 6, A BEAUTIFUL FEMALE COLLEGE STUDENT AND PRIVATE TUTOR BY THE NAME OF MATSUSHIRO RICHIKA POPS INTO THE LIFE OF SHUUSUKE, WHO HAS HAD A FULL STOP PLACED ON HIS SWEET(?) ROMANCE WITH KONDO MAYUKA.

UNFORTUNATELY, MAYUKA HAS MADE HER EXIT, BUT IF YOU ALL TREAT RICHIKA AS KINDLY AS YOU DID MAYUKA, THAT WOULD MAKE ME, AS THE CREATOR OF THIS MANGA, THE HAPPIEST EVER. WELL THEN, I LOOK FORWARD TO SEEING YOU ALL AGAIN IN VOLUME 7! UNTIL THEN!

ON A LUCKY DAY IN JULY,
KOUICHI KUSANO

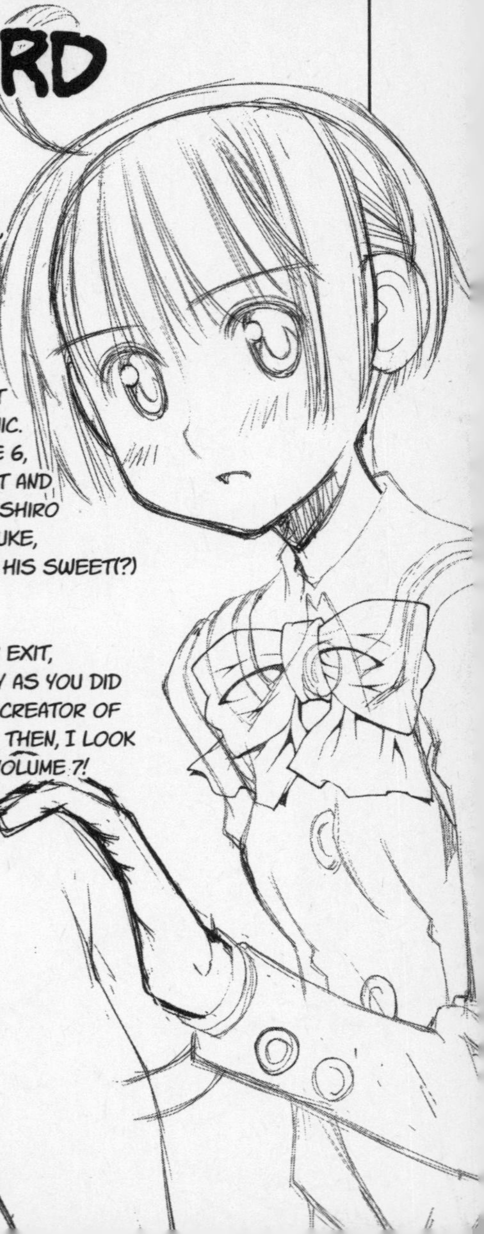

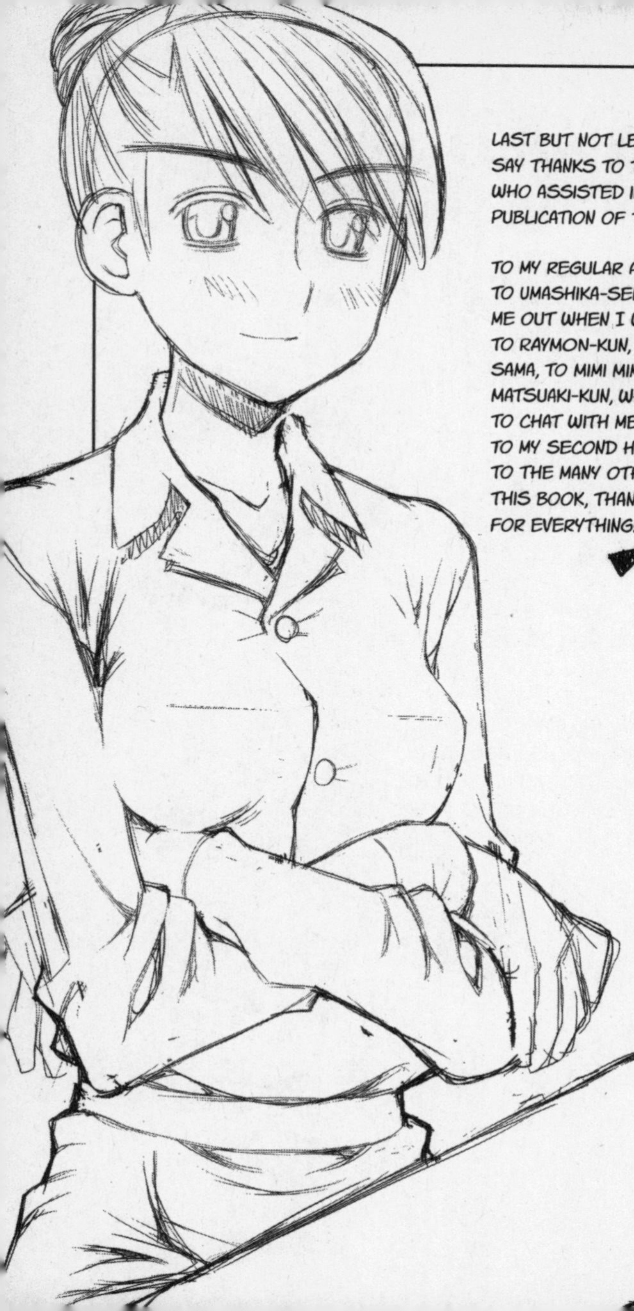

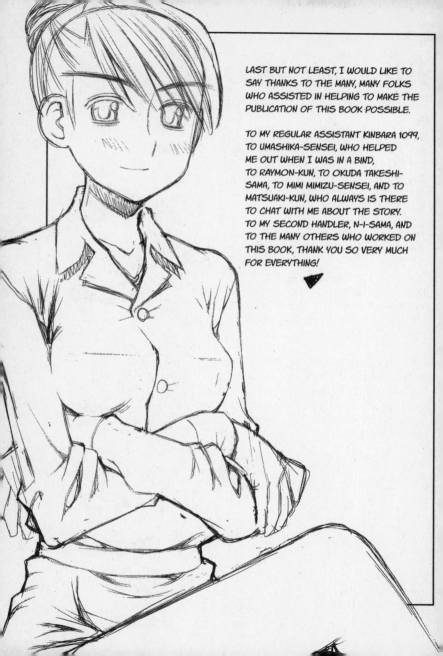

LAST BUT NOT LEAST, I WOULD LIKE TO SAY THANKS TO THE MANY, MANY FOLKS WHO ASSISTED IN HELPING TO MAKE THE PUBLICATION OF THIS BOOK POSSIBLE.

TO MY REGULAR ASSISTANT KINBARA 1099,
TO UMASHIKA-SENSEI, WHO HELPED
ME OUT WHEN I WAS IN A BIND,
TO RAYMON-KUN, TO OKUDA TAKESHI-SAMA, TO MIMI MIMIZU-SENSEI, AND TO
MATSUAKI-KUN, WHO ALWAYS IS THERE
TO CHAT WITH ME ABOUT THE STORY.
TO MY SECOND HANDLER, N-I-SAMA, AND
TO THE MANY OTHERS WHO WORKED ON
THIS BOOK, THANK YOU SO VERY MUCH
FOR EVERYTHING!

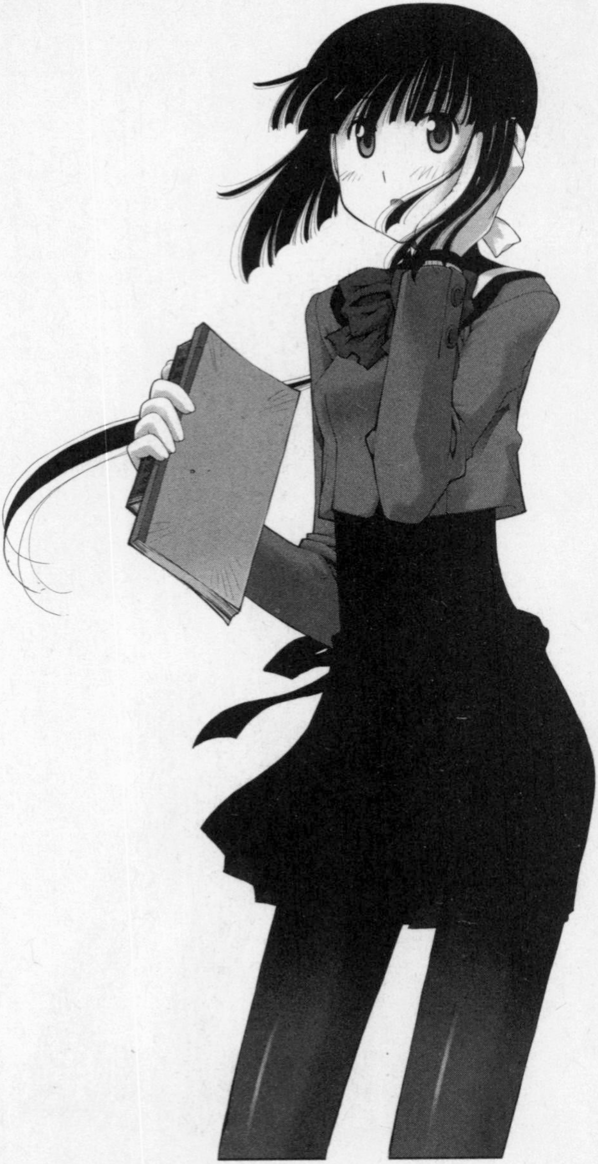

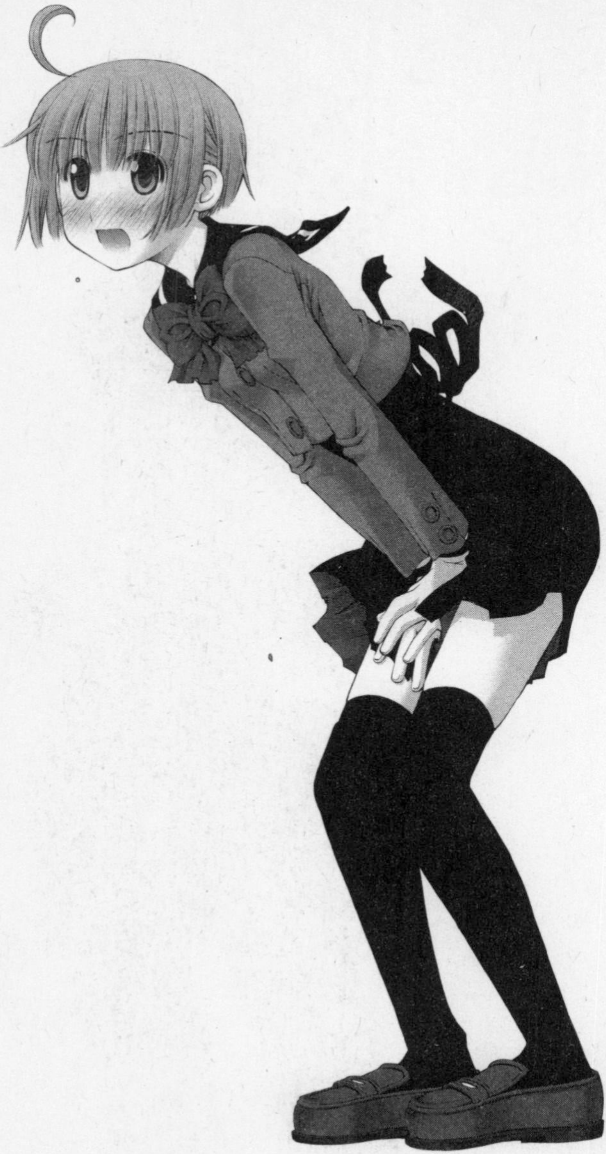

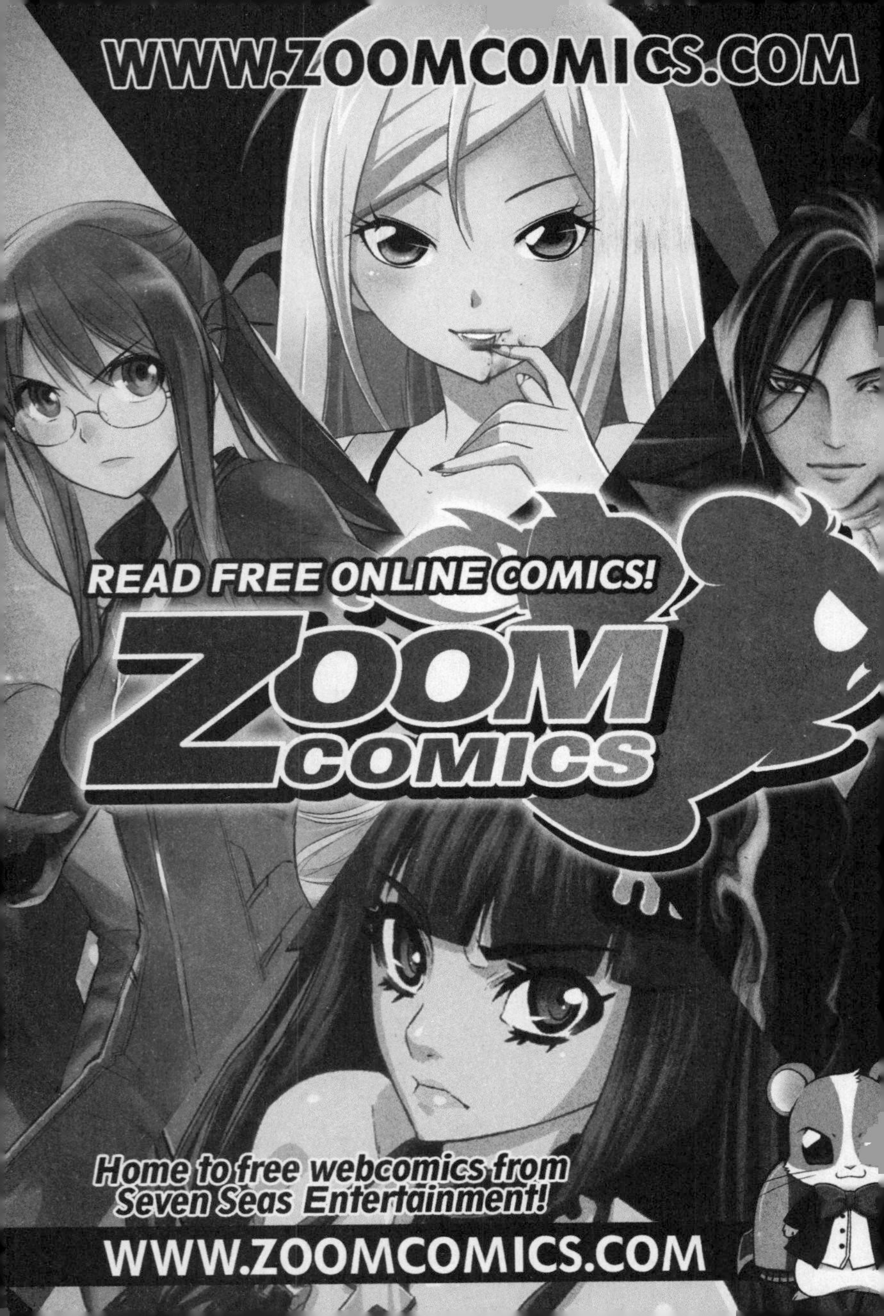

WWW.ZOOMCOMICS.COM
READ FREE ONLINE COMICS!
ZOOM COMICS
Home to free webcomics from Seven Seas Entertainment!
WWW.ZOOMCOMICS.COM